THE ETERNAL TORAH

Living Under God

WILLEM J. OUWENEEL

AN EVANGELICAL INTRODUCTION TO
REFORMATIONAL THEOLOGY
VOL I/2

PART I: SCRIPTURE:
THE REVEALED SOURCE FOR THEOLOGY

AN EVANGELICAL INTRODUCTION TO REFORMATIONAL THEOLOGY

Part I: Scripture: The Revealed Source For Theology
    I/1 *The Eternal Word*: God Speaking To Us
    I/2 *The Eternal Torah*: Living Under God

Part II: God: The Personal Source Behind Theology
    II/1 *The Eternal God*: God Revealing Himself To Us
    II/2 *The Eternal Christ*: God With Us
    II/3 *The Eternal Spirit*: God Living In Us

Part III: Redemption: The Christ-Centered Heart of Theology
    III/1 *The Eternal Purpose*: Living In Christ
    III/2 *Eternal Righteousness*: Living Before God
    III/3 *Eternal Salvation*: Christ Dying For Us
    III/4 *Eternal Life*: Christ Living In Us

Part IV: Consummation: The Lived Shape of Theology
    IV/1 *The Eternal People*: God in Relation To Israel
    IV/2 *The Eternal Covenant*: Living With God
    IV/3 *The Eternal Kingdom*: Living Under Christ

Part V: Method: The Comprehensive Foundation of Theology
    V/1 *Eternal Truth*: The Prolegomena of Theology

THE ETERNAL TORAH

Living Under God

WILLEM J. OUWENEEL

PAIDEIA
PRESS

PAIDEIA
PRESS

The Eternal Torah: Living Under God

This English edition is a publication of Paideia Press (P.O. Box 500, Jordan Station, Ontario, Canada L0R 1S0). Copyright © 2020 by Paideia Press. All rights reserved. Except for brief quotations in critical publications or reviews, no part of this book may be reproduced in any manner without prior written permission from Paideia Press at the address above.

Unless otherwise indicated, Scripture quotations are from the ESV® Bible (The Holy Bible, English Standard Version®). Copyright © 2001 by Crossway, a publishing ministry of Good News Publishers. Used by permission. All rights reserved.

Scripture quotations or references marked as NKJV are taken from the New King James Version®. Copyright © 1982 by Thomas Nelson, Inc. Used by permission. All rights reserved.

Scripture quotations or references marked as NIV are taken from the Holy Bible, New International Version®, NIV®. Copyright © 1973, 1978, 1984, 2011 by Biblica, Inc.™ Used by permission of Zondervan. All rights reserved worldwide. www.zondervan.com. The "NIV" and "New International Version" are trademarks registered in the United States Patent and Trademark Office by Biblica, Inc.™

Book Design by: Steven R. Martins

ISBN 978-0-88815-253-4

Cataloguing-in-Publication data:

Printed in the United States of America

*I will keep your **Torah** continually,*
  forever and ever, . . .
*Oh how I love your **Torah**!*
  It is my meditation all the day.
Your commandment makes me wiser than my enemies,
  for it is ever [or, in eternity] with me. . . .
  I incline my heart to perform your statutes
  forever, to the end. . . .
. . . every one of your righteous rules endures forever.
Psalm 119:44, 97–98, 112, 160

To the Jews I became as a Jew,
  in order to win Jews.
To those under the Torah I became as one under the Torah
  (though not being myself under the Torah)
  that I might win those under the Torah.
To those outside the Torah I became as one outside the Torah
  (not being outside the Torah of God but under the Torah
  of the Messiah)
  that I might win those outside the Torah.
1 Corinthians 9:20–21

Bear one another's burdens,
  And so fulfill the Torah of the Messiah.
Galatians 6:2

Table of Contents

Series Preface		i
Author's Preface		v
Abbreviations		vii
Introduction		1
Chapter 1	What Is the Torah?	9
Chapter 2	Three Views of the Torah	63
Chapter 3	Torah, Hokmah, Logos, and Spirit	109
Chapter 4	The Meaning of the Mosaic Covenant	157
Chapter 5	Is the Mosaic Torah Abolished or Renewed?	207
Chapter 6	The Messianic Torah and the Millennial Torah	259
Chapter 7	A Threefold Torah: Differences and Similarities	315
Chapter 8	New Testament Institutions	377
Chapter 9	Jewish and Gentile Jesus-Believers	427
Appendix I	Is the Church "Spiritual Israel"?	475
Appendix II	The Torah in First-Century Judaism	491
Appendix III	The Sacred Day of the Week	503
Appendix IV	Mosaic and Messianic Ordinances	519
Bibliography		533
Scripture Index		555
Subject Index		581

Table of Contents
Expanded

Series Preface	i
Author's Preface	v
Abbreviations	vii
Introduction	1
1 What Is the Torah?	9
1.1 Jesus-believers and the Torah	10
1.1.1 Pork or Not?	10
1.1.2 Who Is a Jew?	13
1.1.3 Are Messianic Jews Christians?	15
1.2 The Messianic Jewish Movement	18
1.2.1 The Ancient Messianic Jewish Movement	18
1.2.2 The Present Messianic Jewish Movement	24
1.2.3 Types of Jesus-believing Jewry	33
1.3 The Term "Torah" in Scripture	41
1.3.1 The Torah in the Tanakh	41
1.3.2 The Torah in the New Testament	49
1.4 The Two Functions of the Torah	57
1.4.1 The Negative Function	57
1.4.2 The Positive Function	59
2 Three Views of the Torah	63
2.1 The Two Older Theological Views	64

		2.1.1	Covenant and Dispensational Theology	64
		2.1.2	View of the Torah	68
		2.1.3	An Orthodox-Jewish View	73
	2.2	The Two Older Theological Paradigms and the Torah		77
		2.2.1	Questions Concerning the Torah	77
		2.2.2	Important Presuppositions	83
		2.2.3	Essentials	88
	2.3	The Pre-Mosaic Torah		92
		2.3.1	The Adamic Torah, Noahic Torah, and Abrahamic Torah	92
		2.3.2	Abraham *sub lege*, and Jesus-believers *post legem*?	100
		2.3.3	"Torah-lessness"	105
3	Torah, Hokmah, Logos, and Spirit			109
	3.1	The Concept of *Hokmah*		110
		3.1.1	Scripture about *Hokmah*	110
		3.1.2	Tradition About *Hokmah*	116
		3.1.3	Ecclesiastes	124
	3.2	Wisdom in the New Testament		127
		3.2.1	*Sophia*	127
		3.2.2	*Logos:* Ancient Views	131
		3.2.3	*Logos:* Recent Discussion	136
	3.3	Sophia, Torah, Spirit		140
		3.3.1	The Personification of the Sophia	140
		3.3.2	Torah and Spirit	146
		3.3.3	The Torah and the Gods	150

4	The Meaning of the Mosaic Covenant		157
	4.1	The Covenant Concept in General	158
		4.1.1 Description	158
		4.1.2 Conditional v. Unconditional	163
		4.1.3 The New Covenant Today	168
	4.2	The Old Covenant According to the Tanakh	171
		4.2.1 Its Eternal Character	171
		4.2.2 Various Participants	176
		4.2.3 Again: the Torah's Two Functions	179
	4.3	The Old Covenant According to the New Testament	183
		4.3.1 Paul's Letters	183
		4.3.2 Law, Legalism, Ethnocentrism	192
		4.3.3 The Letter to the Hebrews	197
5	Is the Mosaic Torah Abolished or Renewed?		207
	5.1	What Torah Are We Talking About?	208
		5.1.1 Is Messiah the "End" or the "Goal"?	208
		5.1.2 A Part of the Torah?	214
		5.1.3 Reconstructionism	217
	5.2	The Mosaic Torah and the Messianic Torah	220
		5.2.1 Three Questions	220
		5.2.2 Arnold Fruchtenbaum	226
		5.2.3 David Stern	230
	5.3	Jesus and Messianic Jews Kept the Mosaic Torah	232
		5.3.1 Jesus	232

		5.3.2	The Apostle Paul (1)	239
		5.3.3	The Apostle Paul (2)	246

6 The Messianic Torah and the Millennial Torah … 259

   6.1 The One, Eternal Torah … 260
      6.1.1 In Jesus' Words … 260
      6.1.2 In Paul's Words … 269
      6.1.3 Paul's "Ten Commandments" … 273
   6.2 The Torah in Time … 277
      6.2.1 The Torah in the Messianic Kingdom … 277
      6.2.2 Specific Elements … 280
      6.2.3 The Torah for Messianic Jews Today … 286
   6.3 Only the Written Torah? … 293
      6.3.1 The Origin of the Oral Torah … 293
      6.3.2 Jesus and the Oral Torah … 300
      6.3.3 The Book of Ruth: A Piece of Oral Torah? … 311

7 A Threefold Torah: Differences and Similarities … 315

   7.1 A Threefold Torah … 316
      7.1.1 One Torah, Several Manifestations … 316
      7.1.2 The Mosaic Dispensation … 318
      7.1.3 The Davidic-Solomonic Revival … 324
   7.2 Newer Manifestations … 329
      7.2.1 The Messianic Dispensation … 329
      7.2.2 The Millennial Dispensation … 337
   7.3 Similarities and Differences … 344

	7.3.1	The Mosaic Torah	344
	7.3.2	The Messianic Torah	349
	7.3.3	The Millennial Torah	351
	7.3.4	Immanent Differences	354
7.4	The New Torah-Giver		359
	7.4.1	The Torah Is Jesus	359
	7.4.2	*Logos* and *logoi*	363
	7.4.3	Moses and Jesus (1)	368
	7.4.4	Moses and Jesus (2)	372

8	New Testament Institutions			377
	8.1	New Testament *Halakah*		378
		8.1.1	"Do As You Wish"	378
		8.1.2	Tanakhic Freedom of the Spirit	381
		8.1.3	Rabbinic Reasoning	388
		8.1.4	New *Halakhic* Authority	393
	8.2	The Sacraments		398
		8.2.1	Baptism	398
		8.2.2	The Lord's Supper	402
		8.2.3	Anointing the Sick	405
		8.2.4	Moral and/or Ceremonial	407
	8.3	The Four Commandments for Gentile Jesus-believers		412
		8.3.1	What Are They?	412
		8.3.2	Are They Still Binding? (1) No	415
		8.3.3	Are They Still Binding? (2) Yes	418
		8.3.4	Gentiles Invited to Keep the Mosaic Torah?	421

9	Jewish and Gentile Jesus-Believers		427
	9.1	*Kashrut*	428

	9.1.1	Does It Cause Division Between Messianic Jews and Gentiles?	428
	9.1.2	Should the Messianic Jew Never Deviate from *Kashrut*?	434
	9.1.3	Rabbinic *Kashrut*	440
9.2	Is All Food Kosher Since the Messiah?		442
	9.2.1	Acts 10	442
	9.2.2	Mark 7	444
	9.2.3	Other Scriptures	449
9.3	Is Keeping *Kashrut* "Weakness"?		452
	9.3.1	Romans 14	452
	9.3.2	Colossians 2	455
	9.3.3	Summary of Positions	458
9.4	Concluding Considerations		464
	9.4.1	Once More: Circumcision	464
	9.4.2	Epilogue	471
Appendix I	Is the Church "Spiritual Israel"?		475
1)	Romans 11		475
2)	Ephesians 2		482
3)	Other Scriptures		485
Appendix II	The Torah in First-Century Judaism		491
1)	Covenantal Nomism		491
2)	New Testament Judaism		496
Appendix III	The Sacred Day of the Week 503		
1)	Four Positions		503
2)	Relevant Scriptures		510
Appendix IV	Mosaic and Messianic Ordinances		519

1)	Ordinances Preserving Jewish Identity	521
2)	Ordinances of Universal Significance	523
Bibliography		533
Scripture Index		555
Subject Index		581

Series Preface

BY MEANS OF THIS PREFACE, the editor and publisher of this series wish to help the reader both understand and process the content of these volumes.

The capacities and erudition of Dr. Willem J. Ouweneel need no demonstration or defense from us. His voluminous work and prodigious writing stand as a testimony to his love for the Lord Jesus Christ, God's Word, and God's people.

But these volumes present ideas that will surprise some, anger others, and possibly confuse still others. Both the editor and publisher disagree with some of Dr. Ouweneel's assertions and conclusions, but this is not the place for offering our counter-arguments. That requires an altogether different venue. Nevertheless, discerning readers will legitimately wonder why this editor and publisher invested effort and resources in putting these volumes into print.

At least three reasons justify that investment. Each of them is very sensitive.

The first reason is: *self-examination*. Some of our readers may conclude that, in presenting his exegetical, doctrinal, and historical case, Dr. Ouweneel is "coloring outside the lines" of what they have come to believe. He challenges deeply and firmly held convictions and beliefs, like those associated with Israel, with the law of God, with election and reprobation, with infant baptism, with covenant theology, and with justification. At each point, his challenges call us readers to self-examination, regarding our love for Scripture, for the God of Scripture, and for the Truth revealed and incarnated personally in Jesus Christ. One of Ouweneel's challenges is for us believers in Jesus Christ who are Reformed and Presbyterian church members to recognize that there are millions, even billions, of Jesus-believers who disagree with us *and are nevertheless genuine Christians*. And they ought to be acknowledged as such.

The second reason is: *repentance*. Coming, as they do, from one who lives and teaches outside the orbit of many of our readers, Dr. Ouweneel's observations about the state of our (numerous) churches and of our (interminable) doctrinal squabbles ought to embarrass us Reformed and Presbyterian church members. Our incessant polemicizing, our cantankerous stridency, and our offenses against the unity of Christ's church seriously compromise the gospel's witness to the watching world. Brothers and sisters, we must repent of these, for the sake of the gospel, for the sake of the church's witness, and for the sake of our children.

The third reason is: *ecumenicity*. This reason may indeed strike you as strange, but one of the salutary outcomes of reading Dr. Ouweneel's arguments can be this: *not* that you surrender your commitments and convictions that are being challenged, but instead that you come to *respect* and *love* those Jesus-believers who don't share them with you. These Christians are those whose spiritual pilgrimage and gospel-guided history have not brought them to the same place on the road, but who nonetheless are walking the same road as we.

You may well be asking: How, then, is this different from advocating doctrinal relativism? If these distinctive features of Reformed confession and theology are biblical, then why is Dr. Ouweneel being given a microphone for proclaiming his criticisms and rejections of these distinctive emphases of Reformed teaching? The short answer is this: So that from this brother in Christ, this close cousin in the faith, this fellow pilgrim-soldier, we may learn how to lock arms with other Jesus-believers as we face unbelief in our day, even if we can't hold hands. So that we may learn what it means to be Jesus-believers *first*, Reformed or Presbyterian confessors *second*, and only then, *thirdly, theological advocates*.

So we leave you with this challenge: Why do you believe what you believe? What is your biblical warrant? Dr. Ouweneel presents fairly the various positions prevalent within Christianity. The reader will learn why others believe what they believe, and why they don't emphasize certain teachings in the same way that we do.

These books, then, are *not* for the faint of faith. But they *are* for those wanting to grow up and mature into the unity of faith in our Lord Jesus Christ (John 17:20–23; Eph. 4:13).

Nelson D. Kloosterman, editor
John Hultink, publisher

Author's Preface

PART I OF THIS Eternal Series contains two volumes, both dealing with the Bible as such. The first volume is entitled *The Eternal Word*,[1] and deals with the Bible in general. The present volume is Book 2 of Part I, and deals particularly with the "Torah" (Law) aspect of the Bible. It is a translated and heavily edited and expanded version of my Dutch book *Hoe lief heb ik uw wet!: De Eeuwige Torah tussen Oude en Nieuwe Verbond*, published in 2001 by Uitgeverij Medema, Vaassen (Netherlands). The original title was a quotation from Psalm 119: "How I love your law!" (v. 97). Chapter 3 of this volume, "Torah, Hokmah, Logos, and Spirit," is an addition to that earlier book; it is based upon texts from another Dutch book of mine, *De zevende koningin: Het eeuwig vrouwelijke en de raad van God* (Metahistorical Trilogy, vol. 2), published in 1998 by Uitgeverij Barnabas, Heerenveen (Netherlands).

In connection with several matters that are discussed in the present volume, I refer to volumes that will appear later in this series, especially volume IV/2 on the covenant of God and volume IV/3 on the kingdom of God.

Bible quotations in this work are usually taken from the English Standard Version. When other translations are used,

---

1. Ouweneel (2019b).

this is indicated. Quotations from deuterocanonical books are from the Good News Translation. I have taken the liberty of substituting "Torah" for "law," and "Messiah" for "Christ" in these quotations. I explain in the text why I do this.

Houten (Netherlands), Spring 2019
Willem J. Ouweneel

Abbreviations

Bible Versions

ASV	American Standard Version
CEB	Common English Bible
CEV	Contemporary English Version
ESV	English Standard Version
GNT	Good News Translation
KJV	King James Version
NASB	New American Standard Bible
NET	New English Translation
NIV	New International Version
NKJV	New King James Version
RSV	Revised Standard Version

Introduction

TIME AND AGAIN, Messianic (i.e., Jesus-believing) Jewish scholar David H. Stern has written something like this:

> I am certain that the lack of a correct, clear and relatively complete Messianic Jewish or Gentile Christian theology of the Law is not only a major impediment to Christians' understanding their own faith, but also the greatest barrier to Jewish people's receiving the Gospel. . . . [T]he Church hardly knows what to make of the Torah, or how to fit it together with the New Testament. And if the Church doesn't know, don't expect the Jews to figure it out for them! I believe that Christianity has gone far astray in its dealings with the subject and that the most urgent task of theology today is get right its view of the Law.[1]

"Most urgent" is perhaps an exaggeration (the Kingdom of God and the work of the Holy Spirit are other highly neglected, and thus very urgent, topics). Although I differ from Stern regarding several details, as I will show in this book, for the rest I wholeheartedly agree with him.

Other Messianic Jews have recently expressed similar thoughts. For example, Ariel and D'vorah Berkowitz wrote: "If there is one area of misguided theological thinking for be-

---

1 Stern (2009, 39–40; cf. 1997, 1999, 2007).

lievers, it is the study of Torah."[2] On the back cover of a book by Messianic Jewish scholar David Friedman, we read: "Most Christians are disconnected from the Torah; reading this book will reconnect them. Dr. Friedman makes an excellent case for his premise that *all* the first followers of Messiah were not only Torah-observant, but also desired to spread their love for God's *entire* Word [including the Torah] to the Gentiles to whom they preached."[3]

Gentile Jesus-believers have written similar things; for instance, Ron Moseley, of the American Institute for Advanced Biblical Studies, wrote: "Since the first century, the church, for the most part, has misunderstood the law, which both Jesus and Paul dearly loved and by which they both lived."[4] And Thomas Lancaster, of First Fruits of Zion (a Messianic Jewish ministry), wrote: "After all, the Bible is a thoroughly Jewish book. How we Christians ever hoped to understand the Bible without understanding the Torah and Judaism, I do not know."[5] Many more such testimonies could be adduced.

This book aims to contribute to the rediscovery of the Torah by non-Jewish Jesus-believers. It will endeavor to deal with questions like these: What do non-Jewish Jesus-believers (still) have to do with the Law of Moses, the Torah, as the Hebrew Bible calls it? Do Jesus-believers have to live according to the Torah? For instance: why do most non-Jewish Jesus-believers eat pork, and why do most Jewish Jesus-believers not do this? What does "the" Torah actually mean? Does that phrase always refer to the Law of Moses? Is "the Law of Christ," of which the apostle Paul speaks (1 Cor. 9:21; Gal. 6:2), identical with the Law of Moses, or is it a different Law? If it is a different Law, how can there be more Torahs

---

2. Berkowitz (2012, xxi).
3. Friedman (2001; also cf. 2012).
4. Moseley (1998, 39).
5. Lancaster (2011, 9).

than the one and only, eternal Torah of God? If it is the same Law, how can non-Jewish Jesus-believers be under the Law of Christ without being obliged to keep all the commandments of the Law of Moses? In other words: have the Old Covenant and the Law of Moses been abolished, entirely or partly, as many theologians claim? Or have they *not* been abolished, as many others claim? How can there be such entirely opposite positions with respect to such a vital question—a question of great practical significance, since it has everything to do with our daily Christian life? What are the consequences of these contradictory viewpoints?

In this book, I defend the position that in fact both views that I have just mentioned fail in certain important respects. I will try to adduce detailed arguments for the thesis that there *is* only one Torah, the one, eternal Torah of God. However, I do believe that this one Torah has manifested itself, and will manifest itself, in various forms: as the *Mosaic* Torah, as the *Messianic* Torah (including the New Testament commands), and as the *Millennial* Torah. Let me hasten to add that, in fact, these are all three forms of the *Messianic* Torah. First, the Mosaic Torah was given in view of the coming Messiah. When it is said, "the LORD became king in Jeshurun [i.e., Israel]," this was in view of the anointed King that one day would arrive: "Shiloh . . . to Him shall be the obedience of the people" (Gen. 49:10 NKJV). Second, of the Millennial Torah it is said: "the coastlands wait for his law" (Isa. 2:4), that is, "his [i.e., Messiah's] Torah."

In a sense, we might even speak of a Torah of Adam, of Noah and of Abraham, that is, the Adamic Torah, the Noahic Torah, and the Abrahamic Torah (see Gen. 26:5, where God says, "Abraham kept my laws [*torot*, plural of *torah*]." Strictly speaking, none of all these forms of Torah is *the* Torah; they are authentic forms (manifestations) of *the* eternal Torah. This will all be explained in this book.

One peculiar aspect of the one eternal Torah is that it is

directly related with, and in a certain sense identical with, the Wisdom (*Hokmah*) of Proverbs 8 and the Word (*Logos*) of John 1 (see chapter 3). In this sense, the Torah was embodied in the person of Jesus Messiah himself, the Son of God. In a hidden form, it was he who was already present in the Adamic, the Noahic, the Abrahamic, and the Mosaic Torah. In a manifest form, he presents himself in his own New Testament Torah, and one day he will manifest himself in the Millennial Torah. This means concretely that keeping the Torah is the same as reflecting Jesus in our lives. True obedience to God's Torah is never an outward matter of legalism or traditionalism—as all true believers have always known—but essentially means living the life of Jesus Messiah that is within us. All of this will be discussed in detail.

Although in some other respects, the Mosaic form of the one eternal Torah has *not* been abolished, I hope to show that the non-Jewish part of the church, the Body of the Messiah, is not under the Mosaic Torah. However, the apostle Paul and the other Messianic Jews in the early Jesus-believing community, living in the light of the great future of the Messianic Kingdom, consistently kept many, if not almost all, Mosaic commandments. They had good reasons for doing so. At any rate, their keeping the Torah formed a bridge to the new Millennial Torah, which to a great extent—but not entirely—will coincide with the Mosaic Torah. Their keeping the Torah was not obligatory, as it had been for the immature child that is under the commands of his father and has to be checked by a supervisor (cf. Gal. 3:19-4:7). Nor was it weakness, or even sin, or a concession to their Jewish kinfolk. It was the "freedom in the Messiah" (Gal. 2:4), the self-evident consequence of their being Jewish, the consciousness of the fact that accepting Jesus as the Messiah made them even more Jewish than they had been. Keeping the Torah by the early Messianic Jews involved their living both in the light of God's earlier revelations, the Mosaic Covenant in particular, and in the light of the New Covenant.

Introduction

With respect to the place of Israel, there is no cleft between the Old Covenant as it was, and the New Covenant as it will be. In both Old and New Covenants, Israel is still God's covenantal people, even though in the present time, the name *Lo-Ammi* ("Not-My-People") is written above the nation as a whole (Hos. 1:9). Yet, they "are Israelites, and to them belong [not, belonged!] the adoption, the glory, the covenants, the giving of the Torah, the worship, and the promises" (Rom. 9:4). Messianic Jews now belong to the Body of the Messiah, together with the Gentile Jesus-believers; but they have never stopped being Jews. Between the Shabbat, the festivals, circumcision, and the purity laws of the Old Covenant, on the one hand, and the Shabbat, the festivals, circumcision, and the purity laws of the coming Millennium on the other hand, Jewish Jesus-believers today continue to observe Shabbat, the festivals, circumcision, and the purity laws.

The "last days" are the days just before and at the coming of the Messiah (Gen. 49:1; Isa. 2:2; Micah 4:1; 2 Tim. 3:1; James 5:3). It is one of the great divine miracles of these "last days" that a Messianic Jewish movement has appeared that lives out of this reality in a very new way. When I wrote about this movement back around 2000, it was estimated to comprise some 100,000 to 300,000 people, and a few hundred congregations. Today there seem to be over five hundred congregations worldwide, with over a hundred in Israel. There are more than 250,000 members in the United States alone, and perhaps 10,000 to 15,000 in Israel. Only some forty years ago, there were just a handful of Messianic congregations worldwide. However, especially after the conquest of old Jerusalem in 1967, hundreds of Jews came to believe in Jesus as their Messiah. The total number of Messianic Jews still encompasses at best a few percent of international Jewry, but in absolute numbers they constitute by far the majority of Jesus-believing Jews since the first century AD.[6] Since the fall of Communism

---

6. Of course, I am referring here to those Jews who have voluntarily

in the former Soviet Union (1989), many thousands of Jews have come to faith in Jesus. Also, hundreds of Jews from the former Soviet Union, who have made *aliyah* to Israel,[7] have found their Messiah in that land.

Non-Jewish Jesus-believers may rejoice in this development. At the same time, they have to determine what must be their personal attitude toward it. They have never been under the Mosaic Torah. And if current premillennialism—the belief that Jesus will return on the clouds of heaven before the Messianic Kingdom of glory and majesty—is right, they will never be under the Millennial Torah. This is because during the Millennial Kingdom they will be with Jesus in heavenly glory. It is from that *heavenly* side that they will share in the Messianic world empire of *earthly* peace and justice. They are not placed on that uninterrupted line between the Old and the New Covenant, as are their Jewish brothers and sisters.

The Messianic Jews today are part of the Messianic Community—confusingly called the church—in which Jews and non-Jews have been brought together on an equal footing (Eph. 2:11-22). (I will avoid the term "church" because of its negative associations with Gentile religious organizations that are usually foreign to the Jews). At the same time, they are, and remain, part of the nation that was God's covenantal people in the Tanakh (that name by which Jewish Jesus-believers call the Old Testament), and will be God's covenantal people in the Millennium.

This is not the case with non-Jewish Jesus-believers. Formally speaking, the New Covenant is established not even with them, but with the twelve tribes of Israel, as we are explicitly told in Jeremiah 31:31-34 and Hebrews 8:8, 10 (see the next volume in this trilogy). They have been grafted into the tree that is rooted in Israel's patriarchal blessings (see Ap-

---

accepted Jesus as their Messiah and Savior, *not* to those who in the past were forced by Roman Catholic kings to become "Christians."

7. The term *aliyah* (lit., "going up") means immigration to Israel.

pendix I); they are spiritual sons and heirs of Abraham (Rom. 4:11, 16; 11:16–24; Gal. 3:7, 29; 4:28); they live under the blessings of the New Covenant (Luke 22:20; 2 Cor. 3:6). However, they have no decisive reasons to keep commandments that belong to the Mosaic Torah or to the Millennial Torah, *but are obligated to keep commandments that belong to the Messianic Torah*. They are under the commands of the New Testament, numbering more than one thousand, but the great majority of non-Jewish Jesus-believers do not observe Shabbat and the festivals, the law of circumcision, and the purity laws — and I do not believe that they should.

I have written this book to explain in more detail what, in my view, Scripture teaches on all these subjects. Some readers will not (entirely) appreciate my views. Covenantal theologians will discover that I am more on the side of dispensational theology than on theirs. Dispensational theologians will discover that I see more continuity between the Tanakh, the New Testament, and the Millennial dispensations than some of them hold to be correct. And Messianic Jews, at least those who feel that non-Jewish Jesus-believers should get to know the blessings of the *entire* Mosaic Torah and should learn to keep it — voluntarily or because it is their alleged duty — will not be satisfied either. But give me a chance to adduce arguments for the views that I have just alluded to.

In this book, I will avoid the term "Law" because of its legal — if not legalistic — connotations, and the theological one-sidedness usually resulting from it. Therefore, I will nearly always use the term "Torah" (lit., "instruction").

In these chapters, I will refer to Rabbinic Judaism, to Kabbalists, and to liberal Christian theologians. Let me state at the outset that I wholeheartedly disagree with the anti-Jesus attitude of the Jews mentioned, and the anti-revelation attitude of liberal Christians. However, I do agree with the words of Rabbi Simeon ben Zoma (second century AD): "Who is he that is wise? He who learns from every man, as it is said: 'From all who taught me have I gained understanding'" (an unusual rendering of Ps. 119:99).[8] Therefore, I will quote religious authorities with whose theological paradigms I do not agree. I have learned from all of them, just as the apostle Paul had learned from the pagan authors Aratus or Cleanthes (Acts 17:28), Menander (1 Cor. 15:33), and Epimenides (Titus 1:12) without in the least supporting their worldviews.

---

8. Mishnah, Avot 4:1.

Chapter 1
What Is the Torah?

The mouth of the righteous utters wisdom,
 and his tongue speaks justice.
The Torah of his God is in his heart;
 his steps do not slip.
Psalm 37:30–31

Bear one another's burdens,
 and so fulfill the Torah of Messiah.
Galatians 6:2

Summary: *In this book, we are investigating the relationship between Jesus-believers and the Law (the Torah). To that end, we first must know exactly what we mean by the Torah. In the Tanakh, this refers (usually) to the Torah of Moses, but at the same time we learn there that the Torah is much more than just a list of commandments. The Torah is the revelation of God himself, including fatherly, loving instruction to his people. The New Testament, too, speaks extensively of that Torah, but especially with Paul, seemingly in a rather ambiguous way. On the one hand, very negatively: Jesus-believers have been "released from the Torah," and they should rejoice about that. On the other hand, Jesus-believers are now under the "Torah of Christ," and they should rejoice about this as well. The apparent contradiction between these two statements is an important theme in this book.*

1.1 Jesus-believers and the Torah
1.1.1 Pork or Not?

THIS BOOK DEALS WITH the Law—the Torah—and with whether Jesus-believers must keep the Torah. To put it in a simple question: if you are a Jesus-believer, why do you or do you not eat pork? Aside from whether you like pork or not, some of the answers to this question could be:

(1) I eat pork because I am not under the Mosaic Torah—although I *am* under the Messianic Torah, which is something very different. This is the answer that some Evangelical Jesus-believers (more specifically: dispensationalist Jesus-believers) might give.

(2) I eat pork because I admittedly am under the Torah of Moses but only under the moral part of it (which I consider to be identical with the Torah of Christ). This is the answer that many Reformational Jesus-believers (more specifically: covenant-theological or federalist Jesus-believers) might give.

(3) I do not eat pork because I am under the entire Torah of Moses (which I consider to be identical with the Torah of Christ). This is the answer of Seventh-day Adventists, and (for different reasons) of Messianic Jews (Jews who accept Jesus as their Messiah and Savior but retain their Jewish identity), and some non-Jewish Jesus-believers, who sometimes refer to themselves as "Messianic Gentiles."[1]

In the present study, I will argue that to a certain extent all three answers are wrong, or at least inaccurate. Regarding answer (1): the Torah of Moses and the Torah of Christ (Gal. 6:2) are *not* two very different things, because there can basically be only one divine Torah. Regarding answers (2) and (3): the (non-Jewish) Jesus-believer is *not* under the Torah of Moses (in the strict sense of this expression), nor under a part of it. Before Jesus came to earth, Gentiles were never, formal-

---

1. For a presentation of the latter view, see Lancaster (2011).

What is the Torah?

ly or informally, placed under the Mosaic Torah, unless they joined Israel. Gentile Jesus-believers are under the Torah of the Messiah. In their *essence*, these two Torahs, or more accurately, these two manifestations of the one Torah of God, are identical; in their concrete, practical *realization* they are certainly not identical.

Allow me some terminological remarks at this point. I sometimes use the word "Christian" even though I know that Messianic Jews reject this term for historical reasons. That is, they do not want to be associated with the established Christian church, or churches, which in the past persecuted the Jews so fiercely. As Messianic Jew Michael Schiffman put it, "To Jewish people, Christians are the people who have hated and persecuted Jews for two millennia."[2]

I fully understand this. Yet, I remind my Messianic friends of the fact that several times in the New Testament, the people who believed in Jesus of Nazareth as the Messiah of Israel, as their Savior through his atoning work on Calvary, and as the Lord of their hearts and lives, were called "Christians" (Greek *Christianoi*), especially with the latter meaning of people following Jesus as Lord (Acts 11:26). A "Christian" is a follower of "Christ" (i.e., Messiah, Anointed), that is, someone who believes, first and foremost, that Jesus is the Messiah, the anointed King of Israel.

In Acts 26:28, King Agrippa, who through his mother Cypros (a descendant of the Hasmonean high priest Hyrcanus II) was Jewish, complained that the apostle Paul wanted to make him a "Christian," that is, someone who had to believe that Jesus was the Jewish Messiah, and who had to follow him. In 1 Peter 4:16, the apostle Peter discusses the case of some of his readers who as "Christians," that is, as followers of Israel's Messiah, would have to suffer. This reference is important because Peter addresses his Letter to "the elect ex-

---

2.. Schiffman (1996, 5).

iles of the Dispersion," which many take to refer to Messianic Jews.³ This would mean that in two of the three Scriptures where the word "Christian" occurs, Jewish fellow-believers are at least included. Thus, "Christians" are *all* believers in Jesus as Messiah, Savior, and Lord. Yet, I will usually substitute the word "Jesus-believers" for "Christians" (more on this in §1.1.3).

The same Messianic sensitivity exists with respect to the name "Jesus." My Messianic friends prefer the name Yeshuah (emphasis on the second syllable); as one of them told me: "In the name of Jesus, my family in Eastern Europe was persecuted or killed; in the name of Yeshuah I found eternal salvation." Again, I fully understand this, and when I preach among them I also use the name *Yeshuah*. Yet, in the Greek New Testament, Christ is not called *Yeshuah* but *Iēsous*, which in the Vulgate has become *Jesus*. It is this way with many other names: Hebrew *Shaul*, Greek *Saulos*, English *Saul*; Hebrew *Jochanan*, Greek *Iōannēs*, English *John*. Please note in this context:

(1) There is hardly any evidence for the speculation that the New Testament was originally written in Aramaic, as is asserted, for instance, by Andrew Gabriel Roth.⁴ The great majority of scholars is convinced that the New Testament was originally written in Greek. No wonder: most Jesus-believers addressed in the New Testament Epistles would not have understood Aramaic in the first place. The same holds for the Gospels that were mainly addressed to a non-Jewish audience (Mark to the Romans, Luke to the Greek Theophilus).

(2) The Greek name *Iēsous* was not invented by the New Testament authors—or by the supposed translators of the alleged "Aramaic original"—but derived from the Septuagint,

---

3. Of course, 1 Pet. 4:3–4 suggests that a considerable number of the addressees had been pagans.
4. Roth (2012).

the Greek translation of the Tanakh, made by Alexandrian Jews (third/second century BC).[5] It is the Greek rendering of the name Joshua, referring to the successor of Moses. "Joshua" (Heb. *Yehoshuah*) has the same meaning as "Jesus" (*Yeshuah*). In Hebrews 4:8, "Joshua" is in Greek *Iēsous*.

I understand the sensitivity of our Messianic brothers and sisters (see further in §1.1.3), but they will forgive me if I use the far more familiar names Jesus, Paul, John, etc.

1.1.2 Who Is a Jew?

Explaining exactly who is a Christian is less easy than people might expect, especially if one considers the fact that many Messianic Jews do not like the term "Christian" (see §§1.1.1 and 1.1.3). But perhaps answering the question who is a Jew is even more complicated.[6] Rabbinic Judaism considers a person to be a Jew if he is circumcised, if he/she is born of a Jewish mother, and is not a convert to another religion, *or* if a person of non-Jewish descent has converted to Judaism through the *mikveh* (ritual water immersion) and circumcision (if male). One reason why, in the case of an ethnic Jew, the Jewishness of the mother and not that of the father is decisive is that in Ezra's time, Jewish men had to send away their non-Jewish wives as well as the children born of them (Ezra 10). From this, the rabbis concluded that children of Jewish fathers and non-Jewish mothers are not Jewish.

The text does not say that, however. On the contrary, we have much evidence that children of Jewish fathers and non-Jewish mothers, when adopted into and raised in Israel, were considered to be Jewish. At the time, no one would have doubted that the sons Gershom and Eliezer whom Moses had fathered by his Midianite wife Zipporah (Exod. 2:21–22; 4:25;

---

5. Messianic Jewess Welker (2013, 7, 27) seems to be completely ignorant of this fact.
6. See Juster (1995, 191–93); Stern (1997, 16–18).

18:2-4; Judg. 18:30; 1 Chron. 23:15-17; 26:24), or the son Obed whom Boaz fathered through his Moabite wife Ruth, were Jewish (Ruth 4:17-22; 1 Chron. 2:12-17). If it would be argued that Zipporah and Ruth converted to Judaism, this certainly was not the case with Jezebel and her daughter, Athaliah. These women were married to Jewish kings, and Athaliah's son Ahaziah and grandson Joash became kings of Judah on the throne of David (1 Kings 16:31; 2 Kings 8:25-26; 11; 12). Apparently, a child of a Jewish father and a non-Jewish mother was equally considered to be Jewish, if such a child had been circumcised (were he male) and adopted a Jewish identity.

This is in fact the view of most Jewish people. Only Orthodox Jews and most Conservative Jews hold to Jewishness through the mother. The Reform Jews as well as the Messianic Jews will accept as Jews children from either a Jewish father or a Jewish mother. Since most Jewish people in the world are not Orthodox, this means that a good portion of today's Jewish people believe that a person is considered Jewish if born of either a Jewish father or mother.

Confessing to a Jewish identity normally includes circumcising one's sons, keeping Shabbat and the Jewish festivals, observing the Jewish *kashrut* (food laws)[7] and other Mosaic ordinances as far as they can be kept in post-Temple times. In practice, however, particularly in the present state of Israel, many Jews do confess to a Jewish identity — "I am a Jew" — whose adherence to Jewish religious tradition is minimal. It is certainly true that being a Jew is not just an ethnic or racial matter; it is also a religious matter, for people can convert to Judaism through the *mikveh* and circumcision. However, it is equally true that being a Jew is not just a religious matter. The Zionist claim to Palestine is based on the notion that this was

---

7. *Kashrut* is related to *kasher* (Ashkenazi pronunciation: *kosher*), "fit," namely, fit for consumption according to the biblical food laws (Lev. 11; Deut. 14).

the land "of our fathers" (an ethnic concept), which is perfectly biblical: "He will bring you to the land that belonged to your fathers" (Deut. 30:5). Micah 7:20 says of God fulfilling his promises in the latter days: "You will show faithfulness to Jacob and steadfast love to Abraham, as you have sworn to our fathers from the days of old."

"Ethnic" is not to be taken in too strict a sense of common biological descent; many Jewish people have the blood of many other nations coursing through their veins. But it does imply a "nation" that can refer to the patriarchs as its "fathers," and do so not only in some spiritual sense. If Jews do not walk in Abraham's faith, they are not "children of the promise," that is, not "true" children of his; but they *are* "children of the flesh," that is, Abraham's physical descendants (Rom. 9:6–8; cf. John 8:37–40, "offspring," not "children"). On the one hand, the Gentile person going through *mikveh* and circumcision (if male) becomes a Jew in the full sense of the word. On the other hand, even if a person has, say, only one Jewish grandparent but is circumcised (if male) and identifies himself or herself with the Jewish people, that person is a Jew.

1.1.3 Are Messianic Jews Christians?

Messianic Jew David Stern believes that "Kefa [i.e., Peter] directs his Letter primarily to Jewish believers (including Jewish proselytes who later accepted Yeshua), since he was 'an emissary to the Circumcised' (Ga 2:7–8)."[8] Surprisingly, Stern asserts elsewhere that "the term 'Christian,' which appears only three times, apparently denotes being a Gentile believer in Jesus; if this is so, 'Jewish Christian' is a contradiction in terms."[9] Although we understand the historical objections that many Messianic Jews have against the term "Christian," it is obvious that in the New Testament the term *Christianos*

---

8. Stern (1999, 743; cf. 1997, 34). But cf. note 2.
9. Stern (1997, 18; cf. 31–34). He himself (1999, 315) reminds us of the fact that Agrippa was Jewish!

includes both Jesus-believing Jews and Jesus-believing Gentiles (see §1.1.1).

The way Stern tries to circumvent this apparent contradiction is by stating, "We do not learn that Jewish believers are to call themselves Christians, nor do we learn that Gentile believers are to call Jewish believers Christians."[10] But then, we do not learn that *Gentile* believers are to call *themselves* Christians either, or that any believer is to call himself anything. Therefore, according to the practice of many centuries beginning in the New Testament itself, we may call all believers in Jesus, Jew or Gentile, "Christians," which means literally, "followers of the Anointed one (Messiah)." Moreover, the term "Messianic" is not entirely satisfactory because any Jew expecting some sort of Messiah could call himself "Messianic," even if he was not sure if Jesus was that Messiah.

To the Jews, not only terms like Christian and church, as well as the name "Jesus," but also terms like apostle, baptism, cross, etc., are associated with many centuries of persecution. No wonder that David Stern, in his *Jewish New Testament*, preferred to replace such terms by the following terms respectively: Messianic, (Messianic) Community (*qehillah*), Yeshuah, emissary (*shaliach*), immersion (*tevilah*), execution-stake (*tzalav*).[11] Culturally, the term "Christian" is associated with people going to church and celebrating Christmas and Easter—and (in the eyes of many Jews) worshipping some "Christian God"—and not exactly with people going to (Messianic) synagogues and celebrating *Pesach* (Passover), *Yom Kippur* (the Great Atonement Day) and *Sukkot* (the Feast of Tabernacles).[12] This is why I will not refer to Messianic Jews as "Christians." Theologically there would be no objection, but historically, culturally, and emotionally there is every objection.

---

10. Stern (1997, 34).
11. Stern (1989, xix); I have added the Hebrew terms.
12. Berkowitz (1999, 7).

What is the Torah?

The existence of the Messianic Jewish movement is one principal reason for writing this book. For almost two centuries, two theological paradigms have been competing, in which the issue of the Torah played a conspicuous role, as we will see. Today, a third view of the Torah has joined the discussion. To put it briefly: are we bound to keep the Mosaic Torah, that is to say, only its essential (moral) part? This is the view of many covenant theologians. Or are we not bound to keep the Mosaic Torah at all, though bound to keep the Torah of the Messiah, which is something very different? This is the view of many dispensationalist theologians. Today we have a third view, that of a number of Messianic theologians: Jesus-believers, who are to be obedient to Messiah, find the pattern for this obedience in the entire Mosaic Torah (allegedly with a number of exceptions indicated in Scripture itself.). In this view, Gentile Jesus-believers are either considered to be subject to the entire Mosaic Torah, too, or are considered not to be subject, though they are often invited to keep the Mosaic Torah on a voluntary basis. We will investigate this further in §1.2.3.

In passing, I note that even the term "New Testament" may offend some people because it was invented as counterpart of the "Old Testament," a term found in 2 Corinthians 3:14 (the phrase is actually "old covenant"). I like the suggestion by Ariel and D'vorah Berkowitz, to speak not of two parts of the Bible but of seven parts.[13] I list them here, and add their Hebrew names:

(1) The *Torah* (Greek: *Pentateuch*, Gen.–Deut.).

(2) The *Nebiim*: the Prophets (early prophets: Josh., Judg., 1–2 Sam., 1–2 Kings; late prophets: Isa., Jer., Ezek., the twelve Minor Prophets).

(3) The *Ketubim*: the Writings (Ps., Job, Prov.; the five *me-*

---

13. Berkowitz (2012, 26–28).

gillot: Dan., Ezra/Neh., 1–2 Chron.).

(4) The *Beshorot*: the Gospels (Matt.–John).

(5) *Ma'asey haShelichim* (Acts of the Apostles).

(6) The *Iggerot*: the Letters (Rom.–Jude).

(7) The *Chazon* or *Hitgallut* (the Revelation of John)

The first three are abbreviated: T-N-K(h), yielding the well-known acronym Tanakh. Similarly, the last four are abbreviated: B-M-I-Ch, from which the acronym Bamich might be derived; together: Tanakhbamich (although I do not think that this term will become very popular).

1.2 The Messianic Jewish Movement

1.2.1 The Ancient Messianic Jewish Movement

What exactly is the Messianic movement? It is as ancient as the earliest church history, and very recent at the same time. All the first believers in Jesus were Messianic Jews; or they were proselytes, that is, people who, before they had heard the Christian message, had already joined Israel through circumcision (if male) and the *mikveh* (sacred immersion), but these were counted as Jews too. "Proselyte" (Gr. *prosēlytos*) is a New Testament term (Matt. 23:15; Acts 2:11; 6:5; 13:43); presumably, Luke was a proselyte. Even the first Gentiles to be converted to Jesus had belonged formerly to a group already attached to Judaism *without* having undergone circumcision and proselyte baptism (and thus to be distinguished from proselytes): the so-called "God-fearers" (Acts 10:2, 22, 35; 13:16, 26).[14] The early Jesus-believers were called people "who belonged to the Way" (9:2), or "followers of this Way" (22:4), or "the Nazarene sect" (24:5) because they were followers of "Jesus (Messiah) of Nazareth" (2:22; 3:6; 4:10; 6:14; 10:38; 22:8; 26:9.).[15] In Acts 21:20, we hear of literally "many *tens of* thou-

---

14. Gr. *phoboumenos* (or *-noi*) *ton theon*; also see the synonym *sebomenoi* in Acts 13:50; 16:14; 17:4, 17; and 18:7.

15. Regarding their history, see Eusebius (*Ecclesiastical History*, II, 23);

sands of Jews" who had believed,[16] who must have formed a considerable percentage of Judeans at that time. Their leader was James (Jacob, Ya'aqov), "the Lord's brother" (Gal. 1:19), who was well respected by the Jews, but suffered martyrdom in AD 62.[17]

The important thing to note is that these Messianic Jews were never considered by non-Messianic Jews as people that had changed their religion. They were Jews like all the others, and behaved like the other Jews; they were different simply because they believed that Jesus was the Messiah. In this regard they were not conspicuous, because variety within Jewish religion at that time was enormous. Within the scope of the New Testament, think of the Pharisees, the Sadducees, the Zealots, the Herodians, and outside the New Testament, the Essenes.

During the Jewish War (AD 66–70), Messianic Jews remembered the words of Jesus (Luke 21:20–24), and most of them left Jerusalem in time. They fled to the city of Pella across the Jordan, where they perpetuated both their Messianic faith and their Jewish way of life. After AD 70, the Messianic Jews returned to Jerusalem. The destruction of the city in that year had changed the religious situation, though. Just like all other Jews, Messianic Jews could not serve God in the Temple anymore. Variety disappeared; Pharisaic Judaism turned out to be the only school that could maintain itself. The synagogue replaced the Temple, prayers and study of the Torah replaced the sacrifices.

Messianic Jews could not accept this form of official Juda-

Schonfield (1936); Brandon (1957); Klijn and Reinink (1973); Jocz (1979); Rausch (1982); Fruchtenbaum (1993); Pritz (1988); Schiffman (1996, 9–35); and Stern (1997, 49–54, 74–76).

16. It is strange that the ASV, ESV, NIV, and other translations render *myriades* ("tens of thousands") as "thousands," as if they want to belittle the number of believers at the time.
17. Flavius Josephus, *Antiquities*, IX, 1.

ism, which had no room for Jesus the Messiah and his true sacrifice. Heated controversies arose between Messianic and rabbinic Jewry. The rivalry intensified during the Bar Kokhba revolt against the Romans (AD 132–135). At the outset, the Messianic Jews joined this national liberation movement until Rabbi Aqiva declared Bar Kokhba to be the Messiah. Consequently, the Messianic Jews had to withdraw from the revolt, though being accused of desertion and treason for doing so. Many of them were subsequently executed for this alleged treason.

After the revolt had been quashed, the Roman emperor Hadrian forbade all Jews from living in Jerusalem. Messianic Judaism declined, but especially in Syria it survived into the fifth century. In the meantime, the Gentile church developed into a powerful institution, declaring itself to be the sole custodian of salvation. The more Gentile the church became, the more Messianic Jews, who in fact had constituted the early church, were regarded as heretics. Some of the early Messianic Jews indeed held dissentient teachings, particularly with regard to the virgin birth of Jesus and the canonicity of Paul's Epistles (Ebionites, Elkesaites); others did not. Eventually, however, even living in a Jewish manner was considered heretical by the Gentile church. Believers outside the catholic (i.e., universal, worldwide) church were urged, or even forced, especially after the Nicean Council (AD 325), to join this church in order to receive salvation.

Rabbinic Jews said that if you wanted to be a Jew you could not believe in Jesus. The church said that if you wanted to believe in Jesus, you could not live the Jewish way. Consequently, Messianic Jews, that is, Jews who wished to retain their Jewish identity, were cast out both by the Jewish community and by the official church. From the fourth century onward, Jews who came to believe in Jesus as their Messiah and Savior either kept silent and remained within the non-Messianic Jewish community, or joined the church and thereby forfeited their entire Jewish identity. Only a few continued to form

What is the Torah?

small Messianic communities, dwindling as time went by. Some of them died as martyrs under the hands of either the Hellenic church or Rabbinic Judaism. They were squeezed between two powerful religions, until they vanished.

Things got worse when the church developed the disastrous theory that it alone was the true Israel. Already Justin Martyr taught this around AD 140. Consequently, the church became increasingly irritated by the fact that, outside this church there was a nation that kept claiming to be Israel. This anti-Jewish sentiment induced the church to separate from its Jewish roots as much as possible. Notorious examples are Constantine's Sunday Law of AD 321,[18] and the new date of Easter established by the Council of Nicea (325) in order to distinguish it from Jewish Pesach. This anti-Jewish sentiment also turned against the Jewish life-style of Messianic believers. If they claimed to be Christians, they ought to join the Christian church and renounce behaving like Jews. They officially had to give up even the slightest relic of Jewish practices and beliefs. One reason for this attitude appears to have been that, particularly after the Bar Kokhba revolt, when anti-Jewish sentiment ran high in the Roman Empire, the early church fathers made a concerted effort to erase in the official Roman minds all connections to their Jewish roots. If they were to be persecuted (second and third centuries), then it ought to be for believing in Jesus, not for being a Jewish sect. So if Jews wanted to join the Christian movement, they themselves had to abandon all associations with Israel.

Of course, Messianic Jews sometimes committed similar, though opposite, errors. Justin Martyr still "knew of Jews who believed in Christ and who kept the law without insisting that all Jesus-believers should. But he also knew others who not only kept the law themselves, but who also compelled Gentile believers to keep it too."[19] The fact that many Messianic Jews

---

18. See Appendix III on the matter of Shabbat and Sunday.
19. Dunn (1990a, 240).

held tenaciously to the Mosaic Torah was usually not a matter of traditionalism or stubbornness, legalism or ethnocentrism, but of honest conviction. However, there were exceptions, which ruined the reputation of Messianic Jews. This is one of the tragic aspects of church history, continuing until today: on the one hand, Messianic Jews imposing the Mosaic Torah, and even rabbinic traditions, on Gentile Jesus-believers, while on the other hand, the latter imposing their Hellenistic Christianity on the former.[20] Even where Messianic Jews did not press the Mosaic Torah upon Gentile Jesus-believers, eventually a deep cleft developed between the two groups. And because Messianic Jews generally did not accept, or did not fully accept, the oral Torah[21] — the rabbinic traditions — as formally binding, a similar cleft developed between them and Orthodox Judaism.

Pritz made this point, which is central to our investigation: "Just as [the Messianic Jews] rejected the Church's setting aside of the Law of Moses, so they refused the rabbis' expansive interpretations of it."[22] They had fallen between both the Christian church and Rabbinic Judaism, and hardly had an opportunity to develop their own Torah-keeping lifestyle. They were called heretics by both sides; in the Talmud, the terms *minut* ("sectarianism, heresy") and *min(im)* ("sectari-

---

20. Hellenism was the culture and philosophy of the former Greek Empire, still dominating the later Roman Empire. Many early Gentile-Christian dogmas and customs were influenced by Hellenism, although views vary widely regarding how significant this influence was.
21. *Torah sheb'al peh* (*peh* = "mouth"), distinguished from the *Torah shebiktav* (from *k-t-v* = "to write"), the written Torah. According to Maimonides (*Mishneh Torah*), in Exod. 24:12 ("I give you ... the Torah and the *mitzvah*"), Torah is the written Torah, and *mitzvah* is the oral Torah; see, however, Berkowitz (2012, 93).
22. Pritz (1988, 110).

an, heretic") often refer to Messianic Jews.[23] Likewise, many Jesus-believers today, even so-called Hebrew Christians,[24] consider them heretics or sectarians. After everything the church did to Jews in general, also to Messianic Jews, even today many Gentile Jesus-believers are not prepared to at least listen to the views of Messianic Jews—who nevertheless live roughly the way Jesus, and all the apostles, and all the early Jesus-believers lived (see §5.3).

Notice, for instance, the implication in New Testament scholar James Dunn's words: "[H]eretical Jewish Christianity[25] would appear to be not so very different from the faith of the first Jewish believers. . . . [T]he heretical Jewish Christianity of the later centuries could quite properly claim to be more truly the heir of earliest Christianity than any other expression of Christianity."[26] Dunn blames the Ebionites

> because in a developing situation where Christianity had to develop and change . . . its faith did not develop as Christianity developed. It clung to an expression of Christian faith which was acceptable at the beginning of Christianity in a context of Judaism. In the wider environment of the second and third centuries, with the formative documents of Christianity already written, the simple Jewish messianism was no longer adequate. In short, heretical Jewish Christianity was a form of stunted, underdeveloped Christianity, rigid and unfitted to be the mouthpiece

---

23. See, e.g., Berakhot 12a; Sukkah 48b; Sanhedrin 58b, 90b, 99a; 'Avodah Zarah 4a, 4b, 16b, 27b.
24. In this study, the phrase "Hebrew Christians" refers to Christians of Jewish descent who do not practice a Jewish lifestyle.
25. Dunn (1990a, 242–44), refers particularly to the Ebionites, who adhered to the Mosaic Torah, were loyal to James, the brother of Jesus, rather than to Paul, denied the virgin birth of Jesus, and believed in adoptionism (Jesus was adopted as the Messiah and the Son of God at his baptism).
26. Ibid., 242, 244.

of the gospel in a new age.[27]

Of course, Messianic Jews must take into account the full New Testament revelation as we have known it since the closing of the New Testament canon. They would be wise to listen carefully to nineteen centuries of Christian theological thinking (without swallowing all that has been alleged, especially all that has been alleged against the Jews). Yet I believe the views of Messianic Jews are still as valid as they were in the time of the apostles. Might one not safely infer from Dunn's words that he would call present day Messianic Jewry something like an ahistorical return to the primitive past of Christianity? In such a view, the historical development of Christian theology and the Christian church has become *de facto* more important than New Testament thinking. (This is a development similar to that of Rabbinic Judaism, by the way, whose decrees have become *de facto* more important than the Torah as such.) It is one of the aims of the present study to investigate the claims of both the various schools of Messianic Judaism and the various schools of Gentile Christian theology with regard to the Torah.

1.2.2 The Present Messianic Jewish Movement

Throughout the centuries, there has been quite a number of Jewish believers within the church, initially in the Roman Catholic and the Orthodox Churches, later in Protestant churches as well. Most of them had lost contact with Messianic Jewish conviction, that is, they did not live according to the Mosaic Torah anymore. Of course, I am referring to such living not as a way of obtaining salvation but as a consequence of believing in Jesus and his work of atonement, as a matter

---

27. Ibid., 244–45. But note as well: "It is however also possible to draw a firm line of distinction between the Jewish Christianity of the NT and the Jewish Christianity deemed heretical by the great Church in later centuries"—but then *only* "in the assessment of Jesus." (262). The two groups are distinguished more clearly by Bagatti (1971).

What is the Torah?

of faithful obedience to him through the Torah as Jews had always known it. Such Messianic Judaism scarcely existed from the fifth to the nineteenth centuries. However, this fact does not invalidate it. It has never been dead, although it was severely suppressed throughout those centuries. One may safely say that throughout these centuries, there have been far more "converted" Jews, such as the Marranos,[28] who in their hearts *rejected* the faith in Jesus, secretly holding to the Mosaic Torah, than Messianic Jews who truly believed in Jesus as their Messiah and Savior and secretly held to the Mosaic Torah.

It was not until the nineteenth century that Messianic Jewish consciousness awoke again. The following twenty-five men were influential nineteenth-century Hebrew Christians:

(1) *Joseph S. C. F. Frey* (1771–1850, born Joseph Levi), a German Messianic Jew, founded in London in 1809 the *London Society for Promoting Christianity among the Jews* (now called the *Church's Ministry among the Jews*).

(2) *Sir Francis Palgrave* (1788–1861, born Francis Ephraim Cohen), son of a Jewish stockbroker, became an Anglican at age 35, became best known as an English historian and archivist.

(3) *J. August W. Neander* (1789–1850, born David Mendel), was the founder of modern Protestant historiography.

(4) *Joseph Wolff* (1795–1862) was a Christian missionary—especially in the Middle East—and Oriental scholar of German Jewish descent.

(5) *Isaac da Costa* (1798–1860), born into a wealthy Jewish family in Amsterdam, Dutch poet and theologian in the Dutch Reformed Church, turned to Jesus through the Christian scholar Willem Bilderdijk.

(6) *Michael Solomon Alexander* (1799–1845, son of Alexan-

---

28. The Marranos (lit., "pigs") were forced Jewish converts in medieval Christian Spain.

der Wolff.) was a trained rabbi, converted to Christianity at age 26, became an Anglican priest, and in 1841 became the first Anglican bishop at Jerusalem.

(7) *Joachim Heinrich Biesenthal* (1800–1886, born Raphael Hirsch) wrote commentaries on Psalms and Isaiah, and on a large part of the New Testament.

(8) *Marie-Théodor Ratisbonne* (1802–1884, born Théodor R.), grown up in a Jewish banker family, converted to Roman Catholicism and became a priest and the founder of the Notre Dame de Sion congregation (co-founded with his brother *Marie-Alphonse Ratisbonne* [1814–1884], a Jesuit priest and missionary).

(9) *Benjamin Disraeli* (1804–1881), born Jewish, became an Anglican at age 12, a novelist, British prime minister under Queen Victoria, and founder of the modern Conservative Party.

(10) *Francis-Marie-Paul Libermann* (1804–1852, born Jacob L.), a Jewish convert to Roman Catholicism, became the founder of the Congregation of the Sacred Heart and was declared venerable by the Roman Catholic Church in 1876.

(11) *Ridley Haim Herschel* (1807–1864) wanted to become a rabbi but became an Evangelical minister of the Word, founded the British Society for Propagating the Gospel Among the Jews (1842) and the Evangelical Alliance (1845).

(12) *Felix Mendelssohn-Bartholdy* (1809–1847), the great composer and a Lutheran, was a grandson of the Jewish philosopher Moses Mendelssohn.

(13) *Bernard Jean Bettelheim* (1811–1870) wanted to become a rabbi but became the first Protestant missionary in Okinawa (Japan).

(14) *Karl Paul Caspari* (1814–1892), of German Jewish descent, became a Norwegian Lutheran and a well-known Tanakh interpreter.

(15) *Theodore Jonas Meyer* (1819–1894), a converted Jew,

served as a Presbyterian missionary in Italy, and became a peacemaker between Catholics and Protestants there.

(16) *Henry Aaron Stern* (1820–1885), of German Jewish descent, became an Anglican missionary in Abyssinia (Ethiopia), where he was a captive between 1863 and 1868.

(17) *Paulus Stephanus Cassel* (1821–1892, born Selig Cassel), of German Jewish descent, became a historian writing on, and a missionary to, the Jews.

(18) *Ignaz Lichtenstein* (1824–1908, born Isaac L.) was a remarkable Hungarian Orthodox rabbi who accepted Jesus, refused to be baptized all his life, propagated the Christian faith, and yet remained a rabbi until 1892.

(19) *Alfred Edersheim* (1825–1889) became a Presbyterian minister in England; for a while, he was a missionary to the Jews in Romania. He is still known for his *The Life and Times of Jesus the Messiah*.[29]

(20) *Isidor Loewenthal* (1827–1864) was not only a musician, philosopher and mathematician, but also a missionary in what is now Pakistan, and became known especially for having mastered Greek and Latin, the Semitic languages, Pushtu, Persian, and more.

(21) *Jehiel Zvi Lichtenstein* (1827–1912) is known for his *Commentary to the New Testament*, written in Hebrew and published by the *Institutum Delitzschianum* (1891–1904).

(22) *Christian David Ginsburg* (1831–1914), Polish-Jewish born, converted at age 15, and became a great British Bible scholar, especially concerning the Masoretic tradition in Judaism.

(23) *Aaron Adolph Saphir* (1831–1891), of Hungarian Jewish descent, became an English Presbyterian minister and well-known Christian author (e.g., *The Hidden Life*).

(24) Episcopal bishop *Samuel Isaac Schereschewsky* (1831–

---

29. See Edersheim (1971).

1906), of Jewish-Lithuanian descent, became a missionary and translator in China, where he translated the Bible into Mandarin and Wen-li.

(25) *Joseph ben David Rabinowitz* (1837–1899) was a Moldovian Hasidic rabbi who found Jesus in Jerusalem; back in his own country, he founded what has been called the first Messianic Jewish congregation in modern time.

In those times, such Hebrew Christians, although stressing their Jewish identity and feeling a special responsibility with regard to the Jewish people, still belonged to the traditional churches. But in 1866 the first Hebrew Christian Alliance was founded in Great Britain, and in 1867 a Jewish Christian Brotherhood was formed in New York. The American Hebrew Christian Alliance followed in 1915, and the International Hebrew Christian Alliance in 1925. In 1882, Joseph Rabinowitz founded the first Messianic Synagogue in Bessarabia (now in Moldavia), and in 1894 Abram Levi founded a similar congregation in Smyrna. In 1898, a Hebrew Christian Assembly was formed in London, and in 1905 one was founded in Baltimore, Maryland. After that, a great number of Hebrew Christian congregations were instituted in Europe and in the United States. They were orthodox in their Christian beliefs, particularly on sensitive topics such as Christology and soteriology, but at the same time they practiced the Mosaic Torah to a certain extent.

During the Holocaust, many European Messianic congregations were extirpated. After World War II, as the State of Israel arose, the Messianic movement recovered from its heavy blows. Particularly after the re-unification of ancient Jerusalem in 1967, hundreds of Jews came to believe in Jesus as the Messiah, and a number of Messianic congregations originated in Israel (see Introduction). Many Messianic congregations are linked together by the *Fellowship of Messianic Congregations* (FMC), the *International Alliance of Messianic Congregations and Synagogues* (IAMCS, associated with the *Messianic Jewish Alli-*

ance of America), the *Union of Messianic Jewish Congregations* (UMJC), and some smaller organizations.³⁰ By the end of the twentieth century, Baruch Maoz, pastor of the *Chesed weEmet* (Grace and Truth) Christian Assembly at Rishon Letzion (Israel), enumerated 51 Hebrew-speaking congregations, 53 Hebrew-speaking house groups, 23 Russian-speaking congregations, and seven Amharic-speaking congregations (Messianic Jews from Ethiopia) in Israel, together comprising roughly about 6,000 Messianic Jews.³¹ Today, the numbers are perhaps doubled.

The great significance of this new worldwide phenomenon of Messianic congregations is, first, ethnic and social, namely, Jesus-believing Jews reawakening to their own Jewish identity. Second, there is the theological significance: the biblical right, or even duty, of Jesus-believing Jews to preserve their Jewish identity. The best practical way to achieve this is to establish special Messianic congregations, where *both* Jewish and Gentile Jesus-believers are welcome and participate on equal footing, but where the Jewish lifestyle can come to expression, including circumcision, *kashrut*, Shabbats, and Jewish festivals. Third, there is the prophetic significance, which seems to me the most important. God's Spirit is actively leading many Jews to their Messiah and Savior, who give their hearts and lives to Jesus but retain their Jewish identity. There is little doubt in my mind that this is one of the great signs of the last days; God is preparing the greatest awakening among Israel that it has ever seen. It seems Messianic Jew Dan Juster, director of Tikkun Ministries and senior pastor of Beth Messiah Congregation in Washington, DC, was right when he wrote already in 1995: "Messianic Judaism believes in a crucial future for Israel. Furthermore, Messianic Judaism itself may somehow be significantly related to the future."³²

---

30. Stern (1997, 197–98).
31. Quoted in Kjær-Hansen and Skjøtt (1999, 67, 69).
32. Juster (1995, 98).

The position of these Messianic congregations is difficult. They are rejected by the world because they are Jews. They are rejected by Orthodox Jews because of their faith in Jesus Messiah. They are rejected by liberal churches because of their faithfulness to the Scriptures. They are rejected by the established churches and by many Evangelicals because of their loyalty to their Jewish identity. Unfortunately, they sometimes are rejected by one another because of their different views with regard to the Torah (see §1.2.3).

Today there are many kinds of Jews, but perhaps no difference among them is more drastic (and painful) than this one: Messianic and non-Messianic Jews. Please note that both are *Jews*, that is, both belong to the ethnic nation of *Israel*; in other words, they are physical descendants of Abraham, Isaac, and Jacob. We also know basically two kinds of Messianic Jews. On the one hand, those who have largely or fully given up the Mosaic Torah (circumcision, *kashrut*, the festivals, etc.) by having adapted to the ways of the Gentile church. On the other hand, there are Jews who believe in Jesus as the Messiah, and live in a Jewish way by keeping the Mosaic Torah (as far as this is still possible and warranted[33]), and emphasize the planting of Jewish congregations. They do not live this way for traditional reasons, but because they see their Jewish identity and lifestyle as a continuing call from God. The latter are Messianic Jews in the strict sense; the former, still constituting the majority, may be referred to as Jewish (or Hebrew) Christians.[34] They do not support, or they even reject, the planting of Jewish congregations, and see their Jewishness merely as

---

33. See chapters 5–7 below.
34. In the United States, Messianic Jews and Hebrew Christians are often referred to as "Jews for Jesus," but in fact this is the name of just one Hebrew Christian organization, under the former leadership of Moishe Rosen (for the viewpoint of an outsider, see Lipson (1990); cf. Stern (1997, 29).

What is the Torah?

an ethnic identity.[35] Of course, in practice there are all kinds of Messianic Jews and Hebrew Christians and varieties among the two, as we will presently see.

The Messianic Jewish movement is part of a remarkable phenomenon. We live in a time that in many ways mirrors the period described by the book of Acts. That was the period immediately after the first coming of the Messiah; today it is the period immediately prior to the second coming of the Messiah. Today, there is a state of Israel, while the majority of the Jews still live in the Diaspora, as was the case then. Today, there are thousands of Messianic Jews in that state, as there were during the time of Acts, as well as many Messianic Jews outside the Holy Land. Today, they are "zealous for the Torah" (Acts 21:20). Forty years ago, most of them were still Sunday-observers, but today Messianic Jews are Shabbat-observers, as they were during the time of Acts.[36] Just as a particular war, the Jewish War against the Roman oppressors (AD 70), ended the transitional period of the book of Acts, so too the Six-Day War of 1967, which awakened many Jewish souls, seems to have been instrumental in giving the Messianic Jewish movement its great boost. Also, the "signs and wonders and various miracles" that characterized the early Messianic Jewish movement (Heb. 2:3–4) are found today in the present movement.

Between the initial transitional period and the present transitional period, there was no Jewish Messianic movement; there was only the Christian church. The prophetic role that the latter has played during church history has a double aspect, a positive and a negative one. Positively, if there had been no Christian church preaching the gospel until today, no matter how defectively, there would have been no Messianic movement today. If salvation had not come to the Gentiles,

---

35. Juster (1995, 152–53).
36. Bacchiocchi (1998, 278).

there would have been no Gentile Jesus-believers "to make Israel jealous" (Rom. 11:11). Humanly speaking, the Messianic Jewish movement was launched by Gentile Jesus-believers witnessing to Jews. These Jesus-believing Jews are those who "do not continue in their unbelief" but, as "natural branches," have been "grafted back into their own olive tree" (vv. 23–24). They usually received the gospel from Gentile lips, just as Gentiles had initially received the gospel from Jewish lips.

Negatively, generally speaking, the Christian church has been sadly anti-Semitic. This had at least two effects. First, the church played its evangelistic role so badly that in the past only a few Jews have been made jealous. That happened not only because a veil covers the hearts of the Jews (2 Cor. 3:15) and a partial hardening has come upon them (Rom. 11:25), but also because of the unfaithfulness of the church with regard to the principle, "to the Jew first, and also to the Gentile" (Rom. 1:16; 2:10). Second, as mentioned above, the church required Jesus-believing Jews to renounce behaving like Jews and to give up even the slightest relic of Jewish practices and beliefs. The prophetic significance of these two factors was that, although the church is fully responsible for its bad behavior, *God used it to prevent Israel from being swallowed by the church and from forever losing its Jewish identity.* If that had happened, there would have been no Israel anymore whom God could have restored in the Promised Land to bring them under the blessed rule of Jesus the Messiah.[37] Even the most horrible Shoah (lit., "the catastrophe," referring to the Holocaust), for which not God but only wicked human beings were responsible, played a role in God's unfathomable providence. A majority of the Jews were en route to being fully assimilated among the Gentiles. No event, no matter how horrible,

---

37. Thus the Jewish-English sociologist, Ferdynand Zweig, in (1969); see his article included in Kac (1986, 64–65). Also cf. the Jewish author Margarete Susman (1996, 88–89).

created a new Jewish self-confidence along with a longing for a safe country owned by Jews more strongly than the Shoah. Humanly speaking, without this new Jewish self-assurance there would have been no state of Israel, nor a Messianic Jewish movement; and particularly, without this there would be no ultimate restoration of Israel in the Messianic kingdom.

Of course, this is human reasoning. God could have brought about all these facts without making use of human failure. But I find an example of this kind of reasoning in the Talmud: "*And the king removed his ring* [giving it to Haman, thus sealing the latter's persecution of the Jews, Esth. 3:10]. Rabbi Abba ben Kahana said: This removal of the ring was more efficacious than forty-eight prophets and seven prophetesses who prophesied to Israel; for all these were not able to turn Israel to better courses, and the removal of the ring did turn them to better courses."[38] This is a profound statement! Here, a Jewish tradition itself expresses something of the meaning—if we may even use that word—of all persecution of the Jews, which to us is so terribly meaningless. Nothing furthered Israel's preservation of its Jewish self-confidence and identity more strongly, and prevented it from being absorbed by the Gentile nations more effectively, than the persecutions. In the end, these trials may have done more for the rise of the Messianic Jewish movement than gospel preaching by Gentiles. This is by no means an excuse for the outrages committed by the Gentile church; rather, it is evidence of God's wondrous and mysterious ways by which he reaches his goals.

1.2.3 Types of Jesus-believing Jewry

We may now distinguish three groups of *Jews*: non-Messianic Jews (themselves divided into many currents), Messianic Jews, and Hebrew Christians; and three groups of *Jesus-believ-*

---

38. Megillah 14a; cf. Susman (1996, 119).

ers: Gentile Jesus-believers, Hebrew Christians, and Messianic Jews. To avoid misunderstanding I stress the fact that the great majority of all the latter three groups believe that they are all members of the Body of Messiah with absolutely equal rights and standing before God. They differ on the question of the Torah, just as Gentile Jesus-believers differ on it, for that matter.[39]

In contrast with Hebrew and Gentile Jesus-believers, Messianic Jews observe (to a certain extent, which may greatly vary) *kashrut*, Shabbat, and the Jewish festivals, and have their newborn sons circumcised. This is the very minimum. For the rest, I basically distinguish the following *six* main positions with regard to the Torah (although differences are often vague, and transitional or mixed forms are numerous), distributed among two groups:[40]

POSITION 1: *Jesus-believing Jews are basically free from the Mosaic Torah.* Believers holding this view maintain that, since Messianic Jews have accepted Jesus as their Messiah and Savior, they, like all other Jesus-believers, are no longer under the Mosaic Torah but only under the New Testament "Torah of the Messiah." Daniel Yahav, an elder of the Messianic Peniel Fellowship at Tiberias, once said, "We are not under the law, nor have we the duty to observe the whole law." And an elder of a Messianic congregation in Beer-Sheva said, "A Messianic Jew is, when he embraces Jesus, finished with the law."[41] This group of believers differs on the question, though, whether it is desirable or not to observe the Mosaic Torah, particularly as a witness to their non-Messianic Jewish fellowmen:

1.1 *Undesirable:* This the view of Arnold Fruchtenbaum

---

39. Cf. particularly for surveys of Messianic congregations in the state of Israel: Meijer (1997, chapter IV), and Kjær-Hansen and Skjøtt (1999).
40. Cf. Meijer (1997, 46–52); Kjær-Hansen and Skjøtt (1999, 31–33).
41. Meijer (1997, 50).

(§5.2.2), of many of the late Moishe Rosen's *Jews for Jesus*, and of Charles Halff and his *Christian Jew Foundation*. There is a difference, however, as to the desirability of distinct Messianic Jewish congregations:

1.1.1 The congregations of the first group are often of a traditional-Christian nature: Lutheran, Baptist, Evangelical, Charismatic, etc. (most of them baptize believers, some baptize infants). Many of them are Hebrew Christians rather than Messianic Jews, as is indicated especially by the fact that they meet on Sundays, such as the large charismatic King of Kings Assembly at Central Jerusalem.[42]

1.1.2 Particularly in Israel, however, congregations tend to be more specifically Messianic: they follow certain Jewish customs such as the use of the *shofar* (rams' horn) and the *Siddur* (Jewish prayer book). Interestingly, even some congregations of an "imported" denominational type have introduced specific Jewish customs. For instance, some largely Jewish "Brethren Assemblies" in Israel meet on the Shabbat.[43]

Although some allow it, most of these congregations oppose the use of the *kippah* (head cap) and the *tzitziyot* (fringes). Moshe Bar-David, one of the leaders of the Messianic Ramat Gan congregation at Raman Gan (Israel), rejects the *kippah* as being just a rabbinic (non-biblical) tradition. In the new dispensation, he views the *tzitzit* as having been replaced by the Holy Spirit; if in the old dispensation the *tzitzit* reminded the Jews of the commandments, today the Holy Spirit does this and wearing the *tzitziyot* has become superfluous.[44]

1.2 *Desirable:* In order to render an effective testimony to

---

42. See Kjær-Hansen and Skjøtt (1999, 280–81). The English-speaking King of Kings Assembly has been instrumental, though, in founding several Hebrew-speaking congregations meeting on late Saturday afternoons (126–28, 214–17).
43. Kjær-Hansen and Skjøtt (1999, 169, 239).
44. Meijer (1997, 51).

fellow-Jews, especially in Israel, it is very desirable, if not highly desirable, that Messianic Jews observe the Mosaic Torah. Many such congregations use the *shofar* and the *Siddur*, have Torah-scrolls, follow the *Parashot* (the traditional Torah-readings for each Shabbat), and do not object to the *kippah* and/or the *tzitziyot*. However, the things that help to reach Jewish people should never become a hindrance in contacts with Gentile Jesus-believers. David Lazarus, leader of the Messianic Beit Immanuel congregation at Jaffa, said, "I see the law of Moses as a way of preserving the Jewish identity. Especially those laws which were specifically intended for the Jewish people.... We keep certain traditions, but we also have an attitude of freedom and openness. We also know ourselves to be called to contacts with Arabic congregations."[45]

POSITION 2: *It is mandatory that Messianic Jews keep the Mosaic Torah.* Believers holding this view maintain that, because Messianic Jews in coming to Jesus have not lost their Jewish identity, they are to observe the Mosaic Torah. Joseph Shulam, leader of the Messianic Ro'eh Yisrael congregation at Central Jerusalem, said, "Our congregation strives after the restitution of the church at Jerusalem from the first century. Our congregation members wish to live as they lived in that first congregation, as it is mentioned in Acts [21:20; that is, as] 'zealous for the law' ... our congregation resembles far more a synagogue than a church."[46] This group of believers differs, however, on the question:

2.1 Whether it is desirable, or even mandatory, to observe the oral Torah (rabbinic/Talmudic tradition; see §6.3).

2.1.1 *Undesirable:* Messianic Jews may learn a few things from the post-first centuries Rabbis, but because of the latters' anti-Jesus attitude they should largely keep aloof. For instance, this type of Messianic Jew is against the *Kippah* and

---

45. Meijer (1997, 49).
46. Meijer (1997, 45–46); cf. Kjær-Hansen and Skjøtt (1999, 112, 114).

What is the Torah?

most of the *Siddur*.

2.1.2 *Middle position:* Rabbinic traditions can be observed only insofar as they are in harmony with the spirit of the Torah and of the New Testament. This is the view of the Association of Torah-Observant Messianics,[47] of David Stern (§5.2.3), and of Dan Juster, although they may differ in their measure of appreciation of Rabbinic Judaism.[48] This view is similar to that of Conservative Judaism.

2.1.3 *Mandatory:* Some Messianic Jews feel that the rabbis, though blind to Jesus, were led by the Spirit to lead the Jews in their time and that, consequently, Messianic Jews are to observe the so-called oral Torah. This is the view of Haim Levi and his International Federation of Messianic Jews. This view is similar to that of Orthodox Judaism.

In addition to this, Position 2 is also divided on another important matter:

2.2 Whether Gentile Jesus-believers are to keep the Mosaic Torah or not:

2.2.1 *Torah-keeping is obligatory:* Gentile Jesus-believers are to keep the Mosaic Torah, not as a way of building up merit for heaven, of course, but simply because they have become part of the "commonwealth of Israel" (Eph. 2:12; cf. Appendix I). There is only one people of God and one Torah; consequently, if Gentile believers are under the commandments of Jesus, these necessarily include all the Mosaic commandments as well. In fact, Gentile believers are to become full proselytes of Messianic Judaism.

2.2.2 *Torah-keeping is not obligatory but desirable:* Gentile Jesus-believers are not obliged to keep the Mosaic Torah because, though having become part of the people of God, they have in no way become Jews. However, it is highly recommendable that they are taught to study the Torah and learn

---

47. See www.about-torah.org.
48. Cf. Juster (1995, xv).

to keep it on a voluntary basis. Torah-keeping is a great blessing, from which Gentile believers are not to be excluded.

2.2.3 Torah-keeping not obligatory and not desirable: Gentile Jesus-believers are not obliged to keep the Mosaic Torah because they are not Jews, and nowhere in the New Testament are they called to keep the Mosaic Torah, either mandatorily or voluntarily. On the contrary, the "yoke" of the Jews is not to be put on the Gentile believers' "necks" for whatever reason, and life should not be made "difficult" for them (cf. Acts 15:10, 19), as it is for Israel due to their calling from God.

Those holding Position 1.1.1 above are still quite numerous; Hebrew Christians in this category see great dangers in the development of distinct Messianic Jewish congregations. Many Messianic Jewish thinkers who plead for such a development are keenly aware of such dangers but believe — rightly, I think — that they can be overcome. Dan Juster supplies us with such a list of possible dangers threatening Messianic Jews.[49] In line with this, I claim that the Messianic Jewish congregation in the truly biblical sense is *not*:

1. *Legalistic.* We may speak of legalism in cases where (a) people adhere to the fatal letter of the Torah without being led by the living Spirit (cf. Rom. 7:6; 8:4; 2 Cor. 3:6), or (b) want to build up merit for heaven (see Appendix II), or (c) judge other people for not observing the Torah the way *they* think fit, or (d) overestimate human traditions (not immediately based on Scripture), or (e) want to control others around them by their over-spiritual scrupulosity, or (f) are inflexible when it comes to communion with non-Jewish fellow-believers (see §9.1.2), etc. Keeping the Mosaic Torah must never conflict with following Jesus but must be subjected to it. Some Messianic Jews — and some Gentile Jesus-believers as well — are in danger of making Torah-keeping (in whatever way that is to

---

49. Juster (1995, 247–51).

be understood) an aim in itself, as factually taking the place of the Lord Jesus.

2. *Shallow*, which is in some sense the opposite of legalistic. Shallowness, or looseness, is the desire to be free from all traditions and assume the kind of superficiality so characteristic of many free-church Evangelical Jesus-believers who have come from traditionalist Protestant backgrounds. Shallow Messianic Jews throw away the richness of their religious, national, and cultural heritage, as well as neglect to learn from the past mistakes of the Gentile-Christian. Just like so many Evangelical Jesus-believers, they want to reinvent the theological and congregational wheel, or reject theology altogether by creating a false contrast between calling and study. After a while they leave many of their members unsatisfied because the latter begin to remember not only the traditionalism but also the theological depth of the past, particularly the past of traditional Christian denominations, or of Rabbinic Judaism for that matter.

3. *Separatist.* No one should deny the right of Messianic Jews to institute their own congregations, but just the contrary (see §6.3.1). This right as such does not constitute separatism as long as Messianic Jews fully maintain practical fellowship with *all* Jesus-believers as far as possible, and receive Messianic Gentiles in their meetings, even as members of their congregations. Messianic Jews are entitled to maintain their Jewish identity and, since their Gentile members *voluntarily* join such communities, have the right to require the latter to comply with Jewish religious practices. But Messianic Jews' observance of *kashrut* (Jewish food laws) should never come between themselves and their Gentile fellow-believers (see §9.1.2). Messianic Jews should not forget for one moment that together with Gentile Jesus-believers they constitute the one Body of the Messiah. There are distinctions between Messianic Jews and Messianic Gentiles, just as there are between slaves and free men, and between males and females, but in

the Messiah they are all one (Gal. 3:28) — and this should become visible in a very practical way.

4. *Heretical.* In principle, all heresies that have arisen in Christian circles throughout the ages may occur among Messianic Jews. I see one specific example of this, not mentioned by Juster, in the tendency among some Messianic Jews to reject out of hand certain Christian dogmas because they are allegedly not based on Scripture. For instance, the Nazarene Israelite Two House Congregation of Port Elizabeth says in its Statement of Belief "that YHWH reveals Himself in many ways, characteristics and personalities, which include but are not limited to the Heavenly Father, Yahushua the Son, the Word, the Messiah, the Angel or Messenger of YHWH and the Set Apart Spirit (Ruakh HaQodesh)."[50] One wonders in what personalities other than the Father, the Son and the Spirit YHWH has revealed himself! It may be true that the traditional doctrine of the Trinity exhibits Hellenistic influences, that the term "person" (with regard to the three persons of the Godhead) is misleading in the light of modern personality psychology,[51] and that YHWH has revealed himself under many forms such as the *Shekhinah*. But to undercut Trinitarian doctrine, including the deity (not just divinity) of Jesus, without having reflected on seventeen centuries of theological reflection upon it, is unwise, to say the least.[52] This seems

---

50. See nazarene2house.weebly.com/statement-of-beliefs.html.
51. However, the opposite danger of Sabellianism (or modalism, or modalistic monarchianism), which teaches that God has revealed himself in different ages in different modes—thus blotting out the distinctiveness of the Father, the Son, and the Holy Spirit as divine subsistencies—is equally to be rejected.
52. Cf. the Statement of Faith of Jews for Jesus (www.jewsforjesus.org/about-jews-for-jesus/who-we-are/statementoffaith): "We believe in one sovereign God, existing in three persons: Father, Son and Holy Spirit. . . ." See also the helpful chapter by Messianic Jew Schiffman (1996, 93–104).

to me one of the greatest dangers of Messianic Jewry (which is shared with many Evangelical Jesus-believers): on the one hand, throwing out the baby with the bathwater, while on the other hand, trying to reinvent the wheel.

1.3 The Term "Torah" in Scripture

1.3.1 The Torah in the Tanakh

From what I have said thus far, it may have become clear how important it is to define the term "Torah" as accurately as possible. What do we mean with a, or the, Torah? Let us begin with some lexicographical aspects. The Hebrew word *torah* is probably derived from *y-r-h*, "to instruct, to teach."[53] Others derive *torah* from *y-r-h*, "to shoot," i.e., to indicate the direction an arrow is pointing.[54] If we follow the first, more common explanation, *torah* means "instruction, teaching."[55] In the (New) King James Version, the word is always rendered "law," but in newer translations sometimes as "teaching," or something similar, depending on the context (cf. Prov. 3:1; 4:2; 6:20, 23; 7:2 in NKJV and ESV).

The word *torah* can refer to any human teaching, such as that of a homemaker (Prov. 31:26), or to a legal decision (e.g., Deut. 17:11; Hag. 2:11–13; Mal. 2:6–7), or a statute for a special occasion (e.g., Lev. 6:9, 14, 25; 7:1, 7, 11). Already in the case of Abraham, God referred to "my commandments, my statutes, and my laws [*torot*]" (Gen. 26:5), and even before the Torah-giving on Mount Sinai he asked the people of Israel: "How long will you refuse to keep my commandments and my laws [*torot*]?" (Exod. 16:28; cf. 12:49). Torah can even have the broad meaning of "religion," as when Rabbi Eleazar

---

53. Hiphil; cf. Lev. 10:11 ("to teach . . . all the statutes").
54. L. R. Dewitz in Kac (1986, 172).
55. See, e.g., John E. Hartley in Harris et al. (1980, I, 403–405); Robert H. O'Connell in VanGemeren (1997, II, 537–39); Peter Enns in Van-Gemeren (1997, IV, 893–900).

ben Azariah said: "Where there is no Torah there is no good breeding [or, cultured behavior, *derech eretz*]; where there is no good breeding there is no Torah."[56] The footnote in the Soncino edition of the Talmud explains that Torah refers here to "religion in general, any religion that postulates divine authority for moral conduct." And conversely: "religious belief is sterile when it does not express itself in ethical conduct and becoming behavior." Morals presuppose norms, laws that distinguish between moral and immoral behavior.

The most important fact for our purpose is that the word *torah* refers particularly to the body of the divine ordinances given on Mount Sinai: "the Torah of the LORD" (Exod. 13:9), "the Torah of God" (Josh. 24:26), "given by Moses the servant of God" (Neh. 10:29), therefore also called "the Torah of Moses" (Josh. 8:31), contained in "the book of this Torah" (Deut. 28:61). It is the Torah that leads God's people, showing it the right way.[57] In the sense of divine instruction, we find the Torah in Psalm 1:2, where the godly person's "delight is in the Torah [law, instruction] of the LORD, and on his Torah he meditates day and night" (cf. Paul: "I delight in the Torah of God, in my inner being," Rom. 7:22). Or elsewhere: "Blessed is the man whom you discipline, O LORD, and whom you teach[58] out of your Torah" (Ps. 94:12).

As divine instruction, the Torah presents God's thoughts as revealed to Israel, and to a certain extent even to all the nations. We see this in Isaiah 2:3 ("out of Zion shall go the Torah [law, teaching] and the word of the LORD from Jerusalem"; cf. 5:24), where the Afrikaans Bible translation of 1983 has "rev-

---

56. Mishnah, Avoth III.17.
57. Cf. Martin Buber's and Franz Rosenzweig's rendering of *torah* as *Weisung*, from *weisen*, "to point, to show (the way)," in their German translation of the Tanakh.
58. Here "to teach" is *l-m-d*, from which words like *Talmud* ("teaching") and *talmid* ("disciple") are derived.

elation" instead of "Torah." The rendering of Torah as "revelation of God's will" is especially appropriate in Scriptures that refer to God's eschatological *Torah* to all nations, that is, to those who have never known, or been under, the Mosaic Torah (Isa. 2:2-4; 42:3-7; 51:4-9). The Torah is not only the revelation of God's *will* but even of God's *being*, especially of his holiness: "[B]e holy, for I am holy" (variant readings in Lev. 11:44-45; 19:2; 20:7, 26; 21:8; see chapter 4). Through the Torah, which is divine "teaching," but also divine self-revelation, Man learns not only God's will but also God himself. Therefore, he who loves God will also love his Torah, and the reverse. This is a specific theme in Psalm 119: "I will delight in your statutes. . . . Your testimonies are my delight; they are my counselors . . . . Lead me in the path of your commandments, for I delight in it. . . . I find my delight in your commandments, which I love. . . . I delight in your Torah . . ." (vv. 16, 24, 35, 47, 70; cf. vv. 77, 92, 113, 143, 174).

In the *Siddur*, the Jewish prayer book, we find a statement that is recited in the synagogue after the public reading of the Torah scroll, consisting of a combination of Proverbs 4:2 and 3:18: ". . . I give you good precepts; do not forsake my *torah*. . . . She is a tree of life to those who lay hold of her; those who hold her fast are called blessed." In the Bible text, the latter words actually refer to *Hokmah*, wisdom (v. 13), but for Jewish thinking this is the same as the eternal Torah (see extensively chapter 3). It is the wisdom of God that he has submitted the entire cosmos to natural laws—another aspect of his Torah (vv. 19-20; cf. the contrast between Ps. 119:89-91 and vv. 92-96)—and it is the wisdom of Man to submit himself to God's Torah. In this sense, stars, plants, and humans are alike; they are all subject to *Torah* in the broadest sense, whereas God is above the Torah as the Torah-giver.

It is not a harsh king who enforces his law upon Man, but a loving Father (or mother! Prov. 1:8; 6:20), who presents his Torah to his son as the tree of life, that is, the way of true living: "My son, do not forget my *torah*, but let your heart keep my commandments" (3:1). "My son, keep your father's commandment, and forsake not your mother's *torah*. . . . For the commandment is a lamp and the *torah* a light, and the reproofs of discipline are the way of life" (6:20, 23). "My son, keep my words and treasure up my commandments with you; keep my commandments and live; keep my *torah* as the apple of your eye" (7:1–2). "The one who keeps the *torah* is a son with understanding, but a companion of gluttons shames his father" (28:7; cf. vv. 4, 9; 29:18).

Of course, the *torah* of a human father for his child, though an expression of his fatherly affection and feelings, simply means "teaching" or "instruction" concerning the wisest way the child has to live (think, speak, act, function). However, it is a wonderful image of *the* Torah of the heavenly Father. What the human father teaches his child is what the heavenly Father taught his son Israel: "Know then in your heart that, as a man disciplines his son, the LORD your God disciplines you. So you shall keep the commandments of the LORD your God by walking in his ways and by fearing him" (Deut. 8:5–6; cf. 1:31). Here, the Torah is again associated with Wisdom: "See, I have taught you statutes and rules, as the LORD my God commanded me. . . . Keep them and do them, for that will be your wisdom and your understanding in the sight of the peoples, who, when they hear all these statutes, will say, 'surely this great nation is a wise and understanding people'" (4:5–6).

The Mosaic Torah consists of a large number of *torot*: laws, statutes, commandments, precepts, ordinances, rules. Scriptures that use the words *torah* or *torot* more explicitly, in order to explain a certain *torah* or certain *torot* in more detail, give a good indication of the way in which the term is used:[59]

1. *Torot for the sacrificial service:* the *torot* of the burnt of-

---

59. Cf. Enns in Van Gemeren (1997, IV.893–96), for a useful survey.

fering, the grain offering, the sin offering, the guilt offering, the peace offering (Lev. 6:9, 14, 25; 7:1, 7, 11, 37; these are the rules for bringing sacrifices properly). Ezekiel 43:12 (cf. 44:5) speaks of the "*torah* of the house," that is, the precepts for the Temple ministry.

2. *Torot for the Shabbats and festivals:* Nehemiah 8:13–14 speaks of the "words of the Torah" with regard to *Sukkoth* (the Feast of Booths; cf. Exod. 23:16; Lev. 23:34).[60] Specific *torot* are also mentioned in relation to *Pesach* (Passover; see Exod. 12:49; 13:9).[61] Of course, many Scriptures refer to the Shabbats and the festivals without using the term *torah* (see especially Lev. 23; Num. 28–29; Deut. 16).

3. *Torot for a pure life*, that is, clean in a ceremonial (or cultic) sense, which has to do with Israel's sanctified (separated) position in the midst of the nations: *torot* with respect to food (Lev. 11:46), and with respect to various cleansings after giving birth (12:7), after defilement with mildew (13:59), from contagious skin diseases (14:2, 32, 57), after emission of semen, after a woman's monthly impurity, and after sexual contact between a man and a ritually unclean woman (15:32–33), the "water for impurity" for those who have touched death (Num. 19:2, 21), and purification of spoils of war (31:21). Think also of the "*torah* for the Nazirite" (6:13, 21). Ezra 10:3 refers to a *torah* that prohibits marriages with strangers (cf. Deut. 7:3).

4. *Civil, social, and legal torot:* there are *torot* for legal affairs and duties of everyday life (Exod. 18:16, 20). Generally speaking, all legal matters had to be handled according to the Torah (Deut. 17:11). Other specific *torot* refer, for example, to the testing of a woman suspected of adultery (Num. 5:30).

In its widest meaning, the word *torah* in the Tanakh refers to the entire Pentateuch (the five books of Moses). The expression "book of the Torah" (Deut. 28:61), or "book of the

---

60. See Ouweneel (2001, §6.1).
61. Ouweneel (2001, chapter 3).

Torah of Moses" (Josh. 8:31), or "book of the Torah of God" (24:26), might refer to the book of Deuteronomy, or at least to the legal material contained in it (cf. Deut. 1:5; 4:8, 44). In other Scriptures, the expression may also refer to other parts of the Pentateuch (Neh. 10:34 refers to Lev. 6:12–13), even to the Pentateuch as a whole, or at least to the legal material contained in it. Psalm 78:1 ("Give ear, O my people, to my *torah*") introduces an overview of Israel's history as contained in the Pentateuch and later books, and suggests that the term may refer also to the narrative parts of the Pentateuch (also see Wisdom 10 and Sirach 44–50). These are *torot* in that they contain spiritual instruction. In the New Testament, the Greek term *nomos* ("law") in the sense of the Pentateuch has become very common (see §1.2.2).

The Ten Commandments (*Asheret Devarim*, lit., "Ten Words") are not to be isolated from the rest of the Pentateuch and elevated to some domain of timeless, abstract principles.[62] They are placed within the historical framework of Israel's redemption from Egypt: "I am the LORD your God, who brought you out of the land of Egypt, out of the house of slavery" (Exod. 20:2; Deut. 5:6). They are also closely connected with all the other imperatives in historical Pentateuchal narratives, such as: "Go from your country" (Gen. 12:1); "the LORD will fight for you, and you have only to be silent" (Exod. 14:14); "six days you shall gather it [i.e., manna]" (16:26); "you shall be to me a kingdom of priests and a holy nation" (19:6). "Go up into the Negeb . . . , and see what the land is" (Num. 13:17–18); "when the LORD your God gives them over to you, and you defeat them, then you must devote them to complete destruction" (Deut. 7:2). God's commands, no matter how abstract they may seem, are always embedded in concrete *events*, in the *route* that God follows with his people through salvation history.

---

62. Miskotte (1956, 183–84).

Later, we will underscore the fact that it is the God of history, God the Creator and God the Redeemer, who presents himself to Israel and gives Israel his Ten Words (Exod. 19:3-6; 20:2). Ultimately, in this respect the whole Bible is Torah, instruction from the God who leads his people from redemption to the end of the ages. After an introductory song of praise, Psalm 147 says, "The LORD builds up Jerusalem; he gathers the outcasts of Israel" (v. 2; the *redeeming* God). It then also presents to us the *creating* God ("He determines the number of the stars; he gives to all of them their names," v. 4), and finishes with this: "He declares his word to Jacob, his statutes and rules to Israel. He has not dealt thus with any other nation; they do not know his rules. Praise the LORD!" (vv. 19-20; the *leading* God). The Creator-God is the Redeemer-God. The Spirit of God, hovering over the earth (*merakhefet*, Gen. 1:2), is the God who hovers over his people (*yerakhef*, Deut. 32:11). The Shabbat that is celebrated by the Creator (Gen. 2:2-3) is to be celebrated by his own people (Exod. 20:8-11; 31:12-17). The glory that was on the mountain was also to be in the Tabernacle, the "tent of meeting" (24:16-18; 40:34-35), and the model of the Tabernacle was like the model on the mountain (26:30).

Creation, redemption, and Torah belong to the same framework of thought. To this group of three I add a fourth crucial biblical term, namely, the *covenant* (Heb. *berit*, Gr. *diathēkē*). The order of creation is the order of the covenant,[63] just as the Cosmic Torah and the Mosaic Torah are fundamentally one (compare Ps. 119:89-91 with the rest of the psalm, and Prov. 3:19-20 with the rest of that chapter). The Torah cannot be understood outside the framework of the covenant, that is, the *close relationship* between God, who gives the Torah, and his people, who have been placed under the Torah (see chapter 4 below). To put it even more strongly, God gives his Torah

---

63. Miskotte (1956, 188–89).

only to *his own*, from Adam until the end (although while en route, among those who are his there may be many who are this only outwardly, that is, falsely).

James Dunn points out that, indeed, the terms "covenant" and "commands" are closely related.[64] Thus, in Exodus 24:7, the expression "book of the covenant" refers primarily to a collection of commandments (Exod. 20-23). In Exodus 34:38, the "words of the covenant" refer to the Ten Words (Ten Commandments). In Deuteronomy 4:13, Moses says, God "declared to you his covenant, which he commanded you to perform, that is, the Ten Commandments" (cf. v. 8, "all this Torah"). God's commandments are Israel's covenantal duties, as is emphasized many times; thus God, speaks of those who "will not do all my commandments, but break my covenant" (Lev. 26:15). "The Ephraimites . . . did not keep God's covenant, but refused to walk according to his Torah" (Ps. 78:10; cf. Hos. 8:1). The inhabitants of the earth "have transgressed the *torot*, violated the statutes, broken the everlasting covenant" (Isa. 24:5). But, in the end, "this is the covenant that I will make with the house of Israel after those days, declares the Lord: I will put my Torah within them, and I will write it on their hearts" (Jer. 31:33).

This important point—no Torah outside some covenantal framework—will be discussed in more detail. But already at this point I want to say this: the Ten Commandments were *never* intended as a kind of constitution for any Gentile nation state—unless one wishes to believe that, for instance, the white people of the United States, or of South Africa, or of the Netherlands, are "the people of God" in a special sense (these are historical examples!). But God never made a covenant with "the" people in any country except Israel. Gentiles who have become "sons of Abraham" (Gal. 3:7, 29; cf. v. 14) stand in a covenant relationship with God (4:24-26), and are

---

64. Dunn (1998, 132).

under the Torah of Christ (6:2). Redemption, covenant, and Torah belong to the same framework of thought; outside this context, none of these concepts makes any sense anymore. I will return to these points in greater detail.

1.3.2 The Torah in the New Testament

How was the term Torah understood in the time after the Tanakh had been completed? One answer to this question is supplied by the rabbinic tradition. However, this tradition of the elders (the ancient religious authorities) cannot claim divine inspiration as the Scriptures can—even though the rabbis refer to these traditions as the oral *Torah*—and thus its authority does not reach any further than the moral authority of those who have contributed to it. In my view, here and there this tradition even conflicts with the spirit of the Torah, as Jesus himself has made clear (e.g., Mark 7:1-7; see §6.3.2). At the same time, Jesus said of the rabbinic precepts: "The scribes and the Pharisees sit on Moses' seat, *so do and observe whatever they tell you*" —although he had to add: ". . . but not the works they do. For they preach, but do not practice" (Matt. 23:2-3, italics added). If Jesus respected these precepts, Jesus-believers should do so too.

In contrast with the tradition of the elders, the New Testament is not only the best commentary on the Torah ever written, but also the only one that is the inspired Word of God, and thus possesses formal divine authority.[65] For instance, in 1 Timothy 5:18, the apostle Paul refers to Deuteronomy 25:4 and Luke 10:7 equally as "Scripture," and in 2 Peter 3:15-16, the apostle Peter refers, in addition to the Letters of Paul, to "the other Scriptures," thus implying that Paul's Letters were also Holy Scripture.

There is another term that illustrates the character of the New Testament. First, the entire Tanakh is Torah, but the

---

65. Berkowitz (2012, 131).

deepest content of the Torah is also *logos*, "word," namely, Word of God (Rom. 13:9; Gal. 5:14; cf. Lev. 19:18). Second, likewise, the divine revelation that has been granted to us through the apostles is *logos*, that is, Word of God (e.g., Gal. 6:6; Col. 4:3; 1 Thess. 1:6; 2:13; 2 Tim. 2:11; 4:2). The New Testament is just as much Word of God as the Tanakh — no less, but no more either. I emphasize the latter over against the many Jesus-believers who, since Marcion, think the New Testament to be far more important than the Tanakh. However, just as the Tanakh is divinely explained by the New Testament, the New Testament is divinely explained by the Tanakh. Nobody can truly understand and expound the New Testament without a thorough knowledge of the Tanakh. Together they supply us with the *full* understanding of what Torah is.

Already in the Septuagint, the word *torah* is rendered with the Greek word *nomos*, probably in the sense of a living network of traditions and customs of a nation.[66] *Nomos* is derived from the verb *nemō*, which means "to allot, assign," and thus refers to what has been "allotted" to someone, what "fits" him. The term *nomos* therefore refers to a rule, a norm, a standard, as in: "Gentiles ... are a *nomos* [rule, norm] to themselves" (Rom. 2:14). In fact, this is rather different from the actual meaning of the word *torah*. Charles H. Dodd pointed out that *nomos*, since it is not an accurate equivalent of *Torah*, illustrates a change of ideas, a different view of what religion actually is.[67] God's merciful teaching, meant for the faithful maintenance of the covenantal relationship, was gradually replaced by a more formal, legal term, which seems to fit more with the Hellenic than with the Jewish way of thinking.

---

66. Harvey (1972, 1238). Cf. the *Torah–nomos* seminar of the Canadian Society of Biblical Studies, as published in *Studies in Religion/Sciences Religieuses* (1984–86), particularly Segal (1984); Westerholm (1985).

67. Dodd (1954, 25).

Nevertheless, the word *nomos* used in the Septuagint was sanctioned by the New Testament writers as the common rendering of *torah*, and this was not a mistake. *Torah*, too, definitely has (also) a formal-legal content, just like the laws that a king issues for his people. Thus, in Ezra 7:26, "the law (Aram. *dat*) of your God" is placed alongside "the law (Aram., *dat*) of the king" (also see vv. 12, 14, 21, 25). See further Daniel 6:6; 7:25 (*dat* refers to God's Torah) and 2:9, 13, 15; 6:9, 13, 16 (*dat* refers to the king's command). Faithful maintenance of the covenantal relationship involves obedience to God's rules, just as a loyal nation obeys its king.

The apostle Paul uses the word *nomos* 119 times in his Letters, more specifically, 72 times in Romans and 32 times in Galatians.[68] In these 119 cases, *nomos* does not always seem to mean Torah. Sometimes, Paul appears to use the term for an arbitrary law, or even for a general principle. An example may be "the law of faith" in Romans 3:27. Some take this to be the Torah,[69] others think that Paul uses *nomos* here in the sense of a general principle. The term *nomos* can even refer to a certain legal precept, perhaps even Roman law, as in this example: "a married woman is bound by law to her husband while he lives, but if her husband dies she is released from the law of marriage" (Rom. 7:2). This ambiguous meaning—a general principle or the Torah or Roman law—may also be found in this claim of the Jews: "This man [i.e., Paul] is persuading people to worship God contrary to the law" (Acts 18:13; see §7.3.3). Proconsul Gallio thought the Jews were referring to their own Torah ("since it is a matter of . . . your own law," v. 15), but possibly also the meaning "Roman law" was intended, as in Acts 16:21–22 and 17:7, although in these Scriptures other words (*ethos*, *dogma*) are used.

---

68. Dunn (1998, 131n18).
69. Ibid., 634–42, and the references in 639n69, and Dunn (1988, 186); see the discussion of Moo (1996, 247–50).

THE ETERNAL TORAH: LIVING UNDER GOD

With reference once again to Paul's use of the term *nomos*, the way he uses it in the sense of a norm, rule, or principle[70] is demonstrated especially in the following passage: "I find it to be a *nomos* [principle] that when I want to do right, evil lies close at hand. For I delight in the *nomos* [Torah] of God, in my inner being, but I see in my members another *nomos* [principle] waging war against the *nomos* [rule] of my mind and making me captive to the *nomos* [rule] of sin that dwells in my members.... There is therefore now no condemnation for those who are in Christ Jesus. For the *nomos* [rule *or* Torah?] of the Spirit of life has set you free in Christ Jesus from the *nomos* [rule] of sin and death" (Rom. 7:21–8:2).

There are two contrasts here: the "other rule" in the "flesh" (sinful nature) stands in opposition to the "rule" of Paul's mind as renewed by rebirth; and the rule of the Spirit of life stands in opposition to the rule of sin and death. It is possible that, in this last contrast, Paul in fact meant the Torah itself.[71] In this case, the Torah of the Spirit of life stands in opposition to some anti-torah, the torah of sin and death. As David Stern put it: "[S]in is personified as having, so to speak, organized its own Mount Sinai and there given its own '*torah*' which, willy-nilly, we find ourselves devotedly obeying with our old nature."[72] This is the "*torah* of sin," "not a God-given *Torah* at all but an anti-*Torah*. More specifically, it is the Mosaic Law improperly understood and perverted by our old, sinful nature into a legalistic system or earning God's approval by our own works."

By the way, the specificity offered in Stern's final sentence

---

70. The Gr. word *entolē*, "commandment," also sometimes means "principle," as in Matt. 22:36, where the lawyer is actually asking: "Which is the great and first *underlying principle* in the Torah, on which the entire Torah is based?"
71. See (Dunn 1998, 642–49).
72. Stern (1999, 379, 381).

is not accurate because Stern offers two different explanations here. According to the one explanation, the term *nomos* in the expression "the *nomos* of sin and death" refers to some anti-torah (the alternative offered by sin, given on some anti-Mount Sinai, saying "You shall murder," "You shall steal," etc.), say, the torah of the devil. According to the other explanation, the term *nomos* in the expression "the *nomos* of sin and death" refers to *God's own* Torah, but then a Torah distorted by sin into a polity of legalism or Jewish arrogance. Stern's first explanation says: Paul speaks here of the Torah of *God* over against the torah of the *devil*. Stern's second explanation says: Paul speaks here of God's Torah as applied by the Holy Spirit over against God's Torah as applied by sin and death.

Actually, I consider both explanations to be erroneous. The other explanation, which I prefer, is that *nomos* here simply means principle.[73] Two principles may govern the heart and the ways of Man: the principle of the Holy Spirit (in regenerated Man) and the principle of sin and death (in unregenerated Man).

In the remaining passages, Paul uses *nomos* always for the Torah of God (in addition to Rom. 7:22, 26, see v. 12 and 8:7). This is the Torah that God gave to Moses on Mount Sinai (Rom. 2:17-18; 4:13-14, 16; 5:13; 7:1; 1 Cor. 9:8-9; Gal. 3:17, 19; 6:13; Phil. 3:6, 9; Titus 3:9), the "Torah of our fathers" (Acts 22:3), the "book of the Torah" (Gal. 3:10), the Torah "put in place through angels by an intermediary [i.e., Moses]" (v. 19; cf. Acts 7:53; Heb. 2:2), "the Torah of commandments expressed in ordinances" (Eph. 2:15). We will see that Paul speaks of this Torah in a twofold way (see §§1.3 and 4.3.1). On the one hand, he refers to the Torah as the fundamental rule

---

73. See extensively Moo (1996, 460–77), who also deals with a fourth explanation: *nomos* in Rom. 8:2a is principle (in Moo's terms, "binding authority, power"), and in v. 2b is the Mosaic Law taken in the legalistic sense. Moo's final conclusion is basically the same as mine.

for the true people of God (Rom. 8:4; 13:10; Gal. 5:14; 6:2). On the other hand, he describes the Torah's negative function of bringing evil to light (Rom. 3:20; 5:20; 7:5, 7–8; Gal. 3:19; 1 Cor. 15:56; 1 Tim. 1:8–9).[74]

Sometimes, these various ways of using the term can lead to seeming discrepancies, as in Romans 3:19, 21, where we find three or four different meanings of *nomos*:

> Now we know that whatever the Torah [i.e., Tanakh] says it speaks to those who are under [lit., in] the Torah [i.e., under the Mosaic Torah as God's covenant people[75]]. . . . But now the righteousness of God has been manifested apart from the Torah [i.e., beyond God's covenant people, *or* apart from legalism], although the Torah [i.e., the Pentateuch] and the Prophets bear witness to it.[76]

Nomos is the Torah that God gave to Moses on Mount Sinai (Gal. 3:17, 19), and that therefore is called the "Torah of Moses" (e.g., Heb. 10:28) or the "Torah of the Lord" (Luke 2:23–24, 39). Often, the expression refers to the Mosaic Torah in the broadest sense, that is, the entire Pentateuch (see Luke 2:23; 10:26; John 1:45; 1 Cor. 9:9). When Paul says: "Tell me, you who desire to be under the Torah [i.e., to join Israel through circumcision], do you not listen to the Torah?" (Gal. 4:21), he is referring to the history of Abraham. Apparently, the latter use of Torah in this verse refers to the Pentateuch. In the expression "the Torah and the Prophets" (Matt. 5:17; 7:12; 22:40; Luke 16:16; John 1:46; Acts 13:15; Rom. 3:21), the whole Tanakh is meant, whereby Torah means Pentateuch. In Galatians 3:10, the "book of the Torah" (cf. Deut. 27:26) refers

---

74. See also in the Tanakh: Pss. 19, 32, 51, 119; 2 Kings 22–23; Neh. 8–10; Ezek. 20; etc.; also regarding the heathen: Rom. 2:12–15.
75. Others say that "under the Torah" means here: "under legalism (or ethnocentrism, the Jewish-nationalistic arrogance)"; we will return to this in chapter 4.
76. Cf. Moo (1996, 204–205, 222–23).

What is the Torah?

to Deuteronomy or to the entire Pentateuch.

In a still wider sense, the term *torah* can refer to the entire Tanakh. At several places, the word *nomos* (Torah) is used, but in fact quotations from the Psalms and the Prophets are given (e.g., John 10:34; 12:34; 15:25; Rom. 3:19; 1 Cor. 14:21; see also Matt. 5:18; Luke 16:17). Apparently, *nomos* means here the same as Scripture (*graphē*, sometimes *gramma*). Sometimes, the rabbis, too, used *torah* in this sense.[77] For instance, in the Talmud, a representative of Rabbi Hisda said: "Blessed be the Merciful One who gave a threefold Torah," that is, the *Torah* (Pentateuch), *Nebiim* (Prophets) and *Ketuvim* (Hagiographa).[78] Jesus spoke of "the Torah of Moses and the Prophets and the Psalms [as being the first and largest book of the *Ketuvim*]" (Luke 24:44). Because of the close link between Torah and covenant (see chapter 3), the Tanakh can be described as Torah but also as the Old Covenant (2 Cor. 3:14, or Old Testament, [N]KJV). From there comes the usual Christian name for what Jews call the Tanakh; this is an acronym, T-N-Kh, from T = Torah, N = Nebiim (Prophets), and K = Ketuvim (Writings, Hagiographa). "Old Covenant" or "Old Testament" is not necessarily a derogatory expression; it is nothing but the opposite of the Tanakhic term "New Covenant" (Jer. 31:31; cf. Heb. 8:8, 13).

In Romans 4:13–14 (NKJV), "those who are of the Torah" are contrasted with those who are of faith; but in verse 16, the same expression points to those who were born under the Mosaic Torah but have come to faith in Jesus. That is, "being of the Torah" first means "being under the Torah as a legalistic polity" as opposed to faith, and subsequently, it has a natural meaning of "being a Jew," whether Jesus-believing or not. An even starker contrast we find in the short phrase of Galatians

---

77. See Strack-Billerbeck (1922–28) on John 10:34; Rom. 3:19; 1 Cor. 14:21.
78. Shabbat 88a.

2:19, "through the Torah I died to the Torah," that is, "through the true testimony of the Torah I died to the legalistic abuse of the Torah," or perhaps, "to the ethnocentric abuse of the Torah," namely, as the delineation of God's covenantal people, and thus as a ground for ethnocentric arrogance. There are more such passages where *nomos* means two or three different things in one verse, as here, for instance: "Then what becomes of our boasting? It is excluded. By what kind of *nomos* [i.e., principle]? By a *nomos* [i.e., legalistic *or* ethnocentric polity] of works? No, but by the law [i.e., principle *or* Messianic Torah] of faith" (Rom. 3:27). "God sent forth his Son, born of woman, born under the *nomos* [i.e., as one of God's covenant people], to redeem those who were under the law [i.e., legalistic *or* ethnocentric polity], so that we might receive adoption as sons" (Gal. 4:4–5; cf. v. 21, mentioned earlier).

In the New Testament, the term "law" or "commandment" describes the relationship between not only the Master and his disciples (see §6.3.1) but also the Father and his child, as we saw in §1.2.1 with regard to a human father and a human child, and with God the Father and his "son," Israel (Exod. 4:22; Hos. 11:1; cf. Rom. 9:4). Jesus formulated the essence of the Torah as follows: "You therefore must be perfect, as your heavenly Father is perfect" (Matt. 5:48). Be like the Father! Even the relationship of the incarnate Son to the Father was regulated by command(s) (Gr. *entolē*, plur. *entolai*; John 10:18; 12:49–50; 14:31; 15:10; cf. 1 Cor. 15:28). Paul commands us to be "imitators of God, as beloved children" (Eph. 5:1); good children resemble their parents. Good children of God must be blameless and without blemish (Phil. 2:15). "Like newborn infants, long for the pure spiritual milk" (1 Pet. 2:2), where "spiritual" is the Greek word *logikos*, from *logos*, which sometimes has the meaning of *torah*: "long for the pure milk of the Torah" (cf. [N]KJV). True children of God are recognized by the fact that they practice righteousness (1 John 3:10), in that they "love God and obey his commandments. For this is the love of [i.e., toward] God, that we keep his commandment"

(5:2-3). Childhood—being like the Father—and Torah-keeping belong together.

Let me add to this that *each* metaphor describing the relationship between God and his people—not only the covenant metaphor—presupposes its own specific *torot*: Jesus as the Master of his disciples (John 13:13-17), God as the Father of his children (see above), Jesus as the King of his subjects (Ps. 2:6, 10-12), God or Jesus as the Bridegroom of his bride (Jer. 2:2, 8; Ezek. 16:8, 59-63; 2 Cor. 11:2-3; Eph. 5:22-24), God or Jesus as the Shepherd of his flock (Ps. 95:7; 100:3; 119:176; Isa. 53:6; John 10:4; Heb. 13:20; 1 Pet. 2:25), Jesus as the Head of his Body (Eph. 1:22-23; 4:15-16; 5:23; Col. 1:18; 2:19). Disciples are like their Master (Matt. 10:25), children obey their Father, subjects submit to their King, the bride respects her Bridegroom, sheep follow their Shepherd, members of the Body are subject to their Head, etc.

1.4 The Two Functions of the Torah
1.4.1 The Negative Function

As I stated earlier, there are some special ways in which the New Testament generally, and Paul in particular, speaks of the Torah, both in a negative and in a positive sense. I will return to this subject in §3.3.1, but the matter is so important that I wish to make some introductory remarks now.

In a *negative* sense, Paul often refers to the legalistic or ethnocentric (Jewish-nationalistic) meaning of the Torah. Traditionally, theologians have viewed the negative sense of the Torah as a legalistic sense, that is, in the sense of a polity that demands works of the law, done in one's own strength, as the foundation for justification and salvation. According to a newer view, that of James Dunn, Paul's doctrine concerning the negative meaning of the Torah entails Jewish *ethnocentrism*. This involves a polity in which Israel nationalistically boasts in its special status as God's covenant people, based on possessing God's Torah (cf. Rom. 2:17-24; 9:4; Eph. 2:14-16). As a consequence, this carnal Jewish ethnocentrism rejects Jesus

THE ETERNAL TORAH: LIVING UNDER GOD

as Savior for all mankind, *or* this Jewish-Christian ethnocentrism demands that the Gentile believers join Israel through circumcision in order to enjoy the covenant blessings (Rom. 3:19-21, 28-31; 4:14-16; 5:20; 7:5-14; 8:2; 9:30-33; Gal. 2:16, 19, 21; 3:2, 5, 10-13, 17-19, 21, 23-24; 4:4-5, 21; 5:3-4, 18, 23; 6:13). Sometimes, this polity as such—the polity of legalism and/or ethnocentric arrogance—is referred to as *nomos*.

Either this polity involves a keeping the Torah as a way of holiness of works, a way for people to try to obtain God's favor through good works, and even bring about one's own salvation in one's own strength (traditional view). Or this polity implies that the Torah is the delineation of God's covenant people, and is thus a ground for ethnocentric arrogance: "in order to get saved, you have to join us" (Dunn's view). No matter how *nomos* is taken here, *only in this negative meaning* it is said that *nomos* is a ministry of death and condemnation (2 Cor. 3:7, 9), a polity that brings wrath (Rom. 4:15), that brings one under a curse (Gal. 3:10), a polity of hostility by keeping Jews and Gentiles apart (Eph. 2:14-16), a polity that functions as a "record of debt that stood against us with its legal demands" (Col. 2:14).[79]

In *this* sense Paul can say: "Now we know that the Torah[80] is good, if one uses it lawfully,[81] understanding this,

---

79. Assuming that *cheirographon* (lit., "handwriting") does refer to the Torah (cf., e.g., Peake [1979, 527]: "It is generally agreed that the reference here is to the Law"); others, however, take it to mean "our written agreement to keep the law, our certificate of debt to it" (Robinson [1952, 43], followed by Bruce [1984, 109]; cf. Berkowitz [1999, 230]).

80. Here the word *nomos* does not have the article; Paul is referring to the "principle of law" in general. However, in my view, the context indicates that this includes the Torah (in the negative sense just described), so that "law" is not necessarily something different from the Torah (as has been suggested by Berkowitz [1999, 230]).

81. Gr. *nomimōs*, that is, as defined by the Torah itself (Stern [1999, 634]).

What is the Torah?

that the Torah is not laid down for the just but for the lawless and disobedient, for the ungodly and sinners," etc. (1 Tim. 1:8–9), and: "through the law comes knowledge of sin" (Rom. 3:20; cf. 7:7). Because of this negative sense of *nomos*, many Jesus-believers unfortunately insist that they have nothing to do with the law anymore, appealing solely to statements such as 1 Timothy 1:8–9, just mentioned, and to the statement: "[Y]ou are not under law but under grace" (Rom. 6:14), or: "[W]e are released from the law" (7:6). This is a *onesided and therefore wrong appeal to Scripture*. To see this, let us now turn to the positive function of the Torah.

1.4.2 The Positive Function

In a *positive* sense, Paul often refers to the Torah in a more spiritual-transcendent meaning, that is, the Mosaic Torah, or the authoritative, divine revelation—the eternal Torah—that lies behind it (which I will explain later). This is the Torah as something "holy and righteous and good" (Rom. 7:12), "the Torah of God" (vv. 22, 25), the Torah that is "fulfilled in us" through the Spirit (8:4), the Torah of which love is the "fulfilling," and which is therefore also valid for believers (13:10; Gal. 5:14), the "Torah of Christ" under which Jewish and non-Jewish believers have been placed (6:2; 1 Cor. 9:21). This is the Torah whose essence of love Jesus already described as being the "great and first commandment" (Matt. 22:36–40 and par.).

There is no way we could claim that this (essence of the) Torah is not valid for (non-Jewish) Jesus-believers. Jesus said explicitly that he had *not* come to abolish the Torah or the Prophets but to "fulfill" them (Matt. 5:17). The Torah is eternal: "I will keep your Torah continually, forever and ever" (Ps. 119:44). And Paul says, "Christ is the culmination of the Torah" (Rom. 10:4 NIV), or "goal" (CEB), *not* "the end of the Torah," or, even worse: "Christ has brought the Law to an end" (GNT). Christ *fulfilled* the Torah, but he never *ended* it. How can the Torah go forth from Zion (Isa. 2:3; Micah 4:2) one day in the future, if Christ has put it to an end? To quote Paul again: "Do we then overthrow the Torah by this faith? By no means! On the contrary, we uphold [or, establish] the Torah" (Rom. 3:31).

There are more such positive references to the Torah in a New Testament context. The apostle James speaks of its essence of love as "the perfect Torah, the Torah of liberty" (James 1:25; cf. 2:12). For unregenerated Man, the Torah means bondage; for regenerated Man, led by the Holy Spirit, the Torah means freedom because the Torah demands of the believer exactly what his new nature desires to do. James also calls it "the royal [or, kingly] Torah" (2:8), that is, the Torah of the Kingdom of God (cf. v. 5, "heirs of the kingdom"). In this essential meaning, the Torah is the eternal Torah, identical with the *Hokmah* (Wisdom) of Proverbs 8, in a certain sense identical with the *Logos* of John 1 (see chapter 3).[82] The one *Logos* (Word) of Jesus is refracted in his many *logoi* (words), which are his commandments (John 14:23-24), just as the Ten Commandments are actually the Ten Words (*Asheret Devarim*, or, as the rabbis usually said, *Asheret Dibrot*: Exod. 34:28; Deut. 4:13; 10:4; see §6.3.2). In Romans 3:2, Paul uses the term *logia*: "the Jews were entrusted with the *logia* (oracles) of God," which amounts to saying: "the Torah of God."

Indeed, love, the divine *agapē*, is the sum and fulfillment of the Torah in this elevated meaning. Paul says: "Owe no one anything, except to love each other, for the one who loves another has fulfilled the Torah. For the commandments, 'You shall not commit adultery, You shall not murder, You shall not steal, You shall not covet,' and any other commandment, are summed up in this word: 'You shall love your neighbor as yourself.' Love does no wrong to a neighbor; therefore love is the fulfilling of the Torah" (Rom. 13:8-10). Paul speaks of the Torah here as something self-evident, even to his Gen-

---

82. Cf. Ouweneel (1997, 454; 1998, 59-60).

tile-Christian readers, because the essence of the Torah was just as relevant for them as for the Jewish Jesus-believers.

Paul speaks of love in the sense not of some vague sentimental feeling, but of concrete acts of love; truly keeping the Torah consists of *works* of love. Therefore, Jesus does speak of many commandments (John 14:15, 21; 15:10; cf. Matt. 28:19; 1 Cor. 7:19; 14:37; 2 Pet. 3:2; 1 John 2:3-4; 3:22, 24; 5:2-3; 2 John 6), but also of *the* commandment. Apparently, this is the focal point uniting all his commandments: the new Love Commandment (John 13:34; 15:12; cf. 1 John 2:7-8; 2 John 5). All the commandments seem to flow forth from, and to be summarized in, the Love Commandment (see more extensively §§5.1, 6.1, and especially 7.3). In this one commandment, the entire essence of the Torah comes to expression, because God himself is love (1 John 4:8, 16). The essence of God is the essence of the Torah, or, the Torah reflects God. In Jesus, this love has come to manifestation in its perfect form, in his loving person as well as in his work of love. In believers, this love of God comes to manifestation in their keeping his commandments, that is, *the* Love Commandment. This is possible only if God's own love dwells in them: ". . . that the love with which you have loved me may be in them, and I in them" (John 17:26b; cf. 1 John 2:5, 15; 3:17; 4:7-8, 12, 16; 5:3). "God's love has been poured into our hearts through the Holy Spirit who has been given to us" (Rom. 5:5). All these points are explained and unfolded in the following chapters.

Chapter 2
Three Views of the Torah

Give ear, O my people, to my Torah;
*   incline your ears to the words of my*
*   mouth!*
I will open my mouth in a parable;
*   I will utter dark sayings from of old,*
things that we have heard and known,
*   that our fathers have told us.*
We will not hide them from their children,
*   but tell to the coming generation*
the glorious deeds of the L<small>ORD</small>*, and his might,*
*   and the wonders that he has done.*
                            Psalm 78:1–4

Owe no one anything, except to love each other,
*   for the one who loves another has fulfilled the Torah.*
For the commandments,
*   "You shall not commit adultery,*
*   You shall not murder,*
*   You shall not steal,*
*   You shall not covet,"*
*   and any other commandment,*

> *are summed up in this word:*
> *"You shall love your neighbor as*
> *yourself."*
> *Love does no wrong to a neighbor;*
> *therefore love is the fulfilling of the*
> *Torah.*
> Romans 13:8–10

Summary: *The Torah does not stand by itself, but functions coherently with the whole of Scripture. No wonder there are very different views of the Torah, because there are various views of the coherence between the Tanakh and the New Testament. The three most important views are those of covenant theology, dispensational theology, and Messianic theology. Covenant theologians teach that Jesus-believers are still under only the moral part of the Torah of Moses. Dispensational theologians teach that Jesus-believers no longer have anything to do with the Torah of Moses. Messianic theologians teach that at least Messianic Jews are still under the* entire *Torah of Moses. In contrast to these three views, I defend the position that there exists only one, eternal Torah, under which God's people have been placed in every phase of salvation history, but that each phase has its very own form (manifestation) of the Torah.*

2.1   The Two Older Theological Views

2.1.1   Covenant and Dispensational Theology

AS I SAID EARLIER (§1.1), THREE THEOLOGICAL VIEWS with regard to the Torah deserve our attention. The central question I want to raise is this: Are Jesus-believers obligated to keep God's Torah? Of course, the answer depends on how we define "Torah":

(1) Are those dispensational theologians (called dispensationalists) right who claim that we are bound only to the Messianic Torah, the "Torah of Christ" (1 Cor. 9:21; Gal. 6:2), and that, as a matter of principle, this Torah has nothing to do with the Mosaic Torah?

(2) Are those covenant theologians (called federalists, from

Latin *foedus*, "covenant") right who claim that we are bound to obey the Mosaic Torah, but only the essential or moral part of it?

(3) Are those Messianic theologians (confessing Jesus as Messiah and Savior, but maintaining their Jewish identity) right who claim that Messianic Jews, and according to some, *all* Jesus-believers, are bound to keep the entire Mosaic Torah, as far as possible today (since there is no Temple in Jerusalem)?[1]

In summary, the choices are that Jesus-believers must (1) not keep the Mosaic Torah, (2) keep only the moral part of the Mosaic Torah, or (3) keep the entire Mosaic Torah.

Historically speaking, the two most important theological paradigms in question are federalism (covenant theology) and dispensationalism (dispensational theology). In the words of Dan Juster: "Two great theologies have predominated in the interpretation of Scripture in the believing Church over the past seventy-five years [i.e., 1920–1995]. One has been called 'Covenant theology,' the other 'dispensationalism.'"[2] It is interesting to note that Messianic Jews can be found in both camps, although they seem to sympathize more with the latter view, given the fact that most of them are premillennialists; that is, they believe that the second coming of Christ precedes the millennial Messianic kingdom of peace and justice (the *'olam habba*[3]). Covenant theology is linked with Reformational thinking, and dispensational theology with free-church Evangelicalism.

---

1. Stern (2009) refers to this third model as the "Olive Tree" theology; cf. Appendix I.
2. Juster (1995, 43).
3. The "world (or age) to come"; see for the Gk. version of this Heb. expression and its counterpart, *'olam hazeh* (the "present age [or world]"), Matt. 12:32; 13:40; Mark 10:30; Luke 16:8; 18:30; 20:34; Rom. 12:2; 1 Cor. 1:20; 2:6, 8; 3:18; 2 Cor. 4:4; Eph. 1:21; 1 Tim. 6:17, 19; and Heb. 6:5.

Elsewhere I have analyzed the differences between covenant theology and dispensational theology more thoroughly.[4] Here I will summarize those differences that are important for our present purpose.

(1) According to covenant theologians, there is in God's counsel ultimately *only one people of God*, that is, the sum of all believers from Adam to the last day. Tanakhic Israel and the New Testament church are forms of this one people, which is the church (*ekklesia*) of God in the broadest sense of the word. More moderate covenant theologians believe that the Tanakhic prophecies speaking of a future restoration of Israel will be fulfilled in ethnic Israel (in whatever form), but then still in such a way that this future Jesus-believing Israel will become part of the worldwide church.

(2) According to dispensational theologians, there is in God's counsel an essential distinction between the *two peoples of God*, that is, Israel and the church (not including believers from among the Gentiles in the Tanakh and those in the future Messianic kingdom). Though saved through the same blood of Christ, these two peoples have a very different calling, nature, and destination. All Tanakhic prophecies speaking of a future restoration of Israel will be fulfilled literally in future ethnic Israel and in the Gentiles during the Messianic kingdom. According to more moderate dispensationalists, these prophecies can be *applied* to the church, or may find in the church a kind of pre-fulfillment.[5] Moderate dispensationalists have also reconsidered the sharp contrast that had been assumed between the Mosaic dispensation of the law and the present dispensation of grace. There *is* a distinction, since the former points forward to the latter, and the latter fulfills the

---

4. See Ouweneel (2010, 2011, 2012); for a similar treatment, but then from a federalist point of view, see Poythress (1987).
5. Poythress (1987, 31–33) describes those holding this view as "applicatory" dispensationalists; an example is Tan (1974, 180).

former; but in fact, *both* dispensations involve a polity of *both* grace *and* law (in this order).[6]

The actual differences between covenant theology and dispensational theology do not concern the concepts of covenant and dispensation as such. Although extreme dispensationalists see this differently, dispensational theology does *not* necessarily entail that the church has nothing to do with the New Covenant, and thus nothing to do with the (Mosaic or Millennial) Torah. In my view, 1 Corinthians 11:25, 2 Corinthians 3:6, and Hebrews 8 make clear that there *must* be a link between the church and the New Covenant, even if one can view this link in different ways. The problem is not the concept of covenant as such, but a specific tenet of covenant theology, namely, that in God's counsel there can be only one (covenant) people. This means that either Gentile believers are thought to be incorporated into Israel, or that believers from Israel (including the numerous converts in the end time) are thought to be incorporated into the church—if these two alternatives are not basically identical. (In practice there *is* a difference: the former view implies for some Gentile Jesus-believers nowadays that they are obligated to live like Jews, whereas because of the latter view, Jesus-believing Jews throughout the centuries have been forced to surrender their Jewish identity.)

The concept of "dispensation," referring to a specific phase in salvation history, does not constitute the actual problem either, because covenant theology, too, necessarily distinguishes such phases: before and after the promise to Abraham, before and after the Torah-giving on Mount Sinai, before and after the resurrection of Christ, before and after the second coming of Christ.

The point that really matters is the alleged extent of the differences between these two phases. Covenant theology

---

6. See extensively §§4.2 and 4.3, and Appendix II.

emphasizes the *continuity* between the phases, and concludes that in all phases there is only one salvation and one people of God. Dispensational theology underscores the *discontinuity* between the phases, and concludes that, as a result, in the end there are at least two very different peoples of God, namely, Israel and the church.[7] As I said, there are Hebrew Christians in both camps. However, there seems to be a new current within Messianic theology (the theology of Jesus-believing Jews) that is developing its own approach. On the one hand, it believes, together with dispensational theology, in a future millennial kingdom of the Messiah and the future restoration of ethnic Israel in the Holy Land, both spiritually and politically. On the other hand, it believes with covenant theology that in the end there will be only one people of God, the universal people of God from all ages, of which future restored Israel will form a distinct part—distinct, but not separate.[8]

2.1.2 View of the Torah

In §2.1.1, I briefly sketched the three views with respect to the Torah: Jesus-believers must not keep the Mosaic Torah at all (dispensational theology), or only the moral part of the Torah (covenant theology), or ideally the whole Torah (Messianic theology). It is my personal view that, in a certain sense, *all three* views are mistaken. Dispensational theologians, who for a long time took a strongly antinomian position ("Christians have nothing to do with the Law, or any law") are wrong because the substance of the Messianic Torah (also called the "Law of Christ," 1 Cor. 9:21; Gal. 6:2) is identical with the substance of the Mosaic Torah. We are dealing here with manifestations of one and the same eternal Torah. (I will defend this view below.)

Covenant theologians are wrong in claiming that Jesus-be-

---

7. For a balanced discussion of the continuity–discontinuity problem, see the essays in Feinberg (1988).
8. See the summary by Juster (1995, 43–45).

lievers must be under the Mosaic Torah—even if only under the moral part of it—because Gentiles, believers or non-believers, never were and never will be formally under the Mosaic Torah. It is the Torah *of Israel* (and Gentile believers, as we shall see, will never become Israel), or it is "the Torah of the LORD, the God of Israel" (2 Kings 10:31), and the priests "shall teach Jacob your rules and Israel your Torah" (Deut. 33:10); ". . . the Torah or the commandment that the LORD commanded the children of Jacob, whom he named Israel" (2 Kings 17:34; cf. 1 Chron. 16:40; Neh. 8:2). "He . . . appointed a Torah in Israel, which he commanded our fathers to teach to their children" (Ps. 78:5). No Gentile ever came under the Torah of Israel, unless he or she became a proselyte of Israel. Both the claim that Gentile believers have been incorporated into Israel, and thus came under the Mosaic Torah, and the claim that the ceremonial and civil parts of the Mosaic Torah have been abolished, are false. (I will defend this view below as well.) For the same reason, Messianic Jews are mistaken if they believe that Gentile Jesus-believers are under the Mosaic Torah, ideally or formally; that would be the case only if these Gentiles were to join Judaism. All these three views will be discussed further below, and will be contrasted with a view that tries to overcome in a Scriptural way the three errors mentioned.

It is not my intention to enter into all the differences between federalist, dispensational, and Messianic theologies in more detail in the present study. I limit myself to the question of the Torah. However, we do have to consider briefly the prophecies concerning Israel in order to properly understand the Torah. With respect to the Torah, the three views mentioned can be summarized as follows.[9]

(1) *Covenant theology*:[10] Because Israel was, and is, under

---

9. Cf. the extensive study of Fruchtenbaum (1992).
10. Among covenant theologians, representative postmillennialists are Hodge (1960) and Rushdoony (1978); representative amillennialists

the Mosaic Torah, and many covenant theologians consider the church to be the true Israel, they conclude that the church is under the Mosaic Torah. Because this view does not entail that *all* 613 commandments of the Mosaic Torah are valid for the church, covenant theology faces the challenge of drawing a line within the Torah between the commandments that allegedly are valid for the church, and those that supposedly are no longer valid for the church. This line cannot be anything other than an arbitrary line, as we will see. A striking example is found in the argumentation around the Shabbat commandments, which are still thought to be valid, though allegedly transferred to the Sunday (see Appendix III). The problem of the Shabbat also illustrates the difficulties arising when the attempt is made to separate the supposed moral from the ceremonial and civil *torot*. This is impossible because the three types of *torot* are inseparably interwoven within the Shabbat commandments (cf. §7.2.3).

(2) *Dispensational theology*:[11] Because Israel was, and is, under the Mosaic Torah, and many dispensational theologians consider the church and Israel to be fully distinct, they conclude that the church is not at all under the Mosaic Torah. Because dispensational theologians are aware of the fact that the church does stand under the Messianic Torah (the law of Christ), they face the challenge either of keeping the Mosaic and the Messianic Torah entirely separated, or of downplaying the notion of a Christian Torah as such. An example of the latter is offered by Betz, who claims that the apostle Paul adopted the concept of law in Galatians 6:2 from his opponents, and used it here in a polemical way.[12] O'Neill even

---

are Berkhof (1939) and Hendriksen (1978); representative premillennialists are Ladd (1959) and Buswell (1962).

11. Representatives include Chafer (1936, 1948), Ryrie (1965), and Walvoord (1959).
12. Betz (1979, 300–301).

claims that the term *nomos* is so foreign to the context that it must have been interpolated.[13] Räisänen asserts that *nomos* is being used in Galatians 6:2 in a rather loose, almost metaphorical way, more or less as it is used in Romans 3:27 or 8:2. Fulfilling the *nomos* of Christ is simply living the way that a life in Christ has to be lived; the law of Christ is not literally a law.[14] Likewise, Westerholm believes that Paul replaces the Mosaic Law by the Holy Spirit, not by another law; as an analogy with the Mosaic Torah, the expression "law of Christ" is being used loosely to refer to the way of living that is fitting for a Jesus-believer.[15] Again, I notice a certain arbitrariness in this minimizing of the idea of the Torah of Christ, since Paul demands of Jesus-believers that they fulfill the Torah, to which end he even gives literal examples from the Decalogue (the Ten Words)[16] in such a way that a Jesus-believer cannot possibly maintain that formally he has nothing to do with the Decalogue.

(3) *Messianic theology*:[17] In fact, there are many types of Messianic theology; here we are referring to those representatives who advocate observing the entire Mosaic Torah (as far as practically possible). For instance, they are divided over the question whether such an observance is desirable (especially to win not-yet-Messianic Jews), or demanded (because Messianic Jews are still Jews); or over the question whether it is desirable or even demanded that also non-Jewish Jesus-believers learn to observe the Torah; or over the question

---

13. O'Neill (1972, 70); cf. other comments in Fung (1988, 287–89), e.g., on the view that the "law of Messiah" is identical with the Mosaic Torah (288n22).
14. Räisänen (1983, 80–81).
15. Westerholm (1988, 214n38).
16. Rom. 13:8–10; cf. Gal. 5:13–15; Eph. 6:2–3.
17. Representatives of a stricter view include Juster (1995), Stern (1997, 1999, 2009), and Berkowitz (1999, 2012).

whether, and to what extent, Messianic Jews are bound to the rabbinic (Talmudic) interpretation of the Mosaic Torah.

Apparently, Messianic couple Ariel and D'vorah Berkowitz takes a kind of combined position. They hold that God always relates to his people through a covenant.[18] This is a typically covenant-theological view, and though not necessarily wrong, it downplays other relationships between God and his people, such as the (metaphorical) father–son, and husband–wife relationships. Interestingly, in opposition to the common version of covenant theology, the Berkowitzes do view the New Covenant as not realized in the church, which Messianic Jews allegedly would otherwise have to join. On the contrary, they suggest that God allows Jesus-believing non-Jews to join Messianic Jews to keep the Mosaic Torah together with them. It is remarkable that, in a typically federalist way, they quote prophecies that, as they clearly recognize, refer to the *future* Messianic kingdom as evidence that non-Jewish believers may freely keep the Torah *today*.[19]

My own view, which I defend in this book, is this.

(1) It is totally acceptable that Messianic Jews keep the law of circumcision, Shabbat, the Jewish festivals, *kashrut* (food laws), etc., because they are still what they always were: Jews. The Jesus-believing Jews in the book of Acts kept the Mosaic Torah, too (see §5.3).

(2) It is not forbidden that non-Jewish believers keep the Mosaic commandments (to a certain extent, like *kashrut*, Shabbat, and the festivals), at least as long as they do not do this out of legalistic motives but, for instance, out of genuine sympathy and solidarity with the Jews, especially when they live

---

18. Berkowitz (1999, 37); note the word "always" in our formulation, which implies that there were also one or more covenants before Noah (cf. Hos. 6:7, "like Adam they transgressed the covenant"; but cf. other translations).

19. Ibid., 65–77; see also §7.3.3.

in Israel. Moreover, it is certainly commendable for Gentile Jesus-believers to study the commandments, because they form part of God's Word and are full of spiritual lessons.

(3) In general, however, it is undesirable that non-Jewish believers keep the Mosaic Torah.[20] There are at least three important reasons for this. First, they have no New Testament foundation for doing so (shown in Acts 15; see also §8.3), and even less do they have any command. Second, it is unnatural for them to do so because they were not raised under the Mosaic Torah. Third, it is difficult for them to keep the Torah out of genuinely pure motives (no legalism, no sensationalism, no self-complacency, no false philo-Semitism, no discontent with existing churches, etc.). I will discuss all these things later.

2.1.3 An Orthodox-Jewish View

The three views mentioned in the previous sections all tried to answer a question that could be formulated as follows: What is/was the relationship between Jesus and the Torah? Did he abolish it, did he abolish part of it, or did he uphold it? My presentation would not be complete if I did not explain a fourth view: that of Orthodox Judaism with respect to Jesus and the Torah.

I can give only a few examples here, but that of Maimonides (Rabbi Moshe ben Maimon [acronym: Rambam], 1138–1204) should certainly be mentioned. On the whole, he is quite negative about Jesus, and understandably so. Nevertheless, he makes the astounding observation that the purpose of Jesus (and of Muhammad as well, he adds) was "to straighten out the way for the King Messiah, and to restore all the world to serve God together," with reference to Zephaniah 3:9 ("the peoples . . . [will] call upon the name of the LORD and serve

---

20. Welker (2013, 22, 42) deduces from Num. 15:13–16 that anyone who believes in the God of the patriarchs "is to be Torah observant."
The text, however, speaks of the "stranger who sojourns with you," not of Gentile Jesus-believers since Acts 15 (see chapter 8 below).

him with one accord"). Through their efforts,

> the whole world had been be filled with the issues of the anointed one and of the Torah and the Laws, and these issues had spread out unto faraway islands and among many nations uncircumcised in the heart, and they discuss these issues and the Torah's laws. These say: "These Laws were true but are already defunct in these days, and do not rule for the following generations"; whereas the other ones say: "There are secret layers in them and they are not to be treated literally, and the Messiah had come and revealed their secret meanings." But when the anointed king will truly rise and succeed and will be raised and uplifted, they all immediately turn about and know that their fathers inherited falsehood, and their prophets and ancestors led them astray.[21]

Apparently, Maimonides wants to say that Jesus and Muhammad spread the knowledge of Israel's God, of the Messiah, and of the Torah throughout the world. However, their followers misunderstood the Torah, thought that it had been abolished, or that their prophets had given the correct interpretation. But when the true Messiah will come, he can connect with the knowledge that the Gentiles worldwide already possess of the Torah, and supply its right interpretation. Interestingly, Maimonides writes elsewhere that Jesus "interpreted the Torah and its precepts in such a fashion as to lead to their total annulment, to the abolition of all its commandments and to the violation of its prohibitions."[22] In the present book, I am trying to show that this is completely false—but how can we blame Maimonides for asserting what all the Christian and Muslim theologians of his day were asserting?

An Orthodox rabbi who had a much more positive view of Jesus was the astonishing German, Rabbi Jacob Emden (1697–1776). He wrote: "It is therefore exceedingly clear that

---

21. *Hilkhot Melakhim* 11:10–12; quoted by Rudin (2010, 128–29).
22. Halkin (1952, iii–iv).

the Nazarene never dreamed of destroying the Torah."[23] In Emden's opinion, Jesus maintained the Torah for the Jews while he sought to guide the Gentiles toward keeping the Seven Noahic Precepts (see §8.3). This is a view totally different from, and far more correct than, that of Maimonides. Jesus did not annul the Torah, but he maintained it. Later in the same letter Emden wrote: "[T]he Nazarene and his Apostles never meant to abolish the Torah of Moses from one who was born a Jew. Likewise did Paul write in his letter to the Corinthians (1 Cor. 7[:17–20]) that each should adhere to the faith in which each was called. They therefore acted in accordance with the Torah by forbidding circumcision to Gentiles, according to the Halakha, as it is forbidden to one who does not accept the yoke of the commandments. They knew that it would be too difficult for the Gentiles to observe the Torah of Moses. They therefore forbade them to circumcise, and it would suffice that they observe the Seven Noahide Commandments, as commanded upon them through the Halakha from Moses at Sinai.

> It is therefore a habitual saying of mine . . . that the Nazarene brought about a double kindness in the world. On the one hand, he strengthened the Torah of Moses majestically, as mentioned earlier, and not one of our Sages spoke out more emphatically concerning the immutability of the Torah. And on the other hand, he did much good for the Gentiles . . . by doing away with idolatry and removing the images from their midst. He obligated them with the Seven Commandments so that they should not be as the beasts of the field. He also bestowed upon them ethical ways, and in this respect he was much more stringent with them than the Torah of Moses, as is well-known.[24]

These are amazing words for an Orthodox rabbi! Jesus

---

23. Harvey Falk, "Rabbi Jacob Emden's Views on Christianity," *Journal of Ecumenical Studies* 19.1 (1982): 108; cf. Falk (2003, ch. 1).
24. Falk (1982, 109–110).

"strengthened the Torah of Moses majestically"! That is perfectly correct. The only point is that Rabbi Emden falls into wishful thinking: Jesus never presented the Seven Noahide Commandments to the Gentiles. On the contrary, he invited them to accept him as the Messiah of Israel, as the Savior and Lord of all Gentile Jesus-believers. That is, Jesus did not just teach commandments; first and foremost he preached his own person, so to speak. He praised the faith of the Roman centurion and of the Canaanite woman because they had recognized Jesus' greatness (Matt. 8:5–13; 15:21–28). When Greeks came to him and wanted to see *him* (not just hear his teaching), Jesus responded by pointing not to his commandments but to his own glory in his very dying: "The hour has come for the Son of Man to be glorified. Truly, truly, I say to you, unless a grain of wheat falls into the earth and dies, it remains alone; but if it dies, it bears much fruit" (John 12:23–24). Jesus' person was far more important than his teaching, to both Jews and Gentiles.

Another example of an Orthodox rabbi to be mentioned here is the Italian, Rabbi Elijah Benamozegh (1822–1900), who respected Jesus as a wise righteous Jew, but criticized the religious innovations of Paul. He wrote: "Jesus was a good Jew who did not dream of founding a rival church," and thus certainly did not dream of abolishing the Torah.[25] Benamozegh did not object to Christians believing in Jesus as long as they observed the Noahide Precepts. In this regard, Jesus had a mission to the world, though not to Israel, in bringing it back to the Noahic covenant. Judaism and Christianity have a common task: spreading to the world the knowledge of the one true God. I admire the positive appreciation by Benamozegh, but at the same time I have to emphasize again that Jesus did *not* preach *only* the one true God; in the last night of his life on earth he said, "[T]his is eternal life, that they know

---

25. Benamozegh (1995, 329).

you the only true God, *and Jesus Christ whom you have sent*" (John 17:3, italics added). In order to inherit the *'olam habbah* ("the world to come"), you must know not only the one true God — through Jesus or otherwise — but you must know *Jesus in person*.

The ideas of rabbis like Emden and Benamozegh have been picked up, for instance, by the Orthodox Jewish (German-American) philosopher Michael Wyschogrod (b. 1928).[26] He emphasized that in ancient times, there were two ways whereby one could belong to the people of God: by being born a Jew, or by joining Israel as a proselyte, and thus becoming a Jew. He added that Jesus provided a third way: belonging to the people of God *without becoming a Jew*. Indeed, without becoming a Jew — but definitely by being linked with Israel, the people of the Torah.[27] And not only that, again I emphasize that belonging to the people of God is not just a matter of following the *way* that Jesus has indicated — it involves accepting Jesus *in person*: "Believe in God; believe also in me" (John 14:1).

2.2 The Two Older Theological Paradigms and the Torah

2.2.1 Questions Concerning the Torah

We are now able to formulate the central questions that we wish to discuss.

1. *Has the Mosaic Torah been abolished in Jesus?* If yes, then the Messianic Torah, to which all Jesus-believers are subject (1 Cor. 9:21; Gal. 6:2), apparently differs essentially from the Mosaic Torah, which it replaces. If no, then the two must be essentially identical. In other words: *what is the relationship between the Mosaic Torah and the Messianic Torah?* No matter how one answers this question, one always seems to run into trou-

---

26. See Wyschogrod (2000, 2004).
27. Cf. Stern (2009, 78–79).

ble. If there is such a relationship—if the Messianic Torah is essentially the same as the Mosaic Torah—how can Paul say that we have "died to the Torah" and are "released from the Torah" (Rom. 7:4, 6)? If there is no such relationship—if the Messianic Torah is essentially different from the Mosaic Torah—how can Paul tell us that the Torah that Jesus-believers "fulfill" is the Torah as we find it specifically in some Mosaic commandments (Rom. 13:8-10)?

My answer to these questions, as I will expound it in this study, is that the Messianic Torah differs substantially from the Mosaic Torah in many ways, but at the same time *these two are identical in their essence*, which consists of the *k'lal gadol b'Torah* ("greatest principle" of the Torah). To put it in the words of Victor Furnish: both "the law of the Spirit of life" (Rom. 8:2) and "the law of Christ" (Gal. 6:2) refer to "the sum and substance of the law of Moses."[28] Lohse says that the two "law-of" phrases just mentioned, as well as "the law of faith" (Rom. 3:27), involve "the original significance of the Torah," enabling the Torah "once again [to] serve its original purpose of testifying to the 'holy, just and good will of God'" (Rom. 7:12).[29] And Schrage writes: "[T]he law of the Old Testament must first become the 'law of Christ' and be interpreted with respect to its true intention (Gal. 6:2); only then can it be the measure of Christian life."[30] James Dunn recognizes the coherence of the Mosaic Torah and the Messianic Torah because of the close link between Galatians 6:2 and 5:13-14 (cf. Rom. 8:4; 13:8-10).[31] That is not to identify the Messianic Torah with the Mosaic Torah as such, but with its substance, as summa-

---

28. Furnish (1968, 235; cf. 59–65, 191–94); the reference to Rom. 8:2 is doubtful (see §1.2.2).
29. Lohse (1991, 161–62).
30. Schrage (1988, 206–207); as opponents of this view, I quoted Betz, Räisänen, and Westerholm above.
31. Dunn (1998, 631–658).

rized and rephrased by Jesus (Matt. 22:36-40; John 13:34).³² To Dunn, this substance, the Love Command, is not one commandment distinct from the rest, but the precipitate or spirit of the *whole* Mosaic Torah.³³

The way I would like to put it is that the Mosaic Torah is an incomplete manifestation of the one and only eternal Torah, just as the Messianic Torah as contained in the New Testament is a far more complete manifestation of that one eternal Torah. In this study, I will often use the terms "form" or "manifestation" of the one, eternal Torah. Kabbalism would speak here of "emanation"; for instance, Meir ben Gabbai wrote in 1531: "The highest wisdom [*hokmah*] contains as the foundation of all emanations pouring forth out of the hidden Eden [cf. Gen. 2:10; Rev. 22:1-2], the true fountain from which the Written and the Oral Torah emanate and are expressed. . . . On this fountain rests the continued existence of all creatures; it is said of it [Ps. 36:9]: 'For with you is the fountain of life.'"³⁴ God is viewed as the continuous giver of the Torah, which includes, in addition to the Written Torah, the Oral Torah, new *halakhot* (ordinances derived from the Torah), and interpretations of the Written and Oral Torah. This view is the Kabbalist expression of the biblical idea of the continuous cooperation between Holy Scripture and the Holy Spirit expounding it (Hag. 2:5; John 14:26; 16:13; 1 Cor. 2:10-16; 12:7-8; Eph. 3:16-19; 6:17), for the Holy Spirit is the fountain of life (cf. John 4:9, 14; 7:38-39; cf. also Isa. 44:3).

When the New Testament tells us that we "died to the Torah" (Gal. 2:19), then we did not die to this *eternal* Torah, but to the Mosaic manifestation of it, only insofar as this was either viewed legalistically as a way of salvation, a view arising through misunderstanding the statement, "The man who

---

32. See Dunn (1998, 655n134/135).
33. Dunn (1998, 656-57).
34. Quoted by Scholem (1971, 298).

does this will live by them" (Rom. 10:5; Gal. 3:12; cf. Lev. 18:5; Neh. 9:29; Ezek. 20:11, 13), and/or the Mosaic Torah was viewed in an arrogant, ethnocentric manner. Both views were wrong because the true believers mentioned in the Tanakh also received the life of rebirth on the basis of grace and faith, not on the basis of self-righteous works. I will come back to this point extensively.

2. If there is a link between the Mosaic Torah and the Messianic Torah, to what extent are Jesus-believing Gentiles under the Torah? On the one hand, covenant theology says that we are under only the moral part of the Mosaic Torah. On the other hand, some Messianic Jews say that we are under the entire Torah, that is, under all of its 613 commandments (as far as they can be obeyed today, given the fact that there is no Temple). Some of them even say that Gentile Jesus-believers ought to learn to gladly accept the whole Torah and enjoy the blessing of living under it. The problem with the first position is that Scripture does not seem to warrant any dividing up of the Torah into a moral part, on the one hand, and a ceremonial and a civil part, on the other. Such dividing is impossible. The problem with the second position is that there is no positive evidence for it in the New Testament. It even seems to contradict Acts 15:20, which tells us that the Mosaic Torah was not to be placed upon the Gentile Jesus-believers except for a few specific commandments (although v. 21 is taken by some to be an encouragement for Gentile Jesus-believers to get to know the Torah better; see §§8.2 and 8.3).

My own suggestion is to consider the Messianic Torah not as some part of the Mosaic Torah (*contra* the first position) but as identical with the latter's focus and substance, which refers back to the eternal Torah. Jesus-believers are under the *entire* Torah—not under many time-bound regulations of the Mosaic Torah (*contra* the second position), but under the Torah in its *eternal essential transcendent substance*, as well as under the many New Testament precepts, which form the immanent elaboration of the Messianic Torah.

Three Views of the Torah

3. *If Jesus-believers are under the Torah, does this hold in the same manner for both Jewish and Gentile believers?* In other words, if Gentile believers are in fact not bound to a number of so-called ceremonial and civil regulations of the Torah, could it be that Jewish Jesus-believers are still under these regulations? If one severs the Messianic Torah from the Mosaic Torah (see 1. above), then of course the answer is no. But the Mosaic Torah is a manifestation of the one and only eternal Torah, as we now know it more completely in the Messianic Torah. With regard to Israel, to whom the Mosaic Torah was given, this Mosaic Torah was never abrogated, neither by Jesus nor by the apostles (see chapter 5). In other words, the Mosaic Torah still holds for Jewish Jesus-believers because their acceptance of Jesus as the Messiah does not alter the fact that they are still Jews, belonging to the chosen people. Indeed, Paul and all the early (Jewish) Jesus-believers observed the Torah (Acts 21:20-26; 25:8; 28:17; see extensively §5.3). However, again the question whether Jewish Jesus-believers ought to keep the entire Torah cannot be answered with a simple yes or no. Even some Messianic Jews are of the opinion that they need not keep the entire Torah, because in the New Testament some Mosaic decrees have allegedly been abolished, especially the sacrificial laws (see chapter 5).

Again, we encounter the part-whole problem here. Is there really New Testament evidence that only certain ceremonial commandments have been abrogated, so that only a part of the Torah—albeit a very large part—is to be kept by Messianic Jews? Is not such a view contradicted by the fact that the Millennial Torah of the future Messianic kingdom (*'olam habba*) will contain the greater part of the Mosaic Torah, including *all* the sacrifices (see §6.2.2)? It therefore seems that a consistent Messianic position should be either to keep the Torah in its substantial sense (the *Messianic* Torah, the great Love Command, as that is unfolded in hundreds of New Testament precepts), or to keep the entire *Mosaic* Torah without any exceptions (again, insofar as such a keeping of the entire

Torah is at all possible today, in the absence of the Temple).

My own position is that the part-whole problem can be circumvented if we see that the Mosaic Torah, which is just a temporal manifestation of the eternal Torah, is resumed under the New Covenant—the covenant of the future Messianic kingdom—in a newer, richer form: as the Millennial Torah. This view has two interesting implications. On the one hand, it fully allows for the view that a great number of regulations under the Mosaic Torah had only a temporary significance—for instance, in view of the agricultural economy of the Holy Land at the time, or in view of the very limited medical and hygienic knowledge of the time. On the other hand, this view supports Messianic Jews in their observing Shabbat, the great festivals, *kashrut*, and many ceremonial purifications, if only for this reason, that such regulations will also have their place in the coming Millennial Torah.

With regard to the notion of the eternal Torah, I notice that in the *Zohar* (see §3.3.1), the Torah is compared to angels who, when appearing in this world, have to assume some visible form. Likewise, the Torah, when entering the world, was clothed in a "garment," which consists of the narratives relating to events in this world, such as Israel's exodus out of Egypt. David, however, was conscious of the mysteries hidden behind that form: "Open my eyes, that I may behold wondrous things out of your Torah" (Ps. 119:18). The importance of the "garment" lies in the "body" concealed by it, and the importance of the "body" lies in the "soul" concealed by it, says the *Zohar*. The narratives are the "garment," the distinct laws are the "body" of the Torah. It is only the sages who also behold the Torah's "soul," which is the kernel of everything, the original Torah.[35] This primordial Torah (German, *Ur-Torah*), which in the Kabbalist view is "nothing but the great Name of God," is called in the Kabbalah the *Torah q'dumah*, literally "earliest (or primordial, preceding) Torah"

---

35. *Sefer ha-Zohar* (Wilna ed., 1882, III fol. 152a); see further in §8.3.2.

(i.e., long before Sinai), or *Torah q'lulah*, literally "non-unfolded Torah."[36] This is the one "Torah of Creation [*beriah*]," which some Kabbalists contrast with the "Torah of (the World of) Emanation [*atzilut*]" (say, the "Torah of spirituality"), the transcendent kernel of the Torah, or the Messianic Torah.[37]

2.2.2 Important Presuppositions

Of course, all these matters concerning the Torah will be extensively dealt with in the coming chapters. At present, we will consider some presuppositions that are vitally important for our subsequent discussion. This is not the place to deal extensively with them, but they must be carefully stated. I designate my own theological position as moderate dispensational theology.[38] This involves, among other points, the following views:

1. I do not object to ultimately identifying *one single people of God*, consisting of all those who are destined to eternal divine bliss, all sharing the same covenant blessings promised to the patriarchs and the same salvation through Jesus' atoning sacrifice. However, I do believe in a distinction between Millennial Israel and the New Testament Ekklesia, excluding believers from the nations during the Tanakh period—such as Melchizedek (Gen. 14:17-20), Job (Job 42), Heber (Judg. 4), Naaman (2 Kings 5), Ebed-Melech (Jer. 38-39)—and during the future Messianic kingdom. In eternity, Israel and the Ekklesia will remain distinct, just as the New Jerusalem, which is the bride of the Lamb (the Ekklesia), will be distinct from God's people and the nations (Rev. 21:2, 9-10, 24-26).[39] Israel,

---

36. Cf. Scholem (1960, 61, 70, 88–89; 1971, 293–95); see further in §§3.3.1 and 4.1; *q'dumah* is related with *q'dem*, "of old" (primordial time, if not past eternity).
37. Scholem (1960, 91–92, 100, 112–16; 1971, 75–77; cf. 111–12, 115–18, 124, 151).
38. See extensively Ouweneel (2010, 2011, 2012).
39. See, e.g., Kelly (1872, 465–67); Snell (1878, 231–45). Cf. more recent

the wife of YHWH, is essentially different from the Ekklesia, the bride of the glorified Jesus Messiah at the right hand of God.[40] I do not object to calling Millennial Israel the bride of the glorified Jesus Messiah seated on the Millennial throne of David—just as the patriarch Jacob had two brides: he came for Rachel (Israel) and he got Leah (the Gentile church), but in the end he will have Rachel as well.[41]

2. *Israel* consists of all the physical descendants of Abraham, Isaac, and Jacob. Now, "not all who are descended from Israel belong to Israel." That is, all Israelites are Abraham's offspring but only the reborn Israelites are his (true) children; they alone constitute the "Israel of God" (Rom. 9:6; John 8:33, 37, 39; Gal. 6:16). Therefore, the true Israel consists only of the reborn (truly godly) descendants of the patriarchs, who live by grace and love God, and the false Israel consists of the wicked descendants of the patriarchs, whether religious (in the outward sense) or not.

3. The *Ekklesia*, that is, the Body of the Messiah and the spiritual House of God in the present dispensation, consists of all true believers in Messiah from the Day of Pentecost (Acts 2) until the second coming of Christ. (I avoid the word "church" here because to most people this suggests a certain earthly and historical denomination or organization.) The Ekklesia contains both Jewish and Gentile Jesus-believers, with equal rights and equal standing before God (Eph. 2:11-22;

---

dispensationalist commentators, who see a far closer link between the New Jerusalem and the nations on the Millennial earth, such as Walvoord (1966, 313–14).

40. See Fruchtenbaum (2003, Appendix III); cf. the comment by Stern (1999, 838).

41. Interestingly, the church father Ambrose, an adherent of replacement theology (the church is the true Israel), gave the opposite *midrash*: Leah represents the law and Rachel represents grace (*De Jacobo* II. 5. 25); Gregory the Great (*Magna Moralia* XXX, 25, 72) and Irenaeus (*Adversus Haereses* IV, 21, 3), too, saw Rachel as a figure of the church.

cf. 1 Cor. 12:12–13, Gal. 3:28; Col. 3:11). Since Acts 2, all Jesus-believing Jews until the second coming belong to this Ekklesia. Jews who will believe in Jesus *at* the second coming, when the scales will fall from their eyes (cf. Acts 9:18) and they "look on him whom they have pierced" (Zech. 12:10) — when, so to speak, the true Joseph will make himself known to his brothers (Gen. 45:3) — will form the believing remnant of Israel. This will be the nucleus of the saved and justified Israel in the future Messianic kingdom on earth (Rom. 11:26; Isa. 45:25; 60:21). It will be wonderful to be members of the Ekklesia in its heavenly glory, reigning with Messiah during the *'olam habba* in their immortal (resurrected or transformed) body (1 Cor. 15:50–54; Phil. 3:20–21; Rev. 20:4–6). It will be equally wonderful to be members of restored Israel, dwelling in the Holy Land during the *'olam habba* on earth in their mortal bodies, having families under the most blessed conditions under Messiah, each sitting under their vine and their fig tree (Ps. 22:30–31; Isa. 65:20–25; Micah 4:1–4; Zech. 8:4–5).

4. Restored Israel and the Ekklesia exhibit clear-cut similarities, for all believers of all times have been atoned by the same blood of Jesus (Acts 4:12; Rom. 3:25–26; Rev. 5:9), and since Abraham they all are "sons of Abraham," and all share the blessings of the promises made to him (Rom. 4:11–12, 16; Gal. 3:7–9, 14, 29). Nonetheless, the differences between them are quite essential: Israel and the Ekklesia have a different calling, nature, and destination. Thus, believing Jews within the Ekklesia have a portion different from that of believing Jews in the Tanakhic period or in the future Messianic kingdom on earth. Yet, the "heavenly" calling of the Ekklesia and the "earthly" calling of Israel should not be disconnected radically, as was often done by classic dispensational theologians. This is one of the main points on which David Stern attacks dispensationalism,[42] and understandably so. A more moderate dispensationalist such as Kenneth Barker wrote: "[S]trictly

---

42. Stern (1999, 416, 575).

speaking it is also incorrect to call Israel God's earthly people and the Church God's heavenly people, since in the eternal state we will all live together sharing in the blessings of the New Jerusalem and the new earth."[43] The Ekklesia does relate to the Torah and to the Sermon on the Mount (see §2.1.1), and it also has an earthly position and calling (Eph. 5-6; Col. 3; 1 Pet. 2:13-3:7). Likewise, Israel's calling is not just "earthly"; already Abraham knew of a "heavenly country," and was en route to it (Heb. 11:16). Following in his footsteps, all godly Israelites who have passed away are waiting for this same Millennial celestial place.

5. The Ekklesia is not some spiritual Israel, and Gentile Jesus-believers have not been incorporated into Israel.[44] Neither group has been proselytized by the other. The olive tree in Romans 11 is neither Israel nor the church, but the sphere of blessing rooted in the Abrahamic covenant (see Appendix I). It is just as mistaken to assert that Gentile Jesus-believers have been incorporated into Israel as it is to assert that Jewish Jesus-believers have been incorporated into the (Gentile) church. In practice, both ideas amount to the same erroneous view of some spiritual Israel. Believers who were born Gentiles are henceforth distinguished from "the Gentiles" (1 Cor. 5:1; Eph. 4:17; 1 Thess. 4:5), although sometimes they are called "Gentiles" (Rom. 11:13; 16:4; Gal. 2:14; Eph. 3:1; Col. 1:27); they constitute the people taken by God "from the Gentiles for his name" (Acts 15:14). Parallel to this, Jesus-believers who were born Jews are henceforth distinguished from "the Jews" (Acts 16:3; 22:30; 23:20; 25:10; 26:2, 7; cf. 2:40; 1 Thess. 2:14), although on other occasions they are called "Jews" (Acts 16:20; 18:24; 21:20-21, 39; 22:3; Gal. 2:13, 15); they constitute the Jewish "remnant chosen by grace" (Rom. 11:5). Together

---

43. Barker (1982, 12).
44. This despite several Reformed rhymings of Psalm 87 in Dutch: ". . . bij Isrel ingelijfd [grafted into Israel]."

Three Views of the Torah

they constitute something altogether new: the Ekklesia is neither Israelite, nor Gentile, but a totally *novel* community, in which Jewish and Gentile believers, on an equal footing, have been formed into "one new man" (Eph. 2:15). As such, it must be distinguished from both Jews and "Greeks" (Gentiles; 1 Cor. 10:32).

6. With regard to *prophecy*, the present view implies that all unfulfilled (Tanakhic) prophecies pertaining to Israel and the nations are fulfilled solely and literally in future ethnic *Israel* and the nations, respectively. To put it in the briefest possible way: this is obvious from the fact that the Tanakhic promises concerning Israel's restoration to the land are linked with the coming of the Messiah and the establishment of his kingdom (important examples are Isa. 31–32, Dan. 7, and Zech. 14). The same Israel that is cursed in Deuteronomy 29 is restored in chapter 30 (and similarly in many other passages). Concerning Israel's future restoration the Scriptures contain many fine details, which may not, and cannot properly, be spiritualized and applied to the Ekklesia.

The New Testament corroborates this picture. Jesus promises that Jerusalem would not see him again *until* it welcomes him with the words of the psalmist: "Blessed is he who comes in the name of the LORD!" (Ps. 118:26; Matt. 23:37–39; Luke 13:34–35). In Matthew 24 and Luke 21, Jesus unequivocally describes Israel as dwelling in the land at the time of his second coming. Romans 11:26 refers to the future salvation of "all Israel"; this cannot possibly refer to the Ekklesia, because in Romans 9–11 the term "Israel" consistently refers to ethnic Israel. In 2 Thessalonians 2:4, we hear of some new temple at the time of the Antichrist; the text provides no reason to doubt that this will be a literal temple. In Revelation 11:1, we find worshippers in this future temple at Jerusalem.

In summary: Israel is loved on account of the patriarchs, "for the gifts and the calling of God are irrevocable" (Rom. 11:28–29); Israel is restored to the land by Messiah: "if their trespass means riches for the world, and if their failure means riches for the Gentiles, how much more will their full inclusion mean! ... For if their rejection means the reconciliation of the world, what will their acceptance mean but life from the dead?" (vv. 12, 15). "God has the power to graft them in again ... the natural branches [will] be grafted back into their own olive tree" (vv. 23-24).

As to the phrase "ethnic Israel," I do realize that "ethnic" is a questionable term. Jacob Neusner,[45] one of the most prolific and influential Jewish authors on Judaism and its relationships to Christianity, has heavily criticized the notion of Judaism as an "ethnic" religion. He claims that "Israel" is just as much a universal body of converts (those who have accepted the Torah and its commandments) as is the Christian church (those who have accepted Jesus as Messiah and Redeemer). This is one answer to the question "Who is a Jew?" — but there are many other Jewish answers to it.[46] As I argued in §1.1.2, "ethnic" is not to be taken in too strict a sense of common biological descent, but it does imply a nation with the patriarchs as its fathers, and this not only in some spiritual sense. The unsatisfactory but widely accepted rabbinic rule, "A Jew is anyone born of a Jewish mother," is based on an ethnic idea, not a religious notion. What Jews who take their Jewishness seriously would consider the question whether they descend from Abraham — whether through their father or through their mother, or both — to be totally irrelevant?

2.2.3 Essentials

Not all of the six points summarized in §2.2.2 are essential to our view of the Torah. I distinguish between:

---

45. Neusner (1995); see more recently Neusner (1983, 1986, 1990, 1993); Neusner and Chilton (1995).
46. E.g., Jocz (1981, 127–39), who cites a 1961 survey given to thirty-one younger American Jewish intellectuals, who all stressed ethnicity, not religion (141).

(1) *Advantageous aspects:* Distinguishing among essentially different phases in salvation history (dispensations) and between two different peoples of God makes it easier to grasp the idea that the one, eternal Torah assumes different temporal manifestations in subsequent salvation-historical phases. In my view, there are different Torah-manifestations in the Mosaic dispensation, in the present dispensation of the Ekklesia, and in the dispensation of the Messianic kingdom (see chapters 6 and 7). In addition, even in the pre-Mosaic dispensations we can discern specific manifestations of the Torah (see §2.3.1).

(2) *Essential aspects:* The fact that believing Jews in the present dispensation belong to the Ekklesia does not alter the fact that they are, and remain, Jews. In the Messiah, Jewish and Gentile Jesus-believers are united, just as men and women, and slaves and free men, are one (Gal. 3:28). At the same time, in daily life Jewish and Gentile Jesus-believers are just as different from one another as men and women, and slaves and free. Particularly important is the conviction that the prophecies concerning Israel will be fulfilled literally in the future Messianic kingdom. This not only implies a rejection of current covenant theology, but also supplies us with an important element for our discussion of the Torah question. I refer to the way the Torah is presented in view of the future Messianic kingdom.

On the one hand, this presentation is a powerful argument against all those who claim that the Mosaic Torah has been abolished because the Millennial Torah will include the greater part of the Mosaic Torah. On the other hand, precisely the dispensationalist position helps us to discern that the way the Torah will function in the future Messianic kingdom is not necessarily an indication of how it ought to function in the present dispensation of the Ekklesia.

One of the most vital elements in this entire discussion is certainly the question whether there are one or two peoples of God. In a commendable way, David Stern tries to maintain a balance between one-ness and two-ness: "Israel and the Messianic Community [= Ekklesia] are two, yet they are one. Overemphasizing the 'one'-ness [as in common covenant theology. WJO] led Christian theologians to conclude that the Church had replaced the Jews as God's people."[47] Consequently, although replacement (or, displacement) theology (or supersessionism) as such is not anti-Semitic, in practice it easily coincides with anti-Semitism. However, Stern continues, "overemphasizing the 'two'-ness [as in dispensational theology, WJO] yields errors just as serious, and, in their own way, just as potentially anti-Semitic. Messianic Judaism should set for itself the task of elucidating correctly the relationship between the Jewish people and the Messianic Community of Jews and Gentiles by means of 'olive tree theology' (Ro 11:23-24N, 11:26aN; Ga 6:16N)."[48] Dispensational theology is "potentially anti-Semitic" in that it severs the Ekklesia from its Jewish roots. It creates a gap and even a contrast between the heavenly, eternal Ekklesia and the earthly, temporal Israel.

So far, so good. However, I am not convinced that Stern's own solution constitutes the entirely correct middle way between covenant theology and dispensational theology. In my opinion, his "olive tree theology" fails at an essential point. The "olive tree" is *not*, as he believes,[49] Israel. It cannot be Israel, for that would imply that the unbelieving "branches" (i.e., Israelites) were cut off from Israel and that Gentile believers have become Israelites, and it is difficult to believe that Stern would be prepared to uphold either view. On the contrary, he rightly argues that no New Testament passage necessarily

---

47. Stern (1999, 804).
48. The N in the Scripture references refers to Stern's notes on these Scriptures.
49. Stern (1999, 13, 412-17, 471, 576, 582, 803).

teaches that Gentile Jesus-believers have become Jews in any sense of the word.[50]

As a matter of fact, I believe Stern to be somewhat closer to covenant theologians, namely, to those among them who do believe that ultimately there will be basically one people of God but that the prophecies concerning Israel's restoration must be taken literally.[51] Two striking exegetical examples clearly place him in this camp (these are examples he himself mentions in the quotation just given): his interpretation of the olive tree as "Israel," and his interpretation of the "Israel of God" in Galatians 6:16 as the Ekklesia.[52] Of course, Stern fiercely combats any form of replacement theology (supersessionism).[53] But then, not all covenant theologians are supersessionists. In this sense, Stern can be classified with the literal-Israel branch of covenant theology. Other Messianic Jews, such as Charles L. Feinberg and Arnold Fruchtenbaum, belong to the dispensational theological camp instead.[54]

It is interesting to note that in 1987 a survey was conducted by the Messianic Jew Michael Schiffman among thirty Messianic congregations in the United States. Of the spiritual leaders, 27% indicated they had a dispensational theological orientation, 7% were of a covenant theological persuasion, and 23% had a promise-oriented theological conviction.[55] More-

---

50. See, e.g., his comments on Rom. 2:28–29 and Rev. 2:9; 3:9 (Stern 1999, 337–40, 795–96, 799). On "Olive Tree theology," see further extensively Appendix I below.
51. Cf. Berkhof (1939, 716) for the names of some postmillennialist theologians defending this type of view.
52. Stern (1992, 574–76).
53. See Stern (1992, 24–25, 75, 141–42, 216, 404, 410–11, 415–16, 471–72, 571, 575, 689, 747, 806).
54. See especially Feinberg (1961, 1985) and Fruchtenbaum (1992, 2003).
55. See Kaiser (1978, 2008), in whose Old Testament theology the idea of promise functions as a "canonical theological center." His prom-

over, 57% were premillennialists, 43% pre-, 3% mid-, and 7% post-tribulationalists (of course, the percentages overlap). Of the congregation members, 87% claimed to be in full agreement with the leader's theological position, 13% were not.[56]

To a certain moderate extent, the cleft between covenant theology and dispensational theology, two centuries old by now, runs right through present-day Messianic Judaism. This comes to light in minor but highly fascinating details, which are typical of the many theological battles that are still being, or must yet be, fought within Messianic Judaism. A practical and interesting example is the *kippah*, the little cap that religious Jewish men wear on their head. Fruchtenbaum is very much against wearing it, especially during prayer;[57] Stern sees no objection but rather certain advantages under well-specified circumstances.[58]

2.3 The Pre-Mosaic Torah

2.3.1 The Adamic Torah, Noahic Torah, and Abrahamic Torah

In the full, transcendent sense, there is only one, eternal Torah of God; think again of the *Torah atzilut* and the *Torah q'lulah* (§2.2.1). We will attempt to further identify this eternal Torah in chapter 3. However, there are many different immanent manifestations of that one Torah in successive dispensations. The most important ones are those dispensations explicitly mentioned in Scripture.

(1) At the beginning of creation: the *Cosmic Torah*, the

---

ise-theology has been described as a middle road between covenant theology and dispensational theology.

56. Schiffman (1996, 128–29).
57. Cf. 1 Cor. 11:4, "Every man who prays or prophesies with his head covered dishonors his head" (cf. the explanation of Stern 1999, 474).
58. Fruchtenbaum/Stern (1985); cf. Stern (1997, 170–71, 185, 199; 1999, 472, 474, 501, 505).

Three Views of the Torah

law-order or creational order instituted by God for the entire empirical world. This Cosmic Torah is closely linked with the Mosaic Torah. In Psalm 19, there is fundamentally only one Torah, that is to say, one revelation of God, whether it is the Cosmic Torah in the works of nature (vv. 1-7), or the Mosaic Torah for human life (vv. 8-15). In Psalm 119, which is an acrostic poem, the verses 89 to 96 form the stanza *lamed*. This stanza begins with distinctly speaking of the Cosmic Torah (vv. 89-91), but in the same breath the stanza continues with speaking of the Mosaic Torah. Given the parallel between Torah and Hokmah (see chapter 3), we can also refer here to Proverbs 3, where we find a brief reference to the *hokmah* (wisdom) with which God created the world (vv. 19-20) and the *hokmah* expressed in the father's precepts for his son, and the *hokmah* with which the son obeys these precepts (vv. 13-35).

(2) In the Mosaic dispensation: the *Mosaic Torah* as it is unfolded in the 613 commandments found in the Pentateuch. As far as we know, the number 613 was mentioned first by Rabbi Simlai (third century AD).[59] Among the many attempts, the most widely accepted enumeration of these 613 *mitzvot* was construed by the great Rabbi Maimonides (twelfth century).[60]

(3) In the Christian dispensation: the *Messianic Torah*, which in its immanent form includes the many, perhaps more than a thousand,[61] commandments of Jesus and his apostles found in the New Testament.

(4) In the Millennial dispensation: the *Millennial Torah*, of which the Messianic Torah in its transcendent meaning will still be the kernel. For the rest, the Millennial Torah strongly resembles the Mosaic Torah, but there are also conspicuous differences (see chapter 6).

---

59. Talmud, Makkot 23b.
60. Maimonides, *Sefer haMitzvot* (first written in Arabic; first printed in Hebrew in 1497).
61 Finnis Jennings Dake (1996) mentions 1,050 New Testament commandments.

Can there actually be a dispensation without any immanent manifestation of the one, eternal Torah? Can there be any relationship between God and humanity without the expression of God's will in any form? When Paul says, "before the Torah was given" (Rom. 5:13), of course he is referring to the Mosaic Torah. He does not say that before Moses there was no form of Torah at all. The free rendering of verse 14 in the NIV is of interest: "[D]eath reigned from the time of Adam to the time of Moses, even over those who did not sin by breaking a command, as did Adam." Adam broke a "command," which presupposes some form of Torah. Three times we read about the "command" God gave to Adam (Gen. 2:16-17; 3:11, 17; concerning the tree of the knowledge of good and evil). In fact, God had commanded Adam certain things earlier, although the word "command" is not used. In total we may distinguish Seven Commandments in Genesis 1 and 2, which together might truly be called the first manifestation of the Torah — if we wish, the Adamic Torah:

1. "Be fruitful and multiply and fill the earth" (1:28a).

2. "Subdue it [i.e., the earth]" (1:28b).

3. "Have dominion over the fish of the sea and over the birds of the heavens and over every living thing that moves on the earth" (1:28c).

4. "I have given you every plant yielding seed that is on the face of all the earth, and every tree with seed in its fruit. You shall have them for food" (1:29).

5. "The LORD God took the man and put him in the garden of Eden to work it and keep it" (2:15); so the command was, "Work the garden..."

6. "...and keep it" (2:15).

7. "You may surely eat of every tree of the garden, but of the tree of the knowledge of good and evil you shall not eat, for in the day that you eat of it you shall surely die" (2:16-17). Interestingly, a Kabbalistic tradition speaks of the "Torah of the Tree of Knowledge," although it sees this as the Torah to

which Adam became subject after having been driven from Paradise. It is contrasted with the Messianic Torah, which may be called the "Torah of the Tree of Life" (cf. Prov. 3:18; 11:30; 13:12; 15:4). The former is a veiled Torah—its garments consist of the Written and the Oral Torah—and the latter is an unveiled Torah; the former is the "Torah of the Exile," and the latter the "Torah of the Redemption."[62]

In an implicit sense, given the fact that, for instance, marriage and the family were instituted before the fall, the Adamic Torah had a much wider bearing. The institution of marriage under the Adamic Torah implied its lifelong indissolubility. In connection with the matter of divorce, Jesus said, "Have you not read that he who created them *from the beginning* made them male and female . . . ? So they are no longer two but one flesh. What therefore God has joined together, let not man separate. . . . Because of your hardness of heart Moses allowed you to divorce your wives, but *from the beginning* it was not so" (Matt. 19:4–8, quoting Gen. 1:27; 2:24; cf. Mark 10:5–9; italics added). In this regard, the Adamic Torah surpassed the Mosaic Torah; in Juster's words: "Jesus reasserts God's original (Torah) standard of the lifetime commitment to marriage."[63]

After the fall, some of these commandments were changed. As to commands 5. and 6., about working and keeping the Garden of Eden, Adam was banished from the Garden, and from that time on was "to work the ground from which he was taken" (Gen. 3:23). After Noah's flood, command 1. remained the same, but commands 3. and 4. changed into what we might call the *Noahic Torah,* in which I distinguish five commandments.[64] Please note that there is no reference to

---

62. Scholem (1971, 22–24, 40–42, 68–74); on the notion of the Messianic Torah in Talmud and Midrash, see the extensive discussion of Davies (1952).
63. Juster (1995, 52).
64. Not to be confused with what the rabbis, many centuries later, called

subduing and dominion, but God does mention fear of mankind on the part of the animal kingdom.

1'. (cf. 1. above). "Be fruitful and multiply and fill the earth" (Gen. 9:1, 7).

2'. (cf. 3. above). "The fear of you and the dread of you shall be upon every beast of the earth and upon every bird of the heavens, upon everything that creeps on the ground and all the fish of the sea. Into your hand they are delivered" (9:2). In other words, take care of them.

3'. (cf. 4. and 7. above). "Every moving thing that lives shall be food for you. And as I gave you the green plants, I give you everything" (9:3).

4'. (new). "You shall not eat flesh with its life, that is, its blood" (9:3-4).

5'. (new). "And for your lifeblood I will require a reckoning: from every beast I will require it and from man. From his fellow man I will require a reckoning for the life of man. Whoever sheds the blood of man, by man shall his blood be shed, for God made man in his own image" (9:5-6).

The third pre-Mosaic manifestation of the one, eternal Torah is what we could call the *Abrahamic Torah*. God said of Abraham that he "obeyed my voice and kept my charge, my commandments, my statutes, and my laws [*torot*]" (Gen. 26:5). This is the first time the word *torah* occurs in Scripture, in connection not with Moses but with Abraham. We would love to know what that *mishmeret* ("charge"), and all these *mitzvot*, *huqqot*, and *torot* contained. In fact, we find only three commandments specified (apart from Gen. 12:1, of course, which was a one-time command):

1. "Walk before me [i.e., God Almighty], and be blame-

---

the Seven Noahide Commandments for the Gentiles (no idolatry, no murder, no theft, no sexual immorality, no blasphemy, no blood eating, command of maintaining legal courts; see §8.3.3).

less" (Gen. 17:1).

2. "Every male among you shall be circumcised. You shall be circumcised in the flesh of your foreskins, and it shall be a sign of the covenant between me and you" (17:10-11; see further vv. 12-14). For Abraham personally, this was also a one-time command, but at the same time it was an institution for all of Abraham's future male descendants.

3. "I have chosen him [i.e., Abraham], that he may command his children and his household after him to keep the way of the LORD by doing righteousness and justice, so that the LORD may bring to Abraham what he has promised him" (18:19).

In summary, God gave *mitzvot* (from *tz-v-h*, "command") to Adam (Gen. 2:16-17; 3:11, 17) and to Noah (6:22; 7:5, 9, 16), and to Abraham he gave *mitzvot*, *huqqot*, and *torot* (26:6). Therefore, as we said earlier, Romans 5:13 does not mean that no law had been given at all, but that *the* Law, the Mosaic Torah, had not yet been given. Sin cannot be "counted" where there is no law that defines it (cf. v. 13b), as was the case with most sins before Sinai. But that is not to say there was no law at all; already Adam sinned by breaking a command, as we saw (v. 14). Saying "the Law was not there" is not the same as saying "there was no law."[65] The rabbis even concluded from Genesis 26:5 that "our father Abraham observed the whole Torah before it was given."[66] At any rate, they were conscious of the intrinsic coherence of what I call the Abrahamic Torah and the Mosaic Torah.

---

65. Note a similar distinction in Acts 19:2b: "we have not even heard that there is a Holy Spirit" should rather be rendered: ". . . that the Holy Spirit is there" (cf. John 7:39, lit.: "the Spirit was not yet [there]") (Bruce 1988, 363).
66. Mishnah Qiddushin 82a; Shulam (1998, 205n34) also refers to Gen. Rabbah 24.5 and Deut. Rabbah 2.25 in stating that the rabbis either attributed full Torah-observance to Adam, or claimed that Adam and the patriarchs observed only the Noahic commandments.

Let me briefly point out here the significant similarities between the figures mentioned: Adam, Noah, and Abraham. *Noah* after the flood was like a new Adam: he became the father of an entirely new human race, he received commandments similar to those Adam received, he reigned over the animal kingdom, he worked the ground, and he also fell by eating of a forbidden fruit (abuse of the vine); after that, a curse was pronounced. *Abraham*, too, was a kind of new Adam. Canaan was "like the garden of the LORD" (Gen. 13:10), that is, Paradise, the Garden of Eden. He too ruled over numerous animals (v. 2), his offspring was to be like "the dust of the earth" (v. 16), and the "forbidden fruit" through which he fell was sexual intercourse with Sarai's maidservant (Gen. 16), after which the LORD was silent to him for thirteen years (v. 16; 17:1). Adam discovered after his fall that he was naked (Gen. 3:7, 10-11; cf. 2:25), Noah after his fall was discovered naked (9:22-23), and Abraham not only exposed himself to a servant but also denied his marital relationship to his wife (12:10-20; 16:4; 20:1-18).

All three belonged among the greatest men who ever lived, and none of them kept the Torah entrusted to him in a perfect way. Also notice that Adam's sin brought a curse upon the whole human race (Gen. 3:16-19), Noah's sin was the cause of Ham's sin, thus bringing a curse on Ham's offspring, the Canaanites (9:24), and Abraham's sin produced Ishmael, who has been a curse to Israel to this very day (cf. Ps. 83). However, in Jesus Messiah, the "last Adam" (1 Cor. 15:45), there will be a new humanity (cf. Eph. 2:15), he showed God's mercy to a Canaanite woman (Matt. 15:22-28), and Ishmael's offspring will share in the blessings of the Messianic Kingdom (Isa. 60:7; cf. Gen. 25:13).

As a matter of fact, it may surprise us that several commandments that we know from the Mosaic Torah apparently were known before the Torah-giving on Sinai, and sometimes even to the patriarchs. The principle of birthright was known

Three Views of the Torah

to Esau and Jacob (Gen. 25:31-34), as well as the notion of a double portion: Joseph, who was identified as the "firstborn," inherited through his two sons, who were counted as full-fledged tribes in Israel (1 Chron. 5:1; Gen. 48; Josh. 14:4; cf. Deut. 21:17). The levirate principle (a brother-in-law marrying a sonless widow) that was applied by Judah to his sons (Gen. 38:8) is an even more striking example.[67] The blessings of Shabbat are referred to before its formal institution in Exodus 16:23-30 (cf. Gen. 2:2-3). Priests were present in Israel before the institution of the Aaronic priesthood (Exod. 19:22, 24).

By the way, Moses too belonged among the greatest men who ever lived, and he too was not perfect in his obedience. He took God's people to the border of "Paradise" (Deut. 3:25; 8:7-10; 11:8-15), but was not allowed to enter it himself (Num. 20:12).

The only great one who is perfect is Messiah himself, who again will lead the people into the "Garden of Eden." At the "New Exodus," as E. J. Kissane aptly described the content of Isaiah 42:13-44:23,[68] Messiah as the perfect new Moses will lead the nation out of the "wilderness" into "Paradise": "he makes [Zion's] wilderness like Eden, her desert like the garden of the LORD" (Isa. 51:3; cf. Ezek. 36:35; Joel 2:3). Messiah is presented here as the Servant of the Lord (Isa. 42:1-7; 49:1-7; 50:4-11; 52:13-53:12), who has been described by E. Sellin as the "New Moses."[69] In Isaiah 42:1-4, the Servant is the new

---

67. According to Gen. Rabbah on chapter 38, Judah had received the levirate law from his forefathers, but he was the first to put it into practice. Gen. Rabbah 22 tells us that Cain killed his brother Abel in order to be able, as their brother-in-law, to marry Abel's beautiful wives.

68. Kissane (1943, 39–70); especially 43, 3–21 (p. 49–52). Also cf. Jer. 16:14–15; Hos. 2:14–15 (cf. Davies 1952, 8; 1969, 18–27).

69. See Davies (1952, 9–10, 29–34) and references; cf. Davies (1969, 20–25).

Teacher of the Torah, or even the Teacher of a new Torah: ". . . he will bring forth justice [*mishpat*][70] to the nations. . . . He will not grow faint or be discouraged till he has established justice [*mishpat*] in the earth; and the coastlands wait for his law [*torah*]" (vv. 1-4). Notice: not just to Israel but to the nations, to the whole earth. God says of this New Moses: "Behold my servant, whom I uphold, my chosen, in whom my soul delights" (Isa. 42:1). Together with Psalm 2:7 ("You are my Son"), these words reverberate on the Mount of Transfiguration, where Jesus is presented as the New Moses: "This is my Son, whom I love; with him I am well pleased. Listen to him" (Matt. 17:5 and par.; cf. §§6.2.1 and 6.3.3), that is, listen no longer primarily to Moses or Elijah.

2.3.2 Abraham *sub lege*, and Jesus-believers *post legem*?

There is an interesting rabbinic tradition that explicitly says that Abraham was under the Torah, and inadvertently implies that Jesus-believers are not. This tradition claims to be respectably old, for it says that, according to the "school of [the prophet] Elijah" (!), the world "exists for six thousand years, two thousand of them void [*tohu*], two thousand, Torah, and two thousand, the era of the Messiah."[71] The saying

---

70. *Mishpat* can stand for the Torah, the whole of God's ordinances, both ceremonial (2 Kings 17:26–27: "the law [*mishpat*] of the god of the land") and moral (Jer. 5:4: "the justice [*mishpat*] of their God") (Davies 1952, 32).

71. Sanhedrin 97a and 'Avodah Zarah 9a; also see the discussion between Rab Hanan and Rab Joseph (Sanhedrin 97b). In 1531, Melanchthon wrote that the *Dictum Eliae* was very famous among the rabbis, and was generally accepted by the Jews (W.A. 53, 22). Both Luther and Melanchthon refer to Paul of Burgos (1353–1435), a converted Jew, who quoted the *Dictum Eliae* from rabbinic sources. Also cf. Abraham bar Hiyya HaNasi (c. 1100) and Nachmanides (or Ramban, c. 1250), who both believed that Messiah would come at the end of the six thousand years. The same idea was found in the *Zohar*, the famous Qabbalistic work (thirteenth century; §3.3.1) (Froom 1948, 211, 216).

implies that the two thousand years before Abraham—more precisely, from creation until the time when, according to Jewish tradition Abram, at age 52,[72] began teaching the people of Ur that they should worship the only true God—were *tohu*, "void," that is, Torah-less, and therefore from this time of Abraham's teaching there was, in a certain sense, some Torah. At any rate, Abraham allegedly knew "the" Torah, and it was implied in the way he taught people how to live. According to this tradition, the two thousand years of the Torah did not begin with Moses but with Abraham.

It is of interest to note that the saying of Elijah's school just quoted, the *Traditio Domus Eliae* or *Dictum Eliae*, was implied in the Epistle of Barnabas (15:3–5), and that the idea of a world history of six thousand years became very popular among the Fathers (Irenæus, Hippolytus, Lactantius, Hilary, Cyprian, Ambrose, Jerome, and Augustine). It later became renowned among the Reformers, such as Luther, Calvin,[73] and early Reformational authors: Philipp Melanchthon,[74] Johannes Carion, Andreas Musculus, Hugh Latimer, Robert Fleming, David Chythraeus, Theodor Bibliander, and others.[75] The *Dictum* was also quoted by Pico della Mirandola and Andreas Osiander.[76]

One of the Latin forms known from Christian authors reads: *Sex millia annorum mundus, et deinde conflagratio* [or, *destructio*], *duo millia inane* [or, *sine lege*], *duo millia lex, duo millia Messiae. Et propter peccata nostra, quae multa et magna sunt, deerunt anni qui deerunt.* That is, "[S]ix thousand years [lasts] the world, and then [follows] burning [or, destruction], two thousand [years are] empty [or, without law], two thousand

---

72. According to the Talmud, from creation until the time when Abram was 52 was exactly 2000 years ('Avodah Zarah 9a).
73. Institutes of the Christian Religion, 1A.14.1.
74. *Corpus Reformatorum* (Opp. Melanchthon) XIII.977–78.
75. Referred to by Froom (1948, 330, 338, 372, 646).
76. See Froom (1948, 298–99) for references.

[years are under] the law, two thousand [years belong to] the Messiah. And because of our sins, which are many and great, the years that are lacking are lacking." Another version says: *Isti sunt Sex dies hebdomadae coram Deo, Septimus Dies Sabbatum aeternum est.* That is, "There are six week days before God, the seventh day is an eternal Shabbat." The basic idea is that the six thousand years form a parallel with the six days of creation: it took God six days to create the world, it will take him six "days" to restore the world after the fall (cf. Ps. 90:4; 2 Pet. 3:8; see also Slav. Enoch 32:2; 33:1–2).

According to the Jewish calendar, the first four thousand years ended in AD 240, but Messiah did not come. Many Reformational writers, however, arrived at a number of more or less four thousand years for the Tanakhic period,[77] so that in their view, Messiah had indeed come at the time predicted by the *Dictum Eliae.*

Even if they are not always linked with periods of two thousand years each, the partitioning of salvation history into three periods is quite well known. When F. E. Hamilton, distinguished three epochs, the pre-Mosaic, the Mosaic, and the New Testament era,[78] he was following Irenæus, who spoke of three covenants, the first characterized by the Torah written in the heart (i.e., before Sinai; cf. Rom. 2:15), the second, by the Torah as an external commandment given at Sinai, and the third, by the Torah restored to the heart through the operation of the Holy Spirit (cf. Rom. 5:12–21). Augustine held to

---

77. Luther, 3,961 years, Melanchthon, 3,964, Joh. Kepler, 3,984 or 3,993, Lightfoot, 3,960, Playfair, 4,008, Lipman, 3,916, Scaliger, 3,950, Bengel, 3,943, and Ussher exactly 4,000 years (quoted by Bavinck [1928, 451] and Morris [1976, 45]).
78. Hamilton (1942, 26–27); also see Irenaeus (*Adv. Haer.* III, 11, 8): four covenants, one beginning with Adam, one with Noah, one with Moses, and one with Messiah.

Three Views of the Torah

the same tripartite idea.⁷⁹ Similarly, Johannes Cocceius distinguished three dispensations of the covenant of grace, the first *ante legem* (before the Torah), the second *sub lege* (under the Torah), and the third *post legem* (after the Torah).⁸⁰ The latter expression is striking, and seems to imply that in the Messianic era the Mosaic Torah is no longer valid. In opposition to this, other Reformational theologians would prefer to distinguish only two dispensations, that of the Tanakh, and that of the New Testament.⁸¹

Speaking of covenants, in §4.1 we will look at the Torah concept in connection with the covenant concept. Already now, I wish to point out that the Torah manifestations just mentioned usually occur in the framework of a certain divine covenant. The Adamic Torah is congruent with the Adamic covenant,⁸² the Noahic Torah with the Noahic covenant, the Abrahamic Torah with the Abrahamic covenant. Like the Noahic covenant, the Sinaitic covenant (if well understood), the Palestinian covenant, the Davidic covenant, and the New Covenant, the Abrahamic covenant was an unconditional covenant in that ultimately all the promised blessings depend on God's sovereign and electing grace, and these covenants were made with a chosen and redeemed community, and as such included a means of repentance and atonement (cf. §4.1.2) (Gen. 9:8-17; Exod. 20:2; Lev. 16; Deut. 30:1-10; 2 Sam. 7:1-17; Jer. 31:31-34; cf. Rom. 11:29). This has been emphasized by many dispensational theologians (although they usually considered the Sinaitic covenant to be conditional).⁸³

---

79. *Enchiridion* 118 (three stages of the church: before the law, under the law, under grace); also see Migne Patrologia Latina XL, 287.
80. Quoted by Berkhof (1939, 292).
81. Berkhof (1939, 292–301).
82. If such a thing exists (see §4.1.1).
83. See, e.g., Chafer (1948, 313–28); Pentecost (1964, 65–128); Walvoord (1991, chapters 4, 5, 9, 17); Fruchtenbaum (1992, 334–73, 570–87). On this, see further the second volume in the present trilogy.

However, one point needs to be emphasized in particular. Seen from God's standpoint, true believers living under any of the covenants, including even the Sinaitic or Mosaic covenant, ultimately lived by nothing other than God's grace. But seen from the standpoint of human responsibility, each of these covenants contained a certain manifestation of God's Torah, and thus introduced a certain conditionality. This applies to the Noahic and the Abrahamic covenants (see above), and to the Sinaitic covenant, the Palestinian covenant (Deut. 30:10), the Davidic covenant (2 Sam. 7:14), and the New Covenant (Jer. 31:33). Even under the covenant that allegedly is the "unconditional" one *par excellence*, the Abrahamic covenant, God told the patriarch, "I am God Almighty; walk before me, and be blameless, that I may make my covenant between me and you" (Gen. 17:1-2), and, "in your offspring shall all the nations of the earth be blessed, *because* you have obeyed me" (22:18, italics added). I will return to this matter, discussing it extensively in the next volume in the present trilogy, which will deal with the divine covenants.

In summary, from the viewpoint of God's grace, *all* the covenants are unconditional, since ultimately all blessing depends upon God's electing and atoning mercy. From the viewpoint of human responsibility, however, *all* the covenants are conditional. That is, there simply is no relationship between God and Man without any law, any commandment (see further in §4.1). God is always in charge, and Man must always obey. If the Torah in its full, transcendent sense is not only one but eternal, ultimately contained in the Logos, the eternal Son of God (see chapter 3), it will also last eternally. Therefore, it can be said: "I will keep your Torah continually, forever and ever" (Ps. 119:44). Even in the new heaven and on the new earth, the one, eternal Torah will be in force. That is why it is said that even then, in eternity, "his servants will serve him" (Rev. 22:3b).

Three Views of the Torah

2.3.3 "Torah-lessness"

Let me emphasize here, as a kind of appendix, that the matter of being "under the Torah" or not is a confusing one. On the one hand, there is no such a thing as a creature without a, or the, divine Torah between his Creator and himself. Even plants and animals have *torot*—the laws of nature—standing between them and their Creator, and even the most wicked person is under God's Torah (objectively), and has some awareness of moral, judicial, social, and other norms (subjectively). On the other hand, whether one is formally under some explicit Torah of God or not, one may act in utter conflict with God's Torah and thus be "Torah-less."

Perhaps that is why God's greatest human adversary of all times, the Antichrist—who according to many expositors will be a Jew, that is, someone "under the Mosaic Torah"—is called the "man of Torah-lessness" (Gr. *anthrōpos tēs anomias*), the "Torah-less one" (Gr. *anomos*) par excellence (2 Thess. 2:3, 8). That is not simply the transgressor of the Torah, but the rebel denying any Torah over him. In its essence, sin is not just "transgression of the law," as the KJV erroneously renders *anomia* in 1 John 3:4,[84] but "lawlessness" (NIV). That is the rebellious denial of the Torah as such, or any *torah* for that matter. Such a denial is a creature's greatest arrogance conceivable; it is like "grasping equality with God" (cf. Phil. 2:6). Conceit (pride, arrogance) was the sin of the devil, as well as that of Adam (1 Tim. 3:6; Gen. 3:5–6; cf. Isa. 14:13–14; Ezek. 28:17).

The Greek terms *anomos* ("Torah-less") and *anomia* ("Torah-lessness") can mean two very different things: they refer either to one's formal (objective) position or to one's (subjec-

---

84. And not "violation of Torah" either, as Stern (1999, 773) alleges; "transgression of the Torah" is *parabasis tou nomou* (Rom. 2:23), and "transgressor of the Torah" is *parabatēs nomou* (Rom. 2:25, 27; James 2:11).

tive) spiritual attitude. That is, *anomos* and *anomia* can, first, refer to the position of one who has not been formally placed under any explicit Torah of God, without this fact as such saying anything about his spiritual condition (Rom. 2:12; 1 Cor. 9:21). In this sense, *anomos* is similar to, if not identical with, *choris nomou* in Romans 7:8–9.[85] The Gentiles are "Torah-less," that is, they never were, and never will be, under the Mosaic Torah of God. However, this does not say anything about their spiritual condition. Positively, though being formally "Torah-less" they may be "doers of [the] Torah" (Rom. 2:12–13).[86] Negatively, they may be "Torah-less" not only in the formal but also in the moral sense: the people into whose hands Jesus was delivered were *anomoi*, that is, not just Gentiles, but "wicked Gentiles" (Acts 2:23).

Second, *anomos* and *anomia* can refer to the wickedness of the heart, as well as to the anti-Torah acts flowing from such a heart (Matt. 13:41; 24:12; Rom. 4:7; 6:19; 2 Cor. 6:14; 2 Thess. 2:7; 1Tim. 1:9; Titus 2:14; Heb. 1:9; 2 Pet. 2:8; cf. the related word *paranomia* in v. 16). Whereas the Gentiles are "Torah-less" in a formal, positional sense, Jews may be "Torah-less" in a moral, practical sense. Consequently, when the New Covenant will be made the people of Israel will be redeemed from their "Torah-lessnesses" (*anomiai*, Heb. 10:17). Because the people's hearts are "Torah-less," the Torah will be written on, or put in, their hearts (Jer. 31:33; Heb. 8:10; 10:16). Because of the Sinaitic Torah-giving, all Jews are "under the Torah,"[87] but again, this does not say anything about

---

85. The NIV renders the phrase in Rom. 2:12, "apart from the law," and in 7:8–9, "apart from law," as in 3:21.
86. Cf. Baba Kamma 38a (there is also reward for Gentiles who do good things out of free will); Midrash Prov. 17.1 ("the nations can do good and pious deeds, and so escape the judgment of hell"); Sifra 86b ("even a Gentile, if he practices the Torah, is equal to the high priest") (cf. Shulam 1998, 92–93, 108, 116–117).
87. Or, "with the Torah," as one might render the expression *en (tō) nomō* in Rom. 2:12 and 3:19.

their spiritual condition. First, they may be true observers of the Torah. Second, they may overtly act against the Torah as true criminals; this is the sense of *anomoi* in Luke 22:37: those committing crimes against the Torah. Third, there are Jews, even Torah-teachers and Pharisees, who outwardly seem to keep the Torah faithfully but who neglect its essence, and consequently are accused of "Torah-lessness": "[Y]ou outwardly appear righteous to others, but within you are full of hypocrisy and Torah-lessness [*anomia*]" (Matt. 23:23, 28). Even those who confess to be disciples of Jesus but have a wicked heart are called "workers of Torah-lessness" (Matt. 7:23).

In summary, there are Gentiles who are "Torah-less," that is, they never were under the Mosaic Torah (this is objective Torah-lessness), and yet are "doers of the Torah". And, conversely, there are Jews who as such are "under the Torah" but who in their wicked attitude and acts are "Torah-less" (this is subjective Torah-lessness). As a parallel, one might say that true Jesus-believers are not under the Torah (i.e., of Moses), yet keep the Messianic Torah (cf. 1 Cor. 9:21). And conversely, false Jesus-believers, though being under the Torah (i.e., of the Messiah), are "Torah-less," that is, wicked. There are *anomoi* among those who are under, and those who are not under the (Mosaic or Messianic) Torah, that is, wicked Jews and wicked (nominal) Jesus-believers. And there are true Torah-keepers among those who are under, and those who are not under the (Mosaic) Torah: faithful Jews and faithful Jesus-believers, respectively.

Chapter 3
Torah, Hokmah, Logos, and Spirit[1]

Wisdom has built her house;
 she has hewn her seven pillars.
She has slaughtered her beasts; she has mixed her wine;
 she has also set her table.
She has sent out her young women to call
 from the highest places in the town,
"Whoever is simple, let him turn in here!"
 To him who lacks sense she says,
"Come, eat of my bread
 and drink of the wine I have mixed.
Leave your simple ways, and live,
 And walk in the way of insight."
Proverbs 9:1–6

Who is wise and understanding among you?
 By his good conduct let him show his
 works in the meekness of wisdom.
But if you have bitter jealousy and selfish ambition in your hearts,
 do not boast and be false to the truth.
This is not the wisdom that comes down from above,
 but is earthly, unspiritual, demonic.
For where jealousy and selfish ambition exist,

---

1 See extensively Ouweneel (1998, 50–65).

> there will be disorder and every vile practice.
> But the wisdom from above is first pure, then peaceable,
>> gentle, open to reason, full of mercy and good fruits, impartial and sincere.
>
> James 3:13–17

Summary: *In Jewish literature, there is a deep connection between the concepts of* Hokmah *(wisdom; NT:* sophia*) and* Torah *(law; NT:* nomos*). The wisdom with which God created the universe is also the wisdom with which he gave Man his precepts and statutes, and it is Man's wisdom to keep these decrees. In Christian thinking, there is also a deep link between Hokmah/Torah — according to a Jewish tradition, the daughter at God's bosom — and the* Logos *as the Son at the Father's bosom. The similarities are quite striking — and the differences too. In addition, Hokmah/Torah has also been associated with the* Holy Spirit, *by both the rabbis and the church fathers. To say nothing of other alleged linking of Hokmah/Sophia with various feminine figures in the Tanakh (Wisdom literature), or with the Virgin Mary, or (by way of contrast) with the gods of the pagan world.*

3.1   The Concept of *Hokmah*

3.1.1   Scripture about *Hokmah*

SOME OF THE DEEP MEANINGS of the Torah, particularly of the one, eternal Torah, come to light if we compare it with the concept of Wisdom, *Hokmah* in Hebrew, *Sophia* in Greek. The book of Proverbs presents us with God's wisdom in the midst of a world of foolishness, confusion, and wickedness. God's creational wisdom as wonderfully displayed in the cosmos is to be displayed, too, in the smallest details of human life. We find in this book not only the wisdom of God, but also the governmental wisdom of King Solomon. The latter's name, *Shelomo*, comes from the Hebrew *shalom*, "peace." In this,

Torah, Hokmah, Logos, and Spirit

there is a *remez* ("hint")[2] pointing to Jesus as the "Prince of Peace" in the *'olam habba*, the future Messianic Kingdom. Jesus is the greater Solomon (cf. Isa. 9:6; Matt. 12:42); some also assume a link with Shiloh whom the peoples will obey (Gen. 49:10). At the beginning of his kingship over Israel, Solomon prayed for wisdom in view of his royal office: "Give your servant therefore an understanding mind to govern your people, that I may discern between good and evil, for who is able to govern this, your great people?" In answer to this, God made him the wisest king Israel ever had: "Behold, I give you a wise and discerning mind, so that none like you has been before you and none like you shall arise after you" (1 Kings 3:3-12; cf. 4:29-34; 5:12; 10:1-13; Luke 11:31).

In §1.2.1, I quoted some passages in Proverbs in which we find the word *torah* in the sense of "instruction" as given by the wise royal father (or the wise mother) to develop the character of the child (Prov. 3:1, 3, 13, 18-20; 4:2; 6:20, 23; 7:1-2; 28:4, 7, 9; 29:18). Elsewhere, the wise (or sages) are those who live by the Torah, the word of the Lord, and teach it to others (Jer. 8:8-9; see the reverse in Isa. 29:14 and 30:9). True wisdom is not just keeping the Torah, but doing this with the right attitude: in the fear of the Lord. Hence the well-known adage: "The fear of the LORD is the beginning of wisdom" (Prov. 9:10; cf. 1:7; 15:33; Job 28:28; Ps. 111:10; Eccl. 12:13). In Sirach, the scribe is the one who is wise through the constant study of the Torah (38:24-39:11). In rabbinic literature, the wise and the scribes (those who study, observe, and teach the Scriptures; cf. these three verbs in Ezra 7:10) are more or less identical.

The congruencies between Hokmah and Torah are quite obvious. Almost all proverbs in the book of Proverbs can be

---

2. In rabbinic Bible interpretation, a *remez* is a hint at a deeper truth, of which the Bible writers themselves very probably were not aware (cf. 1 Pet. 1:10–11), and which is not normally disclosed by grammatical-historical exegesis.

distributed among the Ten Commandments. There are even references to the Temple service (15:8; 21:3, 27), and God is almost always called by his covenant name, YHWH. The first part of the book (chapters 1–9), which is much more cohesive than most of the rest, clearly follows the Decalogue: the first Five Commandments (true godliness) especially in chapter 3, the Sixth through the Ninth Commandments in many other passages.

The wisdom in this book is given in the form of proverbs (*meshalim*, sing. *mashal*), comparisons, or parables, which do not always yield their wisdom immediately,[3] since, for example, they present us with seeming contradictions (cf. Prov. 10:22 and 14:23; 26:4–5). If it is correct to relate *mashal* to *m-sh-l*, which means "reign," a *mashal* is a "power word" (cf. the "magic" of a *mashal* in Num. 23:7, 18; 24:3, 15, 20–23; cf. 22:6b). This deeper link between wisdom and power comes to light in the great new Torah-giver, Jesus, who is both "the power of God and the wisdom of God" (1 Cor. 1:24; cf. 4:20). Note that Psalm 78 is presented as a *mashal* (v. 2), takes its starting point in God's Torah (v. 5), and reaches its apotheosis in "David his servant" and the sanctuary on Mount Zion (vv. 67–72). Note, too, that Jesus presents the second of his great Kingdom sermons in the form of parables, structuring his teaching in parallel with Psalm 78 (Matt. 13:3, 10–17; especially vv. 34–35). The *remez* in this comparison is quite striking: Proverbs presents us with covert Messianic teaching, Jesus with overt Messianic teaching.

The Prophetic Books contain some hints of the existence of a distinct class of sages, along with the two classes of priests and prophets: "[T]he Torah shall not perish from the priest, nor counsel from the wise, nor the word from the prophet" (Jer. 18:18; cf. Prov. 22:17; 24:23). The prophets maintained the

---

3. Cf. the parallel Hebrew term *hidah* ("riddle, enigma, dark saying, mysterious saying") in Prov. 1:6; also cf. Judg. 14:12–19; Ezek. 17:1.

covenant relationship between God and his people by referring the people back to God's Torah when they had backslid. The priests maintained this relationship by observing the sacrificial ministry, which was the basis for living out and perpetuating God's covenant by repairing all trespasses against it. The sages knew of the ministry rendered by the other classes (cf. Prov. 2:21–22; 11:21; 14:32; 15:11; 24:11 and 15:8; 21:3, 27, respectively). But their main task was to maintain the covenant relationship[4] by applying God's Torah to the smallest details of everyday life, ranging from the ways of kings to those of housewives, and even animals (cf. Prov. 16:12; 20:26, 28; 29:4, 14; 31:10–31; 30:24–31). We are not dealing here with some "folk wisdom" but with God's divine plan for the cosmos as well as for individual human life as laid down in the Torah. For instance, the same "natural law" of sowing and reaping that holds for agriculture holds for human life (cf. literally Prov. 11:18; 22:8; also see John 4:36; 2 Cor. 9:6; Gal. 6:7–8).

The wisdom belonging to the class of the wise is closely linked with the Torah: "How can you say, 'We are wise, and the Torah of the LORD is with us'? But behold, the lying pen of the scribes has made it into a lie. The wise men shall be put to shame; they shall be dismayed and taken; behold, they have rejected the word of the LORD, so what wisdom is in them?" (Jer. 8:8–9). One may have the Torah, and at the same time reject the impact of its message. The wisdom of those falsely called wise will perish because they lack the spiritual insight to read God's Word; in Proverbs these are the fools (Isa. 29:11–14; Prov. 1:7, 22, 32).[5] As Jesus said to the Sadducees:

---

4. Note again that Proverbs almost exclusively calls God by his covenant name, YHWH.

5. Wilson (1989, 284–87) describes several types of fools: the *peti* ("open" fool, i.e., open to instruction), the *kesil* and *evil* ("hardened" fool), the *latzon* ("mocking" fool), and the *naval* ("God-denying" fool);

"You are wrong, because you know neither the Scriptures nor the power of God" (Matt. 22:29). And to his disciples: "Whoever has my commandments and keeps them, he it is who loves me" (John 14:21); true piety involves both having and keeping.

True wisdom is humbly submitting to this Word (cf. Prov. 3:5, 7), living by God's commands in genuine godliness (the fear of the Lord). Very practically: true wisdom is distinguishing between right and wrong: "Behold, the fear of the Lord, that is wisdom, and to turn away from evil is understanding" (Job 28:28; cf. 1 Kings 3:9, 12, quoted above). It is the insight that is known to the mature believers (1 Cor. 2:6), and the mature are those who "have trained themselves to distinguish good from evil" (Heb. 5:14). Those "who are wise"[6] are those who not only know the way of justice but also "turn many [others] to righteousness" (Dan. 12:3). "The wisdom of the prudent is to discern his way" (Prov. 14:8).

The best known and central passage about wisdom in Proverbs is chapter 8:22-31. I quote verses 30-31, where we see Hokmah at God's side supporting him in carrying out the work of creation: "[T]hen I was beside him, like a master workman, and I was daily his delight, rejoicing before him always, rejoicing in his inhabited world and delighting in the children of man." I appreciate in verse 30 the translation of *amon* as "workman" (actually, in this case, "workwoman"!).[7] A similar meaning is encountered in Song of Solomon 7:1 ("master," *amman*) and Jeremiah 52:15 ("artisans, craftsmen," *amon*), where the same root is found. Jewish expositors such as Menachem Meiri and Abraham Ibn Ezra preferred this

---

cf. the biblical Nabal, 1 Sam. 25:25).

6. Here it is the noun *maskilim* (cf. Dan. 11:33, 35; 12:10), from the verb *s-k-l*, "have (give, act with) insight, be wise, act wisely."

7. This translation of *amon* ("workman, craftsman") goes back to the Septuagint (*armozousa*, if taken in the sense of "arranging, constructing") and the Vulgate (*cuncta componens*).

translation, referring to the parallel text in Wisdom 8:6, understanding Hokmah as referring to the one "who has given shape to everything that exists."

The alternative translation, "one brought up" (or "nursling, darling-child"), is derived from Aquila's Greek translation.[8] The Jewish expositor, Rashi, and many after him, preferred this rendering, pointing to a related word in Lamentations 4:5 ("brought up"). Perhaps we may assume here an intentional ambiguity, for Hokmah is both: in the figurative language of Proverbs she is the Lady (1:20; 8:1, 12; 9:1; cf. v. 13) who built the universe and is beloved of God. She is his darling, dwelling with him in the most intimate communion, playing before him, rejoicing as a dancing child, knowing his purposes, counseling him, supporting him in the performance of his works. Or in the words of Fohrer, in Proverbs 8 Wisdom "was created first by Him and was then present at the further and true creation, not as a helper, but as a child playing in its father's workshop. As God's favorite child (*amon* v. 30) it played with creation and with man."[9]

One may wonder whether the word "created" in this quotation is correct (see further in §3.2.3). Verse 22 says, "The LORD possessed [not created; see below] me at the beginning of his way, the first of his acts of old."[10] One may translate: "*as the beginning* [Heb. *reshit*] of his way," which was used by the rabbis as a key to Genesis 1:1, "Through[11] *reshit* God creat-

---

8. According to this interpretation, *amon* is related to *omen*, which means "foster father" (Num. 11:12; 2 Kings 10:1, 5; Esth. 2:7; Isa. 49:23; cf. the feminine form in Ruth 4:16; 2 Sam. 4:4). In that case, the *amon* is a little child who depends on the care and nurture of the parent.
9. Fohrer (1971, 491).
10. See Davies (1955, 151–52, 172), referring to the opening of Gen. Rabbah (Rabbi Hoshaiah on Prov. 8:30).
11. The "through" in these quotations is important. The "by" (Gr. *en*) in Col. 1:16 (NKJV, ESV, CEB, CEV [2x!]) is completely mistaken. The

ed the heavens and the earth," that is, "through (by means of, with the help of.) Hokmah," or "through the Torah." In New Testament language (§3.2), not only were all things created "in the beginning" (Gr. *archē*) through him who is the Logos (John 1:1-3), but he who is the Logos *is* himself "the beginning [*archē*] of God's creation" (Rev. 3:14); he is "the firstborn of all creation. . . . He is the beginning, the firstborn from the dead" (Col. 1:15, 18). Jesus is the *reshit* (*archē*), that is, the one in and through whom God brings about both the old and the new creation.

3.1.2 Tradition About *Hokmah*[12]

Apparently, the Scripture most similar to Proverbs 8, because Wisdom is distinguished from God here as well, is this:

> But where shall wisdom be found? And where is the place of understanding? Man does not know its worth, and it is not found in the land of the living. . . . God understands the way to it, and he knows its place. For he looks to the ends of the earth and sees everything under the heavens. When he gave to the wind its weight and apportioned the waters by measure, when he made a decree for the rain and a way for the lightning of the thunder, then he saw it and declared it; he established it, and searched it out. And he said to man, "Behold, the fear of the Lord, that is wisdom, and to turn away from evil is understanding" (Job 28:12-14, 20-27).

It is worthwhile to compare these Scriptures with some passages in the apocryphal books. These Jewish works arose in the intertestamental period, when the idea of personified

---

world was not created "by" (Gr. *hypo*) but "through" (Gr. *dia*) the Logos/Son.

12. See the many references to Jewish sources in Shulam (1998, 73n53); see further, e.g., Davies (1955, 158–76); Christ (1970, 28–60); Schnabel (1985).

Torah, Hokmah, Logos, and Spirit

Wisdom had come to further development. In general, Jesus ben Sirach stands in the tradition of Job 28 and Proverbs, as is shown in a passage like this one: "Wisdom was created before anything else; understanding has always existed. Has anyone ever been shown where Wisdom originates? Does anyone understand her subtle cleverness? There is only one who is wise, and we must stand in awe before his throne. The Lord himself created Wisdom; he saw her and recognized her value, and so he filled everything he made with Wisdom" (Sirach 1:4-9).[13] Chapter 19:20 says that all wisdom is fear of the Lord and all wisdom is doing the Torah.

Of great interest is chapter 24, where Hokmah/Sophia is fully equated with the Torah. Ben Sirach has Hokmah/Sophia explain how a place was allotted to her among the people of Israel in the form of the covenant Book of Sinai: "I looked everywhere for a place to settle, some part of the world to make my home. Then my Creator, who created the universe, told me where I was to live. 'Make your home in Israel,' he said. 'The descendants of Jacob will be your people.' He created me in eternity, before time began, and I will exist for all eternity to come. I served him in the Sacred Tent and then made my home on Mount Zion. He settled me in the Beloved City and gave me authority over Jerusalem. I put down roots among an honored people whom the Lord had chosen as his own" (vv. 7-12). The Torah is presented here as having existed from before the foundation of the world. Sirach says that all things have been created through Torah's wisdom, that through her all human life is maintained, and that she has obtained a place within temporal reality in her Sinaitic form.

The apocryphal book Wisdom of Solomon arose in Jewish-Hellenistic circles in Egypt. According to some, the book's

---

13. On the relationship between Torah and Hokmah, especially in Jesus ben Sirach, see Marböck (1976).

message was influenced by Egyptian views of wisdom.[14] Yet, in many respects it closely follows Proverbs and Sirach. For instance, the author says that Wisdom "gave shape to everything that exists," and "She is a breath of God's power—a pure and radiant stream of glory from the Almighty. Nothing that is defiled can ever steal its way into Wisdom. She is a reflection of eternal light, a perfect mirror of God's activity and goodness" (Wisdom 7:22a, 25–26), the latter verse implying that Wisdom is the "image of God" (see below on Col. 1:15–17). Even more interesting are statements like these: "She glorifies her noble origin by living with God, the Lord of all, who loves her" (8:3). "Give me the Wisdom that sits beside your throne.... Wisdom is with you and knows your actions; she was present when you made the world. She knows what pleases you, what is right and in accordance with your commands. Send her from the holy heavens, down from your glorious throne, so that she may work at my side, and I may learn what pleases you" (9:4, 9–10). Here Hokmah/Torah is seen as the companion and beloved of God, a heavenly queen sharing in his works, but also as the companion of the alleged writer, King Solomon. She is requested to descend from the holy heavens.[15] This prayer had already been answered when the Torah "descended" upon Sinai, but Solomon desires her as his personal instructor.

In another apocryphal book, Baruch, the concepts of Torah and Hokmah are almost interchangeable. Abandoning the Torah ("the commands that promise life") is abandoning

---

14. See Wilckens (1971, 498–500).
15. "It was one of the very few real dogmas of rabbinic theology that the Torah is from heaven (Heb. *Torah min ha-shamayim*; Sanh. 10:1, et al.; cf. Exod. 20:22 [19]; Deut. 4:36); i.e., the Torah in its entirety was revealed by God" (Harvey 1972, 1239). Paul, linking Deut. 30:11–14 with the descent and ascent of Jesus (Rom. 10:6–7), may have been thinking of the descent and ascent of the Torah/Hokmah (Davies 1955, 153–54).

the "source of Wisdom" (3:9, 12). Baruch describes the greatness of Hokmah in terms reminding us of Job 28, and then tells us that she was granted to Israel "his beloved": "He . . . gave Wisdom to his servant Israel, whom he loved. From that time on, Wisdom appeared on earth and lived among us. Wisdom is the book of God's commandments, the Torah that will last forever. All who hold onto her will live, but those who abandon her will die" (3:36–4:1). That is, the *eternal* wisdom of God has come to Israel in the *earthly* form of the "book of God's commandments," the Mosaic Torah. Ben Sirach tells us explicitly, "Wisdom is the Torah, the Torah which Moses commanded us to keep, the covenant of God Most High, the inheritance of the synagogues of Israel" (24:23).

This tradition began in the Tanakh itself, continued in the deuterocanonical books, and was extended by the rabbis and other Jewish authorities.[16] A Jewish tradition tells us of the eternal Torah that it lay in God's bosom, before the creation of the world, while God sat on the throne of glory.[17] Another rabbinic explanation says that the Torah was God's architectural instrument.[18] A human king does not build a palace according to his own ideas but according to the ideas of a master builder, who consults his own drawings. Similarly, God was the King, and Hokmah/Torah was the Master Builder, looking into the Torah and creating the universe corresponding-

---

16. Harvey (1972, 1236–38) mentions Ben Sirach, Eliezer ben Yose the Galilean, Simeon ben Lakish, Aqiva, Rav Hoshaiah, Philo, Saadiah Gaon, Judah ben Barzillai of Barcelona, Abraham ibn Ezra, Judah Halevi, Maimonides, Isaac ibn Latif, the Qabbalists of Spain, Hasdai Crescas, Joseph Albo, Nachman Krochmal, Franz Rosenzweig, and others, particularly in regard to the question of the alleged pre-existence of the Torah.
17. Midr. Ps. on 90:3 (§12).
18. Mishnah Avot III.14; Sifre Deut. 48 on 11:22; God creating through the Torah is the same as God creating through his own powerful being, for the Torah expresses his being.

THE ETERNAL TORAH: LIVING UNDER GOD

ly.[19] Apparently, the Torah was both God's instrument with which, and God's blueprint according to which, he created the universe. Strack and Billerbeck collected a great number of other quotations presenting the Torah as God's master builder.[20] In some of these quotations, the Torah is described as a person existing before the foundation of the world, and even as a daughter of God. The Torah belongs to seven things that are each two thousand years[21] older than the world.[22]

The Torah lay on God's knee as he sat on the throne of glory. Elsewhere it is said, she lay in God's lap. In a famous Talmudic passage in which the Torah is personified, God addresses her as *bati*, "my daughter."[23] In another passage, its heavenly origin is emphasized: "The following have no portion in the world to come: He who says that the Torah is not from Heaven," etc.[24] Hokmah/Torah is a Lady that has de-

---

19. Gen. Rabbah 1 on 1:1 (see Cohen/Rosenberg 1985, 48; cf. Strack-Billerbeck 1924, 2:356–357).
20. Strack-Billerbeck (1924, 2:357), e.g., Tanchuma B. 2: God took counsel with the Torah before he created the world.
21. This number is derived from the "day [after] day" in Prov. 8:30, a "day" being understood as a thousand years (cf. Ps. 90:4 and Lev. Rabbah on 19:1).
22. In addition to the Torah, these are repentance, the Garden of Eden, Gehenna, the throne of glory, the sanctuary, and the name of the Messiah (Pesachim 54a; Nedarim 39b; Targum Pseudo-Jonathan Zech. 4:7; cf. Gen. Rabbah on 1:4: the Torah was the very first). This is not eternal pre-existence: the Torah and the throne of glory were created before the world (real pre-existence), the others were only conceived of before the world (ideal pre-existence) (cf. Klausner 1955, 460).
23. Sanhedrin 101a; Strack-Billerbeck (1924, 2:353–56) also refer to Lev. Rabbah 20, 10 on Lev. 16:1. So, too, the Jewish-Hellenistic thinker, Philo of Alexandria. However, he also speaks of Wisdom as God's spouse, through whom he created the world, and as the mother of the godly (Wilckens 1971, 500–502; Schipflinger 1988, 40).
24. 'Avodah Zarah 18a.

scended from heaven to this earth, to dwell among the people of Israel.

According to Rabbi Meir, the Torah-giving on Sinai is described by God as the "nuptial joy of my daughter," that is, of the Torah. This joy was endangered when Nadab and Abihu brought strange fire and had to be killed by the Lord (Lev. 10:1–2). God is being compared here to a king, giving his daughter in marriage to Israel, at which the sons of Aaron performed as groomsmen. Thus, Israel is here the bridegroom (God's son-in-law), while the Torah is the bride.[25] This is related to Wisdom 8:2, where Hokmah is called the bride of King Solomon as the representative of the whole nation. Peculiarly enough, rabbinic tradition apparently knows of two opposite metaphors. In the latter, Israel was viewed as the bridegroom of the Torah, but according to a very different metaphor, Israel is the bride of God (cf. Isa. 49:18; 54:6; 61:10; 62:5; Jer. 2:2; Ezek. 16:8–13; Hos. 2:19–20), and the Torah the *ketubah* (written prenuptial agreement; see §4.2.1).

The metaphor of the Torah as the bride of Israel is described in the most beautiful way in a Midrash: "Like a king who had an only daughter. One of the [other] kings came and took her [as wife]; he wanted to go to his country and take his wife with him. The king spoke to him, 'My daughter that I gave you is my only daughter. I cannot separate from her. I cannot tell you, 'Don't take her with you' either, for she is your wife. But show me this goodness that, wherever you go, you prepare me a room, so that I can dwell with you; for I cannot leave my daughter.' Thus God also said to Israel, 'I gave you the Torah. I cannot separate from her. I cannot tell you

---

25. Cf. *Zohar* (II. 99a–b): the Torah reveals her mysterious beauty only to her lovers, who, if they follow her, eventually become her consorts (cf. Scholem 1960, 77–79). At *Simchat Torah* ("Joy of the Torah"), the second day of the *Atzeret* festival (immediately following upon *Sukkot*), one of the members of the congregation is honored as the "bridegroom of the Torah."

THE ETERNAL TORAH: LIVING UNDER GOD

'Don't accept her' either; but wherever you go, prepare me a place in which I can dwell.'"[26] Indeed it is said in Exodus 25:8: "[L]et them make me a sanctuary, that I may dwell in their midst" (cf. 29:42–45). The Torah is a king's daughter, who descended from heaven to become a king's wife. God could not live apart from the Torah, so he came to dwell in Israel too, in a special room prepared for him, and traveled wherever Israel and the Torah went. God sat enthroned upon the cherubs on the atonement cover (Ps. 80:1; 99:1), such that he could not be nearer to his daughter than that.

According to the rabbis, the Torah is the heavenly queen through whom God created all things. When this queen came down from heaven, she materialized, became incarnate, as it were, in the two stone tablets that God gave to Moses and that were kept before God in the ark in the sanctuary (Deut. 10:1–5; 1 Kings 8:9). No matter how strange the word "incarnation" may sound in this context, one Jewish (Kabbalistic) tradition indeed loves to view the Torah as a living organism with body members and joints, a heart, a mouth, etc.[27]

When the Mishnah says, "[M]ake a fence round the Torah,"[28] the Torah is apparently being conceived of as a locked garden and its precepts as precious plants. This reminds us of one of the conspicuous female figures in the Tanakh, the bride in the Song of Solomon: "A garden locked is my sister, my bride, a spring locked, a fountain sealed" (4:12). According to Ben Sirach, after its descent from heaven the Torah said, "I put down roots among an honored people whom the Lord had chosen as his own. I grew tall, like the cedars in Lebanon, like the cypresses on Mount Hermon, like the palm-trees of Engedi, like the roses of Jericho, like beautiful olive-trees in the fields, like plane-trees growing by the water. My breath

---

26. Exod. Rabbah 33 (94a) (quoted by Strack-Billerbeck 1924, 2:356).
27. Scholem (1960, 64–66).
28. Mishnah Avot I.1; see footnote in the Soncino edition; also cf. Avot III.13.

was the spicy smell of cinnamon, of sweet perfume and finest myrrh, of stacte, onycha, and galbanum, the fragrant incense in the sacred Tent. Like an oak I spread out my branches, magnificent and graceful. Like a grapevine I put out lovely shoots; my blossoms gave way to rich and glorious fruit" (Sirach 24:12-17).

To be sure, in Talmudic literature, the bride is seen as portraying not the Torah as much as Israel in relationship with its heavenly bridegroom. However, the two "females," Israel and the Torah, easily blend.[29] For instance, in Song of Solomon 4:13-15 the bride is compared to a garden that is moist with the performance of the Torah. Israel and the Torah are one. A few examples may illustrate this further. Song of Solomon 1 is understood to refer to Israel pondering her early history, first going back to the Torah-giving, symbolized by the kisses of God's mouth (v. 2). In 1:5, the bride says as it were, "Although I am black because I made the golden calf, I am comely because I accepted the Torah." Israel must "follow in the tracks of the flock" (1:8), that is, learn the Torah.[30] Israel delighted to sit in God's shade when he offered them the Torah; in the "banqueting house" (the Tabernacle) she learned many details of the Torah (2:3-4). The bride's two breasts (4:5) are compared by some to the two tablets of the Decalogue because of their alleged precise symmetry. The bride's beauty and flawlessness (4:7) are applied to the Sanhedrin as Israel's choice part, administering justice according to the Torah.[31] Her unwillingness to receive the bridegroom (5:1-7) refers to her departure from the Torah, the Lord's subsequent retreat, and Israel's exile.

In her description of the bridegroom (5:10-16), she views God as he has revealed himself in the Torah; for instance, "his

---

29. See Cohen/Rosenberg (1984, 17-30), particularly following Rashi; also cf. Ibn Ezra and the Midrash Rabbah on the Song of Solomon.
30. Shabbat 33b.
31. Sanhedrin 36b; Yevamot 101a/b.

mouth is most sweet" (5:16) refers to the sweet commandments he gave (cf. Ps. 19:7–11). She speaks of her fragrance for her lover (7:13), "new as well as old": both the earlier precepts of the Torah and the later *halakot* of the rabbis (cf. Matt. 13:52). When she says, "I was a wall, and my breasts were like towers" (8:10; cf. the "fence" mentioned above), she means that she is safely surrounded by the Torah, and that her synagogues and study-halls nurture Israel with the Torah.[32] The bride's companions (8:13) are interpreted as the Torah-scholars;[33] or they are angels listening to Israel's voice when it studies the Torah in its "gardens." In the final verse, Israel pleads with God to hasten and deliver them from the Diaspora, and bring the *Shekinah* to rest again on Mount Zion in the new Temple.[34]

3.1.3 Ecclesiastes

After having considered Proverbs and Song of Solomon, we wonder what we can learn from that other Solomonic wisdom book, the book of Ecclesiastes, in regard to Hokmah and Torah. One key to its understanding is the fact that this book is read on the middle Shabbat of the festival of *Sukkot* (Feast of Booths).[35] One tradition says that this customary reading arose because Ecclesiastes states, "Give a portion to seven, or even to eight" (11:2), thought to be an allusion to the seven days of *Sukkot* and the eighth day of solemn Assembly (*Shemini Atzeret*).[36] *Sukkot* is the Feast of Harvest (Exod. 23:16; 34:22), and thus Solomon's word is taken as an admonition concern-

---

32. Baba Batra 7b.
33. Baba Batra 75a; Shabbat 63a.
34. The imagery strikingly resembles that of many mystical Christian writers; cf., e.g., the Reformed *Kanttekeningen* (marginal notes) of the Dutch *Statenvertaling* (States Translation of the Bible, 1637).
35. See Cohen/Rosenberg (1984, 16–18).
36. 'Erubin 40b.

ing the tithes and other obligations toward the needy.

There must be a better reason, though, for reading this book during *Sukkot*. Its Greek title, *Ecclesiastes*, comes from *ekklesia*, "assembly," and the Hebrew title is *Qohelet*, derived from *qahal*, "assembly." The title thus means: "someone addressing an assembly." The feminine form of the word may refer to *Hokmah*, personified wisdom, as the speaker of the book; or it is to be taken as a neuter adjective meaning "the type of speaker in an assembly."[37] We read of Solomon: "Then Solomon assembled [*q-h-l*] the elders of Israel. . . . And all the men of Israel assembled to King Solomon at the feast in the month Ethanim, which is the seventh month" (1 Kings 8:1-2), that is, at *Sukkot*. When Solomon addressed an assembly during *Sukkot*, what did he say? The most important answer is found in Deuteronomy: "At the end of every seven years, at the set time in the year of release, at the Feast of Booths, when all Israel comes to appear before the LORD your God at the place that he will choose, you shall read this Torah before all Israel in their hearing. Assemble [*q-h-l*] the people, men, women, and little ones, and the sojourner within your towns, that they may hear and learn to fear the LORD your God, and be careful to do all the words of this Torah" (31:10-12). Solomon assembled the people at *Sukkot* and addressed them as the *Qohelet*; Moses assembled the people during *Sukkot* every seven years (i.e., during the Sabbatical Year) to read the Torah to them. If the two are combined, one will understand why Israel read both the Torah and Ecclesiastes during *Sukkot*.

There must still be some deeper connection between the Torah and Ecclesiastes, however, for the closing words of Ecclesiastes are: "The end of the matter; all has been heard. Fear God and keep his commandments, for this is the whole duty of man. For God will bring every deed into judgment, with every secret thing, whether good or evil" (12:13-14). The

---

37. Cohen/Rosenberg (1984, 28).

fascinating thing about Ecclesiastes is that it "is composed of questions and answers from those who have no understanding, to whom the matters of the world appear misleading and distorted but [they] are explained well by the wise man who knows the knowledge of the Most High, and what to answer the heretic. And in addition to this, it labels as futile all matters of this lower world, and leads to straightforwardness and the fear of God and His love."[38]

The Torah tells us what to do. Ecclesiastes speaks about *us*, about the many questions we have as believers thrown into a world that appears in many respects to be absurd, about our stubbornness with respect to discerning the pathway of practical wisdom: doing good, shunning evil. The Torah is the objective side, Ecclesiastes the subjective side, of *Sukkot* preaching. The connection is clearly there: "The Preacher [*qohelet*] sought to find words of delight, and uprightly he wrote words of truth" (12:10), that is, all his words are alluded to in the Torah.[39] "The words of the wise are like goads, and like nails firmly fixed are the collected sayings; they are given by one Shepherd" (12:11). The divine aspect is this: the words of Ecclesiastes are the words of God the great Shepherd, inspired by him. The human aspect is this: the "words of the wise" have been collected "by the masters of assemblies" (KJV, ASV), that is, the sages of the study-halls of the Torah. Their words are like goads, that is, they stir the sheep of the good Shepherd to follow the way of the Torah.

"My son, beware of anything beyond these. Of making many books there is no end, and much study is a weariness of the flesh" (12:12). Some rabbis explain this to mean that it would be impossible to commit the entire Oral Torah to writing.[40] But perhaps it is more obvious to understand these

---

38. Cohen/Rosenberg (1984, 18).
39. Thus Moses Alshich (quoted by Cohen/Rosenberg [1984, 109]).
40. Talmud: Erubin 21b; Metsudath David; Rashi.

words as a warning against the "many books" that go beyond both the Torah and the comments of the sages. The study of God's Word, and of godly comments upon it, refreshes and enlightens the heart; the study of any other books "wearies the body" and wastes time and energy.

One of the central messages of Ecclesiastes could be identified as *joy*: the gift of rejoicing in and enjoying simplicity, the good things of the Lord (2:24-26; 3:12-13; 5:18-20; 9:7-9; 11:8). What festival is more evidently the feast of joy than *Sukkot*? And what festival is more appropriate to remind the people of the great fact that true joy is always linked to keeping God's Torah (Deut. 16:13-15; Neh. 8:17; Ps. 119:14, 111, 162)? "Rejoice, O young man, in your youth, and let your heart cheer you in the days of your youth. . . . But know that for all these things God will bring you into judgment" (Eccl. 11:9). Nothing is more sobering than reading Ecclesiastes, and doing that at one of the merriest moments of the Israelite year. To all of life's difficult and wearisome questions and sorrows, God's sweet Torah is the answer and balm. Down here on earth, all is vanity; up there in heaven, God's words are "like nails firmly fixed."

3.2 Wisdom in the New Testament
3.2.1 *Sophia*

We have seen that the Sophia of Proverbs 8 is personified to a certain extent, and even more so in Jewish tradition. This hypostatization of a divine attribute, wisdom, never turns her into a real creature, like an angel, for example. Yet, it is significant that already in Holy Scripture, Sophia is so clearly presented as a person distinct from God. As Goldberg puts it, "[T]he Bible personifies divine wisdom so that it seems to be a hypostasis of God, but stops just short of giving it separate existence. . . . The figure of wisdom in the OT never came to be regarded as a deity independent of the Lord although some such expressions occur in Prov 8. . . . Wisdom did attain a degree of personification, with features which were by no means abstract."⁴¹ She is the artist, artisan, architect, and master builder who was *with* God in the beginning, and *through whom* he created all things; without her, nothing was made that has been made. God is delighted about *her*, and *her* delight is both in him ("rejoicing before him always") and in mankind ("rejoicing in his inhabited world and delighting in the children of man") (Prov. 8:30-31).

The apostle Paul, too, seems to personify wisdom to a certain extent when speaking, first, of Jesus being the Wisdom of God (1 Cor. 1:24, 30). Second, he speaks of the "manifold wisdom [*polypoikilos sophia*] of God" as displayed in the Ekklesia (Eph. 3:10), as if she were a lady in a robe of many colors. James even speaks of "the wisdom that comes down from above" (James 3:15, 17). This seems to be a clear reference to the Jewish-apocalyptic tradition referring to Sophia's coming down from heaven to God's people in the form of the Torah (§3.1). In fact, the Torah plays an important role in James' reasoning. He refers to it as the "perfect Torah, the Torah of liberty" and as the "royal Torah" (1:25; 2:8, 12). The latter expression is quite interesting in the light of the idea of Sophia, God's daughter, as a supreme queen: "By me [i.e., Wisdom] kings reign, and rulers decree what is just; by me princes rule, and nobles, all who govern the earth."⁴² This interpretation seems to be spoiled by the fact that in the Greek text of James, *nomos* is masculine. It is congruent, though, with the notion of the *lex rex* or *lex regina* (the law as a king or queen) in ancient

---

41. Goldberg (1980, 283).
42. Prov. 8:15-16 (note); in Mishnah Avot VI.1 this verse is explicitly applied to the Torah, thus corroborating the identity of Hokmah and Torah; ibid., II.7 says, "One who has acquired unto himself words of Torah, has acquired for himself the life of the world to come," thus applying the word of Prov. 8:35 about the Hokmah to the Torah (cf. 'Avodah Zarah 17b on Prov. 2:11, and 19a on Prov. 9:3).

literature.[43] James may also have intended to say, "the Torah of the King," or, "the Torah of God's kingdom" (cf. James 2:5).

Worth noting are also the statements of Jesus:[44] "Wisdom is justified by her deeds" (Matt. 11:19), or "by all her children" (Luke 7:35), implying that Wisdom's actions and Jesus' actions coincided.[45] Jesus' statement, "Come to me, all who labor and are heavy laden. . . . Take my yoke upon you, and learn from me . . . and you will find rest for your souls" (Matt. 11:28), is an apparent reference to Sirach 51:23-27 about Wisdom: "Come to me, all you that need instruction, and learn in my school. Why do you admit that you are ignorant and do nothing about it? Here is what I say: It costs nothing to be wise. Put on the yoke, and be willing to learn. The opportunity is always near. See for yourselves! I have really not studied very hard, but I have found great contentment" (in a more negative sense, also cf. Acts 15:10 KJV, NKJV, NIV).

In between these two sayings of Jesus in Matthew 11 are these remarkable words: "I thank you, Father, Lord of heaven and earth, that you have hidden these things from the wise and understanding and revealed them to little children; yes, Father, for such was your gracious will" (vv. 25-26; cf. Luke 10:21). "These things" refers to Wisdom, which is hidden from those who are wise in their own eyes. The entire passage, along with 1 Corinthians 1:24, 30 and 2:6-10, seems to refer to true Wisdom (vv. 19, 25), which is contained in the Son (v. 27).[46]

Jesus introduces Wisdom in a personified way, as a speaking figure: "the Wisdom of God said, 'I will send them prophets and apostles, some of whom they will kill and persecute'" (Luke 11:49). However, in the parallel text, Matthew 23:34,

---

43. Adamson (1976, 114-15).
44. See Davies (1955, 155-57); Schweizer (1987, 39).
45. See Christ (1970, 63-80).
46. Christ (1970, 81-119).

he applies this very saying to himself: "Therefore I send you prophets and wise men...." Perhaps this is the clearest example of hypostatizing in the New Testament: it is Sophia that sends prophets and apostles to the people, and this Sophia has become incarnate in the person of Jesus.[47] This is why he can declare, "I say to you," as opposed to the expression, "You have heard...." (5:22, 28, 32, 34, 39). There can be no actual contrast, for the same Wisdom that spoke to the fathers now addresses the people in the person of Wisdom incarnate. This Wisdom is the *Logos* of John 1 (see the next §§).

The most intriguing *Sophia* saying in the mouth of Jesus appears to be Matthew 23:37-39:[48] "O Jerusalem, Jerusalem, the city that kills the prophets and stones those who are sent to it! How often would I have gathered your children together as a hen gathers her brood under her wings, and you were not willing! See, your house is left to you desolate. For I tell you, you will not see me again, until you say, 'Blessed is he who comes in the name of the Lord'" (cf. Luke 13:34-35, with reference to Ps. 118:26). Many interpreters see personified Wisdom as the speaker here because of the link with verse 34 (prophets, sent ones), because of Jesus' reference to the whole history of Israel (cf. Sir. 24:4, 10, 12, 15; Bar. 4:1-4), and particularly because of the comparison to a female (!) bird. In Sirach 1:15, *Sophia* is literally spoken of as having a "nest" (from Gr. *nossia*; same word in Prov. 16:16 LXX). Descriptions of *Sophia* as a (female) bird are common.[49] This fact underscores the link between Hokmah/Torah and the Holy Spirit (Luke 3:22; cf. Gen. 1:2, the Spirit hovering like a bird [Deut. 32:11]; see further §3.3.2 below).

According to Jesus' prophecy in Matthew 23, "pre-existent Wisdom (as *Shekinah*) dwells in the temple and looks back at all its unavailing efforts: how often it has called Is-

---

47. Christ (1970, 120–35).
48. Christ (1970, 136–52).
49. Christ (1970, 139).

rael to itself (as *Torah*) through messengers, just like the bird tries to protect its young! But Jerusalem kills the prophets and stones the sent ones. Consequently, now judgment is coming: God will abandon the temple, and thus city and nation. With him, Wisdom will not be visible anymore until it (as Son of Man) comes again to judge."[50] Jesus as both the true *Shekinah* and the true Hokmah/Torah calls the people to himself, but because they fail to listen, he withdraws to heaven. This corresponds to what in Wisdom literature is called the Ascent of Wisdom, which is a sign of the approaching end and judgment (cf. Prov. 1:28; 1 Enoch 93:8; 94:5; 4 Ezra 5:9-10; 1 Bar. 48:36). When the people turn back to him, he will come again as the Son of Man (Dan. 7:13).

3.2.2 *Logos:* Ancient Views[51]

There is a clear relationship between the Torah/Hokmah of the Tanakh and Jewish tradition, on the one hand, and the Logos of John 1, on the other. Already in Psalm 119, the Torah is often called *davar*, sometimes *imrah*, both meaning "word" (Septuagint: *logos*). God created the cosmos through his "word" (Ps. 33:6, LXX: *logos*; cf. John 1:3). If John 1 begins by saying that the Logos "was with God,"[52] this clearly seems to point to Proverbs 8:30-31, where the eternal Sophia is with God, and is the craftswoman through whom God created the universe (see §3.1.1). In Proverbs 8, Sophia is God's creational wisdom, not only the Wisdom *through which* he created all things, but also the Wisdom (Torah) that *holds for* created re-

---

50. Christ (1970, 142); regarding the link between *Sophia* and *Shekinah*, see §3.3.2.
51. Recent literature includes Hamerton-Kelly (1973), Schnabel (1985), von Lips (1990), Witherington (1995), Greene (2004), O'Collins (2009), Hillar (2012); cf. Dunn (1998, 266–81) for a brief exposition and many references to ancient Jewish literature.
52. Gr. *pros*: "over against, opposite to," from face to face, in an intimate fellowship with God; cf. *Sophia* as God's daughter sitting on his lap (§3.1.2).

ality; creation *displays* God's wisdom. Likewise, it is said in Colossians 1:17, "He is before all things, and in him all things hold together."[53] And in Hebrews 1:2-3, ". . . his Son . . . through whom also he created the world. He [i.e., the Son] is the radiance of the glory of God and the exact imprint of his nature, and he upholds the universe by the word [*rhēma*] of his power."

In Proverbs 8, we see God's wisdom displayed in the works of his *hands*, in John 1 Jesus as God's Wisdom is, as it were, the Word (*logos*) that went forth from God's *mouth*. All things have been created through, and are submitted to, God's Wisdom, God's Word, God's Torah, God's Logos. Thus, Hokmah/Sophia is the Wisdom that is revealed in God's creational ordinances, both for the cosmos and for human individual and societal life.

Interestingly, the plural in Genesis 1:26 ("Let us make man") is interpreted by one Jewish authority as referring to God and the Torah.[54] Similarly, many Christian authorities have interpreted the plural here as referring to the Father, Son, and Holy Spirit. God created through the Torah, God created through his Son (or through his Spirit; cf. Gen. 1:2; Ps. 33:6; 104:30; in such verses, *ruach* is both "spirit" and "breath"). There are plenty of such correspondences. Jesus is our "advocate with the Father" (1 John 2:1); likewise, the Torah pleads Israel's case before God.[55] All things were created not only *in* and *through* but also *for* Jesus, the "image of God" (Col. 1:15-16). Likewise, the rabbis called Wisdom the "image of God" (cf. Wisd. 7:26), and said that all things were created *for* (the sake of) the Torah.[56] It is like a king who creates a

---

53. See extensively Davies (1955, 150–152) on the relationships between Col. 1:15–18 and Wisdom literature, particularly Prov. 8.
54. Tanchuma Pekudei 3.
55. E.g., Exod. Rabbah on 29:4; *Zohar* (III.35b).
56. Mishnah Avot II.8; III.14; Berakhot 6b; Pesachim 68b; Gen. Rabbah 1 on 1:1; Midr. Ps. 172b (on 78:1); Midr. Exod. 14, 29.

wonderful park for his beloved daughter — as in Hebrews 1:2 in which God's Son is called the "appointed heir of all things" even before it is said that through him God made the universe. It was all for his Son.

It would be too easy to argue that John is suggesting not correspondence but contrast: "the Torah was given through Moses; grace and truth came through Jesus Messiah" (John 1:17). Rather, I believe one may paraphrase this verse as follows: "the gracious Sinaitic manifestation of the one, eternal Torah was given through Moses; so much the more the full grace and truth of the one, eternal Torah came to light through Jesus Messiah."[57] Compare this with verse 14: the Logos, who is in himself "full of grace and truth," became flesh in order that in him the full wisdom of God was revealed.[58] Thus there is a certain juxtaposition of Torah/Hokmah and Logos in the Prologue of John's Gospel. All the common Jewish notions with respect to the Torah, which we know from later rabbinic literature, are attributed by John to the Logos: the pre-existence of the Torah, its being with God, its being divine, its being life and light.[59] In the light of the Tanakh, as well as of early Jewish and later rabbinic literature, one could paraphrase the Prologue as follows:[60]

> In the beginning was the Torah, and the Torah was with God, and the Torah was divine. She was in the beginning with God. All things were made through her, and without her was not anything made that was made. In her was life [cf. Prov. 3:18, 22;

---

57. Note that there is also grace and truth in the Torah (cf. Appendix II)! Midr. Ps. 11 on 25:10: "Truth, the Torah is meant."
58. Cf. Kittel (1967, 134–36).
59. The words of the Torah are life to the world (Sifre Deut. 306 on 32:2; cf. Prov. 8:35; Deut. 32:47); the Torah is light to the world (4 Ezra 14:20–21); the Torah is full of truth (Midr. Ps. on 25:10 [§11]) (cf. Kittel 1967, 135).
60. Cf. Strack-Billerbeck (1922–28, 2:353–358; 3:129–31).

4:13, 22; 6:23; 8:35], and that life was the light of men.⁶¹ The light shines in the darkness, and the darkness has not overcome it. . . . The true light, which gives light to everyone, was coming into the world. She was in the world, and the world [i.e., the entire created reality] was made through her, yet the world [i.e., mankind] did not know [or, acknowledge] her. She came to her own [i.e., Israel], and her own people did not receive her [i.e., truly live by her]. But to all who did receive her, who believed in her, she gave the right to become children of God, who were born, not of blood [i.e., natural descent], nor of the will of the flesh, nor of the will of man, but of God [cf. Deut. 14:1: 'You are the sons [or, children] of the LORD your God']. And the Torah became 'flesh' [i.e., embodied in stone tablets] and dwelt among us [i.e., in the ark of the covenant], and we have seen her glory [cf. the *Shekinah*], glory as of the only daughter from the Father, full of grace and truth. . . . No one has ever seen God; the only daughter, who is in the bosom of the Father, she has made him known [cf. Prov. 8:30-31].

John's message can hardly be misunderstood: the Torah daughter and the Logos Son coincide. In Jesus, the fullness of the one, eternal Hokmah/Torah itself has descended to humanity. At the same time, note the differences: the Torah was "given," grace and truth have "come" (actually, "become"; Gr. *egeneto*). Moses was the intermediary in passing on the Torah, Jesus (the new Moses) is himself the Torah. *Therefore, the true parallel in this passage is not between Moses and Jesus, but between the Torah and Jesus.* The rest of John's Gospel is full of this parallel, too, in expressions such as "living water" (4:10; 7:38), the "bread of life" (6:35), the "light of the world" (8:12), even "the way, the truth and the life" (14:6). If Jesus calls him-

---

61. Cf. Prov. 4:18; 6:23. Cf. Sifre Deut. 306 on 32:2: "the words of the Torah are life for the world." 4 Ezra 14:20–21: "The world lies in darkness, its inhabitants are without light; for your Torah is burned."

self "the way" (John 14:6),[62] in Psalm 119:35 the Torah is "the way" (cf. Deut. 11:22; Ps. 1:6; 17:5; Jer. 6:16). If Jesus calls himself the "true vine" (15:1), in Sirach 24:17 ("Like a grapevine I put out lovely shoots; my blossoms gave way to rich and glorious fruit") it is the Torah that calls itself a vine.[63]

The association between the Hokmah of Proverbs 8 and the Logos of John 1 goes back all the way to the church fathers, such as Origen, John of Damascus, Epiphanius, Methodius, Sophronius, Athanasius, Gregory of Nazianzus, and Augustine.[64] Theodoret (393–c. 460), bishop of Cyrus (near Antioch), distinguished three types of wisdom. First, the wisdom that God has granted to Man as a creational gift, through which humans may know God (see, e.g., Eph. 1:17). Second, the wisdom of God that is reflected in the cosmos that he created (see, e.g., Prov. 3:19-20). And third, the Wisdom that has become manifest in the person of Jesus.[65] Augustine made a similar distinction by distinguishing between uncreated and created wisdom (*Sapientia Increata* and *Creata*). The first Wisdom is the same as the Logos, which became incarnate in the person of Jesus. Augustine connects the second wisdom with the Ekklesia (cf. Eph. 3:10).[66] He explicitly speaks of Wisdom not only as a hypostatization (i.e., turning a divine attribute into a figure, independent of God), but also as a personality, when he speaks of her, for instance, as a "beautiful woman who had kindled thee to ardent love" and "that most chaste

---

62. Cf. Christianity as "the Way" in Acts 9:2; 19:9, 23; 22:4; 24:14, 22. N.B. *halakah* is "going, walking."
63. Cf. Strack-Billerbeck (1922–28, 2:*in locis*).
64. Irenaeus (*Adv. Haer.* IV.20.3: "Wisdom which is the Spirit") and Theophilus of Antioch (*To Autolycus* II.15: the Trinity consists of God, Logos and Sophia) saw in the Sophia (Hokmah) the Holy Spirit (see §3.3.2; see about the church fathers on the Sophia, Schipflinger 1988, 45–60).
65. *Dialogue* III, testimony of Eustathius, bishop of Antioch.
66. Confessiones XII.15.20.

beauty of Wisdom,"[67] or in his prayers, in which he addresses Sophia in an astonishingly direct way.[68]

3.2.3 *Logos:* Recent Discussion

In more recent times, the Sophia–Logos association has not always been accepted.[69] One theologian who did support this identification was Heinrich Windisch.[70] According to him and others, the Logos of John 1 cannot be understood without placing it against the background of the Sophia in Jewish Wisdom literature. Thus the great Jewish-Hellenistic thinker, Philo, in his own way associated the Jewish Sophia idea with the Greek Logos idea developed by the Greek philosopher Heraclitus.[71] Therefore, Harris writes, "[T]he Prologue to the Gospel [of John] can be turned back from a Logos-Hymn to a Sophia-Hymn" (see above, §3.2.2).[72] In principle, I am pleading for such an association, although I hesitate to speak of a full identification. It is no trifling matter that, while in the New Testament Jesus is the (male) Logos, the *Son* of God, Jewish tradition views the (female) Hokmah/Sophia as the *daughter* of God.

This is not simply a matter of the incidental gender of the feminine word Hokmah or Sophia. Rather, in Proverbs itself "the *woman* Folly" (9:13) is explicitly placed over against Wisdom, who also as a *woman* sends out her maids and invites people to her house (9:1-6). In Proverbs 1:20 and 8:1-2 too, she is the Woman (or Lady) Wisdom or Understanding, calling aloud in the city street, the town square, and mountain

---

67. Soliloques I.22.
68. Referred to by Schipflinger (1988, 59); cf. his plead for arriving through hypostatization to personification, and from there to a real person (219–34).
69. See, e.g., Ridderbos (1960, 134).
70. Windisch (1914).
71. See extensively Schipflinger (1988, 36–42).
72. Harris (1917, 39).

heights. In 8:12, she speaks in the first person: "I, wisdom, dwell with prudence," and she continues to do this until she describes her house in chapter 9, standing opposite of Lady Folly's house. Even the "strange woman" (2:16; 5:3, 20; 6:24, 26; 7:5) may contain a reference to this figurative Lady Folly: "He who commits adultery [i.e., with the evil woman of v. 24] lacks sense" (6:32). He who converts to Lady Wisdom is wise, whereas he who converts to Lady Folly is foolish.

According to Ross, one reason why we should be careful to identify the Hokmah of Proverbs 8 with the Logos of John 1 is that the Hokmah of Proverbs 8 turns out to be a creature of God—also according to rabbinic tradition—whereas in the New Testament Jesus is never a creature; precisely in John 1 he is rather the Logos through whom God has created all things.[73] As a matter of fact, Proverbs 8 was abused already by Arius to present Jesus as God's first creature. To this, I object that poetical expressions like "possessed," "fathered," "set up," and "I brought forth" (Prov. 8:22–25, see the notes in the ESV) cannot take away anything from the *eternal* pre-existence of Wisdom. If wisdom is nothing other than a personified attribute of God, and God has necessarily been wise from eternity, Wisdom too must have been "brought forth," "fashioned" and "given birth" from eternity. Therefore, already since Origen[74] the text has been used as an argument for the idea of the *generatio aeterna* of the Son, that is, from eternity the Son has been generated by the Father.

Indubitably, Hokmah in Proverbs 8 is no creature in the sense that at a given point in time, before the world began, she must have originated.[75] Rather, such expressions as "the first of his acts of old," "ages ago," and "at the first" in verses

---

73. Ross (1991, 943).
74. *Peri Archōn* I.2.1–4.
75. It should be added, though, that the Septuagint reads in v. 23, "created me" (Gk. *ektise me*), which in the conflict between Arius and Athanasius embarrassed the latter's adherents considerably.

22–23 point just as much to eternal pre-existence as does the expression, "in the beginning *was* the Logos" in John 1:1. In the Septuagint, the Greek expression *en archē* ("from the beginning," NKJV) in Proverbs 8:23 is exactly the same as *en archē* ("in the beginning") in John 1:1. God could not have created Wisdom as a divine attribute in such a way that before that creation he would not yet have been wise. Through what wisdom could God have created that Wisdom? God's Hokmah, and thus God's Torah too, in its transcendent sense, are necessarily just as eternal as God himself. *This is the most important basis for the notion of the one, eternal Torah.*[76] Every ordinance that God ever instituted, either for the cosmos or for human society, goes back to his eternal wisdom, that is, to the eternal Hokmah/Torah.

The notion of the eternal Torah has an indubitably biblical basis, yet Protestant theology seems to have been hardly conscious of it. In my view, the main reason for this is that this notion is suspect because throughout the centuries it has been encountered in strange settings: Jewish-apocalyptic, Gnostic, Orthodox, and Catholic traditions, which have gone far beyond the biblical data (see §3.3). If we do not want to throw out the baby with the bathwater, we have to regain the biblical notion of the eternal Hokmah/Torah by identifying the foreign elements and purging them from it.

It is of little use to quote Jewish sources for the (inaccurate) claim that the eternal Torah is necessarily identical with the Mosaic Torah.[77] There is a well-known poem, called *Yigdal*, based on the twelfth-century creed of Maimonides and recited regularly in Orthodox synagogues. This poem states that "God gave the Torah of truth to his people through his prophet, who was 'faithful in his house' [Num. 12:7]. God will not alter his eternal Torah or exchange it for another."

---

76. Cf. Torah atsilut and Torah q'lulah or Torah q'dumah (§2.2.1).
77. Cf. Stern (1999, 566).

Torah, Hokmah, Logos, and Spirit

However, some rabbinic sources do claim that alterations in the Torah will be made in the Messianic kingdom (*'olam habba*).[78] Most interesting is a notion in the Kabbalah implying that, "although eternal in its unrevealed state, the *Torah*, in its manifestation in creation, is destined to be abrogated."[79] That is not very far from saying that the one eternal Torah in its unrevealed state exists in various manifestations throughout time within our created reality — a point that plays a main role in my argumentation in the present book.

Let me finish this section with a consideration that appears to corroborate the close association between Hokmah and Logos. The way Psalm 102:25-27 is quoted in Hebrews 1:10-12 strikes us as peculiar because in our Bibles it is God who is addressed in this psalm portion, as clearly distinguished from the suffering Messiah in this psalm. However, the Septuagint, which is quoted almost verbatim in Hebrews 1, reads verses 23-25 as follows: "He answered him in the way of his strength: 'Declare to me the shortness of my days: Bring me not up in the midst of my days. Your years are throughout all generations. You, Lord, in the beginning laid the foundation of the earth. . . .'" Here God is addressing the Messiah, the suffering Man of the Psalm's first part. God says he has only a few days to restore Jerusalem (cf. v. 13), and asks the Messiah not to interfere if he would be half-way in this work of restoration. If we read the Psalm according to the Septuagint, the psalmist in verses 25-27 was presumably thinking along the lines of Proverbs 8:22-32. This time it is not the (female) Hokmah/Torah but the (male) "Lord" (the Messiah), addressed here by God, who is the Instrument through whom God created the world. Likewise, the author of Hebrews implicitly points to him as the Logos of John 1, describing him as the

---

78. Cf. Gen. Rabbah 98,9 (on Gen. 49:11); Lev. Rabbah 9,7 (on Lev. 7:11–12).

79. Quoted from *Encyclopedia Judaica*, s.v. *Torah*, "Eternity (or nonabrogability)" (XV, 1244–46).

Son through whom God made the universe (Heb. 1:2; cf. John 1:3; Col. 1:16).

3.3 Sophia, Torah, Spirit

3.3.1 The Personification of the Sophia

As I said, the Sophia tradition has been loaded with so many unbiblical ideas and notions that the underlying biblical notion of the one, eternal Torah almost got lost. Let us look at some of those foreign elements that have crept in.

In the Gnostic tradition, the Logos and the Sophia were not identified but emphatically distinguished as the masculine and the feminine principle in God. If the relationship between the two had to be described in some way, this was done by defining them as the "father (begetter)" and the "mother (foster-mother, nurse) of the cosmos." The alleged matrimonial Logos-Sophia relationship is called in Greek *hieros gamos*, "holy matrimony."[80] In medieval book painting, on the miniatures and icons of Eastern Orthodox Churches, this matrimony is expressed by all kinds of symbols, based on various legends. Following no one less than Augustine,[81] Russian iconographers, but also some Western artists,[82] loved to depict Sophia, thought to have become incarnate in the Virgin Mary, against the background of the "house with the seven pillars," the house of Lady Wisdom (Prov. 9:1). Of course, the rabbis link this very symbol with the Torah.[83] They speak not only of the house of Lady Torah, but in another metaphor, of the seven pillars of the Torah itself on which the world rests (cf.

---

80. Schipflinger (1988, 242; cf. 195–97, 243, 315–18). In §3.1.2 we found Sophia as the "bride" of Solomon, who is a type of Jesus (the Logos) (ibid., 71–72).
81. De Civitate XVII.20.
82. A good example is the ceiling frescoes of 1734 by C. D. Asam in the church Maria de Victoria, the baroque student church of the University of Ingolstadt (Germany) (Schipflinger [1988, 111–116]).
83. E.g., Lev. Rabbah 11, 3 on 9:1.

Job 9:6; Ps. 75:3). As a midrash states, "The words of the Torah are marble pillars because they are the pillars of the world."[84] The reasoning behind it is that through his statutes God keeps the cosmos together (cf. Ps. 104:19; Jer. 31:35-36; 33:25).

In some art works, Sophia is depicted in a way that is hardly recognizable for those who are not familiar with the Sophia-Mary tradition. One of Michelangelo's famous ceiling frescoes in the Sistine Chapel (in the Vatican) depicts the creation of Adam. God has just finished creating him, and with the fingertips of his right hand almost touches Adam's outstretched hand. That is a well-known picture; but hardly anyone remembers what God's left arm is doing. It is around the shoulders of a young woman, looking with interest in the direction of Adam. She is none other than Sophia, through whom God has created Adam and who later will descend to become the mother and bride of the Last Adam.

In the Capilla Real (Royal Chapel) in the Cathedral of Seville (Spain) — not open for tourists, only for those attending mass — is a large statue of the Virgin Mary, and under it the words of Lady Wisdom: *Per me reges regnant* ("By me kings reign," Prov. 8:15). The suggestion is that Sophia and Mary are identical, or rather, that Mary is the incarnation of Sophia. Only through this identification can the audacious claim be understood that through Mary do the kings of the earth reign.

On the famous altarpiece, *The Lamb of God*, by the brothers Jan and Hubert van Eyck in the St. Bavo Cathedral in Ghent (Belgium), one of the paintings shows the Virgin Mary with the words *Haec speciosior sole et super omnem stellarum dispositionem* ("Wisdom is more beautiful than the sun and all the constellations," Wisd. 7:29). Here again, it is Lady Wisdom speaking, but once again the words are applied to Mary, thought to be the embodiment of this Lady.

In fact, all Sophia-churches of the world (Istanbul, Kiev, Novgorod, Thessaloniki, Polotsk, etc.) are Mary-churches,

---

84. Num. Rabbah 10, 1 on 6:2.

which explains the huge representations of Mary (frescoes, mosaics, statues) in such churches. Such a link between Hokmah/Sophia and the Virgin Mary differs strikingly from the link between Hokmah/Sophia and Logos/Christ, as described above. The process of the incarnation of Sophia in Mary is depicted perhaps nowhere more clearly than in the ceiling fresco in the Maria de Victoria church, the baroque student church of the University of Ingolstadt (Germany).[85] The fresco was painted in 1734 by Cosmas Damien Asam.

Unfortunately, the biblical notion of the eternal Torah has landed in even stranger settings than those just described, namely, outright paganism. Heathen thinking was never satisfied with a feminine hypostatization of a divine attribute. Even in later rabbinic Judaism, we encountered the tendency of viewing Sophia as being so independent that she almost became a divine figure, virtually a pretended goddess—for what else is a "daughter of God"? The Qabbalah took a somewhat different approach. It viewed Hokmah not only as a daughter of God, but also as the feminine aspect in God himself.[86] It spoke of the two "faces," or the two "souls" of God, referring to the masculine and feminine principle in God. The holy book of the Qabbalah, the *Sefer ha-Zohar* ("Book of Lustre," written in Spain by Moses de León, by the end of the thirteenth century, but presumably going back to Shimon bar Yochai, who lived in the first century), argues that only those spiritual images in which the masculine and the feminine are united are of a heavenly nature. God himself allegedly is the highest example of this.

Quite peculiarly, the Qabbalah sees in the *Shekinah* the symbol or expression of the Sophia, the eternal-feminine.[87]

---

85. See Schipflinger (1988, 111–16).
86. For this feminine aspect see, for example, Ps. 131:2; Isa. 49:15; 66:13; Hos. 13:8 (she-bear! lioness!); John 1:13 (cf. Gal. 4:4, "born of woman"); and James 1:18 ("give us birth" [NIV], not "begat us" [KJV]).
87. See extensively Scholem (1977, 135–91); also cf. Schipflinger (1988,

Torah, Hokmah, Logos, and Spirit

The *Shekinah* is the glory[88] of God. She is the queen at the side of the king, daughter as well as bride of God, the mother of every individual Israelite. Qabbalah sees the *Shekinah* as the first of all of God's creatures, just as Wisdom literature witnesses of Sophia. In the *Zohar*, the *Shekinah* is referred to with names used elsewhere for Sophia: "queen," "daughter," "mother," "sister of God," etc. We also find names used for the *Shekinah* which are used in the New Testament for Jesus: "beginning [or, principle] of the world,"[89] "radiance [Heb. *zohar*!] of God's light" (cf. Heb. 1:3), etc. The Qabbalah also associates her with the bride in the Song of Solomon, and calls the Israelites the *Shekinah*'s "members." The *Shekinah* is also the "World Soul" in the Neo-Platonic sense, *ha-Isha ha-Elyona* ("the most high Lady"), the "lady of light in whose mystery is founded all that in the world is feminine." The *Shekinah* appears in various earthly embodiments. Just as one Christian tradition calls Mary the incarnation of Sophia, a Jewish tradition says that the *Shekinah* "at the time of Abraham was called Sarah, at the time of Isaac, Rebekah, and at the time of Jacob, Rachel."[90]

Erich Neumann equates the Sophia with "the Spirit and the bride" (Rev. 22:17).[91] This may surprise us because Spirit and bride are distinguished as two figures (note the plural

---

239–42). The expression "eternal-feminine" (*das Ewig-Weibliche*) comes from the tragedy *Faust* (last part), by Johann Wolfgang von Goethe, and refers there to Love.

88. Literally, the Dwelling (from Heb. *sh-k-n*, "dwell"; cf. *mishkan*, "tabernacle"), i.e., the Presence of God: ". . . personification and hypostatization of the 'indwelling' or 'presence' of God in the world" (Scholem 1977, 136). In many cases, the Gk. *doxa* ("glory") can be rendered as *Shekinah*, as Stern (1989) actually does (e.g., 2 Pet. 1:17).

89. Cf. Rev. 3:14; compare this with Rav Hoshaiah's rendering of Gen. 1:1, "By means of 'the beginning' [i.e., Hokmah/Torah] God created . . ." and Prov. 8:22, "The Lord made me the beginning of his work" (Gen. Rabbah 1 on 1:1) (see §3.1.1).

90. Josef Gikatilla, quoted by Schipflinger (1988, 241).

91. Neumann (1955, 329).

form of the verb "say" in v. 17). Neumann's interpretation becomes more understandable, though, if we realize how much Gnosticism has emphasized the feminineness of the Spirit. The Hebrew word for "spirit," *ruach*, is usually treated as a feminine word. Because of its occurrence in Genesis 1:2, where it performs the typically feminine work of "brooding" (as some render it),[92] Gnosticism called her the first woman. She is often considered to be identical with Sophia.[93] Even some church fathers thought that in Luke 15, we find the Father in the first, the Son in the third, and the Holy Spirit in the second parable, which is about a woman (!) who lost a coin.[94] Not only some Gnostics, but also orthodox fathers viewed both the Spirit and the Sophia as designations for the eternal-feminine.[95] In the apocryphal Gospel of the Hebrews, Jesus calls the Spirit his mother.[96] Cyprian called the virgins of his time who were devoted to God the "most beautiful symbols of the Holy Spirit."

Chrysostom called the Eucharist "the milk from the Holy Spirit's mother breast."[97] The name *Shaddai* ("Almighty") is often read as the plural of *shad*, that is, "my breasts," emphasizing an alleged feminine aspect of God,[98] and some assert that the high priest beheld these (veiled) breasts in the holiest on Yom Kippur. This idea seems to be implied in the Talmu-

---

92. Cf. Ambrose, *Hexaemeron* I. 8. 29; Jerome, *Quest. Heb.*
93. See Layton (1987, 35, 168, 173).
94. Both the Evangelical Arno Gaebelein (1970, 155), and the Reformed Norman Geldenhuys (1983, 402), seem to have no problem with this interpretation.
95. The composer Gustav Mahler in his Eighth Symphony (1906) suggests a link between the Holy Spirit in the first, and the eternal-feminine in the second, parts of the symphony.
96. This "Gospel" is lost, but we know this statement from a quotation by Origen, *Commentary on John* 2.12.87).
97. Quoted by Schipflinger (1988, 321).
98. Cf. the etymological link between *rahum*, "mercy" (of God), and *rehem*, "(mother's) womb" (see Gen. 49:25 in the text).

Torah, Hokmah, Logos, and Spirit

dic reference that the ends of the ark's staves in the sanctuary "pressed forth and protruded [through the veil] as the two breasts of a woman," with a reference to Song of Solomon 1:13, where "my breasts" renders the Hebrew word *shaddai*.[99] Even the word play in Genesis 49:25 seems to support this view: "... because of the Almighty [*Shaddai*], who blesses you with ... blessings of the breasts [*shadaim*] and womb."

In the way just described, the triangle is closed: not only Torah/Hokmah/Sophia and Logos, but also Torah/Hokmah/Sophia and Ruach/Pneuma belong together. In ancient times, the *Shekinah* dwelt in the Tabernacle (Exod. 40:34–38) and the Temple (1 Kings 8:10–12), and today it is the Spirit who dwells in God's Temple, the Ekklesia (1 Cor. 3:16; 2 Cor. 6:16; Eph. 2:22). Therefore, saying that "the tabernacle of God is with men" (Rev. 21:3) is allegedly the same as saying that Sophia, the Lady of Revelation 12:1, that is the *Shekinah*, the Spirit of God,[100] has returned to her "tabernacle."[101] There is always some Christian kernel in such ideas, which at the same time are not far from purely pagan thinking. Here, the Hokmah/Torah is no longer just a gift of God, but an independent feminine figure, not as a metaphor but as a real, divine Lady.

This idea is not far removed at all from the Mother-Goddess of paganism. When in AD 431, at the Council of Ephesus, Sophia/Mary was declared to be Mother of God (Greek *theotokos*), the people were in ecstasy because to them this sounded like the Mother-Goddess. She was the "great Artemis of the Ephesians" (Acts 19:28), the great "Mother of Nature," whom they had lost through the rise of Christianity and whom, in a

---

99. Yoma 54a. Another interpretation (Chagigah 12a) says that *Shaddai* means, "He who [*she*] said, Enough [*dai*]!"
100. For a biblical link between the *Shekinah* and the Spirit, see the expression "the Spirit of glory" (1 Pet. 4:14), that is, "the Spirit of the *Shekinah*."
101. Quispel (1979, 119; cf. 76–77); also cf. Logion 22 and 114 in the Gnostic Gospel of Thomas.

sense, they had now received back in a Christianized form. In the ancient Christian world, Sophia/Mary inherited many of the features of the pagan Mother-Goddess, one of them being the title "Queen of Heaven" (*Regina Coeli*), which had belonged to the Babylonian mother-goddess Ishtar (cf. Jer. 7:18; 44:17–19, 25).

3.3.2 Torah and Spirit

In summary,[102] certain Jewish and Christian traditions have considered the *uncreated* Sophia to be God's feminine side, his feminine self-revelation, reflection of the Eternal Light, the feminine "double" of God, God's intimate advisor and creational partner, master builder of the universe, God's lover and bride, mother of the cosmos, identical with the Holy Spirit and the *Shekinah*. The *created* Sophia has been considered to be the daughter, the firstborn of God, the fullness of God's creational ideas (in the Neo-Platonic sense), the World Soul, sister as well as bride of the Logos (who is the Son), the image (created and animated by the Holy Spirit) of the motherly-feminine principle in the Trinity, the personal Archē of the cosmos. She is the Torah in the sense of world order and harmony, not only of nature but also of human society.[103] In Israel, she has created a people for herself; as such she is the Daughter (of) Zion (e.g., Ps. 9:14; Isa. 62:11; Jer. 6:2, 23; Micah 4:8, 13; Zeph. 3:14; Zech. 2:7, 10; 9:9). She is the Sophia that has found her embodiment in the Virgin Mary, representative of the Ekklesia, or in the Ekklesia itself, the "sophianic" church, the "body" of the Messiah.

Once Hokmah was considered to be identical with the eternal Torah as well as with the divine Spirit, corroboration of such a view could easily be "discovered" in Scripture. The least one can say is that the Bible suggests a clear link between

---

102. Cf. Schipflinger (1988, 65–66).
103. Shabbat 88a, 'Avodah Zarah 3a and 5a contain the idea that, without the Torah, the world must lapse into chaos and anarchy.

Torah, Hokmah, Logos, and Spirit

the Torah and the Spirit. Breaking the Torah is to grieve the Holy Spirit, just as placing the Torah in the midst of Israel was to set God's Holy Spirit among them in the days of Moses (Isa. 63:10-11).[104] The Spirit of the living God writes Messiah on our hearts (2 Cor. 3:3), which is the same as saying that he writes the (Messianic) Torah on our hearts (Heb. 8:10). Having the Torah written on your heart is having the Spirit dwelling in your heart (Gal. 4:6). Living by the Spirit is living by the Messianic Torah, not under legalism (Gal. 5:13-6:2). Living by the Spirit is freedom (2 Cor. 3:17); living by the Messianic Torah is living by the Torah of freedom (James 1:25; 2:12). God puts his Spirit in his people so that they would "walk in my statutes and be careful to obey my rules" (Ezek. 36:27). The "righteous requirement[105] of the Torah" is "fulfilled in us" insofar as we "walk according to the Spirit" (Rom. 8:4).

Just as the Torah led and instructed God's people (*torah* = instruction), the Spirit leads and instructs God's people (John 14:26; 16:13; Rom. 8:14). Just as the Torah gives light to the eyes and renews life (Ps. 19:8; 119:93), the Spirit gives life and enlightens the eyes of the heart (2 Cor. 3:6; Eph. 1:17-18).[106]

---

104. In my view, Dunn (1990a, 68) creates a false contrast in asserting that the expression "law of Christ" (Gal. 6:2) "should not be interpreted as though Paul regarded this [i.e., the Jesus-tradition] as a regulation of binding force on all his converts. Paul's ethic was much too charismatic for that, much too conscious of the Spirit's immediate direction . . . much too dependent on the Spirit's gift of discernment in matters of doubt or dispute." I reply that, whatever rabbinic Judaism made out of this, the Mosaic Torah was just as "charismatic" a matter as the Messianic Torah. There never was any polity of the Torah in which Torah-keeping was not closely linked with a godly life in the power of the Spirit, even though in the Tanakh the Spirit is not referred to as often or as explicitly as in the New Testament.
105. In Gk. "righteous requirement" is one word: *dikaiōma*, i.e., that which the Torah righteously demands of Man.
106. Gen. Rabbah on Gen. 1:3–5: the word "light" occurs five times with regard to the first day of creation, corresponding with the

THE ETERNAL TORAH: LIVING UNDER GOD

The Mosaic Torah was written "by the finger of God" (Exod. 31:18; Deut. 9:10), while Jesus acted "with the finger of God," that is, with the Spirit of God (Luke 11:20; cf. Matt. 12:28). If the Torah convicts people in regard to sin and righteousness and judgment (Rom. 3:20; 5:20; 7:7-11; Gal. 3:19), the Spirit does the same (John 16:8). Rejecting the Torah is the same as resisting the Holy Spirit (Acts 7:38-51). True sons of God are those who keep the Torah (Deut. 8:5-6), that is, who are led by the Spirit (Rom. 8:14). The Word of God—that is, the Torah in its widest sense—is the sword of the Spirit (Eph. 6:17).

Note in particular the important fact that the Holy Spirit was poured out at *Shavu'ot,* or Pentecost (Acts 2). This was not only a harvest feast (cf. Exod. 23:16; 34:2) but later also became the feast of the Torah-giving, because the latter took place in the third month (Exod. 19:1)—according to rabbinic calculation, on the sixth day[107]—while *Shavu'ot* is annually

---

five books of the Torah. As God's being is light, the medieval Jewish scholar, Ezra ben Solomon, commented that the five books of the Torah are *the Name* of the Holy One, the name expressing one's being. The medieval Qabbalist, Joseph Gikatilla, claimed that the whole Torah was an explication of, and a commentary on, the tetragrammaton, YHWH; the expression *Torat YHWH* ("Law of the Lord") thus means "instruction about the tetragrammaton." He also quoted the older Qabbalists saying that God "is in his Name, and his Name in him, and that his Name is his Torah." Likewise, another medieval Qabbalist, Menachem Recanati, inferred from an ancient tradition—"before the world was created, only God and his Name were there" (*Pirqe d'Rabbi Eliezer 3*)—that "the Torah is not something outside him [i.e., God], and he is not something outside the Torah" (Scholem 1960, 58, 61-64). As the Name of God, the *Logos* of God expresses the fullness of his being.

107. Rashi: the "day" in Exod. 19:1 is taken to be the first day of the month, v. 3a is on the second, v. 8b on the third, v. 9b on the fourth, v. 11 ("third day" after this) on the sixth day of the month, i.e., the date of *Shavu'ot* (Cohen/Rosenberg 1985, 451-54).

Torah, Hokmah, Logos, and Spirit

celebrated on the very same day.[108] Thus, God gave the Torah and the Spirit at the same festival.[109] At Mount Sinai, God's redemptive relationship with Israel began, at Mount Zion, his redemptive relationship with the Ekklesia began. At Mount Sinai, God gave his Torah through Moses. At Mount Zion, the Father gave his Spirit through his Son, the new Moses (John 14:16-18, 26; 15:26; 16:13-15; see §7.4.3 about Jesus as the new Moses). In both cases there was a time of preparation, perhaps six days in Exodus 19:10-15, 22,[110] and ten days in Acts 1 and 2.[111] In both cases the people of Israel were stunned (Exod. 20:18-21; Acts 2:6-12, 37).

Quite significantly, at both occasions many "voices" were heard, and fire was seen.[112] Concerning the "voices" some rabbis tell us that the Torah was offered *in* and *to* all the seventy "voices" (languages) of mankind — seventy because of the seventy nations in Genesis 10.[113] God "offered the Torah to

---

108. See, e.g., Yoma 4b. The Sadducees had, and Messianic Jews have, a varying date for *Shavu'ot* because they celebrate *Yom Habikkurim* (exactly seven weeks before *Shavu'ot*) on the day after the Shabbat in the week of *Pesach/Matzot* (cf. Lev. 23:9–16).
109. In §7.2.1, I point to another parallel: between the Torah-giving on Mount Sinai and the Sermon on the Mount of the Beatitudes in Matt. 5–7.
110. See note 107 above.
111. Jesus' ascension was forty days after his resurrection (Acts 1:3), which fell on *Yom Habikkurim* ("Day of the Firstfruits"), while Pentecost (lit. "Fiftieth [Day]") was after fifty days (2:1). This left ten days of prayerful preparation (1:4, 12–14).
112. Exod. 19:16 ("thunders" [plural] is literally "voices"), 18; Acts 2:3–4. Scripture (Jer. 23:29; Eph. 5:26) and Talmud (Ta'anit 7a; Qiddushin 30b; Baba Batra 79a; Mishnah Avot II.10) compare the Torah to fire and also to water, just as the Spirit is compared to fire (Matt. 3:11; Luke 3:16; 1 Thess. 5:19) and water ("pouring," Isa. 32:15; 44:3; Ezek. 39:29; Joel 2:28–29; John 7:38–39).
113. Mekhilta Yitro 5; Sifre Deut. 343; Shabbat 88b; Exod. Rabbah on 5:9; 27:9; in this passage Heb. *lashon* can mean both "tongue" and "language," just like *glōssa* in both Acts 2:3 ("tongue") and 4

every nation and every tongue, but none accepted it, until he came to Israel who received it."[114] Compare Psalm 147:19-20: "He declares his word to Jacob, his statutes and rules to Israel. He has not dealt thus with any other nation; they do not know his rules." While the Torah was offered to all the "seventy voices" but refused by them, at *Shavot* his Spirit came again to all nations: "[H]ow is it that we hear, each of us in his own native language? . . . we hear them telling in our own tongues the mighty works of God" (Acts 2:8, 11).[115] In the end there will be true believers among all the seventy (and many more) nations of the world (cf. Matt. 24:14; 28:19).

3.3.3 The Torah and the Gods

The Torah was "apportioned" to Israel only; it is Israel's "possession" or "inheritance" (Deut. 33:4). By contrast, Deuteronomy 4:19-20 surprisingly tells us that God "apportioned" to the seventy nations the celestial bodies, keeping Israel for himself. Because of the link between the celestial bodies and the "gods,"[116] this is the same as saying that God "apportioned" to each nation its own "god" (i.e., guardian angel) as Deuteronomy 29:16 indeed affirms (the same verb *h-l-q* is used here as in 4:19). Accordingly, when "the Most High gave to the nations their inheritance, when he divided mankind, he fixed the borders of the peoples according to the number of the sons of God. For the LORD's portion is his people, Jacob his allotted inheritance" (Deut. 32:8-9).[117] That is, there were as

---

("tongue" = language).
114. 'Avodah Zarah 2b; Sifre Deut. 343 on 33:2; see extensively Strack-Billerbeck (1922–28, 3:38ff.).
115. In Acts 2:9–11, fourteen geographical districts outside the land of Israel are mentioned, one-fifth of the seventy nations.
116. E.g., the "host of heaven" (celestial bodies, Deut. 17:3; 2 Kings 17:16; Jer. 8:2) can also mean spirits (angels, demons) (1 Kings 22:19). Also cf. Job 38:17; Isa. 14:12.
117. "Sons of God" is the marginal reading based on a damaged Dead Sea Scroll (4Q), which reads *beney el. . .*; cf. Clement of Rome (*1st*

many nations (seventy) as there were "gods" (angelic princes) allotted to them. But his own allotted portion was Israel (cf. Jer. 16:19-20, which says that each nation has a god as its inheritance).

We find the same thought in Sirach 17:17: "[W]hen he divided the nations over all the earth, he placed a ruler over each nation, but Israel is the Lord's portion" — where "ruler" means angelic prince (cf. Isa. 26:13; Dan. 10:13, 20-21; 12:1; 1 Cor. 8:5). The early Jesus-believers knew about this: Pseudo-Clement tells us that God divided the nations of the earth in seventy-two parts,[118] and placed an angel over each of them, but over Israel he placed the greatest of the archangels.[119] According to Clement of Alexandria, God placed angels over the nations and states; he apparently alludes to Deuteronomy 32:8-9 the way we just quoted the text.[120] Origen, too, often interprets this passage as speaking of national angels.[121]

Just as the nations have their "gods," Israel has Michael, the archangel. One could also say, just as the nations have their guardian angels, Israel has the Torah as a kind of "guardian angel," of the sort Paul seems to describe by the notion of the

---

    Ep. Corinthians 29), Septuagint, Symmachus, Vetus Latina, Syrohexaplaris: "angels."

118. The confusion between 70 (7 x 10) and 72 (6 x 12), both including a perfect number (7 = 3 + 4; 12 = 3 x 4), is also present in Luke 10:1, 17, where some manuscripts have 70, others 72. The Masoretic text of Gen. 10 has 70, the Septuagint has 72 nations. "Septuagint" itself means 70, but the Letter of Aristeas mentions 72 translators. See Metzger (1971, 67–76).

119. *Recognitiones* II. 42; thus, too, the Syrian father, Ephraem; cf. Dan. 10:21, "Michael, your prince [*sar*]"; 1 Enoch 20:5: Michael is placed over Israel. Whereas God himself had been the ruler of his people before, since the exile Michael was this ruler (cf. Exod. 32:34–33:3).

120. *Stromateis* VI.17; VII.2.

121. Peri Archōn I.5.2; Kata Kelson IV.8; V.29.

paidagōgos, an attendant of children, in Galatians 3:23-25.¹²² This parallel may throw light upon a difficult passage in Galatians 4. If we accept that the *stoicheia* in verse 3 ("elementary principles") refer to "elemental spirits" and/or astral gods,¹²³ there is a striking connection with the Torah. The expression "under the *stoicheia* of the world" in verse 3 is congruent with "under the Torah" in verse 4. Paul's argument is this: formerly, the Gentile Jesus-believers of Galatia had served the "gods" of the nations; if they now wanted to submit to the Judaizers' legalism,¹²⁴ they would in fact "turn back again to the weak and worthless *stoicheia* of the world."¹²⁵ A slave under the yoke of legalism does not differ essentially from a slave under the pagan idols; both serve basically the same spiritual powers ruling this infidel world. We just saw that God placed the nations under the "gods," special guardian angels; but he placed Israel under the Torah as a *paidagōgos*. Those who substitute legalism and Jewish ethnocentrism for the pure Torah place themselves under the same *stoicheia* as the pagans do. Note that good angels had given the Torah as a guardian to Israel (3:19), but that possibly a satanic angel had seduced the Galatians to their legalism and Jewish ethnocentrism (1:8).

Similarly, Colossians 2:8 says that those drifting away into the worldviews of the Greek and the Judaizing schools come under the power of the *stoicheia*. Verse 15 refers to the (spiritual) "rulers and authorities" disarmed on the cross, verse 16

---

122. See §4.3.1n32 below.
123. See Delling (1971); Bruce (1984, 97–100, 111–12); Fung (1988, 189–93), and the literature mentioned there.
124. I define "Judaizers" as those (Jews or Gentiles) who proclaim that observance of the (entire) Mosaic Torah is a condition for salvation. Those who recommend such observance for various spiritual reasons, but *not* as a condition for salvation, are *not* Judaizers (cf. Wilson 1989, 25–26).
125. Gal. 4:9–10 seems to say that observing a calendar governed by celestial bodies amounts to serving the *stoicheia* (which also refer to the twelve signs of the Zodiac).

may suggest a link between a calendar governed by celestial bodies and the *stoicheia*, and verse 18 speaks of the "worship of angels." Verses 20-23 seem to preach the same message: if you died with Messiah to the *stoicheia* of this cosmos, and then fall into legalism and ritualism, you come again under the power of the *stoicheia*, that is, of those powers of which Messiah had made a spectacle through the cross (v. 15). Thus, there is a tremendous contrast between God's people under the Torah as he intended it and God's people under a legalistic and ethnocentric polity. The former is a lofty picture over against the poor pagans enslaved to the "gods" (which are demons; Deut. 32:17; 1 Cor. 10:19-20; Rev. 9:20): it depicts Israel under the noblest law a nation ever saw, and as thus standing far above the pagans, who are under the meanest idolatry and slavery. But the latter—God's people under legalism and ethnocentrism—is a vile picture of a nation that has degraded itself to the level of the pagans, basically serving the same spiritual powers as they do.

To come back to our subject—Torah and Spirit—God gave angelic princes to the nations but kept Israel for himself, granting his Torah to Israel. To use the imagery given earlier: he entrusted the nations to his *servants*—that was in itself an act of grace (cf. Acts 14:15-17)—but he sent his beloved *daughter* to Israel. However, in Acts 2 he sends his Holy Spirit who, though not at all God's daughter but a divine person of the Trinity, has many links with the Torah. This is the great difference: the Torah was offered to all nations but, as the rabbis claim, refused by all except Israel. The Spirit, however, is offered to all nations and accepted by people from all nations but not by the majority of Israel. In both cases, God carefully chose a shrine for his beloved. The Tabernacle or Temple in Tanakhic times was the dwelling-place of both God (Exod. 25:8; 29:44-45) and the Torah. The "testimony" in Exodus 25:16, 21 is the Torah, that is, the stone tablets that were placed in the "ark of the testimony" (v. 22; 26:33-34). Therefore the tabernacle was called the "Tent of the Testimony" (Num. 9:15;

17:7-8; 18:2) or the Tent of the Torah, so to speak. In the New Testament, the Ekklesia is the "holy temple in the Lord," "a dwelling for God by [or, in] the Spirit" (Eph. 2:21-22; cf. 1 Cor. 3:16).

The outpouring of the Spirit on Mount Zion (Acts 2) is a foretaste of both the Torah-giving and the new Spirit-giving in the age to come: "Come, let us go up to the mountain of the LORD . . . out from Zion shall go the Torah, and the word of the LORD from Jerusalem" (Isa. 2:3; Micah 4:2; cf. Isa. 32:15; 44:3; Joel 2:28). In the day of the Messiah, the Lord will put his Spirit within his people so that they will "walk in my statutes and be careful to obey my rules" (Ezek. 36:27). In light of these and other considerations, any false contrast between the Torah and the Spirit is cut off at its roots. The only allowable contrast is between a Torah without the Spirit — which is a killing letter (2 Cor. 3:6) — and a Torah with the Spirit.[126] The former is the "Torah of sin and death," the latter the "Torah of the Spirit of life" (Rom. 8:2).[127] The righteous requirement of the Torah is fulfilled in us who walk according to the Spirit (vs. 4; cf. Ezek. 36:27).

Can the idea of the *eternal* Torah be stripped of all the foreign elements that have been attached to it? Even if both Jewish and Christian traditions have greatly overplayed their hands, sometimes bordering on paganism, in my view a few things can hardly be denied. There exists unmistakably the one, eternal Hokmah, or Torah, which was from eternity with God. It has come to humanity in various manifestations in successive dispensations, as different appearances of the

---

126. On the basis of the rabbinic principle known as *lifnim mi-shurat ha-din* (described in sources such as Berakhot 7a, Baba Kamma 99b–100a), Shulam (1998, 110, 122–123) rather sees the contrast between the "strict letter" and the "spirit" (small "s"!) of the Torah.

127. Assuming that *nomos* really means "Torah" here, and not simply "principle" (see §1.3.2n73).

"daughter of God," if the expression is acceptable. In view of the close association between the Hokmah/Torah of Proverbs 8 and the Logos of John 1, we may say that the Hokmah/Torah was never manifested in a more lofty way than in the person of Jesus, the eternal Son of God. The Hokmah/Torah comes from God the Father, is embodied in the Son, but is also closely linked with the descent of the Holy Spirit, and at any rate is truly observed only in the power of the Spirit.

Chapter 4
The Meaning of the Mosaic Covenant

He is the L<small>ORD</small> *our God;*
 his judgments are in all the earth.
He remembers his covenant forever,
 the word that he commanded, for a thousand generations,
the covenant that he made with Abraham,
 his sworn promise to Isaac,
which he confirmed to Jacob as a statute,
 to Israel as an everlasting covenant,
saying, "To you I will give the land of Canaan
 as your portion for an inheritance."

Psalm 105:7–11

As they were eating, Jesus took bread,
 and after blessing it broke it and gave it to the disciples,
 and said, "Take, eat; this is my body."
And he took a cup,
 and when he had given thanks he gave it to them,
 saying, "Drink of it, all of you,

> *for this is my blood of the covenant,*
> *which is poured out for many for the*
> *forgiveness of sins."*
>
> Matthew 26:26–28

Summary: *The biblical idea of "law" can be understood only against the background of the idea of "covenant." Here again, we encounter many different views, such as whether there are conditional and unconditional covenants. This issue is closely connected with another difficult issue: the tense relationship between God's electing grace and personal human responsibility. On the one hand, the Bible can say that people are not saved by law-works but only by God's grace, and on the other hand, that in terms of their responsibility, people can be saved only if they walk in God's Torah (or, if you wish, in the way of righteousness, which is the same). In this regard, there is no fundamental difference between the Old Covenant (before Jesus) and the New Covenant (since Jesus). Therefore, there is no opposition whatsoever between these two covenants, for the New Covenant is nothing but the renewal of the Old Covenant. Likewise, the Messianic Torah is nothing but the renewal of the Mosaic Torah.*

4.1 The Covenant Concept in General

4.1.1 Description

So far, we have looked at the notion of the one, eternal Torah and its various manifestations on earth in successive dispensations (salvation-historical epochs). We have looked at the notions of covenant and dispensation as such (chapter 2), and have briefly considered the Adamic, the Noahic, and the Abrahamic Torah (§2.3.1). We now need to pay much more attention to one of the most portentious manifestations of the eternal Torah, that is, the Mosaic Torah. First of all, we will do well to consider this Torah in its proper context, that is, God's covenant with his people.[1]

---

1. Concerning which, consult the following: Kline (1963, 1967), Hillers (1969), McCarthy (1972), Kaiser (1978), Robertson (1981), Nicholson (1986), Kaufmann (1988), Lehne (1990), Lohfink (1991), Wright

The Meaning of the Mosaic Covenant

A biblical covenant, as established by God with humans, has the following features:

(1) It is a *relationship* in the form of a *treaty* (pact, agreement, arrangement), always involving two *parties*, God, on the one hand, and a person (often together with his progeny) or a certain group of persons bound by blood bonds (a family, a nation), on the other hand.

(2) In a covenant, both parties take upon themselves *obligations* that they have to fulfill. God takes his obligations upon himself *voluntarily*, and *imposes* obligations upon Man. Man has to *fulfill* his duties; these are the conditions upon which he, within the covenant, can enjoy concourse with God. These duties are God's *commandments*, his Torah (in whatever specific form). God fulfills his duties that he has taken upon himself, that is, his *promises*, namely, fellowship with Man, along with temporal and eternal blessings for Man.

(3) It is always God who takes the *initiative* to establish a covenant, never Man. Therefore, the New Testament Greek word for "covenant" is not the common word *synthēkē*, implying an agreement between two equivalent partners, but *diathēkē*, an arrangement made by one party for the benefit of another party.

(5) In general (there are a few exceptions; see below), a covenant is made on the basis of *blood*, that is, of a *sacrifice*. The biblical covenants are *blood covenants*. Thus, the Bible speaks of the "blood of the covenant" (Exod. 24:8; Mark 14:24; Heb. 9:20; 10:29), or the "blood of my covenant" (Zech. 9:11), or the "blood of the eternal covenant" (Heb. 13:20).

Much light on this has been shed from ancient treaties

(1991), Medema (1994), Christiansen (1995), Williams (2005), Horton (2006), Enns (2008), Berkowitz (2011, chapter 1), Ouweneel (2011, and references to more recent literature). In the second volume of this trilogy, we will enter much more extensively into the subject of the covenant, but a few points need to be made already now, in connection with the Torah.

that were made by kings with their vassals, and that exhibit similarities to the Mosaic Covenant.² The usual translation of *diathēkē*, which is the common Septuagint rendering of the Hebrew *berit*, is "(last) will, testament" (cf. Gal. 3:15; Heb. 9:16-17). In line with this, Galatians 3:17 speaks of a "covenant previously ratified by God," and compares this with a "man-made covenant [i.e., last will]" that "has been ratified." Just as by means of in his will a man makes arrangements for others, so too, by means of a covenant that he establishes God makes arrangements for others. Compare Acts 7:8, "he [i.e., God] gave him [i.e., Abraham] the covenant of circumcision" (Gen. 17). Just as a human *diathēkē* is effectuated only through the death of the testator, God's *diathēkē* takes effect on the basis of the death of Jesus Messiah, who is — astonishingly enough — both testator and heir, as well as both high priest and sacrifice (Heb. 9:16-17). Even in the Tanakh, a *diathēkē* usually takes effect on the basis of the death of an animal sacrifice (cf. v. 18), and thus is a "blood covenant" or "blood testament."

The Bible speaks of at least seven or eight (or even ten or eleven) such covenants, with at least six or seven covenant partners (between [ ] I add references to the blood basis in each case):

(1) *celestial bodies* (more generally: *creation*; Jer. 33:20, 25; cf. Ps. 89:3-4, 6, 38-40) [no blood basis];

(2) *Adam* (depending on how we read Hos. 6:7³) [no blood basis, although in this connection I think of the "lamb . . . foreknown before the foundation of the world," 1 Pet. 1:19-20];

(3) *Noah* (Gen. 8-9) [8:20-22];

(4) *Abram/Abraham* (Gen. 15; extended in Gen. 17) [15:9-

---

2. Mendenhall (1955); Kline (1963, 1967).
3. "Like Adam, they have transgressed the covenant" (Hos. 6:7). NIV: "As at Adam"; NKJV: "like men" (Targum: "like the men of old"; Septuagint: "as Man," or, "as a man"). In the Talmud (Sanhedrin 38b), in the Vulgate, and by Rashi, Luther, Grotius, and Cocceius, the verse is applied to Adam; many modern expositors reject this translation.

The Meaning of the Mosaic Covenant

10];

(5) *Israel at Sinai* (Exod. 24 and 34; confirmed in Transjordan, Deut. 29) [Exod. 24:5-8];

(6) *Levi* (Mal. 2:4-5; extended to Phinehas, Num. 25:11-13) [Num. 8:5-22, the consecration of the Levites];

(7) *David* (2 Sam. 23:5; 2 Chron. 21:7; Jer. 33:21) [1 Sam. 16:1-13, the sacrificial meal at which David was anointed]; and

(8) *Israel and all nations in the last days* (Isa. 55:1-8; 59:21; 61:8; Jer. 31:31-34; 32:40; 50:5; Ezek. 16:60; 34:25; 37:26; Hos. 2:17; cf. Zech. 11:10) [the blood sacrifice of Jesus himself; Heb. 9-10].

Some of the covenants are characterized by special covenant signs, a phenomenon well-known in ancient Near Eastern covenants.[4] I will follow the numbering just given:

(2) Perhaps one might say that the *tree of life* was the sign of the Adamic Covenant (if there ever was such a covenant), although Scripture never says so.

(3) The sign of the Noahic Covenant was the *rainbow* (Gen. 9:12-13).

(4) The sign of the Abrahamic Covenant was *circumcision* (Exod. 17:11).

(5) The sign of the Mosaic Covenant was the *Shabbat* (Exod. 31:13,17; cf. Ezek. 20:12, 20).

(6) Presumably, the sign of the Levitical-Aaronic Covenant was the Aaronic *high priest* himself, whose family line will never die out (Ezek. 40:46; 43:19; 44:15; 48:11; cf. 1 Sam. 2:35; 2 Sam. 8:17; 1 Kings 2:35; 1 Chron. 18:16; 24:3, 6).

(7) Likewise, the sign of the Davidic Covenant was the Davidic *king* himself, whose line will always occupy the throne of David (cf. 2 Sam. 7:13, 16; 1 Kings 9:5; 1 Chron. 17:12, 14; 22:10; 2 Chron. 6:16; 9:8; Ps. 89:3, 28, 35; 132:11-12; Isa. 9:7; Jer.

---

4. Cf. Berkowitz (1999, 20-21).

33:17, 20–21).

(8) Likewise, we may say that the sign of the New Covenant is Christ himself as both Priest and King.

All of these covenant signs have eschatological significance; God in his judicial glory is compared to the rainbow (Ezek. 1:28; Rev. 4:3; 10:1); the tree of life (Rev. 22:2), circumcision (Isa. 52:1; Ezek. 44:9) and Shabbat (56:1–7; 66:23; Ezek. 44:24; 46:1, 3–4) are perpetuated in the Messianic Kingdom; the Aaronic priest will serve in the Temple (Ezek. 40–44); and the Davidic Messiah will reign on David's throne (Isa. 9:6–7; Jer. 30:9; 33:15–22; Ezek. 34:23–24; 37:24–25; Hos. 3:5; Amos 9:11).

There are basically only *two* covenants made specifically with Israel, ultimately involving all of humanity, because being blessed in Abraham ultimately means being blessed in Israel: "salvation is from the Jews" (John 4:22). Scripture speaks of, or implies, a "first" and a "second covenant," the good and the "better covenant," the temporal[5] and the "eternal covenant," the Old and the New Covenant, that is, the Sinaitic Covenant and the New Covenant of the last days (Heb. 8:7, 13; 9:1, 15, 18; 7:22; 8:6; 13:20; 8:8, 13; 9:15; 12:24).

The covenant characteristics mentioned above are applicable to both the Old and the New Covenants. The alleged difference between the two covenants lies especially in this point: must Man first fulfill certain duties before God fulfills his promises? Under the Old Covenant, God's blessing was *formally* dependent on keeping the Sinaitic Law: "because [or, if] you listen to these rules and keep and do them, the LORD your God will keep with you the covenant and the steadfast love that he swore to your fathers" (Deut. 7:12). If Israel would keep the Torah, God would bless the people (Exod. 19 and 24; cf. Lev. 26; Deut. 29). Under the New Covenant, how-

---

5. Although even this covenant is eternal (§4.2.1) because it is subsumed under the New Covenant.

ever, all God's holy requirements have been met *a priori* in and through Jesus Messiah and his work. No wonder that the Old Covenant has frequently been called a conditional covenant, and the New Covenant an unconditional covenant (cf. §2.3.2). Nonetheless, I am convinced that this idea is utterly wrong. In a sense, the Old Covenant is both a conditional and an unconditional covenant, and the same holds for the New Covenant (see the next §).

4.1.2 Conditional v. Unconditional

First, the *Old* Covenant, too, was rooted in God's *redemptive grace*. As Hebrew Christian Heinz David Leuner put it: "What is new about the new covenant? Like the old covenant, it is a covenant of grace, with love coming from one side only, though there is a broad hint [in Jer. 31] at the mutuality of the new knowledge and at the subjective appropriation."[6] This grace aspect is shown in the preamble of the Decalogue (see below) and in the mercy that God bestowed upon the people after they had broken the covenant right at the outset (Exod. 32-34). The highlight in the latter event is God's proclamation: "The LORD, the LORD, a God merciful and gracious, slow to anger, and abounding in steadfast love and faithfulness, keeping steadfast love for thousands, forgiving iniquity and transgression and sin, but who will by no means clear the guilty, visiting the iniquity of the fathers on the children and the children's children, to the third and the fourth generation" (Exod. 34:6-7).

Second, the *New* Covenant is not without responsible *obedience* either. The very least is that entering into the New Covenant demands obedience to God's call for repentance:

> I will take you from the nations and gather you from all the countries and bring you into your own land. I will sprinkle clean water on you, and you shall be clean. . . . And I will give you a new heart, and a new spirit I will put within you. . . . And

---

6. In Kac (1986, 177).

I will put my Spirit within you, and cause you to walk in my statutes and be careful to obey my rules. You shall dwell in the land that I gave to your fathers, and you shall be my people, and I will be your God. . . . Then you will remember your evil ways, and your deeds that were not good, and you will loathe yourselves for your iniquities and your abominations" (Ezek. 36:24-31).

Under the New Covenant everything involves Jesus Messiah. On the one hand, he bore the curse for his people's transgressions of the Torah, and on the other hand, he laid the just foundation for the covenant's positive blessings. God is free to grant his blessings to all those who stand upon the basis of Jesus' sacrifice, that is, of the "blood of the covenant" (see above). In his *person,* Jesus is the Guarantor, Mediator, and Executor of this New Covenant (Heb. 7:22; 8:6; 12:24). His *work* is that he fulfills God's requirements, and leads Man to God (cf. 1 Tim. 2:5-6; 1 Pet. 3:18), through his blood (Matt. 26:28; Mark 14:24; Luke 22:20; 1 Cor. 11:25; Heb. 9:14-15; 10:29; 12:24; 13:20), that is, his sacrificial death (Heb. 9:14-15, 26-28; 10:10, 14; see further §4.3.3 for the notion of the covenant in the Letter to the Hebrews).

At the same time, we must remember that *all* these elements were already present in the Old Covenant as foreshadowings; otherwise, no one could have been saved at all under that covenant. In other words, under the Old Covenant everything involved the *anticipation* of the Messiah, who would be both priest and sacrifice. People were saved through repentance, through trusting God's grace and the substitutionary sacrifices he had supplied *a priori.* Subjectively, the Sinaitic sacrifices were just as efficacious as Jesus' New Testament sacrifice; objectively, the former derived their significance from the latter.[7] In essence, there is no difference in the way people are saved under the Old and New Covenants, because the Sinaitic sacrifices had meaning only insofar as they point-

---

7. Cf. Freeman (1962).

ed forward to the true and unique sacrifice, that of Jesus: "... Christ Jesus, whom God put forward as a propitiation by his blood, to be received by faith. This was to show God's righteousness, because in his divine forbearance he had *passed over former* sins," that is, in Tanakhic times (Rom. 3:24-25, italics added; cf. Heb. 9:13-14, 22).

It is significant that the Decalogue begins with the words, "I am the LORD your God, who brought you out of the land of Egypt, out of the house of slavery" (Exod. 20:2; Deut. 5:6; cf. Lev. 11:45; 22:32-33). Jewish tradition even considers this to be the first of the *aseret hadevarim*, the Ten Words (in rabbinic literature, *aseret hadibrot*).[8] This "first saying," not an imperative at all but an indicative, places the Decalogue in the context of the covenant by referring primarily to the Redeemer God of the covenant.[9] The Ten Words explicitly address a redeemed nation, if not in the full spiritual meaning (cf. 1 Cor. 10:1-5), then at least in the typological sense (vv. 6-12). Even the famous words, "if a person does them [i.e., my *torot*], he shall live by them" (Lev. 18:5), are not literally speaking to the problem of how to *obtain* eternal life—in spite of that apparent *application* in Romans 10:5 and Galatians 3:12—but to the problem of *how to lead a truly blessed life as part of God's redeemed people*, not in eternity but in the promised land (Deut.

---

8. A Jewish tradition compares the Ten Words one by one with the ten words (*wayyomer Elohim*, "and God said") which God used at the creation of the world: Gen. 1:3, 6, 9, 11, 14, 20, 24, 26, 28–29 (Ginzberg [1968:104–106]).

9. A midrash (Mekhilta of Rabbi Ishmael, Bachodesh 5) explains why the Ten Words were not placed at the beginning of the Torah: a man is readily accepted by a nation as their king if he first confers benefits upon them. Thus, God first led Israel out of Egypt, divided the sea for them, rained manna upon them, opened a well for them, drove quails toward them, and made war against Amalek for them. After that, he told them, "I will be your king" (cf. Exod. 15:18; Num. 23:21; 1 Sam. 8:7), and the people readily accepted him (cf. Exod. 19:8; 24:3,7).

4:40; 5:33; 8:1; 11:9; 16:20; 25:15; 30:16; cf. v. 18). Once again, the saying in Leviticus 18:5 is preceded by the declaration "I am the LORD your God" (v. 4), and by the implicit reminder of the deliverance from Egypt (vv. 1–3). Israel is being addressed as a redeemed and holy nation (Exod. 19:4–6). The saying in Leviticus 18:5 is not about how to *get* holy, but about how to *remain* holy.

In my view, the whole problem of conditional *versus* unconditional covenants can be fruitfully examined only in the light of the two seemingly contrary truths that we find so often in Scripture, namely, on the one hand, God's *unconditional* electing, redeeming, atoning, and preserving grace, and on the other hand, Man's responsibility to obey as a *condition* for any divine blessing. There are no unconditional promises without the claim of a certain obedient response on Man's side—even if this obedience is supported by and proceeds from God's grace—just as there are no conditional promises without God's grace intervening if Man violates the conditions and truly repents of this. In this sense, as I said, the very distinction of conditional and unconditional covenants is off the mark (cf. §2.3.2). Scripture *always* speaks *both* ways, conditionally (that is, from the viewpoint of human responsibility) as well as unconditionally (that is, from the viewpoint of God's sovereign grace).[10]

Viewed from the former standpoint, Israel would be God's treasured possession, a kingdom of priests and a holy nation, *if* they would obey God's covenant, that is, his Torah (Exod. 19:5–6; cf. Deut. 4:29; 6:25; 7:12; 11:13–15, 22–25). Viewed from the latter standpoint, they were encouraged to keep his Torah *because* they were God's redeemed and holy people (Deut. 7:6–11; 14:1–2,21). Viewed from the standpoint of responsi-

---

10. Kaiser (1978:111–12) accuses A. A. Bonar of a one-sided (dispensational theological) interpretation (Torah-keeping leads to eternal life), but he himself falls into the opposite one-sidedness of covenant theology (Torah-keeping always presupposes life).

bility, Israel would lose every blessing if they would disobey God's Torah and thus break his covenant (Lev. 26:14-39; Deut. 11:26-28; 29:19-28). Viewed from the standpoint of sovereign grace, God would preserve a remnant of people for himself even after the nation's greatest failure (Deut. 30:1-10; cf. Lev. 26:40-45; also see Rom. 11:5). Under *all* the covenants, on the basis of human responsibility *all* is always lost, but on the basis of sovereign grace *all* is ultimately restored.

From the conditional viewpoint, the Torah is a means of *obtaining* God's favor, provided this is done with a humble heart, trusting not oneself but God's goodness. From the unconditional viewpoint, it is a means of *praising* God's favor, the response to *having* received God's favor. In the latter sense it presupposes redemption, and deals with the question how the redeemed can live in happy bliss. The answer is, by walking in God's Torah (cf. Lev. 26:3-13; Deut. 10:12-22; 28:1-14). In Gutbrod's words, "Observing the Law does not *create* the relation to God; it *keeps* the people in this continuing relation, e.g., 2 Chron. 33:8 ['I will no more remove the foot of Israel from the land that I appointed for your fathers, if only they will be careful to do all that I have commanded them, all the law, the statutes, and the rules given through Moses']."[11] At the same time, the question of eternal life is not excluded from the picture: one who lives with the Lord on earth, will live with him forever. At least the New Testament makes this extrapolation; Jesus said: "If you would enter life, keep the commandments" (Matt. 19:17), and, "if anyone keeps my word, he will never see death" (John 8:51).

Seen from the conditional viewpoint, no person will ever enter eternal divine bliss who has not performed "good works," that is, acts of obedience to the Torah—although we

---

11. Gutbrod (1967, 1043); he claims, however, that after the exile "the emphasis and concern rest increasingly on the second aspect, so that everything depends on observance of the Law" (cf. Appendix II below).

know very well that such good works can be performed only by a regenerate and humble heart, in dependence on the power of the Holy Spirit (cf. Eph. 2:8–10; Titus 3:4–8; Rom. 8:4; James 2:14–26). Seen from the unconditional viewpoint, no person will ever enter eternal divine bliss in any other way than through God's sovereign electing grace, which leads to rebirth and good works—although this never excludes human responsibility to repent, to trust in God's mercy, and to be eager to do good works (John 6:44; Rom. 2:4; Titus 2:14). "[W]ork out your own salvation with fear and trembling" (Phil. 2:12) because safely reaching the end is one-hundred percent your responsibility, ". . . for it is God who works in you, both to will and to work for his good purpose" (v. 13) because safely reaching the end is one-hundred percent God's preserving grace (cf. Matt. 24:22; 1 Pet. 4:18). Work, since your salvation is entirely *conditioned* by your faithfulness; and know at the same time that your salvation depends entirely on God's *unconditional* faithfulness. And beware of all those who try to play these two sides off against each other.

4.1.3 The New Covenant Today

Jeremiah 31 and Hebrews 8 show that the New Covenant is formally established with the twelve tribes of Israel; only secondarily, through them, this covenant is of significance for the nations as well. Jeremiah 31 and other Tanakhic Scriptures show that the establishment of this covenant is to occur *after* the second coming of Jesus, that is, at the outset of the Messianic kingdom (*'olam habba*, the "age to come").[12] Nonetheless, the New Covenant has great importance already today. It is true that formally the New Covenant has not yet been established, or at least not formally effectuated. But Jewish and Gentile Jesus-believers have, as it were, already been brought "under the roof" of the New Covenant. They have

---

12. The "age to come," following upon "this age," does not commence at the first but at the second coming of Messiah: Matt. 12:32; 13:40; Mark 10:30; Luke 20:34–35; Eph. 1:21.

been brought under the Mediator of the New Covenant, who is their life, and whose blood, on which the New Covenant is based, has cleansed them (Heb. 8:6; 12:24; Luke 22:20; 1 Cor. 11:25).

The present realization of the New Covenant is arguably God's program for the Kingdom of God. In the primary Scripture concerning the New Covenant, Jeremiah 30 and 31, the King takes the central position: "David their king, whom I will raise up for them" (30:9); the one being referred to is the great Son of David. "Their prince shall be one of themselves; their ruler shall come out from their midst. . . . And you shall be my people, and I will be your God" (vv. 21–22). When the King himself instituted the Last Supper for his disciples, he did so in an eschatological context by speaking of both the Kingdom of God and the New Covenant (Luke 22:18, 20). In this context, Jesus-believers celebrate the Lord's Supper. They are not only looking back at the cross by eating and drinking "in remembrance of him" and "proclaiming the Lord's death," but also looking forward to the appearing of the King in glory, in that Jesus-believers eat and drink "until he comes" (1 Cor. 11:24–26), that is, until the Kingdom of God and the New Covenant will be completely consummated.

As I said before, there is much more continuity between the Old and the New Covenants than many dispensational theologians have often realized. Likewise, there is continuity between the pre-Mosaic covenants: the Noahic promises are still in force under the Abrahamic covenant, the Abrahamic promises are still in force under the Mosaic covenant, the Mosaic promises will still be in force under the New Covenant. All of these covenants are based upon God's gracious and unconditional promises. Thus, in Galatians 3:15–4:7 the terms "covenant" and "promises" are used indifferently: the covenant that God made with Abraham (Gen. 15; 17) consisted of unilateral and unconditional ("irrevocable," Rom. 11:29) promises that God granted him. These promises are for those believers who, in the present dispensation, are called "children," "seed," and "heirs" of Abraham (Gal. 3:7, 29). This includes the Gentile Jesus-believers, who are fully included in the Abrahamic covenant (vv. 8, 14).

At the same time, I repeat, none of these covenants was merely unconditional. *Every* covenant between God and Man was based on unconditional grace, but no covenant grace was ever bestowed without being accompanied with the prescription of a way of obedience, in order to live under that grace. This was true even for God's (alleged) covenant with prelapsarian Adam, because all the blessings that the latter had received were not earned, but had been bestowed upon him by pure divine grace (grace is much more than what sinners need; *every* gift of God is pure grace). No Torah of God comes without some measure of grace, nor does any covenant grace come without some Torah. Every manifestation of the one eternal Torah was embedded within some covenant of grace; every covenant was embedded within some Torah, that was always delightful to those who had genuinely learned to live by divine grace. As I said before, Torah and grace are never really contrasted or opposed, not even in Romans 6:14, where grace is being contrasted not with the Torah as such, but with legalism (see chapter 3 and §4.3.2).

This matter has been well summarized by the Messianic Jew, Ludwig R. Dewitz: "In Christ, the two dimensions of service (to God and to Man) become accentuated on the basis of His incarnation, crucifixion, and resurrection. The New Covenant does not prescribe precise commandments in a legalistic sense, but does demand service involving sacrifice. It is clear from the way in which the prophets spoke and in the way Christ observed the law that the law was not meant to become a burden in a legalistic sense, but that it was to be a way of life for God's children. The law was intended to bring out all that is best in Man for giving value to life. Law is always to be seen within the compass of grace, never to be isolated from it as an independent factor, just as grace must be seen as the enabling power to execute the will of God within the compass of the commandment of love."[13]

4.2 The Old Covenant According to the Tanakh
4.2.1 Its Eternal Character

In order to understand the relationship between the Messianic Torah in the present, and the Mosaic Torah in the previous dispensation, we have to investigate the relationship between the Messianic (New) and the Mosaic (Old) Covenants. What exactly was the character of the "Old Covenant" (2 Cor. 3:14), the covenant that God made with Israel at Sinai through Moses and of which the Torah was an essential aspect? The Letter to the Hebrews tells us that the Old Covenant was not "faultless" (Heb. 8:7), and that it was "ready to vanish away" (v. 13). Does that not have consequences for the position of the Mosaic Torah? In order to answer these questions, let us first examine what the Tanakh has to say about the character of the Old Covenant (§4.2), and then what the New Testament adds to this (§4.3).

It cannot be denied that the Mosaic Torah is intimately interwoven with the Old Covenant. Torah and covenant are mentioned in one breath: "And the LORD said to Moses, 'Write these words, for in accordance with these words I have made a covenant with you and with Israel.' So he was there with the LORD forty days and forty nights. He neither ate bread nor drank water. And he wrote on the tablets the words of the covenant, the Ten Commandments" (Exod. 34:27-28; cf. vv. 10-11; Deut. 29:1, 9, 19; 2 Kings 23:3; 2 Chron. 34:30-31). The Ten Words, which are the heart of the Torah, are the "words of the covenant," just as the two stone tablets are the "tablets of the covenant" (Deut. 4:13; 9:9, 11, 15; Heb. 9:4). The ark in which the two stone tablets were put is the "ark of the covenant" (Num. 10:33; 14:44; Deut. 10:8; 31:9, 25-26). Failing to keep the commands is to violate the covenant (Lev. 26:15; Deut. 31:16, 20).

---

13. See the article included in Kac (1986, 173).

As I said, there are two parties in all covenants, each having certain obligations to fulfill. God undertakes to bless the people with every conceivable blessing (Deut. 7:11–20; 11:26–27; 15:4–5; 28:1–14; 30:15–16); Israel undertakes to keep the Torah (Exod. 19:8; 24:3, 7). The Sinaitic covenant is compared to a marriage covenant (Ezek. 16:8; cf. Isa. 54:5–8; 62:5; Jer. 2:2; Hos. 2:18–19; cf. Mal. 2:14, lit. "the wife of your [marriage] covenant"). Therefore, an important way to view the Torah, the bond between God and his people, is to understand it within the framework of the love between God and his people. Without that love, which is possible only in regenerated hearts through the power of the Holy Spirit, the Torah is nothing but an irksome yoke (cf. Acts 15:10), just like marriage is for two married people who do not love each other. "Because Torah-lessness [*anomia*] will be increased, the love of many will grow cold" (Matt. 24:12; see §2.3.3). The more Torah, the more love; the less Torah, the less love.

Moses has summarized this as follows:

> The Lord your God has chosen you to be a people for his treasured possession, out of all the peoples who are on the face of the earth. It was not because you were more in number than any other people that the Lord set his *love* on you and chose you, for you were the fewest of all peoples, but it is because the Lord *loves* you and is keeping the oath that he swore to your fathers, that the Lord has brought you out with a mighty hand and redeemed you from the house of slavery, from the hand of Pharaoh king of Egypt. Know therefore that the Lord your God is God, the faithful God who keeps *covenant* and *steadfast love* [*hesed*] with those who *love* him and keep his commandments. . . . You shall therefore be careful to do the commandment and the statutes and the rules that I command you today. And because you listen to these rules and keep and do them, the Lord your God will keep with you the *covenant* and the *steadfast love* [*hesed*] that he swore to your fathers (Deut. 7:6–12, italics added).

Grant's eisegesis[14] ("The people eagerly, and in ignorant self-confidence, accept the covenant. They have had plentiful proof of their own evil, and of their need of grace, and had been shown grace; yet, in spite of this, do not hesitate to put themselves under law") and that of Scofield[15] ("The Dispensation of Promise ended when Israel rashly accepted the law," Exod. 19:8) is flatly contradicted by God's own joy about Israel's words: "'. . . we will hear and do it.' And the LORD heard your words, when you spoke to me. And the LORD said to me, 'I have heard the words of this people, which they have spoken to you. They are right in all that they have spoken. Oh that they had such a heart as this always, to fear me and to keep all my commandments, that it might go well with them and with their descendants forever!'" (Deut. 5:27–29). It is like a bridegroom who rejoices in the marriage vows of his bride. Of course, Israel was hardly aware of the bearing of its promise ("All that the LORD has spoken we will do") — but the same is true of brides and bridegrooms.

Several important elements of a Jewish wedding were present at the Torah-giving at Sinai.[16] One was the Torah, which functioned as the *ketubah*, that is, the written prenuptial agreement (see §3.1.2). Another element was the *huppah*, a word that originally meant the chamber where the marriage was consummated (Ps. 19:5; Joel 2:16), later the canopy under which bride and bridegroom were wed. At Sinai, this *huppah* was nothing less than the *Shekinah*, the cloud of God's glory, which was over the mountain and the people (Exod. 19:9, 16; 20:21; 24:15–18). In addition, the washed garments of the people at Sinai (19:10, 14) remind us of the bride's wedding dress. Most important of all is the love of bridegroom and bride for each other, representing the covenant love between

---

14.. Grant (1890, 202–203).
15. Scofield (1909, 20).
16. See Wilson (1989, 203–208) and Berkowitz (2011, 6–9) on the similarities between the Sinaitic covenant and Jewish marriages.

God and his people, so magnificently described in the Song of Solomon.

A biblical term that splendidly expresses this mutual relationship of covenant love is the Hebrew word *hasid*, which we know so well from the Jewish movement of the Has(s)idim. The word is derived from *hesed*, which, if used for Man, means "piety, godliness" but if used for God, "benevolence, favor" (see §7.3). The person with *hasid* is both "pious" (in the active sense) and the "object of God's favor" (in the passive sense). In Deuteronomy 7:9, "covenant" and *hesed* ("mercy"; ESV: "steadfast love") are mentioned in one breath. The terms *hesed* and *hasid* always involve the special covenant relationship between God and his people, in that God's *hesed* and Man's *hesed* both refer to the *faithfulness* to that covenant. To put it in more modern terms, *hesed* is the *solidarity* of two parties standing in a relationship with each other, or their *loyalty* to one another. God is *hasid* in that he bestows upon Man all the favors that are implied in his covenant promises. Man is *hasid* in that he, in response to this, faithfully keeps God's Torah. God is loyal to his people by fulfilling his promises, his people are loyal to him by keeping the Torah.

This *hesed* is paralleled by the loyalty within human covenantal relationships. Thus, there is *hesed* within marriage ("kindness" in Gen. 20:13, which is here a loyal service of love). No wonder God's covenant is compared to a marriage, in which God's people like a bride show *hesed* to God ("devotion" in Jer. 2:2). Two friends who have made a covenant between them also know this *hesed* ("kindly" in 1 Sam. 20:8, which is here loyalty). God's covenant is like the covenant between a king and his vassals; thus the subject shows *hesed* to his king ("loyalty," 1 Sam. 20:8 NKJV).

God did not promise his loving loyalty to the people *after* they had obeyed him. On the contrary, he loved them first, *then* asked for their love in return, which they could show by obeying his Torah (Deut. 7:6–14). The Old Covenant was founded upon God's unconditional love, loyalty, and faithfulness. The name of the synagogue benediction referring to the Torah-giving, *Ahavah*, means "love," expressing the fullness of God's love granted to Israel in the Torah. This love is to be reproduced toward one's neighbors: strangers, widows, and orphans, the deaf and the blind, the poor (Exod. 22:21-22, 25; 23:6, 9, 11; Lev. 19:10, 14-15, 33; 23:22; Deut. 10:18-19; 14:29; 15:7-11; 16:11, 14; 24:14, 17-21; 26:12-13; 27:18-19). The non-Messianic Jew, Pinchas Lapide, New Testament scholar by profession, says about even the Talmud, "Basically, the whole Talmud is nothing but one comment on loving one's neighbor, with no other purpose than the full realization of this love to one's fellow man."[17]

Was this covenant with Israel intended only for a certain time? No, for the Lord says, *"I will never break my covenant with you"* (Judg. 2:1). The Sinaitic covenant is an *"everlasting* covenant" (1 Chron. 16:17; Ps. 105:8, 10; cf. Exod. 31:16; Lev. 24:8; Isa. 24:5), just as the Abrahamic covenant (Gen. 17:7, 13, 19) and the Davidic covenant (2 Sam. 23:5). The Lord "remembers his covenant forever," "he has commanded his covenant forever" (Ps. 111:5, 9). This eternal covenant is broken (violated) every time the people sins (Isa. 24:5 NKJV) — but it is never abrogated. At best, it is renewed, and where this happens the renewed covenant is called again an "everlasting covenant" (Isa. 55:3; 61:8; Jer. 32:40; 50:5; Ezek. 37:26). So the New Covenant (Jer. 31:31-32), too, is not the *replacement* but the *renewal* of the Old Covenant. In this New Covenant, the Torah will again take the central position — and in essence that Torah is not a different Torah (v. 33). Therefore the establishment of the New Covenant, too, will have the character of a Torah-giving, as we read literally in Hebrews 8:6b (cf. the same word in 7:11). And because in essence the Millennial Torah will be the same as the Mosaic Torah, the establishment of the New Covenant will essentially be the renewal of the Torah-giving on Sinai.

---

17. Lapide (2004), chapter 4.

"I will remember my covenant with you in the days of your youth, and I will establish for you an everlasting covenant" (Ezek. 16:60). The word "establish" may suggest replacement, but the word "remember" points to renewal.

4.2.2 Various Participants

Already in the Tanakh it is obvious that there are two kinds of human participants in the covenant. There are those who dearly love the Lord, and therefore also his Torah, even if they occasionally transgress the Torah. But there are also those who formally are participants because they belong to Israel but who are foreign to the spirit of the covenant. Because of this dual aspect, from the outset the Torah, too, had a dual aspect. I spoke before of its *double function* (§1.3), but now we have to enter more deeply into this matter.

The one function was that the Torah showed to those who loved God the way to remain in the blessed sphere of the covenant. The other function was that it showed to those who did not love God that they belonged to the covenant only outwardly, not inwardly. The Torah is the joy of the true people of God, but it is a curse for the wicked, for by violating the Torah they break the covenant and in this way jeopardize all the blessings of the covenant (cf. Lev. 26; Deut. 11:26-28; 27:11-28:68). That is not the Torah's fault: "what great nation is there, that has statutes and rules so righteous as all this Torah that I set before you today?" (Deut. 4:8). The words of the Torah are "your very life" (32:47); "the Torah is holy, and the commandment is holy and righteous and good" (Rom. 7:12). No, it is the wicked person's own fault, who apparently prefers death over life:

> I call heaven and earth to witness against you today, that *I have set before you life and death*, blessing and curse. Therefore *choose life*, that you and your offspring may live, loving the LORD your God, obeying his voice and holding fast to him, for *he is your life* and length of days, that you may dwell in the land that the LORD swore to your fathers, to Abraham, to Isaac, and to Jacob,

to give them (30:19–20, italics added).

Just before this passage, Moses told the people that one day curses might come upon them "because you did not obey the voice of the LORD your God, to keep his commands and his statutes. . . . Because you did not serve the LORD your God with joyfulness and gladness of heart. . ." (28:45, 47). This is a negative statement, but in the reversed form it is one of the loveliest descriptions of what Torah-keeping is. It is *"serving the LORD your God with joyfulness and gladness of heart."* True Torah-keeping is not just obedience, even less is it some blind submission—it is serving with a rejoicing heart. That is true life: serving in love. For the true believer the Torah is not a heavy yoke but a light and joyful burden—the "yoke of iron" is the very thing you get on your neck by *giving up* true Torah-keeping (v. 48). Jesus said to his followers: "Take my yoke upon you, and learn from me, for I am gentle and lowly in heart, and you will find rest for your souls. For my yoke is easy, and my burden is light" (Matt. 11:30).

These two ways of Torah-keeping relate to one another as the tree of life is related to the tree of the knowledge of good and evil (Gen. 2:9, 16–17). As Andrew Jukes wrote: "The [latter] tree itself was good, and only evil through Man's weakness; like the law, (and indeed law is but knowledge,) which is 'holy, just, and good,' and yet 'works condemnation.' [Rom. 7:7–13]. But good as it is, let us take heed how we use it. Wisdom [Hokmah/Torah] is the tree of life;—'she is a tree of life to them that lay hold upon her;' [Prov. 3:18] and he that eats of her shall live by her; [John 6:57] but knowledge, even of divine things [such as the Torah], may but reveal our nakedness."[18] Irenaeus made an interesting use of this same imagery against the Gnostics by accusing them of preferring the tree of knowledge (Gr. *gnōsis*) to the tree of life; eating of the former leads to being driven from the "paradise of life."[19]

---

18. Jukes (1875, 54–55).
19. Adversus Haereses V.20.2.

Likewise, the Pharisaic approach to the Torah easily led to a "knowledge" that "puffs up," whereas the way of true life and love "builds up" (cf. 1 Cor. 8:1).

To make things even more complicated, I note that we may distinguish three additional groups within Israel with regard to the Torah:

(1) The *lovers* of the LORD, who are also lovers of the Torah; that is the true Israel. To them he said, I am the LORD "showing steadfast love [*hesed*] to thousands of those who love me and keep my commandments" (Exod. 20:6; Deut. 5:10). "Know therefore that the LORD your God is God, the faithful God who keeps covenant and steadfast love [*hesed*] with those who love him and keep his commandments, to a thousand generations" (Deut. 7:9). "And now, Israel, what does the LORD your God require of you, but to fear the LORD your God, to walk in all his ways, to love him, to serve the LORD your God with all your heart and with all your soul, and to keep the commandments and statutes of the Lord, which I am commanding you today for your good?" (10:12-13). The faithful answer with confessing their love and delight with respect to the Torah (Ps. 119:14, 16, 24, 35, 47, 70, 77, 92, 97, 143, 159, 174).

(2) The *haters* of the LORD (cf. Exod. 20:5; Deut. 5:9), who are also haters of the Torah: "He [i.e., God] will not be slack with one who hates him. He will repay him to his face. You shall therefore be careful to do the commandment and the statutes and the rules that I command you today" (Deut. 7:10-11; cf. 32:40-41). These are those who overtly break the LORD's Torah in a spirit of rebellion, "with a high hand" (Num. 15:30), that is, rebelliously, defiantly, presumptuously.

However, there is also a third group:

(3) The *hypocrites*, who pretend to keep the Torah, but do not really mean it, who keep the Torah only outwardly, who ignore the spirit of the Torah in an attitude of legalism, ritualism, and ethnocentric boasting. We do not yet clearly find them in the Pentateuch, but in the prophetic books they are

clearly identified: "[T]his people draw near with their mouth and honor me with their lips, while their hearts are far from me" (Isa. 29:13; cf. Matt. 15:8). Sometimes, the prophets speak of hypocrites in a way that might suggest that the prophets do not esteem the sacrificial ministry very highly. But what they are obviously opposing is the spirit of hypocrisy. What the prophets emphasize, without ever depreciating the outward keeping of the Torah, is that the LORD seeks the true love of the heart: "For I desire steadfast love and not sacrifice, the knowledge of God rather than burnt offerings. But like Adam they transgressed the covenant; there they dealt faithlessly with me" (Hos. 6:6–7). "I have written for him [i.e., Ephraim] the great things of My Torah, [but] they were considered a strange thing. [For] the sacrifices of My offerings they sacrifice flesh and eat [it], [but] the Lord does not accept them" (8:12–13 NKJV). "I hate, I despise your feasts, and I take no delight in your solemn assemblies. Even though you offer me your burnt offerings and grain offerings, I will not accept them; and the peace offerings of your fattened animals, I will not look upon them. Take away from me the noise of your songs; to the melody of your harps I will not listen. But let justice roll down like waters, and righteousness like an ever-flowing stream" (Amos 5:21–24; cf. Jer. 14:11–12).[20]

4.2.3 Again: the Torah's Two Functions

We can now summarize the *double function* of the Torah as follows. On the one hand, the Torah brings to light the new life in the reborn through the joy and zeal with which they observe it (even though they, too, fail from time to time). On the other hand, the Torah brings to light the corrupt nature of the wicked through the abhorrence with which they treat God's commands ("haters"), or the falsehood with which

---

20. Cf. also Shabbat 30a, where God is said to have told David, "better is to Me the one day that thou sittest and engagest in learning [the Torah] than the thousand burnt-offerings which thy son Solomon is destined to sacrifice before Me on the altar."

they outwardly keep the Torah while their hearts are far from God ("hypocrites"). The former serve God out of true love by keeping his Torah from the inside; they bear the Torah in their hearts (cf. Ps. 37:30-31; 40:8; Rom. 2:15). The latter turn the Torah into a legalistic or ethnocentric system of false Torah-keeping in order to make up to God without a change of heart: "Well did Isaiah prophesy of you hypocrites, as it is written, 'This people honors me with their lips, but their heart is far from me'" (Mark 7:6; cf. Isa. 29:13).

In passing, I note that rabbinic tradition is quite aware of this double function of the Torah as bringing either life to the penitent or death to the wicked (cf. Rom. 7:10; 8:2; 2 Cor. 3:6-8). Rabbi Y'hoshua ben-L'vi said, "If a person is meritorious, [the Torah] becomes for him a medicine that gives life; but if not, it becomes a deadly poison."[21] Another Talmudic Rabbi, named Raba, said something similar.[22] Midrash Tanchuma said: "The Voice of the Lord went forth from Sinai in two ways: it killed the heathen, who would not accept it; but it gave life to Israel, who accepted the Torah."[23] Rabbi Banna'ah said: "Whosoever occupies himself with the Torah for its own sake his learning becomes an elixir of life to him. . . . But, whosoever occupies himself with the Torah not for its own sake, it becomes to him a deadly poison."[24] And elsewhere we read, "[T]he Torah only provided for Man's evil human passions."[25]

Obviously, it would be absolutely incorrect to limit the Torah's function under the Old Covenant to the second, negative function, and thus to restrict the significance of the Old Covenant as being temporary. In doing so, we overlook the fact that the Old Covenant comprised not only the Torah but

---

21. Yoma 72b; cf. the "aroma of Christ": "to one a fragrance from death to death, to the other a fragrance from life to life" (2 Cor. 2:15–16).
22. Shabbat 88b.
23. Exod. Rabbah 5,9.
24. Ta'anit 7a.
25. Qiddushin 21b.

also the sacrificial ministry. Because of the "pleasing aroma" of the daily burnt offering, the LORD dwelt in the midst of his people (Exod. 29:39–46), and on the basis of the reality to which the annual sin offering on *Yom Kippur* pointed, the people's sins were taken away from before the LORD (Lev. 16:16, 21–22). To be sure, the people subjectively shared in this only through true humbling and turning to the LORD (Lev. 16:29, 31; 23:29–32; Num. 29:7; Ps. 51; Isa. 57:15). And surely, the sacrifices had value before God only insofar as they anticipated Jesus' work of atonement; therefore, the renewal or fulfillment of the covenant was required. But this does not imply that the Old Covenant forms a contrast with the New Covenant, even as the Torah does not form a contrast with grace (or with the gospel).

The well-known—particularly Lutheran—dualism of Law and Gospel is basically a false one. The Old Covenant was an integral and self-contained polity of *both* Torah and grace. First, "through the Torah comes knowledge of sin" (Rom. 3:20; see §4.3.1). Second, the sacrificial ministry placed and kept the sinner on the gracious foundation of atonement. And third, that same Torah was written in the heart of the believing Israelite (Ps. 37:30–31; cf. 40:8; Jer. 31:33). The wicked Israelite came under the Torah's yoke of slavery (cf. Gal. 5:1), the believing Israelite lived out of free grace, communicated through the sacrifice, and out of the joy of the Torah. In this sense there is no question of the Old Covenant ever being abrogated; it is only brought to its ultimate consummation in the New Covenant, namely, in Jesus and his atoning sacrifice (see especially §4.3.3).

To be more complete, I would add that the Torah's double function just mentioned concerns only two of several more functions. Fruchtenbaum enumerates nine functions of the Mosaic Torah, of which I will describe six in a rather free way.[26]

---

26. Fruchtenbaum (1992, 591–93). I take his sixth, seventh, and eighth

1. As a self-revelation of God, the Torah reveals God's being, particularly God's holiness. Thus, the essence of the Torah's commands, the *kelal gadol betorah* ("greatest principle" of the Torah), implies becoming holy as the God of the covenant is holy: "Be holy, for I am holy." In several variants, these words are found in Leviticus (11:44-45; 19:2; 20:7, 26; 21:8). In the same context another important expression occurs: "I, the LORD, who sanctify you [i.e., make you holy], am holy" (Lev. 21:8), or more briefly, "I am the LORD who make you/him/them holy" (20:8; 21:15, 23; 22:9, 16, 32; cf. 20:24, 26). To many commandments this brief word is added, "I am the LORD" (many times in Lev. 11 and 18-26). Apparently the LORD intends to say: I am the LORD, and I am holy; and because you are my people I expect you to be holy, too, by obeying my commandments.

2. The Torah was the basic rule for the true people of God; notice what is said above about the lovers of the Torah, those who delight in the Torah. It brings to light the new life in the regenerated through the joy and the eagerness with which they observe the Torah, even though they, too, fail from time to time.

3. The Torah "was to provide for Israel occasions for individual and corporate worship," particularly the Shabbat and the seven appointed times described in Leviticus 23.

4. The Torah was to keep the Jews a distinct people (Exod. 19:5-8; Lev. 11:44-45; Deut. 7:6; 14:1-2). Many of the commandments, such as food laws (Lev. 11), clothing laws (Lev. 19:19; Deut. 22:5,11), sacrificial ministry (Lev. 1-7; Num. 28-29), sexual life (Lev. 12; 18), intended to preserve Israel as a

---

functions together, and I discard the ninth function ("which was to drive one to faith") because I think it is based on an erroneous exegesis of Gal. 3:24–25 in particular (see Fung 1988, 169 and references; Ouweneel 1997, 217–19). Dunn (1998, §§6.3, 6.4, and 6.6) distinguishes three functions of the Torah: nrs. 6, 4/5, and 2 (see our list in the text above).

holy (i.e., separate) nation, distinct from all other nations.

5. In practice, because of Man's evil nature, the polity of the Torah functioned as the "dividing wall of hostility" between Jews and Gentiles (Eph. 2:14).[27] For instance, being circumcised or uncircumcised mattered a great deal and, because of the flesh, the circumcised might boast in their circumcision, and the uncircumcised might despise the circumcised. Under the Old Covenant, that "dividing wall" could be overcome only by the uncircumcised becoming circumcised, and thereby becoming proselytes of Israel.

6. According to its negative function, the Mosaic Torah brings to light the corrupt nature of the wicked through the abhorrence with which they treat God's Torah (as haters), or the falsehood with which they outwardly keep the Torah while their hearts are far from God (as hypocrites) (see more extensively above).

4.3 The Old Covenant According to the New Testament

4.3.1 Paul's Letters

In my opinion, the New Testament's view of the Old Covenant is in full agreement with the Tanakhic view as just described. It is good to emphasize this because many interpreters believe that the New Testament, Paul in particular, speaks mainly or only of the Torah's second function, that is, to unmask and condemn the wicked. Let us see in what way the New Testament handles the concept of *nomos*, usually translated as "law." As we saw in §1.2.2, in the New Testament *nomos* usually refers to the Mosaic Torah. It speaks of this Torah in the double way just described, but also in some other ways (compare one by one the six functions just mentioned in §4.2.3):

1. The New Testament acknowledges the Torah's first

---

27. The expression "dividing wall" reminds us of the *m'chitzah* in the Orthodox synagogue separating men and women, and even more of the wall around the Temple that kept the Gentiles out.

function because Peter quotes God's words about holiness (1 Pet. 1:16) with their full implications: "As obedient children, do not be conformed to the passions of your former ignorance, but as he who called you is holy, you also be holy in all your conduct, since it is written, 'You shall be holy, for I am holy'" (vv. 14-16). In a similar way, Paul points out that (1) God's Spirit is holy (e.g., Rom. 1:4), (2) his Torah is holy (7:12), (3) and our sanctification ("getting holy") is God's will, who gave us his own *Holy Spirit* for this purpose (1 Thess. 4:3-8; cf. Rom. 15:16). He also writes, "[B]e imitators of God, as beloved children" (Eph. 5:1), that is, be as God is. As Jesus said, "You therefore must be perfect, as your heavenly Father is perfect" (Matt. 5:48).

2. Paul refers to the Torah as the basic rule for the true people of God: the Torah as the great Love Command, the Messianic Torah (Rom. 8:4; 13:10; Gal. 5:14; 6:2). As said before, the "*nomos* of faith" (Rom. 3:27) may be the principle of faith, but it could also be the Torah as known by faith. Similarly, the "*nomos* of righteousness" (Rom. 9:31) may be the principle of (one's own alleged) righteousness, but it could also be the Torah as offering a way of attaining, or maintaining, righteousness. For Jesus-believers this means not leaning on their own strength but trusting God in Jesus — weak in ourselves, strong in him (2 Cor. 12:10) — otherwise one does not attain that *nomos*, says the verse.[28]

In this sense, the Torah has not been abrogated or done away with for Paul. In the last verse quoted we saw that he is certainly interested in the question as to how one comes "to the Torah," or to the righteousness that the Torah is concerned about. He maintains the principle, "it is . . . the doers of the Torah who will be justified" (Rom. 2:13). Paul knew himself to be "under the Messiah's Torah" (1 Cor. 9:21). In Greek this

---

28. For the various Pauline passages that speak of the Torah of Love, see Söding (1995, 187-267, where he deals particularly with Galatians and Romans).

is expressed as being *ennomos Christou*, literally, "in-lawed of Messiah," being in a legal bond with Messiah. The whole phrase may be rendered as follows: Paul lived "within [the polity of] the Messianic Torah." Paul called the Mosaic Torah and its commandments "holy, righteous, and good" (Rom. 7:12, 14, 16). Therefore, as such nothing can be wrong with the "righteousness which is of the Torah" (Rom. 10:5 NKJV; cf. Gal. 2:21), for the righteousness of Jesus-believers, too, is none other than the righteousness that satisfies the requirements of the Messianic Torah. What is problematic about the "righteousness which is of the Torah" is that some try to attain it through their own strength, apart from the work of Jesus and the power of the Holy Spirit (traditional view), or that some find a ground for ethnocentric boasting in the Torah maintaining that those wishing to receive the covenantal blessings have to join Israel through circumcision (newer view).[29] In that sense, and *in that sense alone*, the (pretended) "righteousness which is of the Torah" is opposed to the (true) "righteousness of faith" (Rom. 10:6; cf. Gal. 3:11–12). The true righteousness of *faith* is the very righteousness that truly meets the standards of the Messianic *Torah*.

We encounter the same positive meaning of the Torah with James, who speaks of the "royal Torah" and the "Torah of liberty" (1:25; 2:8, 12).[30] As I indicated earlier, the former expression can be rendered as the "Torah of the Kingdom," namely, the Kingdom of God in Jesus (2:5; cf. §3.2.1). James also interprets this Torah as the Love Command: "If you real-

---

29. See particularly Dunn (1998, 128–61, 354–71, 631–58, and references to earlier literature). Dunn's interpretation of expressions like "under the law," "works of the law," "released from the law" in the light of his view of Israel's ethnocentric boasting (my expression) is quite enlightening and fruitful, but seems to me to be as one-sided as the traditional view (see Appendix II).
30. Exod. 32:16 tells us: "the writing of God [was] engraved [*charut*] . . .," but the Midrash Rabbah on this verse tells us that we should read *cherut*, "freedom": the Torah of God is freedom.

ly fulfill the royal Torah according to the Scripture, 'You shall love your neighbor as yourself," [Lev. 19:18] you are doing well.... So speak and so act as those who are to be judged under the Torah of liberty" (2:8, 12). "But the one who looks into the perfect Torah, the Torah of liberty, and perseveres, being no hearer who forgets but a doer who acts, he will be blessed in his doing" (1:25). In itself, the Torah is always necessarily perfect, for it has been given by God. And those who live by God's grace, whether under the Old or under the New Covenants, always know it as a "Torah of liberty." This is a Torah that is in force for the man who has been truly set free by faith in Messiah (cf. Gal. 5:1).

3. The Messianic Torah supplies us with "holy seasons," too. I am not referring to Sunday observance, because in the New Testament there is no such thing as the institution of a holy day, no setting apart of the first day of the week as a mandatory day of rest (see Appendix III). A better example of a "holy season" is the observance of the Lord's Supper (the Eucharist), at whatever moment—even, if so desired, on a daily basis (cf. Acts 2:46). There is nothing wrong with viewing Jesus' exhortation, "Do this in remembrance of me," as a Messianic command, just as, for instance, thanking God (Gr. *eucharisteite*) is a command (Luke 22:19; 1 Cor. 11:24-25; 1 Thess. 5:18). These are a few of the many commands of his Torah, and a few of the sweetest ones at that.

4. In the New Testament, too, the people of God are a "chosen race, a royal priesthood, a holy nation, a people for his own possession" (1 Pet. 2:9; cf. Exod. 19:5-6). As such, being under the Messianic Torah, they must be a nation devoted to God and distinct from all other people when it comes to their eating habits (1 Cor. 8:37; 10:31), clothing laws (1 Tim. 2:9; 1 Pet. 3:3), sacrificial service (Rom. 12:1; Heb. 13:15-16; 1 Pet. 2:5), sexual life (1 Thess. 4:3-8; Heb. 13:4), etc.

5. Today, the "dividing wall" has been destroyed (Eph. 2:14), not by abolishing the Torah as such but by removing

the hostility it had occasioned. Circumcision of the flesh is of no avail anymore if a man wants to know the God of the Bible better (Rom. 3:30; 1 Cor. 7:19; Gal. 5:6; 6:15). At the same time, the Messianic Torah creates a new "dividing wall," so to speak, namely, between the circumcised of heart and the uncircumcised of heart, be they Jews or Gentiles (cf. Rom. 2:28-29; 4:12; Phil. 3:3; Col. 2:11; 3:11).

6. Paul, too, extensively describes the Torah's negative function of exposing wickedness: "through the Torah comes knowledge of sin" (Rom. 3:20). "The Torah came in to increase the trespass" (5:20). "For while we were living in the flesh [the sinful nature; Heb. *yetzer ra*], our sinful passions, aroused by the Torah, were at work in our members to bear fruit for death.... What then shall we say? That the Torah is sin? By no means! Yet if it had not been for the Torah, I would not have known sin. For I would not have known what it is to covet if the Torah had not said, 'You shall not covet.' [Exod. 20:17] But sin, seizing an opportunity through the commandment, produced in me all kinds of covetousness. For apart from the Torah, sin lies dead" (7:5, 7-8). "The power of sin is the Torah" (1 Cor. 15:56). "Why then the Torah? It was added [to the Abrahamic promise] because of transgressions, until the offspring [i.e., Jesus Messiah] should come to whom the promise had been made" (Gal. 3:19). "[W]e know that the Torah is good, if one uses it lawfully [i.e., according to the Torah's own intention], understanding this, that the Torah is not laid down for the just but for the lawless [i.e., those not heeding the Torah] and disobedient, for the ungodly and sinners," etc. (1 Tim. 1:8-9), namely, to unmask them.

For the wicked, the Torah was "weakened by the flesh" (Rom. 8:3), that is, it was weak because of Man's sinful nature. It can place a mirror before the just and the wicked, but by itself it cannot bring salvation to anyone. On the contrary, the Torah is to the wicked a "ministry of death" and "of condemnation" (2 Cor. 3:7-8),[31] a polity that brings wrath (Rom. 4:15), that brings curse because they cannot keep the Torah (Gal. 3:10), a polity functioning as a "record of debt that stood against us with its legal demands" (Col. 2:14). He who is thus condemned by the Torah is condemned even in his ultimate Jewishness, that is, even his circumcision becomes worthless through his actual despising of the Torah (Rom. 2:25; cf. Gal. 5:3).

Instead of recognizing this and humbling themselves under the Torah, the wicked in Israel found in the Torah an opportunity for (individual and ethnocentric) arrogance and self-exaltation. In this way, as I said earlier, the Torah also formed a polity of hostility in separating Jews and Gentiles (Eph. 2:15). Because of this lack of self-knowledge and this self-conceit, hypocrites in Israel believed that through "works of the Torah," accomplished in their own carnal strength, they could be justified and saved. As said earlier, in this context "works of the Torah" involves keeping the commandments in one's own power and thus earning salvation (traditional view), and/or, boasting in one's belonging to God's chosen people and urging others to join them as a condition for sharing the blessings (newer view) (Rom. 3:20, 27-28; 4:2, 6; 9:11, 32; 11:6; Gal. 2:16, 19, 21; 3:2, 4, 10-13, 17-19, 21, 23-24; 4:4-5, 21; 5:3-4, 18, 23; 6:13). Paul calls this a striving for "one's own righteousness" (cf. Rom. 10:3), "my own righteousness, which is of the Torah" (Phil. 3:9 NKJV).

Jesus opposes this hypocritical and arrogant Torah-keeping to the humble, penitent heart-attitude of the Jewish sinner: "He also told this parable to some who trusted in themselves that they were righteous, and treated others with contempt:

---

31. Paul does not use the word *nomos* in 2 Cor. 3, but *gramma*, "letter" (v. 6; cf. Rom. 7:6), which is the polity of the Torah viewed as a system of slavery (Gal. 4:3, 9) and the "ally" of sin (cf. Rom. 5:20). The opposite of *gramma* is *pneuma*, "spirit/Spirit" (2 Cor. 3:3, 6, 8, 16-18; Rom. 7:6; cf. Gal. 4:29; 5:22-25) (Dunn 1998, 149-50).

The Meaning of the Mosaic Covenant

'Two men went up into the temple to pray, one a Pharisee and the other a tax collector [working for the Roman occupiers, WJO]. The Pharisee, standing by himself, prayed thus: "God, I thank you that I am not like other men, extortioners, unjust, adulterers, or even like this tax collector. I fast twice a week; I give tithes of all that I get." But the tax collector, standing far off, would not even lift up his eyes to heaven, but beat his breast, saying, "God, be merciful to me, a sinner!" I tell you, this man went down to his house justified, rather than the other. For everyone who exalts himself will be humbled, but the one who humbles himself will be exalted'" (Luke 18:9–14).

Such a parable, and many similar declarations in the New Testament, do not at all mean that we should *not* endeavor to do "works of the Torah [of the Messiah]," that is, aspire after a righteousness that can stand before the Messianic Torah! On the contrary. However, we should:

(1) *not* attempt this with an unregenerated heart, nor even if regenerated, in our own carnal strength, for in this way we will obtain only a pretended righteousness;

(2) *not* try to ascertain, nor to advance, our salvation through this keeping of the Torah, for we would terribly deceive ourselves (Torah-keeping is not a condition for, but a fruit of, salvation);

(3) *not* think that Gentiles can attain this righteousness that can stand before the Torah only by joining those who are "under the [Mosaic] Torah," that is, Israel. Our pseudo-righteousness would bring us only eternal perdition. Paul said, "[I]t is the doers of the Torah who will be justified" (Rom. 2:13). This is perfectly correct, but only if one keeps in mind that this is possible in the case of regenerated persons alone, and then solely by the power of the Holy Spirit (Rom. 8:4), without Gentile Jesus-believers having to take the full *Mosaic* Torah upon themselves (Gal. 5:2). In this case, "to be justified (i.e., declared righteous)" does not mean acquiring one's own righteousness through keeping the Torah (either of Mo-

ses or of Jesus), but results in manifesting one's God-given righteousness through keeping the *Messianic* Torah in God's strength (cf. James 2:14-26; 2 Cor. 5:21). (This will be dealt with more extensively in the third volume of this trilogy.)

Paul said, "[I]f a Torah had been given that could give life, then righteousness would indeed be by the Torah" (Gal. 3:21); that is to say: the Torah places rightful demands upon Man but cannot help Man to meet those demands because it cannot impart true (divine) life to a person. Therefore, as I said, the Torah was "weakened by [Man's] flesh" (Rom. 8:3), that is, not weakened in its own divine nature — how could that be? — but weakened in its effect. If a mouse is threatened by a cat, it would be good if someone commanded the mouse, "Fly away!," because flying away would deliver the mouse from the cat. The command is both "strong," because obeying it would most surely deliver from death and lead to life, and "weak," because the mouse cannot fly. The command is both true and ineffective.

The unregenerated mass of natural Israel could not "fly," and therefore the nation was "held captive under the Torah, imprisoned until the coming faith would be revealed. So then, the Torah was our guardian until Christ came, in order that we might be justified by faith. But now that faith has come, we are no longer under a guardian" (Gal. 3:23-25). Even this in a certain sense was one of the Torah's positive functions, in that, as a supervisor, an attendant of children (Gr. *paidagōgos*), it guided the godly in Israel and kept a check on wicked Man.[32] It kept the latter under its thumb by reminding

---

32. Dunn (1990a, 98) speaks of a "baby-sitter"; elsewhere (1998, 142-45) he refers to the "guardian angel role" of the Torah; see how Gal. 4:1-5 is parallel with vv. 8-10, where taking upon oneself the Mosaic Torah is viewed as returning to the *stoicheia*, i.e., the "gods" (guardian angels) of the Gentiles (see §3.3.3, and more extensively Ouweneel [2014b, especially §2.1]). Dunn goes too far, though, in suggesting that Israel no longer needs this guardian role of the Torah (see the present study).

The Meaning of the Mosaic Covenant

him constantly of his wickedness. If the mouse boasts that it can fly, then the command "Fly!" is a constant reminder that in fact it cannot. This is positive because it keeps the mouse from boasting, unless the mouse is a fool. Thus, the Mosaic Torah kept natural Israel from boasting in themselves, in contrast to, on the one hand, the self-conceited fools, who boasted anyway, and on the other hand, the meek and humble godly ones, who had already realized that they could live only by the grace and the Spirit of God, and boasted only in this grace and in the Lord himself (Jer. 9:24; 1 Cor. 1:31).

Its job of restraining fools was a negative purpose of the Torah; positively, its goal was to lead the godly to Messiah! Being under the Mosaic Torah *as such* never makes a person a slave. Were Moses and Joshua, Aaron and Phinehas, David and Solomon, Elijah and Elisha, Isaiah and Jeremiah, and also Zechariah and Elizabeth, Joseph and Mary, Simeon and Anna, etc., "slaves"? However, being under the Torah and at the same time being powerless through sin makes one a slave (cf. John 8:34-36). The negative meaning of any Torah—the Mosaic Torah, the Messianic Torah, or the Millennial Torah—is that it enslaves all those who, though outwardly belonging to God's people, are wicked trespassers or "decent" hypocrites, self-confident legalists or arrogant ethnocentrists. But the truly positive function of any Torah—the Mosaic Torah, the Messianic Torah, or the Millennial Torah—is that it is the rule of life for those who, through grace and faith, live out of atonement and forgiveness, possess the life of God, and walk in the power of the Holy Spirit.

Zechariah and Elizabeth were "both righteous before God, walking blamelessly in all the commandments and statutes of the Lord" (Luke 1:6; cf. vv. 74-77). This is the best possible evidence that, also according to the New Testament, *someone can truly be righteous through works of the Torah*—but only in the way of trusting God, living by his grace and power, in true humility and repentance. I repeat, this is what Paul states as a general—and, in itself, perfectly true—principle: "[T]he doers of the Torah will be justified" (Rom. 2:13). This is what Jesus said even more clearly. After an expert in the Torah had asked him about how to inherit eternal life—that is, the bliss of the Messianic Kingdom—Jesus asked him: "What is written in the Torah? How do you read it?" The lawyer answered: "'You shall love the Lord your God with all your heart and with all your soul and with all your strength and with all your mind'; and, '[Love] your neighbor as yourself.' And he [i.e., Jesus] said to him, 'You have answered correctly; do this, and you will live'" (Luke 10:25–28).

If the term "Torah" is used in both a positive and a negative sense, it is well to keep in mind that, strictly speaking, nowhere does Scripture ever ascribe to the Torah a negative function as such. The Torah is always a wonderfully positive instrument of God; it is always "holy, righteous and good" (Rom. 7:13). The Torah as such never was the problem; as Walter Kaiser put it, "That [i.e., in the Torah] is never where the problem ever existed, for Israel or for the Church: the problem always was with people, not the law."[33] The term "Torah" is sometimes used in a negative sense in the New Testament, not because of negative aspects belonging to the Torah as such, but rather because of negative aspects belonging to the people who are under the Torah.

4.3.2 Law, Legalism, Ethnocentrism

I have now arrived at an important point that I will take up more extensively in §5.1.1. Apparently, the Greek language at that time did not have a word for "legalism." By legalism I understand a rigorous and rigid system of Torah-keeping as an end in itself, in one's own strength, often as a ground for boasting and arrogance (see again the Pharisee in Luke 18:9–14), or as a means of power over and oppression of others, often connected with conservatism and formalism.

When Paul uses the expression "under the Torah" in a

---

33. Kaiser in Rudin and Wilson (1987, 132).

negative sense, he may have meant "under the Torah as a legalistic polity," in brief, "under legalism," or according to a newer view, "under the Torah as a ground for ethnocentric boasting," in brief, "under Jewish ethnocentrism" (Rom. 6:14–15; 1 Cor. 9:20; Gal. 3:23; 4:5, 21; 5:18). Actually, Paul uses the expression also in a neutral sense; in that case, being "under the Torah" simply means belonging to Israel (Rom. 2:12; 3:19; Gal. 4:4). But because this belonging to Israel was often an excuse for legalism and/or ethnocentrism, the expression "under the Torah" easily acquired a negative meaning. Likewise, "works of the Torah" often means works through which one tries to earn God's favor by one's own Torah-keeping, and/or works done by those who are "under the Torah," that is, those who belong to God's circumcised people (with the implication that repenting Gentiles are to join them; Rom. 3:20, 28; Gal. 2:16; 3:2, 5, 10). The double meaning of such expressions as "under the Torah" and "works of the Torah" is a cause of much of the confusion surrounding the theological content of the notion of *nomos* in the New Testament.

When Paul says, "[N]ow the righteousness of God has been manifested apart from the Torah" (Rom. 3:21), he does not mean that this righteousness has nothing to do with any Torah. On the contrary, all true righteousness of the Jesus-believer must meet the standards of the Messianic Torah. No, Paul means that the righteousness of God comes to us apart from any system of *legalism* or *Jewish ethnocentrism*, that is, apart from any polity that makes righteousness dependent on one's own good works of the Torah or on one's joining Israel (those "under the Torah"), respectively. Similarly, having "died to the Torah" and having been "released from the Torah" (Rom. 7:4, 6) do not mean "released from *every* tie with *any* Torah," but "released from the duty of attaining righteousness through keeping the Torah in one's own strength," or "from the duty of joining Israel by circumcision," in brief, "released from legalism," or "from Jewish ethnocentrism."

Note here, by the way, that legalism as such does not necessarily *always* imply boasting, religious pride, self-righteousness, or hypocrisy. Räisänen has introduced the distinction between "hard" (or "anthropocentric," or "ethnocentric") legalism, implying such carnal feelings, and "soft" (or "Torah-centric") legalism, not implying such feelings.[34] Westerholm adds "that 'soft' legalists, who try to obey God's law because they believe God has commanded them to do so, may not believe that they are thereby 'earning' their salvation, still less that they are 'establishing a claim' on God based on their own 'merit.' Surely love for God, or even fear of his judgment, are adequate motives for obedience to his commands."[35] This is true, but the question arises whether such an uncommon view of legalism does not lead to terminological confusion. If one wishes to avoid the common pejorative connotations of the term "legalism" it is better to use Sanders' term *(covenantal) nomism* (see Appendix II). Consequently, there are not two, but at least three, forms of Torah-keeping (cf. the tripartition in §4.2.2):

1. There is a fully biblical "(covenantal) nomism" in the sense of God-fearing persons, Jews or Christians, feeling obliged to humbly and faithfully observe God's commandments by the power of his Spirit, not as a condition for entering the covenant but as evidence of faithfulness to the covenant.

2. There is a "soft legalism" in the sense of God-fearing persons, Jews or Christians, feeling obliged to humbly and faithfully observe God's commandments as a *condition* for entering the covenant, or for earning their salvation.

3. There is a "hard legalism" in the sense of persons, Jews or Christians, feeling obliged to observe God's commandments as a *condition* for entering the covenant, or for earning their salvation, and doing so in a spirit of hypocrisy, self-seeking, merit-mongering, boasting, arrogance, or pride, often linked

---

34. Räisänen (1980).
35. Westerholm (1988, 132–33).

with Jewish ethnocentrism.

In my view, the latter attitude is utterly wrong, the middle attitude is wrong, and the former attitude is thoroughly biblical. We are not released from the Torah in the sense that now we can go our own way and do as we please. That would be *anomia* ("Torah-lessness"), if not outright debauchery. No, we are under the Messianic Torah (1 Cor. 9:21; Gal. 6:2). Therefore, "through the Torah I died to the Torah" (Gal. 2:19) means: through the condemnation that the Torah pronounces upon the wicked I have died to that polity whereby one seeks to achieve one's own righteousness by keeping the Torah in one's own strength (traditional view), or that polity which demands my joining Israel through circumcision in order to get "under the Torah" (newer view). But now, the person living through Jesus is gladly under *his* Torah, without having been physically circumcised, because there is no command for this in the Messianic Torah. Through the condemnation of God's Torah over his sinful nature (*yetzer ra*) such a person has died to legalism as well as to ethnocentrism, and now lives under God's Torah in the proper (non-legalistic, non-ethnocentric) way. He has died to all carnal attempts to keep the Torah, and even died to all the impulses to join those "under the Torah" through circumcision, and now humbly endeavors to keep the Messianic Torah through God's Spirit.

The latter is exactly the same as living *by grace* (e.g., Rom. 12:3; 2 Cor. 1:12), following Jesus (e.g., 1 Thess. 1:6), exhibiting the image of Christ (e.g., Rom. 8:29; 2 Cor. 3:18), walking worthily (e.g., Phil. 1:27), bearing the fruit of the Spirit (Gal. 5:22), walking in love (Eph. 5:2), being filled with the Spirit (v. 18), etc. Being led by the *Spirit* (Rom. 8:14) is fundamentally the same as walking according to the pattern of the Messianic *Torah* (13:10). This is nothing else than the Tanakhic principle: "I will put my *Spirit* within you, and cause you to walk in my *statutes* and be careful to obey my *rules*" (Ezek. 36:27).

The indubitable fact that Paul does not discard the Torah

as such is argued by Paul himself: "Do we then overthrow the Torah by this faith? By no means! On the contrary, we uphold the Torah" (Rom. 3:31), that is, we fully maintain it, we place it on an indestructible foundation. For, as we saw, living by the grace of God, through faith, on the basis of a substitutionary sacrifice, was the essence of a godly life under the Torah in the Tanakh, and this has not changed in the New Testament. The *true* Jew has *always* known that the Torah cannot be kept in one's own strength but only by trusting God. As Pinchas Lapide wrote: "That which the Torah means to the Jews is no spasmodic striving after justification, but a life that is lived believingly and full of joy before and with God . . . it is the fullness of divine love expressing itself in the gracious gift of the Torah . . . no rabbi has ever asserted that the Torah is a way of salvation leading to heaven. On the contrary! No world record in the field of Torah-keeping can take away even the least from God's sovereign, loving grace."[36] And elsewhere: "The rabbinate has never considered the Torah as a way of salvation to God. . . . [Jews] regard salvation as God's exclusive prerogative, so we Jews are the advocates of 'pure grace.'"[37] According to the Talmud, salvation can be attained "only through God's gracious love."

A clear-cut first-century Jewish example of this principle of justification by grace alone is found in the Dead Sea Scrolls, namely, in the Community Rule: "For to God belongs my justification [*mishpat*] and the perfection of my way, and the uprightness of my heart are in his hand: by his righteousness are my rebellions blotted out . . . from the fount of his righteousness comes my justification. . . . The fountain of righteousness, the reservoir of power, and the dwelling-place of glory are denied to the assembly of flesh; but God has given them as an everlasting possession to those whom he has chosen. . . . For is Man master of his way? No, men cannot establish their

---

36. Lapide (2011), chapter on the "Joy of the Law."
37. Lapide in Lapide and Stuhlmacher (1984, 37–39).

steps, for their justification belongs to God, and from his hand comes perfection of way.... And I, if I stagger, God's mercies are my salvation for ever; and if I stumble because of the sin of the flesh, my justification is in the righteousness of God which exists for ever.... He has caused me to approach by his mercy and by his favors he will bring my justification. He has justified me by his true justice and by his immense goodness he will pardon all my iniquities.... Truly, this man is a mere frail image in potter's clay and inclines to the dust. What shall clay reply, the thing which the hand fashions? What thought can it apprehend?"[38]

4.3.3 The Letter to the Hebrews

Although the Letter to the Hebrews seems to make strong statements about the abolition of the Old Covenant, in the light of our previous considerations we may now try to understand this Letter's statements. The expositor's difficulties lie especially in the following verses: the Torah is "changed" (7:12), a former regulation is "set aside because of its weakness and uselessness (for the Torah made nothing perfect)" (7:18-19), the New Covenant is "better" than the Old Covenant because "that first covenant" was not "faultless" (7:22; 8:6-7), and the Torah "is but a shadow of the good things to come instead of the true form of these realities" (10:1). Let us consider these points one by one.

Viewed within the context, the "change in the Torah" (7:12) involves a rearrangement (Gr. *metathesis*) of this one and only element of the Torah: the priesthood of Aaron and his progeny is replaced by the Messianic priesthood of Melchizedek (see vv. 11-14). There was nothing new or peculiar about this change, for it had already been announced in the Tanakh; the LORD had said, literally to David, and prophetically to the

---

38. 1QS 11.2–22 (see Shulam 1998, 140; cf. 147, 181, 186–87, 216, 252, 259–260, 262, including references to the Qumran Thanksgiving Hymns [1QH]).

great Son of David, "The LORD has sworn and will not change his mind,'You are a priest forever after the order of Melchizedek'" (Ps. 110:4; see Heb. 5:6; 6:20; 7:17). The high priest of the present dispensation is a priest after the order not of Aaron but of Melchizedek. This will also hold for the future Messianic Kingdom: the Messiah "shall be a priest on His throne" (Zech. 6:13 NKJV), though interestingly on earth represented by the sons of Zadok, a descendant of Aaron (Ezek. 40:46; 43:19; 44:15; 48:11; cf. 2 Sam. 8:17; 1 Chron. 6:3-8).

The rabbis, too, announced certain "changes of the Torah" in connection with the coming of Messiah.[39] The Tanakh itself already mentions several additions to the Torah as Moses had given it, such as the introduction of music into the worship service (1 Chron. 25; cf. Amos 6:5), the introduction of the *Purim* feast (Esth. 9:20-32), and the addition of *Chanukkah* (1 Maccab. 4:52-59; cf. John 10:22). The Torah had never been intended as a rigid system for all time. One of the most striking indications for the basic changeability of the Torah is the evidence in the Talmud that, apparently, an ordinance of the rabbis may supersede even a decree of the Torah.[40] Of course, we cannot agree with this; the inspired Word of God cannot be changed, not even by the greatest servants of God, whether Jewish or Gentile. But I mention this rabbinic view to underscore that the Torah is a flexible matter. The Tanakh itself makes clear that God loves to respond to the suggestions of his people. Thus, it was at their initiative that a second *Pesach* celebration was allowed (Num. 9), that the daughters of Zelophehad were permitted to inherit from their father (Num. 27:1-11), and that Ruth was adopted into Israel (the book of Ruth).

Because the family of Aaron was sinful, like all people, it could not bring about real redemption. In that sense, the "former commandment" was characterized by being "weak

---

39. See Stern (1999, 241-43).
40. Yevamot 89b, 90b; cf. Sanhedrin 46a.

and useless" (Heb. 7:18). That was not God's fault, as if there could be any weakness or fault in him or in his Torah as such, but it was Man's fault. As long as the true high priest in the order of Melchizedek had not come, God had to deal with the sinful and weak family of Aaron. In this way we have to understand the saying, "[T]he Torah made nothing perfect" (7:19). Again, that was not the fault of the Torah as such, for its commands are holy, righteous, and good (Rom. 7:12-13, 16; cf. Deut. 6:18; Ps. 19:7-11; Prov. 2:20), but it was Man's fault. The Torah was able to show sinful Man the right way of salvation. But it had three limitations. Its first limit was that the Torah could not give him the strength to go that way; its second limit was that it could not supply priests who were able to truly help sinful people; and its third limit was that the Torah could not present sacrifices that had inherent power to supply sinful Man with true atonement.

In this way we can also understand that the New Covenant is indeed a "better" covenant than the Old one (7:22; 8:6). Of course, this does not mean that the Old Covenant was a bad or defective one; how could God have established a defective covenant with his people?[41] On the contrary, it was the best covenant that was conceivable under the circumstances. This implies that the Torah necessarily had "but a shadow of the good things to come instead of the true form of these realities" (10:1). The Aaronic priesthood pointed in an imperfect way to Jesus' priesthood, and the animal sacrifices referred in an imperfect way to Jesus' sacrifice. The New Covenant is better than the Old one because it is based on a better priesthood (that of Jesus) and on a better sacrifice (that of Jesus). Something was "wrong" with the Old Covenant (8:7 NIV), not because God would have given an inferior covenant but be-

---

41. To avoid this impression, the Hebrew Christian, Heinz David Leuner, prefers the translation "more powerful," "more glorious," or "stronger" instead of "better" (see article included in Kac 1986, 178).

cause of Man's sinfulness. Here the word "wrong" should be understood to mean "ineffective." In itself the Torah is excellent, and so is the Old Covenant, but again, it cannot guarantee salvation to Man, nor could the Old Covenant's priests and sacrifices as such. Those priests and sacrifices therefore had only a limited value insofar as they anticipated the perfect priesthood and sacrifice of Jesus. Thus, a New Covenant was required.

If only we understand this New Covenant correctly! I repeat: it does not imply a *replacement* but a *renewal* (enrichment, fulfillment) of the Old Covenant. Thus, to the amazement of some, in the future Messianic kingdom, priests from the family of Aaron will again serve in the new Temple (see above), and animal sacrifices will again be offered. This shows afresh that it is incorrect to claim that the Old Covenant has been abolished or abrogated. On the contrary, as we observed earlier, the Old Covenant, too, is called an everlasting covenant (Judg. 2:1; 1 Chron. 16:17; Ps. 105:8, 10), and the covenant with the Aaronic priests was everlasting as well (Num. 25:13; Ps. 106:30–31; cf. Mal. 2:4, 8; 3:3). However, the Levitical priesthood and the animal sacrifices in the Messianic kingdom will have value only insofar as they are based upon, and refer back to, the priesthood and sacrifice of Jesus. The fact that Scripture calls the Old Covenant everlasting and yet speaks of a New Covenant is not necessarily a contradiction, for the New Covenant is nothing but an enrichment and fulfillment of the Old Covenant.

But what about Hebrews 8:13? It says, "In speaking of a New Covenant, he [i.e., God] makes the first one obsolete. And what is becoming obsolete and growing old is ready to vanish away." The author cannot possibly mean that the Levitical priesthood and sacrifices (as well as the Shabbat commandment, the Jewish festivals, *kashrut*, etc.) would be abrogated altogether, for he knew that all these elements of the Old Covenant would be in full force in the future Messianic Kingdom (§6.2.1). But insofar as the Old Covenant was a pol-

The Meaning of the Mosaic Covenant

ity that as such did offer a good Torah but no power to keep it, and in which the priesthood and the sacrifices were imperfect, *this polity* would disappear. This means that, instead of being fully abolished, it would be absorbed in a better covenant, with a better priesthood and better sacrifices.

Of course, in some formal sense, this does mean that the Mosaic Torah and the Old Covenant give way to the Messianic Torah and the New Covenant. But the former's transcendent substance is preserved, and placed within the framework of a "better" polity: founded on the perfect priesthood and perfect sacrifice of Jesus. *In this respect* — and this is what Hebrews 7 and 8 are all about — is there a "change in the Torah" (7:12). But there is no *abolition* of the Torah in its essence, and therefore neither is there an abolition of the Old Covenant in its essence. Just as Jesus does not permit any "jot or tittle" of the Torah to disappear,[42] but "fulfills" the entire Torah (Matt. 5:17-18) — brings it to its "fullness" — likewise, the Old Covenant is not abolished, but is brought to its "fullness" within the New Covenant.[43]

One can easily be entangled by this terminology: abolished, yes or no? "Formally," yes, "substantially," no. Let me put it this way. There is a definite discontinuity, as dispensational theology claims: the Mosaic Torah is *replaced* by the Messianic Torah. At the same time, there is a definite continuity, as covenant theology and many Messianic Jews claim: the Mosaic Torah is absorbed by, and *renewed* in, the Messianic Torah. I myself suggest the following explanation for both

---

42. A Midrash (Exod. Rabbah 6.1) tells us how one day king Solomon replaced a *yod* in the Torah and how the *yod* complained about it to the LORD, saying: "One [letter] today, another tomorrow until the entire Torah is destroyed." God replied: "Solomon and a thousand like him may [attempt to] destroy, but I will not let one tittle from you [i.e., the Torah] be destroyed."
43. On the basis of Hebrew parallels (*l'qayyem*), Bivin (2005, 94) suggests that the word "fulfill" is a rabbinical technical term here, meaning "to sustain by properly interpreting."

this discontinuity and this continuity: *the Mosaic Torah and the Messianic Torah are both manifestations of the one, eternal Torah.*

By way of comparison, it is like the age-old question whether the resurrection body will be the same body as the present one (be it renewed), or a different body, or whether the new earth will be the same earth as the present one (be it renewed), or a different earth. Of course, both statements are true. There is continuity, for it is *this* "mortal body" which is given life in the resurrection (Rom. 8:11), and so it will be *this* earth that will be renewed, not replaced (in spite of the "fled away" in Rev. 20:11, and the "passed away" in 21:1). But there is also discontinuity, for the resurrection body will be as different from the present body as the stalk is different from the seed, or as the imperishable, glorious, powerful, and spiritual is different from the perishable, dishonorable, weak, and natural (1 Cor. 15:37, 42–44). The same holds true, *mutatis mutandis*, for the new earth.

When David Stern claims that "the Torah of Moshe and the Torah of the Messiah are the same,"[44] he is just as right and just as wrong as those claiming that the new body or the new earth is the same as the old one. Stern continues, "Apparent changes are not abrogations, but applications of the eternal *Torah* to the new historical situation resulting from the Messiah's first coming. The central requirement of the Torah remains unchanged, 'trust and faithfulness expressing themselves in love' ([Gal.] 5:6). Yes, there is a Law of Love;[45] Moses brought it to God's people." So far, so good. But a bit later Stern says, "One considers the United States constitution to be 'the same' as when it was promulgated, although it has been amended many times, and specific provisions have even had their meaning reversed by court interpretation."[46] All

---

44. Stern (1999, 569).
45. As the "Law of the Messiah" in Gal. 6:2 has been interpreted (WJO).
46. Stern (1999, 570).

right, but with metaphors one can "prove" a lot. In France, the whole republic "changes" when the constitution is altered. In 1814, the First Republic began, in 1848 the Second, in 1870 the Third, in 1946 the Fourth, and in 1958 the Fifth Republic. The United States always had the "same" constitution, and the five French Republics all had "different" constitutions. But one could just as well say that the United States has "changed" its constitution many times, and that since 1814 France always had basically the "same" constitution.

Stern says that despite the many *differences* between the Mosaic Torah, the New Testament Messianic Torah, and the Millennial Torah, they are basically *one and the same* Torah. I say, in spite of the many *similarities* between the Mosaic Torah, the New Testament Messianic Torah, and the Millennial Torah, they are basically *different* manifestations of the one, eternal Torah. The New Covenant will not be a replacement but a renewal of the Old Covenant, yet it will be really *new*. This is the very argument of Hebrews 8:13. And if the covenant will be new, then the Torah of the New Covenant will be new. Not in the sense of replacement but of renewal—yet new. Therefore, what Stern says is inaccurate: "[The Torah under the New Covenant] is not some new Torah, different from Tanakh *Torah*."[47] The weakness of Stern's position is exhibited by what follows: "Christian theology all too often tries to escape or water down the plain sense of what is said here, so that what is required is very little, usually a vague 'sensitivity to God's will' that becomes impossible to pin down." Stern should not need such a caricature of his average opponent because he implicitly but mistakenly judges the latter's motives, which is forbidden by the Messianic Torah (Matt. 7:1-2). One may firmly stress that the Jesus-believer must keep all the—perhaps more than thousand!—commandments of the New Testament Messianic Torah, and yet emphasize that this is a Torah-manifestation different from the Mosaic Torah.

---

47. Stern (1999, 686).

Likewise, the Millennial Torah will be basically new, for "the coastlands *wait* for his [i.e., Messiah's] Torah" (Isa. 42:4).

A very good example of how the New Testament handles this matter of the "newness" of the Messianic Torah is John 13:34, where Jesus says, "A new commandment I give to you, that you love one another: just as I have loved you, you also are to love one another." Compare this with 1 John 2:7-8: "Beloved, I am writing you no new commandment, but an old commandment that you had from the beginning. The old commandment is the word that you have heard. At the same time, it is a new commandment that I am writing to you, which is true in him and in you, because the darkness is passing away and the true light is already shining."

How is this to be understood? Jesus' command to love one another was "new" with respect to the similar command under the "old" Torah (Lev. 19:18) in at least two ways. First, Jesus is not speaking here of love toward all men but of the special brotherly love within the Christian community (which does not exclude our duty, of course, to show love to all people; cf. Rom. 12:17-18; Phil. 4:5; Titus 3:2). Second, the "old" Torah commands one to love the other "as yourself," whereas Jesus commands one to love the other "as[48] I have loved you." The former ties in with Man's natural self-love, the latter is a supernatural love, which is possible only through rebirth and the power of the Holy Spirit. Rabbi Aqiva taught the "old" command, namely, our own life comes before our friend's life; God commands you to love your neighbor as yourself, not more than yourself.[49] But Jesus teaches, "This is my commandment, that you love one another as I have loved you. Greater love has no one than this, that someone lay down his life for his friends" (John 15:12-13; cf. 1 John 3:16).

In my view, the contrast between "old" and "new" in 1 John

---

48. Not "because," as C. Plummer (quoted by Morris 1971, 633) renders it.
49. Quoted by Stern (1999, 771).

2:7-8 is not the same as in John 13.[50] By the time John wrote about our Lord's new commandment, it had itself become an "old" command, well-known to his readers, as is clear from this statement: "And now I ask you, dear lady — not as though I were writing you a new commandment, but the one we have had from the beginning — that we love one another" (2 John 5; cf. 1 John 3:23; "beginning" here refers to the start of Jesus' ministry; 1:1; 2:7, 13-14; 3:11; only in 3:8 does it refer to the "beginning" of history). Yet, John argues that the command was now being realized in a new way because the darkness was passing away and the Age of Light had begun. In John 13, Jesus gave the new command to his disciples; now, since the Day of Pentecost, the new commandment had become "true," not only *"in* him" but also *"in* you" (1 John 2:8), through the power of the Holy Spirit. The new command is new, first, because it has a new *form* (". . . as I have loved you"); second, because it is addressed to a newly founded *community* (". . . love one another"); and third, because it is realized *in* the believers through the Spirit (cf. Rom. 5:5; 8:4).

At this point we need to ask a fundamental question: What theological *interest* — I do not speak of psychological motives — is being protected by a certain type of theology that stresses either the "same" or the "different"? The answer is obvious. Dispensational theologians (e.g., Jewish Arnold Fruchtenbaum) have every interest in emphasizing the *differences* between the Mosaic Torah, the New Testament Messianic Torah, and the Millennial Torah, because they believe in essentially different dispensations. Covenant theologians, and Messianic Jews like David Stern, have every interest in emphasizing the *identity* of the three Torah manifestations, because they believe that Jesus-believers are under the Mosaic Torah, either the moral part of it or its entirety. I am attempting to defend a virtually impossible middle position by stressing both the "one-ness" and the "three-ness." I have every in-

---

50. Cf. Marshall (1978, 129); *contra* Stern (1999, 771).

terest doing so, because the notion of the one-ness is a strong weapon against the erroneous idea that the Mosaic Torah has been abolished. And the notion of the three-ness is a strong weapon against the erroneous idea that Gentile Jesus-believers are, for example, under the Shabbat commandment or *kashrut*. They are *not* under these latter commandments, not even under the moral part of the Mosaic Torah; happily they are under the commandments of the New Testament Messianic Torah. In certain respects, the position of Stern, a Messianic Jew, is quite different. This will be dealt with specifically in chapter 5 and subsequent chapters.

Chapter 5
Is the Mosaic Torah Abolished or Renewed?

My son, keep your father's commandment,
    and forsake not your mother's Torah.
Bind them on your heart always;
    tie them around your neck.
When you walk, they will lead you;
    when you lie down, they will watch over you;
    and when you awake, they will talk with you.
For the commandment is a lamp and the Torah a light,
    and the reproofs of discipline are the way of life

Proverbs 6:20–23

Do not think that I have come to abolish the Torah or the Prophets;
    I have not come to abolish them but to fulfill them.
For truly, I say to you, until heaven and earth pass away,
    not an iota, not a dot, will pass from the Torah until all is accomplished.
Therefore whoever relaxes one of the least of these

> commandments
>> and teaches others to do the same
>> will be called least in the kingdom of heaven,
> but whoever does them and teaches them
>> will be called great in the kingdom of heaven.
>>> Matthew 5:17–19

Summary: *If the one, eternal Torah manifests itself in every dispensation — albeit each time in a somewhat different form — there cannot be any question of the Torah having been abolished (cf. Matt. 5:17). What Jesus-believers have been freed from is not the Torah as such — on the contrary, in each dispensation the true* tzaddiq *lives according to God's Torah — but from legalism, from a holiness based on works, from the most pious Torah-keeping that has no room for Jesus Messiah. Every manifestation of the Torah, whether it is the Mosaic Torah, the Messianic Torah of the present dispensation, or the Millennial Torah of the Messianic Kingdom to come, is both a moral and a ceremonial, civil, and juridical Torah. To be sure, opinions about these matters greatly differ, even among Jewish Jesus-believers. One thing is clear: during their entire life, Paul and the other apostles kept not only the Messianic Torah but — because they had remained Jews — also the Mosaic Torah, as long as it did not conflict with the Messianic Torah.*

5.1 What Torah Are We Talking About?
5.1.1 Is Messiah the "End" or the "Goal"?

In chapter 4, I argued that neither the Old Covenant nor the Torah was abolished with regard to their essence. If the Mosaic Torah essentially has not been abolished, then it is essentially still in force. What does this essence, this *kelal gadol betorah* ("greatest principle" of the Torah), involve? Are Jewish Jesus-believers still under the 613 commandments of the Torah? Have Gentile Jesus-believers come under the 613 commandments of the Torah? We have seen that Jesus-believers are under the commandments of Jesus (John 13:34; 14:15, 21; 15:10, 12), that is, under the Messianic Torah (1 Cor. 9:21; Gal.

6:2). I have also introduced my thesis that the Messianic Torah is essentially not a different Torah than the Sinaitic Torah, which was concentrated in the Ten Words. These Words have been elaborated and deepened especially in Jesus' Sermon on the Mount (Matt. 5–7), and in the Letters of the apostles, who quote and apply them in a direct way (Rom. 7:7; 13:8–10; Eph. 6:2–3; James 2:8, 11; also see Gal. 5:14). The Ten Words themselves find their focal point in Messiah's great Love Command. In this respect at least, "the" Torah was never abolished.

Related to this is the question as to how we are to read Romans 10:4: "Christ is the end [NIV: culmination; CEB, NASB note: goal] of the Torah." The Greek word for "end," *telos*, can mean either "goal (aim, outcome)" (e.g., 1 Tim. 1:15; 1 Pet. 1:9), or "termination" (1 Pet. 4:7). Both meanings make good sense here.[1] First, Jesus is the goal, the aim, the meaning, the fulfillment, the consummation of the Torah, as he himself has declared: "Do not think that I have come to abolish the Torah or the Prophets; I have not come to abolish them but to fulfill them" (cf. Matt. 5:17).[2] And Paul says, "Do we then overthrow the Torah by this faith? By no means! On the contrary, we uphold [or, establish] the Torah" (Rom. 3:31).

Second, in Jesus, the polity of the Torah *as a legalistic or ethnocentric polity* has terminated. That which he brought to an end is a polity in which salvation is made entirely dependent upon sinful Man's own keeping of the Torah, or on joining the people of Israel. "You are not under Torah, but under grace" (Rom. 6:14); that is, "You are not under a *legalistic/ethnocentric*

---

1. In addition to the commentaries and the translations, see Badenas (1985) and Linss (1988); see the numerous references and comments in Oegema (1999, 217–44).
2. A comparison of Rom. 10:4 and Matt. 5:17 is wasted on Dunn (1990a, 245–246), who asserts that Matthew's Gospel gives "clear expression to a Jewish Christian attitude to the law," and this "in contrast to the Pauline view."

polity, but under grace." For your salvation, you are not dependent upon your own sinful Torah-keeping but upon the grace of God as revealed in Jesus.

In §4.3.2, I mentioned that Greek at that time did not have any words for legalism. As Cranfield put it: "[T]he Greek language of Paul's days possessed no word-group corresponding to our 'legalism,' 'legalist' and 'legalistic.' This means that Paul lacked a convenient terminology for expressing a vital distinction, and so was surely seriously hampered in the work of clarifying the Christian position with regard to the law. In view of this, we should always, we think, be ready to reckon with the possibility that Pauline statements which at first sight seem to disparage the law were really directed not against the law itself but against that misunderstanding and misuse of it for which we now have a convenient terminology."[3]

This view has not remained uncriticized.[4] It does not answer the question why Paul, even if he had no term for legalism, did not use other linguistic means to distinguish between *nomos* in the negative sense and *nomos* in the neutral or positive sense. Perhaps Paul's negative statements with respect to *nomos* are *not* directed against a certain misunderstanding and misuse of it. He rather turns against the idea that, since the coming of Jesus, one might retain and observe the Torah — proudly or humbly — thus attempting to earn the promised covenantal blessings, while leaving out Jesus altogether. Therefore, when Paul uses the expression "under the Torah" in a negative sense, he apparently means "under the Torah *only*, apart from Messiah," which in a sense is legalism

---

3. Cranfield (1981, 853).
4. Westerholm (1988, 131–35); Dunn (1992) (in response to Cranfield [1991]) (but Dunn himself is criticized by Schreiner [1993, 99–100; cf. 138–39]). Dunn (in Dunn and Suggate [1993, 3–42]) understands "justification by faith" as being Paul's view that, in order to be justified, one does not have to be "under the law," i.e., be part of Israel.

(Rom. 6:14–15; 1 Cor. 9:20; Gal. 3:23; 4:5, 21; 5:18.). Similarly, "works of the Torah" often means "legalistic works," that is, works through which one tries to earn heaven by one's own defective Torah-keeping *apart from Jesus' salvation* (Rom. 3:20, 28; Gal. 2:16; 3:2, 5, 10). Similarly, "released from the Torah" (Rom. 7:6) does not mean "released from every tie with the Torah," but "released from legalism/ethnocentrism," that is, true or pretended faithfulness to the Torah, or claiming the need of being proselytized into Israel, while rejecting Jesus (see further §4.3.2 and Appendix II).

In conclusion, "the" Torah has not come to an end at all. Jesus himself is the eternal Torah; how then could it have been abolished? There is a thing called the Messianic Torah; how then could "the" Torah have been abolished? Impossible! What came to an end was a polity in which the Torah was severed from Jesus. Not the Torah as such was abolished, but Jesus was introduced into the sphere of the Torah as its fulfillment, meaning, sense, aim, and goal. The point was not that first-century Judaism had misunderstood the Torah and that Paul was correcting their view, but that Judaism had believed that one could remain within the covenantal sphere of the Torah without believing in Jesus. The (Jewish) apostles did not give up the (Mosaic) Torah for Jesus, but they continued to observe the (Messianic) Torah *on the basis of* their faith in Jesus, and not apart from it.

As we will see, the apostles kept the *entire* (Mosaic) Torah during their *entire* life (§§5.2 and 5.3). Shortly after Paul said that we have been "released from the Torah," he told his readers that we have been redeemed "in order that the righteous requirement [one word: *dikaiōma*] of the Torah might be fulfilled in us, who walk not according to the flesh, but according to the Spirit" (Rom. 8:4). Thus, Gentile Jesus-believers are definitely required to meet the standard of the Torah (according to its essence), but this is possible only in the power of the Holy Spirit, which all true Jesus-believers possess (v. 9).

THE ETERNAL TORAH: LIVING UNDER GOD

Also compare this other statement of the apostle Paul: "Owe no one anything, except to love each other, for the one who loves another has fulfilled the Torah" (Rom. 13:8). Shortly after the verse where Paul says, "[A]ll who rely on works of the Torah are under a curse . . . the Torah is not of faith" (Gal. 3:10, 12), we hear: "the whole Torah is fulfilled [CEV: summed up] in one word: 'You shall love your neighbor as yourself'" (5:14), and: "Bear one another's burdens, and so fulfill the Torah of the Messiah" (6:2). If correctly understood, there is no contradiction in this: we have been redeemed from legalism, the polity that makes salvation dependent upon one's own defective Torah-keeping apart from Jesus. We have been redeemed also from ethnocentrism, the polity that makes salvation dependent upon being part of Israel, again, apart from Jesus. Consequently, we now serve God by keeping the Messianic Torah through the power of the Holy Spirit as those who belong to Jesus (Rom. 8:9).

Thus, one of the ways to describe the essence of the Christian life is that we fulfill the righteous demands of the Messianic Torah by God's Spirit working within us (Rom. 8:4). The Torah is a "Torah of righteousness" (9:31), and there is nothing wrong with pursuing it, as long as it is done not in a carnal but in a spiritual way, that is, not in the power of the flesh but of the Spirit. One who faithfully keeps the Torah is the true *tzaddiq*, the "righteous" person. In Israel, Jesus was the eminent *Tzaddiq* (Matt. 27:19, 24; Acts 3:14; 7:52; 22:14; 1 Pet. 3:18; 1 John 2:1; perhaps also James 5:6), who had the Torah within his heart[5] (Ps. 40:8). In a sense, Jesus is the eternal Torah in his own person, as we saw earlier (§3.2).

Martin Buber tells about Rabbi Löb, the "hidden *Tzaddiq*," who wanted to visit the "great *Maggid* of Mezhirech,"[6] and

---

5. Heb. *mê'ai*, sing. *mê'eh*, "bowel," "inmost part."
6. *Maggid* = preacher; the great *Maggid* was Dov Baer of Mezhirech (d. 1772), successor to the Ba'al Shem Tov, the founder of the Hasidic movement.

explained that he went to him not to learn from him words from the Torah, but to see how he put on and took off his felt shoes. His reason was that a genuine *Tzaddiq* is not one who (only) *speaks* Torah but he who *is* Torah.[7] This is the best Jewish way of describing Torah-keeping that I could imagine. With regard to the greatest *Tzaddiq* and *Maggid*, Jesus Messiah, it means that everything he did and said *was* "perfect Torah" because the righteousness of the Torah was his very being (see §7.3). This is the true example for every Jesus-believer in the sense that Jesus is the goal, the aim, the essence, the meaning, the significance, the *kelal gadol* ("greatest principle" or "summary") of the Torah—he *is* the Torah. We find his person in every "jot and tittle" of the Torah, just as, conversely, we find the Torah in every fiber of his person. He preached Torah, and he was what he preached (John 8:25). Likewise, the Messianic Torah is imprinted upon every thought, word, and deed of the Messianic believer in this world.

This reminds us of what James says, "[I]f anyone is a hearer of the word and not a doer, he is like a man who looks intently at his natural face in a mirror. For he looks at himself and goes away and at once forgets what he was like. But the one who looks into the *perfect Torah*, the Torah of liberty, and perseveres, being no hearer who forgets but a doer who acts, he will be blessed in his doing" (1:23–25; italics added). One can understand these words in two ways. The first is: the mirror of the Torah shows me my failures and shortcomings, and teaches me to do something about it.[8] I prefer the second explanation: the mirror of the Torah shows me the ideal picture of what the true *tzaddiq* is before God, and challenges me to answer to it.[9] The saying, Jesus *is* Torah, means: he perfectly answered and answers to the picture that the Torah presents to God's people.

---

7. Buber (1963, 224).
8. E.g., Stern (1999, 727).
9. E.g., Adamson (1976, 82–83); Berkowitz (2011, 80–81, 125).

Gershom Scholem gave the following presentation of the true *hasid*: "Hasidism does indeed teach that Man meets God in the concreteness of his dealings in the world. . . . Hasidism denied in principle the existence of a purely secular sphere of life which would have no significance for the religious task of Man. . . . The contemplative mind can . . . transform even what is essentially profane into something that possesses immediate religious significance. The motto for this attitude was provided by Proverbs 3:6, 'In all thy ways acknowledge Him,' which the Hasidim interpreted to mean: Through every single action in which you are engaged you are enabled to gain knowledge of God, you are enabled to meet Him. . . . The Hasidic writers placed special emphasis on such 'forgotten' realms of simple and insignificant action, and Hasidim's transformation of them into vehicles for the sacred was one of the most original aspects of the movement."[10]

This notion, implying that spiritual life may in no way be severed from so-called "secular life," from everyday life (including, as the Rabbi of Polnoye emphasized, "such earthly actions as eating, drinking, and sexual intercourse, yes, even business transactions"), is also essentially Christian; it is "living Jesus"; as the apostle Paul put it, "[T]o me to live is Christ" (Phil. 1:21); "Christ is your life" (Col. 3:4).

5.1.2 A Part of the Torah?

Yet, one vital question remains unanswered. If "the" Torah has not been done away with, what exactly does this imply for the *Mosaic* Torah? Are the purification laws, or the ceremonial and the civil laws that we find in the Mosaic Torah, still in force? If yes, for whom, then? Or are they not in force anymore? Can we make a biblically responsible distinction between the *moral* Torah, on the one hand (which allegedly is still in force), and the *ceremonial* and *civil* laws, on the other? It might seem obvious that, if Jesus is Torah and if what matters

---

10. Scholem (1971, 238–39).

is the righteousness of the Torah, it is solely the moral Torah that concerns us. But where do we find a distinction, let alone a separation, between the moral laws and the ceremonial-civil laws in the Bible? Where do we find that a part of the Torah has been abrogated, and another part has not? Moreover, what moral command is there that has no ceremonial aspects and consequences, and what ceremonial command is there that has no moral root? Whatever the answer may be, what are its practical consequences?

When in the rest of this chapter we speak of Torah-keeping, we mean more than keeping the "moral Torah," say, the central Love Command. We are always including such typically Abrahamic or Mosaic matters as the commandments requiring circumcision, keeping Shabbat and the Jewish festivals, *kashrut* (the laws concerning *kosher* and *treif* [non-*kosher*][11] food), other purification laws, etc.

Two things may be clear. First, keeping the Mosaic Torah was never enforced upon the Gentile Jesus-believers, or even recommended to them, with the exception of the four commandments of Acts 15:20, 29 (see §8.3). But second, parallel to this, keeping the Mosaic Torah was never forbidden to the Jewish Jesus-believers. Rather, particularly the Messianic Jews living in Judea carefully observed the Torah, without any rebuke for this from any side (Acts 21:20). According to a certain (probably wrong) interpretation of Romans 14, some might call such Torah-keeping "weak" (see §9.3), but being weak is very different from being reprehensible. Scripture is very clear as to what *is* reprehensible:[12]

---

11. *Kosher* (lit., "fit") is the Ashkenazic pronunciation, which is almost universal among Western Jews. The Sephardic and Israeli pronunciation is *kasher* (emphasis on the last syllable), from which the word *kashrut* is derived. *Treif* literally means "torn"; it originally referred to meat that had been torn off by wild animals, and therefore was not *kosher*; later, this meaning was extended to all non-*kosher* food.
12. Cf. Stern (1999, 634).

THE ETERNAL TORAH: LIVING UNDER GOD

(1) To consider the "traditions of the elders" to be Torah, thereby declaring them to be equal with, or sometimes even superior to, the written Torah (Matt. 15:1–20; Mark 7:1–23). This is all the more serious when such traditions turn out to actually contradict the spirit of the Torah (cf., e.g., Mark 7:9–13). There is nothing wrong with traditions as such if they are part of Scripture, or at least are in line with Scripture (cf. literally in 1 Cor. 11:2; 2 Thess. 2:15; 3:6).

(2) The doctrine that keeping the Torah *as such* is a, or the, necessary ground for salvation, and thus, that faith in Jesus is insufficient, or not even required (Rom. 3:19–26; Gal. 2:16; 3:23).

(3) To require of Gentile Jesus-believers that they keep certain parts of the Torah which were intended for Jews only (Acts 15:20–21; Gal. 2:11–6:16; Col. 2:16–23), thereby in effect proselytizing them.

More points could be mentioned. One thing is sure, though: what is never called reprehensible is a Messianic Jew keeping the Mosaic Torah, just as every religious Jew is accustomed to doing. At the same time, this does not answer the question as to how precisely Jesus-believers are to view a Torah-keeping Messianic Jew. Is this simply up to them, and therefore should be of no concern to Gentile Jesus-believers? That seems to me too easy, and actually incorrect. Gentile Jesus-believers read the New Testament, too, and they too try to understand its doctrines and their intentions. It is a theological question that involves the whole Body of the Messiah, and its practical unity. Is it only "not reprehensible" that Messianic Jews keep the Torah, or is it *good*, yes, even *mandatory* that they do so? This question is important for Gentile Jesus-believers, too, for it requires a correct understanding of the Mosaic Torah, of its possible place in the present divine polity, and of its possible relevance for their own Christian life.

Therefore again, how are we to view a Torah-keeping Messianic Jew? Is it a "weakness" that Gentile Jesus-believers, as "strong" believers, have to tolerate in him (cf. Rom. 14)? Or is it *good* that a Jew who has come to faith in Jesus as the Messiah keeps the Torah, and continues doing so? Is he *obliged* to do so? Should Gentile Jesus-believers, if their opinion is asked at all, modestly encourage the Messianic Jew to continue keeping the Torah? But then, to what extent should the latter keep the Torah? These are some of the difficult questions we have to face.

5.1.3 Reconstructionism

One of the most remarkable and controversial answers to the question as to what part of the Mosaic Torah is still in force today has been given by so-called "Christian Reconstructionism," or "Theonomy," or "Kingdom Now" Theology. This is largely a North American movement developed by some Reformed theologians.[13] Outside North American Reformed and evangelical circles it is not very well known, but within these circles it has caused considerable discussion. The best known authors among them hold a postmillennial eschatology, involving the expectation of some Messianic Kingdom of peace and righteousness *before* the second coming of Jesus. Although not all people within this future Kingdom are going to be Jesus-believers, all nations of the world will have Christian governments during this age. In addition to this eschatology, Reconstructionists insist that Mosaic laws should be the basis for the modern legal order. That is, in any country where a Christian government has the power to enforce them, Mosaic laws are to be introduced.

The great issue among Reconstructionists involves precisely which Mosaic laws are to be enforced. They generally distinguish a number of Mosaic laws which they consider to have been fulfilled in Jesus and thus to have been abolished.

---

13. See especially Rushdoony (1973) and Bahnsen (1977); see comments by Barker and Godfrey (1990; various essays), Schreiner (1993, 30–31, 141–43), and Juster (1995, xv–xviii).

This includes the law of circumcision, *kashrut*, and of course the sacrificial laws. The so-called moral as well as civil laws, however, are considered to have continuing validity, not just in the lives of individual believers but also in civil society as a whole. Theonomists call these laws *standing laws*. These are laws that were not given to particular individuals or groups for particular occasions but are applicable to all people, individually and collectively, for all time. It is interesting to note the following distinctions:

[0] Most dispensationalist Jesus-believers believe that *no* element of the Mosaic Torah is still applicable today (except perhaps for Messianic Jews).

[1] Most Reformed Jesus-believers believe that only the *moral* statutes of the Mosaic Torah are still applicable today, not only for Jewish but also for Gentile Jesus-believers.

[1-2] Reconstructionists (or theonomists) believe that the *moral* and the *civil* Mosaic laws, but not the ceremonial laws, are still applicable today, not only individually but also collectively; not only for Jesus-believers but for all people.

[1-2-3] Messianic Jews believe that the entire Mosaic Torah, including the *moral*, the *civil*, and the *ceremonial* laws, is still applicable today, not only for (Messianic and non-Messianic) Jews but, as some believe, also for Gentile Jesus-believers.

It would be consistent, if one wishes to introduce the Mosaic standing laws, to claim that the corresponding penalties are to be enforced as well. This is indeed the view of some theonomists. Throughout this recent debate, some theonomists have insisted that homosexuals, adulterers, rapists, kidnappers, blasphemers, and practitioners of witchcraft should receive the death penalty for their sins. Theonomists argue that God does not change; if he once commanded such trespassers to be executed, there is nothing that has changed his mind in the present time. To put it even more strongly, some theonomists insist that the large increase of such heinous sins is allegedly due to society's disobedience in refusing to enforce the God-willed death penalty against those who rebel against God's Torah.

Reconstructionism illustrates in a very practical way the importance of determining whether the entire Mosaic Torah, or a certain part of it, is still in force. Of course, more is involved here than just a certain view of the Torah as such; theonomy also involves a certain Christian, or allegedly Christian, view of the nation state and of politics.[14] For instance, most Messianic Jews, believing that the Mosaic Torah is still applicable to them, and is perhaps even an ideal to be pursued by Gentile Jesus-believers, would never think of urging state governments to inflict the death penalty on trespassers. But is this consistent? Was it not the authorities in ancient Israel who executed professional criminals? Why not the authorities today?

Thomas Schreiner followed the easier way of refuting theonomy; he claimed that the Mosaic covenant was abolished, so the civil laws are no longer applicable.[15] Messianic Jews, who believe that the entire Mosaic Torah, including its civil laws, is still in force, have to refute theonomy the harder way. However, Schreiner supplied them with another valid argument: no contemporary nation state—I would include the present state of Israel—possesses the unique position of ancient Israel as a covenantal nation: "The nation of Israel was a unique entity as a covenant people. Today no nation has the unique privilege of a state and a religion ordained by God. This does not mean that the Old Testament law should not be consulted by nations today, nor does it deny that the nations are held responsible for failing to observe God's laws [Lev. 18:26-28; Deut. 2:10-23; Amos 1-2]. Moral principles found in the law of the Old Testament are normative for all states in all places. But the standing laws of the Old Testament should

---

14. Cf. Ouweneel (2014a).
15. Schreiner (1993, 141–42).

not necessarily be accepted as normative for modern states simply because they hail from the Old Testament." Schreiner points to Vern Poythress for a more careful, though perhaps not always satisfactory, attempt to apply the Mosaic Torah to modern states.[16]

5.2 The Mosaic Torah and the Messianic Torah
5.2.1 Three Questions

I now return to the heart of my argument, which involves the questions I asked in §2.2.1. My questions were:

1. *What is the link between the Mosaic Torah and the Messianic Torah?* My answer was that the Mosaic Torah is an incomplete manifestation of the one and only, eternal Torah as we now know it more perfectly in the Messianic Torah. Jesus-believers did not die to this eternal Torah but to the Mosaic manifestation of it, and then only insofar as it was misunderstood to be a way of salvation to be traveled in one's own strength. This misunderstanding specifically involves altering the covenant promise of Leviticus 18:5, "Keep my decrees and laws, for whoever obeys them will live by them. I am the LORD," from being a way *of* life into a way *to* life (even though Paul seems to *apply* this verse this way; cf. Rom. 10:5; Gal. 3:12). Clearly, in the Tanakh true believers also received eternal life on the basis of grace and faith, not on that of works as such.

2. If there is a link between the Mosaic Torah and the Messianic Torah, *to what extent are Jesus-believers under "the" Torah?* My answer was to consider the eternal Torah not as some part of the Mosaic Torah but as its focus and essence. We are under the entire Torah—not under the many temporary regulations contained in the Mosaic Torah but under the Torah in its eternal essence, as it has now been unfolded in the many regulations of the Messianic Torah.

3. If Jesus-believers are under "the" Torah, *does this hold in the same manner for Jewish and Gentile Jesus-believers?* My an-

---

16. Poythress (1991); cf. Karlberg (1986, 187–90).

swer was that the Mosaic Torah, as simply a temporary manifestation of the eternal Torah, is manifested under the New Covenant in a newer, richer form. This position has two interesting implications. On the one hand, it fully allows for the view that a great number of regulations under the Mosaic Torah had only a temporary significance, for example, in view of the agricultural economy of the Holy Land at the time, or in view of the very limited medical and hygienic knowledge of the time. On the other hand, this view supports Messianic Jews in their keeping Shabbat, the great festivals, *kashrut*, and many ceremonial purifications, because such regulations will also have a place in the future Messianic Kingdom *('olam habba*), that is, in the Millennial Torah (see extensively Ezek. 40–46).

What I am offering here is a kind of middle path between two opposing views. One view is that the Mosaic Torah was not abolished, and that it is essentially the same as the Messianic Torah. The other view is that the Mosaic Torah *was* abolished, and that the Messianic Torah is something essentially different. Both views agree in seeing all Jesus-believers to be under the Messianic Torah. They disagree about whether the Mosaic Torah has been abolished or not. Although there seems to be no third possibility, both views suffer a major defect. If the former position were true, I cannot see why in principle *all* commandments of the Torah would not pertain to *all* Jesus-believers, for they are *all*, Jews and Gentiles alike, under the Messianic Torah. If the latter position were true, the Mosaic Torah and the Messianic Torah are severed in a way not warranted at all by Scripture (see below). There are not two or more different "Torahs." It seems to me that both positions mentioned are untenable; in previous chapters, I suggested this way of reconciling the two: *There is only one (eternal) Torah, though appearing in different forms in successive dispensations.* I must now enter more deeply into this matter.

First, let me briefly summarize why I think that the Mosaic Torah, the Messianic Torah, and the Millennial Torah cannot be fully identical (some of these points are discussed further elsewhere in this study, especially in chapters 6 and 9).

1. *Circumcision*

* Under the *Mosaic* Torah, all males are to be circumcised (Lev. 12:3).

* Under the *Messianic* Torah, it is of course not forbidden to circumcise Gentile Jesus-believing males—if it is done without any motives of legalism or religious pride—but they are not required to be circumcised, as is clearly testified in 1 Corinthians 7:18b ("Was anyone at the time of his call uncircumcised? Let him not seek circumcision").

* Under the *Millennial* Torah, it seems that all believers on earth, Jews and Gentiles, will be circumcised (Isa. 52:1; Ezek. 44:9). (This does *not* hold for the Ekklesia of the present dispensation, for during the Messianic kingdom *she will be with Christ in glory, in glorified bodies.*)

2. *The Jewish festivals*

* Under the *Mosaic* Torah, all God's people must celebrate the Jewish festivals (Lev. 23).

* Under the *Messianic* Torah, Gentile believers do not have such a duty; it is not prohibited either, but the festivals could easily become a spiritual snare to them (Col. 2:16–23).

* Under the *Millennial* Torah, it seems that all believers on earth, Jews and Gentiles, will celebrate the Shabbat and the Jewish festivals (Isa. 56:1–7; 66:23; Ezek. 44:24; 45:18, 21–25; 46:1, 3–4, 6; Hos. 12:9; Zech. 14:16–19).

3. *The promised land*

* Under the *Mosaic* Torah, the promised land is the Holy Land of Israel (e.g., Gen. 15:18).

* Under the *Messianic* Torah, the promised land is, so to speak, the "heavenly places" (Eph. 2:6), an "inheritance . . . kept in heaven" (1 Pet. 1:4), "in the light" (Col. 1:12); our "citizenship" is not in ethnic Israel but "in heaven" (Phil. 3:20).

* Under the *Millennial* Torah, the people of Israel will again inherit the Holy Land (e.g., Deut. 30:1–10), but the nations will have their own countries (e.g., Isa. 19:23–25).

4. *The blessings*

* Under the *Mosaic* Torah, the specific blessings for those fulfilling it were primarily earthly and physical (Lev. 26:3–13; Deut. 28:1–14).

* Under the *Messianic* Torah, those fulfilling it have been "blessed in Christ with every spiritual blessing in the heavenly places" (Eph. 1:3). Of course, there is no strict division: there are spiritual blessings for Torah-observant Israel, and physical blessings for Messianic believers. But there is a difference in character, in emphasis. The specific nature of the blessings under the Mosaic Torah is different from the specific nature of the blessings under the Messianic Torah.

* Under the *Millennial* Torah, the specific blessings for those fulfilling it will again be earthly and physical, not excluding the spiritual, of course (Isa. 30:23–26; 32:15–20; 51:3; 60:13; 66:12–14; Jer. 31:12; Joel 2:23–27).

5. *The sanctuary*

* Under the *Mosaic* Torah, there was a physical sanctuary, first the Tabernacle, later the First and Second Temples.

* Under the *Messianic* Torah, there is a spiritual sanctuary, the Temple or House of God, of which Jewish and Gentile believers are the spiritual stones, namely, the Ekklesia, the Messianic Community (1 Cor. 3:16; 2 Cor. 6:16; Eph. 2:20–22; 1 Tim. 3:15; Heb. 3:6; 1 Pet. 2:4–5; 4:17).

* Under the *Millennial* Torah, there will be an earthly, physical sanctuary again, called the Third Temple (Ezek. 40–46).

6. *The priesthood*

* Under the *Mosaic* Torah, only the sons of the house of Aaron were priests (Exod. 28:1) — although it is true that all Israel was to be a "kingdom of priests" (Exod. 19:6). The priests

brought animal sacrifices.

* Under the *Messianic* Torah, all Jesus-believers are priests bringing spiritual sacrifices (Rom. 12:1-2; Heb. 13:15; 1 Pet. 2:5; Rev. 1:6; 5:10; 20:6), a fact that demanded a "change in the Torah" (Heb. 7:12). That is, the order of Aaron has been replaced with that of Melchizedek, so that Jesus, son of David, of the tribe of Judah, could become the High Priest under God's new polity (vv. 11-28). As such, he is the "great priest over the house of God" (10:21), which is "us" (3:6).

* Under the *Millennial* Torah, Jesus will be the celestial King and Priest, but the earthly priests will again be of the house of Aaron only, more specifically of the house of Zadok (Ezek. 40:46; 43:19; 44:15; 48:11; cf. 1 Chron. 6:3-10; see also Isa. 66:21; Jer. 33:18, 21; Mal. 3:6), and again will bring animal sacrifices (Ezek. 44-46) — although in a wider sense all Israel will be priests (Isa. 61:6), bringing spiritual sacrifices.[17]

After having outlined some differences between the Mosaic Torah, the Messianic Torah, and the Millennial Torah, I must emphasize one important point. Strict dispensationalists strongly emphasize the essential differences between the present dispensation, on the one hand, and the previous dispensation (from Moses to Jesus) and the following (Millennial) dispensation, on the other hand. But they hardly take into account the *transitional period* of the book of Acts, just as they seem to have little understanding for the *transitional period* that we apparently are entering today, just before the second coming of the Messiah (cf. §1.2.2). By "transitional" I mean that there was a time, from the Day of Pentecost (Acts 2), when Jewish and Gentile Jesus-believers did indeed form one Body of the Messiah, one Messianic Community, but when the myriads (tens of thousands) of Messianic Jews, particularly those in the Holy Land, nevertheless fully retained

---

17. Cf. Hos. 14:2, lit. "the calves of our lips" (KJV; Septuagint: "fruit of our lips"; cf. Heb. 13:15, "a sacrifice of praise to God, that is, the fruit of lips that acknowledge his name").

Is the Mosaic Torah Abolished or Renewed?

their Jewish identity (Acts 21:20). Today, I believe, it is God who is bringing about a significant Messianic Jewish movement, in which Messianic Jews, particularly those in the Holy Land, again retain their Jewish identity, and even cordially welcome Gentile Jesus-believers to join them and receive the blessings of keeping the Mosaic Torah.

No matter what we may think of this, strict dispensational theologians struggle with the fact that this Messianic Jewish movement exists at all, and exists *today*. Dispensationalists whole-heartedly believe in a spiritual future for a restored Israel in the Holy Land, but in the nineteenth and early twentieth centuries they were sure that God would lead the Jews back to their land only *after* the rapture of the Ekklesia.[18] And until some decades ago, dispensationalists were convinced that at least the formation of the believing Jewish remnant could occur only after the rapture.[19] They could afford to wholeheartedly believe in Israel's glorious future without bothering about Israel *today*—because it was all going to happen after the Christians would not be on the scene anymore. Today, however, dispensationalists have to rethink their position because the remnant of Israel—a remnant retaining its Jewish identity, even refusing to be called "Christians,"

---

18. Voorhoeve (1922, 164–65): "The first event we have to expect is the coming of the Lord Jesus in the air to take his Church to himself. . . . After that . . ., a part of the Jews . . . goes to Jerusalem in unbelief, rebuilds the temple there, and reintroduces its religious ceremonies." Cf. Kelly (1872, 221). Of course, this discussion makes sense only if pretribulationism (the doctrine that the Ekklesia will be raptured *before* the Great Tribulation; see Ouweneel 2012, chapter 10) is true.

19. Scott (1920, 162): "Immediately after the translation of the heavenly saints (1 Thess. 4. 15–17) God will work in grace among His ancient people." Pentecost (1964, 214): "[It is] necessary [to have] the pretribulation rapture of the church, so that God may call out and preserve a remnant [of Israel] during the tribulation in and through whom the promises may be fulfilled." Cf. Walvoord (1966, 139–43).

though recognized as belonging to the Body of the Messiah—is already appearing.

What are we to make of this? Are we to believe that present-day Messianic Jews are to be raptured with the rest of the Ekklesia, so that afterward God will need to start forming a Jewish remnant all over again, or are we to believe that Messianic Jews do not belong to the Ekklesia? As David Stern has put it: ". . . Nor is it thinkable that Messianic Jews are to be faced with the decision of whether to identify with their own people the Jews and stay to suffer, or with their own people the believers (the Messianic Community, the Church) and escape."[20] Of course, this is more an emotional than a theological argument, but it will help dispensationalists to think again. My subject now is not the pre-, or mid-, or post-tribulationist position (see §2.2.3). But the least we can say is that the rise of the present-day Messianic Jewish movement is a great challenge to all types of Christian theology.

Interestingly, some Jesus-believing Jews are strict dispensationalists themselves; a conspicuous example is the Russian-American Jew, Arnold Fruchtenbaum (see §5.2.2). In opposition to this group, we find Messianic Jews who maintain that Messianic Jews must fully retain their Jewish identity and are bound to the Mosaic Torah. A conspicuous example is the American-Israeli Jew, David H. Stern (see §5.2.3). Let us look more closely at their positions.

5.2.2 Arnold Fruchtenbaum

As far as I can determine, Arnold Fruchtenbaum (b. 1943) and David Stern (b. 1935) represent two main streams in today's Messianic Jewish theology. It is striking to note that their names hardly appear in recent writings about the Torah by Gentile Christian theologians. There is great interest in the matter of the Torah in the Pauline Letters, especially since the

---

20. Stern (1999, 623; cf. 575: "Is a Jewish believer, then, going to flee with the Jesus-believers or stay behind to suffer with the Jews?").

sensational studies by Ed Sanders, and in subsequent studies such as those by Tom Wright and Frank Thielman.[21] But in these studies, the voice of Messianic Jews is hardly heard, although the latter take a special interest in the matter because of the Mosaic Torah's practical relevance to them. Both Fruchtenbaum and Stern are professional theologians.

In his extensive study and PhD dissertation, *Israelology*, Fruchtenbaum made the following allegations, either directly or by means of references to other writers with whom he apparently agrees on these points.[22]

1. "The Mosaic Torah was given to Israel and not to the Church. Just as Israel belonged to a dispensation different from that of the Church, there is a different Torah in each dispensation. The Mosaic Torah holds for Israel, the Messianic Torah holds for the Church. This is indicated in Galatians 3:16–25: the Mosaic Torah was in force till the Messiah would come. The Dispensation of Faith (or, Grace) follows upon the Dispensation of 'the' Torah. Since Jesus, the Mosaic Torah is not in force anymore, not even for Israel."

My response: Scripture does not know of two or more Torahs; there is only one, eternal Torah, although it may assume different forms in successive dispensations. This is not a play on words. I firmly believe that *essentially* the Mosaic Torah and the Messianic Torah are one and the same Torah. This is shown by the fact, mentioned earlier, that the Old Covenant is not a conditional but definitely an unconditional as well as an everlasting covenant; the New Covenant is not a replacement but a renewal of the Old Covenant. Israel's priesthood is everlasting (Exod. 29:9; 40:15; Num. 25:13), and its *torot* are everlasting (Lev. 3:17; 16:34; 24:9; Num. 19:21); that is, they will last as long as Israel lasts.[23]

---

21. Sanders (1977, 1983; see Appendix II); Wright (1991, 1997); Thielman (1995).
22. Fruchtenbaum (1992, 373–80, 476–94, 588–601, especially 640–80).
23. The Jewish scholar, Saadiah Gaon (tenth century), argued that

2. "The Mosaic Torah was a unity, so that, if this Torah is not in force anymore, formally speaking the Decalogue is not in force anymore either. The fact that under the Messianic Torah we are not allowed to steal, to kill, or to lie either does not mean that the two Torahs are identical, or that the Decalogue is still in force. This is corroborated by the fact that at least one commandment, that of the Shabbat, has no meaning anymore in the Messianic Torah. The Mosaic Torah was the rule of life for the believer in the Tanakh, the Messianic Torah is the rule of life for the believer in the New Testament."

My response: When Paul shows that we are under the Messianic Torah, specifically, the Love Command, he quotes the Mosaic Torah as evidence for that claim (Rom. 13:8-10; Gal. 5:13-15; Eph. 6:2-3). This clearly shows the basic unity and continuity of the Mosaic Torah and the Messianic Torah. If Paul wanted to say that we should not murder or steal, and that we should honor our parents, it would have been improper and misleading to quote the Ten Commandments as evidence for this if these commandments had been formally replaced by other commandments.

3. "Many passages clearly and explicitly show that the Mosaic Torah has come to an end, such as Romans 7:4, 6; 10:4, 2 Corinthians 3:2-11; Galatians 3:23-4:7; Ephesians 2:14-15, Hebrews 7:11-18."

My response: The verses mentioned do not necessarily show anything more than that the legalistic polity has come to an end. Translations are sometimes misleading, though. For instance, the NIV says in Ephesians 2:14-15 that Jesus "destroyed the barrier, the dividing wall of hostility, by setting aside in his flesh the Torah with its commands and regu-

---

Israel is a nation only by virtue of the Torah, that God has stated that Israel will endure as long as heaven and earth (Jer. 31:35–36), and that therefore the Torah will last as long as heaven and earth (*Emunot v'dê'ot* 3:7). Philo and Maimonides were of the same opinion (Harvey 1972, 1244–45).

lations." In my view, this is not at all what Paul intended. What was "set aside" was not the Torah but the hostility. ESV makes the same mistake: ". . . by abolishing the Torah of commands . . ." (v. 15). Compare NKJV: Jesus "has broken down the middle wall of separation, having abolished in His flesh the enmity, [that is], the law of commandments [contained] in ordinances." Here, the phrase needing to be supplied in our English translation, "[that is]," is best understood to mean "occasioned by." Because of Jews' and Gentiles' sinful nature (*yetzer ra*), the Torah, proudly hailed by Jews and despised by (pagan) Gentiles, had occasioned hostility between the two. By dying to sin, Jesus abolished this hostility; factually he did this by bringing those Jews and Gentiles who believed in him together into one Body, the Ekklesia, the Messianic Community.

4. "In Matthew 5:17-18, Jesus refers to the Mosaic Torah including even the least commandments of it. Now, it is clear that many of these commandments have become obsolete (a good example is offered in Mark 7:19, in which Jesus abolishes kashrut), so that Jesus cannot mean that this Torah is still in force. Apparently, he only means that he obeyed this Torah during his life on earth, and that he brought out its true meaning."[24]

My response: It is hard to believe that if Jesus wanted to say only that he kept the Torah during his life or wanted to bring out its true meaning, he would have said that he did not want to "abolish" the Mosaic Torah. In my view, Matthew 5-7 shows the very opposite. Precisely by bringing out its true meaning he showed how "the" Torah would function in the new dispensation. It would indeed function in a new way;

---

24. The Jewish scholar, Hans Joachim Schoeps (1950, 61), claims that it is possible to deduce virtually the entire history of dogma from the attempts to interpret Matt. 5:17. All such attempts in the early church (at least six) presupposed a positive attitude of Jesus to the Mosaic Torah.

however, that does not make the Messianic Torah a different Torah, but at best a new manifestation of "the" (one, eternal) Torah.

5. "Several Scriptures only demonstrate that the Jesus-believer is free to keep parts of the Mosaic Torah if he so wishes, not that he is required to keep this Torah as such (e.g., Acts 18:18; 20:16; 21:17–26)."

My response: The Scriptures mentioned do not show that the Jesus-believer is free to keep parts of the Mosaic Torah if he so wishes, but they and other passages show rather that Paul and the other apostles consistently kept the Mosaic Torah throughout their lives (see §5.3). Was this merely to demonstrate their freedom? Where does Fruchtenbaum find evidence for this idea? Do not the passages show instead that it was completely natural to the Messianic Jews to keep the Mosaic Torah as they had done before? I will supply ample evidence for this.

5.2.3 David Stern

Another significant Messianic Jewish theologian, David Stern, presented a view that in many respects is diametrically opposed to that of Fruchtenbaum. I suppose Stern would largely agree with my brief responses just given. Yet, at some points he seems to go to the other extreme:[25]

1. "There is only one Torah, so the Messianic Torah is nothing but the continuation of the Mosaic Torah. Not being under the Torah anymore but under grace, does not mean that the Mosaic Torah is not in force anymore, but that the legalistic principle has been replaced with the grace principle."

My response: I take a middle position here, between Fruchtenbaum and Stern: the Messianic Torah is not a different Torah (*contra* Fruchtenbaum), nor is it identical with the Mosaic Torah (*contra* Stern), but the two are different manifestations

---

25. Stern (1997, 125–187), and see Stern (1999) on various relevant Scriptures.

in successive dispensations of the one, eternal Torah.

2. "A gospel without the Torah is no gospel at all; if the Torah would no longer be in force, the line of communication with rabbinical Judaism is simply cut."

My response: This is hardly a compelling argument; if the Torah were no longer in force, we simply would have to honestly acknowledge this to Jews in the rabbinical tradition (non-Messianic orthodox Jews), just as we Christians must honestly confess to them that Jesus is the Messiah, which they are not pleased to hear either. But fortunately, that line of communication is not severed.

3. "If the Mosaic Torah is still in force there are two restrictions: some elements of the Mosaic Torah have been abolished, especially the duty to bring sin offerings, and the ceremonial and civil parts of it are not binding for Gentile Jesus-believers."

My response: There are no restrictions in the Mosaic Torah whatsoever as it is in force today. Even the Torah of the sin offerings has not been abolished, as is shown by the fact that in the future Messianic Kingdom sin offerings will be sacrificed in the Third Temple (§6.2.2). Therefore, Messianic Jews who really believe that they are under the Mosaic Torah should be consistent; if today a temple would be built in Jerusalem, they should be willing to take part in the complete sacrificial service.

4. "However, it is God's desire that the latter Jesus-believers, too, get to know the Torah and learn to enjoy its blessings by learning to keep it (cf. Acts 15:21)."

My response: There is not the slightest indication in the New Testament that Gentile Jesus-believers are encouraged to get to know the Mosaic Torah and to come to enjoy its blessings by learning to keep it. At least, Acts 15:21 ("from ancient generations Moses has had in every city those who proclaim him, for he is read every Sabbath in the synagogues") does not necessarily point into this direction (§8.3.3). Stern himself supplies us with six very different interpretations of this difficult verse.[26]

5. "The precise nature of the restrictions with regard to keeping the Mosaic Torah, and the way the other commandments have to be observed, is to be determined by appropriate *halakhic* authorities, appointed by Messiah himself."

My response: Appropriate *halakhic* authorities cannot be anyone else than the apostles, and that only insofar as their decrees are contained in the New Testament. Apart from the New Testament, there are no authorities that can formally prescribe how Jesus-believers should live. Elders of a local congregation have authority only over congregational life, and only insofar as their regulations are in agreement with the New Testament. They are to expound the New Testament, and they may determine in what way specifically they are going to apply this or that rule in their congregation. But they can hardly make genuinely new *halakah*.

5.3 Jesus and Messianic Jews Kept the Mosaic Torah
5.3.1 Jesus

Perhaps the best way to analyze the matters raised in §5.2 further is to start with the indubitable fact that Messianic Jews in the New Testament, including the great "apostle to the Gentiles" (Rom. 11:13), have consistently kept the Mosaic Torah during their lives. To begin with, this was naturally true of Jesus himself.[27] He may be called a "Messianic Jew" in the sense that he was a Jew who believed that he himself, Jesus, is the Messiah. This self-identification has been denied, but in Matthew 16:17 Jesus fully accepted the confession by Simon Peter: "You are the Messiah, the Son of the living God."[28] Je-

---

26. Stern (1999, 279).
27. See extensively Friedman (2001, 3–43).
28. Of course, one can always deny this biblical proof by claiming such a passage to be an inauthentic saying of Jesus. Vermes (1973, 141–43) refers to the five passages where Jesus himself teaches

sus also acknowledged this before Caiaphas, the high priest ("Again the high priest asked him, 'Are you the Messiah, the Son of the Blessed?' And Jesus said, 'I am'," Mark 14:61-62), and even publicly before "the Jews," or more correctly, "the Judeans": "the Jews gathered around him and said to him, 'How long will you keep us in suspense? If you are the Christ, tell us plainly.' Jesus answered them, 'I told you, and you do not believe'" (John 10:24-25).

Of course, this was revolutionary. Jesus said other stunning things. For instance, he denied that a Jew as such, purely because he belonged to the chosen people, would have access to the Kingdom of God, and Jesus made repentance and rebirth a condition for entering the Kingdom (Matt. 5:3, 10, 19-20; 6:33; 7:21-23; 13:19-23; 17:25-26 ["sons" vs. "others"]; 18:3-4; 19:14; 21:31; Luke 5:32; 15:7; John 3:3-5). Though recognizing Israel's election (Matt. 10:5-6; 15:21-28), Jesus opened up this way of repentance and rebirth into God's Kingdom even for so-called "outlaws" — the "sinners" (Matt. 9:10-13; 11:19 and par.) — and the Gentiles, without ever demanding that they would repent in the way prescribed by the rabbis, namely, by observing the Mosaic Torah (Matt. 8:10-12; 12:38-42; 13:37-38; 21:43; Luke 11:29-32; 13:28-30). He even claimed that his own physical body was the true Temple of God on earth (John 2:19-22). But here is one thing Jesus never did: he never attacked, or even questioned, the Torah, not to mention that he would never have trespassed the Torah.

To many Jesus-believers this is self-evident, but they think this applies only to the Written Torah. However, in fact Jesus did not attack the Oral Torah either. On the contrary, he said, "The scribes and the Pharisees sit on Moses' seat, *so do and observe whatever they tell you*, but not the works they do. For they

---

on the subject of the Messiah (Mark 9:41; 12:35-37; 13:6; Luke 24:26,46), but claims that only the one in Mark 12 "can be counted as authentic." At least in this passage, then, "Jesus' rhetorical statements imply a veiled self-affirmation" (Lane 1974, 438).

preach, but do not practice. They tie up heavy burdens, hard to bear, and lay them on people's shoulders, but they themselves are not willing to move them with their finger" (Matt. 23:2-4, italics added). Thus, Jesus definitely advised the people to faithfully keep the instructions of the Torah-teachers. For instance, he accepted the great significance of the *Shema* as part of the commandments for Israel (Mark 12:29); the *Shema* is a creed to be recited twice a day, according to the rabbis (cf. Deut. 6:4, 7). The prayer Jesus taught his disciples, which we know as "the Lord's prayer" (Matt. 6:9-13), was entirely in line with rabbinical prayers in his day; it exhibits clear similarities to the *Qaddish* and the *Amidah* or *Shemoneh-Esreh*. Another example is that, as David Bivin and Roy Blizzard have shown, many difficult sayings of Jesus can be easily explained from contemporaneous Jewish writings.[29]

Several Jewish writers of the twentieth century (Hans-Joachim Schoeps, Jacob Neusner, David Flusser, Pinchas Lapide, etc.[30]) have indeed attempted to show that none of what Jesus taught was essentially new, that is, was not already contained in rabbinic teaching that preceded his. Rabbi Harvey Falk wrote that Jesus "never wished to see his fellow Jews change one iota of their traditional faith. He himself remained an Orthodox Jew to his last moment."[31] Of course, this is not entirely correct; it certainly did not hold for what Jesus taught about *himself*, not only his Messiahship but also his divine Sonship (in the synoptic Gospels, especially Matt. 11:27).

Yet, the rabbis have a point in stressing that Jesus' Torah

---

29. Bivin and Blizzard (1984). An interesting example (144–45) is the "good eyes" and the "bad eyes" (Matt. 6:22–23; Luke 11:34); apart from rabbinic literature, we would not have known that the former refers to a generous, and the latter to a greedy, person (cf. Wilson 1989, 121; Stern 1999, 32).
30. See, e.g., Schoeps (1949), Neusner (1983, 1986), Flusser (1988, 1998), Lapide (2004, 2011).
31. Falk (2003, 158).

Is the Mosaic Torah Abolished or Renewed?

teaching hardly *deviated* essentially from general rabbinic tradition. E. P. Sanders has underlined this in several of his studies.[32] He rightly rejected Eduard Schweizer's reprehensible view that Jesus "again and again ostentatiously transgressed the Old Testament commandment to observe the Sabbath and had little concern for the Old Testament laws relating to ritual purity."[33] And Sanders accepted Geza Vermes' belief that Jesus never broke a biblical commandment or opposed a basic Jewish belief (except the Sadducees' denial of the resurrection of the dead, Matt. 22:23-33 and par.), though he clashed with others over customs, particularly those which the Pharisees had "invested with a quasi-absolute value, but which to him were secondary to biblical commandments."[34] Vermes later wrote: "Nowhere in the Gospels is Jesus depicted as deliberately setting out to deny or substantially alter any commandment of the Torah *in itself*. The controversial statements turn either on conflicting laws where one has to override the other, or on the precise understanding of the full extent of a precept."[35]

Here is Sanders' summary:[36] "The synoptic Jesus lived as a law-abiding Jew. He accepted Deut. 6.5 and Lev. 19.18 as the 'two greatest' commandments, and his epigram, 'Do unto others,' is based on Lev. 19.18 + 19.34 . . . in choosing them Jesus fixed on the passages which others of his time also saw

---

32. Sanders (1985, 245–69); Sanders (1990).
33. Schweizer (1971, 32).
34. Vermes (1973, 35); see Sanders (1990, 2). Vermes' examples of clashes over customs come from Mark 2:16, 24; 7:1 and par.
35. Vermes (1993, 21). Cf. Daube (1956, 55–62) who, on the basis of rabbinic tradition, argues that "You have heard . . . but I tell you" does not mean, ". . . I tell you something else [than the Torah]," but may mean (in my words), "You have literally understood (or, You might understand literally). . . . But rather take it in the following way"—which does not affect the Torah as such but only our (broadened) understanding of it.
36. Sanders (1990, 90).

as central. He attended the synagogue [this was his custom, Luke 4:16. WJO], he did not eat pork, he did not work on the sabbath in any obvious way. He accepted the sacrificial system as atoning (Matt. 5.23f.) and purifying (Mark 1.40-44). In common with other teachers, he cautioned his followers not to sacrifice until wrongdoing had been rectified and grievances assuaged [Matt. 5.23-26]. He also paid the temple tax — by a very curious means [17.24-27]. On the sabbath there are two minor infringements: his disciples pick grain [Mark 2.23-28], he puts his hand on a sick woman to heal her (Luke 13.10-17).[37] In both cases there is a legal defense: hunger overrides the law, and the sabbath is made for people, not people for the sabbath; everyone unties and leads animals to water on the sabbath."[38]

On what other points might Jesus' views seem to be at variance with the Torah? The most significant cases appear to be the following:

(1) *Purity*. In the parable of the Good Samaritan (Luke 10:30-35), Jesus implicitly "criticizes a priest and a Levite for not being willing to risk coming into contact with a corpse."[39] They did not know whether the man by the side of the road was dead; touching a corpse would have made them ritually unclean, and would have hampered them in their Temple ministry.[40] This was true for the priests (Lev. 21:14), but possibly the Levites had accepted some of the restrictions laid on the priesthood. Jesus in fact required priests and Levites to

---

37. There are more than two cases: see Matt. 12:10–13 (and par.) (the man with the shriveled hand) and Luke 14:1–6 (the man suffering from dropsy).
38. Cf. Sanders (1990, 22): "[T]hese incidents on the sabbath, even if taken as literally true in all their aspects, were extremely minor in the context of the period."
39. Sanders (1990, 41).
40. We have to note, though, that the priest was "going *down* that road" (v. 31), that is, traveling from Jerusalem to Jericho; his Temple service was over.

Is the Mosaic Torah Abolished or Renewed?

risk transgression of the Torah when there was a chance of helping an injured person. In this way, Jesus did not reject the Temple ministry as such, nor the purification laws as such, but the attitude of being too squeamish with regard to them, at the expense of mercy and the love of God (cf. Matt. 23:23; Luke 11:42).

(2) *Tithes*. In Matthew 23:23 Jesus did not condemn tithing mint, dill, and cumin as such, for he explicitly said that one should not neglect this. But he argued that one should not spend "too much time making sure that the tithing laws were kept,"[41] thus neglecting the more important things: justice, mercy, and faithfulness. Jesus does not turn against the Torah of tithing (Num. 18:24-28; Deut. 14:22-29; 26:12-13), but against a wrong (one-sided) attitude toward tithing.

(3) *Oaths*. The Torah mentions several kinds of oaths (Exod. 22:10-11; Lev. 5:4; Num. 5:19, 21; 30:2, 10, 13; Deut. 6:13; 10:20), but also warns against swearing falsely (Lev. 5:1, 4; 6:3; 19:12; cf. Exod. 20:7). When Jesus told his disciples not to swear oaths at all (Matt. 5:16-22), this was no contradiction of the Torah as such, "since the person who does not swear obviously would not transgress the law which forbids swearing falsely."[42] At the same time, Jesus' new command appeared to go beyond the Mosaic Torah. Compare this with the matter of divorce, which, though not recommended, was tolerated in the Mosaic Torah "because of your hardness of heart" (Matt. 19:8), but as a matter of principle was prohibited in the Messianic Torah (vv. 4-6, 9). Likewise, oaths were tolerated in the Mosaic Torah but were basically prohibited in the Messianic Torah. In these cases, the Messianic Torah does not contradict the Mosaic Torah but surpasses it.

(4) *Phylacteries and tassels*. The former are boxes containing Scripture verses, worn on the forehead and arms (Heb. *tefillin*; Deut. 6:4-9; 11:13-20; cf. Exod. 13:9, 16), the latter are

---

41. Sanders (1990, 48).
42. Ibid., 55.

fringes (Heb. *tzitziyot*) on the corners of the *tallit*, the prayer shawl (Num. 15:37-41). In Matthew 23:5 Jesus did not reject wearing *tefillin* or *tzitziyot* as such; in fact, he himself appears to have worn the latter.[43] Rather, he protested against making the *tefillin* "broad" and the *tzitziyot* "long," thus exaggerating obedience, probably to make a show of it (cf. vv. 6-7). "We note that the criticism has to do with a matter of degree, not the practice itself."[44]

In summary, we may conclude with Sanders: "Jesus did not seriously challenge the law as it was practiced in his day, not even by the strict rules of observance of pietist groups — except on the issue of food [Mark. 7:15, 19]."[45] I do not agree with the latter exception, as I will show in §9.2.2; in my view, Jesus did not protest against *kashrut* at all. For points other than those dealt with by Sanders, which might be taken to suggest that Jesus did not faithfully observe, or even acknowledge, the Mosaic Torah, I refer to §6.3.2. For the time being, I conclude that Jesus never criticized the Mosaic Torah as such, but always lived in strict observance of it, even according to the generally accepted interpretations of the Torah. This was not simply because this was all before Calvary and before Pentecost (Acts 2), as if things drastically changed after that. In the next sections, I will attempt to show that even *after* Pentecost, Paul and the other apostles lived precisely as Jesus had done all his life: as Torah-observing Jews.

I therefore do not agree with Dunn's allegation that if "Jesus' attitude to tradition was radical the attitude of the ear-

---

43. Matt. 9:20; 14:36 and par.: "the fringe of his garment"; "fringe" (Gr. *kraspedon*) is the same as the "fringes" in 23:5. Vermes (1993, 16) is convinced that, here too, *kraspedon* = *tzitzit*. Only in this way can we understand why the woman touched precisely this part of Jesus' clothes. Likewise, the robe of a Jew that will be taken hold of by Gentile men (Zech. 8:23) may refer to the *tzitzit* attached to it (Berkowitz 1999, 71-72).
44. Sanders (1990, 72).
45. Ibid., 96.

Is the Mosaic Torah Abolished or Renewed?

liest Jerusalem Christians seems to have been much more conservative,"[46] nor with his theory about "a much deeper divide between Paul and the Jewish Christianity emanating from Jerusalem than at first appears,"[47] and "a deepening rift between Paul and the Jerusalem church . . . the sharpness of the antagonism between Paul and Jerusalem can hardly be overstated,"[48] nor that Paul "was rejected totally by the Jewish Jesus-believers."[49] Dunn even goes so far as to say that it "was probably inevitable that Paul should become associated with a Gnostic anti-Judaism."[50] I do not believe there is any convincing evidence for any of these statements.

5.3.2 The Apostle Paul (1)

Messianic Jews in the New Testament, including the great apostle to the Gentiles, have consistently kept the Mosaic Torah throughout their lives.[51] On the one hand, no one was more strongly opposed to enforcing Torah-keeping, including circumcision, upon the Gentile Jesus-believers than the apostle Paul. He did not even recommend it to them, but quite the contrary (1 Cor. 7:18). On the other hand, we read no more clearly and extensively about anyone keeping the Mosaic Torah than we read concerning this very apostle, who never opposed Torah-keeping by Messianic Jews, as long as they did not do it for legalistic and similar reasons. Rather, Paul himself always frankly confessed that he had remained a Jew (Acts 21:39; 22:3; Rom. 11:1; 2 Cor. 11:22).

To be sure, he stated that in Messiah there "is neither Jew nor Greek, there is neither slave nor free, there is no male and female, for you are all one in Messiah Jesus" (Gal. 3:28). And

---

46. Dunn (1990a, 64).
47. Ibid., 254.
48. Ibid., 255.
49. Ibid., 296.
50. Ibid., 295; see further §5.3.3.
51. See extensively Friedman (2001, 47–75).

surely, "in one Spirit we were all baptized into one body—Jews or Greeks, slaves or free" (1 Cor. 12:13). And surely, Jesus Messiah made Jewish and Gentile Jesus-believers "one," creating "in himself one new man in place of the two," reconciling "us both to God in one body through the cross," and "through him we both have access in one Spirit to the Father" (Eph. 2:14–18). But just as in everyday Christian living the distinction between male and female, and between slave and free, was perpetuated, the same held for the distinction between Jew and Gentile.

Within the Ekklesia, it would be utterly wrong to try to ignore sexual and social differences. It would be equally wrong to try to ignore the differences between Jew and Gentile. Why would it be incorrect for Messianic Jews to behave in a Jewish way, if believing Gentiles are free to keep behaving in a self-consciously Greek (or American, or Dutch) way?[52] There is nothing wrong with the latter—as long as the distinction between Jesus-believers and unbelievers is maintained—so what could be wrong with Messianic Jews retaining their Jewish identity? And then, living the American or Dutch way was never divinely prescribed to the Americans or the Dutch—but living the way of the Torah was definitely prescribed by God to the Jews. And when they come to believe in Jesus as Messiah, Savior, and Lord, they do not become less Jewish but more Jewish than ever before.

Paul wrote, "Was anyone at the time of his call already circumcised? Let him not seek to remove the marks of circumcision. Was anyone at the time of his call uncircumcised? Let him not seek circumcision. For neither circumcision counts for anything nor uncircumcision, but keeping the commandments of God. Each one should remain in the condition in which he was called" (1 Cor. 7:18–20). When one's eternal salvation or one's position in the Ekklesia is at stake, being circumcised (Jew) or uncircumcised (Gentile) means noth-

---

52. Berkowitz (1999, 224–25).

Is the Mosaic Torah Abolished or Renewed?

ing. First, both are equally saved by the grace of God and the blood of Jesus alone (Rom. 10:12). Second, within the Ekklesia the two are on perfectly equal footing (Eph. 2:19). Third, their practical value before God is not measured by their being Jew or Gentile, but by their faithfulness to the Messianic Torah, that is in fact, to Jesus himself (Rom. 8:4; 13:8–10). All the same, the Jew remains a Jew, and the Greek remains a Greek, like a man remains a man, and a woman remains a woman. Neither of them should try to change that; let the Messianic Jew by all means remain a Jew, and the Gentile Jesus-believer by all means remain a Gentile.[53]

Paul himself never made it a secret that after he accepted Jesus as Messiah, he remained a Jew. He called non-Messianic Jews his "brothers," his "kinsmen according to the flesh" (Rom. 9:3; cf. Acts 13:26, 38; 22:1, 5; 23:1, 5–6; 28:17), as did other Messianic Jews (Acts 2:29; 3:17; 7:2). Paul said of non-Jesus-believing Jews, "Are they Hebrews? So am I. Are they Israelites? So am I. Are they offspring of Abraham? So am I" (2 Cor. 11:22, present tense). He even did not reckon himself among Israel only, but also still among the Pharisaic party in Israel: "My brothers, I *am* a Pharisee [*egō Pharisaios eimi*], the son of Pharisees" (Acts 23:6, present tense; italics added), that is, a member of "the strictest party of our religion" (26:5). He still felt bound to the civil Torah because he appealed to the Torah over against his judge (23:1–5). In other words, some twenty years after his conversion Paul still numbered himself among the strictest Torah-keepers in Israel—a real *shomer-mitzvot* ("keeper of the commandments").

To be sure, elsewhere he said that he was "circumcised on the eighth day, of the people of Israel, of the tribe of Benjamin, a Hebrew of Hebrews; as to the law, a Pharisee; as to zeal, a persecutor of the church; as to righteousness under the

---

53. This is true quite apart from the fact that American Jews and Dutch Jews—Messianic or not—in general are very American and very Dutch, respectively.

Torah, blameless. But whatever gain I had, I counted as loss for the sake of Christ" (Phil. 3:5-7). In other words, there was something that surpassed his noble descent, namely, his relationship with Jesus. And insofar as his descent had included legalism this descent was only "loss": "Indeed, I count everything as loss because of the surpassing worth of knowing Christ Jesus my Lord. For his sake I have suffered the loss of all things and count them as rubbish, in order that I may gain Christ and be found in him, not having a righteousness of my own that comes from the Torah, but that which comes through faith in Christ, the righteousness from God that depends on faith" (vv. 8-9). But please note: it was not Paul's Jewishness and circumcision as such that was "loss" and "rubbish" — for God himself had granted him these privileges and attached great value to them — but it was his ethnocentric and legalistic arrogance that had been associated with these privileges and had kept him from Jesus for a certain amount of time.

What Paul's practical Jewishness meant to him is obvious from some other examples. During his second missionary journey he found at Lystra a young man, Timothy, "a son of a Jewish woman who was a believer, but his father was a Greek" (Acts 16:1). Paul wanted to take this young Jesus-believer, who "was well spoken of by the brothers at Lystra and Iconium" (v. 2), along with him on the journey. However, he realized that, because Timothy had a Jewish mother, according to Jewish custom he was considered to be a Jew. Therefore, we read that he "circumcised him because of the Jews who were in those places, for they all knew that his father was a Greek" (v. 3).

Of course, one might object that this was only a concession to the non-Jesus-believing Jews. But first, Paul was not the type of person who made such concessions to please other people but which actually violated his own convictions (cf. Gal. 1:10). Second, for Paul, circumcision did not contribute anything whatsoever to one's salvation and one's standing before God (Gal. 5:6; 6:15). Third, we should remember that

Is the Mosaic Torah Abolished or Renewed?

Paul was dead set against forcing Gentile Jesus-believers to get circumcised (Gal. 5:2). All the same, in this case Paul just as decisively circumcised a Jewish young man. Whatever his motives may have been, this example shows at least that no one could honestly forbid a Messianic Jew to have his sons circumcised. Rather, every Messianic Jew should feel as much attached to the people of Israel, of which he is still a part, as Paul did. And such a Jew should realize just as much that he would forfeit that attachment if he would not have his sons circumcised.

The reason for having these sons circumcised is not because this would add anything to their salvation, or to their parents' salvation. They are circumcised simply because they were born of Jewish parents, and thus belong to God's ancient covenant people. The parents' faith in Messiah does not change that at all; on the contrary, through that faith they reached the true fulfillment of their Jewishness. As I said, the Jew who believes in the Messiah is not less a Jew, but *more* so, and more *truly* so. From a redemptive point of view, circumcision in itself does not "count for anything," as we just saw in 1 Corinthians 7 and Galatians 5. Therefore, the circumcision of a Jew who rejects the Messiah amounts to nothing more than identifying him as a Jew. Faith in Messiah does not render a Jew's circumcision worthless, however, but gives circumcision its true meaning: "For no one is a Jew who is merely one outwardly, nor is circumcision outward and physical. But a Jew is one inwardly, and circumcision is a matter of the heart, by the Spirit, not by the letter. His praise is not from man but from God" (Rom. 2:28–29).[54]

If Paul really wanted to say that, viewed from any viewpoint whatsoever, circumcision for a Messianic Jew did not

---

54. For now I am disregarding the question whether, according to Paul, the believing Gentile in a sense is also a true "Jew," or whether he is speaking solely of natural born Jews (cf. Stern 1999, 336–40). See Appendix I.

mean a thing, he would not have circumcised Timothy. What he wanted to say in Romans 2 is that circumcision *without faith in Messiah* had no meaning. We find the very same thing in the Tanakh, namely, that what matters is that the Jew has not only his male sexual organ circumcised but also his heart (Lev. 26:41; Deut. 10:16; 30:6; Jer. 4:4; 6:10; 9:26; Ezek. 44:7, 9) as well as his ears (Jer. 6:10; Acts 7:51) and lips (Exod. 6:12, 30).[55] Without the circumcision of heart, ears, and lips, the circumcision of the sexual organ is worthless. But God never says that Jews who have the circumcision of the heart do not need (any longer) the circumcision of the sexual organ. That is a false contrast, which is never made in the Tanakh or in the New Testament. Circumcision was *forbidden* in the case of Gentile Jesus-believers if it was viewed as essential to salvation, which it wasn't, or if they wanted to become full proselytes, for which there was no reason. Gentile Jesus-believers join not Israel but the Ekklesia, and they remain Gentiles; Jewish Jesus-believers join the Ekklesia too, and at the same time remain Jewish (see Appendix I). Therefore, circumcision was not forbidden in the case of Messianic Jews; on the contrary, it was required if a Jew wanted to remain part of the people of Israel. Paul the Jew certainly wanted to remain part of Israel. And he wanted Timothy, too, to live like a real Jew, that is, with circumcision administered not only to his heart, but also to his sexual organ.

How self-evident Paul considered both his Jewishness and his Jewish lifestyle can be seen in Acts 18:18: "At Cenchreae he had cut his hair, for he was under a vow." The passage does not tell us what kind of vow this was, for which he had his hair cut off, but we do know that the so-called Nazirite vow involved letting one's hair grow during the time of the vow, after which one's hair was cut off (Num. 6:1–21). According

---

55. Cf. Pirqe de R. Eliezer 29; a Qumran source (1QS 5.1–5) speaks of the circumcision of "the foreskin of the [evil] inclination and disobedience" (see Shulam 1998, 107–8, 111–12).

Is the Mosaic Torah Abolished or Renewed?

to the rules of the Torah, this can hardly have been a true Nazirite vow, because in that case Paul would have had his hair cut off only in Jerusalem (cf. Num. 6:22), where it would have been placed on the altar along with the sacrifices assigned to accompany it (cf. §5.3.3 about Acts 21:23-24). We therefore do not know precisely whether this was indeed a Nazirite vow; perhaps it was an adapted form of it, which could have become customary in the Diaspora. At any rate, the verse shows that, also after his conversion to Jesus, Paul continued observing certain Jewish customs. Even long after his conversion, he could testify that he had never done anything against the "Torah of the Jews" (Acts 25:8), or even against the "customs of our fathers" (the rabbinic regulations, Acts 28:17). This is the clearest testimony one could imagine. *Paul never transgressed the Mosaic Torah, and not even the rabbinic traditions* (as long as they agreed with the Torah in spirit and letter).[56] Therefore, he could say, "I always take pains to have a clear conscience toward both God and man" (Acts 24:16), that is, both before and after his conversion to Jesus.

Paul's faithfulness to the Torah is evident as well from his desire to travel to Jerusalem in order to celebrate there the Feast of Pentecost (Acts 20:16). This is the Jewish Feast

---

56. I therefore strongly disagree with Dunn's allegation (1990a, 64) that Paul felt "that the traditions of Judaism were shackles which imprisoned faith." In my view, the Scriptures being discussed here show that Paul went much further than just going "along with his old traditions when in the company of orthodox Jews" (65). Dunn is right in stating that, according to Paul, "faith in Christ could not and must not be made to depend on the observance of certain traditions" (65), but he does not see that Paul may have had other reasons for following the Mosaic Torah, and even many Jewish traditions, than legalism or accommodation. Following the present-day theological custom of ascribing the Pastoral Letters to a later generation, Dunn can even suggest, falsely so, in my opinion, that in the Pastorals "we seem closer to the Pharisees' attitude towards the oral law than to the attitudes of Jesus and Paul towards the tradition of their time" (69-70).

of Weeks (*Shavu'ot*) (Lev. 23:15-21), which every Jewish man was supposed to celebrate in the Holy Land (Deut. 16:9-12, 16). According to the Western text in Acts 18:21, on another occasion Paul was eager, too, to travel to Jerusalem for one of the festivals (NKJV: "I must by all means keep this coming feast in Jerusalem"), possibly *Pesach*. To be sure, Paul was flexible in this matter if the circumstances in the Lord's work required so (cf. 1 Cor. 16:8-9); but this was entirely within the limits of the Mosaic Torah (see §8.1). Presumably, Paul also observed the Day of Atonement (*Yom Kippur*), for this is the Jewish festival described in Acts 27:9 as "the Fast" (see ESV note). This day falls between the middle of September and the middle of October, a time at which shipping on the Mediterranean Sea became too dangerous. For someone like Luke — presumably a proselyte of Gentile descent — it was apparently still customary to measure time by the Jewish calendar, which seems to imply that he and Paul indeed still observed *Yom Kippur*. Just as naturally, Luke referred to *Matzot*: "we sailed away from Philippi after the days of Unleavened Bread" (20:6). Paul apparently kept *Shavu'ot* and *Pesach*.

The apostle also regularly attended the synagogue services, not explicitly as a missionary but as a common Jewish man; otherwise he would not have been invited to speak a word during such services (13:14-47; 14:1; 17:1-4). According to H. L. Ellison, Paul must have worn the *tzitziyot* (see §5.3.1); otherwise no synagogue would have allowed him to speak.[57]

5.3.3 The Apostle Paul (2)

There seem to be other signs that Paul never denied his Jewish origin, and remained attached to Jewish tradition all his life. In light of Acts 20:6, just quoted, it is quite possible that Paul was referring to the early Jesus-believers' literal observance of *Pesach*:[58] "Messiah, our Passover [*Pesach*] lamb, has

---

57. Quoted by Juster (1995, 86, 214–15, 306, 310).
58. Cf. Stern (1999, 447–49).

been sacrificed. Let us therefore celebrate the festival [*Seder*], not with the old leaven [*chametz*], the leaven of malice and evil, but with the unleavened bread [*matzah*] of sincerity and truth" (1 Cor. 5:7-8; see on this point §8.2).[59]

A second obscure sign of Paul's continued Jewishness is that he said, "I have fought the good fight, I have finished the race, I have kept the faith. Henceforth there is laid up for me the crown of righteousness, which the Lord, the righteous judge, will award to me on that Day" (2 Tim. 4:7-8). Paul is using the expression "righteous Judge" (Heb. *dayan tzedeq*) here, which is still used in the Jewish burial service. The expression is found in 2 Maccabees 12:6, 41, in connection with the good fight of faith against God's enemies, and with those who had fallen in this fight.

Here is a third example: Paul spoke of "the fragrance of the knowledge of him. For we are the aroma of Messiah to God among those who are being saved and among those who are perishing, to one a fragrance from death to death, to the other a fragrance from life to life" (2 Cor. 2:14-16). Here the gospel gives us knowledge of God as the Torah did for Israel. Presumably this was a well-known expression in Judaism, for in the Talmud the Torah is called a flavor of life for one man, and a flavor of death for another.[60]

Here is a fourth example: in the Letter to the Hebrews,

---

59. If Paul is writing in 1 Cor. 5 about the literal *Pesach*, he probably wrote the Letter briefly before this festival, and not after it, as Stern suggests (1999, 488). It is interesting that in this one Letter, Paul writes about all the seven festivals of Lev. 23: *Pesach* (5:7-8), *Shavu'ot* (16:8), Jesus the firstfruit in resurrection as typified in the *'Omer Reshit*, the "sheaf of the firstfruits" (Lev. 23:10), presented to God on the first day of the week after *Matzot* (1 Cor. 15:20, 23) (the literal day on which Jesus rose from the dead). The *Shofar* in 15:52 reminds us of *Rosh HaShanah*, Israel's "New Year" (Lev. 23:23–25), while his "coming" (v. 23) points to *Yom Kippur*, and "the kingdom" (v. 24) to *Sukkot*.

60. Yoma 72b.

THE ETERNAL TORAH: LIVING UNDER GOD

whose author I believe may have been Paul, it is interesting that the author in a Jewish way avoids the name of God[61] by using such a typical euphemism as the "Majesty on high [or, in the heavens]";[62] in Hebrew, *HaG'dulah BaM'romim* or *HaG'dulah BaShamayyim* (cf. Matt. 26:64, "at the right hand of Power [*dynamis*]").

Interestingly, Paul was not only familiar with current and older non-canonical Jewish writings, but he did not hesitate to refer to them. Besides the many apparent references to the common apocryphal books, Paul seemed to hint at 1 Enoch 46:3 (Col. 2:3), 3 Maccabees 5:35 (1 Tim. 6:15) and 4 Maccabees 2:5 (Rom. 7:7). In 1 Corinthians 10:4 ("the spiritual Rock that followed them") Paul appeared to be familiar with a Jewish tradition that speaks of the "Well of Miriam, which was the rock that Moses had struck and that rolled and went along with Israel during their travellings."[63] Also compare references to the book known as Ascension of Isaiah 5:11-14 (Heb. 11:37), and 1 Enoch 70:1-4 (Heb. 11:5).[64]

Paul's continuing Jewishness comes to light also in his frequent use of the midrashic way of reasoning by freely applying certain Tanakhic passages "out of context." Striking examples are found in Romans 9:25-26 (free application of Hos. 1:10; 2:23); Romans 10:6-8 (Deut. 30:12), 18 (Ps. 19:4); 1 Corinthians 9:9-10 (Deut. 25:4); 1 Corinthians 14:21 (Deut. 28:49;

---

61. Cf. John, who speaks of those who went out "for the sake of the name" (3 John 7; cf. Acts 5:41), which is a well-known Jewish euphemism (*HaShem*) for YHWH.
62. Heb. 1:3, megalōsynē en hypsēlois; 8:1, megalōsynē en tois ouranois.
63. Tana'it 9a; Shabbat 35a. Philo (*Legum Allegoriae* 2.21) interpreted the rock in Deut. 8:15 as follows: "The rock of flint is the Wisdom of God from which he feeds the souls that love him." Possibly, "Paul in equating Christ with the Rock was thinking of Him as the Divine Wisdom" (Davies 1955, 153).
64. See further references to Assumption of Moses (Jude 9), 1 Enoch 1:2 (1 Pet. 1:12), 1:9 (Jude 14–15), 60:8 (Jude 14). For all these references, see Aland et al. (1983, 910).

Isa. 28:11); 2 Corinthians 3:3 (Exod. 24:12; 34:1; Deut. 10:2; Jer. 31:33; Ezek. 11:19; 36:26), 2 Corinthians 7 and 13 (Exod. 34:30, 35); Galatians 3:16 (Gen. 22:18); Galatians 4:21–31 (Gen. 16:15; 21:2, 9–10; Isa. 54:1); and Hebrews 7:3 (Gen. 14:18–20).

There is also similarity between some of his prayers and common Jewish prayers, particularly the *Shemoneh-Esreh* (= "Eighteen"), the principal synagogue prayer (also called *'Amidah*, "Standing," because of the required position when it is prayed), recited three times a day. We find reminiscences of several of its nineteen (formerly eighteen) petitions in the New Testament Letters:

 * First blessing ("Praise be to you, Lord, our God and God of our fathers, God of Abraham, God of Isaac and God of Jacob"; cf. 2 Cor. 1:3; Eph. 1:3; also Acts 3:13; 24:14; 1 Pet. 1:3).[65] Romans 11:28 reminds us of the phrase: "Remember the pious deeds of the patriarchs." The phrase "God our Savior" in the Pastoral Letters reminds us of God being called in this first blessing "King, Helper, Savior and Shield."

 * Second blessing ("You cause the dead to live . . . you bring death, bring life, and bring salvation to spring forth, therefore you can be counted on to cause the dead to live"; cf. Rom. 4:17; Heb. 11:19).

 * Fourth blessing ("You grant knowledge to mankind and teach people understanding. Grant us knowledge, understanding and insight from yourself"; cf. Eph. 1:8, 17; Col. 1:9).

 * Fifth blessing ("Praise to you, Lord, who is gracious to forgive abundantly"; cf. Rom. 5:15, 20; Eph. 1:7–8; 1 Tim. 1:14).

 * Tenth blessing ("sound the great trumpet for our freedom . . . and gather us into one from the four corners of the earth"; cf. 1 Cor. 15:52; 1 Thess. 4:16; also cf. Matt. 24:31; Rev. 11:15).

---

65. Also compare the phrase "he chose us . . . in love" (v. 4) with the close of the *Ahavah* benediction (referring to the revelation of the Torah): "Praise be to you, Lord, who has chosen your people Israel in love."

THE ETERNAL TORAH: LIVING UNDER GOD

* Fifteenth blessing ("speedily cause the Branch of David your servant to flourish. Exalt his horn by your salvation.... You... cause the horn of salvation to flourish"; cf. Acts 13:23; Luke 1:69).

* Nineteenth blessing or *Sim shalom* ("Put peace, goodness, blessing, grace, kindness and mercy upon us and upon all Israel, your people"; cf. Gal. 6:16; 1 Tim. 1:2; 2 Tim. 1:2; also cf. Heb. 4:16; 2 John 3; Jude 2). This blessing also refers to the "book of life" (cf. Phil. 4:3; also Rev. 3:5; 13:8; 17:8; 20:15; 21:27).

Another famous synagogue prayer is the *Qaddish*, whose phrase "Praise be to God forever and ever" reminds us of Romans 9:5; 11:36; 16:27; Galatians 1:5; Philippians 4:20; 1 Timothy 1:17; 2 Timothy 4:18 (cf. Heb. 13:21; 1 Pet. 1:23; 4:11; 5:11; 2 Pet. 3:18; Rev. 1:6; 5:13; 7:12). The petition "May he who makes peace in his high places [quoted from Job 25:2] make peace for us and for all Israel" reminds us of Romans 15:33; 16:20; Philippians 4:9; 1 Thessalonians 5:23; and especially 2 Thessalonians 3:16 (cf. Luke 19:38; Heb. 13:20-21).[66]

In Acts 22:12, the apostle Paul is able to inform the Jewish crowd that Ananias, the Jewish disciple of Jesus (cf. 9:10) who had visited Paul (then Saul) after his Damascus experience, was "a devout man according to the Torah [NIV: devout observer of the Torah], well spoken of by all the Jews who lived there." At that time, it was apparently normal that Messianic Jews diligently kept the Torah; moreover, it was still possible for a Messianic Jew to be highly respected by all the non-Messianic Jews for Torah observance. Obviously, it did not occur to Messianic Jews in those days, both in Israel and abroad,

---

66. It has often been noted that the opening phrases of the *Qaddish* ("Magnified and hallowed be his great name throughout the world, which he has created according to his will, and may he establish his Kingdom during your life and during your days, and during the life of the whole house of Israel, speedily and soon; and say ye, Amen") strikingly corresponds to those of the Lord's Prayer.

to live differently from the way all godly Jews had always lived. It was said of Zechariah and Elizabeth, the parents of John the Baptist, that they were "righteous before God, walking blamelessly in all the commandments and statutes of the Lord" (Luke 1:6). Who told the Messianic Jews after the Pentecost event of Acts 2 that henceforth they were not supposed to observe the Mosaic Torah anymore? If anyone might have told them it would have been the apostle Paul. In fact, his Letters are often quoted precisely to prove that Messianic Jews should not keep the Mosaic Torah anymore. But surely, Paul himself is the best interpreter of his own Letters. And surely, his own behavior showed exactly the opposite, since he was a strict Torah-keeper all his life.

Finally, please note that for Paul the Torah was so self-evident that even to a *Gentile* audience he loved to quote the Torah, and thereby implicitly encouraged his largely Gentile readers to study the Pentateuch. It was to the *Gentile* Galatians that he posed the question: "Tell me, you who desire to be under the Torah [i.e., the Mosaic Torah], do you not listen to the Torah [i.e., the Pentateuch]?" (Gal. 4:21). For the rest, see the following (not necessarily complete) survey of Torah passages that Paul quotes to a largely Gentile audience as a self-evident source of divine knowledge:

Gen. 2:7	1 Cor. 15:45
Gen. 2:24	1 Cor. 6:16; Eph. 5:31
Gen. 12:3	Gal. 3:8
Gen. 15:5	Rom. 4:18
Gen. 15:6	Rom. 4:3, 22; Gal. 3:6
Gen. 16:15	Gal. 4:22
Gen. 17:5	Rom. 4:7–8
Gen. 17:10–11	Rom. 4:11
Gen. 18:10, 14	Rom. 9:9
Gen. 21:2, 9	Gal. 4:22
Gen. 21:10	Gal. 4:30

THE ETERNAL TORAH: LIVING UNDER GOD

Gen. 21:12	Rom. 9:7
Gen. 22:18	Gal. 3:8
Gen. 25:23	Rom. 9:12
Exod. 9:16	Rom. 9:17
Exod. 12:40	Gal. 3:17
Exod. 13:21; 14:22	1 Cor. 10:1
Exod. 16:15; 17:6	1 Cor. 10:3
Exod. 16:18;	2 Cor. 8:15
Exod. 20:12	Eph. 6:2–3
Exod. 20:13, 17	Rom. 13:9
Exod. 29:45	2 Cor. 6:16
Exod. 32:6	1 Cor. 10:7
Exod. 33:19	Rom. 9:15
Exod. 34:33	2 Cor. 3:13
Lev. 11:44–45	1 Pet. 1:16
Lev. 18:5	Rom. 10:5; Gal. 3:12
Lev. 19:18	Rom. 13:9; Gal. 5:14
Lev. 26:11–12	2 Cor. 6:16
Num. 9:18	1 Cor. 10:1
Num. 11:4	1 Cor. 10:3
Num. 14:2, 36	1 Cor. 10:8, 10
Num. 20:11	1 Cor. 10:3
Num. 21:4; 25:1, 9	1 Cor. 10:8, 10
Num. 26:64–65	1 Cor. 10:3
Num. 35:30	2 Cor. 13:1
Deut. 1:33	1 Cor. 10:1
Deut. 5:16–21	Rom. 13:9; Eph. 6:2–3
Deut. 10:14	1 Cor. 10:28
Deut. 10:16	Col. 2:11
Deut. 10:17	Gal. 2:6; Eph. 6:9; Col. 3:25
Deut. 13:5; 17:7,9	1 Cor. 5:13

Deut. 19:15	2 Cor. 13:1
Deut. 19:19; 24:7	1 Cor. 5:13
Deut. 21:23	Gal. 3:13
Deut. 25:4	1 Cor. 9:9
Deut. 27:26	Gal. 3:10
Deut. 29:3-4	Rom. 11:8
Deut. 30:12-14	Rom. 10:6-8
Deut. 32:17	1 Cor. 10:20
Deut. 32:21	Rom. 10:19
Deut. 32:35	Rom. 12:19
Deut. 32:43	Rom. 15:10

5.3.3 Other Messianic Jews

In Acts 21:20, we read that the Messianic Jews said the following to the apostle Paul: "You see, brother, how many thousands [*myriades*, lit., tens of thousands] there are among the Jews [or, Judeans] of those who have believed. They are all zealous for the Torah." Paul is told here as a most natural thing that the tens of thousands of Messianic Jews in Judea were zealous keepers of the Torah. As James Dunn put it: "They apparently continued to observe the law without question, not interpreting their traditions of Jesus' words and actions in a manner hostile to the law. Hence the Pharisees seem to have seen in them little or nothing of the threat which Jesus posed (Acts 5:33-39) and not a few became members of the Jesus-sect while still remaining Pharisees (Acts 15:5; 21:20).... They evidently continued to be firmly attached to the temple, attending daily at the hours of prayer (Acts 2:46; 3:1) ... since Judaism has always been concerned more with orthopraxy than with orthodoxy (right practice rather than right belief) the earliest Jesus-believers were not simply Jews, but in fact continued to be quite 'orthodox' Jews. . . . Altogether it is a form of Christianity which we today would scarcely recognize"⁶⁷ (except among Messianic Jews).

In Acts 21, Paul did not protest the fact that the Messianic Judeans zealously kept the Torah; on the contrary, he was pleased to demonstrate that he himself, too, was a Jew who was still faithful to the Torah. The brothers presented the following matter to him (v. 21): "[T]hey have been told about you that you teach all the Jews who are among the Gentiles to forsake Moses, telling them not to circumcise their children or walk according to our customs." Please note carefully what is said here. Many Gentiles and even quite a few Jewish Jesus-believers find it self-evident that Jews who have faith in Messiah no longer circumcise their sons or observe Shabbat, the Jewish festivals, *kashrut*, and other purification laws. They *teach* the very thing of which the Judean Jesus-believers *falsely accused* Paul.

If Paul held the same view, this would have been the moment to inform the Messianic Judeans: Let me be honest about this, brothers, I do indeed teach the Jews in the Diaspora not to circumcise their sons or live according to our customs. But no, this was not at all what Paul did.⁶⁸ What people had been told about Paul was pure slander. He had *not* told the Jews who had come to faith in Jesus not to circumcise their sons or live according to Jewish customs anymore. To put it more strongly, he apparently taught believing Jews that they *should* circumcise their children and live according to the customs, or *at least he did not object to this*. Actually, he hardly had to stress this matter. For in the light of the Tanakh, what is more obvious than that a Jew wanting to serve God observes the Mosaic Torah? And if a Jew gets to know the Messiah and accepts him in faith, does this make him a better or a worse Jew?

---

67. Dunn (1990a, 238–39).
68. This seems to have been totally overlooked by Dunn (1990a, 256), who uses the episode precisely as an argument for alleging "a fundamental antipathy on the part of the Jewish Jesus-believers to Paul himself and to what he stood for," even after this episode.

Is the Mosaic Torah Abolished or Renewed?

Some things that always remain the same are so self-evident that they do not have to be explicitly emphasized in the New Testament.

The same Paul who fought against imposing the Mosaic Torah on Gentile Jesus-believers kept that Mosaic Torah himself, just like all other Messianic Jews. This was not mandatory, in the sense of the immature child that is under his father's commands and is constantly monitored by the supervisor (cf. Gal. 3:19–4:7). Nor was it weakness, sin, or concession. It was the "freedom in the Messiah" (cf. 2:4), the self-evidence of being Jewish, of being even more Jewish than before by having accepted Jesus as the Messiah. The early Jewish Jesus-believers' Torah-keeping involved living in the light of both God's earlier revelation, particularly the Old Covenant, and also in the light of the New Covenant. There is no gap between the Old Covenant, on the one hand, and the New Covenant as it will be established with Israel in the future, on the other hand. Between the Old Covenant and that future establishment of the New Covenant with Israel, Israel is still God's covenantal people, even if *Lo-Ammi* ("Not My People") is written on the nation for the time being. "To them belong the adoption [i.e., as son, Exod. 4:22], the glory [i.e., the *Shekinah*], the covenants, the giving of the Torah [Heb., *Matan Torah*], the worship [i.e., the Temple service] and the promises" (Rom. 9:4).

Jewish Jesus-believers belong to the Ekklesia, the Messianic community of Jewish and Gentile Jesus-believers. But they have never stopped being Jews. In between the Shabbat and the festivals, the circumcision and the purification laws of the Old Covenant, on the one hand, and the Shabbat and the festivals, the circumcision and the purification laws of the New Covenant, on the other hand, Jewish Jesus-believers self-evidently observe the Shabbat and the festivals, the circumcision and the purification laws. It is one of the wonders of these last days that a Messianic Jewish movement has arisen that grasps this natural matter in a fresh way.

Paul was pleased to demonstrate his loyalty to the Torah by practicing, in a way visible to all, one of the Jewish customs. The brothers proposed, "What then is to be done? They will certainly hear that you have come. Do therefore what we tell you. We have four men who are under a vow; take these men and purify yourself along with them and pay their expenses, so that they may shave their heads. Thus all will know that there is nothing in what they have been told about you, but that you yourself also live in observance of the Torah" (Acts 21:22–24). In other words, prove that you are still a good Jew, an observer of the Mosaic Torah! To reassure Paul, the brothers added, "As for the Gentiles who have believed, we have sent a letter with our judgment that they should abstain from what has been sacrificed to idols, and from blood, and from what has been strangled, and from sexual immorality" (v. 25; cf. Acts 15:20, 29). In other words, as truly as we believe that only these four commandments are to be imposed upon the Gentile Jesus-believers, we believe that the Jewish Jesus-believers are to keep the Mosaic Torah.

Paul did what they asked: "Then Paul took the men, and the next day he purified himself along with them and went into the temple, giving notice when the days of purification would be fulfilled and the offering presented for each one of them" (v. 26). Here again, a Nazirite vow was probably involved, accompanied by the burnt offering, the sin offering, and the peace offering (Num. 6:14). Paul not only paid the expenses of these four apparently poor brothers, but because of his participation he himself, too, had to be accepted and ritually purified by the priests. According to verse 27, the entire process lasted seven days. By his participation Paul demonstrated before everyone that he was a good Jew, who lived in obedience to (lit., walked on the right path of keeping) the Torah (v. 24).

Paul did not do this merely as a concession to the Messianic Jews in Judea, for, as we saw, in Acts 18:18 he had followed a similar Jewish custom entirely voluntarily. Nowhere in Acts

Is the Mosaic Torah Abolished or Renewed?

is Paul's action here condemned or branded as weakness. Such condemnation and branding of Paul's behavior arises simply from the theological prejudices of some expositors; Scripture nowhere teaches that. On the contrary, what else would we expect from these tens of thousands of Messianic Jews, living among other, non-Messianic, Jews? For them, living according to the Torah was just as natural as it was for the early believers to keep meeting together in the Temple courts (Acts 2:46), for Paul to pray in the Temple after his conversion (Acts 22:17), and for Peter and John to go "up to the temple at the hour of prayer, the ninth hour" (3:00 p.m.; Acts 3:1). At that hour the evening burnt offering (*Minchah*) was sacrificed in the Temple. As long as this Temple remained standing, Messianic Jews apparently participated in the ministry of the Temple, including even the sacrificial ministry. If shortly afterward Peter referred to "the God of Abraham, Isaac and Jacob" (Acts 3:13), he was quoting from the evening prayers that had just been uttered during *Minchah*.

As I said, the early believers also kept attending synagogue services (Acts 9:20; 13:5, 14; 17:1–2, 10, 17; 18:4, 19, 26; 19:8). Of course, someone like Paul went there to share the gospel with fellow Jews. Yet, as I said earlier, he could have attended there only if he behaved like a Jew and participated in the service (see §5.3.2). This included using *tefillin*, *tallit*, and *tzitzit*, and praying the fixed Jewish prayers. The Messianic Jews obviously had their own synagogues, too. In James 2:2, a Letter addressed "to the twelve tribes in the Dispersion" (i.e., the Israelites scattered among the nations; 1:1), it literally says, "If a man comes into your synagogue. . . ." Although the word can indeed mean "assembly" or "meeting," elsewhere in the New Testament it is *always* translated "synagogue." One must have very strong reasons to deviate from this customary translation in a Letter addressed to Jews.[69]

---

69. I found the translation "synagogue" in the Darby Translation and the Complete Jewish Bible. The Orthodox Jewish Bible renders it

As I mentioned in §1.2.1, even after the destruction of the Temple, communities of Messianic Jews ("Nazarenes") continued to exist until the fifth century. They continued observing the Torah as well as they could. Under the pressure of a church that became more and more anti-Semitic and consisted almost exclusively of Gentile Jesus-believers, these Messianic Jewish communities gradually died out. They were absorbed into the church and lost their Jewish identity. For centuries, the world became accustomed to Jewish Jesus-believers who gave up their Jewish identity under pressure, or who themselves adapted to the Gentile life-style. As a consequence, we find it perfectly normal and appropriate that Jewish Jesus-believers no longer keep the Torah. However, it seems that we should instead consider this kind of conduct by such Jewish Jesus-believers to be very *abnormal*. Jewish Jesus-believers are Jews par excellence—and faithful Jews are Torah-keepers. Not the Torah-keeping Jewish Jesus-believer, but the non-Torah-keeping Jewish Jesus-believer, is anomalous—"anomalous" being related, in both etymology and meaning, to the word "lawless."

"Beit HaKnesset (House of Assembly, shul, synagogue, shtibel)."

Chapter 6
The Messianic Torah and the Millennial Torah

The Torah of the L<small>ORD</small> is perfect,
   reviving the soul;
the testimony of the L<small>ORD</small> is sure,
   making wise the simple;
the precepts of the L<small>ORD</small> are right,
   rejoicing the heart;
the commandment of the L<small>ORD</small> is pure,
   enlightening the eyes.

Psalm 19:7–8

Give attention to me, my people,
   and give ear to me, my nation;
for a Torah will go out from me,
   and I will set my justice for a light to the
   peoples. . . .
Listen to me, you who know righteousness,
   the people in whose heart is my Torah.

Isaiah 51:7, 7a

Summary: *The Messianic Torah does not form a contrast with the Mosaic Torah, but is rather the spiritualization, the deepening and enrichment of it. Both Jesus and the apostles have made this clear in* *their teaching. This can be beautifully illustrated by means of the Ten Commandments. The Millennial Torah, which will be in force during the Messianic Kingdom, differs from both the Mosaic Torah and the Messianic Torah in that it contains many of the moral, civil, and ceremonial precepts of the Mosaic Torah, but along with the deepening and enrichment of the Messianic Torah. This has consequences for the way of life of Messianic (Jesus-believing) Jews today, a matter on which they do not always agree among themselves.*

6.1 The One, Eternal Torah

6.1.1 In Jesus' Words

SO FAR, WE HAVE CLAIMED THAT THE MESSIANIC TORAH, Jesus' Love Command worked out in the many concrete New Testament commandments, is not essentially different from the Mosaic Torah, but it is not identical with it either. The Messianic Torah must not be identified with the temporary and limited Sinaitic form of the Torah as concentrated in the Ten Words. The latter could never be the complete and final form of "the" (eternal) Torah, if only for the simple reason that eight of the Ten Commandments are negative. They are prohibitions in the form of "You shall *not*. . . ." The primary purpose of this form is apparently not to encourage the faithful but rather to discourage the sinner.[1] Yes, this form *proves* to him that he is a sinner: "[T]hrough the Torah comes knowledge of sin" (Rom. 3:20; cf. 5:20; 7:5, 7-8; 1 Cor. 15:56; Gal. 3:19; 1 Tim. 1:8-9). This negative aspect has now come to an end: it has been fulfilled and absorbed by Jesus (cf. John 1:17). From *that* legal polity, as an externally imposed way of life, capable of being turned into a path of self-redemption, we have been released (Acts 15:10; Rom. 6:14-15; 7:4-6; Gal. 2:19; 4:5; 5:18).

---

1. This does not necessarily imply, though, that the addressees of the Decalogue are viewed as *only* sinners. As Gutbrod (1967, 1037) points out, in the Decalogue there "is not commanded what establishes the relation to Yahweh, but prohibited what destroys it." See chapter 4 above.

However, that does not mean that Jesus abolished the Sinaitic Torah; rather, he fulfilled it, brought it back to its divinely intended fullness. This is the central message of the Sermon on the Mount: "Do not think that I have come to abolish the Torah or the Prophets; I have not come to abolish them but to fulfill them" (Matt. 5:17). This "fulfilling" can indeed refer to his own keeping of the Torah in his human life; he always kept the Mosaic Torah. It can also refer to his "fulfilling" the Tanakh as prophecy: "[T]ruly, I say to you, until heaven and earth pass away, not an iota, not a dot, will pass from the Torah until all is accomplished" (v. 18). But the context suggests that the import of Jesus' words is much broader. In particular, it appears to mean: "extending, deepening" (cf. Matt. 7:12; 22:40). Several of the Ten Words are taken as examples of how they are not abrogated but revealed now in a form that is both more positive and more profound. In this way, the limited, temporary Mosaic Law was *elevated to* and *absorbed into* the Messianic Torah. A polity was abrogated, but an eternal substance was preserved and continued.

In the Sermon on the Mount, Jesus did not abrogate any Mosaic commandment, despite the fact that some expositors have thought so.[2] What he did is this. First, if necessary, he unmasked the traditional additions and distortions by the ancestors, which obscured the deep meaning of the Torah. Second, he brought to light the more profound, moral content of the Torah. Some examples may illustrate the tremendous contrast between the literal form of the Mosaic Torah and the Messianic Torah. On the one hand, the Messianic Torah is much more *severe*, on the other hand, it is much more *lovely* and *sublime* than the Mosaic Torah. As W. D. Davies put it: "[W]e cannot speak of the Law being annulled in the antith-

---

2. My claim is supported by, e.g., Vermes (1993, 37): "[I]t is to be concluded that ... the six 'antitheses' [Matt. 5:21–22, 27–28, 31–32, 33–34, 38–39] ... in no way can ... be identified as a frontal attack by [Jesus] on the Law of Moses or on traditional Judaism."

eses [of Matt. 5:22, 28, 32, 34, 39, 44: 'But I say to you . . .'], but only of its being intensified in its demand, or reinterpreted in a higher key."[3] Or as Messianic Jew Dan Juster put it: "Matthew 5–7 seeks to distill the essence of Torah insofar as it reflects God's eternal standards of love and truth. It is not the Old Testament dispensation exposited nor the millennial ethic;[4] it is God's eternal law made clear and applied to human life in this unjust world . . . *so far as the Books of Moses reflect God's eternal law*, they will never pass away."[5]

To underscore this, let me quote from what to my knowledge is the very first book devoted by a modern non-Messianic Jewish scholar to Jesus, a book by Joseph Klausner: "In [Jesus'] ethical code there is a sublimity, distinctiveness and originality in form unparalleled in any other Hebrew ethical code. . . . If ever the day should come and this ethical code be stripped of its wrappings of miracle and mysticism [sic], the Book of Ethics of Jesus will be one of the choicest treasures in the literature of Israel for all time."[6]

I will now mention seven examples of Mosaic commandments dealt with by Jesus, and in each case I will note *three* things: in the Messianic Torah, the negative commandment is (1) sharpened even further, but then also (2) turned into a positive commandment, for the performance of which (3) Jesus himself provides the great example. The result is that all of these commandments turn out simply to be variations of the one, central Love Command.

First Commandment:[7] "You shall have no other gods before

---

3. Davies (1969, 29).
4. Juster (1995, 50) gives the example that, in the Millennium, Jews will no longer "be constrained by Roman soldiers to carry their load a mile as in the first century" (Matt. 5:41).
5. Juster (1995, 51).
6. Klausner (1925, 414).
7. According to the usual Christian numbering; in Jewish numbering, this is the Second Word.

me." Under the Old Covenant, this is a negative commandment, that is, a prohibition; not even this one could be kept by natural man. Under the New Covenant, this commandment is applied the more sharply. Thus, even greed,[8] or disowning Jesus, is considered to be idolatry (Eph. 5:5; Col. 3:5; 1 John 5:20-21; cf. 1 Sam. 15:23, regarding "presumption"). Of course, the Tanakh also knew the positive form of this commandment, that is, to serve God alone (Exod. 23:25; Deut. 6:13-15; 10:12, 20; 11:13; 13:4; Josh. 24:20-22). But in the New Testament this commandment extends to serving Jesus and, in a sense, forms the heart of the Messianic Torah: "[A]lthough there may be so-called gods in heaven or on earth—as indeed there are many 'gods' and many 'lords'—yet for us there is one God, the Father, from whom are all things and for whom we exist, and one Lord, Jesus Messiah, through whom are all things and through whom we exist" (1 Cor. 8:5-6). Jesus himself is the great example of giving all due honor to God, of serving and loving him, and doing his will alone (Matt. 4:10; Luke 4:8; John 4:34; 5:30; 6:38), just as we do the will of God and of Jesus Messiah alone (Rom. 12:2; Eph. 5:17; 6:6; Col. 1:9-10; 4:12; 1 Thess. 4:3; 5:18; Heb. 13:21; 1 Pet. 4:2-3; 1 John 2:17).

Positive Messianic commandment: *"You shall love and serve only the one God, the Father, and the one Lord, Jesus Messiah, and do his will."*

Third Commandment: "You shall not take the name of the LORD *your God in vain."* This commandment is explained elsewhere in the Torah: "You shall not swear by my name falsely, and so profane the name of your God" (Lev. 19:12). It became a habit in Israel to soften this prohibition in that people did not swear by the name of YHWH or God, but by "heaven" (cf. Luke 15:18,

---

8. The Gr. *pleonexia* ("greed") is man's striving for getting, by all possible means, an advantage over others, for reaching his own goals without reckoning with God or his fellow-man (cf. Rom. 1:29; 1 Cor. 6:10-11; 2 Cor. 2:11; Eph. 5:3; see Selter [1986]). He turns himself into an idol, desiring to subject all men and all things to himself.

21), or even by "the earth," or by "Jerusalem." About this practice Jesus said, "Again you have heard that it was said to those of old, 'You shall not swear falsely, but shall perform to the Lord what you have sworn.' But I say to you, Do not take an oath at all, either by heaven, for it is the throne of God, or by the earth, for it is his footstool, or by Jerusalem, for it is the city of the great King. And do not take an oath by your head, for you cannot make one hair white or black. Let what you say be simply 'Yes' or 'No'; anything more than this comes from evil [or, the evil one]" (Matt. 5:33-37). "Swearing" takes place when people wish to reinforce their statements by appealing to God, so that other people will the more readily believe them. Jesus argues that his disciples should not need to do this; they should be known as thoroughly trustworthy. Instead of taking the name of the Lord in vain, "we should use the holy name of God only with reverence and awe, so that we may properly confess God, pray to God, and glorify God in all our words and works."[9] Paul applied the requirement of this commandment in terms of Jesus in a special way: "Do I make my plans according to the flesh, ready to say 'Yes, yes' and 'No, no' at the same time? As surely as God is faithful, our word to you has not been Yes and No. For the Son of God, Jesus Christ, whom we proclaimed among you, Silvanus and Timothy and I, was not Yes and No, but in him it is always Yes. For all the promises of God find their Yes in him. That is why it is through him that we utter our Amen to God for his glory" (2 Cor. 1:17-20).

Positive Messianic commandment: *"You shall love and serve God so much that you only use his name to confess him, pray to him, praise him, worship him."*

Fifth Commandment: "Honor your father and your mother." This and the Fourth Commandment are the only ones not beginning with "You shall not," so they cannot be turned from negative into positive commandments. But Jesus did unmask

---

9. Heidelberg Catechism, Q&A 99.

the negative ways in which this command was sometimes observed. On one occasion, Jesus said to a man, "Follow me." But the man replied, "Lord, let me first go and bury my father." Jesus said to him, "Leave the dead to bury their own dead. But as for you, go and proclaim the kingdom of God" (Luke 9:59-60; cf. Matt. 8:21-22). This is *the* example in recent decades supplied by authors who endeavor to demonstrate that, at least in this case, Jesus disregarded or overruled the Torah.[10] However, if the disciple-to-be "intended to suggest that he would not throw in his lot with Jesus at once, and used his eventual filial duty to bury his father (old and sick?) as an excuse for procrastination, Jesus' sharp rejoinder would surprise no one."[11]

Even if this interpretation would be too far-fetched, the Fifth Commandment as such is not necessarily at stake. The duty to honor one's parents remains fully intact. Attempts to circumvent this command—for instance, by sequestering the financial means needed to support one's parents by placing them under *corban* (a gift devoted to God)—Jesus calls "making void the word of God by your tradition that you have handed down" (Mark 7:8-13). However, the duty to genuinely serve and obey God—which includes following Jesus!—always surpasses the duty to care for one's neighbor, including even one's parents (cf. Matt. 10:37; 12:47-50; Luke 14:26). This is not contrary to the Torah, but entirely in line with it; Messianic times presuppose disrupted family ties, which one day will be restored; see Micah 7:6 (quoted in Matt.10:36; cf. Luke 12:51-53) and Malachi 4:7 (hinted at in Matt. 17:11). Moreover, the apparent antithesis involved should instead be taken as a comparison: "hating" one's parents in Luke 14:26 is

---

10. Vermes (1993, 28) refers to A. Schlatter, N. Perrin, M. Hengel, A. E. Harvey, and Sanders (1985, 252–55; cf. 267: "We have found one instance in which Jesus, in effect, demanded transgression of the law: the demand to the man whose father had died").
11. Vermes (1993, 29); cf. Stern (1999, 35–36).

generally understood to mean "loving them less than Jesus" (cf. Deut. 21:15, where the "hated" wife is really the one that is "less loved" than the other). So the command actually says: Love your parents, but love Jesus even more, so that, if you would ever have to choose between them, you would rather follow Jesus. Again, Jesus himself is the great example: he never allowed his mother to interfere in his divine task (Matt. 12:46-50; John 2:3-4), but at the cross, when his work was almost finished, he showed his unlimited filial affection to her (John 19:26).

Positive Messianic commandment: *"You shall love your parents at all costs — although you shall always love God more — and take care of them even in your own most difficult circumstances."*

Sixth Commandment: "You shall not murder." Again we have a negative prohibition, which under the New Covenant is applied in a much more severe way: even hating and despising one's fellow human being is viewed as manslaughter (Matt. 5:22). At the same time, in the Messianic Torah the prohibition is turned into a positive commandment: "By this we know love, that he laid down his life for us, and we ought to lay down our lives for the brothers" (1 John 3:16). That is, not only should we not take the other's life, but we should be prepared to lay down our lives for the other. Jesus himself is our great example here, for he laid down his life for his sheep (John 10:11), that is, for his friends (15:13).

Positive Messianic commandment: *"You shall love your fellow Christian so much that you shall be prepared to lay down your life for him."*

Seventh Commandment: "You shall not commit adultery." Here is another negative prohibition, which is sharpened further in the Messianic Torah: even adulterous thoughts are counted as adultery (Matt. 5:28). Under the New Covenant, this prohibition is turned into a positive commandment: "Husbands, love your wives, as the Messiah loved the Ekklesia and gave himself up for her" (Eph. 5:25). That is, not only should husbands not deceive their wives, but they must show them the greatest love, a love even unto death, if need be. Jesus himself is again our great example here, for he literally went into death for his "wife," as the verse shows. He became a "bridegroom of blood" to her, if we may freely apply Exodus 4:25-26 this way.

Positive Messianic commandment: *"You shall love your wife so much that you shall be prepared to lay down your life for her."*

Eighth Commandment: "You shall not steal." This negative prohibition is actually sharpened already within the Decalogue itself, namely, in the Tenth Commandment: "You shall not *covet* . . . ." That is, even the hidden craving for what belongs to one's neighbor is already to be called theft. Under the New Covenant, this prohibition is turned again into a positive commandment: "Let the thief no longer steal, but rather let him labor, doing honest work with his own hands, so that he may have something to share with anyone in need" (Eph. 4:28; cf. Prov. 3:27-28). That is to say, not only should we not steal from each other, but we should share as much as possible with each other (cf. 1 John 3:17). Again, Jesus himself is our great example here. He set the example for our own readiness to sacrifice, for "though he was rich, yet for your sake he became poor, so that you by his poverty might become rich" (2 Cor. 8:9).

Positive Messianic commandment: *"You shall love your fellow Christian so much that you shall be prepared to share everything you have with him."*

Ninth Commandment: "You shall not bear false witness against your neighbor," that is, you shall not lie about him. This negative prohibition is sharpened in Scripture in such a way that not only should we not tell untrue things *about* and *to* each other, but we should not tell true things with an untruthful attitude either. God has "pleasure in uprightness" (1 Chron. 29:17); "you delight in truth in the inward parts" (Ps. 51:6; cf. Rom. 3:4). From this follows automatically the positive form of this commandment under the New Covenant: "Therefore, having put away falsehood, let each one of you speak the truth with his neighbor, for we are members one of another" (Eph. 4:25). That is, not only should we not lie to each other, but we should serve each other with the truth because of our loving attachment to each other as members of the same Body of the Messiah. Again, Jesus is our great example here, for he came "to bear witness to the truth," and he did so, out of love for us, even before his judges, yes, even unto death (John 18:37).

Positive Messianic commandment: *"You shall love your fellow Christian so much that you shall be prepared to serve him with the truth, in a truthful way."*

In a general way, we notice the striking fact that the language of Matthew's Gospel so closely resembles that of the Mosaic Torah.[12] He is the only evangelist to use the word *anomia*, "Torah-lessness" (7:23; 13:41; 23:28; 24:12); he uses the term "righteousness" (*dikaiosynē*) seven times in the typically Jewish sense of fulfilling God's commandments (3:15; 5:6, 10, 20; 6:1, 33; 21:32; elsewhere in the Gospels only in Luke 1:75 and John 16:8, 10); and he uses the characteristic verb "doing" (*poiein*) about forty times, twenty-two times in the Sermon of the Mount alone (see in particular 5:19; 7:21, 24; 12:50; 19:16–17; 25:40, 45).

It is of great interest that rabbinic tradition, too, has attempted many times to formulate the essence (*k'lal gadol*, "greatest principle") of the Mosaic Torah. If Jesus (Matt. 19:19; 22:39) as well as Paul (Rom. 13:9; Gal. 5:14) and James (2:8) quoted Leviticus 19:18 as the vital Love Commandment with respect to one's fellow human being, the Talmud and the Midrash Rabbah do the very same. In the Talmud, the great rabbi Hillel said, "What is hateful to you, do not to your neighbor: that is the whole Torah, while the rest is the commentary

---

12. Cf. Dunn (1990a, 246–47), who, by the way, uses this as one of his arguments for creating a contrast between Matthew and Paul.

The Messianic Torah and the Millennial Torah

thereof; go and learn it."[13] One Midrash says, "All that you do, do only out of love."[14] Rabbi Simlai made his own summary of the Torah's substance: it can be summarized in eleven, six, three, two commandments, or even one commandment. He is quoted as having said that "David came and reduced [the 613 *mitzvot*] to eleven [Ps. 15:2-5] . . . Isaiah came and reduced them to six [Isa. 33:15] . . . Micah came and reduced them to three [Micah 6:8]. . . . Again came Isaiah and reduced them to two [principles], as it is said, *Thus saith the Lord, [1] Keep ye justice and [2] do righteousness* [Isa. 56:1]. Amos came and reduced them to one [principle], as it is said, *For thus saith the Lord unto the house of Israel, Seek ye Me and live . . .* [Amos 5:4]. But it is Habakkuk who came and based them all on one [principle], as it is said, *But the righteous shall live by his faith."* [Hab. 2:4][15] "Faith" is to be taken here as loving confidence in God.

6.1.2 In Paul's Words

The apostle Paul provides the following summaries and substances of the Torah: "Owe no one anything, except to love each other, for the one who loves another has fulfilled the Torah. For the commandments, 'You shall not commit adultery, You shall not murder, You shall not steal, You shall not covet,' and any other commandment, are summed up in this word: 'You shall love your neighbor as yourself.' Love does no wrong to a neighbor; therefore love is the fulfilling of the Torah" (Rom. 13:8-10). "[T]hrough love serve one another. For the whole Torah is fulfilled in one word: 'You shall love your neighbor as yourself'" (Gal. 5:13-14). "Bear one another's burdens, and so [i.e., through this act of love] fulfill the

---

13. Shabbat 31a (cf. Matt. 7:12!); Gen. Rabbah 24,7 (Rabbi Aqiva); Lev. Rabbah 24,5 (Rabbi Chiyya).
14. Sifre Deut. 41 (on 11:3). The Torah was identified with love (e.g., Midr. Ps. on 1:18). Also cf. Shulam (1998, 481n10).
15. Makkot 23b–24a; interestingly, Paul arrives at the same ultimate conclusion: the essence of living under God's Torah is expressed in Hab. 2:4 (Rom. 1:16–17; Gal. 3:11; cf. Heb. 10:38).

Torah of the Messiah" (6:2). "Children, obey your parents in the Lord, for this is right. 'Honor your father and mother' (this is the first commandment with a promise), 'that it may go well with you and that you may live long in the land'" (Eph. 6:1-3). And James says of "the perfect Torah of liberty" (1:25): "If you really fulfill the royal Torah according to the Scripture, 'You shall love your neighbor as yourself,' you are doing well" (2:8; cf. v. 9-12). The substance of the Mosaic Torah is identical with the substance of the Messianic Torah: love God and love your neighbor.

Karin Finsterbusch has drawn our attention to the fact that the notion of the Messianic Torah appears much more often in Paul's Letters than the few explicitly positive references to *nomos* may suggest.[16] Following the principles laid down especially by Klaus Berger,[17] she identified a semantic field that she called the "Torah field," which describes Christian conduct according to the Messianic Torah (she did so without making virtually any formal distinction between the Mosaic Torah and the Messianic Torah). This "Torah field" contains the words *peripateō* ("to walk"), *phroneō* ("to have a certain mind about") and *aphrōn* ("unmindful, unwise"), *areskō* ("to please") and *euarestos* ("pleasing, acceptable"), *agathos* ("good"), *teleios* ("perfect"), *thelēma* ("will") and *pneuma* ("spirit"). Three of these terms occur in Philippians 3:15-21, five of them in Ephesians 5:6-20, and four of them elsewhere (Rom. 8:1-8; 12:1-2; 2 Cor. 5:1-10; Col. 1:9-10; 1 Thess. 4:1-8). Colossians 1:9-10 contains *sophia* ("wisdom") and *synesis* ("understanding"), which parallels *phroneō* and *aphrōn*. Only in Romans 8 are the terms being employed explicitly related to the Torah (v. 4).

In Jewish literature, all seven terms, often in combination, are related to conduct according to the Torah. This occurs so frequently that one may assume that Paul also used them in

---

16. Finsterbusch (1996, 108-84).
17. Berger (1984, 137-59).

The Messianic Torah and the Millennial Torah

order to describe such conduct faithful to the Torah. In fact, 1 Thessalonians 4:4–6 contains a clear reference to the seventh commandment, while Romans 12:1 challenges us to present a sacrifice (see the rest of Romans 12, which is an exposition of the Messianic Torah), and in 2 Corinthians 5:10 the criterion for judging good and evil must be the Torah (corroborated by the parallel in Rom. 2:6-16). Of special interest are the references to the Holy Spirit in most passages.[18] Just as in the rabbinic and Qumran literature of the time, the Torah is rarely referred to explicitly; Paul seems to be more interested in the practical exposition of the Torah's intentions than in the literal formulation of the Torah's commandments.

In a particularly beautiful way the Messianic Torah comes to light in the establishment of the New Covenant. God says that he will put his Torah in the minds of the Israelites "and write it on their hearts" (Jer. 31:33; also cf. Heb. 8:10). This refers to the one, eternal Torah, but not in the exact form of the Sinaitic Torah, for that was the limited, temporary manifestation of the Torah under the Old Covenant. In the New Covenant we receive the Torah in its completion and consummation, its fullest, deepest meaning, as it has been manifested in Jesus Messiah. Here, there is no longer any essential difference between the ideas that the *Torah* of God is written in their hearts, or that the *love* of God is poured out into their hearts, or that the *Spirit* of God is poured out into their hearts (cf. Rom. 5:5; 13:8-10, 14; Gal. 4:6). We see this in quite an amazing manner when Paul applies this teaching concerning the New Covenant to us, freely replacing "Torah" with "Messiah": "[C]learly you are an epistle of [i.e., concerning, representing] Christ, ministered by us [as ministers of a New Covenant (v. 6)], written not with ink but by the Spirit of the living God, not on tablets of stone [as under the Old Covenant] but

---

18. Rom. 8:4–7 (cf. "the *nomos* of the Spirit of life" in v. 2); 2 Cor. 5:5; Eph. 5:18; 1 Thess. 4:8; cf. Phil. 3:3; Col. 1:8 (cf. *pneumatikos* in v. 9). See Reinmuth (1985) on the relationship between Spirit and Torah.

on tablets of flesh, [that is,] of the heart" (2 Cor. 3:3 NKJV).[19]

The Torah in its fullest and deepest meaning, as intended by Jeremiah, is congruent with Jesus, as intended by Paul, written on the "fleshy tables" (KJV) of our hearts. The substance of the Mosaic Torah was the Ten Words, written on tablets of stone; the substance of the Messianic Torah is Jesus himself, written on tablets of flesh. If the angel says, "[T]he testimony of Jesus is the spirit of prophecy" (Rev. 19:10), we may certainly apply this to the Torah: the tenor of the Torah is to testify of Jesus.

Speaking of the heart, we may point out how Paul emphasizes obedience in connection with a pure heart: "The aim [Gr. *telos*] of our charge is love that issues from a pure heart and a good conscience and a sincere faith" (1 Tim. 1:5). The command was specifically related to Timothy's "charge" (vv. 3, 18; cf. 6:13-14), but we may give it a wider application: the aim of the *Messianic Torah* is love from a pure heart, with a good conscience, and with faith unfeigned: "pursue righteousness, faith, love, and peace, along with those who call on the Lord from a pure heart" (2 Tim. 2:22). Observing the Messianic Torah is indeed a genuine pursuit (Gr. *diōkō*): "Pursue love" (1 Cor. 14:1); "always seek [or, pursue] to do good to one another and to everyone" (1 Thess. 5:15). "Pursue righteousness, godliness, faith, love, steadfastness, gentleness" (1 Tim. 6:11). "Strive for [or, Pursue] peace with everyone, and for the holiness without which no one will see the Lord" (Heb. 12:14). There is nothing wrong with pursuing (seeking to keep) "a Torah of righteousness"; on the contrary, in a real sense, this is the essence of Christian life—as long as it rests on the principle of faith, that is, entrusting oneself to God's grace, Jesus' work, and the Holy Spirit's power (Rom. 9:31-32).

Paul's arguments contain numerous examples of his awareness of the *k'lal gadol b'Torah*, the "greatest principle in the Torah." Sometimes this *k'lal gadol* seems to be in conflict

---

19. Cf. the link between *Torah, Hokmah,* and *Logos* (chapter 3 above).

with the *shurat hadin*, the "wall of the law," sometimes called the "letter of the Torah" (Rom. 2:27, 29; 7:6; 2 Cor. 3:6). But in such cases, just like the rabbis often did, Paul argued that a certain deed is *lifnim mishurat hadin*, "within the line of the law,"[20] that is, not according to the letter of the Torah but according to its spirit, its more fundamental moral principle. Certain deeds of love might literally seem to infringe upon the Torah, but in fact were considered by the rabbis to be in line with the Torah's underlying principle of love and respect for one's neighbor and for God himself. Joseph Shulam found hints of this in Romans 2:27, 29; 7:14; 8:4; 13:8–10; and 14:15, 17.[21]

6.1.3 Paul's "Ten Commandments"

It is not difficult to find implicit, and sometimes even explicit, references to the Ten Commandments in Paul's Letters (see on the Fourth Commandment extensively, Appendix III); obvious examples for the other commandments are:

First Commandment ("You shall have no other gods before me"): "[A]lthough there may be so-called gods in heaven or on earth—as indeed there are many 'gods' and many 'lords'—yet for us there is one God, the Father, from whom are all things and for whom we exist, and one Lord, Jesus Messiah, through whom are all things and through whom we exist" (1 Cor. 8:5-6); "what pagans sacrifice they offer to demons and not to God. I do not want you to be participants with demons" (10:20).

Second Commandment ("You shall not make for yourself a carved image . . . ."): "Do not be idolators . . . flee from idolatry," that is, do not bow down before idols (idolatrous images) to worship them (1 Cor. 10:7, 14; also see 5:10–11; 6:9; 2 Cor. 6:16; Gal. 5:20; Eph. 5:5; Col. 3:5; 1 Thess. 1:9). (In fact, the

---

20. Cf. Berakhot 7a.
21. Shulam (1998, 110, 112, 250, 441, 471–73, cf. 122n59, 123n62, 314n11, 317n35, 450n11, 450n14, 484n40).

second commandment also implies that no images of the true God must be made.)

Third Commandment ("You shall not take the name of the LORD *your God in vain . . . ."):* "[Y]ou must put them all away: anger, wrath, malice, slander (Gr. *blasphēmian*), and obscene talk from your mouth" (Col. 3:8; also see 1 Tim. 1:20; 2 Tim. 3:2-4; Titus 2:5). Paul wishes "that the name of God and the teaching may not be reviled" (1 Tim. 6:1).

Fifth Commandment ("Honor your father and your mother . . . ."): "Children, obey your parents in the Lord, for this is right. 'Honor your father and mother' (this is the first commandment with a promise), 'that it may go well with you and that you may live long in the land'" (Eph. 6:2-3; also see Col. 3:20; 2 Tim. 3:2).

Sixth Commandment ("You shall not murder"): ". . . understanding this, that the Torah is not laid down for the just but for the Torah-less and disobedient, for the ungodly and sinners, for the unholy and profane, for those who strike their fathers and mothers, for murderers, . . ." (1 Tim. 1:9). "Let all bitterness and wrath and anger and clamor and slander be put away from you, along with all malice" (Eph. 4:31; also see Col. 3:8).[22]

Seventh Commandment ("You shall not commit adultery"): "[D]o you not know that the unrighteous will not inherit the kingdom of God? Do not be deceived: neither the sexually immoral, nor idolaters, nor adulterers . . . will inherit the kingdom of God. . . . Flee from sexual immorality" (1 Cor. 6:9-10,

---

22. Direct prohibitions of murder are conspicuously lacking in Paul, even in lists found in 1 Cor. 5:9-10 and 6:9-10; the word "murders" does not occur in Gal. 5:21 in important manuscripts. In the Scriptures mentioned Paul does refer, though, to utterances of hatred and malice; cf. Matt. 5:22: "everyone who is angry with his brother will be liable to judgment," and 1 John 3:15: "Everyone who hates his brother is a murderer, and you know that no murderer has eternal life abiding in him."

18; cf. 10:8); "sexual immorality and all impurity or covetousness must not even be named among you" (Eph. 5:3-4). "Put to death therefore what is earthly in you: sexual immorality, impurity, passion, evil desire, and covetousness, which is idolatry" (Col. 3:5). "For this is the will of God, your sanctification: that you abstain from sexual immorality; that each one of you know how to control his own body in holiness and honor, not in the passion of lust like the Gentiles who do not know God; that no one transgress and wrong his brother in this matter, because the Lord is an avenger in all these things, as we told you beforehand and solemnly warned you. For God has not called us for impurity, but in holiness. Therefore whoever disregards this, disregards not man but God, who gives his Holy Spirit to you" (1 Thess. 4:3-8; cf. Rom. 13:9; 1 Cor. 5:1, 9-11; 6:13; 7:2; 2 Cor. 12:21; Gal. 5:19; 1 Tim. 1:10.).

Eighth Commandment ("You shall not steal"): "Let the thief no longer steal, but rather let him labor, doing honest work with his own hands, so that he may have something to share with anyone in need" (Eph. 4:28; also see Rom. 13:9; 1 Cor. 5:10-11; 6:10; 1 Tim. 1:10).

Ninth Commandment ("You shall not bear false witness against your neighbor"): "Therefore, having put away falsehood, let each one of you speak the truth with his neighbor, for we are members one of another" (Eph. 4:25). "Do not lie to one another, seeing that you have put off the old self with its practices and have put on the new self, which is being renewed in knowledge after the image of its creator" (Col. 3:9-10; also see Rom. 13:9; 1 Cor. 6:10-11; 1 Tim. 1:10).

Tenth Commandment ("You shall not covet . . . ."): "For you may be sure of this, that everyone who is sexually immoral or impure, or who is covetous (that is, an idolater), has no inheritance in the kingdom of Christ and God" (Eph. 5:5). "Put to death therefore what is earthly in you: sexual immorality, impurity, passion, evil desire, and covetousness, which is idolatry" (Col. 3:5). "For the love of money is a root of all

THE ETERNAL TORAH: LIVING UNDER GOD

kinds of evils. It is through this craving that some have wandered away from the faith and pierced themselves with many pangs" (1 Tim. 6:10; see also Rom. 7:7-8; 13:9; 1 Cor. 5:10-11; 6:10; 2 Tim. 3:2).

Here, then, are the New Testament Ten Commandments in brief (compare them with the positive commandments in §6.1.1):

1. "I do not want you to be participants with demons." Instead, have fellowship with the true God. That is, *love God*.

2. "Do not be idolaters." Instead, serve the true God. That is, *love God*.

3. "You must rid yourselves of blasphemy." Instead, revere and worship God. That is, *love God*.

4. "Let no one judge your Shabbat observance." *That is, love God*, for whom sacred days have been set apart and who alone decides how they are to be observed.

5. "Children, obey your parents in the Lord." That is, *love your parents*; but also, recognizing that all human authority is derived (received) authority, *love God*.

6. "Get rid of all bitterness, rage, and anger." Instead, serve your brother. That is, *love your brother*.

7. "We should not commit sexual immorality." Instead, serve your wife. That is, *love your wife*.

8. "He who has been stealing must steal no longer." Instead, share with your brother. That is, *love your brother*.

9. "Do not lie to each other." Instead, minister truth to your brother. That is, *love your brother*.

10. "Put to death evil desires and greed." Instead, bring sacrifices for the benefit of your brother. That is, *love your brother*.

In summary: love God, love your neighbor (parent, wife, brother, etc.), the latter being nothing but a special form of the love toward God: "[I]f anyone has the world's goods and sees his brother in need, yet closes his heart against him, how does

The Messianic Torah and the Millennial Torah

God's love abide in him?" (1 John 3:17); "[T]his we know that we love the children of God, when we love God and obey his commandments" (5:2).

6.2 The Torah in Time
6.2.1 The Torah in the Messianic Kingdom

In both the Old Covenant and the New Covenant, the Torah occupies the central position:

> It shall come to pass in the latter days that the mountain of the house of the LORD shall be established as the highest of the mountains, and shall be lifted up above the hills; and all the nations shall flow to it, and many peoples shall come, and say: 'Come, let us go up to the mountain of the Lord, to the house of the God of Jacob, that he may teach us his ways and that we may walk in his paths.' For out of Zion shall go the Torah and the word of the Lord from Jerusalem" (Isa. 2:2–3; cf. Micah 4:1–2).

The servant of the LORD, that is, the Messiah, "will not grow faint or be discouraged till he has established justice [*mishpat*] in the earth; and the coastlands wait for his Torah" (Isa. 42:4). "Give attention to me, my people, and give ear to me, my nation; for the Torah will go out from me, and I will set my justice for a light to the peoples. . . . Listen to me, you who know righteousness [*tzedeq*], the people in whose heart is my Torah" (Isa. 51:4, 7). In view of the coming Messianic Kingdom (*'olam habba*), the Tanakh says in the last prophetic book (last page), "Remember the Torah of my servant Moses, the statutes and rules that I commanded him at Horeb for all Israel" (Mal. 4:4).

This selection of Scriptures makes clear that the Mosaic Torah can hardly be viewed as having disappeared, because many of its basic elements will occupy a central place in the future Messianic Kingdom. It is therefore too one-sided when Hebrew Christian Arthur W. Kac wrote: "The Mosaic Law, or the Sinai covenant, consists of three parts: The Decalogue

(Ten Commandments); the Levitical code; and the civil code. The civil code was designed for a people engaged in agriculture and living in a certain geographical area at a certain stage of history. The Levitical code with its sacrificial system was bound up with the existence of the Jerusalem Temple. . . . The Decalogue alone has a universal character and is capable of serving as a religious and moral standard for the peoples of the world, irrespective of time and place."[23] This is not correct; the Millennial Torah will contain far more than the Ten Commandments. However, Messianic Jews Ariel and D'vorah Berkowitz move a little too far to the other extreme in saying, "We are not a theocratic community living in the Land of Israel. Therefore, we will find that some of the commandments are impossible to perform. It goes without saying [sic] that the situation will be completely rectified when Messiah returns."[24] Rather, I believe that the Millennial Torah and the Mosaic Torah will have much in common but will not be identical.

W. Harvey wrote in the *Encyclopaedia Judaica* that the "rabbis taught that the Torah would continue to exist in the world to come (e.g., Eccles. R. 2:1), although some of them were of the opinion that innovations would be made in the messianic era (e.g., Gen. R. 98:9; Lev. R. 9:7)."[25] To be more precise, the form that the one, eternal Torah will assume in the Messianic Kingdom—what I call the Millennial Torah—will have very much in common with the form that the one, eternal Torah possessed under the Old Covenant (the Mosaic Torah), al-

---

23. Kac (1986, 276; also cf. 288).
24. Berkowitz (1999, 242).
25. Harvey (1972, 1244). Rare passages, however, suggest that most sacrifices (Lev. Rabbah 9.7) or most festivals will be annulled (Yalqut on Prov. 9:2), or that *kashrut* will be lifted (Midr. Ps. on 146:7), or at least that the Torah will be changed (Davies 1952, 54–66).

though they will not be identical.[26]

Ralph Alexander came very close to this position, although he identified the Mosaic Torah and the Millennial Torah: "The Mosaic covenant would find its fruition in the messianic kingdom in that Israel finally would be God's people and he would be their God in a relationship that was to exist under the Mosaic covenant. That the pictorial sacrifices had their reality in the work of Jesus does not nullify the relationship with the Mosaic covenant that is a holy one. The Mosaic covenant showed Israel how to live a holy life in a relationship with God, and that type of life is still valid under the new covenant (cf. Jer 31:33-34; Rom 8:4). Therefore, for the Mosaic covenant and the New Covenant to be fulfilled side by side is not incongruous."[27] Ralph Alexander is more outspoken here than Dan Juster:[28] "When Messiah reigns, a whole new order will exist, certainly true to the universal principles reflected in the Mosaic constitution. But there will not be a return to the Mosaic constitution which accommodated the needs and limitations of the people in the ancient Near East over three thousand years ago."[29] The latter may be true to a certain extent (see §5.2.1), but I see far more correspondence between the Mosaic Torah and the Millennial Torah than Juster appar-

---

26. Gershom Scholem (1971, 53–56, cf. 65–72) describes views maintaining that the Messianic Torah will be identical with the Mosaic Torah as well as views maintaining that the Messianic Torah will be a "new" Torah. Isa. 51:4, "Torah [without the article!] will go out from me," is understood as: "A new Torah will go out from me"; there seem to have been Bible manuscripts in which the verse occurred in this form. Several sources tell us that in the age to come the Messiah will give a new Torah to Israel; Edersheim (1971, II, 765) refers to Midr. Song of Sol. 2:13; Targum on Isa. 12:3; Lev. Rabbah 13.
27. Alexander (1986, 986).
28. Juster (1995, 33).
29. Notice that Juster alleges the opposite of what the Berkowitzes claim (see above)—and, in my view, both go too far.

ently does.

Not just the moral dimension but ceremonial parts too will be preserved in the Millennial Torah. In Isaiah 42:1-4, the Servant of the Lord (the Messiah) is described as the Teacher of the *mishpat* to all the nations, that is, of both the ceremonial and the moral ordinances. In 2 Kings 17:26-27, *mishpat* is ceremonial: "the law [*mishpat*] of the god of the land," namely, the kind of ceremonies demanded by the deity. In Jeremiah 5:4, *mishpat* is moral: "the justice of their God."[30] As the bringer of the Millennial Torah, the Servant is both a kingly and a prophetic figure,[31] and a priestly one as well, so that his Torah will include all the usual elements, namely, moral, civil, and ceremonial.

6.2.2 Specific Elements

The Tanakh describes many specific elements of the Millennial Torah, particularly in Ezekiel 44-46. The discrepancies between the Mosaic Torah and the Millennial decrees as implied in Ezekiel's description were an embarrassment to the rabbis. Some held the view that, as Fisch writes, "[O]nly the prophet Elijah, who will herald the ultimate redemption [see §7.2.2], will elucidate these chapters. They added the observation that had it not been for Rabbi Chanina ben Hezekiah, who explained several of these difficulties, the Book of Ezekiel would have been excluded from the Scriptural canon."[32] Other rabbis felt that many problems in these chapters can be solved by assuming that the ceremonies described refer only to the dedication of the new Temple.[33]

Leaving these doubts aside, we may enumerate some important Millennial *torot*, new and old, as follows:

---

30. Davies (1952, 32) (cf. §2.3.1).
31. See Davies (1952, 32-34) and references.
32. Fisch (1950, 265; cf. 270, 316), with reference to Menachot 45a; cf. Shabbat 13b, Chagigah 13a.
33. Fisch (1950, 316-19).

The Messianic Torah and the Millennial Torah

(1) *Circumcision.* "Awake, awake, put on your strength, O Zion; put on your beautiful garments, O Jerusalem, the holy city; for there shall no more come into you the uncircumcised and the unclean" (Isa. 52:1). "No foreigner, uncircumcised in heart and flesh, of all the foreigners who are among the people of Israel, shall enter my sanctuary" (Ezek. 44:9). In the Messianic Kingdom, no uncircumcised men will be allowed into the new Temple.

(2) *The Shabbat and the New Moon.* "Keep justice, and do righteousness, for soon my salvation will come, and my righteousness be revealed. Blessed is the man who does this, and the son of man who holds it fast, who keeps the Sabbath, not profaning it, and keeps his hand from doing any evil. . . . To the eunuchs who keep my Sabbaths, who choose the things that please me and hold fast my covenant, I will give in my house and within my walls a monument and a name better than sons and daughters; I will give them an everlasting name that shall not be cut off. And the foreigners who join themselves to the LORD, to minister to him, to love the name of the LORD, and to be his servants, everyone who keeps the Sabbath and does not profane it, and holds fast my covenant—these I will bring to my holy mountain, and make them joyful in my house of prayer; their burnt offerings and their sacrifices will be accepted on my altar; for my house shall be called a house of prayer for all peoples" (Isa. 56:1-7).[34]

"'From new moon to new moon, and from Sabbath to Sabbath, all flesh shall come to worship before me" (66:23).

In the Messianic Kingdom consummated at Messiah's return, the priests of Israel shall "keep my *torot* and my statutes in all my appointed feasts, and they shall keep my Sabbaths

---

34. The Lord prescribed the blowing of the trumpet (Num. 10:10; Ps. 81:3) and certain sacrifices (Num. 28:11–15) to celebrate the beginning of the months. In the rest of the Tanakh we find several hints that the appearance of the new moon was celebrated (1 Sam. 20:5, 18, 24; 2 Kings 4:23; Isa. 1:13; Amos 8:5).

holy" (Ezek. 44:24). "Thus says the Lord God: 'The gate of the inner court that faces east shall be shut on the six working days, but on the Sabbath day it shall be opened, and on the day of the new moon it shall be opened.... The people of the land shall bow down at the entrance of that gate before the Lord on the Sabbaths and on the new moons. The burnt offering that the prince[35] offers to the Lord on the Sabbath day shall be six lambs without blemish and a ram without blemish.... On the day of the new moon he shall offer a bull from the herd without blemish, and six lambs and a ram, which shall be without blemish'" (46:1, 3–4, 6).

(3) *The Jewish festivals.* The following pertains to the Messianic Kingdom: "In the first month, on the first day of the month, you shall take a bull from the herd without blemish, and purify the sanctuary.... In the first month, on the fourteenth day of the month, you shall celebrate the Feast of the Passover [*Pesach*], and for seven days unleavened bread shall be eaten. On that day the prince shall provide for himself and all the people of the land a young bull for a sin offering. And on the seven days of the festival he shall provide as a burnt offering to the Lord seven young bulls and seven rams without blemish, on each of the seven days; and a male goat daily for a sin offering. And he shall provide as a grain offering an ephah for each bull, an ephah for each ram, and a hin of oil to each ephah. In the seventh month, on the fifteenth day of the month and for the seven days of the feast [*Sukkot*, the Feast of Booths], he shall make the same provision for sin offerings, burnt offerings, and grain offerings, and for the oil" (Ezek. 45:18, 21–25).[36]

---

35. The "prince" (more correctly, "leader") in Ezek. 44–46 and 48 must be an earthly ruler, who cannot be Messiah himself because he needs sin offerings for himself (45:22) and has natural children (46:16); presumably he is Messiah's earthly representative (cf. Alexander 1986, 974).

36. Several festivals seem to be conspicuously absent in Ezekiel. However, "the appointed feasts" in 46:9 likely include *Shavu'ot* (Pentecost),

The Messianic Torah and the Millennial Torah

"I am the Lord your God from the land of Egypt; I will again make you dwell in tents, as in the days of the appointed feast" (Hos. 12:9), that is, the Feast of Booths.

"Then everyone who survives of all the nations that have come against Jerusalem shall go up year after year to worship the King, the Lord of hosts, and to keep the Feast of Booths [*Sukkot*]. And if any of the families of the earth do not go up to Jerusalem to worship the King, the Lord of hosts, there will be no rain on them. And if the family of Egypt does not go up and present themselves, then on them there shall be no rain; there shall be the plague with which the Lord afflicts the nations that do not go up to keep the Feast of Booths. This shall be the punishment to Egypt and the punishment to all the nations that do not go up to keep the Feast of Booths" (Zech. 14:16–19).[37]

(4) *Kashrut and other purification laws.* "Those who sanctify and purify themselves to go into the gardens, following one in the midst, eating pig's flesh and the abomination and mice, shall come to an end together. . . . For I know their works and their thoughts, and the time is coming to gather all nations and tongues. And they shall come and shall see my glory" (Isa. 66:17–18).

During the Messianic Kingdom, the priests "shall teach my people the difference between the holy and the common, and show them how to distinguish between the unclean and the clean. . . . They shall not defile themselves by going near a dead person. However, for father or mother, for son

---

and some Jewish commentators identify the "feasts" in 46:11 as the three pilgrim festivals, including *Shavu'ot*, and "the appointed festivals" of *Rosh haShanah* (New Year) and *Yom Kippur* (Day of Atonement) (Fisch 1950, 319–20). Note "all my appointed feasts" in 44:24.

37. The rabbis realized the significance of *Sukkot* for all nations; therefore, some linked the seventy bulls to be sacrificed during the festival (Num. 29:13–32) with the seventy nations of Gen. 10 as an atonement for them (Sukkah 55b).

or daughter, for brother or unmarried sister they may defile themselves" (Ezek. 44:23, 25).

(5) *The sacrificial ministry*. The following regards the Temple service during the Messianic Kingdom: "It shall be the prince's duty to furnish the burnt offerings, grain offerings, and drink offerings, at the feasts, the new moons, and the Sabbaths, all the appointed feasts of the house of Israel: he shall provide the sin offerings, grain offerings, burnt offerings, and peace offerings, to make atonement on behalf of the house of Israel" (Ezek. 45:17; also see extensively chapters 43–46, especially 43:27; 45:23–24; 46:12–15).

"'[F]rom the rising of the sun to its setting my name will be great among the nations, and in every place incense will be offered to my name, and a pure offering. For my name will be great among the nations,' says the LORD of hosts" (Mal. 1:11). "And the Lord whom you seek will suddenly come to his temple. . . . But who can endure the day of his coming, and who can stand when he appears? . . . [H]e will purify the sons of Levi and refine them like gold and silver, and they will bring offerings in righteousness to the LORD. Then the offering of Judah and Jerusalem will be pleasing to the LORD as in the days of old and as in former years" (3:1–4).

"And on that day there shall be inscribed on the bells of the horses, 'Holy to the LORD.' And the pots in the house of the LORD shall be as the bowls before the altar. And every pot in Jerusalem and Judah shall be holy to the LORD of hosts, so that all who sacrifice may come and take of them and boil the meat of the sacrifice in them" (Zech. 14:20–21).[38]

(6) *Civil justice*. The Messianic Kingdom will be a polity of justice; peace and righteousness will be characteristic of Messiah's throne: "Of the increase of his government and of

---

38. Strangely enough, Lev. Rabbah 9.153.1 and 27.168.4 claim that "in time to come" (i.e., in the days of the Messiah) "all sacrifices shall cease, except the sacrifice of thanksgiving."

peace there will be no end, on the throne of David and over his kingdom, to establish it and to uphold it with justice and with righteousness from this time forth and forevermore" (Isa. 9:7).

> He shall not judge by what his eyes see, or decide disputes by what his ears hear, but with righteousness he shall judge the poor, and decide with equity for the meek of the earth; and he shall strike the earth with the rod of his mouth, and with the breath of his lips he shall kill the wicked. Righteousness shall be the belt of his waist, and faithfulness the belt of his loins (11:3–5)

"[T]hen a throne will be established in steadfast love, and on it will sit in faithfulness in the tent of David one who judges and seeks justice and is swift to do righteousness" (16:5). "Behold, a king will reign in righteousness, and princes will rule in justice" (32:1). "The Torah will go out from me, and I will set my justice for a light to the peoples" (51:4).

"In those days and at that time I will cause a righteous Branch to spring up for David, and he shall execute justice and righteousness in the land" (Jer. 33:15). It is prophetically said of the LORD during the coming Kingdom: "The LORD within her is righteous; he does no injustice; every morning he shows forth his justice; each dawn he does not fail" (Zeph. 3:5). Although we may naturally assume that there will be a complete system of higher and lower courts of justice, the Lord himself will be the highest Judge.

An important example of civil justice is the administration of the death penalty during the Messianic Kingdom: "No more shall there be in it an infant who lives but a few days, or an old man who does not fill out his days, for the young man shall die a hundred years old, and the sinner a hundred years old shall be accursed," i.e., shall undergo the death penalty at the age of hundred (Isa. 65:20). Prophetically referring to the great Son of David during the Messianic Kingdom, David tells us, "Morning by morning I will destroy all the wicked in the land, cutting off all the evildoers from the city of the LORD" (Ps. 101:8).

6.2.3 The Torah for Messianic Jews Today

It is of great importance to note that, during the future Messianic Kingdom (*'olam habba*), Israel will keep the Millennial Torah. Although not all commandments are mentioned in the prophecies concerning that Kingdom, it seems that the Millennial Torah contains the Mosaic Torah to a large extent. The people of Israel, to the extent that it will experience that Kingdom, will all be saved (Rom. 11:26); "[I]n the LORD all the offspring of Israel shall be justified and shall glory" (Isa. 45:25). "Your people shall all be righteous; they shall possess the land forever, the branch of my planting, the work of my hands, that I may be glorified" (60:21). This nation of Israel, that will know Jesus as its Messiah, will be ruled by him, the Son of David. The Lord of hosts will have renewed his covenant with them: "Behold, the days are coming ... when I will make a new covenant with the house of Israel and the house of Judah. ... For this is the covenant that I will make with the house of Israel after those days. ... : I will put my Torah within them, and I will write it on their hearts. And I will be their God, and they shall be my people. And no longer shall each one teach his neighbor and each his brother, saying, 'Know the LORD,' for they shall all know me, from the least of them to the greatest. ... For I will forgive their iniquity, and I will remember their sin no more" (Jer. 31:31–34).

Those who believe that Jews who belong to Jesus are no longer obligated to keep the Torah may be shocked when studying such passages. At the second coming of Jesus, the wicked will be cut off from Israel (Isa. 33:14; 56:9–57:13; 66:17; Zech. 13:8–14:5; Matt. 11:20–24; 24:37–41; Luke 10:13–16; 13:22–30). During the Messianic Kingdom, the faithful of Israel will serve Jesus and keep the Torah. For many Christians today, the most shocking aspect is discovering that Israel will be performing the sacrificial ministry, that is, burnt offerings, grain offerings, drink offerings, sin offerings, and peace offerings. There is no point at which the two theological paradigms (see §2.1) clash more intensely than here. If the "literal Israel" view implies that during the Messianic Kingdom Israel will again bring sin offerings, the "spiritual Israel" view might reply: That is the best proof that the "literal Israel" view is untenable. But the opposite seems to me to be true: there is no way for the "spiritual Israel" view to be able to do justice to the sacrificial ministry as it is described here, and even less can it do justice to its many details.

Indeed, there seem to be only two alternatives for the expositor. Either it is nonsense that sin offerings will be sacrificed again on a literal altar in a literal Temple at Jerusalem; but then, the reason for giving such a detailed description of a future sacrificial ministry remains completely open. Or Israel will, at God's command, keep the Torah during Messiah's Kingdom, but then the entire Torah, including the sacrificial ministry. If the latter is the case, the conclusion just mentioned must be reversed: if the "literal Israel" view implies that during the Messianic Kingdom Israel will again bring sin offerings, that is excellent proof that the "spiritual Israel" view is untenable.

Even Messianic Jews sometimes shrink from the notion that during the Millennium *every* kind of sacrifice will be brought. For example, Ariel and D'vorah Berkowitz write, "[I]s it really fair to the Torah to say that one will only follow the ethical sections, while ignoring the civil? More importantly, does Torah itself give us the right to make such distinctions? The only exception is that made by the Brit Chadasha [the New Testament] itself: the sacrifices would no longer be necessary in this age."[39] These closing words, "in this age," were absent in the original edition. Presumably, they have been added to make room for the sacrifices in the Millennial age.

David Stern writes, "Has the Levitical system of sacrifices

---

39. Berkowitz (2011, 46).

been abolished by the New Covenant? The New Testament book of Messianic Jews [i.e., the Letter to the Hebrews] is devoted to the subject, but a careful reading shows that only the sin offering has been canceled, replaced by Jesus himself [cf. Heb. 10:18]. It appears that if and/or when the Temple is rebuilt (the propheteers have varying opinions on this), the other sacrifices (continual offering, thank offering, grain offering, etc.) would continue."[40] This is an astonishing statement because Ezekiel 40–46 mentions the sin offering as part of the Millennial sacrifices no fewer than fourteen times (40:39; 42:13; 43:19, 21–22, 25; 44:27, 29; 45:17, 19, 22–23, 25; 46:20)! Jesus is both the true sin offering and the true burnt-, grain-, and peace-offering (Heb. 10:5–10; cf. Ps. 40:6–8). Why, then, would only the sin offering have been abrogated? Because it brings atonement? But other offerings bring atonement as well (Lev. 1:4; Ezek. 45:15, 17).

In my opinion, the truth is that Jesus' sacrifice is sufficient once and for all, and has shown that all animal sacrifices *in themselves* have no value whatsoever, neither the Mosaic nor the Millennial ones (Heb. 7:27; 9:12, 26–10:14). The sacrifices in the Tanakh had value only because, and only insofar as, they *foreshadowed* the one, true sacrifice of Jesus. But then there can be no fundamental difference between Tanakh sacrifices that point *forward*, and Millennial sacrifices that point *back*, to the sacrifice of Jesus. What on earth could be the meaning of the precise and detailed prescriptions for the *future* sacrificial ministry in Ezekiel 40–46 if all these sacrifices must be viewed as fulfilled in the one sacrifice of Jesus? When Hebrews 10:18 says, "Where there is forgiveness for these [sins], there is no longer any offering for sin," this surely means that the "shadow" (cf. v. 1) has given way to the fulfillment. However, David Stern rightly says, "Even the sin-offering ritual could theoretically [on the basis of Ezek. 40–46 also practically!] be continued, but only if it were regarded as a memorial and not

---

40. Stern (1997, 97).

as effective in itself. Just as it was never more than 'a shadow' (v. 1andN), so now, if it should be resumed (which would presuppose the rebuilding of the Temple at some future time; see 2 Th 2:4N), it could not be more than a reminder of the great deliverance provided in Jesus' death as our final and permanently effective sin offering and his resurrection as our *cohen gadol,*" that is, "great priest" (13:20).[41]

This is correct, but notice the false distinction Stern makes here between "memorial" and "effective." Neither the Mosaic sacrifices nor the Millennial sacrifices are effective in themselves; they are effective only because, and insofar as, they point to the one and only truly effective sacrifice of Jesus. And both the Mosaic sacrifices and the Millennial sacrifices are "memorials," so to speak, looking either forward in anticipation or backward in commemoration, respectively; that is, both sacrificial systems call to mind the one, unique sacrifice of Jesus. In these regards there is no fundamental difference at all between the Mosaic sacrifices and the Millennial sacrifices.

The ultimate implication of all this appears to be none other than this: if Messianic Jews are supposed to keep the Mosaic Torah, it necessarily must be the entire Torah, and if the entire Torah, it necessarily must include, if practically feasible, the sacrificial ministry. We already saw that Peter and John went "up to the temple at the hour of prayer, the ninth hour" (Acts 3:1), that is, at the hour when the evening burnt offering was sacrificed in the Temple. As long as this Temple existed, Messianic Jews apparently participated in its ministry, including the sacrificial ministry. And Paul participated in the ritual purification and the sacrifices that had to be brought in connection with a Nazirite vow (Acts 21:26); these were a burnt offering, a peace offering, and even a sin offering (Num. 6:14; see §5.3.2). Because of the destruction of the Temple in AD 70, the Jews have no longer had the opportunity to bring sacrifices. But if indeed the Third Temple will one day be rebuilt, the

---

41. Stern (1999, 704).

sacrificial ministry will be restored there as well. As a matter of fact, the New Testament prophet John tells us that in this Temple at Jerusalem sacrifices will be brought again: "Rise and measure the temple of God and the altar and those who worship there, but do not measure the court outside the temple; leave that out, for it is given to the nations, and they will trample the holy city [i.e., the earthly Jerusalem, cf. v. 8] for forty-two months" (Rev. 11:1).[42]

Without going more deeply into the details I suggest the following state of affairs.[43] The temple involved here in Revelation 11 apparently is not yet the Temple of Ezekiel 40–44, but a temple that will be built even before the second coming of Jesus. This may be an existing building, or a temple built by Israelis, perhaps at the place of the Dome of the Rock, or very nearby. It will be a building that, for the time being, God will acknowledge as his temple, where an altar will be found and where initially his faithful will bring sacrifices and worship. After this, the outer court of the temple, and even the whole city, will be given to the Gentiles for forty-two months, or three and a half years, that is, a half "week" (Dan. 9:27). Initially, the "little horn" of Daniel 7:8, 25 (i.e., the "prince who is to come"[44]) will allow the temple worship, but as soon as the devil will have taken possession of him he will put an end to the temple ministry, and set out to heavily persecute the saints (Dan. 7:21, 25: the horn arising on the head of the fourth [Roman] beast). Daniel 9:27 speaks of this, too: "In the middle of the week[45] He shall bring an end to sacrifice and offering"

---

42. Cf. Ouweneel (1995, 295–304).
43. Cf. Ouweneel (1999, 61, 78, 81, 94, 197; 2012, 261–64, 294–95, 300–301).
44. Dan. 9:26; in my view, the ruler of the fourth, i.e., the Roman Empire that is to be restored in the last days (see Ouweneel 1999, 2012, 2014b passim).
45. That is, a period of seven years, for half of the "week" is 42 months (Rev. 11:2; 13:5), or 1,260 days (Rev. 11:3; 12:6; cf. Dan. 12:11–12), or "time, times, and half a time" (Rev. 12:14; Dan. 7:25; 12:7), i.e.,

(NKJV). In the Holy Place of the temple, "the abomination that makes desolate" will be erected (cf. Matt. 24:15; Rev. 13:11–18). From that moment, God can no longer acknowledge this temple as his, and will abhor it (Isa. 66:1–6). Ultimately, he will destroy it at the second coming of Jesus (Ps. 74:3, 7; 79:1; Isa. 66:5–6). Perhaps it may be concluded from Daniel 12:11 that the time between the erection of the abominable ministry until the rebuilding of the new and final Temple, that of Ezekiel 40–44, will be 1,290 or 1,335 days.

Not only will an end be made to the sacrificial ministry in the temple, but in 2 Thessalonians 2:4 we also hear of a person who "exalts himself against every so-called god or object of worship, so that he takes his seat in the temple of God, proclaiming himself to be God [or, a god]." In this passage, he is called the "man of Torah-lessness [*anomia*]," the "son of destruction," and "the Torah-less one [*anomos*]" (vv. 3, 8–9). Strikingly enough, two of these three expressions refer to the Torah; this man is someone who dissociates himself from the Torah. He is just as anti-Torah as he is anti-Messiah.[46] Initially, the future temple will be a sign of true Jewish devotion; afterward, it will be the scene of the most vehement Jewish apostasy. Within a few years, the place will witness both the faithful keeping of the Torah, and the most abominable spurning of the Torah.

Such a prospect—if my picture approximates the true course of future events—may arouse mixed feelings among Messianic Jews. On the one hand, they may not like to render service in a temple that soon will be occupied by the An-

---

three and a half years. Interestingly, the Talmud (Sanhedrin 97a) speaks of a period of seven years prior to the Messiah's coming, during which events are to take place that Jesus himself described in Matt. 24.

46. "Antichrist" (1 John 2:18, 22; 4:3; 2 John 7); see Ouweneel (1999, chapters 3 and 6; 2012, chapter 8); cf. Stern (1999, 627–28) for Jewish traditions about this figure.

ti-Messiah. On the other hand, if they believe they are bound to the Mosaic Torah, a temple at Jerusalem is the natural place for them because it is the only place where the Torah can be kept in its entirety. That includes the civil part of the Torah, which regulates the death penalty and other judicial matters. When the temple will have been rebuilt one day at Jerusalem, Orthodox as well as Messianic Jews, if they wish to keep the entire Torah, will have no excuse anymore not to "make *aliyah*" (emigrate) to the land of Israel, or at least to make a pilgrimage to Jerusalem in order to attend there the three great festivals, *Pesach*, *Shavu'ot*, and *Sukkot*. Only there will they be able to participate in the restored sacrificial ministry. Even if Messianic Jews have motives and customs very different from those of Orthodox Jews (see chapter 8), this does not change the fact that the sacrificial ministry is part and parcel of the complete Torah, which the Messianic Jew believes he should keep. As a matter of fact, I know Messianic Jews who look forward to the Third Temple and take it for granted that they will participate in the sacrifices there.

It is of interest to note that those "who worship there" (Rev. 11:1), that is, in the future temple, appear to be the same as "those who keep the commandments of God and hold to the testimony of Jesus" (12:17), or "the saints, those who keep the commandments of God and their faith in Jesus" (14:12).[47] Perhaps this is the most beautiful description that one could imagine with regard to Messianic Jews; they are saints who both observe the Mosaic Torah and believe in Jesus (just as Gentile believers observe the Messianic Torah and believe in Jesus).

---

47. See Ouweneel (1995, *in loco*; 1999, 66, 92); contra Stern (1999, 826), who thinks this refers to Gentile Christians; in commenting on 14:12 (ibid., 830) he does apply the expression to the people of Israel!

6.3 Only the Written Torah?
6.3.1 The Origin of the Oral Torah

We have tried to establish that Messianic Jews keep the entire Torah as a matter of course, not to earn points for heaven but simply because this is an essential part of both the Old and the New Covenants that God has made with Israel. We also saw that the "entire Torah" includes the moral as well as the ceremonial, civil, and purity precepts. Israel still needs the ceremonial commandments in view of the sacrificial ministry that will be reinstituted in the Third Temple. In the land of Israel, the people also need the civil laws again (although in the present highly secularized state of Israel they can be implemented only in a limited way). And the purity commandments, for instance, *kashrut* and the use of the *mikveh*, the Jewish ritual bath, have remained important to Israel throughout the centuries.

Yet this does not sufficiently indicate what exactly is involved in the "entire Torah" as it is to be kept by Messianic Jews. Is that (1) solely the Written Torah as comprised in the Pentateuch? Or is it (2) the Written Torah and the Oral Torah together? Or is it (3) the Written Torah with some New Testament commandments added to it? The answer to this question is less easy than it may seem. Let us first consider the answer suggested under (1).

It may seem obvious to many that the "entire Torah" contains only the Written Torah. The argument for this could be, first, that the Oral Torah,[48] that is, the "tradition of the elders," must be rejected because Jesus seemed to do so too (Mark 7:1–13). Second, one might argue that, strictly speaking, the New

---

48. The term "Oral Torah" (*Torah sh'be'al peh*) seems to have been used first by Hillel (Shabbat 31a; see note, Soncino ed., 139). *Torah sh'be'al peh* means the Torah implied in the phrase *al pi*, "by the mouth" (so literally in Exod. 34:27) (cf. Gittin 60b). The Written Torah was called Torah *sh'bi khetav*, the Torah implied in the word *ketav*, "write," as, e.g., in the same verse, Exod. 34:27.

Testament could not contain any commandments involving an extension of the Mosaic Torah because Moses has said: "You shall not add to the word that I command you, nor take from it, that you may keep the commandments of the LORD your God that I command you" (Deut. 4:2). "Everything that I command you, you shall be careful to do. You shall not add to it or take from it" (12:32). In other words, the Mosaic Torah is a closed and complete entity.

However, we cannot get rid of the Oral Torah that easily. In the Mishnah we read: "Moses received the Torah from Sinai and handed it down to Joshua, and Joshua to the elders, and the elders to the prophets, and the prophets handed it down to the men of the Great Assembly,"[49] referring to the 120 leaders who returned from the Babylonian exile with Ezra. In this tradition there could very well be a kernel of truth, for it is clear that the Written Torah does not contain all the regulations that Israel required in order to be able to carry out God's commandments. It is natural to assume that Moses orally instructed the people concerning numerous matters without all these instructions having been written down.

One possible example of this we find in Deuteronomy 12:21: "If the place that the LORD your God will choose to put his name there is too far from you, then you may kill any of your herd or your flock, which the LORD has given you, as I have *commanded* you, and you may eat within your towns whenever you desire" (italics added).[50] However, we find no such command (or permission) elsewhere in the Torah.[51] Moses commanded this orally but did not register it in writing. Another example: Moses could not have accurately constructed the tabernacle according to the written instructions alone; but a pattern of the tabernacle was shown to him on the moun-

---

49. Mishnah Avot 1:1.
50. Cf. Stern (1997, 148).
51. Unless v. 21 simply refers back to v. 15, as several expositors have suggested.

The Messianic Torah and the Millennial Torah

tain (Exod. 25:9, 40). From the Written Torah we know only the instructions, not the pattern, the blueprint. Not only at such points but also at hundreds of other points, the instructions of the Torah are too vague for direct use; they had to be explained and specified. It is therefore a matter of course that for centuries, the teachers of the Torah have applied themselves to this elaboration. We may well assume that a number of oral interpretations of the Written Torah go back all the way to Moses.

We just quoted the name of Ezra. In the Tanakh he is the most important example of a scribe (*sophêr*), a Torah-scholar: "Ezra . . . was a scribe skilled in the Torah of Moses that the LORD, the God of Israel, had given. . . . Ezra had set his heart to study the Torah of the LORD, and to do it and to teach his statutes and rules in Israel" (Ezra 7:6, 10). Ezra was an authoritative teacher of the Torah, from whom the people could ask for advice if there was a question about the correct application of some commandment. In the Talmud, Rabbi Jose even said, "Had Moses not preceded him, Ezra would have been worthy of receiving the Torah for Israel."[52] He argued: as Moses "went up to God" on Mount Sinai (Exod. 19:3), Ezra "went up from Babylonia" (Ezra 7:6), that is, to God on Mount Zion (cf. 1:3), and as Moses taught the Torah to Israel (Deut. 4:14), Ezra taught the Torah to Israel (Ezra 7:10). In fact, there are some striking similarities between the exodus from Egypt and that from Babylon. The "dragon," in whose power the Israelites were being held, was defeated on both occasions (Isa. 51:9–11; Jer. 51:34, 44); and they traveled through the waters and the desert, where the Lord gave them to eat and to drink (Isa. 40:3; 41:18; 43:2, 16, 19–20; 48:20–21; 49:9–12; 50:2; 63:11–14). Subsequently, both Moses and Ezra, both of them Amram's descendants (Exod. 6:19; Ezra 7:1–5), brought them under the Torah (cf. Ezra 9–10; Neh. 8–9). Being in exile is like being away from God (cf. Ps. 42); going up out of Egypt or Baby-

---

52. Sanhedrin 21b.

THE ETERNAL TORAH: LIVING UNDER GOD

lon, respectively, is to meet God (Exod. 7:16; 10:9, 25-27; Ezra 1:3-5).

There is even a tradition saying that by Ezra's time the Torah was totally lost, and that it was restored to him letter by letter.[53] Such a legend served to underscore Ezra's significance as a "second Moses." One tradition identifies him with Malachi, who was the last prophet, as Moses had been the first.[54] ("Malachi," which means "my messenger" [cf. Mal. 3:1], might not be a name but just a description.) Another tradition describes him as a disciple of Baruch, the scribe of Jeremiah (Jer. 36:4).[55] Travers Herford wrote about the congruency between Moses and Ezra: "[Ezra] marks . . . a new stage of development, as important as the rise of prophecy, and only less important than the work of Moses. If Moses were the real founder of the Jewish religion, giving to it the power to rise above and draw away from the religions of 'the peoples round about,' Ezra stood forth at a most critical period to save the Jewish religion, and with it the national life, from relapsing into decay through contact with Gentile ideas and practices."[56]

The wisdom that Ezra possessed was not based on his intelligence or his common sense, or even some direct revelation, but undoubtedly on tradition; that is, he knew how the ancestors had interpreted the commands. And again, why could this tradition in some cases not go back all the way to Moses? In the first six centuries since Ezra, c. 430 BC to c. AD 200, the rabbinic interpretations were handed down entirely orally through memorization.[57] After AD 70, when the scattering of the Jews intensified, the need for some codification

---

53. Sukkah 20a; cf. 4 Ezra 14:22.
54. Megillah 15a.
55. Megillah 16b.
56. Herford (1962, 18).
57. See for this part more extensively Ouweneel (2000a, §§6.3.2 and 9.1.4).

The Messianic Torah and the Millennial Torah

came up. Only around AD 200, the "definitive" Mishnah[58] was put together by Rabbi Yehudah HaNasi ("the Prince"); the final editorial work took place later. It was a mixture particularly of *halakah* (juridical interpretation[59]), and some *haggadah* (narrative interpretation[60]) or *midrash* (homiletic interpretation[61]). The interpretation of the Mishnah was written down in the so-called *Gemarah*,[62] which together with the Mishnah constitutes the Talmud. The Babylonian Talmud, finalized c. AD 500, acquired a much higher reputation than the Palestinian Talmud, finalized c. AD 425.

(Ultra-)Orthodox Jews declare everything in the Talmud to be sacred, and they try to erase from it all contradictions and to canonize all juridical opinions contained in it. Less strict Jews are of the opinion that the Talmud must be studied, but need not be believingly accepted in all points. This distinction is comparable to that between Roman Catholics, to whom church tradition is sacred, and Protestants, who assume a more critical attitude toward church tradition.

At any rate, to every serious student of the Tanakh—Jewish and Christian—the Talmud is a tremendous storehouse of discussions and interpretations highlighting certain aspects of Scripture. No wonder that many Messianic Jews follow certain customs which are not explicitly taught in the Torah

---

58. *Mishnah*, "learning (through repetition)," comes from *sh-n-h*, "repeat."
59. *Halakhah* comes from *h-l-kh*, "go, walk," and refers to the right way of life as intended in the Torah. *Halakhah* is also a legal decision, or the whole of legal decisions, taken by a legitimate authority and derived from the Torah with regard to a certain domain of life.
60. *Haggadah* (or Aram. *aggadah*) comes from *n-g-d* (hi. "make known, disclose, declare").
61. *Midrash* comes from *d-r-sh*, "seek, search," namely, searching the text, seeking its interpretation.
62. *Gemarah*, "completion," comes from Aram. *g-m-r* (Heb. *n-m-r*), "complete."

but which they believe to be in line with the Torah.[63] However, there are many differences of opinion about this among them; here are four points that divide Messianic Jews:

(1) *Men wearing the head cap* (called *kippah* or *yarmulke*). Not only is this not a biblical tradition, but it is not even a Talmudic tradition. It became mandatory first in the sixteenth century (*Shulchan 'Arukh*), although it had become common practice some centuries earlier. 1 Corinthians 11:2–16 is no argument against wearing the *kippah* because, according to the best expositors, that passage goes much further; that is, it forbids men to veil themselves and thus to behave like women.[64] Positive arguments for wearing the *kippah* are that it identifies with Jews who want to be faithful to the Torah, and it is a witness to non-Messianic Jews.

(2) *The Siddur*. Besides the Tanakh and the Talmud, the Siddur, which is the Jewish prayer book for daily use and particularly for the Shabbat and the festivals, is one of the most important Jewish books. Many Messianic Jews use it, or use considerable parts of it, others do not. Arguments against using the Siddur could be, first, that its use seems to be at odds with the free expression of the heart under the guidance of the Holy Spirit; the New Testament knows of many such free prayers.[65] Second, the Siddur does not contain New Testament truth. Third, the Siddur contains rabbinic elements that are not in accord with the spirit and the contents of the Tanakh and/or the New Testament. Arguments for using the Siddur could be, first, that its use is important for every Messianic Jew wishing to identify with his fellow-Jews and to be a wit-

---

63. Cf. Juster (1995, 227–38).
64. Fee (1987, 495–517); cf. Juster (1995, 215–18); Stern (1997, 170–71; 1999, 474).
65. Matt. 5:44; 24:20; 26:39, 42; Luke 18:11–13; John 15:7; Acts 1:24–25; 4:24–30; 8:15, 22, 24; 26:29; Rom. 1:10; 1 Cor. 14:13; 2 Cor. 13:7, 9; Eph. 6:18–19; Phil. 1:9; Col. 1:3, 9; 4:3; 1 Thess. 3:10; 5:25; 2 Thess. 1:11; 3:1; Heb. 13:18; James 5:14, 16–18; 1 John 3:22; 5:14–16.

ness to them. Second, the use of the Siddur does not exclude free prayers at all. Third, there is a striking congruity between some prayers in the Siddur (the Qaddish, the Amidah or Shemoneh-Esreh) and certain New Testament portions (see §§5.3.1 and 5.3.2). People have attempted to reconcile some of the pro and con arguments by devising a special Messianic version of the Siddur.[66]

(3) *The formation of Messianic Jewish congregations.* A common argument against such formation is that in this way Messianic Jews separate from Gentile Jesus-believers. Although separatism is a real danger — and as far as I can see, one that is not always avoided — there can be no fundamental objection to the establishment of Messianic Jewish congregations as long as they fully maintain practical fellowship with all Jesus-believers as far as possible.[67] Baptists have their own congregations because of their specific views on baptism, Pentecostals because of their views on the gifts of the Spirit, and Lutherans or Calvinists because of their specific Reformational Creeds, etc. If these differences are not recognized in Scripture at all, then Messianic Jews have all the more right to have their own congregations because their specific identity *is* recognized in the New Testament.

They may even speak of "synagogues" because James 2:1-2 explicitly refers to a Messianic Jewish "synagogue" (although many translations do not acknowledge this). They do have the duty to receive Messianic Gentiles in their meetings, and even as members of their congregations, if these Gentile believers so wish. But in order to maintain their Jewish identity they have the full right to require of such Gentile members, since they voluntarily join such communities, to comply with Jewish religious practices. These primarily include biblical ordinances; in addition to the many dealt with in this study, we may mention *Pidyon-haben* ("redemption of the

---

66. See Fischer and Bronstein (1988); Fischer (1992).
67. Juster (1995, 220-23; cf. 249-50); Stern (1997, 167-70, 181-83).

[first-born] son").⁶⁸ There are also Jewish customs not based on direct biblical data but on meaningful traditions, such as *Bar-Mitzvah* ("son of the commandment"), the medieval ceremony through which a Jewish boy, at the age of thirteen, comes of age religiously. Jesus' first visit to Jerusalem, at the age of twelve (Luke 2:41–50), has been presumed to anticipate this custom.⁶⁹

(4) *Calling Messianic leaders "rabbis."* Matthew 23:8 seems to be an argument against this practice: "[Y]ou are not to be called rabbi, for you have one teacher [or, master], and you are all brothers." However, do we not call a person "father" or "instructor" (or "teacher") (vv. 9–10)? Paul calls himself both (1 Cor. 4:15; 1 Thess. 2:11; 1 Tim. 2:7; 2 Tim. 1:11)! Apparently, Jesus is not forbidding these titles as such but forbidding his followers from accepting unearned honors, particularly honors that are due to the Lord alone.⁷⁰ If the title "rabbi" is used at all in Messianic congregations, it should be reserved for those who have had a proper rabbinic (theological and practical) training and a proper ordination (*semikah*). This raises practical (and difficult) questions regarding which accredited agencies supply proper rabbinic training, and which legitimate authority grants proper rabbinic ordination.

6.3.2 Jesus and the Oral Torah

It would be shortsighted if Messianic Jews desiring to keep the entire Torah would set aside the Talmudic literature. There is a host of useful material in the Oral Torah (the Talmud and related writings) with regard to keeping the Torah, at least insofar as this material does not contradict the Torah as such nor the New Testament. Studying all the Talmudic literature

---

68. Exod. 13:2–16; when the son is a month old he is "redeemed" for a price of five sanctuary-shekels (Num. 3:15; 18:16). Joseph and Mary followed this practice (Luke 2:22–24) (cf. Stern 1999, 108–9).
69. Stern (1999, 110); also cf. Juster (1995, 232–33).
70. Juster (1995, 224–25); Stern (1997, 172; 1999, 68–69).

The Messianic Torah and the Millennial Torah

and comparing it with the New Testament is a gigantic enterprise. Some may wonder whether it is really worth the effort. Did not the Lord Jesus himself reject the "tradition of the elders"? Indeed, he often turned against tradition, but we have to carefully note the way he did this (see above in §5.3.1). He never turned against the tradition of the elders as such; on the contrary, he said: "The scribes and the Pharisees sit on Moses' seat, *so do and observe whatever they tell you*, but not the works they do. For they preach, but do not practice. They tie up heavy burdens, hard to bear, and lay them on people's shoulders, but they themselves are not willing to move them with their finger" (Matt. 23:2-4, italics added).[71]

Thus, Jesus definitely advised the people to faithfully keep the instructions of the teachers of the Torah. In fact, John 7:37-39 presents us with an example of how Jesus himself honored a specific element of the Oral Torah, namely, the water-drawing ceremony (*Simchat Beit-haSho'evah*) of *Hoshana Rabbah* ("Great Hosannah"), performed on the last, "great" day of Sukkot. The ceremony is not prescribed in the Tanakh but in the Mishnah.[72] Jesus connected with the tradition by applying the ceremony to himself as the true source of living water, thus presenting himself as the Messiah (cf. vv. 40-43).

The traditions as such never were the problem, as long as they, or their use, truly reflected the spirit of the Torah. In fact, several Jewish traditions not prescribed by the Written Torah but by the Oral Torah are apparently taken for granted in the New Testament. Interesting examples are:

(1) The ceremonial washings (John 2:6; 13:3-5; cf. Matt. 15:2).[73]

---

71. Dunn's claim is therefore too one-sided that "the only references to tradition as such in the Gospels show Jesus as radically opposed to it" (1990a, 63). See also extensively §5.3.1.
72. See Jer. Mishnah Sukkot V.1.55a.
73. See the sixth and final order of the Mishnah: Seder Toharot.

(2) The avoidance of spoiled food (John 6:12).[74]

(3) Mary "remained seated" in the house (John 11:20), that is, "sitting *shiv'ah*," sitting in mourning for seven days following the death of a spouse or a close relative.[75]

(4) The mentioning of a "Shabbat day's journey" (Acts 1:12), that is, the maximum of two thousand cubits outside the city walls that were allowed by the rabbis.

(5) Also note that, according to a *haggadah*,[76] David ate the consecrated bread on Shabbat (1 Sam. 21:6) — a fact that renders Matthew 12:1–8 more understandable.

(6) I may add that, when Jesus was asked what is the most important commandment of the Torah, he surprisingly answered by first quoting from Deuteronomy 6:4 the *Shema*: "Hear, O Israel: The LORD our God, the LORD is one,"[77] although for his reply this was not necessary at all (Mark 12:29). It was not so much the Tanakh as it was the rabbinic tradition that had turned saying the *Shema* into a commandment, namely, the foremost Jewish creed to be cited twice daily.[78]

Dan Juster validly distinguishes between what I would call pre-Jesus and post-Jesus Oral Torah. Jesus spoke in a positive way of much in the Oral Torah of his days, but could the same be done with regard to post-first century Rabbinic Judaism? Juster writes: "I have become convinced that Rabbinic Judaism is a more severe departure from Biblical faith than I had ever realized in my early days of Jewish recovery.... I believe that the heart essence of Rabbinic Judaism is the rejection of the prophetic Spirit that forms the essence of

---

74. Cf. Shabbat 50b, 147b.
75. The word "sit" in Gk. (*ekathezeto*) is rather strange here, unless "sitting *shiv'ah*" is meant, which literally means sitting on the floor or a low stool, unshod and abstaining from any work.
76. Yalqut 1 Sam. §130 (referred to by Schoeps 1950, 66).
77. Or, "The LORD our God is one LORD," or, "The LORD is our God, the LORD is one," or, "The LORD is our God, the LORD alone."
78. Moseley (2000, 13).

The Messianic Torah and the Millennial Torah

the Hebrew Scriptures and the New Covenant Scriptures. . . . Rabbinic Judaism is the child of the first century pharisees who added the prayer of condemnation against Jewish believers and Jesus to the Synagogue liturgy. . . . I am convinced to no longer use post first century Rabbinic prayers." [79] Juster continues with a brief discussion of some post-Jesus Jewish customs and their propriety in Messianic Jewish individual and community life.[80]

To quote another testimony from Noam Hendren, one of the leaders of the Messianic *Keren Yeshu'ah* congregation at Tel Aviv: "We must understand that certain elements in the rabbinic instructions and the *halakah* were developed in opposition to the faith in Jesus. Sometimes believers inadvertently take over a beautiful prayer from the synagogue without realizing that the original intention of the prayer was anti-Christian. Several congregations, for instance, sing the hymn *Adon 'olam* ['Lord of the universe'], a song written with the intention of excluding the divinity of the Messiah." [81] I cannot judge whether this is historically correct but the general point is well taken: post-Jesus Rabbinic Judaism was and is consciously opposed to Jesus. It is all the more astonishing that the International Federation of Messianic Jews could write: "[A] growing number of Messianic Jews believe, as the Orthodox, that God vested appointed men of Israel with rabbinic and judicial authority, and that, therefore, the writings of our Jewish fathers are an essential and inseparable ingredient of Torah observance."[82]

Once again, a comparison between Roman Catholics and Protestants may help. Understandably, after the Reformation

---

79. Juster (1995, xi–xii).
80. Juster (1995, xv) says that the "tone" of his friend David Stern's *Manifesto* (1997; first ed., 1988) "is too positive concerning that which we have to gain from Rabbinic Judaism."
81. Meijer (1997, 50).
82. On an earlier website, now removed.

(beginning in 1517), many Roman Catholics wrote against the Protestants, often vehemently. However, that does not render all the theological treatises of such Catholics worthless. They can be very useful, as long as they are analyzed carefully. But this is something we should do with *all* theological works.

I repeat: there is nothing wrong with many Jewish traditions as such. The New Covenant, too, knows of "traditions" (thus literally in 1 Cor. 11:2; 2 Thess. 2:15; 3:6) that provide certain rules for practical spiritual life,[83] just as the Old Covenant did. But what Israel had to guard against was, first, the legalism, ritualism, ethnocentrism, and hypocrisy of many teachers and, second, any tradition, or the interpretation of it, that ran counter to the spirit of the Torah (see below). Jesus was so outraged at this attitude that he even accused the teachers of the Torah and the Pharisees of *anomia*, "Torah-lessness" (Matt. 23:28).

We should remember here, though, that such protests against a false way of handling the Torah were also leveled by many Jews themselves. Thus, for instance, the Talmud warns against the seven types of false Pharisees, which presumably can be interpreted as follows:[84] the "wait-a-moment" Pharisee (who wants the people to wait while he performs a commandment), the "pestle" Pharisee (the excessively humble one, whose head is bowed like a pestle in a mortar), the "shoulder" Pharisee (the self-complacent one, proudly carrying his good deeds on his shoulder so that all can see them), the prudish (or "reckoning") one (who commits a sin, then does a good deed and balances the latter against the former), the bruised Pharisee (refusing to face reality, e.g., running into a wall while looking at the ground to avoid seeing women), the Pharisee fearing punishment, and the Pharisee from love (either loving reward, or really loving the Torah as such).

---

83. Also see the verbal root (*paradidōmi*) in 1 Cor. 11:23, and cf. 4:17; 7:10, 17; 9:14; 14:37 (Dunn 1990a, 67–70).
84. Sotah 22b; Jer. Berakhot 14b; Jer. Sotah 20c (see Shulam 1998, 102).

The Messianic Torah and the Millennial Torah

Jesus strongly resented the many Torah teachers and Pharisees who turned religion into an outward matter, practiced not out of love to God but out of self-love: the craving for the praise of men (Matt. 6:1-2, 5, 16-18). In John 5:44-47 Jesus said: "How can you believe, when you receive glory from one another and do not seek the glory that comes from the only God? Do not think that I will accuse you to the Father. There is one who accuses you: Moses, on whom you have set your hope. For if you believed Moses, you would believe me; for he wrote of me. But if you do not believe his writings, how will you believe my words?" In such terms Jesus explained that the hypocrites, who accepted praise from men, were accused by the very Moses on whom they had set their hopes but whom they did not really believe with their hearts. Again, Jesus did not at all reject the traditional interpretation as such, but the hypocritical attitude with which the Torah was often taught. It is striking that he appealed to none other than Moses himself to support his verdict. Jesus never opposed Moses, as has been falsely asserted,[85] but rather appealed to Moses in opposition to the hypocrites.

Stephen did exactly the same. He was accused of speaking "blasphemous words against Moses" and "against the Torah,"

---

85. Cf. the astonishing statements by A. B. Bruce (1979, 106): "Christ's position as fulfiller entitled Him to point out the defects of the law itself," and (389) on Mark 7:19: "The idea throughout is that ethical defilement is alone of importance, [and] all other defilement, whether the subject of Mosaic ceremonial legislation or of scribe tradition, a trivial affair. Jesus here is a critic of Moses as well as of the scribes, and introduces a religious revolution." Likewise, Dunn (1990a, 97–98) asserts that at times "Jesus clearly sets his own revelation and insights into God's will over against the Torah—not just the oral Torah . . . but even the written Torah itself . . . in Matt. 5.33–37 he in effect sets aside the regulations about swearing . . . and in 5.38–42 he abolishes the *ius talionis*. . . . Perhaps most striking of all, his teaching on the causes of impurity as recalled in Mark 7 in effect cuts at the root of the whole ritual law (as Mark perceives—7.19b)." Regarding the latter point, see §9.2.2 below.

and of wanting to "change the customs that Moses delivered to us" (Acts 6:11-14). In reply to this, he acknowledged Moses as the God-sent "ruler and redeemer," who, however, had been rejected by the people (7:35, 39-40). Moreover, Stephen recognized the Torah as God-given "living oracles," which had been rejected by the people (7:38-43). The real situation was exactly the opposite: it was not Stephen who spoke and acted against Moses, but the mass of the people who did this, particularly their leaders.

In Matthew 23:23-24 Jesus pointed out the folly of meticulously obeying the finest details of the Torah—like giving a tenth of one's spices—while at the same time neglecting the essence of the Torah: justice and mercy and faithfulness. Thus, these "blind guides" literally strained out a gnat but figuratively swallowed a camel. The metaphor used here involved the decree that all wine had to be strained through a sieve to prevent the drinker from swallowing *treif*, vermin. It is striking that even in the latter case Jesus says, "These [things] *you ought to have done*, without neglecting the others [that is, justice, mercy and faithfulness]," that is, the Torah as well as its traditional interpretation and elaboration (v. 23b, italics added). Jesus did not question the fact that the Torah has to be interpreted, and that, as time goes by, certain interpretations become traditional. What Jesus resented in Matthew 5, and again in chapter 23, was never the Torah itself, nor even the inevitable "tradition of the elders" as such, but every unwarranted expansion or mitigation of the Torah, or interpretations contravening the spirit of the Torah.

Let me give some examples of each.[86]

(1) *Expansion*. Tradition insisted on a large number of ritual purifications that went far beyond the Torah and to which Jesus did not feel bound (Mark 7:1-7) (see §9.2.2 below). In

---

86. See Ouweneel (2000a, §6.3.2). Juster (1995, 56): "when tradition went against God's Word and when religious leaders missed the true essence of the Torah, Jesus was severe in His criticism."

the course of time, the Shabbat commandment, too, had been expanded with many unwarranted stipulations—a tendency that Jesus resented on the principle that man was not made for the Shabbat but the Shabbat for man (2:27). It is worth noting, though, that Jesus in fact did not criticize these stipulations as such, but appealed to the accepted convention that a more important principle may override a less important one: intense hunger overrides the Shabbat law (see §5.3.1).

David Stern mentioned an interesting modern example.[87] The Torah forbids making fire on Shabbat (Exod. 35:3). When electricity was introduced the rabbis forbade lighting electrical lamps on Shabbat because pressing the button may produce a tiny spark. For the same reason a Jew is not to use an elevator on Shabbat. However, Orthodoxy invented the "shabbat elevator," which automatically goes up and down all day, stopping on each floor. An Orthodox Jew is permitted to use it because no "fire" is produced. Stern comments, "The majority of Jews, even those who understand the above logic, think that something is peculiar about a system that produces this rule, that such a rule neither enhances human spirituality nor expresses God's will."

Sometimes the rabbis no longer realized the difference between the (Written) Torah and their traditions (the Oral Torah), for in John 5:10 (NIV) they say to the healed invalid, "It is the Sabbath, and it is not lawful [Gr. *ouk exestin*] for you to take up your bed"—whereas the Torah does not say anything of the kind. It was Jewish tradition that forbade this.[88] (Jeremiah 17:21-22 apparently opposes carrying merchandise; cf. Nehemiah 13:19.) One could also say that the scribes were not referring to the Written Torah but to the Oral Torah.

(2) *Mitigation.* One Jewish interpretation referred a person accused of manslaughter to a lower court of justice, and there-

---

87. Stern (1997, 152).
88. Cf. Talmud, Shabbat 6a.

by mitigated the seriousness of this crime.[89] Jesus did the opposite by declaring even the *thought* of manslaughter to be a transgression of the commandment (Matt. 5:21-26). Another example involved the way some Jews circumvented honoring one's father and mother by granting the means to support them the status of *Corban* (a gift devoted to God, and thereby removed from use) (see §6.1.1).

With regard to divorce, too, some Pharisees of the school of Hillel interpreted the Torah in a rather lenient way. They believed that a man could divorce his wife for anything that caused annoyance or embarrassment. In opposition to their laxity Jesus placed a stern "no divorce," which was entirely in the spirit of the Torah (Matt. 19:3-9; cf. Mal. 2:16). He explained that any alleged leniency on the part of Moses was based on the hardness of the people's hearts, not on God's primary intention (cf. Deut. 24:1-4 and Jesus' appeal to Gen. 2:24). What the Mosaic Torah did not recommend but at best tolerated is not tolerated in the Messianic Torah. Thus, the latter brings out the spirit of the one, eternal Torah better than the Mosaic Torah did.[90]

(3) *False interpretation.* Jesus indicated that the rule of "an eye for an eye and a tooth for a tooth" was not to be viewed as a principle indicating the way people were to deal with one another in their daily life (Matt. 5:38-42).[91] That is, people should not take revenge on their own initiative and on their own behalf. As far as the magistrates were concerned, however, he did not contradict this principle of retaliation (cf. Paul: the ruler is "an avenger who carries out God's wrath on the wrongdoer," Rom. 13:4). Nevertheless, his argument

---

89. At least, this is the way Ridderbos (1965, 109) understands Jesus' intention in Matt. 5;21.
90. This does not mean that Jesus directly defied the Mosaic Torah: "It is a general principle that greater stringency than the law requires is not illegal" (Sanders 1985, 256).
91. Cf. Ridderbos (1965, 116–17).

The Messianic Torah and the Millennial Torah

does *not* proceed like this: If someone slaps you on the right cheek, don't slap him back but leave the matter to the judge. Rather, while accepting judges and tribunals (Matt. 5:25), and even the precept "an eye for an eye and a tooth for a tooth," Jesus recommends relinquishing the right of appealing to that precept. Instead, the disciple is to turn to the striker the other cheek also (v. 39). Thus, he is not to "resist" in a court of law.

Once again, we see that the Messianic Torah surpasses the Mosaic Torah: the latter allows someone who has been slapped to appeal to a court of law, but the former recommends abandoning that right and seeking to win the brother instead.[92] Compare the apostle Paul: "Why not rather suffer wrong? Why not rather be defrauded?" (1 Cor. 6:7). Likewise, the Mosaic Torah allowed a person to receive his required cloak back before sunset (Exod. 22:26-27; Deut. 24:12-13), but the Messianic Torah prescribes gladly parting with something that is legally protected (Matt. 5:40). Gentleness, mercy, and love do not displace justice, but they often surpass justice.

Another false but probably popular interpretation was to view the "neighbor" as the fellow countryman or only one's friend (Matt. 5:43-47). Consequently, the unbiblical "hate your enemy" was added by some rabbis to the biblical "love your neighbor."[93] The Mosaic Torah itself had already emphasized that one was to love others as oneself, including strangers residing in the land, and that one should be concerned about one's enemies (Lev. 19:33-34; Exod. 23:4-5; Deut. 21:10-14). Jesus explained that your "neighbor" could also be your enemy, as he showed particularly in the parable of the Good

---

92. Carson (1984, 155–56).
93. Cf. Yomah 22b–23a: "Any scholar, who does not avenge himself and retain anger like a serpent, is no [real] scholar" (a line differently explained, though). In the Qumran [Q] Community Rule [Serek, abbr. QS], found in Qumran Cave I [IQ], loving the sons of Light is coupled with hating the sons of Darkness (IQS I.9–10) (see LaSor 1972, 200–201, 240–41).

Samaritan (Luke 10:25-37).

Two things must be clear. On the one hand, it would be both unwise and, in the light of Jesus' advice, unbiblical to set aside the "tradition of the elders." For centuries, the rabbis have investigated numerous *halakhic* problems, and it would be foolish to reinvent the wheel time and again. Jesus himself accepted the Oral Torah as far as it went. On the other hand, it could not be fairly claimed that the Oral Torah has any formal-divine authority comparable to that of the Written Torah.[94] Therefore, the term "Oral Torah" itself is misleading because it suggests a parity with the Written Torah. In light of Deuteronomy 17:8-13, we are surely allowed to say that God gave the priests and judges in Israel a certain formal authority to interpret the Written Torah. In a sense, as a matter of principle this authority exists until this very day; interpreting Scripture is the duty of the teachers of God's church on earth (1 Cor. 12:28; Eph. 4:11-13), and applying it to daily congregational life is the duty of the elders of any congregation (Acts 20:28; Phil. 1:1; 1 Thess. 5:12-13; 1 Tim. 3:1-7; 5:17; Titus 1:5-9; Heb. 13:7, 17; 1 Pet. 5:1-5). But there is nothing in the Torah that gives us the right to refer to these interpretations as an "Oral" Torah, and even less to declare them to possess an authority equal to that of the Written Torah.

The Tanakh nowhere bestows any authority upon some kind of Oral Torah; instead, the people are always referred back to the Written Torah. For instance, the king is bound to the Written Torah (Deut. 17:18-19). Joshua referred the people back solely to the Written Torah, and not, for instance, to his own oral interpretations of it (Josh. 23:6-8). In King Josiah's days the Written Torah was rediscovered (2 Kings 22-23) and imposed upon the people without the slightest reference to any authoritative Oral Torah. The very fact that so many false elements had come to be included in the "tradition of the elders," as Jesus brought to light, clearly shows that this tra-

---

94. See on this point Berkowitz (1996, chapter 6).

dition was not a divine work but a mass of "human [i.e., humanly flawed] commands" (Matt. 15:19–20; Mark 7:7–8; Gal. 1:14; Col. 2:8, 22; Titus 1:14; cf. Isa. 29:13: "a commandment taught by men").

The same principle is found in the New Testament era. At the end of his career, the apostle Paul committed believers not to some formal *halakhic* authority ("the" church, elders, bishops, theologians) but "to God and to the word of his grace, which is able to build you up and to give you the inheritance among all those who are sanctified" (Acts 20:32). The "word of God's grace" includes both the Tanakh and the preaching of the apostles (cf. 1 Thess. 2:13) — but nothing more than that. As Peter wrote at the end of his career: "This is now the second letter that I am writing to you, beloved. In both of them I am stirring up your sincere mind by way of reminder, that you should remember the predictions of the holy prophets and the commandment of the Lord and Savior through your apostles" (2 Pet. 3:1–2). We certainly must interpret God's Word, and surely, as time goes by, certain interpretations may become traditional. But they never acquire some formal authoritative status alongside the prophetic and apostolic Scriptures. In the widest sense, Torah encompasses the entirety of Holy Scripture. It may be a rabbinic view that all authoritative interpretation of the Torah is also Torah, but that is not a scriptural view; interpretations of, and extrapolations from, Scripture never become Scripture itself.

6.3.3 The Book of Ruth: A Piece of Oral Torah?

One of the most interesting pieces of Oral Torah, so to speak, may well be the Scroll of Ruth — interesting, of course, for several reasons, among them that this may be a piece of Oral Torah that eventually ended up being included in the Written Torah![95] In Israel, the question was raised whether David was qualified to be king of the nation because his great-grand-

---

95. See Cohen/Rosenberg (1984, 89–93).

mother, Ruth, was a Moabitess, and Moabites were not allowed to enter the assembly of the LORD (Deut. 23:3). According to the rabbis, David's eligibility to be king was openly contested by Doeg the Edomite (cf. 1 Sam. 21:7; 22:9).[96] Samuel was still alive at that time; tradition tells us that he composed the Scroll of Ruth,[97] allegedly in order to explain the *halakah* that provided the basis for Ruth becoming accepted among Israel.

Interestingly, this is the way the rabbis interpreted Psalm 40:7, "Behold, I have come; in the scroll of the book it is written of me." That is, I have come with a scroll that is written about me, allegedly referring to the Scroll of Ruth, which included David's lineage (Ruth 4:18-22; cf. 1 Chron. 2:3-15), as well as his legal right to a place among Israel, and even to the kingship through his descent in the male line of Judah (cf. Gen. 49:10). The *halakah* established in this Book involved Ruth's admission to the assembly of the LORD through her marriage with Boaz. The *halakah* was legitimately established by Boaz—who according to the rabbis was the head of the Sanhedrin at that time—together with ten elders (4:2, 4, 9, 11). Generally speaking, two types of *halakah* were accepted in Israel: what was derived from the Torah through the thirteen rabbinic rules of exposition, and what could be traced directly to Moses. The *halakah* established by Boaz and the elders was given the latter classification. It was a piece of Oral Torah that, according to the rabbis, was written down by Samuel and, because of its great importance with regard to David's kingship, eventually received a place in the canon.

It is of special interest that the Scroll of Ruth is read in the synagogues during the festival of *Shavu'ot*. We remember that *Shavu'ot* is both a harvest feast (cf. Ruth 3) and the feast of the Torah-giving (Exod. 23:16; see §5.3). This helps us understand why the Scroll of Ruth is read at this festival.

---

96. Yevamot 76b, 77a; also see Midrash Lekach Tob.
97. Cf. Baba Bathra 14b:

(1) The Book is a harvest idyll. Naomi and Ruth arrived at Bethlehem "at the beginning of barley harvest" (1:22). Jewish literature (Midrash, Targum, Rashi) has pointed out that this marked "the beginning of Passover, when the reaping of the *omer* (Lev. xxiii. 10) took place."[98] In Ruth 2:23, we hear that Ruth gleaned "until the end of the barley and wheat harvests" (the barley is ripe before the wheat, Exod. 9:31-32). The beginning of the wheat harvest—seven weeks after the beginning of the barley harvest—is marked by *Shavu'ot* (cf. Exod. 34:22), the "feast of the firstfruits" (*chag habbikkurim*). I see Ruth 3 as suggestive of the merriment of *Shavu'ot* (cf. vs. 7). I know of no rabbinic tradition pointing to such a link, but this may be because *Shavu'ot* is at the beginning, and the event of Ruth 3 occurred nearer to the end, of the wheat harvest.

(2) *Shavu'ot* is also the feast of the giving of the Torah, not only the Written but also the Oral Torah. Perhaps Ruth is read to remind the people of the significance of the Oral Torah.[99] As the *Midrash L'kach Tov* reminds us, the Torah is the "Torah of loving-kindness"; both the Torah and the Scroll of Ruth are "composed entirely of kindness."[100] Ruth is a book about the joy of the Torah (*Simchat-Torah*). Sometimes its decrees may seem to be against us, as Deuteronomy 23:3 was against Ruth, but the latter verse was "overruled" by the levirate law of Deuteronomy 25:5-10.[101] The questions whether this law applied also to close kinsmen other than the deceased man's own brothers, and whether this law could be applied to the Moabite wife of a deceased Israelite, were settled by the *hal-*

---

98. Cohen/Rosenberg (1984, 121).
99. Cohen/Rosenberg (1984, 92).
100. Cohen/Rosenberg (1984, 93).
101. The Targum expressly mentions the levirate marriage in connection with Ruth 4, although not all rabbis agree that the "redemption" in this chapter is indeed synonymous with the levirate. The "overruling" was possible because many rabbis argued that Deut. 23:3 speaks of the Moabite, not of the Moabitess.

akah that Boaz and his *minyan* formulated.

(3) Another Jewish source, *B'sorath Eliyahu,* reminds us of a tradition telling us that at Mount Sinai, when the Torah was given, the souls of all Jews as well as of all future proselytes were present. The reading of the book about Ruth the proselyte at *Shavu'ot* may be an allusion to this.

(4) The reading of Ruth is also a reminder of the fact that, if God has mercy on someone from a rejected nation who sought his mercy, he certainly will show mercy to any Jew who loves God's Torah. The way of the Torah is not easy; Ruth's experiences "on the thorny path of righteousness" show that "the Torah can only be acquired by those who tread the road of hardship and want."[102]

---

102. Cohen/Rosenberg (1984, 104).

Chapter 7
A Threefold Torah:
Differences and Similarities

How can you say, "We are wise,
> *and the Torah of the* Lord *is with us"?*
But behold, the lying pen of the scribes
> *has made it into a lie.*
The wise men shall be put to shame;
> *they shall be dismayed and taken;*
behold, they have rejected the word of the Lord*,*
> *so what wisdom is in them?*
> > > > > > Jeremiah 8:8–9

You show that you are a letter from Christ
> *delivered by us,*
written not with ink
> *but with the Spirit of the living God,*
not on tablets of stone
> *but on tablets of human hearts.*
Such is the confidence
> *that we have through Messiah toward God.*
Not that we are sufficient in ourselves to claim anything as coming from us,
> *but our sufficiency is from God,*
who has made us sufficient to be ministers of a new

covenant,
not of the letter but of the Spirit.
2 Corinthians 3:3-6

Summary: *It is worthwhile to compare the Mosaic Torah, the Messianic Torah, and the Millennial Torah with one another concerning the following issues: the place of the king, the priest (and the Temple ministry plus priestly teaching), and the prophet, the introductory rite, the central mountain, the characteristic Theophany (manifestation of God), the basic sacrifice (and its associated redemption), the place of angels, the central song, the central banquet, and the specific blessings. What is the place of key concepts such as love, righteousness, covenant loyalty, and peace in all three manifestations of the Torah? And what is the specific meaning of Jesus Messiah as the "new Moses," the new Torah-giver? He is more than Moses, for in a sense in his own person he is the one, eternal Torah.*

7.1 A Threefold Torah

7.1.1 One Torah, Several Manifestations

IN CHAPTER 4, I EMPHASIZED THAT IN THE FUTURE Messianic Kingdom *('olam habba)* the entire Torah will be still in force, that is, that specific form of it that I have called the Millennial Torah. This form of the Torah includes most but not all of the Mosaic Torah. At least, we cannot prove that literally every element of the Mosaic Torah will be in force. There are some interesting omissions in the prophetic books. For instance, of the various festivals only *Pesach* and *Sukkot* are mentioned (Ezek. 45:21, 25; Zech. 14:16; cf. Hos. 12:9). *Shavu'ot* and *Yom Kippur* are omitted, although "(all) the appointed festivals" in Ezekiel 44:24; 45:17; 46:9, 11 might very well include them (see note 36 in §6.2.2). Interestingly, Yalqut Shimeoni on Proverbs 9:2 asserts with regard to the Messianic age: "All festivals will one day be abolished, except for Purim which will never be abolished.... Rabbi Eleazar said: 'Also the Day of Atonement will never be abolished.'" Probably there is a studied contrast here between the most joyful and playful day and the most holy and ascetic day on the Jewish calendar, as well as a pun on Purim and Yom haKippurim.[1]

On the one hand, vital elements of the Mosaic Torah seem to be lacking—at least, they are not mentioned in Scripture—whereas, on the other hand, Ezekiel 40-44 contain a number of elements foreign to the Mosaic Torah. A conspicuous example consists of the commandments concerning "the prince," in whom I can discern no other than the earthly representative (probably from the house of David) of the Messiah (see again §6.2.2).

This leads to the following important conclusion. On the one hand, the Millennial Torah has much more in common with the Mosaic Torah than many covenant theologians seem to realize. To them it must be a shocking idea that dispensational theologians believe that, during the Messianic Kingdom, so much of the Mosaic Torah will still be in force, even the sacrificial ministry. On the other hand, the Millennial Torah and the Mosaic Torah have less in common than some Messianic Jewish theologians, and certainly Orthodox Jews, seem to believe. The reason is simply that *the two forms of the Torah are not identical.* As I summarized it in §6.2.1, the form that the one, eternal Torah will assume in the Messianic Kingdom will have very much in common with the Mosaic Torah. But they will be sufficiently different to recognize the Millennial Torah and the Mosaic Torah as different manifestations of *the* (one, eternal) Torah. Moderate dispensational theology has every reason to distinguish the following three manifestations of the one, eternal Torah, each linked with a specific *king*, specific *priests*, a specific *prophet*, a specific *mountain*, a specific *theophany*, a specific role of *angels*, a specific *song*, a specific *ministry*, and a specific *banquet*, in addition to the specific *blessings* mentioned in Romans 9:4-5 (see the next §§).

---

1. Scholem (1971, 54–55).

7.1.2 The Mosaic Dispensation

Let us first look at the various characteristics of the Mosaic polity.

1. *The king.* In Deuteronomy 33:3-5, this is said to God: Your holy ones "followed in your steps, receiving direction from you, when Moses commanded us the Torah, as a possession for the assembly of Jacob. Thus he became king in Jeshurun,[2] when the heads of the people were gathered, all the tribes of Israel together." Opinions are divided about whether it is God or Moses who is this "king in Jeshurun"; Rashi said the former (followed by many recent Christian expositors); Philo, Ibn Ezra, and Maimonides said the latter (followed by many older Christian expositors). At any rate, this kingship is connected with the giving of the Torah: God is its Author, Moses its mediator. Craigie explained: "[T]he people acclaim their leader, namely, God (the lawgiver): Let there be a King in Jeshurun. The kingship of God in early Israel rests on three basic premises: (i) the liberation of his people in the Exodus (see Exod. 15:18 [also cf. Num. 23:21-22; 1 Sam. 8:7; Ps. 47:6-7. WJO]); (ii) the giving of the law at Sinai; (iii) the victory (still lying in the future) by which God would grant to his people the promised land."[3]

2. *Priests and Temple ministry.* No Mosaic dispensation, including the Mosaic Torah, would have been conceivable without a sanctuary ministry, and thus without the Tabernacle, afterward the Temple, ministry. The Mishnah says: "The world is upheld by three things: Torah, Temple worship, and acts of mercy."[4] These three things belong together: Temple worship implies serving God, acts of mercy imply serving people, and the Torah prescribes and regulates both. Temple ministry is not only worship but also a provision for the sinful and pen-

---

2. That is, "The Upright One," namely, Israel (see Deut. 32:15; 33:26).
3. Craigie (1976, 393-94).
4. Mishnah Avot I.2.

itent people of God. The Torah decrees how a person must live, but also what one must do after having failed. Torah and Temple ministry together keep God's people in fellowship with him. In a sense, Moses was Israel's priest par excellence; he had direct and permanent access to God.[5] In practice, his brother Aaron and the latter's descendants functioned as priests (Exod. 28:1; 30:30; 40:13; Num. 3:3-4; 25:11-13).

3. *Teaching.* In addition to the sacrificial ministry, another task of the priests was teaching the Torah: "You are to distinguish between the holy and the common, and between the unclean and the clean, and you are to teach the people of Israel all the statutes that the LORD has spoken to them by Moses" (Lev. 10:10-11). The Levites (i.e., the priests) "shall teach Jacob your rules and Israel your Torah" (Deut. 33:10). Priests and Levites "helped the people to understand the Torah. . . . They read from the book, from the Torah of God, clearly, and they gave the sense, so that the people understood the reading" (Neh. 8:7-8). "True instruction [or, the Torah of truth] was in his [i.e., Levi's] mouth . . . he turned many from iniquity. For the lips of a priest should guard knowledge, and people should seek Torah from his mouth, for he is the messenger of the LORD of hosts" (Mal. 2:6-7). Note the essence of Leviticus 10, namely, teaching the Torah is basically nothing but teaching the difference between the holy and the common, and between the unclean and the clean (cf. Ezek. 44:23).

4. *The prophet.* If God was the King in Jeshurun (see point 1), Moses was his prophet, as he himself acknowledged (Deut. 18:15, 18; 34:10; cf. Num. 12:6-8).[6] He bore the title

---

5. Lev. 8–9 makes clear that Moses was the first priest in Israel; cf. Exod. 24:4–8; 25:22; 32:30, 32; 33:9, 11; Num. 7:89; 12:8; Ps. 99:6.
6. Hebrew Christian Aaron Judah Kligerman (in Kac [1986, 216–18]) wrote about Moses' threefold function (king, priest, prophet): "Moses was the first mediator between God and Israel. . . . A mediator incorporates three functions: that of king, prophet, and priest... Moses was an uncrowned king. He exercised more power over Israel than any king in Israel's history. The uniqueness of Moses' position

"man of God" (Deut. 33:1; Josh. 14:6; 1 Chron. 23:14; 2 Chron. 30:16; Ezra 3:2; Ps. 90 title). Under the Old Covenant, another prophet, a "man of God" too, played a great role in restoring the people to the Torah and to the covenant of the Lord: Elijah (1 Kings 17:18, 24; 19:10, 14; 2 Kings 1:9-13). As such, he will play an eschatological role as well (see §7.2.1 and 7.2.2).

5. *Admission rite.* In the name *b'rit milah*, "covenant of circumcision," the link between circumcision and the covenant—first the Abrahamic covenant (Gen. 17:10-14), later the Mosaic covenant (Lev. 12:3; cf. John 7:22)— is maintained. Circumcision created an *outward* separation between the *mul b'arlah* ("circumcised man," lit., "circumcised in the foreskin") and the *arêl* ("uncircumcised man," lit., the "one having the foreskin"; cf. Acts 11:3, Gr. "having [the] foreskin"). Morally, however, there was no distinction between the Gentile *arêlim* and the Israelite Torah-trespassers, who were "uncircumcised of heart" (Jer. 9:25-26; cf. 4:4; Deut. 10:16; 30:6; Rom. 2:29).

6. *Mountain.* The Mosaic Torah was given on Mount Sinai, also called the "mountain of God" (Exod. 3:1; 4:27; 18:5; 24:13; 1 Kings 19:8) and the "mountain of the LORD" (Num. 10:33). However, at other places it is called the "mountain of the LORD" is Zion (Ps. 24:3; Isa. 2:3; 30:29; Micah 4:2; also cf. Gen. 22:14) (see §7.1.3), which points forward to the Millennial Torah (§7.2.2). A Jewish tradition[7] tells us why Mount Sinai was preferred above all other mountains.

7. *Theophany.* The Torah-giving was accompanied with thunder and lightning, clouds, fire, and smoke (Exod. 19:16-19; 20:18; cf. 24:17). As Deuteronomy 33:2 says: "The LORD came from Sinai and dawned from Seir upon us; he shone forth from Mount Paran; he came from the ten thousands of holy ones, with flaming fire [NKJV: a fiery law] at his right

---

as a prophet is spelled out in [Num. 12:6-8a]. . . . As the great mediator, Moses discharged also the functions of a priest."

7. E.g., Gen. Rabbah 99 (see Ginzberg 1968, 83-85).

A Threefold Torah: Differences & Similarities

hand." The phrase "fiery law" is unclear,[8] but in any case, the Torah is referred to in verse 4. New divine manifestations included the descent of the "pillar of cloud," the *Shekinah*, upon the first "tent of meeting," that is, upon the Tabernacle, and upon the "mercy seat" (the atonement cover), as well as fire descending upon the first burnt offering (Exod. 33:9-10; 40:34-38; Lev. 9:23-24; 16:2; Num. 7:89; also cf. 14:10; 16:19, 42; 20:6: the *Shekinah* in judgment). The "pillar of cloud" was the sign of the LORD's glory (Exod. 16:10; cf. 24:16; 34:5; Num. 12:5), it pointed the way to Israel (Exod. 13:21-22), it stood between the people and the pursuing Egyptians (14:20), it enshrouded the top of the Sinai (Exod. 19:9; 24:15-18; Deut. 5:22), and it led the people through the desert (Num. 9:15-22; 10:11-12, 34; 11:25; 12:5; 14:14; Deut. 1:33; 31:15; Ps. 78:14; 99:7).

8. *Initial sacrifice and redemption.* The Mosaic Torah was founded upon redemption from the bondage of Egypt—see the opening phrase of the Ten Commandments (Exod. 20:2; Deut. 5:6)—and upon the blood of the *Pesach* lamb put on the doorframes (Exod. 12:7, 22). The actual establishment of the Mosaic covenant was confirmed by burnt offerings and sacrificed oxen offered as peace offerings to the LORD. Half of the blood was "thrown" on the people as the "blood of the covenant that the LORD has made with you" (24:4-8).

9. *Angels.* Deuteronomy 33:2 refers to "ten thousands of holy ones," which are angels. Note as well the link between Sinai and the tens of thousands of "chariots of God" in Psalm 68:17, which some rabbis explained as angels.[9] Interestingly, the New Testament refers several times to the role of angels at

---

8. Heb. *eshdat*, in the (N)KJV reads as *esh-dat*, "decree of fire" (so also the rabbis: a Torah revealed in fire, Exod. 19:18; 24:17; Deut. 4:12, 15, 33, 36; 5:4–5, 22–25); cf. the NIV: "mountain slopes."

9. Exod. Rabbah 29,2. The angel who actually gave the Torah to Moses is called Yefefiyah, the "prince of the Torah" (Ginzberg 1968, 114; also see 94, 109–114 and the many references in Strack/Billerbeck 1922–28 on Acts 7:53).

the Torah-giving (Acts 7:53; Gal. 3:19; Heb. 2:2). A Talmudic tradition tells us that Moses ascended into heaven to capture the Torah from the angels.[10]

10. *Song.* The Torah-giving led to the great Song of Moses in Deuteronomy 32. According to chapter 31:19–22, this Song was to serve as a witness for God against Israel when it would break his covenant. Deuteronomy 32:44–46 explains that the purpose of the Song was to remind the people of the Torah. In the Talmud, the Song of Moses sometimes stands for the entire Torah.[11] There are many haggadic allusions to song as the symbol of the Torah. In fact, part of the commandments is given in metrical form (Exod. 21:12–17; Deut. 27:15–26), almost as a song. When after Israel's long winter in Egypt, the bridegroom in the Song of Solomon says: "Arise, my love, my beautiful one, and come away . . . the time of singing has come" (2:10–12), this is God's appeal to Israel to leave Egypt and his "invitation to receive the Decalogue."[12]

11. *Banquet.* The Torah-giving on Sinai is connected with a remarkable meal: "Then Moses and Aaron, Nadab, and Abihu, and seventy of the elders of Israel went up, and they saw the God of Israel. There was under his feet as it were a pavement of sapphire stone, like the very heaven for clearness. And he did not lay his hand on the chief men of the people of Israel; they beheld God, *and ate and drank.* The LORD said to Moses, 'Come up to me on the mountain and wait there, that I may give you the tablets of stone, with the Torah and the commandment, which I have written for their instruction'" (Exod. 24:9–12, italics added).

12. *Blessings.* In Romans 9:4–5 Paul mentions the following eight specific prerogatives of Israel, God's ancient covenant people. Notice that six of these eight are mentioned in a Mid-

---

10. Shabbat 89a.
11. Sanhedrin 21b; see footnote in the Soncino edition.
12. Cohen/Rosenberg (1984, 20).

rash[13] as having been "created," either actually (real pre-existence) or as ideas (ideal pre-existence), before the world (see the additions between {} to each point). To Israel belong:

(a) The *mishpat* (or *ma'amad*) *habbanim* (adoption as sons) (Exod. 4:22; Deut. 14:1) {"[The creation of] Israel was contemplated, as it is written: 'Remember your congregation, which you have purchased of old,'" Ps. 74:2}.

(b) The *kavod*, more specifically, the *Shekinah* (divine glory) (Exod. 40:34–38) {"The Throne of Glory [was created] as it is written: 'Your throne is established from of old,'" Ps. 93:2}.

(c) The *b'ritot* (the covenants) (Exod. 24; Deut. 29).

(d) The *mattan hatTorah*, "giving of the Torah" (Exod. 20) {"The Torah [was created] for it is written: 'The LORD possessed me [i.e., *Hokmah* = *Torah*; see chapter 3 above] at the beginning of his work, the first of his acts of old (*qedem*),'" Prov. 8:22}.

(e) The *'avodat haShem*, "service of God" (Temple worship) (Exod. 25–31; Lev. 1–16) {"[The creation of] the Temple was contemplated, as it is written: 'A glorious throne set on high from the beginning is the place of our sanctuary,'" Jer. 17:12}.

(f) The *havtachot* (promises) (Gen. 12) {I might add that Titus 1:2 speaks of a promise "before the ages began"; cf. 1 John 2:25; also cf. the "grace, which he [i.e., God] gave us in Christ Jesus before the ages began," 2 Tim. 1:9}.

(g) The *avot*, "fathers" (patriarchs) (Gen. 12–50) {"The creation of the patriarchs was contemplated, for it is written: 'Like the first fruit on the fig tree in its first season, I saw your fathers,'" Hos. 9:10}.

(h) "[F]rom their race, according to the flesh, is the Christ, who is God over all, blessed forever" (Rom. 9:5) {"The name

---

13. Gen. Rabbah 1.4. Cf. similar references in Shulam (1998, 339n6). Pesachim 54a and N'darim 39a give a somewhat different list of seven items: the Torah, repentance, the Garden of Eden, Ge-Hinnom (i.e., hell), the throne of glory, the Temple, and the name of the Messiah.

of Messiah was contemplated: 'May his name endure forever, his fame continue as long as the sun,'" Ps. 72:17; also cf. Micah 5:2: ". . . whose coming forth is from of old [*miqqedem*], from ancient days [*mimê 'olam*]"}.

The sixth pre-existing element in the Midrash is repentance, which is thought to date from before the foundation of the world because of Psalm 90:2-3 in the following rendering: "Before . . . you had formed the earth and the world . . . you turned Man to humiliation [lit., dust]." I do not want to force this point into Paul's list, but surely [c] the covenants and [f] the promises can only be fulfilled by the way of repentance (Deut. 30:1-10).

7.1.3 The Davidic-Solomonic Revival

It would be incorrect to explain the Mosaic dispensation solely in terms of its Mosaic beginnings. Just as the Mosaic covenant was enlarged by the Davidic covenant, the Mosaic dispensation was widened and deepened by the Davidic (and Solomonic) revival. Without the characteristics of the latter, the Messianic and Millennial dispensations could not be grasped in their full scope.

1. *The king.* David was the king "after God's own heart" (1 Sam. 13:14), "his servant" (2 Sam. 3:18; 7:5, 8; 1 Kings 8:66; 11:13, 32, 34, 36, 38; 14:8; 2 Kings 8:19; 19:34; 20:6; 1 Chron. 17:4, 7; Ps. 78:70; 89:4, 21; Isa. 37:35; Jer. 33:21-22, 26; Ezek. 34:23-24; 37:24-25), "his anointed" (Heb. *mashiach*; 2 Sam. 22:51; Ps. 18:51; 132:17; cf. 20:7; 28:8), "the LORD's anointed" or "the anointed of the God of Jacob" (2 Sam. 19:21; 23:1), and as such not only the Messiah's great ancestor (Isa. 11:1; Jer. 23:5; 33:15, 17; cf. Rev. 5:5; 22:16: "the root and the descendant of David") but also his great royal type. The Messiah is even called by the name "David" (Jer. 30:9; Ezek. 34:23-24; 37:24-25; Hos. 3:5; Amos 9:11). From the time of David's kingship, Israel's future is forever linked with that of the house of David (2 Sam. 7:13, 16; 22:51; 1 Kings 2:4; 2 Kings 8:19; 2 Chron. 6:16; Ps. 72:17; Isa. 55:3; Jer. 33:17; Ezek. 37:25; Luke 1:33; Acts 2:30). Likewise,

Solomon, the great son of David, is a type of the Messiah, who is David's greatest Son (Matt. 1:1; 9:27; 12:23; 15:22; 20:30-31; 21:9,15 and par.; cf. 12:42; Luke 1:32).

2. *Priests and Temple ministry.* A few great Israelites functioned as priests without belonging to the house of Aaron: in addition to Moses, they were David and his son, Solomon. In them, a special link between royalty and priesthood was forged, which will be fulfilled in the Messiah (see §7.2.2). David offered sacrifices when he brought the ark up to Zion, being dressed as a priest (2 Sam. 6:13-18). At the future site where the altar of burnt offering would stand in the Temple to be built by Solomon, "David built an altar to the LORD, and offered burnt offerings and peace offerings" (2 Sam. 24:25). Literally, 2 Samuel 8:18 tells us that "David's sons were priests" (see, however, the parallel text, 1 Chron. 18:17: "David's sons were the chief officials in the service of the king"). It is the Davidic king to whom the LORD swore, "You are a priest forever after the order of Melchizedek" (Ps. 110:4) (see point 9). Young Solomon offered sacrifices on the bronze altar belonging to the Tabernacle (2 Chron. 1:6). After having finished the Temple, King Solomon gave the people the priestly blessing, and offered sacrifices on their behalf on the new altar of burnt offering (1 Kings 8:14-15, 55, 62-64) — a task normally reserved for the priest (Deut. 33:10; 1 Chron. 6:49; 23:13). His authority extended over the high priest (1 Kings 2:27, 35). The Tabernacle had been a preliminary sanctuary; the Temple of Solomon was the actual sanctuary intended by God (Deut. 12:5-6, 11; 14:23; 16:2-11; 26:2). Its purpose was to maintain God's covenant with his people through sacrifices that covered their transgressions of the Torah.

3. *Teaching.* I explained in §7.1.2 that, in addition to the sacrificial ministry, another task of the priests was teaching the Torah. I noted that the essence of this was teaching the difference between the holy and the common, and between the unclean and the clean (Lev. 10:10; Ezek. 44:23). This is the true *hokmah*, as young King Solomon was clearly aware:

"Give your servant an understanding mind to govern your people, that I may discern between good and evil," and God answered, "I now do according to your word. Behold, I give you a wise and discerning mind" (1 Kings 3:9, 12). "Behold, the fear of the Lord, that is wisdom, and to turn away from evil is understanding" (Job 28:28).

4. *The prophet.* As an almost perfect type of the Messiah, David himself occupied the offices of king, priest, and prophet. The latter function comes out clearly in 2 Samuel 23:1: "The oracle of David, the son of Jesse, the oracle of the man who was raised on high," which "oracle" (Heb. *n'um*) contained the "oracle of the LORD" whispered to the prophet, or the "oracle" of the prophet receiving the whisper of the Lord. Think especially of the many prophetic (Messianic, millennial) Psalms of David. Acts 2:30 tells us explicitly that David was a prophet.

5. *Admission rite.* In a derogatory way, David referred to Goliath as "this uncircumcised Philistine" (1 Sam. 17:26, 36). King Saul emphasized, though in a carnal way, the significance of circumcision by asking David to provide one hundred foreskins of Philistines, *the* enemies of Israel at the time (18:25–27). The prophets underscored the fact that the Gentiles were uncircumcised, thus emphasizing the meaning of circumcision for Israel (e.g., ten times in Ezek. 32:19–32).

6. *Mountain.* As stated earlier (§7.1.2), Mount Sinai, the mountain of the Torah-giving, was called the "mountain of God" and the "mountain of the LORD" (Exod. 3:1; 4:27; 18:5; 24:13; 1 Kings 19:8; Num. 10:33), but afterward, these names were transferred to Zion (Ps. 24:3; Isa. 2:3; 30:29; Micah 4:2). This is the place up to which David brought the ark of the covenant, namely, Zion, the City of David (2 Sam. 5:7; 6:10, 12, 16). Since then, these three are indissolubly linked: David–the ark[14]–Zion. Henceforth, Zion was to be the center of God's

---

14. Or, "the Temple"; although 1 Kings 8:1 distinguishes Zion from the Temple mount, "Zion" is often used as the name of the latter: Ps. 9:11; 20:2; 48:2–3, 11–12; 65:1; 74:2; 76:2; 84:7; 99:2; 128:5; 135:21;

covenant with Israel, the final place within the Holy Land that served as the home of the Sinai Torah (Ps. 2:6; 78:67-72; 132:10-18)

7. *Theophany.* We saw that God revealed himself to Moses and the people in the "pillar of cloud," the *Shekinah,* descending upon the Tabernacle, and the fire descending upon the first burnt offering. Likewise, the cloud of God's glory later filled the Temple of Solomon, as fire came down from heaven upon the burnt offering in this Temple (1 Kings 8:10-11; 2 Chron. 5:13-14; 7:1-3; Ps. 80:2).

8. *Initial sacrifice and redemption.* The Mosaic dispensation began after the exile in Egypt, the Messianic dispensation after the exile in Babylon, and the Millennial dispensation will begin after the third and final exile. It is striking to note that the Davidic revival also began after an "exile," namely, that of the ark of the covenant. When the ark was captured, the glory of the LORD left the Holy Land and went into exile in the land of the Philistines (1 Sam. 4:21-22, *Ikavod,* "the glory is gone"). The return of the ark and its being "hidden" in Kiriath Jearim (1 Sam. 7:2)[15] occasioned Samuel's revival in 1 Samuel 7. Both this revival and the restoration of the ark in Zion, first under David, then under Solomon, were accompanied by special sacrifices (see point 2). Particularly those sacrifices offered in the Temple, the new sanctuary, placed the people on a new footing before the LORD (cf. 1 Kings 8:22-52; 2 Chron. 6:12-42; also see Ps. 78:68-72). Notice how the new resting place of the ark and God's covenant with his people were linked together (1 Kings 8:1, 6, 9, 21, 23; 2 Chron. 6:1, 10-11, 14; Ps. 132:11-14).

9. *Angels.* Through an angel, God identified for David the place where the Temple was to be built. Contrary to God's will, he counted the fighting men of Israel, and was punished for it by means of the three-day plague that came over the

---

Isa. 2:3; 8:18; 18:7; Joel 3:17, 21; Zech. 2:10; 8:3; 9:9.

15. Cf. the remarkable verse in Ps. 132:6, where David "found" the ark in "Jaar" (i.e., Kiriath Jearim; Jearim is the plural of Jaar).

land. The plague was stopped at the moment when the angel of the LORD was about to slay the inhabitants of Jerusalem: "And the angel of the LORD was standing by the threshing floor of Ornan the Jebusite. And David lifted his eyes and saw the angel of the LORD standing between earth and heaven, and in his hand a drawn sword stretched out over Jerusalem" (1 Chron. 21:15–16; cf. 2 Sam. 24:16–17). David bought the threshing floor and built an altar on it. Later, "Solomon began to build the house of the LORD in Jerusalem on Mount Moriah, where the LORD had appeared to David his father, at the place that David appointed, on the threshing floor of Ornan the Jebusite" (2 Chron. 3:1).

10. *Song.* King David introduced music and singing in the sanctuary of God (1 Chron. 25). To this end, he even invented new musical instruments, if we may interpret Amos 6:5 this way (see the NIV for a different version). At the dedication of Solomon's Temple the Levites used "the instruments for music to the LORD that King David had made for giving thanks to the LORD—for his steadfast love endures forever—whenever David offered praises by their ministry" (2 Chron. 7:6; cf. 5:13; 20:21; 1 Chron. 16:34, 41). David the poet was the greatest provider of songs to be sung during the Temple ministry: the Psalms of David. He was "the sweet psalmist of Israel" (2 Sam. 23:1). See, for instance, Psalm 30: "A song at the dedication of the temple," or Psalm 122: "A song of ascents [to the temple]"; see further Psalms 5, 26, 27, 36, 52, 65, 68, and 138.

11. *Banquet.* After David had brought the ark up to Zion he marked the special occasion of the revival by distributing "among all the people . . . a cake of bread, a portion of meat, and a cake of raisins to each one in the whole crowd of Israelites, both men and women" (2 Sam. 6:19; cf. 1 Chron. 16:3). One day long before this, the priest-king Melchizedek had brought out bread and wine to Abraham and his men, and "in" Abraham he gave it to all Israel, who were still in the "loins" of the patriarch (Gen. 14:18; Heb. 7:1–10). David and his royal descendants, serving as priest-kings "after the order

A Threefold Torah: Differences & Similarities

of Melchizedek" (see point 2), were administering bread and wine — divine blessing — to the people.

12. *Blessings.* Israel's prerogatives mentioned in Romans 9:4-5 may be applied to the Davidic revival in the following way:

(a) The adoption as son is granted in a particular way to the Davidic king (2 Sam. 7:14; 12:24-25; 1 Chron. 17:13; Ps. 2:7; 89:26-27).

(b) The divine glory: the *Shekinah* rested on the ark in the Temple (see point 5).

(c) The covenants: within the context of the Mosaic covenant the LORD established a special covenant with David and his house (2 Sam. 23:5; Ps. 89:3-5, 35-37; Jer. 33:21; cf. Ps. 111:9; 132:11-12; Isa. 55:3).

(d) The Mosaic Torah was reinforced upon the Davidic king (1 Kings 2:3; 1 Chron. 22:11-13; 2 Chron. 6:16).

(e) The Temple worship: see point 2.

(f) The promises: special promises to David and his house (see [c]).

(g) The patriarchs: invoked during the Davidic revival (1 Chron. 16:12-18; 29:18).

(h) The human ancestry of the Messiah: see point 1.

7.2 Newer Manifestations

7.2.1 The Messianic Dispensation

We now come to the new form that the one, eternal Torah has taken during the Messianic dispensation.

1. *The King.* The so-called Sermon of the Mount (Matt. 5-7), which supplies us with the essence (*k'lal gadol*) of the Messianic Torah, is given to us in the Gospel of Matthew, the Gospel that particularly introduces us to the anointed King, the Messiah of Israel (cf. Matt. 1:1, 6, 16-18, 20; 2:2, 4; 11:2; 16:16, 20; 21:5; 22:42-45; 23:10; 24:5, 23; 25:34, 40; 26:63, 68; 27:11, 17, 22, 29, 37, 42). See point 3 above, where the Messianic Torah is connected with the Messianic Kingdom. Living under the

Messianic Torah means rendering humble service in the kingdom of God (Rom. 14:17-18).

2. *Priests and Temple ministry.* The Ekklesia (the Messianic community) is the new Temple of God, in which the Holy Spirit dwells (1 Cor. 3:16; 2 Cor. 6:16; Eph. 2:20-22) and where sacrificial ministry takes place (Heb. 10:19-22), namely, a "sacrifice of praise to God, that is, the fruit of lips that acknowledge his name" (13:15; cf. Hos. 14:2). Under the Messianic Torah, the entirety of a Jesus-believing life constitutes a sacrifice to God (Rom. 12:1), a "life of love," a "fragrant offering and sacrifice to God," just as Jesus gave himself up for us (Eph. 5:2). Even when we repent after having sinned, it is like coming to the "Temple" with a "sin offering," that is, coming before God on the basis of the true sin offering of Jesus: "If we confess our sins, he is faithful and just to forgive us our sins and to cleanse us from all unrighteousness.... [I]f anybody does sin, we have an advocate with the Father, Jesus Messiah the righteous. He is the propitiation for our sins" (1 John 1:9; 2:1-2). He is also "priest forever after the order of Melchizedek" (Ps. 110:4; cf. Heb. 5:6, 10; 6:20; 7:11, 15, 17, 21), the high priest of the New Covenant (Heb. 2:17; 3:1; 4:14-15; 5:1, 5; 7:23-28; 8:1; 9:11, 25; 10:11-12, 21), and his people are the priests: "a holy priesthood, to offer spiritual sacrifices acceptable to God through Jesus Messiah" (1 Pet. 2:5; cf. v. 9; Rev. 1:6; 5:10; 20:6).

3. *Teaching.* I explained in §7.1.2 that, in addition to performing the sacrificial ministry, the priests were assigned to teach the Torah. I noted that the essence of this was teaching the difference between the holy and the common, and between the unclean and the clean (Lev. 10:10; Ezek. 44:23). This is the true *hokmah*, true wisdom, as I explained in §7.1.3. The apostle Paul said, "[A]mong the [spiritually] mature we do impart wisdom" (1 Cor. 2:6), and the mature are "those who have their powers of discernment trained by constant practice to distinguish good from evil" (Heb. 5:14; cf. Job 28:28). Under the Messianic Torah it is no different than under the Mosaic

Torah, that is, the wisdom of the Torah entails, also today, following the good (the things of the Spirit) and avoiding evil (the things of the flesh). As James said, "Religion that is pure and undefiled before God, the Father, is this: to visit orphans and widows in their affliction, and to keep oneself unstained from the world" (James 1:27). The "righteous requirement of the Torah" is to be "fulfilled in us, who walk not according to the flesh but according to the Spirit. For those who live according to the flesh set their minds on the things of the flesh, but those who live according to the Spirit set their minds on the things of the Spirit. . . . For the mind that is set on the flesh is hostile to God, for it does not submit to God's Torah; indeed, it cannot. Those who are in the flesh cannot please God" (Rom. 8:4–8).

4. *The prophet.* Under the Old Covenant, God was King in Jeshurun, and Moses was his prophet. Under the New Covenant, Jesus is King in Jeshurun, and John the Baptist was his prophet (Matt. 11:9; 14:5; 21:26; Luke 1:76). He was the "voice of one crying in the wilderness" (Isa. 40:3 note; cf. Matt. 3:3; Mark 1:3; Luke 3:4; John 1:23), and "my messenger," said the Lord, the one who prepared "the way before me" (Mal. 3:1; cf. Matt. 11:10; Mark 1:2; Luke 1:76; 7:27; John 3:28). The context suggests that the latter "messenger" is Elijah:[16] "Behold, I will send you Elijah the prophet before the great and awesome day of the LORD comes. And he will turn the hearts of the fathers to their children and the hearts of the children to their fathers" (Mal. 4:5–6; cf. Sir. 48:10–11). John the Baptist was the fulfillment of that prophecy: ". . . he will go before [the Lord] in the spirit and power of Elijah, to turn the hearts of the fathers to the children" (Luke 1:17). At least, he was that fulfillment only if the people were "willing to accept it"; but he was rejected precisely in his quality as "Elijah" (Matt. 11:14; 17:12;

---

16. However, Jewish exegetes like Kimchi and Ibn Ezra distinguished between the two: the former saw in Mal. 3:1 an angel, the latter, Messiah ben Joseph.

Mark 9:12–13). This is probably the reason why already at the outset of the Fourth Gospel, John denied that he was "Elijah" (John 1:21). Thus, there remains an ultimate fulfillment of the Elijah-prophecy (see §7.2.2).

In addition to this, of course Jesus himself was the great Prophet (see §7.3.3). Jesus called himself a prophet (Matt. 13:57 and par.; Luke 13:33), he was viewed by the masses as a prophet (Matt. 14:5; 21:46; Mark 6:15; Luke 7:16; 9:8, 19; 24:19; John 4:19; 9:17), and even as *the* Prophet in the sense of Deuteronomy 18:15, 18 (Matt. 21:11; John 6:14; 7:40; Acts 3:22–23; 7:37). He was compared to the great prophets of the Tanakh, and at the same time he surpassed them (Heb. 1:1–3). "The testimony of Jesus is the spirit of prophecy" (Rev. 19:10), that is, the Spirit who spoke through the prophets was the Spirit of Jesus[17] (cf. 1 Pet. 1:11); he himself was God's "faithful and true witness" on earth (Rev. 3:14; cf. 1:5).[18]

5. *Admission rite.* Under the Messianic Torah, Jesus-believing Jews continued the practice of circumcising their boys (cf. Acts 16:3; 21:10; 28:17). The strictest of them even blamed Peter for entering the house of uncircumcised men and eating with them (11:3). Meanwhile, for both Jewish and Gentile Jesus-believers a common admission rite had been introduced: a *mikveh* (called *baptisma*) "into the name of the Father and of the Son and of the Holy Spirit" (Matt. 28:19), or, "in the name of Jesus Messiah for the forgiveness of your sins" (Acts 2:38; cf. 8:16; 10:48; 19:5), or, "into [the death of] Messiah Jesus" (Rom. 6:3–4; cf. Gal. 3:27). This time, the rite was not limited to men but those who were baptized were "both men and women" (Acts 8:12). Only in Colossians 2:11–12, a direct link is seen between circumcision and baptism in the sense that the "circumcision [i.e., atoning death] of Messiah" is applied to the hearts of the believers, that is, God's judgment in Jesus

---

17. Another exegesis is also possible: "The tenor of prophecy is to witness of Jesus."
18. See Ouweneel (1995, 455).

A Threefold Torah: Differences & Similarities

of our "flesh" (sinful nature); this *inner* circumcision of the heart finds its counterpart in the *outer* rite of baptism.[19]

6. *Mountain*. As has been often noted,[20] one might say that the Messianic Torah was also given on a particular mountain,[21] that is, in the Sermon on the Mount. Compare this mountain episode featuring the *principles* of the Messianic Kingdom with another mountain episode featuring the *blessings* of the Kingdom (Matt. 15:29-30),[22] the mountain episode featuring the *glory* of the Kingdom (17:1-6),[23] and the mountain episode featuring the *subjects* of the Kingdom (28:16-20).[24] These four references to "the mountain" function as *r'mazim*:[25] the first and fourth *r'mazim* hint at the Torah-giving on Sinai.[26] The second *remez* hints at Exodus 15:26, where God is called the Healer for those who keep the Torah. The third *remez* hints at God's Sinaitic theophany, and presents Jesus as greater than Moses (cf. §7.3.3). The similarities here are significant:[27] on Mount Sinai Moses was commanded to build the Tabernacle (Exod. 25-26), on the Mount of Transfiguration Peter offered to build three tabernacles (Matt. 17:4). In both cases, only a few people were allowed on the mountain, while the crowd was left behind; but ultimately it was Moses or Jesus alone up there, each with a shining face (Exod. 24:9-15; 34:29-35; Matt.

---

19. See extensively Ouweneel (2011, chapters 5–8).
20. See Dunn (1990a, 248) and references there.
21. Traditionally Har haSimcha, or Mount of Beatitudes, near Tabgha, northwest of the Sea of Galilee.
22. Is this the same mountain as the one in Matt. 14:23 and John 6:3?
23. Since Cyril of Jerusalem (fourth century), some have considered this to be Mount Tabor; others have thought of one of the Hermon mountains.
24. Presumably one of three mountains mentioned previously.
25. A *remez* is a hint within the text to be deciphered by the reader (see §3.1.1n2).
26. Davies (1969, 16–17).
27. Davies (1969, 20–25).

17:1-2, 8, 14). On both occasions, the divine voice came from the "cloud" that "overshadowed" (Exod. 24:16; 40:34; Matt. 17:5).

7. *Theophany.* First, Jesus himself was "theophany," that is, "God manifested in the flesh" (1 Tim. 3:16 note); "the Word was God . . . the Word became flesh" (John 1:1, 14); "the Son of God appeared" (1 John 3:8). Second, God came into this world in the person of the Holy Spirit. There is a clear parallel between the Torah-giving on Mount Sinai in Exodus 20 and the outpouring of the Spirit on Mount Zion in Acts 2, as we see in the fire and the voices (cf. §§3.3.2 and 3.3.3 on the general links between the Torah and the Holy Spirit).

Equally important is the scene in Matthew 17, on the Mount of Transfiguration, not only because it revealed Jesus' glory, but also because the "cloud" was manifested again (Matt. 17:5 and par.). That this is a reference to the *Shekinah* is obvious from the fact that it is described as "the Majestic Glory" from which God's voice was heard (2 Pet. 1:17). The remarkable verb *episkiazō* ("overshadow") is found not only here but also in Exodus 40:35 (Septuagint): the cloud "overshadowed" the Tabernacle (cf. Ps. 105:39). The verb is also used in Luke 1:35, where the angel said to Mary, "The Holy Spirit will come upon you, and the power of the Most High will overshadow you; therefore the child to be born will be called holy—the Son of God." Here, the *Shekinah* descends upon Mary, the "cloud" overshadows her to beget Jesus in her. This "cloud" is the Holy Spirit, or the power of the Most High.

From the moment Jesus was baptized by John, the *Shekinah* rested upon him. His body was the tabernacle or temple in which the *Shekinah* dwelt. Therefore, he could say of his body: "Destroy this temple, and in three days I will raise it up" (John 2:19). He "dwelt" [lit., "tabernacled," Gr. *eskēnōsen*] among us, and we "have seen his glory [*Shekinah*], glory as of the only Son from the Father" (John 1:14; cf. Luke 3:21-22; 4:1,

14; John 1:33). That is, the divine *Shekinah* dwelt among us in the tabernacle of Jesus' body. It dwelt in him as it had dwelt before upon the ark in the Tabernacle and the Temple. In this connection the condemnation of Jesus is important. He told the Sanhedrin: "[F]rom now on you will see the Son of Man seated at the right hand of Power and coming on the clouds of heaven" (Matt. 26:64). This basically implied that the *Shekinah* did not dwell in Herod's Temple, but in him, Jesus, and would depart with him from this earth to heaven. In the eyes of the Jewish judges, this was desecration of the Temple, a trespass liable to punishment by death (cf. Acts 6:14).

When, after his resurrection, Jesus returned to his Father, the *Shekinah* did not leave the earth altogether because ten days after Jesus' ascension, the Holy Spirit descended. Today, in every meeting of the Ekklesia, if it really takes place in the power of the Spirit, the *Shekinah* is present in her midst (Matt. 18:18-20;[28] cf. 1 Cor. 14:24-25).

8. *Initial sacrifice and redemption.* The Messianic Torah is founded upon deliverance from the bondage of sin (Rom. 6:19-20) and upon the blood of the Passover lamb (1 Cor. 5:7, "Christ, our Passover lamb, has been sacrificed"). "Behold, the Lamb of God, who takes away the sin of the world" (John 1:29). When Jesus developed Passover into the Lord's Supper, he himself explained how the New Covenant was to be founded upon his own blood: "[T]his is my blood of the covenant [Luke 22:20: the new covenant], which is poured out for many [including Gentile believers] for the forgiveness of sins" (Matt. 26:28). "[Y]ou were ransomed . . . with the precious blood of Christ, like that of a lamb without blemish or spot" (1 Pet. 1:18-19). "Worthy are you [i.e., the Lamb] . . . for you were slain, and by your blood you ransomed people for God from every tribe and language and people and nation" (Rev. 5:8-9).

---

28. Cf. Talmud, Berakhot 6a: if three are sitting as a court of judges the *Shekinah* is there with them.

9. *Angels.* In the case of Jesus as the new Torah-giver, angels seem to be absent. But again we find a *remez*, or should I say, a *midrash*, for those who are prepared to see it, this time in the resurrection story. As the Torah came through Moses, grace and truth came through the dead and risen Jesus Messiah (cf. John 1:17). There were two cherubs on the "mercy seat" (the atonement cover on the ark), between whom dwelt the *Shekinah* (Exod. 25:22; 1 Sam. 4:4; 2 Sam. 6:2; 2 Kings 19:15; Ps. 80:1; 99:1) and who "looked down" upon the Torah, the stone tablets put into the ark (Exod. 25:16-20). Likewise, there were two angels in the empty tomb of Jesus "looking down," as it were, at the place where his body — the dwelling place of both the Torah (Ps. 40:8) and the *Shekinah* — had been (John 20:12; cf. Luke 24:4-6). Angels played a conspicuous role just before and during the life of Jesus (Matt. 1:20; 2:13, 19; 4:11; Mark 1:13; Luke 1:11, 26; 2:9; 22:43), as well as in the early church (Acts 5:19; 8:26; 10:3, 22; 12:7-11, 23; 27:23).

10. *Song.* Under the new dispensation of Jesus, there is a New Song, in which the Lamb is praised for having bought his own with his blood: "Worthy are you to take the scroll and to open its seals, for you were slain, and by your blood you ransomed people for God from every tribe and language and people and nation, and you have made them a kingdom and priests to our God, and they shall reign on the earth" (Rev. 5:9-10; cf. 14:3). Being filled with the Spirit leads to "addressing one another in psalms and hymns and spiritual songs, singing and making melody to the Lord with your heart" (Eph. 5:18-19; cf. Col. 3:16).

11. *Banquet.* The new Messianic Torah is embedded in the New Covenant, whose blessings are enjoyed by the Ekklesia even before it is formally established with the twelve tribes of Israel. The specific meal pertaining to this new Torah and this New Covenant is the Lord's Supper, which was derived from the Seder meal of *Pesach*: "And he took bread, and when he had given thanks, he broke it and gave it to them, saying, 'This is my body, which is given for you. Do this in remem-

brance of me.' And likewise the cup after they had eaten, saying, 'This cup that is poured out for you is the new covenant in my blood'" (Luke 22:17–20; cf. 1 Cor. 11:23–25).

12. *Blessings.* Israel's prerogatives mentioned in Romans 9:4–5 may be applied to the Ekklesia in the following way:

(a) Adoption as God's children (Matt. 5:9, 45; Luke 6:35; 20:36; Rom. 8:14–15, 19, 23; 2 Cor. 6:18; Gal. 3:26; 4:5–6; Eph. 1:5; Heb. 2:10; 12:5–8; Rev. 21:7).

(b) The divine glory: the *Shekinah* is now in the Ekklesia (see point 5).

(c) The covenants: the Ekklesia is under the blessings of the New Covenant (see point 9) (Luke 22:20; 1 Cor. 11:25; 2 Cor. 3:6; Heb. 8).

(d) The Torah-giving: the Ekklesia is under the Messianic Torah (1 Cor. 9:21; Gal. 6:2).

(e) The Temple worship (see point 2).

(f) The promises: the believers of the Ekklesia are the new heirs of the promises (Gal. 3:14, 22, 29; 4:28; Eph. 3:6; Titus 1:2; Heb. 4:1; 6:12, 17; 8:6; 9:15; 10:36; James 2:5; 2 Pet. 1:4; 1 John 2:25).

(g) The patriarchs: the believers of the Ekklesia are Abraham's children and heirs (Rom. 4:11–12, 16; Gal. 3:7, 9, 14, 29).

(h) The human ancestry of the Messiah: literally this does not apply to the Ekklesia; on the other hand, even if we had natural kinship with Jesus, what counts now is being a new creation in him (2 Cor. 5:16–17). That is to say, the spiritual link of any believer with Jesus is more essential than the blood bond of a Jew with Jesus.

7.2.2 The Millennial Dispensation

We now come to the new form that the one, eternal Torah will assume during the Millennial dispensation.

1. *The King.* The Millennial Torah is associated with the appearance of the Messiah, the anointed King of Israel: "I have set my King on Zion, my holy hill. . . . I will make the nations

your heritage.... You will rule them with a rod of iron" (Ps. 2:6–9 note). "For to us a child is born, to us a son is given; and the government shall be upon his shoulder.... [He will reign] on the throne of David and over his kingdom, to establish it and to uphold it with justice and with righteousness" (Isa. 9:6–7). "There shall come forth a shoot from the stump of Jesse ... with righteousness he shall judge.... Righteousness shall be the belt of his waist" (Isa. 11:1, 4–5). "Behold, a king will reign in righteousness, and princes will rule in justice" (32:1). "The Torah will go out from me [i.e., the Messiah], and I will set my justice for a light to the nations" (51:4).

2. *Priests and Temple ministry.* The Temple worship of the Old Covenant finds its sequel in that of the New Covenant as described in Ezekiel 40–44, where we have the description of both the Millennial Temple in Jerusalem and the new ministry that will take place there. In contrast with the ministry in the present dispensation, it will be a ministry in a literal Temple with literal sacrifices. In this sense, there is a clear overlap with the ministry under the Torah of Moses, but there are also conspicuous differences (see §6.2). The priests of the new Temple are the descendants of Zadok, who himself was a descendant of Aaron (Ezek. 40:46; 43:19; 44:15; 48:11; cf. 2 Sam. 8:17; 1 Chron. 6:3–8; cf. §4.3.3). Jesus Messiah, the high priest in the order of Melchizedek, "shall be a priest on His throne, and the counsel of peace shall be between them both" (Zech. 6:13 NKJV), that is, between the Messiah's kingship and priesthood.

3. *Teaching.* I explained in §7.1.2 that, in addition to the sacrificial ministry, the priests were also given the task of teaching the Torah. This was so under the Mosaic Torah ("You are to distinguish between the holy and the common, and between the unclean and the clean, and you are to teach the people of Israel all the statutes that the LORD has spoken to them by Moses," Lev. 10:10–11), and it will be thus under the Millennial Torah; the priests "shall teach my people the difference between the holy and the common, and show them

how to distinguish between the unclean and the clean" (Ezek. 44:23). Teaching the Torah is basically nothing but teaching the difference between the holy and the common, between the clean and the unclean, between the godly and the ungodly. The Temple will be the ideal place for this, because the Temple area will have a wall "to make a separation between the holy and the common" (42:20).

4. *The prophet.* We have seen earlier (§7.2.1) that John the Baptist could have been the "Elijah" announced in Malachi 4:5 but was rejected as such. So the prophecy's fulfillment was deferred until the latter days. As Chief Rabbi J. H. Hertz wrote, "Far more than the prophet of zeal and fire of the Biblical narrative, he is to later generations the helper and healer, the reconciler and peace-bringer, the herald of the days of the Messiah."[29] Eli Cashdan wrote, "According to Jewish tradition, Elijah's mission is to bring peace to the world, solve all difficulties, settle legal disputes, herald the advent of the Messiah, and turn mankind to their Father in heaven."[30] This herald is not literally Elijah, but a prophet acting "in the spirit and power of Elijah" (cf. Luke 1:17).[31] As such, he will be not only a new Elijah but also a new Moses.[32] They were the only men in the Tanakh who argued with God on Mount Sinai or Horeb (Exod. 32:31–34; 33:12–23; 1 Kings 19:9–18). It was these two who appeared with Jesus on the Mount of Transfiguration, speaking with him about his "exodus" (Luke 9:30–31), as a foreshadowing of the Millennial glory. (Notice that Moses, the leader of the exodus, spoke with Jesus about his exodus.) The "two witnesses" in Revelation 11:5–6, appearing shortly

---

29. Hertz (1938, 970).
30. Cashdan (1957, 356).
31. Cf. the prophetic reference to the Messiah as "David" (Jer. 30:9; Ezek. 34:23–24; 37:24–25; Hos. 3:5), though he is not literally David but acts in the spirit and power of David, so to speak.
32. This is not to be confused with Jesus himself as the "new Moses" (§§2.3.1 and 3.3.2).

before the second coming of Jesus, exhibit the characteristics of Moses and Elijah.[33] Jewish tradition has made much of the parallels between the two.[34]

5. *Admission rite.* Amazingly, the Tanakhic prophets rarely referred to circumcision in an eschatological context. Apparently, the prophets took it for granted that in the Messianic Kingdom the male Israelites would be circumcised: "[T]here shall no more come into you [i.e., Jerusalem] the uncircumcised and the unclean" (Isa. 52:1). "No foreigner, uncircumcised in heart and flesh . . . shall enter my sanctuary" (Ezek. 44:9; cf. Hab. 2:16). "Behold, the days are coming . . . when I will punish all those who are circumcised merely in the flesh . . . and all the house of Israel [who, though circumcised in the flesh,] are uncircumcised in heart" (Jer. 9:25–26; cf. the eschatological meaning of "the days are coming" in 16:14; 23:5, 7; 30:3; 31:31, 38; 33:14).

6. *Mountain.* The Millennial Torah is given on "the mountain of the LORD . . . out of Zion shall go forth the Torah" (Micah 4:2; Isa. 2:3; cf. Ps. 24:3; Zech. 8:3). Zion is also the place of the LORD's and the Messiah's dwelling (Ps. 2:6; Isa. 24:23; 33:5; 59:20; 60:14; Joel 3:16; Obad. 17, 21; Micah 4:2, 7). In Hebrews 12:18–22, Mount Zion, the mountain of the new Torah-giving and of divine grace in Jesus, is contrasted with Mount Sinai, the mountain of divine wrath on trespassers (cf. Gal. 4:24–26).

7. *Theophany.* Here, the theophany is nothing less than the appearance of God-Messiah himself. His future descent is linked with either Mount Zion or the Mount of Olives (Isa.

---

33. See Ouweneel (1995, 302–4).
34. Edersheim (1971, II, 705–9): Targum Pseudo-Jonathan on Exod. 40:10 calls Elijah a Levite, even the high priest in the Messianic era. He allegedly will anoint the Messiah with sacred oil (Tanchumah on Exod. 23:20). Yalqut II.32d compares him with Moses step by step. Both met the Lord on Horeb, allegedly in the same cave (Exod. 33:21–23; 1 Kings 19:9, 13) (Sifre on Deut.). In the Messianic era, Moses and Elijah will come together "as one" (Deut. Rabbah 3).

31:4–5; cf. 2:3; 30:29–30; Zech. 14:3–5; cf. Ezek. 43:1–5; Acts 1:11; also see Dan. 7:13, 22; Zech. 12:10.). One could also think here of a verse such as Revelation 7:15, which refers to the saints who will enter into the Millennial Kingdom: "[H]e that sitteth on the throne shall spread his tabernacle over them" (ASV). This refers to the Tabernacle of the Tanakh, and thus to the *Shekinah* that had dwelt in it.[35] "Spread his tabernacle" is one word (*skēnōsei*), the same verb as the one that means "to tabernacle," which we found above in John 1:14 (§7.2.1). In fact, we could render the verse as follows: "he who sits on the throne will place his *Shekinah* over them." In Revelation 21:3 we find the same verb: when the new heaven and the new earth have arrived, "the tabernacle [*skēnē*] of God is with men. He will dwell (*skēnōsei*) with them," that is, he will place his *Shekinah*, his divine glory, in the midst of his people.

8. *Initial sacrifice and redemption.* At the outset of the Millennial Kingdom, the LORD tells his people, "I will make with you an everlasting covenant, my steadfast, sure love for David," and, "as for me, this is my covenant with them. . . . My Spirit that is upon you, and my words [i.e., my Torah] that I have put in your mouth, shall not depart out of your mouth" (Isa. 55:3b; 59:21). Shortly before this, the prophet had pointed out the foundation for this everlasting covenant, namely,

> [H]e has borne our griefs and carried our sorrows . . . he was pierced for our transgressions; he was crushed for our iniquities; upon him was the chastisement that brought us peace, and with his wounds we are healed . . . when his soul makes an offering for guilt, he shall see his offspring; he shall prolong his days; the will of the LORD shall prosper in his hand (Isa. 53:4–10).

And then with a direct reference to the Millennial Kingdom (v. 12): "Therefore I will divide him a portion with the

---

35. Note that Heb. *mishkan* ("tent, tabernacle") and *Shekinah* (lit., "dwelling") are both derived from *sh-k-n*, "to dwell"; cf. Ezek. 37:27 (ASV): "my tabernacle shall be with them."

great, and he shall divide the spoil with the strong, because he poured out his soul to death and was numbered with the transgressors; yet he bore the sin of many, and makes intercession for the transgressors." The beginning of the Messianic Kingdom is the moment for God "to finish the transgression, to put an end to sin, and to atone for iniquity, to bring in everlasting righteousness" (Dan. 9:24). In the prophetic application, this was the moment when the high priest, during the First and the Second Temple, came out of the sanctuary after having presented the blood of the bull and the goat (Lev. 16:17).

9. *Angels.* The references to angels at the appearance of God-Messiah are numerous (Matt. 13:41; 16:27; 24:31; 25:31; Mark 8:38; 2 Thess. 1:7; cf. Zech. 14:5). Some would also interpret "his saints [or, holy ones]" in 1 Thessalonians 3:13 and the "armies of heaven" in Revelation 19:14 as angels (cf. Ps. 89:6-7); others view them as believers (cf. Col. 3:4; Rev. 17:14).

10. *Song.* Here again, there is a New Song (Isa. 42:10; cf. Ps. 33:3; 40:3; 96:1; 98:1; 144:9; 149:1), closely linked with the Millennial Torah (Isa. 42:4, 21). This Song is the perpetuation of the Song of Moses, and at the same time it is genuinely new because it is associated with the Lamb: "the song of Moses, the servant of God, and the song of the Lamb" (Rev. 15:3). It is sung by those who obey the Torah: "It is these who have not defiled themselves with women, for they are virgins. It is these who follow the Lamb wherever he goes . . . in their mouth no lie was found, for they are blameless" (14:4-5).

11. *Banquet.* Isaiah 24:5-9 describes a time in which there is no banquet anymore because the Torah has been broken: "The earth [or, land] lies defiled under its inhabitants; for they have transgressed the laws [*torot*], violated the statutes, broken the everlasting covenant. Therefore a curse devours the earth [or, land]. . . . The wine mourns, the vine languishes, all the merry-hearted sigh. . . . No more do they drink wine with singing; strong drink is bitter to those who drink it." But a chapter lat-

er, when God's salvation has appeared and the covenant has been restored, the prophet, referring to God's mountain, says: "On this mountain the LORD of hosts will make for all peoples a feast of rich food, a feast of well-aged wine, of rich food full of marrow, of aged wine well refined. And he will swallow up on this mountain the covering that is cast over all peoples, the veil that is spread over all nations. He will swallow up death forever; and the LORD God will wipe away tears from all faces, and the reproach of his people he will take away from all the earth, for the LORD has spoken. It will be said on that day, 'Behold, this is our God; we have waited for him, that he might save us. This is the LORD; we have waited for him; let us be glad and rejoice in his salvation.' For the hand of the LORD will rest on this mountain" (Isa. 25:6–10).

12. *Blessings.* Israel's prerogatives mentioned in Romans 9:4–5 are applied to the Millennial people of God in the following way:

(a) Adoption as God's children (Hos. 1:10).

(b) The divine glory: the *Shekinah* will return to the new Temple (Ezek. 43:1–5).

(c) The covenants: a New Covenant will be established with Israel, the blessings of which will be extended to all the nations (Jer. 31:31–34; Isa. 55:3–5; 56:4–7).

(d) The Torah-giving (Isa. 2:3; Micah 4:2).

(e) The Temple worship (see point 2).

(f) The promises: God will make good all his promises to Israel and the nations (Jer. 32:42; 33:14).

(g) The patriarchs: "as regards election, they [i.e., Israel] are beloved for the sake of their forefathers. For the gifts and the calling of God are irrevocable" (Rom. 11:28–29); the promises made to the patriarchs will be the foundation of the Messianic Kingdom.

(h) The human ancestry of the Messiah: just as he was once born in Bethlehem as one of Israel (Micah 5:2), so too he will one day "come from Zion" as the Deliverer, and "will banish ungodliness from Jacob" (Rom. 11:26; cf. Isa. 59:20-21): "Behold, the man whose name is the Branch: for he shall branch out from his place, and he shall build the temple of the LORD. It is he who shall build the temple of the LORD and shall bear royal honor, and shall sit and rule on his throne. And there [or rather, he!] shall be a priest on his throne, and the counsel of peace shall be between them both" (Zech. 6:12-13).

7.3 Similarities and Differences

The three manifestations of the one, eternal Torah described above in §§7.1.2, 7.2.1, and 7.2.2 exhibit essential *transcendent similarities* as well as conspicuous *immanent differences*. The main similarity is that they all three center around (1) the one, transcendent Love Command (Heb. *ahavah*, Gr. *agapē*), which can be summarized with a single word from 1 John 4:19: "we love," or even "let us love."[36] Likewise, the three manifestations of the Torah can be summarized in (2) the biblical concept of "righteousness" (Heb. *tzedaqah*, Gr. *dikaiosynē*), (3) that of "covenant loyalty" (Heb. *hesed*, Gr. *hosiotēs*), and (4) that of "peace" (Heb. *shalom*, Gr. *eirēnē*). Let us consider these things in more detail, comparing in each case the covenant God and the covenant people.

7.3.1 The Mosaic Torah

(1) *Love (ahavah)*

* *Covenant God*: ". . . because he loved your fathers and chose their offspring after them and brought you out of Egypt with his own presence, by his great power" (Deut. 4:37); "[I]t is because the LORD loves you and is keeping the oath that he swore to your fathers, that the LORD has brought you out with a mighty hand and redeemed you from the house of slavery, from the hand of Pharaoh king of Egypt. Know therefore that the LORD your God is God, the faithful God who keeps covenant and steadfast love [*hesed*] with those who love him and

---

36. One word, *agapōmen*, in the best manuscripts lacks a specified object.

keep his commandments, to a thousand generations" (7:8-9). "Yet the LORD set his heart in love on your fathers and chose their offspring after them, you above all peoples, as you are this day" (10:15).

* *Covenant people:* Love is the sum and fulfillment of the Mosaic Torah, as Jesus himself made clear: "[O]ne of the scribes came up and heard them disputing with one another, and seeing that he answered them well, asked him, 'Which commandment is the most important of all?' Jesus answered, 'The most important is, "Hear, O Israel: The Lord our God, the Lord is one. And you shall love the Lord your God with all your heart and with all your soul and with all your mind and with all your strength [cf. Deut. 6:4-5]".' The second is this: "You shall love your neighbor as yourself." [cf. Lev. 19:18] There is no other commandment greater than these.' And the scribe said to him, 'You are right, Teacher. You have truly said that he is one, and there is no other besides him. And to love him with all the heart and with all the understanding and with all the strength, and to love one's neighbor as oneself, is much more than all whole burnt offerings and sacrifices.' And when Jesus saw that he answered wisely, he said to him, 'You are not far from the kingdom of God'" (Mark 12:28-34). The latter sentence is noteworthy: grasping the essence of God's Torah is grasping the essence of God's Kingdom.

The apostolic writers summarize the Mosaic Torah similarly: "[T]he one who loves another has fulfilled the Torah. For the commandments . . . are summed up in this word: 'You shall love your neighbor as yourself.' Love does no wrong to a neighbor; therefore love is the fulfilling of the Torah" (Rom. 13:8-10); "[T]hrough love serve one another. For the whole Torah is fulfilled [or, summed up] in one word: 'You shall love your neighbor as yourself'" (Gal. 5:13-14). "If you really fulfill the royal Torah [the Torah of the Kingdom] according to the Scripture, 'You shall love your neighbor as yourself,' you are doing well. But if you show partiality, you are committing sin and are convicted by the Torah as transgressors

[Torah-breakers]. For whoever keeps the whole Torah but fails in one point has become accountable for all of it. For he who said, 'Do not commit adultery,' also said, 'Do not murder.' If you do not commit adultery but do murder, you have become a transgressor of the Torah" (James 2:8–11).

Loving God and one's neighbor is not merely an (immanent) "part" of the Mosaic Torah. Rather, the Love Command is the transcendent substance and heart of the entire Mosaic Torah. Everything is rooted in love: the purification laws, which are nothing other than devotion to God; Shabbat and the Jewish festivals, which for the greater part are days of joy and worship; and even *kashrut*, which is based on loving commitment to this central principle: striving for the clean, shunning the unclean, for the glory and honor of God.

(2) *Righteousness (tzedaqah)*

* *Covenant God:* The Torah is the expression of God's righteousness: "The LORD was pleased, for his righteousness' sake, to magnify his Torah and make it glorious" (Isa. 42:21). We see this in a beautiful way in the great Torah-psalm: "I know, O Lord, that your rules [sing. *Mishpat*][37] are righteous [*tzedeq*]. . . . My eyes long for your salvation and for the fulfillment of your righteous promise [lit., the word of your righteousness]. . . .You have appointed your testimonies in righteousness. . . . Your righteousness is righteous forever, and your Torah is true. . . . Your testimonies are righteous forever . . . all your commandments are righteous" (Ps. 119:75, 123, 138, 142, 144, 172). "And what great nation is there, that has statutes and rules so righteous as all this Torah that I set before you today?" (Deut. 14:8). "The Rock, his work is perfect, for all his ways are justice [*mishpat*].A God of faithfulness and without iniquity, just [*tzaddiq*] and upright is he" (32:4). The Torah and the Prophets testify to the "righteousness of God" (Rom. 3:21), the "righteousness that is based on [lit., is out of] the

---

37. *Mishpat* is derived from *sh-p-t*, "decide, settle, judge, punish."

Torah" (10:5), or, "in the Torah . . . of the Torah" (Phil. 3:6, 9).

Covenant people: In Psalm 119, the Torah is the expression of *God's* righteousness, but keeping the Torah is *man's* righteousness: "I have done what is just [*mishpat*] and right [*tzedeq*]" (Ps. 119:121), that is, I have kept your Torah. He who truly observes the Mosaic Torah is the true *tzaddiq*, the "righteous one": "The mouth of the righteous [*tzaddiq*] utters wisdom [*hokmah*], and his tongue speaks justice [*mishpat*]. The Torah of his God is in his heart; his steps do not slip" (Ps. 37:30-31). *Mishpat* is a related term, which excellently expresses the true spirit of the Torah: "He has told you, O man, what is good; and what does the LORD require of you but to do justice [*mishpat*], and to love kindness [*hesed*], and to walk humbly with your God?" (Micah 6:8). The "distinction between the righteous and the wicked" is the difference "between one who serves God and one who does not serve him" (Mal. 3:18). In the New Testament, Zechariah, Elizabeth, Simeon, Joseph (Mary's husband), John the Baptist, Joseph of Arimathea, and Cornelius are described as *dikaioi* (Heb. *tzaddiqim*; Luke 1:6; 2:25; Matt. 1:19; Mark 6:20; Luke 23:50; Acts 10:22), while Jesus is the *Dikaios* (*Tzaddiq*) par excellence (Matt. 27:19, 24; Luke 23:47; Acts 3:14; 7:52; 22:14; 1 Pet. 3:18; 1 John 2:1; perhaps even James 5:6).

(3) *Covenant loyalty (hesed)*

Covenant God: "The LORD, the LORD, a God merciful and gracious, slow to anger, and abounding in steadfast love [*hesed*][38] and faithfulness, keeping steadfast love [*hesed*] for thousands" (Exod. 34:6-7; cf. Num. 14:18). "And because you listen to these rules and keep and do them, the LORD your God will keep with you the covenant and the steadfast love [*hesed*] that he swore to your fathers" (Deut. 7:12). Notice here the link between covenant and *hesed* (also see v. 9; 1 Kings 8:23; 2

---

38. In the ESV, *hesed* is consistently translated as "steadfast love"—not necessarily the most fortunate choice (NET Bible, "loyal love," is more accurate).

Chron. 6:14; Neh. 1:5; 9:32; Dan. 9:4), which implies that God's *hesed* (covenant loyalty) is an essential aspect of the covenant.

* *Covenant people:* The objects of God's *hesed* are themselves *hasidim*, that is, the pious, or godly, or holy ones (saints), who are loyal to the covenant: "Turn away from evil and do good; so shall you dwell forever. For the LORD loves justice; he will not forsake his saints [sing. *hasid*]" (Ps. 37:27-28). "Gather to me my faithful ones [sing. *hasid*], who made a covenant with me by sacrifice!" (50:5). Like always, the human *hasid* is not only the one who is godly, holy, and loyal to the covenant, but also the object of God's *hesed*, that is, of the object of *God's* loyalty to the covenant (cf. 12:1; 32:6; 132:16; 149:1, 5).[39] God is *hasid* by bestowing upon Man all favors that are part of his covenant promises. Man is *hasid* in that, in answer to God's favors, he faithfully and devotedly keeps God's Torah. God is loyal (*hasid*) toward his people by fulfilling his promises. His people are loyal (*hasidim*) toward him by observing the Torah.

(4) *Peace (shalom)*

* *Covenant God:* A key verse is Psalm 119:165: "Great peace [*shalom*] have those who love your Torah," that is, God grants them true peace. "If you walk in my statutes and observe my commandments and do them, then I will give you your rains in their season. . . . I will give *peace* in the land, and you shall lie down, and none shall make you afraid' (Lev. 26:3-6).

* *Covenant people:* The wise man says, "My son, do not forget my Torah, but let your heart keep my commandments [*mitzwot*], for length of days and years of life and peace [*shalom*] they will add to you" (Prov. 3:1-2). If people pay "attention to [God's] commandments [*mitzwot*]," their peace is "like a river," their "righteousness like the waves of the sea"

---

39. In such cases, Dutch translations often have *gunstgenoten* or *gunstelingen* ("favorites"), objects of God's *gunst* ("favor"). Given the Calvinistic background of the oldest translations, one can understand that the emphasis is more on God's sovereign loyalty than on human loyalty.

A Threefold Torah: Differences & Similarities

(Isa. 48:18). Over against these Torah-keepers stand the wicked, for whom "there is no peace" (48:22; 57:21) and who do not know the "way of peace" (59:8; cf. Jer. 4:10; 6:14; 8:11, 15; 12:12; 16:5; 30:5; Ezek. 13:10, 16; Micah 3:5).

7.3.2 The Messianic Torah

(1) *Love (ahavah, agapē)*

　* *Covenant God:* The starting-point for all reflection on love as the essence of the Messianic Torah is the fact that God himself is love: "And this is his commandment, that we . . . love one another, just as he has commanded us. Whoever keeps his commandments abides in God, ... Beloved, let us love one another, for love is from God, and whoever loves has been born of God and knows God. Anyone who does not love does not know God, because God is love" (1 John 3:23-24; 4:7-8; cf. v. 16).

　* *Covenant people:* Love is the substance of the Messianic Torah, for the Messiah himself said, "A new commandment I give to you, that you love one another: just as I have loved you, you also are to love one another. By this all people will know that you are my disciples, if you have love for one another" (John 13:34-35). "My command is this: Love each other as I have loved you" (15:12; cf. 1 John 3:23; 4:21; 2 John 5). By the very keeping of his commands we are to demonstrate our love to Jesus as well: "If you love me, you will keep my commandments" (14:15). "Whoever has my commandments and keeps them, he it is who loves me" (14:21). "If you keep my commandments, you will abide in my love" (John 15:10; cf. 1 John 5:3; 2 John 6).

(2) *Righteousness (tzedaqah, dikaiosynē)*

　* *Covenant God:* Living according to the Messianic Torah is striving for God's righteousness: "seek first the kingdom of God and his righteousness, and all these things will be added to you" (Matt. 6:33). The revelation of the Messiah and of the way of salvation, which is rooted in him and his work of atonement, is the revelation of God's righteousness (Rom. 1:17; 3:5, 21-22, 25-26; 10:3).

* *Covenant people:* Jesus compared the false *tzedaqah* of the Pharisees and the scribes with that of his disciples; the latter should exceed the former (Matt. 5:20). The *tzedaqah* under the Messianic Torah is greater because Jesus himself is our *tzedaqah* (1 Cor. 1:30). Consequently, the believers have in person become "*tzedaqah* of God" in Jesus (2 Cor. 5:21). Believers under the Messianic Torah are the new *tzaddiqim* (Acts 24:15; Rom. 5:19; James 5:16; 1 Pet. 4:18). They have not only been justified ("made *tzaddiqim*") by faith, once and for all, but in practice they show themselves to be true *tzaddiqim* by performing the works of the Messianic Torah through the power of God's Spirit, as was the case with Abraham and Rahab (James 2:14-26; cf. Rom. 2:13; Titus 2:11-14; 1 John 2:29; 3:7; Rev. 22:11).

(3) *Covenant loyalty (hesed, hosiotēs)*

* *Covenant God:* From Tanakhic quotations like in Acts 13:34-35 it appears that the Greek equivalents of *hasid* and *hesed* are *hosios* and *hosiotēs* (the latter word occurs only in Luke 1:75 and Eph. 4:24). The words are often rendered "holy" and "holiness" but should not be confused with *hagios* (Heb. *qadosh*) and *hagiotēs* (*qodesh*). God himself is the *hosios* in the sense of the benevolent (Rev. 15:4; 16:5); his *hosia* (Acts 13:34) are his benevolent acts toward his covenant partners.

* *Covenant people:* Under the Messianic Torah, the believer is the "godly one" (*hosios*), usually rendered as "holy one" (Acts 1:27; 13:35; Titus 1:8; Heb. 7:26). The believer is called upon to serve God "without fear, in holiness (*hosiotēs*) and righteousness before him all our days" (Luke 1:74-75); the believer is "to put on the new self, created after the likeness of God in true righteousness and holiness (*hosiotēs*)" (Eph. 4:24). In spite of the translation "holy," we maintain that the basic meaning is "covenant loyalty."

(4) *Peace (shalom, eirēnē)*

* *Covenant God:* If the believer will fulfill the Messianic Torah, the "God of peace" will be with him (Phil. 4:9; cf. Rom. 15:33; 16:20). In this attitude he will sanctify us and keep us blameless (1 Thess. 5:23). The "God of peace who brought again from the dead our Lord Jesus, the great shepherd of the sheep, by the blood of the eternal covenant," will "equip you with everything good that you may do his will, working in us that which is pleasing in his sight, through Jesus Christ" (Heb. 13:20-21). Note here the link between some important elements: the God of peace, the eternal covenant, the performance of God's will (i.e., the Messianic Torah).

* *Covenant people:* "The righteous requirement [one word: *dikaiōma*] of the Torah" is "fulfilled in" the Jesus-believers, "who walk not according to the flesh but according to the Spirit . . . to set the mind on the Spirit is life and peace" (Rom. 8:4, 6). The fruit of the Spirit is "love, joy, peace," etcetera (Gal. 5:22); there is "peace and mercy" for those who walk by the "rule" of Messiah (6:16). The Kingdom of God, in which we serve Christ, is "righteousness and peace and joy in the Holy Spirit" (Rom. 14:17-18). Those who keep the Messianic Torah, live in peace with all men" and are "holy" (Heb. 12:14; cf. Matt. 5:9; Mark 9:50; Luke 1:79; John 14:27; 16:33; Rom. 12:18; 14:19; 2 Cor. 13:11; Eph. 4:3; Phil. 4:7; Col. 3:15; 1Thess. 5:13; 2 Tim. 2:22; 1 Pet. 3:11; 2 Pet. 3:14).

7.3.3 The Millennial Torah

(1) *Love (ahavah, agapē)*

* *Covenant God:* Of course, love is also the vital element in the Millennial Torah: "I have loved you with an everlasting love; therefore I have continued my faithfulness to you. Again I will build you, and you shall be built, O virgin Israel! . . . For this is the covenant that I will make with the house of Israel after those days . . . : I will put my Torah within them, and I will write it on their hearts. And I will be their God, and they shall be my people" (Jer. 3:3-4, 33). "On that day it shall be said to Jerusalem: 'Fear not, O Zion; let not your hands grow weak. The LORD your God is in your midst, a mighty one who will save; he will rejoice over you with gladness; he will quiet you by his love; he will exult over you with loud singing. I will gather those of you who mourn for the festival'" (Zeph. 3:16–18).

* *Covenant people:* Isaiah speaks of the time when the Temple will again be a center of attraction for all the nations. Foreigners will come "who join themselves to the LORD, to minister to him, to love the name of the LORD, and to be his servants, everyone who keeps the Shabbat and does not profane it, and holds fast my covenant" (56:6). Micah 6:8, quoted earlier, supplies us with the golden rule for the coming kingdom: "He has told you, O man, what is good; and what does the LORD require of you but to do justice [*mishpat*], and to love kindness [*hesed*], and to walk humbly with your God?"

(2) *Righteousness (tzedaqah, dikaiosynē)*

* *Covenant God:* Under the Millennial Torah, the Messiah himself will be the "sun of righteousness [*tzedaqah*]" (Mal. 4:2); and a Midrash says, "What is the name of King Messiah? Rabbi Abba ben Kahana said, His name is 'the Lord'; as it has been said, 'And this is the name by which he [i.e., the Davidic King of Jer. 23:5] will be called: "The LORD is our righteousness"'" (Jer. 23:6).[40] One could even argue that apparently the Messiah himself is here called YHWH *Tzidqênu*, "The LORD our righteousness."

* *Covenant people:* God's people will be those who have been "justified" (made *tzaddiqim*) by God's "righteous" (*tzaddiq*) Servant (Isa. 53:11); the whole nation will be *tzaddiqim*, that is, all walking in the ways of his Torah (45:25; 60:21). Then, God's people will pay attention to the LORD's commands, so that their righteousness will be like the waves of the sea; those

---

40. Lam. Rabbah 1.16.51; Midrash Ps. 21.2; cf. 1QH 2.8–18, 6.10–12 (see Shulam 1998, 135–37).

who know righteousness (*tzedeq*) will be the same as those who will have God's Torah in their hearts (Isa. 48:18; 51:7; cf. 58:2).

(3) Covenant loyalty (hesed, hosiotēs)

* *Covenant God:* "For the LORD has called you like a wife deserted and grieved in spirit, like a wife of youth when she is cast off, ... For a brief moment I deserted you, but with great compassion I will gather you. In overflowing anger for a moment I hid my face from you, but with everlasting love I will have compassion on you, ... [M]y steadfast love [*hesed*] shall not depart from you, and my covenant of peace shall not be removed" (Isa. 54:6-10). "And I will betroth you to me forever. I will betroth you to me in righteousness and in justice, in steadfast love [*hesed*] and in mercy. I will betroth you to me in faithfulness. And you shall know the LORD" (Hos. 2:19-20). *The* great call to worship during the Messianic Kingdom will be: "Give thanks to the LORD of hosts, for the LORD is good, for his steadfast love [*hesed*] endures forever!" (Isa. 54:10,13; Jer. 33:11; cf. also see Ps. 100:5; 107:1; 118:2-4, 29; 136).

* *Covenant people:* The Psalms often refer to God's "holy ones" (or, "saints," *hasidim*) in a way that clearly anticipates the Messianic Kingdom: "Turn away from evil and do good; so shall you dwell forever. For the LORD loves justice; he will not forsake his saints [*hasidim*]. They are preserved forever, but the children of the wicked shall be cut off. The righteous [*tzaddiqim*] shall inherit the land and dwell upon it forever" (37:27-29). "Arise, O LORD, and go to your resting place, you and the ark of your might. Let your priests be clothed with righteousness, and let your saints [*hasidim*] shout for joy" (132:8-9). "All your works shall give thanks to you, O LORD, and all your saints [*hasidim*] shall bless you! They shall speak of the glory of your kingdom and tell of your power, to make known to the children of man your mighty deeds, and the glorious splendor of your kingdom. Your kingdom is an everlasting kingdom, and your dominion endures throughout all

generations" (145:10-13). "Let the godly [*hasidim*] exult in glory; let them sing for joy on their beds. Let the high praises of God be in their throats and two-edged swords in their hands, to execute vengeance on the nations and punishments on the peoples, to bind their kings with chains and their nobles with fetters of iron, to execute on them the judgment written! This is honor for all his godly ones [*hasidim*]. Praise the LORD!" (149:5-9).

(4) *Peace (shalom, eirēnē)*

* *Covenant God:* During the *'olam habba*, the Messiah will be the *sar-shalom*, "Prince of peace"; "of the increase of his government and peace there will be no end" (Isa. 9:6-7). He himself will be "Peace" (Micah 5:5), and he "will proclaim peace to the nations" (Zech. 9:10).

* *Covenant people:* The believer "whose mind is stayed on you, because he trusts in you," will be kept "in perfect peace" (Isa. 26:3; cf. v. 12). The righteous will have "peace" through the chastisement that was upon Messiah (53:5). God's "covenant of peace" will be for them, and great will be the peace of their children (Isa. 54:10, 13; cf. Ezek. 34:25; 37:26). "The righteous man . . . enters into peace" (Isa. 57:2; cf. 55:12; 57:19; 66:12). "I will bring to it [i.e., Jerusalem] health and healing, and I will heal them [i.e., my people] and reveal to them abundance of prosperity [*shalom*] and security" (Jer. 33:6; cf. v. 9).

7.3.4 Immanent Differences

In addition to love, righteousness, loyalty, and peace as the *transcendent* substance of every manifestation of the Torah, there are numerous *immanent* differences. Thus, there are some down-to-earth reasons why the Millennial Torah *cannot* be identical with the Mosaic Torah. This has to do with the obviously temporary character of the Mosaic Torah. We mention only a few examples.

(1) A number of provisions of the Mosaic Torah were intended mainly for Israel's forty-year journey through the wil-

derness, particularly for the Tabernacle with all the utensils and services associated with it. In due time, the Tabernacle was to be replaced by the Temple, but the latter is referred to in the Pentateuch only in an indirect way; see Exod. 15:13, 17, and the many references in Deuteronomy (12:5, 11; 14:23; 16:2, 6, 11; 26:2) to the place the LORD would choose as a dwelling for his Name.

(2) Some other provisions in the Mosaic Torah apparently had only a temporary significance as well, such as those concerning the cities of refuge (Num. 35:6-34; Deut. 19:1-13; Josh. 20). The concept of the "avenger of blood" seems to have been a relic from the past, for which God still made allowance, but which in due time was superseded by regular courts and tribunals. After the Pentateuch and the book of Joshua we never hear of the "avenger of blood" again, except in 2 Samuel 14:11, although we might have other exceptions in Job 19:25 and Isaiah 47:3-4, where *goel* may (partly) imply the idea of the *goel haddam* ("avenger of blood").[41]

(3) Some other Mosaic regulations concern the typical situation of the early state of Israel, such as its still rather primitive agricultural economy and social-judicial structure. To this belong, for instance, the laws concerning the Sabbatical Year (*Shemitah*) and the Year of Jubilee, about which we do not hear again in the Millennial Torah. (Sabbatical Years in the present state of Israel are, e.g., 2007-08, 2014-15 and 2021-22. The widespread claim that 1917-18 [when Jerusalem was freed from the Turks], 1966-67 [when Old Jerusalem was re-captured] and 2015-16 are Years of Jubilee is nothing but Christian imagination.)

(4) Some other Mosaic decrees concern medical problems that, with the medical knowledge that we now possess, would be dealt with today in a very different way. Think of the regulations about leprosy, which is to be interpreted as infectious skin diseases and mildew (Lev. 13-14). Even the early trans-

---

41. See Ouweneel (2000b, §5.3.2).

lators of the Hebrew Old Testament did not yet know exactly what kind of diseases were involved. At the time of the exodus, the decrees mentioned were remarkably advanced measures compared with the cures employed by other nations. But it is hard to imagine that such diseases would not be dealt with in a far more efficient way during the Messianic Kingdom.

(5) We definitely see some progress, already within the Tanakh, as to the way women were treated. The commandment "You shall not commit adultery" (Exod. 20:14; Deut. 5:18) was concerned not so much with one's own straying wife but with the straying husband of the woman with whom adultery was committed: "If a man commits adultery with *the wife of his neighbor*, both the adulterer and the adulteress shall surely be put to death" (Lev. 20:10, italics added). This law also applied in a case where the woman was betrothed; in this case, too, the straying man was dishonored (Deut. 22:23-24). This is in line with the other commandments: "Do not touch the *life* of your neighbor" (Sixth Commandment), "Do not touch the *wife* of your neighbor" (Seventh Commandment), "Do not touch the *freedom* of your neighbor" (cf. Gen. 40:15; Exod. 21:16; Deut. 24:7; "men-stealers" in 1 Tim. 1:10 NKJV; Eighth Commandment), "Do not touch the *reputation* of your neighbor" (Ninth Commandment), and "Do not touch the *property* of your neighbor" (Tenth Commandment). In this latter commandment, even the wife is mentioned as part of the neighbor's property: "You shall not covet your neighbor's house; you shall not covet your neighbor's wife, or his male servant, or his female servant, or his ox, or his donkey, or anything that is your neighbor's" (Exod. 20:17).

Within the Mosaic Torah one's own straying wife remains entirely out of the picture. The Torah also implicitly teaches that sex with a female slave is not as blameworthy as sex with a free woman, because the former is only a slave (Lev. 19:20). Our morals have changed very much, to the extent that we would rather argue the opposite way: sex with a subordinate person is *worse* than sex with a person who can act according to his/her own free will. It was good that, if a woman was taken captive from the enemies and an Israelite wanted to marry her, the Torah allowed her to first lament her parents—but whether she herself was willing to marry that Israelite was apparently irrelevant (Deut. 21:10-13).

However, in Malachi 2 the situation is very different. Here, the wife is called "the wife of your youth . . . your companion and your wife by covenant" (v. 14; cf. Prov. 2:17). In this chapter, adultery or divorce is a matter of hurting not another man *but one's own wife*. It is breaking a covenant in a way that is just as bad as breaking the covenant between God and his people. Don't be faithless to the wife of your youth (v. 15)! "'For the man who does not love his wife but divorces her,' says the Lord, the God of Israel, 'covers [or, The Lord . . . says that he hates divorce, and him who covers] his garment with violence'" (v. 16).

This is also the view of the Messianic Torah: "What therefore God has joined together, let not man separate. . . . Whoever divorces his wife and marries another commits adultery against her, and if she divorces her husband and marries another, she commits adultery" (Mark 10:9-12). I do not believe that Matthew 5:32 and 19:9 ("except for sexual immorality") imply that in cases of sexual immorality someone *is* allowed to divorce his or her spouse, because in such cases the adulterous persons were supposed to be put to death (see further on this subject Luke 16:18; Rom. 7:2-3; 1 Cor. 7:10-16).

In the Messianic Kingdom, God himself will give the supreme example: "[T]he Lord has called you like a wife deserted and grieved in spirit, like a wife of youth when she is cast off. . . . For a brief moment I deserted you, but . . . with everlasting love I will have compassion on you" (Isa. 54:6-8). We have to understand here that it was Israel who deserted the Lord first and committed adultery with the false gods and their servants (Ezek. 16; Hos. 2), and that God let her go for a time. So much greater is the miracle, then, that in the end he will accept her again to be his wife. There can never be any permanent divorce between God and his people. This sets the standard: under the Mosaic Torah adulterers have to be stoned to death; under the Millennial Torah, repentant adulterers and adulteresses receive forgiveness and are restored to their spouses.

It is worth noting that several Mosaic decrees involved not things that were prohibited or commanded by God, but things he allowed only "because of your hardness of hearts," as Jesus told the Jews (Matt. 19:8; Mark 10:5; cf. Deut. 24:1-4). In other words, these regulations did not really reflect God's mind on the matters concerned; for the time being he was merely accommodating the weakness of the people. In the Scriptures just referred to, this involved the matter of divorce, where the prophets as well as the Messianic Torah better express God's thought than the Mosaic Torah at the time could have done. The Sinaitic Torah was adapted to the "childhood" of Israel (Exod. 19:4; Num. 11:12; Deut. 1:31; 8:5), since at the time Israel was still under the *paidagōgos*. In contrast to this, the Messianic Torah belongs to the time of adulthood and maturity (Gal. 3:23-4:7). What God allowed his people in their childhood was no longer permitted to them in their adulthood.

Another example of this is slavery. Israel was *allowed* to buy slaves from other nations—not from their own midst, though (Lev. 25:39-46)—but this does not mean that slavery as such ever reflected God's mind. In the Messianic Torah there is no permission to buy and sell people as slaves: masters and slaves are only commanded to behave in a Christian way (Eph. 6:5-9; Col. 3:22-4:1; 1 Tim. 6:1-2; Titus 2:9-10; 1 Pet. 2:18), believing slaves are encouraged to seek to be released if possible (1 Cor. 7:21), just as believing masters are sometimes encouraged to release believing slaves (Philem. 10-16). Under the Millennial Torah, only those who had enslaved Israel will, as a punishment, themselves be slaves of Israel instead of being killed (Isa. 14:2).

Interestingly, as I stated earlier, rabbinic tradition was clearly conscious of the fact that the Messiah would change the Torah.[42] Some of the most striking statements are the following: "The Torah which one learns in this world is vanity in comparison with the Torah of the Messiah."[43] The ninth-century *Alphabet Midrash* of Rabbi Aqiva says: "In the future the Holy One . . . will expound to [the godly] the meanings of a new Torah which he will give them through the Messiah." Some rabbis have stressed, however, that a new Torah could never mean a Torah essentially different from the Mosaic Torah. One view was that the very same letters of the Mosaic Torah will be rearranged, so that the new Torah will thus be identical with the Mosaic Torah.

7.4 The New Torah-Giver

7.4.1 The Torah Is Jesus

The one, eternal, transcendent Torah is in force throughout the history of humanity, from the creation of Adam to eternity. At the same time, there are immanent commandments, that is, commandments regulating humanity's temporal, earthly existence, which are valid for only a certain dispensation. Every manifestation of the Torah contains some commandments that other manifestations of the Torah do not contain. The Mosaic Torah contains elements that none of the other manifestations contains, such as certain festival, agricultural, hygienic, medical, social, and purification regulations. The Millennial Torah, too, contains elements that none of the other manifestations contains, such as regulations for "the prince" (see §6.2.2 above). In the same vein, we expect to find immanent commandments in the Messianic Torah that none of the other forms contains, such as regulations for the practical life of the New Testament *Ekklesia*, including baptism and the Lord's Supper. The most portentious aspect of the Messianic

---

42. Cf. Stern (1999, 241–43, 566).
43. Eccl. Rabbah on 11:8 ("Torah of the Messiah": cf. Gal. 6:2).

Torah, however, is that it is not simply a distinct mass of new commandments. *The Messianic Torah is primarily the transcendent manifestation of Jesus himself in the lives of believers.*

Living out the Messianic Torah is living out Jesus. Jesus is the new Torah-giver and the teacher of the Torah *par excellence*. But one does not become his disciple (that is, pupil, student, follower) by simply learning his commandments by heart and trying to carry them out as best as one can. No, the great desire of the true student is "to be *like his teacher*" (Matt. 10:25). The "fully trained" pupil is the one who is "like his teacher" (Luke 6:40). The student does not simply obey; no, he "abides" in the teacher's word.[44] This word is the atmosphere in which he dwells, breathes, and moves. Dwelling in his word is actually dwelling in the teacher himself (cf. John 15:3: "Abide in me") and in his love: "If you keep my commandments, you will abide in my love" (John 15:10). After the rich young ruler had stated that he had kept all the commandments, Jesus showed him how to become perfect: "[G]o, sell what you possess and give to the poor, and you will have treasure in heaven; and come, follow me" (Matt. 19:21; cf. Mark 10:21; Luke 18:22). Through the parable of the Good Samaritan, Jesus showed one Torah-scholar the essence (*k'lal gadol*) of the Torah: unselfish service to fellowmen out of love (Luke 10:25-37), even if these fellowmen are enemies, just as Jesus himself did.[45]

Following the Messianic Torah is having "put on" Jesus (Rom. 13:14). It is being "transformed into the same image" as the Lord (2 Cor. 3:18; see the whole of 2 Cor. 3 in connection with the New Covenant). It is having "Messiah formed in you" (Gal. 4:19; see the scope of the whole Letter, e.g., 4:5, 19 and 6:2). It is attaining "to mature manhood, to the mea-

---

44. John 8:31; "abide," *menō*, is more correct and profound than the NIV's "hold to."

45. It is striking that Jesus himself was called a "Samaritan" in a derogatory way (John 8:48).

sure of the stature of the fullness of the Messiah" (Eph. 4:13). Following the teacher is developing the same mind as he has (Phil. 2:5). It is "being renewed in knowledge after the image of its creator. Here . . . Messiah is all, and in all" (Col. 3:10-11).

The Messianic Torah thus constitutes a full polity of a teacher and his disciples containing at least the following important factors:

* The *commandments* as such: the teacher commands his disciples to do certain things, avoid certain things, and be certain things.

* The *example* of the teacher: there is no commandment that he gives which he has not fulfilled himself by being totally obedient to his Father (John 4:34; 5:30; 6:38; 8:29; 10:18; 12:49-50; 14:31; 15:10) and by lovingly giving himself up for him and for his own (Gal. 1:4; 2:20; Eph. 5:2, 25; 1 Tim. 2:6; Titus 2:14; see specific examples in §6.1.1). This is why obeying Jesus' commandments entails identification with him; obedience is following a way that he himself walked first.

* The *strength* that the teacher gives: the teacher not only tells the pupil what to do, not only gives him his own example, but also grants him the strength to carry out the teacher's commands. Though he does not exclude the pupil's own responsibility, we might say that in a sense it is the teacher himself who brings about the fulfillment of the commandments. "Whoever abides in me and I in him, he it is that bears much fruit, for apart from me you can do nothing" (John 15:5). "I have been crucified with Messiah. It is no longer I who live, but Messiah who lives in me" (Gal. 2:20). Elsewhere, the Holy Spirit—who is, by the way, the Spirit of Jesus (Acts 16:7), of Messiah (Rom. 8:9; 1 Pet. 1:11), of Jesus Messiah (Phil. 1:19), of God's Son (Gal. 4:6)—is the power by which the commands are carried out (Rom. 8:2, 4; Gal. 5:16-18, 25; Eph. 3:16-19; Phil. 3:3).

If fulfilling the Messianic Torah involves following and reflecting Jesus, it is obvious that the emphasis in this fulfillment is not only upon acts but especially upon the spiritual, Jesus-like attitude behind the acts. It is rather a matter of *being* than of *doing*, rather *being* like Jesus than imitating the *acts* of Jesus. A good biblical term to express this is fruit-bearing. "By this my Father is glorified, that you bear much fruit and so prove to be my disciples" (John 15:8). "The wisdom [Heb. *hokmah*] from above is first pure, then peaceable, gentle, open to be reason, full of mercy and good fruits, impartial and sincere. And a harvest [or, fruit] of righteousness is sown in peace by those who make peace" (James 3:17-18). The term "fruit" refers not just to the act but also to the attitude behind the act: purity, peacefulness, gentleness, submission, mercy, impartiality, truthfulness, and righteousness; also holiness, goodness, and thankfulness (Rom. 6:22; 2 Cor. 9:10; Eph. 5:9; Phil. 1:11; Heb. 12:11; 13:15).

Over against the "*works* of the flesh" Paul places the "*fruit* of the Spirit" (Gal. 5:19,22a): love, joy, peace, patience, kindness, goodness, faithfulness, gentleness, self-control. He even adds surprisingly, "Against such things [or, such persons] there is no *nomos*" (v. 23b). This phrase has been interpreted in several ways.[46] With other exegetes, I believe that Paul is referring here not to any (principle of) law in general but to the Mosaic Torah, just as in verse 14: "The whole Torah is fulfilled [i.e., summed up] in one word . . . ," and 6:2: ". . . and so fulfill the Torah of the Messiah." Thus, a rather free but correct rendering of verse 23b may be: The Torah is not against such things as love, joy and peace, etc. (or, such persons as exhibit such characteristics); on the contrary, the fruit of the Spirit reflects the very essence of the Torah. More than anything, this is love (§6.1), but also joy (Ps. 119:111), peace (Prov. 3:17), goodness (Prov. 4:2), etc. The Torah is not just about right *acts* but about something far more essential: the loving, joyful, peaceful (etc.) *attitude* of the Torah-keeper's heart.

This is not a particularly New Testament idea; it is the very

---

46. Cf. Fung (1988, 273).

thought of Psalm 1: the godly man's "delight is in the Torah of the LORD, and on his Torah he meditates day and night. He is like a tree planted by streams of water that yields its fruit in season, and its leaf does not wither" (vv. 2-3). Good fruits are viewed here as the result of one's delight in the Torah. Fruit as a metaphor refers not primarily to any activity as such; a fruit-producing tree does not groan or sweat, so to speak. Fruit-bearing is the natural result of simply being a tree, as long as it stands near an adequate source of water. Note that this delight in the Torah flows forth from love for the LORD himself: "Blessed is the man who fears the LORD, who greatly delights in his *mitzwot*" (Ps. 112:1). Thus, the prophet can say, "Blessed is the man who trusts in the LORD, whose trust is the LORD. He is like a tree planted by water, that sends out its roots by the stream . . . it does not cease to bear fruit" (Jer. 17:7-9). Similarly, in New Testament language, we learn that he who delights in Jesus will never fail to bear fruit—that fruit which exhibits nothing but the very nature of Jesus himself.

7.4.2 Logos and logoi

In summary, Jesus brought to light the true, profound meaning of the Torah, and that meaning is Jesus himself. He is the *telos* (goal, purpose, sense, meaning, fulfillment, consummation) of the Torah (Rom. 10:4); this ultimately means that he is in person the one, eternal Torah. The Torah is God's Word; God reveals himself by speaking. Therefore, the Sinaitic Torah in its briefest form, in which God reveals himself (cf. Exod. 20:2), is called the "Ten Words" (Exod. 34:28; Deut. 4:13; 10:4). They were ten revelational statements of God, which together constituted his first explicit covenantal will toward Israel.

In the singular, the Torah is also called "the LORD's word" (Num. 15:31 Septuagint: *rhēma*; Deut. 5:5 Sept.: *rhēmata*). Now, in the New Testament Jesus is, in his own person, the Word, the *Logos* (John 1:1-3). As the God-Man, Jesus Christ *is* the meaning of the Torah; that is, he is that point where we found an inner coherence between (1) the Mosaic Torah, (2) the Tanakhic Hokmah, and (3) the Logos of the New Testament, namely, Jesus. We have also seen (chapter 3) that the Torah, she whom some rabbis called the "daughter of God," who materialized in the Sinaitic Torah, is related to the Son of God, who became incarnate in the person of Jesus Messiah, the "wisdom of God" (1 Cor. 1:24), "Messiah, in whom are hidden all the treasures of wisdom and knowledge" (Col. 2:2-3) (see chapter 3).

According to John 1:3, creation exists through the Logos, "the Word." We have seen that Logos involves thinking, but then in the sense of expressing that which was thought before. God expresses himself in his Word, and this Word is Jesus. God reveals himself in Jesus. Therefore Jesus is the eternal Logos, for in him God expressed, or revealed, himself in a perfect way from the time there were beings to whom he could reveal himself. Jesus is the revelation of God in word and work. And because God's word is law, and God's law is word, Jesus is in the same sense the eternal Torah. If he is the eternal Logos, he is the eternal Torah. A comparison of John 14:21 ("my commandments") and verses 23-24 ("my word," *logos*) shows how Jesus considered the Logos (the Word) of God always as Command (*Mitzwah*) of God.[47] Similarly, John 12:49-50 ("his commandment is eternal life") is parallel with 1 John 1:1-2 and 5:20: Jesus himself is eternal life. He *is*, as it were, the *Mitzwah* of God.

This is not easily understood because in its divine, eternal, transcendent fullness, the Torah is indeed one, singular, but in its immanent diversity within our temporal reality, it comes to expression in many different commandments. Thus, the one, eternal *Logos* within earthly, temporal reality diversifies into many different *Logoi* (statements of God; cf. again John 14:23-24). We can hear the Word (the *Logos*) only in the many different words (*logoi*) that God or Jesus speaks to us.

---

47. This point was not grasped by Kittel (1967, 134), who construed a contrast between *logos* and *nomos* in John's Prologue (1:1–18).

Likewise, the one, eternal Torah was manifested at Sinai in 613 commandments, concentrated in the Ten Words: distinct commandments for temporal life (see Appendix IV). They are like the many colors in which the one, white light of the eternal Torah, the eternal Logos, is refracted. We easily fall into the snare of thinking that this is the Torah: a mass of many laws. However, in its eternal form the Torah transcends both its Sinaitic form and its Millennial form, as well as the many immanent commandments of the New Testament. In this divine, eternal form it is the Messianic Torah in the loftiest transcendent sense. Jesus is the meaning and fulfillment of the Torah. As we stated earlier, he did not abolish the Sinaitic Torah but fulfilled it, brought it back to its eternal fullness as intended by God (Matt. 5:17).

Even the way in which this Torah is refracted into many commandments in the Sermon on the Mount and the rest of the New Testament implies that we are dealing here only with an earthly-temporary manifestation of this Torah, no matter how much loftier it may be than its Sinaitic manifestation. Jesus as the eternal Torah even transcends his own, highest, but temporal-immanent, commandments. This is not difficult to understand, for how many of the New Testament commandments will still be required in eternity? Does this mean that in eternity we will not need any Torah anymore? No, the Torah is eternal. We will still be bondservants in eternity; we will eternally serve God and one another in and through love (cf. Rev. 22:3). What remains is the eternal Love Command. But in our everyday life on earth today, this Messianic Torah must refract into many concrete regulations. Therefore, Jesus speaks in a very real way of his "commandments" that must be kept. Having Jesus in one's heart as the eternal Torah (cf. again Jer. 31:33 and 2 Cor. 3:3) means in a tangible way observing the commandments of Jesus in one's daily life, otherwise it does not mean anything at all. He explicitly told us about his commandments so that we would keep them (Matt. 28:19; John 13:34; 14:15, 21; 15:10, 12; cf. 1 Cor. 7:10–11, 19;

9:14; 14:37; 2 Pet. 3:2).

There are numerous examples of very concrete new commandments in the New Testament (see chapter 8). But the important thing is first to discern Jesus' way of bringing to light the deeper spirit of the Torah. He condemns the outward sinful *act* as such, but he also exposes the heart's sinful *orientation*, the *motivation* behind the concrete act, and the heart's *attitude* in general. If such a teacher were to be found anywhere, then here was a good teacher who taught his students as the father in Proverbs taught his son (see §1.3.1 above), climaxing his instructions in this word: "My son, give me your heart" (Prov. 23:26). Here was a teacher who could really probe people's hearts, and read people's most secret thoughts (Matt. 12:25; 27:18; Luke 6:8; John 2:24–25; 6:61, 64; 13:11; 16:19).

No wonder we read that "the crowds were astonished at his teaching, for he was teaching them as one who had authority, and not as their scribes [Torah-scholars]" (Matt. 7:28–29). The full impact of this has not always been realized. Some have suggested that the Torah-scholars (Greek, *grammateis*) were not rabbis but wise men from the *'am-ha'aretz*, the unschooled, ordinary people (Acts 4:13), the "crowd that does not know the Torah" (John 7:49). This means, according to this view, that they were Torah-teachers without *semikah* (formal authority that came with ordination, literally, "laying on [of hands]"), and therefore could not bring *hiddushim* ("new things," sc. interpretations) or make *halakah* (juridical judgments).[48] However, Jesus himself described a Torah-teacher "who has been trained for the kingdom of heaven" as follows: he "is like a master of a house, who brings out of his treasure [of knowledge] what is new [*hiddushim*, relating to the Messiah and the New Covenant] and what is old [relating to the Old Covenant]" (Matt. 13:52).

The scribes definitely were ordained theologians. The as-

---

48. Thus, D. Daube, quoted by Lane (1974, 72); cf. Stern (1999, 10, 87–88, 180).

A Threefold Torah: Differences & Similarities

tonishment of the crowds is far more impressive because they realized that Jesus had a teaching authority (Heb. *semikah*, Greek *exousia*) that surpassed that of formal rabbinic ordination. This is why the chief priests and the elders of the people, who knew Jesus never had any formal training (John 7:15), came to inquire by what *semikah* he acted the way he did and who had given him that *semikah* (Matt. 21:23).

The practice of laying on of hands goes back to Moses' ordination of Joshua (Num. 27:23 and Deut. 34:9: *s-m-k*, "lay on"). Who laid hands on Jesus so as to grant him the right to make *halakah*? Well, who had laid hands on Moses? No one; he had been directly ordained by God himself. This is the daring answer of Jesus concerning his own *semikah* (see implicitly in Matt. 21:23-27, and explicitly in John 5:27, 36-47; 7:28-29; 8:16-19, 28-29; 12:44-50). Jesus had received his *semikah* at the moment he was baptized by John the Baptist, and at the same time was anointed with the power of the Holy Spirit (Acts 10:38), while the Father said from heaven: "This is my beloved Son, with whom I am well pleased" (Matt. 3:13-17). No person in human history ever had such a *semikah*, not even Moses.

Jesus had the *semikah* to bring out *hiddushim* and to make new *halakah* (cf. Matt. 12:1-12; 15:1-20; 16:19; 18:18-20). He had all *semikah*, not only on earth but even in heaven, and thus had the authority to send out his emissaries to have his Torah taught to all nations on the earth (28:18-20). Jesus' *semikah* surpassed even that of Moses, since he had the authority to forgive sins, whereas Moses could only intercede for trespassers (Exod. 32:32; Num. 12:13). When the people saw this, "they glorified God, who had given such *semikah* to men" (Matt. 9:8). He equally had the *semikah* to cast out demons. When the people saw this, they asked each other, "What is this? A new teaching [and this even] with *semikah*! He commands even the unclean spirits, and they obey him" (Mark

1:27).⁴⁹

7.4.3 Moses and Jesus (1)

Jesus was the second Moses, the new Torah-giver, and at the same time greater than Moses: *Christus Iesus novus Moses*, "Messiah Jesus the new Moses."⁵⁰ This is clear from Matthew 17:3-5: "Listen to him" — that is, listen no longer only to Moses, who mediated in giving the Sinaitic Torah, or to Elijah, who restored the people to the Torah. This divine word is a direct allusion to Deuteronomy 18:15 (cf. Acts 3:22): "The LORD your God will raise up for you a prophet like me from among you, from your own brothers — it is to him you shall listen." The words "like me" (Heb. *kamoni*) underline the similarity between Moses and Jesus (cf. Acts 3:22; 7:37). Philip tells Nathanael that Jesus is the one "of whom Moses in the Torah . . . wrote" (John 1:45), and Jesus himself tells us: "Moses . . . wrote of me" (5:46). The people exclaimed, "This is indeed the Prophet who is to come into the world" (John 6:14; cf. 7:40).⁵¹ Just as Moses, the mediator of the Old Covenant, in a sense was king, prophet, and priest in Israel (see §7.1.2), Jesus, the Mediator of the New Covenant, was and is King, Prophet, and Priest. And just as Jesus is the true *Hokmah*, the true spirit of the Torah, some rabbis equated the "soul of Moses" — after his death, his body not having been found — to *Hokmah*, which is nowhere to be found except with the LORD.⁵²

The New Testament mentions the following similarities:

---

49. Even Yochanan ben Zakkai, founder of post-Temple Rabbinic Judaism, who studied the speech of the demons, had no power over the demons (Sukkah 28a; cf. Acts 23:13–17).
50. See Davies (1969, 10–16); for a Jewish view, see Schoeps (1949, 87–116).
51. Schoeps (1949, 90–91) pointed to the remarkable fact that the early Mishnah scholars (Tannaim and almost all Amoraim) refrained from interpreting Deut. 18:15, 18!
52. *Avot de-Rabbi Nathan* (version B) 25 (cf. Saldarini 1975, 151–52; Shulam 1998, 349, 358–59n13); also cf. Shabbat 89a.

A Threefold Torah: Differences & Similarities

* Moses lifted up the snake in the desert; so too the Son of Man was lifted up (John 3:14).

* Moses gave the bread from heaven; the Father gave his Son as the bread from heaven (6:32).

* Moses was a prophet; Jesus was one too.

* Moses was rejected by his people (cf. Acts 7:23-29); Jesus was too.

* It could be said about each of them that he was "mighty in his words and deeds" (Acts 7:22; see vv. 20-28, 51-52).

* Israel was baptized into Moses (1 Cor. 10:2; cf. Isa. 63:11), and Jesus-believers are baptized into Messiah (Rom. 6:3).

* The Egyptian magicians, Jannes and Jambres,[53] opposed Moses (2 Tim. 3:8), and the heretics of today oppose (the doctrine concerning the) Messiah (2 John 9).

* The song of Moses is parallel to the song of the Lamb (Rev. 15:3).

* Moses was accompanied by twelve princes of Israel's tribes and seventy(-two) elders (Num. 1:44; 11:16, 24-25; Exod. 24:1, 9); Jesus was accompanied by, and sent out, twelve apostles, corresponding to Israel's tribes, as well as seventy(-two) messengers (Matt. 19:28; Luke 22:30; 10:1).[54]

* Some rabbis believed that the *Shekinah* rested on Moses;[55] similarly, the *Shekinah* rested on Jesus (see §7.2.1).

* Interestingly, the Targum (Aramaic paraphrase) of the Psalms applies Psalm 68:18 ("You ascended on high, leading a host of captives in your train and receiving gifts among

---

53. Mentioned in the Targum Jonathan 7:11–8:19.
54. Cf. Pseudo-Clement, *Recognitiones* I.40–41, on this parallel. Rabbinic tradition tells us (referred to by Schoeps 1949, 96) that Moses originally had seventy-two elders (including Eldad and Medad); similarly, some manuscripts have seventy in Luke 10:1, 17, but others have seventy-two messengers, six for each tribe (see chapter 3 note 134 above).
55. Sanhedrin 11a.

men") to Moses ("You, prophet Moses, ascended to the sky, you took captives captive, you taught the words of the Torah, and gave them as gifts to the children of men"), whereas Ephesians 4:8 applies the verse to Jesus ("When he ascended on high he led a host of captives, and he gave gifts to men").

There are also *a fortiori* arguments:

* "Moses permitted . . . I tell you [however]" (Matt. 19:8-9).

* Those who do not listen to Moses will listen even less to someone rising from the dead (especially Jesus) (Luke 16:31).

* "The Torah was given through Moses; grace and truth came through Jesus Messiah" (John 1:17).

* Those who do not listen to the writings of Moses will listen even less to the Lord (John 5:45-47).

Scripture also mentions contrasts:

* Moses was the mediator of the Old Covenant, Jesus of the New Covenant (Deut. 5:5; Gal. 3:19; 1 Tim. 2:5; Heb. 8:6; 9:15; 12:24).

* Moses brought the "ministry of death," Jesus brought the "ministry of the Spirit" (2 Cor. 3:7-8).

* Moses was a servant in God's house, Jesus is Son over God's house (Heb. 3:1-6).

* The covenant of Moses was consecrated with the blood of animals, that of Jesus with his own blood (Heb. 9:18-23).

* Moses was connected with Mount Sinai, the mountain of judgment, Jesus with Mount Zion, the mountain of grace (Heb. 12:18-22).

* In Moses' case Sinai was the mountain of the Torah-giving, Jesus gave his at another mountain (Matt. 5-7; see §7.2.1).

Let me add a Jewish tradition here. "The Talmud and Midrash name Moses 'the first redeemer' in contrast to Messiah, who is 'the last redeemer,'" wrote the Jewish scholar, Joseph

A Threefold Torah: Differences & Similarities

Klausner, in his *The Messianic Idea in Israel*.[56] Apparently, this refers to a Jewish tradition, which may go back to New Testament times, based on Ecclesiastes 1:9 ("What has been is what will be"), saying, *kego'el rishon kego'el acharon*, "As was the first redeemer, so will be the last redeemer."[57] Rabbinic expositors elaborated this as follows: Moses and his family rode on a donkey (Exod. 4:20); the last redeemer will do the same (Zech. 9:9). The first redeemer rained bread from heaven (Exod. 16:4); the last one will do the same (cf. Ps. 132:15). The first one opened up a source of water (Exod. 17:6); the last one will do the same (Joel 3:18).

These Jewish expectations were each fulfilled in Jesus. He entered Jerusalem on a donkey (John 12:14-15 and par.), he identified himself as the Prophet by supplying the people with bread (6:11, 14), and he did the same by promising that "streams of living water" would flow from within his followers (7:38, 40). Micah (7:15) expected the people to see God's wonders in Messiah's time as "in the days when you came out of Egypt." The rabbis even thought of ten Messianic miracles matching the ten plagues of Egypt.[58] As a matter of fact, after having depicted Jesus as the second Moses on the new "Sinai" (Matt. 5-7), Matthew describes exactly ten miracles of Jesus (8:1-9:34).[59]

If Moses' Torah begins with Ten Commandments preceded by a Prologue (Exod. 19:3-6; 20:1-17), Jesus' Torah begins

---

56. Quoted by the Hebrew Christian theologian T. H. Bendor-Samuel (see his essay included in Kac 1986, 257).
57. Schoeps (1949, 91-93).
58. Mishnah Avot V.5.
59. Similarities in Matthew noted by P. Dabeck ("siehe, es erschienen Moses und Elias," *Biblica* 1942, 176; quoted by Schoeps 1949, 95): Matt. 2:20 ~ Exod. 4:19; Matt. 26:1 ~ Deut. 32:45; Matt. 28:20 ~ Deut. 32:46; the (first) seven beatitudes and the seven woes of Matt. 5:3-9 and 23:13-29 allegedly correspond with the seven blessings and curses of Deut. 28.

with the Beatitudes followed by an Epilogue (Matt. 5:2-16). Edersheim counted ten,[60] but I count only nine beatitudes; did he see a tenth one in verse 12? At any rate, the comparison is enchanting: the true purpose of the Ten Commandments is to make us *makarioi*, "blissful, happy," by following the Messiah (cf. Ps. 1:1-2; 94:12; 106:3; 112:1; 119:1-2; 128:1; Prov. 3:13; 8:32, 34; 16:20; Isa. 30:18; 56:1-2). Each of them could be reworded as a beatitude: "Blessed [lit., blissful, happy] are you if you have only me, and no other gods besides me," "Happy are you if you remember the Sabbath," "Happy are you if you honor your father and mother," etc.

Another similarity: if Matthew tells us that Jesus' "face shone like the sun" (Matt. 17:2), he seems to be connecting here with an ancient Jewish tradition[61] telling us that the light of Messiah's face would be brighter than that of Moses' face (cf. Exod. 34:29-30, 35, "the skin of Moses' face was shining").

7.4.4 Moses and Jesus (2)

There may even be a parallel between the five books of the Pentateuch and five parts in Matthew's Gospel before the Passion of Jesus. It seems that, as Dunn wrote, Matthew deliberately "gathered together Jesus' teaching into five blocks (5-7; 9.36-10.42; 13.1-52; 17.22-18.35; 23-25), each block preceded by narrative material and its conclusion marked by the repeated formula, 'When Jesus finished these words/parables/teaching. . .' (a feature which can hardly be accidental - 7.28; 11.1; 13.53; 19.1; 26.1). A not implausible explanation of this feature is that Matthew intends thereby to suggest that Jesus' teaching parallels the five books of Moses."[62]

Already Papias (early second century) pointed out that there are five "books" in Matthew, corresponding with the five books of Moses and each consisting of narrative material,

---

60. Edersheim (1971, I, 529).
61. Midrash Psalms 21.179.
62. Dunn (1990a, 248).

A Threefold Torah: Differences & Similarities

a collection of Jesus' teachings, and a closing formula: "When Jesus had finished these sayings, . ." or similar words. Some of the books of the Torah (almost) end in a similar way: "When Jacob finished commanding his sons . . . " (Gen. 49:33), "And when Moses had finished speaking with them . . . " (Exod. 34:33), "So Moses finished the work" (40:33). "And when Moses had finished speaking all these words to all Israel . . . " (Deut. 32:45).

According to this ancient suggestion, the five "books" in Matthew's Gospel, preceded by a prologue (1-2) and followed by an epilogue (26-28), would roughly consist of Matthew 3-7; 8-10; 11-13; 14-18; 19-25.[63] One objection against this scheme is that the first "book" seems to correspond with Exodus, rather than with Genesis. Therefore, Edersheim made a different division; he identified a "Genesis-part" (Matt. 1-4) and an "Exodus-part" (Matt. 5-7).[64] Indeed, Matthew 1 ties in with Genesis 1 in that it literally begins with the words, "Book of the *genesis* of Jesus Messiah . . . " (1:1) and with the activity of the Holy Spirit, "hovering" over Mary as it were (1:18-25; cf. Gen. 1:2).[65] Continuing this thought, one might suggest that Matthew 8-12, with its references to priests (8:4; 12:4-5), sacrifices (8:4; 9:13; 12:7), and cleansing (8:2-3; 9:20-22; 10:8; 11:5), forms the Leviticus-part, and Matthew 13:1-20:28, which describes the consequences of Jesus' having been rejected by Israel, forms the Numbers-part, while Matthew 20:29-25:46, describing the fulfillment of God's ways with Israel and the nations, forms the Deuteronomy-part. Matthew 26-28, leading into the promised land of resurrection, forms the fitting Joshua-part. In this way, Matthew's Gospel seems to be a real Hexateuch.

If we now consider Moses and Jesus especially in terms of

---

63. See Davies (1969, 6–16).
64. Edersheim (1971, I, 527; cf. Stern 1999, 47).
65. Davies (1969, 12–13).

their births, we again discover several conspicuous parallels.

(1) The book of Exodus begins with a genealogy before the circumstances of Israel and the birth of Moses are described; Amram was a grandson of Levi, and a great-grandson of Jacob (Exod. 1:1-5; 6:15-19). The Gospel of Matthew also begins with a genealogy before the birth of Jesus is described (Matt. 1:1-17); Joseph was a son of Jacob, and a great-grandson of Levi (Matt. 1:16; Luke 3:24).

(2) At the time of Moses, Israel suffered under foreign oppression; it was a nation of slaves under the power of Egypt, with Pharaoh at its head, who promulgated despotic decrees, including the requirement of heavy forced labor (Exod. 1:11,14; 5:6-9). At the time of Jesus, Israel suffered again under foreign domination; it was a nation of slaves (cf. Ezra 9:8-9; Neh. 9:36-37) under the power of the Romans, with the emperor at their head (emphasized by Luke) as well as the Edomite king, Herod (emphasized by Matthew). Israel was subjected to the despotic decrees of Augustus, requiring that the registration involved a census and a valuation in view of heavy taxes (Luke 2:1).

(3) Against the background of Moses' birth we hear of a terrible massacre of little boys (Exod. 1:16, 22); the Pharaoh had all the newborn boys thrown into the Nile. Moses, however, was kept hidden by his parents. Against the background of Jesus' birth we also hear of a terrible massacre of little boys (Matt. 2:16); King Herod had all the boys in Bethlehem from up to two years old slaughtered. The child Jesus, however, was whisked away by his parents as they fled to Egypt.

(4) Jochebed saw that her child was beautiful, that is, "beautiful to God" (Exod. 2:2; Heb. 11:23; Acts 7:20), and hid him for three months. During her pregnancy Mary spent three months in quietness with Elizabeth (Luke 1:56); after the birth of Jesus others honored her child, and she herself "treasured up all these things, pondering them in her heart" (2:19, 51).

(5) Jochebed put her child into an exceptional cradle, a pa-

pyrus basket, because there was no room for the boy in society; a young woman stayed near the basket: Miriam (Gr. *Maria[m]*) (Exod. 2:3-4). Mary (Gr. *Maria[m]*) put her child into an exceptional cradle: a manger, that is, a food-trough for animals, because there was no room for the boy in the inn; the young Mary sat by the manger (Luke 2:7, 16).

(6) Strangers came to see the child of Jochebed in his unusual cradle: the daughter of Pharaoh with her servants discovered little Moses (Exod. 2:5). Strangers came to see the child of Mary in his unusual cradle: the shepherds came to the child, whose manger functioned as one of the signs given to them (Luke 2:12,16); later the wise men from the Orient came as well (Matt. 2:1-12).

(7) Moses spent the first years of his life in Egypt. The striking fact is that Jesus, too, spent the first years of his life in Egypt (Matt. 2:13-15).

I add to this that Flavius Josephus supplies us with several other details about the birth of Moses, which are not mentioned in the Tanakh, but with which Matthew, and his Jewish readers as well, were probably familiar:[66]

(1) An Egyptian astrologer predicted the birth of a Hebrew boy, who would defeat Egypt and deliver Israel.[67] Because of this, Pharaoh decreed that all Hebrew boys were to be killed. Wise men (Gr. *magoi*, i.e., astrologers) from the East predicted the birth of a Jewish boy, who would be king over Israel (which also implied that he would deliver his people from the Romans). Because of this, Herod decreed the massacre of the innocents at Bethlehem (Matt. 2:1-18).

(2) Amram was a distinguished man among his people.

---

66. Jewish Antiquities II.9.
67. Exod. Rabbah 31 tells us that when Moses was a little boy, he one day grabbed the crown from Pharaoh's head and put it on his own. Some counselors told the king, "We are afraid that this is the man of whom we have since long predicted that he would be out for your crown."

THE ETERNAL TORAH: LIVING UNDER GOD

Joseph was of the house of David (Matt. 1:20; Luke 2:4).

(3) God appeared to Amram in a dream to enlighten him about the significance of the child that his wife expected, including the words: "[H]e will deliver his people from the slavery." An angel of the Lord appeared to Joseph in a dream to enlighten him about the significance of the child that his wife was expecting (Matt. 1:20-23), including the words: "[H]e will save his people from their sins" (v. 21).

(4) Josephus calls Moses the greatest personality that has ever arisen among the Hebrews. Jesus is the greatest personality of the New Testament, even of the whole Bible, even of all humanity.[68]

---

68. Jewish tradition tells us that just before Moses' death, God told his soul, "Leave him, and I will lift you up into the highest heavens, and grant you a place beside my throne, beside Cherubim and Seraphim" (cf. Luke 23:46; Eph. 1:20–21; Heb. 8:1; 12:2; 1 Pet. 3:21–22).

Chapter 8
New Testament Institutions

The L*ord* *was pleased,*
> *for his righteousness' sake*
to magnify his Torah
> *and make it glorious.*
>> Isaiah 42:21

My judgment is
> *that we should not trouble those of the Gentiles who turn to God,*
but should write to them to abstain
> *from the things polluted by idols,*
> *and from sexual immorality,*
> *and from what has been strangled,*
> *and from blood.*
For from ancient generations Moses has had in every city those who proclaim him,
> *for he is read every Sabbath in the synagogues.*
>> Acts 15:19–21

Summary: What are the specific characteristics of the Messianic Torah? It contains its own typical commandments, which cohere directly with its central Command of Love. It knows its own authorities who, on the basis of the Messianic Torah, are entitled to provide *new ordinances. It contains its own new ceremonies ("sacraments": baptism, the Lord's Supper, anointing the sick), which are carefully correlated with those of the Old Covenant. In addition to this, what is the meaning of the four special commands that in Acts 15 were imposed upon the non-Jewish Jesus-believers? What is their meaning for today? Moreover, the question will be answered regarding the extent to which non-Jewish Jesus-believers are obliged, or entitled, to keep the ceremonial commandments of the Mosaic Torah (circumcision, kashrut, Shabbat, festivals).*

8.1 New Testament *Halakah*
8.1.1 "Do As You Wish"

In the New Testament, numerous commandments can be identified that are binding on *all* Jesus-believers. Some people claim to have found more than one thousand commandments.[1] To mention only a few categories, there are commandments with regard to:

(1) *The regulation of congregational life:* church discipline (1 Cor. 5:12–14), appointment of elders (1 Tim. 3:1–13; Titus 1:5–9; Heb. 13:17), orderly meetings (1 Cor. 14), the use of spiritual gifts and ministries (Rom. 12:3–8; 1 Cor. 12; Eph. 4:7–16; 1 Thess. 5:12–13).

(2) *Practical aspects of congregational life:* social communion, peacefulness, like-mindedness, unity (Rom. 12:16; 15:5; 1 Cor. 1:10; Gal. 5:20–22; Eph. 4:1–6; Phil. 2:1–4).

(3) *The authorities and our submission to them* (Rom. 13:1–7; 1 Tim. 2:1–2; Titus 3:1; 1 Pet. 2:13–14); Stern[2] refers to the interesting saying by Rav Shmu'el,[3] *Dina dimalkuta dina*, "The law of the [secular] kingdom [one lives in] is Law," that is, *halakah*. The law of the nation state is, for a Jew, also "Torah," to be obeyed as if God himself had commanded it, except in cases where this "Torah" (secular law) conflicts with God's biblical

---

1. Dake (1961, 313–16) came up with 1,050.
2. Stern (1999, 65, 429).
3. Nedarim 28a.

New Testament Institutions

Torah (cf. Acts 4:19; 5:29).

(4) *Divorce and remarriage* (Mark 10:1-12; 1 Cor. 7:10-16).

(5) *Social communion with non-believers* (Rom. 12:18; 1 Cor. 8-10; Gal. 6:10; Titus 3:2).

(6) *Sexual purity* (Rom. 13:13; 1 Cor. 6:9-20; Gal. 5:19; Eph. 5:5; 1 Thess. 4:3-7; Heb. 13:4).

(7) *Care for the poor and needy* (Rom. 12:13a; 15:26; 2 Cor. 8-9; James 2:1-16).

(8) *Hospitality* (Rom. 12:13b; Heb. 13:2; 1 Pet. 4:9).

(9) *Abstaining from the love of money* (Luke 12:15; 1 Tim. 6:6-10; 2 Tim. 3:2; Heb. 13:5).

(10) *Abstaining from worldliness* (Rom. 12:2; James 4:4; 1 Pet. 2:11-12; 1 John 2:15-17; 5:19-21), etc.

These many hundreds of New Testament commands do not conflict whatsoever with the notion of Christian freedom. Rather, the Messianic Torah *is* the "Torah of freedom" (James 1:25; 2:12). True freedom is always a freedom under norms, otherwise it would only be debauchery. But true freedom implies that what the Torah demands is the very thing that the new nature desires to do. The statement, "All things are lawful [or, permissible] for me," is in principle correct although it can be easily abused "as an opportunity for the flesh [*yetzer ra*]" (Gal. 5:13; cf. 1 Pet. 2:16). The Torah identifies what is of the flesh and what is not: "All things are lawful for me, but not all things are helpful. All things are lawful for me, but I will not be dominated by anything" (1 Cor. 6:12). Freedom entails doing what I wish—but the Messianic Torah knows exactly what the new nature desires. This is what Augustine meant: *Dilige et quod vis fac;*[4] if you truly love, in the biblical sense of the word—serving one another in love as intended by the Torah (Gal. 5:13-14)—you may do as you wish.

In the present study, we have found several examples of Jesus-believing thinkers who believed in some essential dif-

---

4. *Homily* 7.8 (on 1 John 4:4–12).

ference between the Mosaic Torah and the Messianic Torah. It has been alleged that the Mosaic Torah necessarily contained hundreds of different commandments because the Holy Spirit had not yet been poured out. Believers did not yet know the freedom of the Holy Spirit, and therefore supposedly were bound to numerous, very specific, regulations. Under the New Covenant, by contrast, believers possess the indwelling of the Holy Spirit, and thus supposedly do not need very specific regulations anymore; in principle, the Love Command suffices for them. If they are driven by their new nature alone, which produces fruits of love, and if they are simply led by the Holy Spirit, all will be fine.

There is some truth in this view, yet it is off the mark for several obvious reasons.

(1) The Messianic Torah also contains hundreds of very specific regulations (see above for a number of examples).

(2) We are still "in the flesh" (i.e., dealing with sinful inclinations, *yetzer ra*) in us, which flesh needs to be regulated and subdued not only by the power of the Holy Spirit but by specific guidelines of the Word of God. The Holy Spirit does not operate apart from God's Word; we would not even be able to distinguish acts of the flesh from acts of the Spirit without the explicit regulations of God's Word. Everybody might claim to be led by the Spirit; but the fences that the Messianic Torah erects determine to what extent this is true.

(3) True believers before the Day of Pentecost had the Holy Spirit, too, although not in the same fullness and with the same permanency as they had that Day; but they certainly knew what it was to be led by the Spirit.[5]

---

5. Exod. 31:3; Deut. 34:9; Judg. 3:10; 6:34; 11:29; 13:25; 14:6, 19; 15:14; 1 Sam. 10:6; 16:13–14; 2 Sam. 23:2; 2 Chron. 20:14; Ps. 51:13; Isa. 11:2; 61:1; 63:10–11, 14; Ezek. 11:5; Micah 3:8; Mark 12:36; 13:11; Luke 1:15, 41, 67; 2:25; Acts 1:16; 4:25. Notice particularly Isa. 63:11, where it is said of the people who had just passed through the Red Sea that God "put in the midst of [or, within, cf. the same

(4) Believers in the Tanakh definitely knew the freedom of the Spirit, too. It is this latter point that I would like to clarify a little further.

8.1.2 Tanakhic Freedom of the Spirit

The Mosaic Torah was never intended as a rigid system of detailed decrees that never allowed for any initiative of the Holy Spirit that might surpass them. Even in the Tanakh, the Spirit from time to time broke through the fence of the Torah. The fierceness with which God punished any such Torah-breaking if it were done in a carnal and rebellious spirit was matched by his gracious reward of the true spiritual initiatives of those believers who really practiced their liberty in the Spirit. Let me give five examples, corresponding with five of the Ten Words.

Fourth Commandment: "Remember the Shabbat day." Fleeing from Saul, David came to Ahimelech the priest, and asked him for bread. The only bread that the priest had on hand was the "bread of the Presence, which is removed from before the LORD, to be replaced by hot bread on the day it is taken away" (1 Sam. 21:6). Some rabbinic sources tell us that this occurred on a Shabbat,[6] which is quite likely, since this was the day when the showbread was exchanged (Num. 4:7; 1 Chron. 9:32), and verses 5-6 suggest that this had just happened. There are several trespasses here. First, David lied about his mission (1 Sam. 21:2). Second, the priest gave the bread to David and his men, whereas only priests were supposed to eat it (Lev. 24:9). Third, if it indeed was a Sabbath, David was not resting on this day. In fact, the priest and he had to pay dearly for these trespasses when King Saul had Ahimelech and eighty-four other priests killed for their treason (22:11–19).

Yet, Jesus uses this event as an example to show that cer-

---

word, *qêrev*, in Ps. 103:1] them his Holy Spirit."

6. Yalqut 1 Sam. §130; Rabbi Shim'on in Menachot 65b. Also see Strack and Billerbeck (1922–28, I, l) and Lohse (1971:22).

tain situations surpass even the Shabbat commandment. David and his companions could eat the consecrated bread because, on their cumbersome flight, this was a matter of life and death for them. How much more could the companions of the Son of David, who is "Lord of the Shabbat," eat the grain on the Shabbat (Matt. 12:1-8). In some small measure, David foreshadowed the "Lord of the Shabbat." Also note Jesus' next words (v. 5): "Or have you not read in the Torah how on the Shabbat the priests in the temple profane the Shabbat and are guiltless?" Profaning—and yet being guiltless! As Carson comments: "Formally speaking the Levitical priests 'broke' the Sabbath every week (v. 5), since the right worship of God in the temple required them to do some work . . . the law that established the Sabbath also established the right of the priests, formally speaking, to 'break' it."[7] Similarly, it was required to "break" the Shabbat in order to circumcise a male infant if Shabbat fell on the eighth day after the child's birth (John 7:22-23). Apparently, such a child was born on the Shabbat before; who could have forbidden the mother to "labor" on that day, and the midwife to help her?

Fifth Commandment: "Honor your father and your mother." On one occasion, none other than Moses himself commanded certain people to disregard one of his own commandments. After the idolatry of the golden calf, he told the faithful Levites to each kill "his brother and his companion and his neighbor" (Exod. 32:27). In Deuteronomy 33:9, Moses recapitulated this event: "[Levi] said of his father and mother, 'I regard them not'; he disowned his brothers and ignored his children. For they observed your word and kept your covenant." Listen to what is said here: the Levites showed outright disrespect for their own parents—in flat contradiction to the Fifth Commandment—and were praised for it! This was because they put God's Word and God's covenant above a scrupulous Torah-observance. It reminds us of Jesus' word: "If anyone

---

7. Carson (1984, 281).

comes to me and does not hate his own father and mother [i.e., does not love me more than he loves them] . . . he cannot be my disciple" (Luke 14:26). Because of what Levi did, God's "covenant with Levi" will "stand. . . . My covenant with him was one of life and peace, and I gave them to him. It was a covenant of fear, and he feared me. He stood in awe of my name. . . . He walked with me in peace and uprightness, and he turned many from iniquity" (Mal. 2:4–6).

Sixth Commandment: "You shall not murder." Phinehas, son of the high priest Eleazar, was so outraged about Israel's idolatry and sexual immorality with the Moabites that he killed an Israelite man together with the Midianite woman he slept with; he pierced both of them with his spear (Num. 25:8). Now this was not his duty; it was not even his right to do so. Killing a person was forbidden by the Sixth Commandment; any judicial killing was reserved to the courts and the executioners. But at this vital moment in Israel's history, where God had already commanded Moses to kill the people's leaders (v. 4), Phinehas felt this was the right thing to do—and God agreed: "Phinehas . . . has turned back my wrath from the people of Israel, in that he was jealous with my jealousy among them, so that I did not consume the people of Israel in my jealousy. Therefore say, 'Behold, I give to him my covenant of peace, and it shall be to him and to his descendants after him the covenant of a perpetual priesthood, because he was jealous for his God and made atonement for the people of Israel'" (Num. 25:10–13; cf. 1 Chron. 9:20; Ps. 106:28–31).[8] By "breaking" the Torah, Phinehas atoned for Israel and received an everlasting "covenant of peace."

Seventh Commandment: "You shall not commit adultery." There is the amazing story of Tamar in Genesis 38, who offered herself as a prostitute to Judah because she had been

---

8. Ezra, who was also zealous for the Torah, was a descendant of this Phinehas (Ezra 7:5), who was the high priest after his father (Josh. 22:13, 30–32; Judg. 20:28).

married to two of his sons, and he had refused to give her his third son. Now, even if Judah was a widower at the time, their intercourse was a sin against the Seventh Commandment in the broader sense of prohibiting all sexual immorality. Such a commandment was certainly implied in the creation order even before the Mosaic Torah had been given. But Tamar resorted to this strange deed for a purpose: she was entitled to Judah's third son because her previous husbands had left her without sons. Apparently, the law of levirate marriage (Deut. 25:5-10) was already practiced in those days. Tamar trespassed the lesser commandment, so to speak, in order to gain the blessing of the greater commandment. In this case, it was not the LORD who explicitly praised Tamar; but Judah himself, Jesus' forefather, had to admit: "She is more righteous than I, since I did not give her to my son Shelah" (v. 26). Moreover, the LORD rewarded her in that she became pregnant and gave birth to twins, the eldest of whom, Perez, became the forefather of the Davidic dynasty, and thus of the Messiah (cf. Ruth 4:12, 18-22; 1 Chron. 2:4-15; Matt. 1:3).

Ninth Commandment: "You shall not bear false witness against your brother." Surprisingly, James presents "Rahab the prostitute" to us as an example of true faith, which expressed itself in good deeds: she was "justified [i.e., shown to be righteous] by works when she received the messengers and sent them out by another way" (James 2:18-20, 25-26). According to a strict interpretation of the Torah, Rahab committed a sin against the Ninth Commandment (here taken in its broader sense of prohibiting lying and deception) in telling lies to the king's messengers (Josh. 2:3-5). I leave aside her prostitution, and the fact that she betrayed her own country, which was high treason. In spite of all this, what was her reward? "Rahab the prostitute and her father's household and all who belonged to her, Joshua saved alive. And she has lived in Israel to this day, because she hid the messengers whom Joshua sent to spy out Jericho" (Josh. 6:25). "By faith Rahab the prostitute did not perish with those who were disobedient, because she had given a friendly welcome to the spies" (Heb. 11:31). Just as Phinehas received an everlasting priesthood — so that even the Millennial priests in Jerusalem will be his descendants (1 Chron. 6:3-12; 16:39; 18:16; Ezek. 40:46; 43:19; 44:15; 48:11) — so too Rahab, like Tamar, received a place in the ancestry of the Messiah: she became a (fore)mother of Boaz, David's great-grandfather (Matt. 1:5-6). The prominent places in the Millennium will be reserved for the descendants of a killer, a whore,[9] and a liar, who by breaking certain commandments obeyed the *spirit* of the Torah in a better way than many meticulous Torah-observers.

In all cases where a person is confronted with two conflicting commandments, where he cannot obey both at the same time, he is to follow the higher commandment (although, admittedly, it may not always be easy to establish which of the two *is* the higher commandment, or to establish objective criteria for such a choice). Obedience to the Lord, seeking his honor and glory, seeking the highest blessing for the neighbor, in short, following the Love Command, always surpasses the strict observance of any concrete commandment of the Torah. Even Tamar's longing for sons, which ultimately implies the longing to be a (fore)mother of the Messiah, can be viewed as falling under the Love Command.

We find illustrations of the principle of seeking the higher commandment also in some reverse cases. Sometimes, people did *not* break any explicit commandment, yet acted altogether against the *spirit* of the Torah, and were punished for it. One might say that, in these cases, in some sense they wrongly chose the lesser commandment. Thus, the two sons of Aaron "each took his censer and put fire in it and laid incense on it and offered strange fire before the LORD, which he had

---

9. Even more than one (or two) people: in addition to Tamar and Rahab, Matt. 1 mentions Ruth, who at least fell under the suspicion of fornication by "offering" herself to Boaz (Ruth 3), and Uriah's wife, with whom David committed adultery (2 Sam. 11).

not commanded them" (Lev. 10:1). They may have wished to follow the general rule of serving the Lord, but they ignored the rule whereby the Lord himself prescribes how he wishes to be served (cf. John 4:24). They did not act "contrary to his command" (as the NIV wrongly renders it), but they did something that had *not* been commanded, that is, they acted on their own initiative. I think that the Lord loves the *spiritual* initiatives of his people, but there are always fixed boundaries for such initiatives.

Sixteen times we read in Leviticus 8 and 9 about things that the Lord had commanded Moses, Aaron, and his sons to do. Subsequently, Nadab and Abihu added a certain offering to all these things that the Lord had commanded. But adding to the commandments on their own initiative was acting against the spirit of all the precise commandments the Lord had given them. They brought "strange fire," that is, unauthorized fire, which probably implied fire that had not been taken from the altar (cf. 16:12). The fire on the altar was the fire "from before the Lord," which had been given by the Lord himself. No "strange fire," that is, fire from any other origin, would please him. Consequently, Nadab and Abihu themselves were consumed by fire that "came out from before the Lord" (10:2). They had brought the wrong fire, so God consumed them by the right fire. They had broken the highest commandment, that is, to seek the honor and glory of the Lord out of love for him, and thus the Lord honored *himself* by judging *them* (v. 3).

We have identified some people who broke a commandment, yet were rewarded, and some who did not break a specific commandment, yet were punished. There is an important third group: those who ventured to alter the Torah, or at least ventured to ask for alterations. Israelites were supposed to celebrate *Pesach* on the fourteenth of the first month. But when some could not celebrate it on that day because they were ceremonially unclean, the Lord at their request gave new *halakah*: he allowed them to celebrate it on the fourteenth of the second month (Num. 9:6–12).

Similarly, the five daughters of the Manassite Zelophehad came to Moses with the request: "Why should the name of our father be taken away from his clan because he had no son? Give to us a possession among our father's brothers" (Num. 27:4) — although they knew that the Torah allowed only sons to inherit land. (Notice that Job did something similar [42:15], even though his daughters had brothers.) The LORD answered: "The daughters of Zelophehad are right. You shall give them possession of an inheritance among their father's brothers and transfer the inheritance of their father to them" (v. 7).[10] Interestingly, at a later stage, some Manassite family heads came to Moses with the request that Zelophehad's daughters were not to marry outside their tribe so that their land would not be lost to the tribe (Num. 36:3-4). This time the LORD gave a similar answer: "The tribe of the people of Joseph is right," and commanded the five daughters to marry "within the clan of the tribe of their father" (vv. 5-6).

This is an important example of the development of *halakah* even within the Torah itself. It was never God's intention that the Torah would be a rigid block of moral concrete. Under specific circumstances, commandments could be broken if in so doing a higher purpose was served; or people could ask the LORD to exempt them from certain commandments, thus asking him for special *halakah*. This continued after the closing of the Torah as well; the admission of Ruth into the people of God constitutes an excellent example (see §6.3.3). The new elements that David introduced into the temple ministry constitute another (see §7.1.3). Those who were truly led by the Holy Spirit, even in Tanakhic times, often rose above the strict commandments as such, if these hindered them in observing the highest commandment: "You shall love the LORD your God with all your heart and with all your soul and

---

10. Cf. Num. 26, which numbers only sons, to whom the land was to be allotted "as an inheritance based on the number of names" (vv. 52–56).

with all your might" (Deut. 6:5).

8.1.3 Rabbinic Reasoning

As I explained earlier, the way New Testament *halakah* is formed is along the lines of both the Tanakh and rabbinic tradition much more than many seem to recognize. Let us emphasize this point a little more strongly by dealing with a few examples of typical rabbinic reasoning in the New Testament.

A good example with which to begin is the *qal v'chomer* argument.[11] In John 7:23, Jesus gives a beautiful example of what the rabbis would call a *din-Torah*, a prescription about the practical application of the Torah. Jesus' argument is that, if tradition allows a child to be circumcised on a Shabbat, so much the more can a person be healed on the Shabbat. The *qal v'chomer* ("light and heavy") argument, in philosophy called an *a fortiori* argument, was characteristic of the rabbis' work. They are described as those who "weighed the light and the heavy in the Torah," that is, they expounded the Torah according to the hermeneutical rule of *qal v'chomer*.[12] This rule applies when two commandments collide — in this case, the Shabbat commandment and the command to do well — and allows the "heavier" command (here, the healing) to prevail over the "lighter" command (here, the prohibition to work). In verse 22, Jesus seems to point to a rule already known in Judaism for ages: if a child was born on a Shabbat he was allowed to be circumcised eight days later, that is, on the next Shabbat, although this would involve work (see §8.1.1).[13] In fact, the Talmud uses the same argument: "Rabbi El'azar answered, If circumcision, which involves only one of the 248 parts of the human body, suspends Shabbat, how much more must [saving] the whole body suspend Shabbat!"[14]

---

11. Cf. Stern (1997, 159; 1999, 177–78).
12. Chagigah 15b.
13. See Shabbat 128a, and so on.
14. Yoma 85b.

I will simply quote some other examples without further comments: "[I]f God so clothes the grass of the field, which today is alive and tomorrow is thrown into the oven, will he not much more clothe you?" (Matt. 6:30). "For if they do these things when the wood is green, what will happen when it is dry?" (Luke 23:31). "Is it not written in your Torah, 'I said, you are gods'? [Ps. 82:6] If he called them gods to whom the word of God came—and Scripture cannot be broken—do you say of him whom the Father consecrated and sent into the world, 'You are blaspheming,' because I said, 'I am the Son of God'?" (John 10:34-36).[15]

Paul also uses this type of *qal v'chomer* argument, for example, in 1 Corinthians 9:9-10, where he quotes Deuteronomy 25:4: "You shall not muzzle an ox when it is treading out the grain." He argues that, if God is concerned about oxen—and he is—then he is all the more concerned about his children: "It was written for our sake, because the plowman should plow in hope and the thresher thresh in hope of sharing in the crop."

Some other Pauline examples without further comment: "[I]f while we were enemies we were reconciled to God by the death of his Son, much more, now that we are reconciled, shall we be saved by his life" (Rom. 5:10; see further vv. 11-21). "Now if their [i.e., Israel's] trespass means riches for the world, and if their failure means riches for the Gentiles, how much more will their full inclusion mean! . . . For if their rejection means the reconciliation of the world, what will their acceptance mean but life from the dead?" (11:12, 15). "For if you were cut from what is by nature a wild olive tree, and grafted, contrary to nature, into a cultivated olive tree, how much more will these, the natural branches, be grafted back into their own olive tree" (v. 24). To the Corinthian believers: "If to others I am not an apostle, at least I am to you, for you are the seal of my apostleship in the Lord" (1 Cor. 9:2).

---

15. See Stern (1999, 32, 45, 117, 189, 933).

"Now if the ministry of death, carved in letters on stone, came with such glory... will not the ministry of the Spirit have even more glory? For if there was glory in the ministry of condemnation, the ministry of righteousness must far exceed it in glory.... For if what was being brought to an end came with glory, much more will what is permanent have glory" (2 Cor. 3:7–11; also cf. Rom. 8:23; 10:6–8).

Also see the Letter to the Hebrews: "For if the blood of goats and bulls, and the sprinkling of defiled persons with the ashes of a heifer, sanctify for the purification of the flesh, how much more will the blood of Christ, who through the eternal Spirit offered himself without blemish to God, purify our conscience from dead works to serve the living God" (Heb. 9:13–14). "For if they did not escape when they refused him who warned them on earth, much less will we escape if we reject him who warns from heaven" (12:25).[16]

The *qal v'chomer* argument was one way of establishing new *halakah*. Another example was the matter of the social interaction and fellowship between Jewish and Gentile Jesus-believers. We will see (§9.1.2) that Jesus, and Paul as well, supplied us with important rules concerning the social interaction and fellowship between Jewish and Gentile Jesus-believers (Acts 10:9–16, 28; Gal. 2:11–14). If the Jewish Jesus-believers keep *kashrut*, this may not impede either their social life with Gentiles to whom they bring the gospel, or their eating together with Gentile Jesus-believers. This is again a *qal v'chomer* argument: when two commands collide, the "higher" command is to prevail over the "lighter" command. Thus, the command to eat freely with Gentiles prevails over *kashrut*. Another example of the same principle is found in Acts 20:16: "Paul had decided to sail past Ephesus, so that he might not have to spend time in Asia, for he was hastening to be at Jeru-

---

16. See Shulam (1998, 191, 297); Stern (1999, 358–59, 373, 400, 414–15, 460–61, 497, 694, 719).

New Testament Institutions

salem, if possible, on the day of Pentecost." This seems to imply that the command to be at Jerusalem to celebrate *Shavu'ot* occasionally had to prevail over the command to preach the gospel (cf. 1 Cor. 16:8-9, "I will stay in Ephesus until Pentecost [*Shavu'ot*], for a wide door for effective work has opened to me, and there are many adversaries").

Another example of Jewish aspects of the Messianic Torah involves the use of certain typical rabbinic rules of exegesis in the New Testament. It was Rabbi Hillel who, in the first century BC, constructed certain rules for the exposition of the Tanakh. One of these rules was that of *g'zerah shavah* or "verbal analogy," meaning that, if in two Scriptures the same characteristic expression occurs, the meaning of that expression in the one Scripture is identical with that in the other. The New Testament supplies us with several examples of the apostles applying this rule. In Acts 2:25-28 and 34-35, Peter first quoted Psalm 16:8-11, and then Psalm 110:1. Both passages contain the expression "at my right hand," so that these Scriptures may be linked together. Consequently, if Psalm 110 is undeniably Messianic, then so too is Psalm 16. Paul followed a similar type of reasoning in Acts 13:34-35. First, he quoted Isaiah 55:3, and then Psalm 16:10; both passages contain the Greek word *hosios*, "holy, faithful, pious" (Heb. *hesed*). Through this common expression the two Scriptures are linked together, so that they can both be applied to the resurrection of Jesus.

We are especially interested in examples of this typical rabbinic technique that relate to the Torah. In Romans 4, Paul argues that "righteousness" — that is, the "righteousness that is based on the Torah" (Rom. 10:5; cf. Phil. 3:6, 9) — is not obtained through one's own strength but through faith and divine forgiveness. In verses 3 and 6-8, Genesis 15:6 and Psalm 32:1-2 are linked together because they both contain the word *logizō*, "count toward, impute to, reckon to." Thereby the principles of faith and forgiveness are linked as well. In verses 7-9, Psalm 32:1-2 ("Blessed is the one . . . ") is implicitly linked with Genesis 12:3, the blessing of Abraham, thus establishing that true blessing comes only through faith and forgiveness.[17] The majority of Israelites had not obtained this righteousness because they were blind to the true way of acquiring it. Paul establishes this through another application of *g'zerah shavah*. In Romans 11:8–10, he links Isaiah 29:10 and Psalm 69:22–23 because they both contain the expression "closed eyes" or "darkened eyes." In Galatians 3:10 and 13, Paul links Deuteronomy 27:26 and 21:23 because they both contain the word "cursed." In the first passage, those are cursed who try to obtain the righteousness of the Torah by their own strength; in the second Scripture, it is Messiah who is cursed on the cross in order to release the legalists from the "curse of the Torah," which they inevitably incur.

I emphasize that in cases like these, common grammatical-historical exegesis would not necessarily have associated such passages, which apparently in Paul's mind are clearly linked. He did not follow modern Western rules of exposition but, interestingly, he did apparently accept well-known rabbinic rules, in which he had been "educated at the feet of Gamaliel" (Acts 22:3; this was the highly regarded Rabban Gamaliel I, grandson of the famous Hillel the Elder).

Another rabbinic exegetical principle is called *binyan av mishnei k'tuvim*, or *binyan av*, for short. This refers to an analogy between two Scriptures, each of which contains a related, though slightly different notion. Thus, in Romans 10:4–8, from a combination of Leviticus 18:5 (life is through Torah-observance) and Deuteronomy 30:12–13 (life is through faith, viz., in Messiah) Paul establishes the truth of verse 4: Messiah is the goal of the Torah.[18]

Yet another principle is called *middah k'neged middah*, "measure for measure" (cf. Matt. 7:2). See, for example, Romans 2:1, where Paul argues that if the majority of Israel engages

---

17. Shulam (1998, 163).
18. Shulam (1998, 345, 357–58).

New Testament Institutions

in the same sins as the Gentiles, they are liable to the same judgment, despite the fact that they possess the Torah. But also, positively, because believers are associated with Messiah, what is true for him is true for them: life, sonship, resurrection, the righteousness of the Torah (Rom. 6:5–8; 8:10–11, 29; Gal. 2:20; 2 Cor. 5:14–15; Eph. 2:4–6; Phil. 3:9).[19]

There are other such typically rabbinic passages in Paul's epistles, using techniques familiar to us through later rabbinic writings that argue about the Torah in order to establish *halakah*. Paul uses expressions such as "What shall we say?" (*ti eroumen*; Rom. 3:5; 4:1; 6:1; 7:7; 8:31; 9:14, 30; cf. Heb. *mah nafqa minah*, "What comes out of [this]?"), "By no means!" (*mē genoito*, lit. "May it not be"; Rom. 3:4, 6, 31; 6:2, 15; 7:7, 13; 9:14; 11:1, 11; 1 Cor. 6:15; Gal. 2:17; 3:21; 6:14; Heb. *chas v'chalilah*), "as it is written" (*kathōs gegraptai*; Rom. 1:17; 2:24; 3:4, 10; 4:17; 8:36; 9:13, 33; 10:15; 11:8, 26; 15:3, 9, 21; 1 Cor. 1:31; 2:9; 10:7; 2 Cor. 4:13; 8:15; 9:9; Heb. *k'mo sh'n'amar*), and "I am speaking the truth" (*alētheian legō*; Rom. 9:1; 2 Cor. 7:14; 12:6; Gal. 4:16; 1 Tim. 2:7; Heb. *divrei emet ani m'dabbêr 'imkha*),[20] which we know from Talmudic arguments about the Torah. Again, we note that Paul's way of establishing New Testament *halakah* in many aspects reminds us more of rabbinic exegesis than of modern grammatical-historical exegesis.

8.1.4 New *Halakhic* Authority[21]

In Matthew 16:19 Jesus told Peter: "I will give you the keys of the kingdom of heaven, and whatever you bind on earth shall be bound in heaven, and whatever you loose on earth shall be loosed in heaven." Binding and loosing have been explained as "binding" someone's sins, or even someone's demons, upon him, and as forgiving those sins (cf. John 20:23),

---

19. Shulam (1998, 78–79, 315).
20. Shulam (1998, 6; cf. 126, 147, 339n3).
21. Cf. extensively Sigal, who calls Jesus a "proto-rabbinic halakhist" (1987, 6).

or driving out those demons, respectively. However, it is only the Jewish context that can supply us with the right interpretation. In rabbinic tradition, "binding" and "loosing" (Heb.: *asar v'hittir*, or *asar v'sh'ra*) mean "forbidding" and "permitting."[22] Jesus granted to Peter the divine authority to establish new *halakah*, as we see him functioning particularly in his prominent position among the apostles (Acts 1:15; 2:14, 38; 3:4, 12; 4:8; 5:3, 8, 15, 29; 8:20; 9:32, 38; 10:5; 11:2; 12:3; 15:7; Gal. 2:7-8) and in his two New Testament Letters. Entrusting the keys to Peter made him a kind of Jewish *shammash* ("steward, deacon") and *dayan* ("judge").[23] Jesus thereby invested this "uneducated, common fisherman" (Matt. 4:18; Acts 4:13) with the same authority that previously the learned teachers of the Torah and the Pharisees had possessed in the Jewish community. In Matthew 23:4, we find corroboration that this is the meaning of "binding" and "loosing": "They [= the Torah-scholars and the Pharisees] tie up heavy burdens, hard to bear, and lay them on people's shoulders."

In Matthew 18:18-20 Jesus extended this *semikah* to all the apostles (in every instance here, the "you" is plural): "Truly, I say to you, whatever you bind on earth shall be bound in heaven, and whatever you loose on earth shall be loosed in heaven. Again I say to you, if two of you agree on earth about anything they ask, it will be done for them by my Father in heaven. For where two or three are gathered in my name, there am I among them." In verses 15-17 Jesus spoke about how his followers were to deal with a sinning brother. If personal efforts did not help, the case had to be presented to the congregation, which would have to make a decision. To this, Jesus attached the quoted verses, in which he conferred the power of "binding" and "loosing" to the "two or three"

---

22. See, e.g., the Talmud tracts Chagigah 3b, Ta'anit 12a, and Makkot 23b (cf. Bivin and Blizzard 1984, 143-49; Stern 1997, 149-50; 1999, 56-58).

23. Stern (1999, 54).

who are together in the name of Jesus, that is, to render their verdicts in his name.

Contrary to what people often think, verses 19–20 do not speak of the meetings of believers, especially prayer meetings, although the passage may be applied this way in the manner of a homiletic midrash. Rather, these verses speak of the "two or three" who are gathered together with Jesus to establish *halakah*: to forbid actions, or to permit actions, or to impose actions. This interpretation is supported by the fact that Jesus seems to allude to rabbinic tradition here. Certain Talmud tracts derive from Malachi 3:16 the notion that, where two are together and occupy themselves with the Torah (!), or even more specifically, where three sit together as a court of justice, that is, to apply the Torah (!), the *Shekinah* is among them.[24] Thus, Jesus is saying that, where two or three of his followers are poring over the Messianic Torah, to derive *halakah* from it, he himself will be with them; that is, of course, through his Spirit (cf. §3.3.2 about the supposed relationship between the *Shekinah* and the Holy Spirit). Naturally, in practice these followers are specifically the Messianic community leaders, first the apostles, afterward the teachers and elders in the congregations (Matt. 28:20; Eph. 4:11–16; 1 Tim. 3:2; 5:17; Titus 1:9; Heb. 13:7, 17). The early Jesus-believers followed the teaching (*didachē*) of the apostles, who had just been filled with the Holy Spirit (Acts 2:4, 42). Remembering that *torah* means "teaching," one understanding of the expression is that the believers followed the apostles' *halakah* or Oral Torah, that is, their exposition and practical application of the Tanakh in view of the new (post-Easter and post-Pentecost) situation.

Peter Tomson has made a special study of *halakah* in the Pauline epistles.[25] All of the examples he has found belong to the mode of what he calls "*halakah* cited in support of a hor-

---

24. Mishnah Avot III. 2; Gemara: Berakhot 6a (see Edersheim 1971, II, 124).
25. Tomson (1990).

tatory argument." I freely present his categories in my own way, examples of which I find particularly in 1 Corinthians.

(1) Explicit *halakah* of the Lord: rules going back to direct commandments of Jesus. Some of these agree with Pharisaic-rabbinic *halakah*, such as: "the Lord commanded that those who proclaim the gospel should get their living by the gospel" (1 Cor. 9:14; cf. Matt. 10:10; Luke 10:7); and: ". . . the women should keep silent in the churches. For they are not permitted to speak, but should be in submission, as the Torah also says" (1 Cor. 14:34). There is no such rule in the Mosaic Torah (see §8.2.4), so this may go back to the Messianic Torah (cf. v. 37: "the things I am writing to you are a command of the Lord"). Other rules are non-Pharisaic but rather seem to be similar to Essene *halakah*, such as: "To the married I give this charge (not I, but the Lord): the wife should not separate from her husband (but if she does, she should remain unmarried or else be reconciled to her husband), and the husband should not divorce his wife" (7:10-11); and: "For I received from the Lord what I also delivered to you, that the Lord Jesus on the night when he was betrayed took bread," etc. (11:23-25).

(2) Pauline *halakah*, such as: "To the rest I say (I, not the Lord) that if any brother has a wife who is an unbeliever, and she consents to live with him, he should not divorce her," etc. (7:12-14); "concerning the betrothed, I have no command from the Lord, but I give my judgment as one who by the Lord's mercy is trustworthy" (v. 25); "Eat whatever is sold in the meat market without raising any question on the ground of conscience," etc. (10:25-27). Consider 11:2-16 as well (see v. 16: ". . . we have no such practice, nor do the churches of God"). I add that this *halakah* is specifically Pauline but explicitly applies to all Jesus-believers (cf. 1 Cor. 1:2; 4:17; 7:17; 11:16; 14:34), in contrast to Pauline occasional commands given to individual churches or persons. Note the "instructions" (Gr. *entolas*) given to the church in Colossae concerning Barnabas (Col. 4:10), and the charge to Timothy "to keep the

[not "this"] commandment" (Gr. *entolēn*),[26] that is, the Messianic Torah (cf. the expression "guard the deposit entrusted to you," 1 Tim. 6:14, 20; cf. 1:5; 2 Tim. 1:14).

(3) General *halakah*, that is, not typically apostolic, such as: "sexual immorality among you . . . , for a man has his father's wife" (5:1); "each man should have his own wife and each woman her own husband. The husband should give to his wife her conjugal rights, and likewise the wife to her husband" (7:2-3); "it is written in the Law of Moses, 'You shall not muzzle an ox when it treads out the grain.' [Deut. 25:4] Is it for oxen that God is concerned? Does he not certainly speak for our sake? It was written for our sake, because the plowman should plow in hope and the thresher thresh in hope of sharing in the crop" (9:9-10, *halakhic* midrash); "I testify again to every man who accepts circumcision that he is obligated to keep the whole Torah" (Gal. 5:3, the proselyte *halakah*).

In his second Letter Peter has some interesting expressions indicating that in some sense the whole of the New Testament message is *halakah*. He writes of the apostates who had turned "back from the holy commandment [Gr. *entolē*] delivered to them" (2 Pet. 2:21). This is more or less the same as saying that they had turned their backs on the entire apostolic New Testament teaching, the Messianic Torah. "It is characteristic of this writer to emphasize the aspect of Christianity, not only as faith, but as the moral law," says Strachan, who views "the command given by our Lord and Savior through your apostles" in 2 Peter 3:2 as the "teaching of our Lord on the fulfillment of the moral law" (cf. John 12:50).[27]

Hans-Helmut Esser says of 2 Peter 2:21, "This refers to the entire Christian teaching, above all in ethical practice which is described in the same verse as 'the way of righteousness' (cf. Prov. 21:16; Job 24:13; Matt. 21:32). The sole defense against

---

26. The article might be viewed as deictic here, but I prefer the explanation given.
27. Strachan (1979, 141–42).

libertinism is to recall Tanakhic prophecy and 'the commandment of the Lord and Savior through your apostles' (3:2). In both passages the way is prepared to understand Jesus as the proclaimer of a new Torah and Christian doctrine as the summary of it."[28] He also points out that, in the Septuagint, *entolē*, or the plural *entolai*, is sometimes the rendering of the Hebrew word *torah* (Deut. 17:19; 2 Kings 21:8; 2 Chron. 30:16),[29] thus underscoring the truth that for Peter, in a sense, the whole Christian faith is Torah.

8.2 The Sacraments

8.2.1 Baptism

Just like the Lord's Supper and the anointing of the sick, baptism was based on the Lord's direct command. One might say, they are royal commandments, for all three are placed in a clear-cut Kingdom context (cf. Matt. 10:7-8; 26:26-29; 28:19-20; Luke 10:9). They may be called part of the "royal Torah" (James 2:6, 8). Baptism is based on the royal command to baptize, or to be baptized, as an introduction to the Kingdom of God (Matt. 28:18-19; Mark 16:15-16; Acts 2:38; 8:36; 10:48; 22:16). The Lord's Supper is based on the royal command of Jesus: "Do this in remembrance of me" (Luke 22:19; 1 Cor. 11:24-25), in connection with his coming again and the establishment of his Kingdom (Mark 14:25; 1 Cor. 11:26). Healing the sick is based on the royal command of Jesus: "Heal the sick," in the context of preaching the Kingdom of God (Matt. 10:7-8; Luke 10:9; cf. Matt. 4:23; 9:35; 12:28). It is the application of the "powers of the age to come" (Heb. 6:5), when no one will say, "I am sick" (Isa. 33:24).

Interestingly, all three institutions are rooted in Jewish customs. Baptism (Rom. 6:3-4; Gal. 3:27; Eph. 4:5; Col. 2:12; 1 Pet. 3:21) is the obvious continuation and elaboration of the Jewish *mikveh*, the immersion bath for ceremonial purifica-

---

28. Esser, in VanGemeren (1997, I, 339).
29. Ibid., 335.

tion.³⁰ Baptism is a specific, New Testament form of a Jewish *baptismos*, or "washing."³¹ There are quite a few references to such washings or purifications (Heb. *toharot*; sing. *tohar*, "ceremonially clean"). The *toharot* often were the subject of heated disputes (cf. John 3:25) because the Oral Torah decreed down to the finest details when and how they had to be applied. The sixth part of the Mishnah, called Toharot, was devoted entirely to this subject. Some New Testament examples involve only the washing of hands; before a meal, water was used for ceremonially cleansing the hands (Matt. 15:2-3; Mark 7:3; John 2:6). Other cases involve washings of the whole body. Those who wanted to celebrate *Pesach* but were ceremonially unclean had to use the *mikveh* (John 11:55; cf. Num. 9:10, 13). Luke 2:22 tells us: "[W]hen the time came for their purification according to the Torah of Moses...." This refers to the commandment of Leviticus 12:1-4, according to which a mother is ceremonially unclean for forty days after having given birth to a son; in the case of a daughter this was eighty days. After this interval, the mother had to offer an animal sacrifice in the temple (vv. 6-8). After the destruction of the Temple, Jewish women were no longer able to fulfill this duty. Therefore, the sacrifice was replaced by immersion in a *mikveh*.

The *mikveh* most important for our subject was proselyte baptism, the rite through which, together with circumcision in the case of males, Gentiles were admitted into Judaism. It was also one of the means of introducing new members into the Qumran community.³² Ritual immersion does not seem to have occurred in the Tanakh, but Rabbi Joshua found a hint in

---

30. This is one important argument against the ancient Christian notion that baptism has replaced circumcision; the two have very different backgrounds, and consequently different meanings, in Israel's religion (Berkowitz 1999, 250–51).
31. See *baptismos* ("[ceremonial] washing") in Mark 7:4; Heb. 6:2; 9:10. The word for "baptism" in its usual meaning is rather *baptisma*.
32. See 1 QS 2.25–3.9 (quoted by Shulam 1998, 213).

Exodus 19:10, where the people, about to be admitted into Judaism, were told to wash their clothes: "[I]f where washing of the garments is not required ablution [purifying immersion] is required, how much more should ablution be required where the washing of the garments is required" (*qal v'chomer* argument). This appeal to Exodus 19 was rejected by others because the purpose of the washing might have been merely for cleanliness. More decisive in the eyes of the rabbis was Exodus 24:8, "Moses took the blood and threw it on the people," and, the rabbis added, "we have a tradition that there must be no sprinkling without ritual ablution." So they were convinced that Israel underwent the *mikveh* at Sinai.[33] There is no way that a person can enter into the covenant relationship with the LORD other than by being born of an immersed nation, or by being immersed himself. Note the difference with the Ekklesia; here, it is not sufficient to belong to an immersed community; every new member has to be baptized personally, both Jews and Gentiles.

A special, spiritualized example of the *mikveh* in the New Testament is found in Ephesians 5:25-27: "Husbands, love your wives, as Christ loved the church and gave himself up for her, that he might sanctify her, having cleansed her by the washing of water with the word, so that he might present the church to himself in splendor, without spot or wrinkle or any such thing, that she might be holy and without blemish." These verses possibly refer to the Jewish bride's ritual bath shortly before the wedding, called *qiddushin* ("sanctification"). Similarly, before the bride of the Messiah—that is the Messianic Ekklesia—is presented to her heavenly bridegroom, she undergoes her spiritual *mikveh*, that is, her sanctification and her cleansing through the spiritual washing by means of the Word of God.

Another spiritualized example of the *mikveh* is found in Hebrews 10:19-22: "Therefore, brothers, since we have con-

---

33. Yevamot 46b (cf. Shulam 1998, 214).

fidence to enter the holy places . . . and since we have a great priest over the house of God, let us draw near to God with a true heart in full assurance of faith, with our hearts sprinkled clean from an evil conscience and our bodies washed with pure water." The latter phrase is a clear reference to the washing during the consecration of the priests, Aaron and his sons (Exod. 29:4; Lev. 8:6), or the washing of the high priest on *Yom Kippur* before he entered the Most Holy Place (Lev. 16:4). The verb used implies immersion of the whole body. We may assume that the author of Hebrews 10 was thinking of baptism.[34] Although this author never explicitly says so, he presents the Jesus-believers as priests in this passage and elsewhere (Heb. 2:11; 4:16; 7:25; 13:15). Therefore, he can apply the washing of the Tanakhic priests to New Testament believers.

In Colossians 2:11-15 Paul says: "In him [i.e., Jesus] also you were circumcised with a circumcision made without hands, by putting off the body of the flesh [*yetzer ra*] . . . having been buried with him in baptism. . . . God made [us] alive together with him, having forgiven us all our trespasses. . . . He disarmed the rulers and authorities . . . by triumphing over them in him [or, in it, i.e., the cross]." Note in these verses three basic elements of the Jesus-believer's initiation, which are the same as those which literally played a role in the initiation of a proselyte: first, circumcision (here in its spiritual meaning); second, the *mikveh* (baptism);[35] and third, the offering of a sacrifice in the Temple (here applied to Jesus' sacrifice at the cross).[36]

---

34. Bruce (1985, 250–51). This is an argument against replacing baptismal immersion by sprinkling: the sprinkling with blood (cf. Heb. 9:13–14) is figurative, the washing with water both figurative and literal.
35. This shows, by the way, that in Paul's mind (spiritual) circumcision and baptism are clearly distinguished as subsequent steps (contra many covenant theologians, who identify the two).
36. Stern (1999, 608).

Interestingly, Jewish use of the *mikveh*, including proselyte baptism, always implies self-immersion, in contrast with New Testament baptism. Some believe there is an exception in Acts 22:16, where the middle voice of the imperative, *baptisai*, is supposed to mean, "immerse yourself."[37] However, we know from Acts 9:18 that Paul was baptized (passive voice), probably by the Damascene disciple Ananias. Because we do not have any indication of self-immersion in the New Testament, it is natural to interpret the middle voice in Acts 22:16, to mean not merely receiving something but doing something for oneself, but then simply in the sense of submitting oneself to New Testament baptism: "get yourself baptized."[38]

8.2.2 The Lord's Supper

Like baptism, the Lord's Supper (*Shulchan haAdon*) is rooted in a Jewish institution. This is obvious from the fact that it consisted in an adaptation of the Jewish Passover (Matt. 26:17–29; Luke 22:7–20).[39] When celebrating *Pesach*, Jews commemorate their deliverance from the Egyptian bondage through the death of the Pesach lamb. Likewise, Jesus-believers celebrating the Lord's Supper "proclaim the Lord's death" (1 Cor. 11:26), implying their deliverance from the "Egyptian" bondage of sin through Jesus, their Passover lamb, who was sacrificed for them (1 Cor. 5:7; also see John 1:29, 36; 19:33, 36 [referring to Exod. 12:46]; 1 Pet. 1:19; Rev. 5:6–13). In *Pesach*, deliverance is central; in the Lord's Supper, the Deliverer is central.

David Stern thinks it was likely that the early Jesus-believers, including those of Gentile descent, observed *Pesach*, and

---

37. Stern (1999, 307).
38. Knowling (1979, 459); Bruce (1988, 418). A famous case of self-baptism in early church history was Thecla (*Acts of Paul and Thecla* 9–10).
39. See extensively on the links between Pesach and the Lord's Supper, Wilson (1989, 237–52), and the many references there.

that Paul is referring to this in 1 Corinthians 5:7–8: "Cleanse out the old leaven [*chametz*, i.e., any product with leaven in it[40]] that you may be a new lump, as you really are unleavened. For Messiah, our Passover [*Pesach*] lamb, has been sacrificed. Let us therefore celebrate the festival [*Seder*], not with the old leaven [*chametz*], the leaven of malice and evil, but with the unleavened bread [*matzah*] of sincerity and truth."[41] I do not object to the idea that the early Jesus-believers may have observed the Seder. I wonder, though, whether Paul is referring to this here, because he clearly uses the terms *chametz* and *matzah* in a figurative sense. Paul is not "passing back and forth between the literal and the figurative";[42] instead, I think he is referring only to the figurative.

The bread that Jesus used was the common *matzah*, the unleavened *Pesach* bread. Concerning the breaking of the *matzah*, Stern observes: "In the modern Seder [Passover meal] three pieces of *matzah* are placed in a three-part cloth bag called a *matzah tash*. Early in the service the middle piece of *matzah* is broken. Half is divided into enough pieces for everyone at the table and eaten. The other half, called the *afikoman*, is hidden, to be found by children later and eaten by everyone as the last food of the meal (Heb. *afikoman* may come from a Greek word meaning 'dessert'). . . . [M]any scholars believe this ritual was added to the Seder service by Messianic Jews, for whom the three *matzot* represent Father, Son and *Ruach HaQodesh* [the Holy Spirit]. The second *matzah*—representing the Son, who called himself the 'bread of life' [John 6:41, 48] and who in

---

40. The evening before *Pesach*, Jews were to have gotten rid of all leaven. The last bits of leavened products were to be burned the next morning (*bi 'ur-chametz*). In the evening of that day, the Seder is celebrated. At that meal and throughout the following week, the only bread eaten is *matzah*, unleavened bread (cf. Exod. 12:15–20; 13:3–7; Deut. 16:3).
41. Stern (1999, 447–49); cf. Welker (2013, 25).
42. Thus Stern (1999, 448).

[Matt. 26:26] says of the *matzah*, 'This is my body' — is broken for all and given to all (symbolically representing his death for all mankind). Yet there is a mystery, a hidden part, similar to the hidden *afikoman*: like the middle *matzah* at the Pesach meal, the Messiah appears twice in history, in a first and a second coming."[43]

The Seder includes four cups of wine, two before the meal and two after. Each is traditionally identified with one of God's four promises in Exodus 6:6-7, the third one corresponding with God's promise, "I will redeem you. . . . " Two of the four cups are referred to in Luke 22:17, 20, where Jesus applied them in a fresh way. The cup of verse 17 must have been the first or second of the four, since the breaking of bread (v. 19) came just after the second cup. The cup of verse 20 must have been the third one, thus called the "cup of salvation" (cf. Ps. 116:13), or the "cup of blessing" or "thanksgiving" (cf. 1 Cor. 10:16).[44] Jesus used this cup to introduce the New Covenant, which involves the final redemption from the "Egyptian" bondage of sin (Luke 22:20; Matt. 26:28).[45] Interestingly, according to David Daube,[46] the fourth and last cup was also alluded to indirectly in that Jesus refrained from taking it: "I tell you I will not drink again of this fruit of the vine until that day when I drink it new with you in my Father's kingdom" (Matt. 26:29). If Daube is right, Jesus deliberately postponed the last part of the liturgy until the arrival of the actual, final Kingdom. The Father's Kingdom is just as much the Kingdom of the Son of Man (Matt. 13:41), and thus the same as the Messianic Kingdom; it is the "kingdom of our Lord and of his Messiah" (Rev. 11:15).

---

43. Stern (1999, 80).
44. Paul used the rabbinical expression, *kos shel beraka, kasa debhirketha* (Berakot 51a) (Daube 1956, 330).
45. Stern (1999, 144).
46. Daube (1956, 330–31).

8.2.3 Anointing the Sick

It is my personal conviction that the New Testament refers not to two but to three sacraments, that is, ecclesial ritual ceremonies. I am referring not only to baptism and the Lord's Supper but also to anointing the sick. My reasons for this are the following.[47]

(1) Anointing the sick was instituted by Jesus himself, just as baptism and the Lord's Supper were. The latter was instituted during Jesus' last night before his death, baptism after his resurrection, and the anointing during his ministry on earth. Jesus told the Twelve, "Heal the sick, raise the dead, cleanse lepers, cast out demons" (Matt. 10:5, 8). And later he also told the Seventy: "Heal the sick" (Luke 10:1, 8-9). This healing took place by means of oil: the disciples "anointed with oil many who were sick and healed them" (Mark 6:13). It is hardly believable that the disciples would have done this anointing work on their own initiative, that is, without a specific commandment from the Lord. Later, this sacrament was explained by the apostle James: "Is anyone among you sick? Let him call for the elders of the church, and let them pray over him, anointing him with oil in the name of the Lord. And the prayer of faith will save the one who is sick, and the Lord will raise him up" (James 5:14-15). This explanation and command were not only for Jewish Jesus-believers of the first century AD (cf. James 1:1), but remain in force until the coming of the Lord (see 5:7-8). Jesus-believers accept this as inspired Scripture so that, again, this word cannot be anything other than a direct command of Jesus.

(2) In all three sacraments a material element is involved: in baptism it is water, in the Lord's Supper it is bread and wine, in the anointing it is oil. In each case the material element is a sign: the water of baptism points to the death — more specifically, the tomb — of Messiah, bread and wine to the

---

47. See extensively Ouweneel (2011a, chapters 5-7).

body and blood of Messiah, oil to the healing power of (the Spirit of) Messiah. All three sacraments point to the death of Christ: baptism (Rom. 6:3-4), the Lord's Supper (1 Cor. 11:26), and the anointing (cf. Isa. 53:4-5; according to Matt. 8:17, the prophet was speaking here of literal diseases).

(3) All three sacraments involve the forgiveness of sins: baptism (Acts 2:38; 22:16), the Lord's Supper (Matt. 26:28), and the anointing: "[T]he prayer of faith will save the one who is sick, and the Lord will raise him up. And if he has committed sins, he will be forgiven. Therefore, confess your sins to one another and pray for one another, that you may be healed" (James 5:15-16).

(4) As I said, all three sacraments are rooted in Jewish ceremonies: baptism in the *mikveh*, the Lord's Supper in *Pesach*, and the anointing in common Jewish practice. There is no doubt that, when Jesus commanded his disciples to apply oil to the sick, he was following Jewish custom. A Midrash tells us about Rabbi Joshua helping a nephew who was under a spell: "Rabbi Joshua anointed him with oil, and he recovered."[48] The Talmud quotes this saying of the rabbis: "It is forbidden [on *Yom Kippur*] to anoint part of the body. . . . If, however, one was sick or had scabs on his head, he may anoint himself the usual way without fear."[49] In the latter case, oil was apparently considered a medicine; but in the former case, it was considered a divine antidote against demonic influence.[50] The Jerusalem Talmud speaks of anointing a sick person with oil mixed with wine on a Shabbat,[51] and of lifting spells by applying oil to the head of the sick person.[52]

Baptism is applied once, at the start of someone's disci-

---

48. Eccl. Rabbah (see on 1:8).
49. Yoma 77b; cf. Maimonides, *Hilchot Shebitat Ashur* 3.9.
50. See for other examples of this use of oil, Strack/Billerbeck, 1922–28, I, 428–29; II, 11–12.
51. Jer. Berakhot 1.3a.9.
52. Jer. Ma'aser Sheni 2.53b.48.

New Testament Institutions

pleship, and the Lord's Supper is celebrated as often as God's people desire (cf. Acts 2:46; 20:7; 1 Cor. 11:26), whereas the anointing of the sick is applied as often as there is (serious) illness ("Is anyone among you sick . . ." James 5:14).

In my view, the sacramental anointing of the sick can hardly be severed from the Tanakhic anointing of kings, priests, and prophets. This anointing always involved their special election as it sovereignly pleased God (cf. Ps. 89:19-20; cf. Isa. 42:1 with 61:1), and their preparation for the royal, priestly, or prophetic office. Anointing here signifies dedication, consecration. The name of the heavenly Bridegroom is as oil poured out (Song 1:3); that is to say, at the anointing, God's name (i.e., his glory and power) is laid upon the sick person. Putting God's name on a person means blessing (Num. 6:22-27). The sick person is not only blessed with healing but also dedicated to the Lord.[53]

8.2.4 Moral and/or Ceremonial

The fact that at least the Lord's Supper is such a clear continuation of a Mosaic institution, while baptism and anointing the sick are continuations of ancient Jewish customs, should make us suspicious of the facile claim of covenant theologians that only the moral part of the Mosaic Torah is still in force. They haven't the slightest New Testament ground for splitting up the Torah into a moral as well as a ceremonial and civil Torah in this way. On the contrary, how could, for instance, the moral *torot* be maintained if there were not the ceremonial *torot* to compensate for breaking the former?

It is no use saying that, after having broken the moral *torot*, in Jesus we do not need ceremonies anymore. Confessing a sin before God, realizing in our souls that Jesus had to die for that sin, and consciously accepting God's forgiveness, is the New Covenant counterpart to bringing an animal sin offering under the Old Covenant. Excommunication from the

---

53. See more extensively Ouweneel (2006).

Messianic community because of impenitence for severe trespasses, and restoration into it after repentance, correspond to certain ceremonial and civil laws under the Old Covenant (John 20:23; 2 Cor. 2:2-11; and see below). Another example is the Fourth Commandment concerning the Shabbat (see Appendix III), which is both a moral and a ceremonial-civil commandment. If covenant theologians believe the Shabbat commandment to be vital they should also take its ceremonial and civil aspects seriously (and some of them do meticulously apply the Sabbath precepts to their Sunday observance).

In my opinion, the reasoning of covenant theologians is not consistent. Either the *entire* Mosaic Torah is still in force — not just a rather arbitrary (moral) selection of it — or the New Testament Messianic Torah contains not only moral but also ceremonial and civil elements. Some of the latter elements are again directly adopted from the Mosaic Torah and find their legitimate place in the Messianic Torah, in either a literal or a figurative sense. In other words, the Messianic Torah, whether viewed as identical with the Mosaic Torah or as a new (manifestation of the eternal) Torah, is a moral as well as a ceremonial and civil Torah. The moral commandments are the *mishpatim* (lit. "judgments"), the ceremonial commandments are the *'eduyot* (lit. "witnesses"), and the judicial commandments are the *chuqqim* (lit. "decrees").[54] Excellent examples of such adaptations are found in the Letters to the Corinthians (even though the specific classification of one or another in terms of the three categories mentioned may be debatable).

1. *Mishpatim* (moral commandments)

(a) *Sexual immorality.* The Mosaic decree, "A man shall not take his father's wife, so that he does not uncover his father's nakedness" (Deut. 22:30; cf. Lev. 18:8; 20:11) is confirmed in 1 Corinthians 5:1, "[T]here is sexual immorality among you . . . a man has his father's wife."

---

54. Cf. Moseley (2000, 19).

(b) *Marital duties.* The Mosaic decree, a man "shall not diminish her [i.e., his wife's] food, her clothing, or her marital rights" (Exod. 21:10), is confirmed in 1 Corinthians 7:3, "The husband should give to his wife her conjugal rights."

(c) *Idolatry.* The Mosaic decree, "[K]now that the LORD is God; there is no other besides him" (Deut. 4:35), is confirmed in 1 Corinthians 8:4, "[W]e know that an idol has no real existence, and that there is no God but one."

(d) *Concern.* The Mosaic decree, "You shall not muzzle an ox when it is treading out the grain" (Deut. 25:4), is figuratively confirmed in 1 Corinthians 9:9–10: after the quotation, Paul says, "Is it for oxen that God is concerned? Does he not certainly speak for our sake?"

(e) *Unequal yoke.* The Mosaic decree, "You shall not plow with an ox and a donkey together" (Deut. 22:10), is figuratively applied in 2 Corinthians 6:14, "Do not be unequally yoked with unbelievers."

(f) *Generosity.* The Mosaic decree, "You shall give to him [i.e., your poor brother] freely, and your heart shall not be grudging when you give to him" (Deut. 15:10), is confirmed in 2 Corinthians 9:7, "Each one must give as he has decided in his heart, not reluctantly or under compulsion, for God loves a cheerful giver."

2. *'Eduyot* (ceremonial commandments)

(a) *Desecration.* The Mosaic decree not to profane the sanctuary of God (Lev. 21:12, 23; cf. Ezek. 5:11) is confirmed in 1 Corinthians 3:17, "If anyone destroys God's temple, God will destroy him. For God's temple is holy, and you are that temple."

(b) *Living on contributions.* The Mosaic decree that the Levites "shall eat the LORD's food offerings as their inheritance" (Deut. 18:1), is referred to in 1 Corinthians 9:13–14 and applied to "those who proclaim the gospel" in order that they "get their living by the gospel."

(c) *Sharing in altar service.* The Mosaic decree that allows Israelites to eat the meat of the peace offerings (Lev. 7:15-18) is referred to in 1 Corinthians 10:18 ("Consider the people of Israel: are not those who eat the sacrifices participants in the altar?") and applied to those who "partake of the table of the Lord" (v. 21; note that the altar is called the "Lord's table" in Ezek. 41:22; 44:16; Mal. 1:7, 12).

3. *Chuqqim* (judicial commandments)

(a) *Expelling evil.* The Mosaic decree, "You shall purge the evil from your midst" (Deut. 13:5; 17:7, 12; 19:19; 21:21; 22:21-22, 24; 24:7) is confirmed in 1 Corinthians 5:13: "Purge the evil person from among you."

(b) *Ample testimony.* The Mosaic decree that legal truth shall be established on the testimony of two or three witnesses (Num. 35:30; Deut. 17:6; 19:15) is confirmed in many places; for example, in 2 Corinthians 13:1 we read, "Every charge must be established by the evidence of two or three witnesses" (also see Matt. 18:16; 1 Tim. 5:19; Heb. 10:26-28).

At the same time, these examples show that the Messianic Torah in fact is not identical with the Mosaic Torah; in many ways the latter is only a *type* of the former (1 Cor. 10:6, 11). "Does not the [Mosaic] Torah say the same [as the Messianic Torah]?" (1 Cor. 9:8b). To be sure, the *principle* is the same, but often the application is not. For instance, 1 Corinthians 5:13 applies a rule from Deuteronomy but not in a literal way: the death penalty is replaced by excommunication. 1 Corinthians 9:9 and 1 Timothy 5:18 apply a rule from Deuteronomy 25:4 but in a figurative, and thus more elevated, way. The same is true for Leviticus 21:12, 23, Deuteronomy 18:1, and 22:10, which are referred to in 1 Corinthians 3:17, 9:13-14, and 2 Corinthians 6:14, respectively. The ceremonial law of Leviticus 7 is applied to the ceremony of the Lord's Supper. In contrast to covenant theologians, we claim that Jesus-believers are under a moral as well as a ceremonial and a civil-judicial Torah. Over against covenant theologians as well as Messianic Jews, we claim that this is not literally the Mosaic Torah but the New Testament Torah of Jesus. In contrast to dispensational theologians, we claim that there is a definite continuation of the Mosaic Torah in the Messianic Torah, and clear congruence between the Mosaic Torah and the Messianic Torah, and even direct adoption of Mosaic *torot* within the Messianic Torah. No wonder: they are both manifestations of the one and only eternal Torah.

The most peculiar usage of the Mosaic Torah in the Corinthian Letters is found in 1 Corinthians 14:34: "[T]he women should keep silent in the churches. For they are not permitted to speak, but should be in submission, as the Torah says." It has often been pointed out that in fact the Mosaic Torah says nothing of the kind. Usually, Genesis 3:16 ("your husband . . . shall rule over you") is appealed to, but this verse speaks rather of an undesired consequence of the Fall, not of a divine command, even less of a command for women to remain silent. Therefore, others have presumed that Paul is referring to the Oral Torah (cf. §6.3), or to put it in a more New Testament way, "an oral understanding of Torah such as is found in rabbinic Judaism."[55] A similar reference is found in Flavius Josephus: "The woman, says the Torah, is in all things inferior to the man. Let her accordingly be submissive."[56]

Let me give two examples of rabbinic understanding of the Torah in this regard. One is supplied by Rabbi Eleazar ben 'Azariah, who said with respect to Deuteronomy 31:12 (men, women, and children come to hear the Torah): "If the men came to learn [i.e., to study by discussion], the women came to hear," that is, to listen to the debate but not to participate in it.[57] The other example comes from Rabbi Judah: "[T]he Sages

---

55. Fee (1987, 707), referring to an article by S. Aalen. Incidentally, Fee sees this reference to the Torah as one piece of evidence for the non-Pauline origin of vv. 34–35.
56. *Contra Apion* II. 200–201.
57. Chagigah 3a (see Stern 1999, 484).

said that a woman should not read in the Torah [i.e., aloud in the congregation] out of respect for the congregation."[58] This does not mean, however, that the rabbis forbade women to read the Torah for themselves. Some of them forbade them to study the Torah—but perhaps this referred to the Oral Torah[59]—but others recommended it. The Talmud gives the example of "Beruriah, wife of R. Meir [and] daughter of R. Hanina b. Teradion, who studied three hundred laws from three hundred teachers in [one] day."[60] Study of the Torah as such was not the problem, but reading aloud and learning aloud, in the synagogue, was out of the question. Although the Tanakh contains no prohibition of the sort, it is amazing that 1 Corinthians 14:34 seems to understand the Torah the way the rabbis apparently did.

8.3 The Four Commandments for Gentile Jesus-believers

8.3.1 What Are They?

In Acts 15, we hear of a painful conflict in the early church. There were Judaizers, that is, people who wanted to "Jewishify" Gentile Jesus-believers, by telling them, among other things: "Unless you are circumcised according to the custom of Moses, you cannot be saved" (v. 1). Some Jesus-believers of the Pharisee party rose up and said, "It is necessary to circumcise them and to order them to keep the Torah of Moses" (v. 5). The apostles Paul and Barnabas in particular were strongly opposed to this. They were against enforcing the Mosaic Torah upon Gentile Jesus-believers. During the convention at Jerusalem, Peter argued along the same lines: "[W]hy are you putting God to the test by placing a yoke on the necks of the disciples that neither our fathers nor we have been able to bear?" (v. 10).

---

58. Megillah 23a.
59. See Nedarim in the Soncino ed., 107n2.
60.. Pesachim 62b.

This does not necessarily mean that he calls the Mosaic Torah as such a heavy yoke. A Torah reviving the soul, giving joy to the heart, and giving light to the eyes (Ps. 19:7-8), cannot possibly be experienced as a heavy burden. On the contrary, John says of God's Torah, "[H]is commandments are not burdensome" (1 John 5:3). The Torah is heavy only for a carnal Jew who abuses the Torah as a ground for boasting, or a carnal Jew or Gentile who turns the Torah into a legal system, that is, a way to earn credits for heaven. Indeed, *that* system is a "yoke of slavery" (Gal. 5:1). However, of him who truly loves and serves God it is said, "The Torah of his God is in his heart" (Ps. 37:31), and he or she can say, "Oh, how I love your Torah" (Ps. 119:97; cf. 1:2; 19:9). To such people Jesus says, "Take my yoke upon you, and learn from me, for I am gentle and lowly in heart, and you will find rest for your souls. For my yoke is easy, and my burden is light" (Matt. 11:29-30).[61]

This matter of the "heavy" Mosaic Torah and the "light" Messianic Torah is so important that I interrupt myself for the following quotation from the Jesus-believing Jew Nahum Levison: "The law and the precepts of the Rabbis only increase the tendency to fatalism, for the more one tries to realize them, the more conscious he becomes of the impossibility of doing so.... Through Jesus the Messiah it is realized that the struggle is not a hopeless one, that God is very near, and that He is actively interested in life. He is always by one's side, ready to aid in the conflict and to make life victorious.... It must be admitted at first the teaching of Jesus frightens. The shifting of the struggle from the material to the spiritual makes it appear even more difficult. Love thy enemy. Do not allow the mind to covet or possess that which is not thine—this is much harder than, Thou shalt not steal or commit adultery. But when one turns from the teaching to the Teacher, to that

---

61. The rabbis called the Torah a "yoke," specifically the "yoke of the kingdom of heaven" (Mishnah Avot III. 5.6; Sifre Deut. 323.128b).

pure, sinless and blameless life, one realizes that these are the things that make life's warfare a joy and life itself worthwhile. The coming of Jesus into the life of the Jew means that the [Mosaic] Law and precepts, which only say to you, 'You cannot realize us, we are too high and lofty for human attainment,' are swept away, and a higher and nobler conception and ideal come in their place with the blessed assurance that through Jesus the Messiah we can attain, we can realize them, and we can be victorious. The life of defeat with which the [Mosaic] Law confronts you is exchanged for a life of victory through Jesus the Messiah, the Lord of life."[62]

Let us return to Acts 15; after Peter's words and the travel report by Barnabas and Paul, James began to speak: "Simon has related how God first visited the Gentiles, to take from them a people for his name" (v. 14). In other words, in order to belong to God's people, henceforth the Gentile does not have to become a Jewish proselyte, whereby he would be taking the Mosaic Torah upon himself, for God gathers from the Gentiles a people who are his own without becoming Jewish (cf. Titus 2:14; 1 Pet. 2:9). James continues, "Therefore, my judgment is that we should not trouble those of the Gentiles who turn to God, but should write to them to abstain from the things polluted by idols, and from sexual immorality, and from what has been strangled, and from blood" (vv. 19-20). Here we encounter the well-known four commandments for Gentile Jesus-believers.[63]

* *Abstaining from food polluted by idols:* that is, according to verse 29, abstaining "from what has been sacrificed to idols" (see 1 Cor. 8:4-13 on this subject). In its widest meaning, this

---

62. See the essay included in Kac (1986, 167). Cf. Hebrew Christian Harcourt Samuel (ibid., 260): "The yoke of the Law was indeed a heavy one. Peter's testimony was that it was a yoke that neither he nor his fathers had ever been able to bear. Christ took that yoke upon Himself that it might be lifted from our shoulders."
63. Cf. Stern (1999, 277–79).

is abstinence from everything that is still linked with pagan idolatry, although not in too scrupulous a manner: "Eat whatever is sold in the meat market without raising any question on the ground of conscience" (1 Cor. 10:25).

* *Abstaining from sexual immorality:* every form of illegitimate sex, including adultery, homosexual behavior, (temple) prostitution. According to many expositors, the prohibition of illegitimate sex is so self-evident for any godly person that this can hardly be intended here. Indeed, if illegitimate sex were intended, why did the gathering not add some other self-evident sins forbidden by the Ten Commandments, such as swearing, killing, stealing, and lying? Such expositors think the Greek word *porneia* refers here to marriages with close family members as had been forbidden in Leviticus 18.[64]

* *Abstain from meat of strangled animals:* that is, meat of animals that were not slaughtered in such a way that the blood flowed out fully. This prohibition is a specific form of the fourth and last prohibition. (This is possibly the reason why the words "and from what has been strangled" [v. 20] are lacking in some manuscripts.)

* *Abstaining from animal blood:* that is, drinking animals' blood, eating blood foods; according to some expositors this refers (also) to bloodshed (i.e., murder).[65]

8.3.2 Are They Still Binding? (1) No

The great majority of modern expositors consider the four prohibitions to be purely ritual, not moral: (1) participation in pagan ceremonies, (2) marriages with close relatives, (3) consumption of blood food, including (4) eating strangled animals. *In concreto*:

* Do not irritate your Jewish brothers by dealing too casually with what is linked with idolatrous practices. More

---

64. Cf. Metzger (1975, 434); Longenecker (1981, 448); Bruce (1988, 299) and references.
65. Cf. Knowling (1979, 323, 325).

generally this involves the question: how far can I go in my contacts with pagan fellow-countrymen?

* Do not irritate your Jewish brothers by marriages with close relatives, which to them are an abomination. More generally this involves the question: what kind of marriage can I enter without giving offense?

* Do not irritate your Jewish brothers by eating blood in any form. More generally this involves the question: what food can I eat without giving offense?

If those are right who view the four prohibitions only as a concession to Jewish scruples, it is not required of Gentile Jesus-believers to eat only kosher food. Stern says, "Today, when Messianic Jews are a small minority in the Body of the Messiah, and few if any of them take umbrage at Gentiles' eating habits, the issue is irrelevant, and there is no need for Gentile Jesus-believers to obey a command never intended as eternal. However, in Israel, Gentile believers may find it convenient to keep at least a semblance of kosher, simply to fit in with a pattern widespread in the Land, or to be able to invite tradition-keeping Jews to dinner; and there are not a few Gentile Jesus-believers who do so."[66]

Others agree that the four commandments did not constitute anything more than a kind of minimum standard for practical intercommunion of Jewish and Gentile Jesus-believers—a requirement that, at least outside the state of Israel, largely lost its relevance many centuries ago. R. J. Knowling has an extensive discussion on the matter, with many details that we cannot discuss here.[67] He feels that "the Decree was ordained for the Churches which are specifically mentioned, viz., those of Antioch . . . , Syria and Cilicia. In these Churches Jewish prejudice had made itself felt, and in these Churches with their constant communication with Jerusalem the Decree would be maintained. . . . [But] in what may be called strict-

---

66. Stern (1999, 278–79).
67. Knowling (1979, 335–37).

ly Gentile Churches, in Churches not only further removed from Palestine, but in which [Paul's] own Apostleship was adequate authority, he may well have felt that he was relieved from enforcing the Decree. In these Churches the stress laid upon such secondary matters as 'things strangled and blood' would simply have been a cause of perplexity, a burden too heavy to bear, the source of a Christianity maimed by Jewish particularism."[68]

F. W. Grosheide sees James' proposal involving whether "Jewish and Gentile Christians may associate in one congregation, may serve God together, without one group continually irritating the other. . . . The Jewish Christian is not to demand that the Gentile Christian be circumcised. But it may be required of the Gentile Christian that he will impose upon himself certain restrictions, in order that the Jewish Christians will not find it too hard to serve God together with the Gentile Christians."[69] Richard Longenecker views these prescriptions "not as being primarily theological but more sociological in nature; not as divine ordinances for acceptance before God but as concessions to the scruples of others for the sake of harmony within the church and the continuance of the Jewish Christian mission."[70]

Bruce Metzger believes that, "in order to avoid giving unnecessary offense to Jewish Jesus-believers (and to Jews contemplating becoming Jesus-believers), the Council asked Gentile converts to make certain concessions for prudential reasons, abstaining from those acts that would offend Jewish scruples and hinder social intercourse, including joint participation in the Lord's Supper."[71] F. F. Bruce adds: "At a later time, when the issue dealt with by the apostolic council was no

---

68. Ibid., 336–37. He refers to Lightfoot, Hort, Zöckler, K. Schmidt, Wendt, and others.
69. Grosheide (1963, 22–23).
70. Longenecker (1981, 448).
71. Metzger (1975, 430).

longer a live one, the provisions moved by James and adopted by the other leaders were modified so as to become purely ethical injunctions; the Western text [Codex D, 11 minuscules, etc.] makes James propose that Gentile converts 'abstain from idolatry, from fornication and from bloodshed, and from doing to others what they would not like done to themselves.'"[72] Metzger argues: "[T]his reading can scarcely be original, for it implies that a special warning had to be given to Gentile converts against such sins as murder, and that this was expressed in the form of asking them to 'abstain' from it—which is slightly absurd! It therefore appears to be more likely that an original ritual prohibition against eating foods offered to idols, things strangled and blood, and against *porneia* [fornication] (however this latter is to be interpreted) was altered into a moral law by dropping the reference to *pniktou* [the strangled] and by adding the negative Golden Rule, than to suppose that an original moral law was transformed into a food law."[73]

8.3.3 Are They Still Binding? (2) Yes

Many older expositors[74] took a very different viewpoint. According to them, the four commandments of Acts 15 are a variant of the Seven Precepts of Noah, six of which were said to have been given by God to Adam, and the seventh was given as an addition to Noah (cf. Gen. 9:1–17; also see 1 Cor. 5:10; 6:10; Rev. 21:8).[75] According to the Talmud, God imposes these Noahic Commandments upon every *ger toshav*, that is, every sojourner among Israel: practicing justice by appoint-

---

72. Bruce (1988, 296).
73. Metzger (1975, 431–32). For literature supporting the Western text, see Metzger (1975, 433–34).
74. Including a rabbi such as Jacob Emden (18th century); see Falk (2003, chapter 1).
75. See Davies (1955, 112–19), who argues that Paul must have been familiar with the Seven Precepts of Noah; see further extensively Lichtenstein (1981); Novak (1983); and Müller (1994).

ing judges (cf. Deut. 16:18), abstaining from blasphemy, idolatry, sexual immorality, bloodshed, theft, and eating "living flesh," that is, flesh with the blood in it (Gen. 9:4; Lev. 3:17; 7:26-27; 17:10, 14; 19:26; Deut. 12:16, 23; 15:23; cf. 1 Sam. 14:33; Ezek. 33:25).[76]

If this explanation were correct, it is difficult to see why the apostles mentioned only three out of the six or seven Noahic Precepts. Were the other three viewed as self-evident for Gentile believers? But why would blasphemy, bloodshed, and theft have been self-evident, whereas idolatry and sexual impurity would not have been? Others, leaving out "the strangled" (which is lacking in certain manuscripts of Acts 15), see here the very three prohibitions for which a Jew should rather die than transgress them: idolatry, sexual immorality, and murder.[77]

If we really are dealing here with a selection of the Seven Precepts of Noah, or with the three capital offenses just mentioned, Gentile Jesus-believers should definitely still refrain from marrying close relatives and eating blood-sausage, and should eat meat only from animals slaughtered in a kosher way. In both cases, these commandments are not ritual but moral in nature, not temporary but permanent. As F. W. Grant put it: "The last two [things strangled and blood] are connected together, and go back beyond Moses to God's covenant with Noah and his posterity, — therefore are not simply Jewish, though incorporated in the Jewish law, but apply to the whole present race of men. . . . Man has, of course, set it aside, and the world at large has forgotten it; but the good of

---

76. Baba Kamma 38a; Sanhedrin 56a; 'Avodah Zarah 2b; Gen. Rabbah 34; also see Maimonides in his *Mishneh Torah*; see comments by Knowling (1979, 335–36).

77. Sanhedrin 74a. Cf. more generally, Shabbat 83b, where Resh Lakish says: "The words of the Torah can endure only with him who sacrifices himself for it," i.e., only when a man is prepared to die for it. Cf. Bruce (1988, 296n62).

that which is from God abides, and this is the duty and privilege of the Church to maintain, — the rights of the Creator, as well as the grace of the Redeemer."[78]

It is of interest to note that Jewish tradition, too, has presented us with several views about which decrees were to be imposed on the Gentile converts in the Messianic era. One extreme view was that they would be subjected to the whole Mosaic Torah.[79] Another extreme view was that only three ordinances were to be imposed, two connected with *Sukkot*, one with the *tefillin*.[80] A third view suggests that there are thirty original Noahic commandments, allegedly enumerated in Leviticus 19, which are to be made binding to the Gentiles.[81]

I have made a contrast between a ritual interpretation (§8.3.2) and a moral interpretation (this §) of the four commandments. Let me add an argument that seems to plead more for the latter than for the former view. It is amazing to see how often the consumption of blood is forbidden in the Mosaic Torah (Lev. 3:17; 7:26-27; 17:10-14; 19:26; Deut. 12:16, 23-25; 15:23). Even those who hold that Jesus-believers are not under the Mosaic Torah should be impressed by the fact that, already in God's covenant with Noah, blood, and meat containing blood, are strictly forbidden (Gen. 9:4). What ground is there to assume that this covenant does not hold for Gentile Jesus-believers? Not even "strangers" in Israel were to eat blood (Lev. 17:12). There is not just a ritual motive but also a moral reason for this great emphasis on the blood prohibition. A creature's "life" (*nefesh*) is in the blood, the very blood that, when it is poured out at the altar, makes atonement for the people (Lev. 17:11). Life belongs to God; not eating "lifeblood" (Gen. 9:4) is a token of revering God as the Origin, the

---

78. Grant (1901, 100–101).
79. Chullin 92a.
80. Midr. Ps. 31:1.
81. Stein (1867–1910), referred to by Edersheim (1971, II, 765; cf. 437–38).

Giver, and the Restorer of life.

It is "right in the sight of the LORD" to stay away from blood (Deut. 12:25). Even carnal king Saul was angry with those who had eaten meat that contained blood (1 Sam. 14:33–34). In the last days of the kingdom of Judah, one of the reasons why they were no longer allowed to possess their land was that they ate meat containing blood (Ezek. 33:25). I find it hard to believe that the reason why blood was forbidden in Acts 15 was *merely* to respect the consciences of Jewish believers.

8.3.4 Gentiles Invited to Keep the Mosaic Torah?

Acts 15:21 states something very remarkable: "For from ancient generations Moses has had in every city those who proclaim him, for he is read every Sabbath in the synagogues." What does James want to say by this? Does he mean that everywhere in the Roman Empire there are Jews, and that Gentile Jesus-believers should not be a stumbling block to them (cf. 1 Cor. 10:31)? Does he mean that there are everywhere enough Gentiles who hear the Mosaic Torah in the synagogues and therefore decide to become proselytes, so that non-Jesus-believing Judaism will not suffer loss of numbers? Or does he mean that Gentile Jesus-believers heard the Torah in the synagogues, and that one has to respect it if they nonetheless decide not to become proselytes? Or does he mean that Gentile Jesus-believers heard the Torah in the synagogues, and that they would thus be the more inclined to accept the four commandments? Or does he mean that Jewish Jesus-believers will keep hearing the Mosaic Torah in the synagogues, and that Gentile Jesus-believers therefore would have to adapt a little to them in order to enable communion with them? Or does he mean that Gentile Jesus-believers will keep hearing the Mosaic Torah in the synagogues, and in this way as a matter of course will get to know the other aspects of living with the Torah, aspects beyond the four prohibitions mentioned?

There are all kinds of possible interpretations. In my view, it is therefore too far-fetched when Ariel and D'vorah Berkowitz want to deduce from this single verse the notion that, according to God's mind, Gentile Jesus-believers too may be expected to gradually develop the desire to keep the entire Mosaic Torah.[82] In itself, there can be hardly any serious objection against Gentile Jesus-believers desiring to keep the entire Torah,[83] as long as this desire is accompanied by the right motives. First, it must be done on an entirely voluntary basis, for example, out of solidarity with the Jewish people — especially when living in the state of Israel — or as a practical reminder of the spiritual lessons of the Mosaic Torah, the Jewish festivals in particular.[84]

Second, every idea that keeping the entire Mosaic Torah is a way of contributing to one's salvation is to be utterly rejected (as the Berkowitzes themselves do emphasize). On the other hand, however, I do not know of any clear-cut indication in the New Testament that Gentile Jesus-believers are indeed encouraged, or advised, to adopt for themselves the entire Mosaic Torah. On the contrary, how easily could the problems of Galatians 2:11-14, for example, have been solved if Gentile Jesus-believers had learned before, or had been taught by Paul, to keep the Mosaic Torah on a voluntary basis (see further §9.1.2).

Astonishingly, Chumney tells us that the Jewish festivals are also for non-Jews: in Deuteronomy 16:10-11, 14-16, the "stranger" refers to "the non-Jew (Bible-believing Gentile) who has joined himself to the Jewish people."[85] Thus,

---

82. Berkowitz (1999, 91–95; 2011, 69–71); cf. Stern (1997, 157).

83. As A. and D. Berkowitz (1999, xvii) put it: "[T]he non-Israelite believers have divine permission to freely and fully participate in the lifestyle taught in the Torah."

84. Gentile Jesus-believers are not obliged to celebrate, but may well join in with Jesus-believing Jews in celebrating, the Jewish festivals, in spite of the fact that the early church condemned this and called those who did so heretics (Synod of Laodicea, sometime between 341 and 381).

85. Chumney (1994, 7).

is it the case that what held for the strangers living in Israel is now applicable to all Gentile Jesus-believers worldwide? Chumney will have difficulties, then, with Exodus 12:43–49, which emphasizes that *Pesach* is only for the circumcised, such that thereby all uncircumcised foreigners and strangers were excluded from it. Of course, some may argue that Gentile Jesus-believers may take part in *Pesach* because they are circumcised of heart,[86] but that is a typically New Testament argument. If one wants to argue from the Tanakh, then circumcision of the heart can never be enough; the strangers who may have been circumcised in their heart but not in their flesh were not permitted to participate in Pesach.

Ariel and D'vorah Berkowitz have some more arguments for inviting—not importuning!—Gentile Jesus-believers to keep the Mosaic Torah. They quote prophecies that, as they themselves clearly recognize, refer to the future Millennial Kingdom as evidence that Gentile Jesus-believers may decide to keep the Torah today.[87] They also understand the expression "God-fearing" (Gr. *phoboumenos* [or *-noi*] *ton theon*; Acts 10:2, 22, 35; 13:16, 26; synonym *sebomenoi*, Acts 13:50; 16:14; 17:4, 17; 18:7; cf. §1.2.1) to refer to Gentiles attached to Judaism without having undergone circumcision and proselyte baptism.[88] The first Gentiles who believed in Jesus came from this group, and consequently were already familiar with keeping the Torah: "[T]he Scriptures give no indication that any of the God-fearers mentioned in the book of Acts gave up their Torah observance after becoming believers in the Messiah of Israel."[89]

---

86. Berkowitz (1999, 248–49).
87. Berkowitz (1999, 65–77); see §2.1.2 above.
88. Stern (1999, 257, 268). Judaism knows them as *ger toshav*, "resident stranger," the "proselyte of the gate," who lives among Jews, follows some of their customs, without having been circumcised and without having to fulfill the whole Torah.
89. Berkowitz (1999, 89–91).

Now I think such an argument *ex silentio* seems to be a bit shaky. First, why had the God-fearers not been circumcised in the first place? One good reason seems to be that they felt more attracted to the moral content than to the ritual decrees of the Mosaic Torah.[90] Second, after having come to faith in Jesus they were not urged to be circumcised either; so what impetus was there for them to decide to keep the ritual decrees? Third, after a large number of God-fearers had come to Jesus — notice the Jews as well as the (apparently God-fearing) Greeks in the synagogue of Corinth (Acts 18:4) — some Jews publicly charged Paul with "persuading people to worship God contrary to the Torah" (Acts 18:13). From these Jews' point of view, there must have been at least some basis for this accusation, one reason being that Paul's converts were never circumcised.

It is not impossible, as the Berkowitz couple suggests, that in Acts 18:13 *nomos* refers not to "Jewish or rabbinic law, as opposed to the Torah," but to "Roman law," just like in Acts 16:21-22 and 17:7. But this is not a very strong argument. First, in the latter verses different words (*ethos, dogma*) are used; in Acts *nomos* always seems to refer simply to the Mosaic Torah (6:13; 7:53; 13:15, 39; 15:5; 21:20, 24, 28; 22:3, 12; 23:3, 29; 24:6, 14; 25:8; 28:23). Second, it is quite clear how proconsul Gallio understood the term: ". . . your own law" (v. 15).

As self-evident as it is that Jewish Jesus-believers continue to observe the entire Torah, it seems equally self-evident that Gentile Jesus-believers observe only the New Testament commandments (which obviously encompass the transcendent substance of the Mosaic Torah; see Appendix IV). I appreciate the wisdom of David Stern here: "[R]ules concerning *kashrut* and celebrations are external impositions for non-Jews. Messianic Jews, since they are part of the Jewish people, have reason enough for observing these rules, which for them are pleasant shadows, even as through trust in Jesus they have

---

90. Cf. Bauer (1971, 1478).

New Testament Institutions

the substance as well [Col. 2:17]. But since these shadows are irrelevant to Gentiles, since God did not give these commands to Gentiles, Sha'ul [i.e., Paul] urges the Colossians not to be bound legalistically to them. For that matter, he elsewhere urges Jews as well not to fall into the trap of perverting the Torah into a legalistic system."[91]

As argued earlier, the central Love Command, the transcendent heart of the Torah, holds for all those who are born again, in whatever dispensation they live. Or rather, in principle this holds for all mankind. But the immanent, temporal commandments of the Mosaic Torah do *not* hold for all. In itself there is nothing strange about this.[92] In the Pentateuch, too, we find commandments that are in force only for priests, or only for men or women, or only for baby boys, or only for the king. Likewise, the New Testament contains commandments that apply only to elders or to ordinary congregation members, or only to widows, or only to men or women, or only to parents or children, or only to masters or slaves. In the same vein, there are commandments that apply to Jews but not to Gentiles. In Messiah, there is "neither Jew nor Greek, there is neither slave nor free, there is no male and female" (Gal. 3:28; cf. 1 Cor. 12:13; Col. 3:11). But in daily practice, there are different commandments for slaves and free people, for males and females—so why not for Jews and Gentiles?

The fact that Gentile Jesus-believers are not under the Mosaic Torah does not make their duty "lighter." Do Jews have to keep 613 commandments, and Gentile Jesus-believers only the Love Command (see Appendix IV)? As we saw, F. J. Dake identified no fewer than 1,050 New Testament commandments. However, the 613 commandments of the Mosaic Torah and the 1,050 commandments of the Messianic Torah are nothing if they are not kept in the spirit of the great Love Command. That command is an impossible yoke for those

---

91. Stern (1999, 611–12).
92. See Stern (1997, 156).

who lack the willingness, capacity, and desire to love (Acts 15:10). By contrast, it is the lightest burden conceivable for those who, in Jesus and through the Spirit, *can* love, and *love* to love (Matt. 11:29–30; 1 John 5:3; cf. Rom. 5:5).

Chapter 9
Jewish and Gentile Jesus-Believers

Keep this Book of the Torah always on your lips;
  meditate on it day and night,
so that you may be careful to do everything written in it.
  Then you will be prosperous and successful.
                                               Joshua 1:8

Then what becomes of our boasting?
  It is excluded.
By what kind of Torah?
  By a Torah of works?
  No, but by the Torah of faith.
For we hold that one is justified by faith
  apart from works of the Torah.
Or is God the God of Jews only?
  Is he not the God of Gentiles also?
Yes, of Gentiles also, since God is one —
  who will justify the circumcised by faith
  and the uncircumcised through faith.
Do we then overthrow the Torah by this faith?
  By no means!
  On the contrary, we uphold the Torah.
                                               Romans 3:27–31

THE ETERNAL TORAH: LIVING UNDER GOD

Summary: *This final chapter deals with the exceptional position of "Messianic" (i.e., Jesus-believing) Jews, who keep not only the Messianic Torah but also the Mosaic Torah. First, the question is raised in how far the latter point may be a hindrance for full fellowship between Jewish and non-Jewish Jesus-believers, and how this can be avoided. Second, various Scriptures are discussed which are often – in my view, wrongly – adduced as arguments that Messianic Jews should not keep the food laws anymore. Third, the various viewpoints are compared: may, or should, Messianic Jews keep the Mosaic Torah? May, or should, Gentile Jesus-believers to a certain extent become proselytes of Israel?*

9.1   Kashrut

9.1.1   Does It Cause Division Between Messianic Jews and Gentiles?

IN THIS FINAL CHAPTER WE INVESTIGATE the special difficulties that Messianic Jews face who want to keep the Mosaic Torah. We found that the numerous Messianic Jews in Judea who were "zealous for the Torah" (Acts 21:20) are never criticized for in the New Testament for their zeal (see §5.3). On the contrary, the apostle Paul himself was a meticulous Torah-keeper. Nonetheless, the zealous Torah-keepers in Judea sometimes exhibited specific weaknesses, if not outright sinful behavior. Their problem was not Torah-keeping as such, but subscribing to some (or many?) of the following two errors. First, some of them secretly insisted that Gentile Jesus-believers ought to keep the entire Mosaic Torah too, which in fact meant they ought to become full-fletched Jewish proselytes. Second, some believed that a Jew, whether Jesus-believing or not, should under no circumstances depart from keeping the Mosaic Torah, not even in his fellowship with Gentile Jesus-believers (cf. §9.1.2). As to Paul, he never refused to personally keep the Mosaic Torah wherever he could; but with all his strength he combated the two errors just mentioned.

The occurrence of the first error is confirmed by Acts 15:1, 5, quoted in the previous chapter: "[S]ome men came down from Judea [to Antioch] and were teaching the [Gentile] brothers, 'Unless you are circumcised according to the custom of Moses, you cannot be saved'. . . . [S]ome believers who belonged to the party of the Pharisees rose up and said, 'It is necessary to circumcise them [i.e., the Gentile believers] and to order them to keep the Torah of Moses.'" The discussions at the apostles' convention in Jerusalem resulted in strong resistance to this group. Only the well-known four commandments (see §8.3) were imposed upon Gentile Jesus-believers, and therefore not the entire Mosaic Torah, which would have included circumcision. Apparently, the apostles did not object to the Messianic Jews' "zeal for the Torah" (Acts 21:20), the more so because the latter did not want to impose upon Gentile Jesus-believers anything more than the four commandments agreed upon in Acts 15:20, 29 (cf. 21:25). It is natural to assume, though, that not all Judaizers had been convinced by the decisions of the Jerusalem convention. But we should not confuse two points: Judaizers were severely criticized, Jews who are "zealous for the Torah" were not criticized at all.

Yet one might wonder whether the Judaizers were not right about at least one point. If *kashrut* continued to be in force for Messianic Jews but was not to be imposed upon Gentile Jesus-believers, was there not the danger of a bipartite development within the Jesus-believing community? It would result in two parties: a *kashrut*-keeping and a non-*kashrut*-keeping party. How could one prevent this bipartite development from leading to a real division? In other words, how could rebuilding the "dividing wall of hostility" (Eph. 2:14) be prevented? There seem to be two wrong answers and one right answer to this question. The correct answer is that Messianic Jews, in their social intercommunion with Gentile Jesus-believers, ought not to cling too strictly to kashrut, which would render that intercommunion impossible (see further in §9.1.2).

The two wrong answers are diametrically opposed. One answer arose in Messianic Jewish minds, and argued as follows: impose *kashrut* upon Gentile Jesus-believers as well, for then there will be no division anymore. The other answer arose in Gentile-Christian minds, and is frequently heard to this day. It argued as follows: Messianic Jews ought to give up *kashrut*, for by clinging to it they re-erect the "dividing wall." Indeed, if Messianic Jews would refuse to eat with Gentile Jesus-believers due to *kashrut*, that would in many cases be wrong (§9.1.2). But if they were to observe *kashrut* in their personal lives, that fact would not be sufficient reason to accuse them of re-erecting the "dividing wall."

Besides, it should be kept in mind that Ephesians 2 does not deal with this question at all.[1] Paul's point here is that, as a consequence of the one faith in Jesus, the Jewish Messiah, there is not the slightest hindrance for Gentiles to form one faith community with Messianic Jews. Paul argues that, because the "dividing wall" has been broken down, the Gentiles can now join the Messianic Jews without feeling hampered, that is, without being obliged to become Jewish proselytes. However, many Gentile Jesus-believers to this very day argue exactly the opposite way: the "dividing wall" has been broken down, so that now Messianic Jews can join "us" — on the condition that they give up the Mosaic Torah. That is to turn things upside down. Paul says, the "dividing wall" is gone, so the Gentiles can participate without having to become Jews. If one indeed wishes to reverse the statement, it should be done consistently: the "dividing wall" is gone, so believing Jews can participate without having to become Gentiles!

In 1 Corinthians 7:18, Paul indeed argues that if someone has become a believer as a Jew, let him not try to become a Gentile — and if someone has become a believer as a Gentile, let him not try to become a Jew. The fact that a Jew or Gentile has accepted Jesus as his or her Savior is no reason to stop being a Jew or Gentile, respectively. On the contrary, the Jesus-believing Jew has never been more of a "Jew" than since

---

1. Cf. Stern (1997, 144; 1999, 581–88).

his conversion to Jesus. Who is a truer Jew than the one who has learned to embrace the Messiah of the Jews and now loves the Torah more than ever before? In other words, the fact that the "dividing wall" is gone does not imply that every distinction is gone. Jesus-believing Jews and Gentiles have, and keep having, different callings and lifestyles, as we have argued time and again in the present study.

Messianic Jew Dan Juster rightly argued that the "dividing wall" was not a wall of distinction but a wall of *hostility*.[2] In Messiah, the hostility is gone but the distinction remains, just as in Messiah there are no *disparities* between slaves and free men, or between males and females anymore (cf. Rom. 10:12; Gal. 3:28; Col. 3:11), which does not imply, however, that all social and sexual distinctions are gone. Likewise, Jews remain Jews and Gentiles remain Gentiles within the Messianic community (the Body of the Messiah), just as Americans remain Americans and Dutch remain Dutch, even in the style of their church life. Besides, differences between American and Dutch people are only of a historical and cultural nature, but the Jewish lifestyle is based upon divine calling. Therefore, the same apostle who says, "[T]here is no distinction between Jew and Gentile" (Rom. 10:12), says a few verses later, "I myself *am* [not, *was*] an Israelite" (11:1). There is no difference whatsoever when it comes to salvation in Jesus—but there is a great difference when it comes to Jesus-believing lifestyles.

A lot of confusion must be swept away here. Unfortunately, most non-Messianic Jews and most Hebrew and Gentile Jesus-believers are of the opinion that, when a *Jew* comes to faith in the *Jew* Jesus as *Israel's* Messiah, he has converted to a non-Jewish "religion," namely, "Christianity," or what is practiced by the church of the Gentiles. What a foolish, sad, and fatal mistake with dramatic historical consequences, which can hardly be overestimated! I just quoted Acts 15: "[S]ome men came down from Judea and were teaching the [Gen-

---

2. Juster (1995, 112–13).

tile] brothers, 'Unless you are circumcised . . . you cannot be saved.'" Conversely, from the fourth to the twentieth centuries, some men came down from "Rome" (later from "Wittenberg," "Geneva" and "Canterbury" as well) who were teaching the Jewish brothers: Unless you *deny* your circumcision (as well as your *kashrut*, your Jewish festivals, etc.), you cannot be saved!

Just as the Judaizers had Gentile friends who astonishingly supported their view, there are Hebrew Christians today who have been captured by "Rome," "Wittenberg," "Geneva," and "Canterbury," so as to publicly abhor of the Messianic Jewish lifestyle. They are only playing into the hands of non-Messianic Jews who assert that Messianic Jews have converted to a different religion. This viewpoint of Hebrew Christians has become, even if inadvertently, one of the greatest hindrances for Jews to accept Jesus as their Savior and Messiah. In Acts 15:2, "Paul and Barnabas had no small dissension and debate with" the erring teachers identified in verse 1. It is time that we too have no small dissension and debate with the erring teachers — Gentiles and even Jews — from "Rome," "Wittenberg," "Geneva," and "Canterbury," insofar as they still maintain their ancient errors. If they do so, they resist the present work of the Holy Spirit among the Jewish people.

A Jew who believes in Jesus has not changed his religion at all, but has come to the fulfillment of his own religion, *to the true and complete fulfillment of his Jewishness*. Only such a Jew has really come to the essence (*k'lal gadol*) of the Torah. Gentile Jesus-believers ought not to become Jews, or desire to become Jews (1 Cor. 7:18b); but it should be stressed just as strongly that Messianic Jews ought not to become Gentiles, or desire to become Gentiles. Unfortunately, in the past this has happened far too frequently. This was due to the rejection of the Jews by non-Messianic Jewry as well as to the strong Gentile character of the church. However, in the present "last days," in which Messianic Jews constitute a considerable and respectable movement to be reckoned with, there is not the slightest excuse for a *Jew* to give up his *Jewishness* when accepting the *Jewish* Messiah of the *Jews*. As the Hebrew-Christian historian, Bernard B. Gair, put it, "When a Jew accepts the Messiah, Jesus, he is not less a Jew, but rather becomes a 'completed' Jew, for he has found in his life and spirit the fulfillment of the promises made by God to our fathers. He becomes, together with all believers—Jew and Gentile—a redeemed son of God, a spiritual Israelite."[3]

The number of prejudices in this respect is tremendous, among both Gentile- and Hebrew-Christians as well as Messianic Jews—and non-Messianic Jews, too, for that matter. It is not at all normal for a Messianic Jew to give up his Jewishness; it is perfectly normal if he does *not* do so. First, such a Jesus-believing Jew who continues living like a Jew is not thereby being "legalistic" or "weak"; he would be so only if he were to keep the Jewish customs with the purpose of earning points for eternity, thus trying to contribute to his salvation. Second, a Messianic Jew is not a Judaizer either; he would be so only if he were to attempt to impose Jewish customs upon Gentile Jesus-believers by presenting these customs as a condition for salvation. Third, a Messianic Jew is not being shrewd, as if he were keeping the Torah only in order to mislead non-Messianic Jews and to win them over to his "religion." Fourth, a Messianic Jew does not try to re-erect the "dividing wall of hostility"; that would be the case only if his Jewishness were so rigid as to prevent him from eating with Gentile Jesus-believers (see the next §).

Let me quote here a testimony by Eitan Shisskoff, leader of the Messianic congregation *Olahei Rachamim* in Kiryat Yam (Israel): "God has given the Torah to the Jewish people forever. There is a New Covenant, but the New Covenant is a part of the law of Moses . . . . The Torah is a fundamental

---

3. In Kac (1986, 269); I take issue with this last phrase, however; see Appendix I.

revelation. The authors of the New Testament, Jesus himself, quoted it often and lived according to the law.... I see no reason to change that as a twentieth-century Jew.... I was born as a Jew and my rebirth in the Messiah did not take away my Jewishness from me."[4] Shisskoff would love to develop "a Messianic *halakah*, not one that is binding but one that can convey what it means, as a believer in Jesus, to lead a Jewish life." Joseph Shulam of the *Ro'eh Yisrael* congregation in central Jerusalem feels that the study of God's Word "ought to develop a Messianic *halakah*, that is a practical New Covenant system of living among the Jewish community."[5]

9.1.2 Should the Messianic Jew Never Deviate from *Kashrut*?

The second error mentioned in §9.1.1 involved the idea that a Jew, Messianic or not, under no circumstances ought to deviate from *kashrut*, not even while enjoying fellowship with Gentile Jesus-believers. The occurrence of this error is confirmed by Galatians 2:11-13, where Paul relates: "But when Cephas [i.e., Peter] came to Antioch, I opposed him to his face, because he stood condemned. For before certain men came from James, he was eating with the Gentiles; but when they came he drew back and separated himself, fearing the circumcision party. And the rest of the Jews acted hypocritically along with him, so that even Barnabas was led astray by their hypocrisy."

James Dunn describes three alternative explanations of this passage, the third of which he himself prefers: (1) The congregation at Antioch had entirely given up *kashrut*; the men from James insisted on the decree of Acts 15:29. (2) The congregation did maintain *kashrut*; the men from James insisted that the Gentile believers became full proselytes of Judaism. (3) The Gentile believers did observe *kashrut* to a certain ex-

---

4. Meijer (1997, 48).
5. Quoted by Kjær-Hansen and Skjøtt (1999, 114).

tent; the men from James insisted on a much more scrupulous observance.[6] In my view, none of these alternatives is plausible because none is rooted in a clear distinction between the duties of Jewish and Gentile Jesus-believers.

For quite some time, Paul and Barnabas, and the other Messianic Jews at Antioch, had been eating freely with the Gentile Jesus-believers (Acts 11:26). This means that to enjoy this fellowship, the *kashrut* custom with which they had been brought up had to be put aside — at least to a certain extent. In fact, God had already prepared Peter for this before he went to the house of Cornelius (Acts 10:10-16; 11:5-10; see §9.2.1). This new code of behavior did not involve the abrogation of *kashrut* as such, but the decree that *kashrut* should not impede fellowship with Gentile Jesus-believers. The new code was not just an invention of the Messianic Jews in order to be able to commune more freely with Gentile Jesus-believers. No, it went back to a direct revelation of God, given to none other than Peter himself (Acts 10:10-16). It was all the more sad, then, that he was the very one who ignored it at Antioch.

The reason Peter did so was not that he had become uneasy about the underlying principles. The Lord had shown him too clearly how he was supposed to act. Before the men of James arrived he did eat with the Gentile believers. At first, he therefore behaved at Antioch just like the other Messianic Jews had done for a long time: "eating with the Gentiles." Refusing to eat with the Gentile Jesus-believers, *including the celebration of the Lord's Supper with them,* implied a denial of the fellowship of the one Body of the Messiah (1 Cor. 10:16-17). In principle, this implied the acceptance of two Messianic communities: one comprised of Jews, the other of Gentiles. There is nothing by which the Messiah is more "divided" (cf. 1 Cor. 1:13) than by such an attitude of unilateral or mutual exclusion. But the mere refusal to eat common meals together is serious enough. *This* is a genuine example of the threatening

---

6. Dunn (1990b, 151-58).

possibility that the Torah will still remain, or become anew, a "dividing wall of hostility" (Eph. 2:14) between Jews and Gentiles, even within the Ekklesia.

Peter's reason for reconsidering his behavior later was not of a principled but of a diplomatic nature. Paul perceived this; he saw that Peter was driven by abject fear of the Judaizers. Therefore, Paul stood up in the meeting and directed his angry rage at the Messianic Jews who were eating separately, particularly at the one most responsible—Peter. Paul said: "If you, though a Jew, live like a Gentile and not like a Jew, how can you force the Gentiles to live like Jews?" (v. 14b). More literally, "If you being a Jew live Gentile-like (*ethnikōs*) and not Jew-like (*Ioudaïkōs*). . . ." At Jerusalem, Peter had undoubtedly lived like the other Messianic Jews, that is, as a Torah-keeper (cf. Acts 3:1; 21:20). But here at Antioch, in his fellowship with Gentile Jesus-believers, he lived like them, as he had done earlier in the house of Cornelius (Acts 10). Paul asked, "How can you force the Gentiles to live Jewishly?" The word "force" may amaze us. Peter had stopped living "Gentile-like" (*ethnikōs*); but is that not something very different from *forcing* the (believing) Gentiles to live "Jew-like" (*Ioudaïkōs*)? Paul seems to mean that, although Peter had not urged the Gentile Jesus-believers to adapt, the consequence of his behavior would be that, if Jewish and Gentile Jesus-believers wished to continue living together, the latter would have to adapt to the former.

I repeat here what I said earlier in §8.3.3: I do not know of any clear-cut indication in the New Testament that Gentile Jesus-believers are encouraged, or advised, to follow the entire Mosaic Torah. On the contrary, how easily could the problems of Galatians 2:11-14 have been solved if Gentile Jesus-believers had learned to follow the Mosaic Torah on a voluntary basis. Instead, Paul blamed Peter for forcing Gentile Jesus-believers to live "Jew-like." Of course, if Messianic Jews sometimes have to adapt to Gentile Jesus-believers, the latter sometimes have to adapt to the former. They do so by not dishing up *treif* (i.e., non-kosher) food for their Jewish friends, and by not giving offense to them by treating the latter's biblical scruples carelessly. But nowhere do the apostles even implicitly suggest that the noblest way for the Gentile Jesus-believer would be to submit to, for instance, *kashrut*. On the contrary, the Messianic Jew, who has every right, if not duty, to keep *kashrut*, also has the duty to never let *kashrut* come between him and his Gentile fellow-believer.

Paul's words in 1 Corinthians 9:19–21 seem closely related to this: "[T]hough I am free from all, I have made myself a servant to all, that I might win more of them. To the Jews I became as a Jew, in order to win Jews. To those under the Torah I became as one under the Torah (though not being myself under the Torah) that I might win those under the Torah. To those outside the Torah I became as one outside the Torah (not being outside the Torah of God but under the Torah of Messiah [*ennomos Christou*]) that I might win those outside the Torah." The text does not mean that Paul behaved like a hypocrite; that was the very behavior he had found blameworthy in Peter (Gal. 2). Nor was Paul interested in cunning evangelism methods, for he said about his own preaching (2 Cor. 4:2): "[W]e have renounced disgraceful, underhanded ways. We refuse to practice cunning, or to tamper with God's word." Another thing that is often inferred from 1 Corinthians 9 is that Paul himself no longer continually observed the Torah, but if he did so at all, he kept Torah only when he was among Jews.

In fact, this passage is not at all about whether a Messianic Jew is to keep the Torah, but about how far a (Jewish or Gentile) Jesus-believer ought to go to win other people, Jews or Gentiles.[7] Otherwise, how could Paul say that he "became like" a Jew to the Jews when in fact he *was* a Jew all along (Acts 22:3; 23:6; Rom. 9:3; 11:1; 2 Cor. 11:22)? "Becoming like" does not mean here, "*behaving* like," for he already behaved

---

7. Cf. Stern (1999, 464–67); also cf. Dodd (1968, 134–48).

like a Jew (Acts 28:17). Instead, it means "placing himself in the position of." This is not a matter of imitation but of empathy. Whenever he preached the gospel he tried not to cause anyone to stumble, whether Jews or Greeks (cf. 1 Cor. 10:32). Rather, he put himself in the position of the non-Messianic Jews or the Gentiles, and as far as possible he honored and accommodated their own views and feelings, their wishes and questions, their norms and values, their needs and cravings.

Which one of the apostles had such a great gift in this regard? Paul sensed the legalism and traditionalism of the "weak" (1 Cor. 9:22a; cf. 8:7-12). He understood the Hellenistic thinking of the Greeks (Acts 17:16-31, especially v. 28; cf. Titus 1:12). He knew the feelings of the Jews who rejected the Messiah, for he had once done the same (Acts 9:4-5). "I have become all things to all people, that by all means I might save some. I do it all for the sake of the gospel, that I may share with them in its blessings" (1 Cor. 9:22b-23). But he never separated from Gentile Jesus-believers with a view to observing *kashrut* for the sake of pleasing the Judaizers or non-Messianic Jews. Nor did he ever denigrate *kashrut* in order to please the Greeks. Paul tried to get as close to his listeners as he could — but he never denied or compromised his principles.

As a present-day example of Paul's attitude, I quote the view of Chuck Cohen, one of the leaders of the Messianic *King of Kings* Assembly in central Jerusalem: "I eat biblical kosher, I eat no pork or shrimp. But when somebody has invited me and entirely in good faith has dished up ham for me, I eat it. I do not want to give offense in the unity of believers. It is something I do but which I do not want to impede unity with other believers."[8]

---

8. Meijer (1997, 49). From a Messianic Jewish standpoint, the congregation is exceptional: though located in Jerusalem, it is English-speaking and meets on Sundays (Kjær-Hansen and Skjøtt 1999, 280-81). Hebrew meetings are held late Friday afternoon, just before Shabbat.

Particularly in Israel, Messianic Jews face a double problem. In addition to their religious duty as such with regard to the Torah—on which they have varying views—on the one hand they have to be good witnesses to non-Messianic Jews by making the cleft between themselves and other Jews as small as possible. On the other hand, there should be no hindrances whatsoever in their fellowship with Gentile Jesus-believers, or with Gentile not-yet-believers. On the one hand, Messianic Jews do not eat pork, either because they believe that to be their God-given duty, or if they no longer view it as a duty, because of their non-Messianic Jewish friends, colleagues, and neighbors. On the other hand, though many Gentiles may respect such Jewish consciences, Messianic Jews should be prepared, when they are guests of ignorant Gentiles, either Jesus-believers but especially non-Jesus-believers, to eat what is set before them.

Although the case is quite different, there is a general moral principle in Paul's words: "Eat whatever is sold in the meat market without raising any question on the ground of conscience. For 'the earth is the Lord's, and the fullness thereof [Ps. 24:1].' If one of the unbelievers invites you to dinner and you are disposed to go, eat whatever is set before you without raising any question on the ground of conscience. But if someone says to you, 'This has been offered in sacrifice,' then do not eat it, for the sake of the one who informed you, and for the sake of conscience—I do not mean your conscience, but his. For why should my liberty be determined by someone else's conscience?" (1 Cor. 10:25-29). The practical application for a Messianic Jew could be: don't eat pork, but if you could save a man's life through eating pork (as his guest), then do it; but if you could help him spiritually by explaining to him why you want to keep God's Torah, then don't eat his pork. Do not go by rigid rules but by the principle of love, altruism, and empathy, under the guidance of the Holy Spirit.

9.1.3 Rabbinic *Kashrut*

I have argued that Messianic Jews have the right, if not the duty, to observe biblical *kashrut*. But that is not the same as rabbinic *kashrut*. For Messianic Jews it is no use keeping biblical *kashrut* just to please their Orthodox fellow-Jews, because the latter's traditions go far beyond what can be warranted on the basis of the Torah. Messianic Jews are to observe biblical *kashrut* in its own right, that is, keep the food laws of Leviticus 11 and Deuteronomy 14. Rabbinic *kashrut* is much more severe than that, and offers a striking example of how tradition can start with a statement in the Bible and then, following its own imagination, can go wildly astray.

One of the most conspicuous elements in rabbinic *kashrut* is based on this single statement in the Torah: "You shall not boil a young goat in its mother's milk" (Exod. 23:19b; 34:26b; Deut. 14:21b). Presumably, the background of this prohibition was some fertility cult among the Canaanite people, which was an abomination to the LORD, but that background is of little importance for own present considerations. Rabbinic tradition took the prohibition so seriously and literally that it extended it in the widest sense imaginable: the young goat became any goat, the goat became any animal, the mother's milk became any milk, cooking became touching. Ultimately, the prohibition came to be understood as follows: "You shall not boil any meat in any milk; do not even let any meat come into contact with any dairy product."

Apparently the underlying argument is this: be so careful not to cook a young goat in its mother's milk that you are better off not cooking any meat in any milk. This resembles the prohibition of pronouncing the Lord's name, YHWH, which came about along the same lines: in order to avoid taking the name of YHWH in vain (Exod. 20:7), you are better off not pronouncing the name at all. There may be some validity to such an argument, just like Jesus told his disciples not to swear at all in order not to risk breaking any oath (Matt. 5:33–37). But never was a decree expanded to such an extent as the prohibition to cook a young goat in its mother's milk. It almost sounds like an imaginary prohibition that a person ought not to marry at all in order not to risk marrying the wrong spouse; or not to eat at all in order not to risk eating the wrong thing.

Rashi (Rabbi Solomon ben Isaac) and his grandson, Rashbam (Rabbi Samuel ben Meir), both alleged that this Torah-statement forbids every mixture of milk and meat.[9] Here we see the power, not of sound exegesis but of *halakah*, carried to its extreme. To do justice to the rabbinic reasoning involved here, we may reconstruct it as follows: How do we know for sure that the animal we cook in milk was not born of the mother from which we got the milk? To be absolutely sure, one simply never cooks meat in milk. To be absolutely sure that one never cooks meat in milk, one never eats meat and milk together. And to be absolutely sure that one never eats meat and milk together, one never prepares and serves them together. Consequently, the Orthodox Jewish family has virtually two different kitchens: cooking utensils plus tableware for meat, and cooking utensils plus tableware for dairy products, and they are never mixed.

Humanly speaking, I can understand that the Orthodox Jew is proud of such a strict observance of the Torah. However, one may wonder if something is not peculiar about a tradition that produces such an exaggerated complexity. Is not the only question that really matters this one: Is such a system truly what God intended for the people of Israel? To what extent does this type of Torah interpretation reflect a truly spiritual mind? As far as I understand the Messianic Torah, such a "great burdensome legalism"[10] would be irreconcilable with its spirit and tenor.

To say the very least, there is no duty for Messianic Jews in this rabbinic *kashrut*. Some of them, living among Orthodox

---

9. Cohen/Rosenberg (1985, 490–91).
10. Juster (1995, 231).

Jews and wishing to receive them in their homes, may feel led by the Lord to observe rabbinic *kashrut*. Joseph Ben-Zvi, the pastor of a Reformational type of Messianic congregation, Bat Tzion (in the vicinity of Jerusalem), says, "The *halakah* is not binding on us but it is appropriate to keep parts of it, especially in a Jewish society. Some laws are biblical, but some go further, for instance, a kosher household. We eat kosher because people around us eat kosher. We are not as strict as the Orthodox Jews but we go further than so-called biblical kosher. We do not mix meat and milk, for example."[11]

In my view, there is nothing wrong with this, as long as they do not feel obliged to do so for biblical, traditionalist, or legalistic reasons. It is like Protestants eating beef on Fridays. Should they feel guilty because the Roman Catholic Church has prohibited this? Or should they realize that what is forbidden by Roman Catholic tradition is not necessarily forbidden in Scripture? In many ways, the Messianic Jew is to rabbinic tradition what the Protestant is to Catholic tradition: there may be much in it that is worth considering, and even adopting, but only Scripture is binding, and only sound exegesis can help here. Sometimes, Protestants may have uncritically and inadvertently taken over Roman Catholic but unscriptural customs, or, conversely, may have thrown out the baby with the bathwater, and Messianic Jews may have done similarly. But the underlying principle must remain clear: the norm is Scripture alone.

9.2 Is All Food Kosher Since the Messiah?
9.2.1 Acts 10

In §9.1.2 we briefly referred to Peter's vision: "[H]e became hungry and wanted something to eat, but while they were preparing it, he fell into a trance and saw the heavens opened and something like a great sheet descending, being let down by its four corners upon the earth. In it were all kinds of ani-

---

11. Quoted in Meijer (1997, 49).

mals and reptiles and birds of the air. And there came a voice to him: 'Rise, Peter; kill and eat.' But Peter said, 'By no means, Lord; for I have never eaten anything that is common or unclean.' And the voice came to him again a second time, 'What God has made clean, do not call common.' This happened three times, and the thing was taken up at once to heaven" (Acts 10:10–16; cf. 11:5–10).

Expositors agree that through this vision the Lord prepared Peter for his visit to Cornelius' house. But they do not agree on the precise import of this vision. They have usually been of the opinion that the Lord abolished once and for all the distinction between kosher and treif food here.[12] But the context has little to do with this distinction.[13] On the contrary, in the sheet "were all kinds of animals and reptiles and birds of the air." Was it really the Lord's intention to tell Peter that from now on he was free to eat snakes, crocodiles, lizards, spiders, beetles, mice, dogs, cats, vultures, and owls? When the Lord said, "kill and eat" (v. 13), if *kashrut* had been the issue, Peter could have ritually slaughtered the kosher animals that were on the sheet and eaten their meat. But Peter was undoubtedly perplexed by the fact that the kosher animals formed an unholy mixture with treif animals. That was his very problem: the unholy mixture with "unclean" people such as Gentiles. The Lord's point was not at all to declare all *foods* kosher, but to declare all *people* "clean," as Peter himself understood far better than many expositors: "You yourselves know how unlawful[14] it is for a Jew to associate with or to visit anyone of another nation, but God has shown me that I should not call any person common or unclean" (v. 28). Note that Peter does not say, "any animal," but "any person." The point was not that in his personal life Peter had to give up *kashrut* but that

---

12. Cf. Knowling (1979, 253–55); Longenecker (1981, 388); more balanced is Bruce (1988, 205–206).

13. Cf. Stern (1997, 161; 1999, 257–58); Berkowitz (1999, 203–206).

14. Gk. *athemitos*, here equivalent to "against our Torah" (cf. NIV).

kashrut should not be an impediment to preaching the gospel to an "unclean" Gentile in his own house, and even eating with him.

The rigid prejudice of expositors that this passage is dealing with the abrogation of *kashrut*, while Peter's real problem was with the propriety of a Jew entering a Gentile house, can lead to strange conclusions. Martin Dibelius was sure that, on the one hand, Peter's problem was whether and how he could enter a Gentile's house—which is correct—and, on the other hand, the vision was about the matter of kosher and treif food—which is incorrect. On the basis of his own prejudice, Dibelius concluded that Luke inserted the story of Peter's vision here to explain why Peter could enter Cornelius' house, although, in his view, the vision as such had nothing to do with this.[15] It did not occur to him that the opposite view might fit the context better, namely, that Peter's vision was not about the abrogation of *kashrut* at all, but about the very problem of a Jew entering a Gentile's house.

9.2.2 Mark 7

However, as some will object, in Mark 7:19 we do read that Jesus "declared all foods clean." Arnold Fruchtenbaum refers to this verse time and again to argue that the Mosaic Torah has been abolished, and he does not even attempt to interpret the verse; apparently he feels no need for any further exegesis.[16] But does the verse really say that Jesus abrogated *kashrut*? How then could he, in spite of his objections to the teachers of the Torah, say of them, "[D]o and observe *everything* they tell you" (Matt. 23:3)? And to these teachers themselves he said: "[Y]ou tithe mint and dill and cumin, and have neglected the weightier matters of the law: justice and mercy and faithfulness. These you ought to have done, *without neglecting the oth-*

---

15. Dibelius (1956, 111–12).
16. Fruchtenbaum (1992, 640, 648, 650, 884, 908); cf. Lane (1974, 256); Bruce (1988, 206).

ers" (v. 23, italics added). That is, he did *not* tell them to stop tithing mint and dill and cumin, or to cease keeping any of the Torah's other commandments. Jesus never cancelled the distinction between kosher and treif foods, but fully maintained the Mosaic Torah,[17] and even the "traditions" as long as they did not contravene the spirit of the Torah (see §6.3.2 above). For this reason alone, it is quite inconceivable that Mark 7:19 would involve the abrogation of *kashrut*.[18]

However, equally important is the question: Is Mark 7 really about *kashrut* at all? Hardly. Jesus is speaking of the "tradition of the elders" (v. 3), the Oral Torah, as Jews would say, which would later be written down mainly in the Mishnah. In the tract Yadayyim ("Hands") the rules of the so-called *netilat-yadayyim*, the ritual washing of hands, are recorded (cf. Matt. 15:2-3; Luke 11:38; John 2:6). Mark explains them to his Gentile readers: "[T]he Pharisees and all the Jews do not eat unless they wash their hands properly, holding to the tradition of the elders, and when they come from the marketplace, they do not eat unless they wash. And there are many other traditions that they observe, such as the washing of cups and pots and copper vessels and dining couches" (vv. 3-4).

Such a washing has little to do with hygiene. Jews view this action as being parallel to the action of the priests washing their hands and feet in the bronze basin before beginning their service (Exod. 30:18-21). The idea is that every family head is priest in his own house, that his dining table is like an altar (cf. Ezek. 41:22; 44:16; Mal. 1:7, 12, where the Temple altar is called the Lord's "table"), and that his food is an offering.[19] The *berakah* that he utters is like the praise of God in the tem-

---

17. Cf. on this verse Stern (1997, 160–61; 1999, 93–94).
18. Cf. Lindars (1988) on this verse.
19. Of course, the similarities are limited: the very things that are placed on the altar—blood, the meat of the burnt offering (Lev. 1), the fat of the peace offering (Lev. 3)—are never to be eaten by the Israelite.

ple. During the wilderness journey, every meal of meat was probably supposed to have the character of a peace offering, so that such a meal was in fact a sacrificial repast even if eaten at home (Lev. 7:11-34). Just as the priest washed his hands before performing his ministry, the Oral Torah demanded the same of every ordinary Israelite before eating his meal. This also explains why Torah-keeping Jews sprinkle salt on their bread before giving thanks for it: this is to observe the ancient commandment that no offering on the altar should be without salt (Lev. 2:13). Likewise, because Jesus-believers should present themselves as living sacrifices (Rom. 12:1), Jesus said, "Have salt in yourselves" (Mark 9:50).

E. P. Sanders told us that he could not believe that Jesus would have really rejected the notion of (ritually) unclean animals. That is, on the one hand, Sanders was following the traditional interpretation that Mark 7:15-19 is "denying the Jewish dietary code. . . . [T]his statement, if it really means what it appears to mean, nullifies the food laws and falls completely outside the limits of debate about the law in first-century Judaism." On the other hand, he rightly realized that such a "saying makes Jesus the direct source of a rupture with ordinary Judaism"—which to Sanders is inconceivable: "[T]he saying attributed to Jesus . . . appears to me to be too revolutionary to have been said by Jesus himself."[20] Sanders also spoke of "a strong contravention of the law,"[21] and wrote: "Jesus rejects . . . the law itself (food). . . . Jesus did not seriously challenge the law as it was practiced in his day, not even by the strict rules of observance of pietist groups—except on the issue of food."[22] Similarly, Cranfield wrote: "Jesus speaks [in Mark 7] as the one who is, and knows himself to be, *telos nomou* ['the end of the law'] (Rom. 10.4)."[23] And Dunn al-

---

20. Sanders (1990, 28).
21. Sanders (1990, 91).
22. Sanders (1990, 95-96).
23. Cranfield (1959, 244).

leged: "[Jesus'] teaching on the causes of impurity as recalled in Mark 7 in effect cuts at the root of the *whole* ritual law (as Mark perceives—7:19b)."[24]

Sanders did attempt a different interpretation of the verse, so that "it can be saved as an authentic logion [saying of Jesus]," by suggesting that the "nothing . . . rather" argument in Mark 7:15 is to be taken as meaning, "What comes out is much more important" than what goes in,[25] "leaving the food laws as such untouched. In this case there is no conflict with the law." Sanders added, "This interpretation of the saying, however, grants the point that as it is intended in Mark 7 it is unauthentic." In other words, verse 15 may be an authentic saying of Jesus, but the Gospel writer's conclusion in verse 19 allegedly misrepresents Jesus' intention. In my view, Sanders' former claim is correct, the latter is not. Because of the same misunderstanding, Dunn can say that Matthew in chapter 15:1-20 "(1) softens Mark's version (Mark 7.15)—he was not prepared to have Jesus affirm that unclean foods cannot defile; (2) he completely omits Mark's interpretation that Jesus' saying implied annulment of the law on clean and unclean foods. . . . Matthew was less than willing to abandon the dietary laws himself and less than happy with the suggestion that Jesus' words amounted to an abrogation of the law."[26]

My position is that there is no such contrast between Mark and Matthew at all. In my view, *Mark 7 is not about food laws* but about the *netilat-yadayyim*;[27] there is absolutely nothing to

---

24. Dunn (1990a, 98); cf. Dunn (1990b, 37–60).
25. Sanders finds examples for this type of argument in Exod. 16:8c (cf. v. 2) and in Mark 9:37: "whoever welcomes me does not welcome me but the one who sent me" means "not only me but also . . ."; in Sanders' words: "receiving me is tantamount to receiving God."
26. Dunn (1990a, 247–48).
27. Even concerning this matter, Sanders (1990, 41) states: "[T]hat handwashing was to most Jews a relatively unimportant matter, [which] leads to the conclusion that Jesus was not in serious dispute with his contemporaries over laws of purity."

suggest that *kashrut*, the distinction between kosher and treif, is involved here. As Geza Vermes wrote: "[W]hatever [Jesus] meant to convey by [the words of Mark 7:14–15], it was surely not an abrogation of the dietary laws."[28] However, his way of maintaining this is to identify the clause, "In saying this, Jesus declared all foods clean" (v. 19), as "a gloss introduced by the redactor of Mark, having nothing to do with the original narrative, and even less with Jesus." My own explanation does not need such an escape. In my view, the point that Jesus made was that the "tradition of the elders" concerning the washing of hands should not be more strict than the Torah demanded. In other words, the point is not that treif foods are declared kosher here, but rather the reverse: kosher foods do not become treif if eaten with unwashed hands. Dan Juster pointed out that Jesus did not declare all *animals* clean, but all *foods*, that is, that which had already been defined as "food" in Leviticus 11: "[I]n Mark 7, what God calls food is clean, whether or not rabbinical ritual and washing has been followed."[29]

In fact, Jesus was not even concerned with the *netilat-yadayyim* as such, but with making the basic claim that "cleanness" is not primarily a ritual or physical, but a spiritual, matter. The Jews were so occupied with the "tradition of the elders" that they were in danger of overlooking the essence, namely, the heart's inward attitude. But on no occasion did Jesus turn the Torah 180 degrees around as if it is *only* the heart that matters, and not outward behavior. The "weightier matters of the Torah" are "justice and mercy and faithfulness" (Matt. 23:23), but that does not mean that the outward customs are totally irrelevant (see again v. 3a and §6.3.2).

Take the example of circumcision. The Tanakh acknowledges that it is the circumcision of the heart that matters — but it never abolishes the circumcision of the body (see §5.3.2

---

28. Vermes (1993, 25).
29. Juster (1995, 55, 126); cf. Berkowitz (1999, 201–203).

above). Even in the Messianic Kingdom, circumcision will be the condition for participation in the Temple ministry: "O Jerusalem . . . there shall no more come into you the uncircumcised and the unclean" (Isa. 52:1; see §6.2.1). More than ever, during the Messianic Kingdom it will be essential to be "circumcised of heart" — but this will not replace the circumcision of the flesh, not only for the Israelites but even for the "foreigners": "No foreigner, uncircumcised in heart and flesh . . . shall enter my sanctuary" (Ezek. 44:9).

Likewise, more than ever it will be the cleanness of heart that will matter — but this fact will not abolish the *torot* referring to the cleanness of foods; on the contrary: "Those who consecrate and purify themselves to go into the gardens, following one who is among those who eat the flesh of pigs, rats and other unclean things — they will meet their end together with the one they follow.... And I, because of what they have planned and done, am about to come and gather the people of all nations and languages, and they will come and see my glory" (Isa. 66:17–18 NIV).

9.2.3 Other Scriptures

Occasionally a few other passages are believed to teach that God has done away with *kashrut* in the present dispensation.[30] The apostle Paul condemned those heretics who require "abstinence from foods that God created to be received with thanksgiving by those who believe and know the truth" (1 Tim. 4:3). It is quite possible that these heretics had included some elements of *kashrut* in their teachings. However, when the Letter condemns these people this does not imply that it condemns *kashrut*. If that were the case, the Letter would also be condemning abstinence from marriage as such, because this is mentioned in the same verse. This would flatly contradict Paul's words in 1 Corinthians 7:8 and 38. Paul did not condemn abstinence from foods or from marriage as such;

---

30. E.g., Fruchtenbaum (1992, 925) refers to 1 Tim. 4:4.

the context clearly points to the sin of viewing asceticism as a mandatory way of holiness. Let us remember that Paul himself carefully observed *kashrut* all his life (see §5.3.2 above), just as he also abstained from marriage. Neither *kashrut* nor abstinence from marriage as such were the problem, but the contempt for God's good creation was the essence of the heresy involved (see vv. 4–5).

Another example is 1 Corinthians 8:8, where Paul says: "Food will not commend us to God. We are no worse off if we do not eat, and no better off if we do." No wise and God-fearing Jew would have ever thought that keeping *kashrut* as such would make him more pleasing to God. Likewise, Gentile Jesus-believers should not think that *not* keeping *kashrut* would make them more pleasant to God. Actually, this verse is not about *kashrut*, of course, but about food that had been sacrificed to an idol and that had been offered for sale at the public meat market (1 Cor. 8:7; cf. 10:25). Believers with a "weak conscience" (8:10) had scruples against buying such food, "stronger" believers did not. But the latter should take care that the exercise of their freedom (namely, to buy) would not become a stumbling block to "weaker" believers, who might see them buy such food and might thus themselves be enticed into idolatry.

A third relevant passage is Hebrews 9:9–10: "gifts and sacrifices . . . deal only with food and drink and various washings, regulations for the body imposed until the time of reformation." This verse may seem to suggest that, now that the "time of the new order" has arrived, the Mosaic regulations concerning "food and drink and various [ceremonial] washings" do not apply anymore. Actually, this verse is not about *kashrut* but about the food and drink that was involved in the sacrificial ministry. We are under the present "new order," literally, the "time of the re-arrangement (*kairos diorthōseōs*)," that is, under the Messianic Torah. In this polity, there is no longer any question of the ancient sacrificial ministry with its foods and drinks and washings. These could not provide the repentant sinner a "perfect conscience" anyway (Heb. 9:9; cf. 7:11, 19; 10:1, 14), as is now possible through the sacrifice of Jesus.

A fourth example is Hebrews 13:9: "[I]t is good for the heart to be strengthened by grace, not by foods,[31] which have not benefited those devoted to them." *Kashrut* can hardly be involved here because the author is speaking about the use of foods, not about abstinence from them. Some thought that eating certain foods enhanced their spirituality. Several suggestions have been made as to what foods the author has in mind. The best explanation, supported by verse 10, may be that the Hebrew believers still thought that partaking of peace-offering meals and the like (cf. Lev. 7) would bring them to a higher spiritual level. At any rate, there is no indication that the passage has anything to do with *kashrut*.

Similar misunderstandings have been attached to verse 13: "Therefore let us go to him outside the camp and bear the reproach he endured." This verse is not saying that the "Hebrews" — Messianic Jews — were to leave the Jewish people or to stop being Jews, just as Jesus, who had "suffered outside the [city] gate" (v. 12), had not stopped being a Jew. Nor does the verse suggest that Messianic Jews had to abandon Jewish practices, that is, had to stop serving God through keeping his Torah. What the verse does say is that the Messianic Jews had to side with their rejected Messiah, even if that would imply practical separation from non-Messianic Jews and from that Judaistic polity which believed it could maintain the Torah while rejecting the Torah's Messiah. Abandoning Jewish practices is the last thing Messianic Jews should, and do, want. But if clinging to the despised Messiah implies expulsion by the majority of the Jewish people, then they will have to accept this.

---

31. The addition of the adjective "ceremonial" (NIV), which is not in the Gk., is unnecessary eisegesis.

9.3 Is Keeping *Kashrut* "Weakness"?
9.3.1 Romans 14

The matter of Messianic Jews keeping *kashrut*—as well as keeping the Jewish festivals and circumcising their sons for that matter—may elicit at least four different reactions.

(1) "Such behavior is to be rejected because it is unscriptural." We have already refuted this reply: even the apostles kept the Jewish customs, and Paul circumcised Timothy. In Acts 21, Paul took great pains to refute the slanderous rumors that he was teaching the Messianic Jews "to forsake Moses, telling them not to circumcise their children or walk according to our customs" (v. 21). Paul did not teach such things; on the contrary, he not only tolerated their observance by Messianic Jews, but he could say himself, "I had done nothing against our people or the customs of our fathers" (28:17). As a Messianic Jew, he kept both the Written and the Oral Torah as much as he could.

(2) "Torah-keeping by Messianic Jews is to be demanded because it is Scriptural." This is the view of many modern Messianic Jews. They believe that their acceptance of Jesus as the Messiah does not mean they have stopped being Jews, and that therefore they are bound to the conditions of God's covenant with Israel. That holds not only for the Old Covenant, but also for the New Covenant, which is also based upon a Torah-giving. The word "enacted" (or "established") in Hebrews 8:6 is derived from a verb that literally means, "give as law."[32] At the conclusion of the New Covenant, which the LORD makes "with the house of Israel and the house of Judah" (Jer. 31:31), he says: "I will put my laws[33] into their minds, and write them on their hearts" (Heb. 8:10). The major difficulty with this view, however, is that many Messianic Jews identify

---

32. The verb is *nomotheteō*, related to *nomos*, "law"; see this or related words, always referring to the Torah, in Rom. 9:4; Heb. 7:11; James 4:12.

33. Heb. *torot*; in Jer. 31:33 we find the singular, *torah*.

the latter Torah as the Mosaic Torah, which it is not. It is the Millennial Torah. The latter does include the Shabbat and the Jewish festivals, circumcision and *kashrut*, but not necessarily *all* the elements of the Mosaic Torah (see §6.2 above). Among these are many elements that ought to embarrass Messianic Jews because in fact they do not, or cannot, keep these themselves, such as many economic and agricultural, not to mention sacrificial, *torot*.

(3) "Torah-keeping by Messianic Jews is to be encouraged." Particularly many Gentile Jesus-believers see position (2) as going too far; they often even view it as legalistic. But they do occasionally see a certain desirability for Torah-keeping by Messianic Jews, for example, as a means to win non-Messianic Jews for Jesus. This seems to me a half-hearted attitude. If Torah-keeping by Messianic Jews is wrong, they ought not to do it, even if it were to win their Jewish brothers. If something is really wrong in itself, people should try to avoid it under any circumstances. But if Torah-keeping by Messianic Jews is right, they ought to pursue it, not only as a means useful for evangelism but simply because they are Jews.

(4) "Torah-keeping by Messianic Jews is to be tolerated." This is the view of those who actually disapprove of Torah-keeping by Messianic Jews, but believe that this is to be viewed as a temporary "weakness," until Messianic Jews have reached a better understanding. For this view they appeal to Romans 14:1–15:7, where the "strong" and the "weak" are described as follows: "One person believes he may eat anything, while the weak person eats only vegetables. . . . One person [i.e., the "weak" one] esteems one day as better [i.e., more sacred] than another, while another [i.e., the "strong" person] esteems all days alike" (Rom. 14:2, 5). Note verse 21, which also mentions drinking wine. Many take for granted that the expression "weak" refers to Messianic Jews who still hold to Jewish customs. James Dunn is one interpreter who sees it as self-evident that Romans 14 and Colossians 2 (see §9.3.2)

refer to Messianic Jews still following Jewish traditions.[34] But then Paul himself would be "weak" (Acts 21:21-26; 25:8; 28:17)! Besides, where does Romans 14 suggest that Messianic Jews are in view? Nowhere. On the contrary, why would a Torah-keeping Jew eat only vegetables, and not kosher meat as well? As if there were no *shoch'tim*[35] at Rome, with its large Jewish community (cf. Acts 28:17)! And further, why would a Torah-keeping Jew not drink wine? There is not a single prohibition to that effect (on the contrary, see, e.g., Deut. 14:26), except for Nazirites during the time of their voluntary vow (Num. 6:3, 20) and for priests on duty (Lev. 10:9). In other words, it appears to be impossible to view the "weak" of Romans 14 as Torah-keeping Messianic Jews.[36]

Nor can the "weak" be Judaizers as intended in Galatians 2:11-14 either, because Paul does not call those persons "weak" at all, but absolutely reprehensible. It seems rather that the "weak" are Jesus-believers, Jewish or Gentile, still clinging to all kinds of ascetic practices and holy days, particularly out of some inward fear and insecurity. These may have been Messianic Jews dealing with Jewish customs in a wrong way, by believing, for instance, that they would thereby get on God's good side, or by an obsessive attitude hampering them in their fellowship with Gentile Jesus-believers. But the "weak" could just as well have been Gentile Jesus-believers who came under a Judaizing influence, or whose lifestyle was an overreaction to their former idolatrous walk. All kinds of interpretations are possible. Joseph Shulam thinks of the various attitudes toward eating meat offered to idols, and other pagan practices.[37] But there is nothing in Romans 14 and 15 that compels us to view Paul as speaking of Messianic Jews

---

34. Dunn (1990a, 64–65).
35. *Shochêt*, i.e., kosher butcher; from *sh-ch-t*, "to slaughter."
36. Cf. Murray (1968, 172–74, 260–61); Moo (1996, 826-33); Stern (1999, 431–36).
37. Shulam (1998, 456-57, 461–62).

who were simply doing what all good Jews do: keeping the Mosaic Torah.

9.3.2 Colossians 2

Once we have grasped the previous arguments, other Scriptures fall into place as well, such as Colossians 2:16-17: "[L]et no one pass judgment on you in questions of food and drink, or with regard to a festival or a new moon or a Sabbath. These are a shadow of the things to come, but the substance [or, reality] belongs to Messiah." Here again it is not said that Messianic Jews may no longer keep the Mosaic Torah.[38] Rather, the text is probably not referring to Messianic Jews at all, but to Gentile Jesus-believers who had fallen into the hands of Judaizers or Gnostics. What is being rejected here, just as in Romans and Galatians, is a *legalistic* or *ascetic* attitude toward the Torah, that is, an attitude *inserted between the believer and Jesus* (cf. Col. 2:6-8, 20-3:4; also see Appendix III). Paul is not at all concerned with the Mosaic Torah as such, but with "empty deceit, according to human tradition" (v. 8), with "human precepts and teachings" (v. 22). That is something quite different from the Mosaic Torah, which is God's own Word.

In my opinion, the whole context of Colossians 2 shows a concern with a legalism that Judaizers or Gnostics considered necessary for salvation, or at least enriching their spiritual life. However, he who died with Messiah, and was buried, raised, and made alive with him (vv. 11-13), does not need these "human traditions"; to him, Jesus and his atoning work suffice. *Of course* the Mosaic Torah is a "shadow" (Col. 2:17) — however, not a "mere shadow" (NASB), or "only a shadow" (CEB, CEV, GNT), as some translations add in a deprecating way. The Mosaic Torah is a "shadow" in a very positive sense: it is the mold that was filled by Jesus (cf. Matt. 5:17). A shadow refers to — sometimes, points forward to — an object casting that shadow. That "object" is "the Messiah"; this is what we

---

38. Cf. Bruce (1984, 113–29); Stern (1999, 610–12).

read literally in verse 17. Compare this with the same positive meaning of "shadow" in Hebrews 8:5 and 10:1. The object is greater than the shadow—but that does not turn the shadow into nothing. Rather, the object casting the shadow will continue doing so as long as that object exists. Since the coming of Jesus, the shadow continues. He who prefers the shadow to the object, namely, Jesus, is seriously mistaken. But the same holds for one who believes he can sever the object from the shadow.

There is nothing wrong with a great Jewish—and Gentile-believing!—respect for the "shadows," for (1) God himself gave them in a perfect form to Israel. (2) To the Jew, they remain equally beautiful, whether he has come to know the Messiah or not. And (3) from early childhood, the "shadows" are woven into the Jewish lifestyle in such a strong way that, if Jews would be forced to give them up, it would be like telling a man to give up his masculinity, or telling a white person to give up his "Caucasianness." This would imply a terrible loss of identity with which Gentile Jesus-believers unfortunately are rarely able to empathize. In Colossians, Paul may be telling the Gentile Jesus-believers: Do not adopt out of a legalistic-ascetic mentality Jewish customs that are perfectly natural to *Messianic Jews*. If the latter practice them, that need not be for legalistic-ascetic reasons at all. If it is, such practice is utterly wrong; but it does not need to be for such reasons. But if you, Gentiles, would start practicing these customs, because of your different mentality they could become a spiritual danger to you. As Paul says a bit later: "If with Messiah you died to the elemental spirits of the world, why, as if you were still alive in the world, do you submit to regulations—'Do not handle, Do not taste, Do not touch' (referring to things that all perish as they are used)—according to human precepts and teachings? These have indeed an appearance of wisdom in promoting self-made religion and asceticism and severity to the body, but they are of no value in stopping the indulgence of the flesh" (vv. 20–23).

To summarize: because the great majority of the Colossian Jesus-believers were Gentiles, these people had never been under the *Mosaic* Torah at all. And they will never be under the *Millennial* Torah because at that time they will be with Jesus in heavenly glory. As we have seen, it is "from that side" that they, like all the other members of the Ekklesia, will experience the Messianic Kingdom (*'olam habba*). The members of the Ekklesia will not be *earthly subjects* of the King in that Kingdom, as restored Israel and the nations will be, but will be *heavenly co-rulers* with the King (2 Tim. 2:12; Rev. 5:10; 20:6; 22:5).[39] The Ekklesia will not dwell in the earthly Jerusalem and the earthly promised land, as restored Israel will, but in the heavenly Jerusalem (Gal. 4:26; Heb. 12:22; Rev. 3:12; 21:2, 10; cf. the heavenly "city" in Heb. 11:10, 16; 12:22; 13:14) and the heavenly promised land (Heb. 11:14, 16; cf. our position in the "heavenly realms" in Eph. 1:3; 2:6 [cf. 1:20]; 3:10; 6:12, and "our citizenship in heaven," Phil. 3:20). No wonder: restored Israel and the nations will dwell on the Millennial earth[40] in great bliss, yet in their mortal bodies. What else could Isaiah 65:20, 22b possibly mean when it speaks of dying during the Messianic Kingdom? But the Ekklesia—all those who "share in the first resurrection" (Rev. 20:4-6)—will be with the Lord in their resurrection bodies (cf. 1 Cor. 15:50-55; 1 Thess. 4:13-18; Phil. 3:20-21). Therefore, it is hardly relevant to quote Millennial prophecies as evidence for what Messianic Jews and Gentile Jesus-believers are supposed to do in the present age, while still living on earth before the second coming of the Messiah.

The Colossian Gentile Jesus-believers will never be under the Millennial Torah, just as they had never been under the Mosaic Torah. They were under only the Messianic Torah.

---

39. The verb "reign" (related to Latin *rex*, "king") is Gr. *basileuō*, related to the noun *basileus*, "king."

40. This is not yet the renewed earth of the eternal state (2 Pet. 3:13; Rev. 21:1) (see Ouweneel 1995, *in loco*).

They were not standing on the continuous covenant line between the Tanakh and the New Testament, as the Jews are. The believing Jew today is part of the Ekklesia, in which Jews and Gentiles have been brought together on perfectly equal footing. "Here there is not Greek and Jew, circumcised or uncircumcised, barbarian, Scythian, slave, free, but Messiah is all, and in all" (Col. 3:11). But that is true on a transcendent level *in Jesus*. In the immanent reality of human history, as I argued earlier, every member of the Ekklesia is either circumcised or uncircumcised, either slave or free, either male or female. Likewise, the Jew remains a Jew, the Gentile remains a Gentile. The Jew is, and remains, part of the nation that was God's covenantal people in the Tanakh and that will be God's covenantal people in the Messianic Kingdom.

Not so the Gentile Jesus-believers. Formally, the New Covenant is not even established with them but with Israel. The Gentile Jesus-believers have been "grafted into" the sphere of Israel's patriarchal blessings (Rom. 11:16–24), they are spiritual children and heirs of Abraham (4:11, 16; Gal. 3:7, 29; 4:28; Luke 22:20; 2 Cor. 3:6), they live under the blessings of the New Covenant. But they have neither a formal nor a practical reason to keep commandments that belong to the Mosaic Torah and/or the Millennial Torah. These practices may be a blessing to them—if observed in a proper manner and with the proper motivation—but they could also be a spiritual danger to them if observed improperly.

9.3.3 Summary of Positions

In §1.2.3, I described the various theological positions of Messianic Jews (as far as I have been able to identify them) with regard to Torah keeping by both them and Gentile Jesus-believers. In the light of everything we have discussed, let us now briefly review these positions.

1. Jesus-believing Jews who hold that *Messianic Jews are basically free from the Mosaic Torah* will claim the same, per-

haps even more strongly, with regard to Gentile Jesus-believers. They do not invite the latter to join them; on the contrary, such believing Jews are rather "Hebrew Christians," who have come to follow the ways of the Gentile Jesus-believers, for all intents and purposes. That is, they have each accepted one of the various traditional Gentile Jesus-believing paradigms, especially covenant theology or dispensational theology, and have joined traditional Christian movements, such as Lutheran, Reformed, Baptist, Evangelical, and Charismatic in particular.

2. Jesus-believing Jews who hold that *it is mandatory that Messianic Jews keep the Mosaic Torah* do so because they maintain that in coming to Jesus, Messianic Jews have in no way given up their Jewish identity. We have seen that these Messianic Jews differ on the question as to whether it is desirable, or even mandatory, to observe the Oral Torah (rabbinic/Talmudic tradition). In addition to this, they also differ on the question whether Gentile Jesus-believers should also learn to observe the entire Mosaic Torah or not. There seem to be basically three options, which I designate in my own way:

2.1 *The Proselyte View:* There is only one Torah, which is the Mosaic or Sinaitic Torah; Gentile Jesus-believers, too, have been brought under the "Torah of the Messiah" (1 Cor. 9:21; Gal. 6:2), which is none other than the Torah of Moses. Neither for Messianic Jews nor for Gentile Jesus-believers is the Torah ever a meritorious way of salvation. Consequently, neither Acts 15 nor Galatians can be used as an argument against Torah keeping by Gentile Jesus-believers. Even if Acts 15 seems to impose only four commandments upon Gentile Jesus-believers, this can never mean that the "Torah of the Messiah" is limited to these four.[41] On the contrary, verse 21 seems to suggest that, by attending services in the syna-

---

41. In Appendix IV, I myself claim that dozens of commandments of the Mosaic Torah are literally applicable to Gentile Jesus-believers.

gogues, Gentile Jesus-believers will gradually come to learn the blessings of all the other Mosaic commandments as well. Gentile Jesus-believers have been "grafted into" the commonwealth of Israel, and thus must learn the ways of Israel, just like all the proselytes of old. The ultimate consequence of this view is that it is God's purpose that Gentile Jesus-believers are to undergo, not only the proselyte *mikveh* ("baptism") but, if they are males, also circumcision (see §9.4.1). This is the view, for instance, of Andrew Gabriel Roth of the *Aramaic English New Testament* and of Messianic Jewess Carmen Welker,[42] and others.

There is definitely a certain consistency in this position, which is lacking in several intermediate positions (see below). Yet, I cannot accept it, as I will explain in §9.4.1.

2.2 The Distinction View: Gentile Jesus-believers are to keep the "Torah of the Messiah," which is not identical with the Mosaic Torah, or at least not identical with the ceremonial, civil, and judicial parts of it. Matters like circumcision, *kashrut*, Shabbat, and the Jewish festivals define the Jewish identity of both Messianic and non-Messianic Jews; Gentile Jesus-believers have nothing to do with these matters. It is unnatural for them to follow the ways of Israel. What binds together Messianic Jews and Gentile Jesus-believers are the patriarchal promises, the one redemptive work of Jesus, the one faith in him, the common bond of belonging to the Ekklesia, the one Body of the Messiah. But for the rest, Messianic Jews and Gentile Jesus-believers pursue different paths. Those Gentile believers who insist on becoming part of a Messianic Jewish congregation, because they feel specifically called to do so, may be received after having been proselytized. But I know of Messianic Jewish congregations that are very reluctant to do so, or even do not allow Gentile Jesus-believers to attend their meetings.

---

42. Roth (2012); Welker (2013).

Jewish and Gentile Jesus-Believers

My main counter-arguments are briefly the following:

(a) This view can hardly serve to realize the "unity of the Spirit" within the Ekklesia (Eph. 4:3); on the contrary, it is virtually re-erecting the "dividing wall of hostility" (2:14).

(b) The New Testament features many local congregations including as members both Messianic Jews and Gentile Jesus-believers. This may at times have been difficult, but the believers found ways to meet and function together (see Gal. 2:11-16).

(c) Due to so many persecutions in the past, emotional arguments of Messianic Jews with regard to Gentile Jesus-believers and to practical contacts with them must be taken very seriously — but ultimately these arguments should not determine the attitude of Messianic Jews within the Ekklesia, the Messianic community.

2.3 *The Intermediate View:* Each of the previous views is rather extreme (which in itself does not prove them wrong, for that matter; "extreme" is always a relative judgment). Several authors have therefore suggested a middle path. The New Testament supplies no proven requirement that Gentile Jesus-believers are obliged to submit to circumcision, *kashrut*, Shabbat, and the Jewish festivals, but neither does it supply an exemption whereby they have absolutely nothing to do with these matters. The New Testament is strongly preoccupied with heretics preaching these matters as a necessary way of salvation, for legalistic, ethnocentric, ascetic, or Gnostic reasons. But it hardly touches upon the question as to how particularly the Shabbat and the Jewish festivals could function, not as a condition of salvation for Gentile Jesus-believers, but as a practical blessing to them.

In this view, Gentile Jesus-believers are warmly invited to "take hold" of the Jew by the *tzitzit* ("fringe") of his clothes to come along with him (Zech. 8:23).[43] Traveling this path is not

---

43. Cf. the title of Berkowitz, *Take Hold: Embracing Our Divine Inheri-*

considered mandatory for Gentile Jesus-believers but rather a potential blessing for them. The Jewish Torah-scholar Resh Lakish has argued that, if ten men are grabbing one fringe, and there are four fringes on every Jew, and traditionally (based on Gen. 10) there are seventy nations, we then have 10 x 4 x 70 = 2,800 men accompanying one godly Jew.[44] A thousand godly Jews could thus attract almost three million Gentiles!

The "take hold" argument goes something like this: non-Messianic Jews have the "shadows" (pictures) but not their fulfillment in the Messiah, and Gentile Jesus-believers have the fulfillment but not the pictures. Messianic Jews have both the pictures and their fulfillment. Gentile Jesus-believers may argue that they do not need the pictures, and to some extent this may be true. But did not Jesus himself still give them baptism, the Lord's Supper, and anointing with oil as beautiful and helpful pictures? Many Gentile Jesus-believers have forgotten all about the Jewish roots of these sacraments. Why should they receive baptism, and not at the same time become interested in the other forms of Jewish *mikveh*? Why should they receive the Lord's Supper, and not become interested in the full *Pesach Seder*, of which the Lord's Supper was just a part? Why should they receive the anointing with oil, and not become interested in Jewish customs in this matter, from which present-day church customs were derived?

True, Gentile Jesus-believers are never commanded to be concerned in this manner with Jewish practices, but neither are they ever prohibited from such interest. What is mandatory for Messianic Jews, and is a great blessing to them, could, without ever becoming mandatory, become a great blessing for Gentile Jesus-believers as well. If "there remains a Shabbat rest for the people of God" (Heb. 4:9), there cannot be anything against the weekly enjoyment of the picture of that Mil-

---

tance with Israel (1999). This book is an excellent presentation of the intermediate view; also cf. Berkowitz (2011).

44. Talmud, Shabbat 32b (see the Soncino edition note).

lennial rest by keeping Shabbat. If believers can never have sufficient reminders of the atoning work of Jesus, why not enjoy the annual blessing of observing *Yom Kippur*? If many Gentile Jesus-believers love to celebrate Pentecost because they love to remember the outpouring of the Holy Spirit, why not celebrate it in the prescribed biblical way—that is, by observing *Shavu'ot*? And so on.

To a certain extent, I can sympathize with this intermediate view. I see some problems with it, however.

(a) Again, one would like to find the slightest indication in the New Testament that this is indeed a commendable path for Gentile Jesus-believers to take. Acts 15:21 will not suffice, because this verse has many plausible interpretations, as we have seen.

(b) Even though I admit that the New Testament does not point to it as a non-commendable path—except, of course, if one seeks to earn points for heaven through it—I wonder if Scripture supplies the refined distinction between mandatory and commendable. What things, under the Messianic Torah, are commendable but not mandatory? Is not what the Master "recommends" to the *talmid* (disciple) an absolute command for him? "Your wish is my command," says the German proverb.[45] But this renders the objection to the problem identified above as (a) all the more urgent.

(c) If the Lord gave us baptism, the Lord's Supper, and the anointing of the sick, why could he not also have explicitly given us so much more: *kashrut*, Shabbat, the Jewish festivals? It is incorrect to suggest that baptism, the Lord's Supper, and anointing the sick were new institutions, and *kashrut*, Shabbat, and the Jewish festivals were not. Baptism and the Lord's Supper were the ancient *mikveh* and *Pesach* in a new, Messianic form, just as the Lord could have given us *kashrut*, Shabbat, and the Jewish festivals in a new, Messianic form. But he didn't, and the apostles didn't either.

---

45. Dein Wunsch ist mir Befehl.

(d) To what extent do we still need the pictures, given the fact that since Acts 2, the Holy Spirit dwells in believers in a new and special way? What can the pictures add to the way in which the Holy Spirit introduces us to their spiritual significance?

(e) Is it at all possible for Gentile Jesus-believers to begin following Jewish ways without a sense of sensationality, or even traces of legalism? As I said earlier (see §9.3.1 above): what comes so naturally for Messianic Jews is so unnatural for Gentile Jesus-believers. Can we ever trust their deepest motives if they begin to indulge in what some have denigratingly called "pro-" or "philo-semitism"?

Yet, that is not all, for I admit:

(a) The pictures are still beautiful and helpful, and may be a blessing, not only for Messianic Jews but also for Gentile Jesus-believers, *as long as their motives are pure.*

(b) The New Testament might not recommend the ways of Israel to Gentile Jesus-believers, but it does not forbid them either, *as long as these Jesus-believers' motives are pure.* How could something that is a blessing to Messianic Jews be wrong, and thus be a non-blessing for Gentile Jesus-believers?

(c) If we have received Messianic rituals like baptism, the Lord's Supper, and anointing the sick, which were explicitly derived from Jewish rites, I can see no *a priori* reason why Gentile Jesus-believers could not at least profit from other appropriate Messianic Jewish ceremonies, *as long as their motives are pure.* One should be careful in arguing that what is not explicitly prohibited in Scripture is permitted—but one should be equally careful in arguing that what is not explicitly permitted in Scripture is prohibited.

9.4   Concluding Considerations

9.4.1   Once More: Circumcision

Let me conclude, by way of summary, by mentioning once more a subject that brings together many subjects we have

Jewish and Gentile Jesus-Believers

been discussing. It involves the subject of circumcision (the ritual cutting away of the foreskin). Quite amazingly, there are Messianic Jews who are of the opinion that *all male Gentile Jesus-believers are to be circumcised*. In §9.3.3 I gave some examples of such Jews. In addition, some Gentile Jesus-believers have adopted this very view, and have begun to proclaim it, sowing great confusion among believers. The arguments of these people are simple—and simply wrong. They are basically two:

(1) *The first argument:* Every Gentile Jesus-believer has been grafted into Israel. It is impossible for any male to be part of the commonwealth of Israel without having been circumcised. Take, for instance, Exodus 12:48, "If a stranger shall sojourn with you and would keep the Passover to the LORD, let all his males be circumcised.... But no uncircumcised person shall eat of it." That is, for a male believer it is impossible to take part in *Pesach*, or in its New Testament counterpart, the Lord's Supper, without having been circumcised in the flesh.

My reply to this argument is that *nowhere in Scripture is it claimed that Gentile Jesus-believers have become part of Israel* (see Appendix I, on the olive tree in Rom. 11). On the contrary, Paul keeps distinguishing between Israel and the Ekklesia as two different entities (1 Cor. 10:32, "Jews ... Gentiles [lit., Greeks] ... the church of God"; Gal. 6:16, "as for all who walk by this rule, peace and mercy be upon them, *and* upon the Israel of God" [italics added]). Even during the Millennial Kingdom, Israel and the nations remain distinct. In other words, Gentile Jesus-believers have *not* become proselytes of Israel, in any sense of the word.

(2) *The second argument:* Jesus told his followers, both Jewish and Gentile, that they were supposed to keep his "commandments" (John 14:15, 21; 15:10-17; cf. 2 Pet. 3:2). Jesus was sent by God; his commandments cannot be different from God's commandments—which are eternal—and God's commandments are none other than the Mosaic Torah. Thus,

Jesus implicitly told his disciples to obey the Mosaic Torah. If Gentile Jesus-believers have become "sons of Abraham" (Gal. 3:7), then they have come under the command of Genesis 17:10–14: *all* Abraham's descendants had to be circumcised, as well as the foreigners within his household.

My reply to this argument is that it does not distinguish properly between the Mosaic Torah and the Messianic Torah. The differences are conspicuous (see §5.2.1 above): they involve different ceremonies, different views on "holy days," a different "holy land," different promised blessings, a different sanctuary, a different sacrificial ministry, and a different priesthood. At least a number of the New Testament commandments cannot possibly be viewed as an addition to Mosaic commandments because they differ in an essential way. Many literal Mosaic commandments have received a figurative-moral application (see Appendix 4, category 2.2.3): the death penalty has been replaced by excommunication, physical battles have been replaced by spiritual battles, and physical circumcision has, in the case of Gentile believers, been replaced by the spiritual circumcision of the heart (see below). How could Paul speak of "a circumcision made without hands" (Col. 2:11) if the Colossian believers actually had been circumcised "with hands"?

In this book, I have shown in what way this type of argument *cannot* be answered, namely, by asserting that both the Mosaic Torah and physical circumcision have been abolished. Neither of them has been abolished; they remain fully in force—for Israel. Gentile Jesus-believers never were under the Mosaic Torah, and never will be; they are under the Messianic Torah, just as, in the Messianic Kingdom, they will be under the Millennial Torah. Messianic Jews have every right, if not duty, to circumcise their little sons. Gentile Jesus-believers have this right too,[46] *but not the duty*. A male Gentile

---

46. Coptic, Ethiopian, and Eritrean Orthodox Christians, the Nomiya Christians in Kenya, and some other African denominations, require

Jesus-believer has a circumcised heart, but not necessarily a circumcised male organ. There is not the slightest New Testament evidence that he should.

To further corroborate this view, let us briefly look at a few key passages.

(1) It is amazing that anyone can find some room in Acts 15 for the *mandatory* circumcision of Gentile Jesus-believers, when the whole purpose of the chapter was to *combat* those who asserted that it was "necessary to circumcise them [i.e., male Gentile believers] and to order them to keep the Torah of Moses" (v. 5). Gentile believers were told that they had to abstain only from "things polluted by idols, and from sexual immorality, and from what has been strangled, and from blood" (vv. 20, 29; 21:25). That is, circumcision (and *kashrut*, etc.) was *not* imposed on them. The legalistic party said, "They have to be circumcised"; the apostles replied, "No, they have to abstain only from the four things mentioned," and circumcision was not one of them. (The difficult verse 21 can be interpreted in many different ways [see §5.2.3 above], so that it is hardly possible to draw far-reaching conclusions from it; cf. §8.3.3 above.)

(2) In Acts 16, we read that the apostle Paul took Timothy, the son of a Jewish mother, and "circumcised him because of the Jews who were in those places, for they all knew that his father was a Greek" (v. 3). Everybody understands this: According to the rabbis, Timothy was a Jew (though he had a Gentile father), and thus had to be circumcised. However, what purpose would have been served by mentioning this fact if *all* the newly converted Jesus-believers—Jews and Gentiles—were circumcised anyway? The answer is that, apparently, Gentile Jesus-believers were *not* circumcised; and the fact that Timothy *was* circumcised was only "because of the Jews," that is, in order not to offend them.

(3) Paul told the Roman believers: "[N]o one is a Jew who

---

circumcision for membership.

is merely one outwardly, nor is circumcision outward and physical. But a Jew is one inwardly, and circumcision is a matter of the heart, by the Spirit, not by the letter. His praise is not from man but from God" (Rom. 2:28-29). Astonishingly, some people read this as if every person having a "circumcised heart" is a Jew. However, the text does not say so;[47] this understanding would not even fit the context. Paul is referring here to the difference between a true Jew and a false Jew. Both are circumcised in the flesh, but the former is also circumcised in his heart (cf. Lev. 26:41; Deut. 10:16; 30:6; Jer. 4:4; 9:25-26; Ezek. 44:7; Acts 7:51). Paul does not make any statement here about non-Jews.

(4) Paul told the Corinthian believers: "Was anyone at the time of his call already circumcised? Let him not seek to remove the marks of circumcision. Was anyone at the time of his call uncircumcised? Let him not seek circumcision. For neither circumcision counts for anything nor uncircumcision, but keeping the commandments of God" (1 Cor. 7:18-19). What could be clearer than this? Paul is arguing time and again that Gentile Jesus-believers are not to join Judaism, whether Messianic or not.[48] There is nothing in this chapter, or in the rest of this Letter, to relativize this statement by Paul. He is simply saying: if you were uncircumcised when you came to Jesus, stay that way; there is no obligation for you to be physically circumcised. I therefore read verse 19 this way: It does not really matter whether you are circumcised or not (if you are a circumcised Jew—fine; if you are an uncircumcised Gentile—fine); the thing that really matters is whether you walk in obedience to the Messianic Torah. Part of this is

---

47. This logical error is called the fallacy of the undistributed middle, like arguing: a sheep is a mammal; a cow is a mammal; therefore, a cow is a sheep (a true Jew has a circumcised heart; a true Gentile believer has a circumcised heart; therefore, a true Gentile believer is a true Jew).

48. Stern (1999, 456).

having a circumcised *heart*, as well as *ears* (Jer. 6:10; Acts 7:51) and *lips* (Exod. 6:12, 30).

(5) Paul told the Galatian believers: "[E]ven Titus, who was with me, was not forced to be circumcised, though he was a Greek" (Gal. 2:3); that is, the Messianic leaders in Jerusalem did not urge Gentile believers to have themselves baptized. Paul referred to those who thought otherwise as the "circumcision party" (2:12; lit., "those of the circumcision"). He taught, "[I]f you accept circumcision, Christ will be of no advantage to you. I testify again to every man who accepts circumcision that he is obligated to keep the whole Torah. You are severed from Christ, you who would be justified by the Torah; you have fallen away from grace. For through the Spirit, by faith, we ourselves eagerly wait for the hope of righteousness. For in Christ Jesus neither circumcision nor uncircumcision counts for anything, but only faith working through love" (5:2–6). It is a distortion of Paul's argument, and of the entire message of this Letter, to conclude from this that, *as long as you do not want to be justified by the Torah*, it is okay for you to be circumcised and place yourself under the whole Mosaic Torah, or that you are even *obliged* to do that. In verse 11 Paul flatly *denies* that he "still preach[es] circumcision," that is, the obligation of male Gentile Jesus-believers to be circumcised, *for whatever reason*. Twice Paul says here what he says in 1 Corinthians 7:19: "[I]n Christ Jesus neither circumcision nor uncircumcision counts for anything" (Gal. 5:6); "neither circumcision counts for anything, nor uncircumcision, but a new creation" (6:15). Nowhere does Paul give the slightest hint that Gentile believers should actually be circumcised; on the contrary, in his view, what has value is not the circumcision of the flesh (except for Messianic Jews, of course), but only the circumcision of the heart.

(6) Paul told the Philippian believers: "Look out for the dogs [i.e., heretics], look out for the evildoers, look out for those who mutilate the flesh. For we are the circumcision, who worship by the Spirit of God and glory in Christ Jesus and put

no confidence in the flesh" (Phil. 3:2–3). Paul uses a word play here, which does not come to light easily in the English translation. The KJV tries to maintain the word play: "[B]eware of the *concision* [Greek *katatomē*, "cutting down"]. For we are the *circumcision* [Greek *peritomē*, "cutting around"]." Paul warned against the Judaizers, whom he called "dogs" and "evildoers"; they taught that no salvation was possible without circumcision. Their "circumcision," says Paul, is nothing but a mutilation of the flesh, whereas *we*, the true Jesus-believers (Jew or Gentile) have received the true "circumcision," not one in the flesh but one of the heart.[49]

(7) Paul told the Colossian believers: "In him [i.e., Messiah] also you were circumcised with a circumcision made without hands, by putting off the body of the flesh, by the circumcision of Christ, having been buried with him in baptism, in which you were also raised with him through faith in the powerful working of God, who raised him from the dead. And you, who were dead in your trespasses and the uncircumcision of your flesh, God made alive together with him, having forgiven us all our trespasses" (Col. 2:11–13). Please note carefully the gist of Paul's argument to these Gentile Jesus-believers: Before your conversion you were uncircumcised in the flesh. After your conversion, you did *not* receive circumcision in the flesh, "made with hands." No, you received *only* the circumcision of your hearts, *"made without hands."* In the words of Stern: "Sha'ul [i.e., Paul] explains that this spiritual circumcision consisted in the Messiah's **stripping away** not the literal foreskin but what it stands for, **the old nature's control over the body**. Verse 13a makes the metaphor explicit by equating **'foreskin'** with a person's **sins** and his **old nature**."[50]

In summary: it is very sad that for centuries, the Gentile church—including even some "Hebrew Christians"—has forced believing Jews to abandon their Jewish identity and

---

49. Cf. Stern (1999, 598–600).
50. Stern (1999, 608).

assume a Gentile identity, in that they abjured their circumcision, Shabbat, *kashrut*, etc. Today, we meet the opposite: Jewish Jesus-believers — and even some Gentile Jesus-believers — forcing believing Gentiles to abandon their Gentile identity and assume a Jewish identity, including not only Shabbat, *kashrut*, etc., but even circumcision. I do not know what is worse: forcing Jews to become Gentiles, or Gentiles to become Jews. *The New Testament never does either*. Jews remain Jews, and Gentiles remain Gentiles, even though Jesus-believing Jews and Jesus-believing Gentiles have become one in Jesus Messiah, and have been brought together into one Ekklesia. But that does not make them identical, just as men and women, slaves and free, do not become identical in Jesus. They are *one* in Jesus, not the same.

9.4.2 Epilogue

Messianic Jews may, and should, express the continuity between the Old Covenant and the New Covenant by keeping Shabbat and the festivals, circumcision and the purification laws. But most Gentile Jesus-believers do not do so, and I do not believe they should — although I believe they could. Gentile Jesus-believers, as well as Messianic Jews for that matter, are under the more than one thousand commandments of the New Testament. They are under the Messianic Torah. Among all the immanent manifestations of the one, eternal Torah there is none greater than this one: the Messianic Torah. Gentile Jesus-believers have no reason to be jealous of circumcision, *kashrut*, Shabbat, and the Jewish festivals, and the many other Mosaic (ceremonial and civil) *torot*. They, as well as Messianic Jews for that matter, have the best Torah possible. Nothing will ever surpass being a *talmid* of Jesus Messiah on earth in the "present age" (*'olam hazzeh*), and share his heavenly bliss during the "age to come" (*'olam habba*) in the Messianic Kingdom.

"Truly, I say to you, among those born of women there has arisen no one greater than John the Baptist. Yet the one who is least in the kingdom of heaven is greater than he. From the days of John the Baptist until now the kingdom of heaven has suffered violence [or, has been coming violently], and the violent take it by force. For all the Prophets and the Law prophesied until John" (Matt. 11:11-13). The Tanakh (Torah and Prophets) pointed forward to John the Baptist as the greatest of all the prophets (Isa. 40:3; Mal. 3:1; Matt. 11:10; Mark 1:1-3; Luke 16:16). But now that the Messiah himself has arrived, even the least disciple in God's Kingdom is greater than the great John. So great is belonging to the Messianic community of the present age! It is great that the Torah pointed to John; it is greater that John pointed to Jesus. It is the greatest to belong to Jesus.

"[B]lessed are your eyes, for they see, and your ears, for they hear. For truly, I say to you, many prophets and righteous people [*tzaddiqim*] longed to see what you see, and did not see it, and to hear what you hear, and did not hear it" (Matt. 13:16-17; cf. Luke 10:23-24). What his followers saw was Jesus in the glory of his person and of his actions. What they heard was his word, his commandments, his instruction, his Torah, and more than that: Jesus himself. The rabbis speculated about the Messianic Torah—that is, about the way the Messiah would alter the Mosaic Torah—and the prophets and *tzaddiqim* longed to hear the Messianic Torah. Today, even the simplest *talmid* of Jesus knows him and his Torah: "Whoever has my commandments [*mitzvot*] and keeps them, he it is who loves me. And he who loves me will be loved by my Father, and I will love him and manifest myself to him. . . . If anyone loves me, he will keep my word [*logos*, Heb. *torah*], and my Father will love him, and we will come to him and make our home with him" (John 14:21, 23). Today, God's *Shekinah* does not dwell in the dark, behind a closed veil, but makes its home with even two or three of the simplest *talmidim* studying and observing his Torah.

For the time being, even the greatest non-Messianic Jew is without a Davidic king, without a temple, without a sacrifice, and without the *Shekinah* (cf. Hos. 3:4; Rom. 9:4-5). Literally, at the moment such a Jew is outside the sphere of covenantal blessings because these blessings are sustained only by a truly acceptable sacrificial ministry. No matter how painful it may be, in a sense he is even without Torah, for two reasons. First, the Mosaic Torah has given way to the Messianic Torah. Second, he who does not have the Messiah, who is the essence of the Torah, does not really possess the Torah but only an empty shell. At the moment, the non-Messianic Jew is outside the sphere of the promises made to the patriarchs because, though these promises are irrevocable with respect to Israel (Rom. 11:29), they can be received and enjoyed only in the spirit of repentance (Deut. 30:1-10; Ezek. 36:24-32), above all, repentance with regard to their rejected Messiah (Zech. 12:10-14).

For the time being, even the greatest non-Messianic Jew is still far from these things. But the least *talmid* of the Messiah, even if he is of the least Gentile descent, has it all: the Davidic King sitting at the right hand of God, the Temple of God (in the present day, that is the Ekklesia), the true sacrifice of the Messiah offered to God at Golgotha, the *Shekinah* (the glory of God as presented to us in Jesus Messiah), the adoption as sons of God, the promises made to the patriarchs, the blessings of the New Covenant, and the Messianic manifestation of the Torah. Godly non-Messianic Jews are looking forward to the New Covenant that will be made with *Jews*—but the least *talmid* of the Messiah enjoys its blessings already today, even if he is a poor Gentile. Godly non-Messianic Jews are wondering about the new Torah of the Messiah—but the least *talmid* of the Messiah already knows this Torah, even if he is a poor Gentile. Blessed is he, Jew or Gentile, who knows the Messianic Torah, and above all, knows the Messiah himself!

Let me quote a post-Holocaust *non*-Messianic Jewish scholar, the English sociologist Ferdynand Zweig, who spent five years in Israel and, like so many Israelis, developed a tremendous interest in Jesus of Nazareth. He wrote in 1969: "The

THE ETERNAL TORAH: LIVING UNDER GOD

Jewish religion seems to be at present to the large mass of Israeli Jews uninspiring and uninspired. Could it be that Jesus could give it a new lease of life? Could a new, Israeli stage of Jewish religion escape from the Ghetto wall made up of 613 bricks, and instead *incorporate the personality and message of Jesus*, the Jew from Nazareth, as a major prophet for Israel, *of course excluding all Christianized stylization of Jesus as Christ*? These are perhaps the most exciting, the most portentious questions, most pregnant with potentialities, affecting not only the people of Israel, but also those of the world at large."[51] These seem to me to be prophetic words; they are a direct call, as it were, to replace the Mosaic Torah with the Messianic Torah, in Israel and around the world.

At the same time, the inherent weakness of these words is obvious: the presentation of "Jesus as Christ," that is, as Israel's Messiah, is not just a matter of "Christianized stylization" but of the way the New Testament portrays him. No wonder the Lithuanian-Canadian theologian Jacob Jocz, a Messianic Jew, responded to Zweig's article with these words: "To a Jewish believer in Jesus as Savior and Lord, Zweig's concern strikes a deep and sympathetic cord. However, his emphasis upon the 'message' reveals the typical naïve Jewish optimism, which can have no place after the Holocaust. . . . The path to the new life Zweig is seeking for his people is the one that leads through the atoning death and resurrection of Jesus. Here lies the secret of power on the part of the Man of Nazareth."[52]

---

51. See the essay quoted in Kac (1986, 68; italics added).
52. See the essay quoted in ibid., 152.

Appendix I
Is the Church "Spiritual Israel"?

1) Romans 11

In every discussion about the place of the Torah, the Tanakh and the New Covenant, and the position of Jewish and Gentile Jesus-believers with respect to them, the matter of the olive tree in Romans 11:16-24 arises. This passage seems to be a proof text for the view that believers from the Gentiles have been incorporated, or to use Paul's language, "grafted" into Israel. Covenant theologians use this as evidence that the New Testament considers the Ekklesia to be the true, spiritual Israel, the "Israel of God" (replacement theology or supersessionism; cf. Gal. 6:16).[1] Please note: in this view, the Ekklesia is some kind of "Israel" *without* anything specifically Israelite: without Shabbat, festivals, circumcision, *kashrut*. It is a *Gentile* "Israel," which has little or nothing to do with the biblical Israel. This peculiar idea proceeded from a double mistake. First, the mistake was to think that the Jewish festivals, physical circumcision, and *kashrut* had been *abolished* and that Shabbat had shifted to Sunday. Nothing could be further from the truth. Second, the mistake was to think that

---

1. See Fruchtenbaum (1992, 94–97, 198–201, 290–95) for a discussion of this view; see also Stern (1999, 572–76) for different views on Gal. 6:16; also see §3 of this Appendix.

THE ETERNAL TORAH: LIVING UNDER GOD

the Ekklesia is some kind of "spiritual Israel."

Some Messianic Jews use this interpretation of Romans 11 for the opposite purpose, namely, for judaizing the Gentile believers. They believe the metaphor of the olive tree shows that Gentile Jesus-believers now belong to the "commonwealth of Israel," as Messianic Jew David Stern put it,[2] which subsequently can be used as an argument for inviting Gentile Jesus-believers to keep the entire Mosaic Torah.[3] Messianic Jew Dan Juster used similar words: "The Church is grafted into the true ancient people of God: Israel."[4] Messianic Jew Joseph Shulam wrote, "The root and its (original) branches are Israel."[5] The Messianic Jewish Berkowitz couple said the same: Jesus-believing Gentiles "have now been brought near and 'grafted in' to Israel . . . grafted into the olive tree of Israel"; they "became *fellow heirs* with Israel"; they "have become honorary, grafted-in, citizens with Israel."[6] Messianic Jewess Carmen Welker wrote, "*believing Gentiles who are grafted into the Olive Tree (Israel) automatically become part of Israel!*"[7]

I suppose, though, that I do understand what Stern, Shulam, Juster, the Berkowitzes, and Welker are really trying to say. It would seem logical to infer that if the Gentile Jesus-believers have been grafted into Israel, the Ekklesia has become Israel in some way, some kind of "spiritual Israel," though not in the sense of replacement theology, such that ethnic Israel does not play any specific role anymore in the plan of God. The authors mentioned maintain the conviction that ethnic Israel remains pivotal in God's counsel. However, both Juster

---

2. Stern (1997, 32, 49–52; 1999, 413–17); the reference is to Eph. 2:12. He often claims that the olive tree is Israel (1999, 13, 412–17, 471, 576, 582, 688, 803).
3. Berkowitz (2011, 71–72, 132–34).
4. Juster (1995, 35; cf. vii).
5. Shulam (1998, 374).
6. Berkowitz (1999, 104, 111, 120).
7. Welker (2013, 22, italics original).

and Stern deny, and I think rightly so, that Jesus-believing Jews are ever called "spiritual Jews" or "spiritual Israel," in these or similar terms. Both argue that Romans 2:28-29 ("a man is a Jew if . . . ") and Galatians 6:16 ("the Israel of God") literally refer only to people of Jewish descent (see §3 in this Appendix).[8] Likewise, the Berkowitzes say that "being grafted into Israel does not mean that the gentiles have become Jewish. Jewishness is a term which is both a cultural and a genealogical title reserved only for the physical family of Abraham, Isaac, and Jacob"; and, "Being part of the Remnant of Israel does not make a gentile into a Jewish person. Likewise, adopting Jewish cultural habits and/or customs is not what being fellow-citizens with Israel means."[9]

Rightly so! Even Messianic Jews who believe that having been grafted into the olive tree implies that Gentile believers, too, ought to submit to *kashrut* and even circumcision would hesitate to say that Gentile believers have become Jews. One interesting consequence would be that the hundreds of millions of Gentile believers, too, would have to attempt to make *aliyah* (immigrate to Israel as Jews)! Carmen Welker identifies the olive tree with Israel, but hastens to add, "That doesn't mean they [i.e., Gentile Jesus-believers] become 'Hebrews' or 'Jews' — but it does mean they are in royal company and complete God's Family!"[10] Similarly, the Berkowitzes say, "gentiles . . . 'grafted in' to the olive tree of Israel . . . does not mean that gentile believers are now Jews."[11]

Although, as I quoted, when all six Messianic Jewish authors say that Gentile Jesus-believers have been grafted into "Israel," they actually appear to mean: grafted into the sphere of spiritual patriarchal blessings of Israel.[12] These authors also

---

8. Juster (1995, 104–105); Stern (1999, 336–40, 571–76).
9. Berkowitz (1999, 107, 121; cf. 185; 2011, 33–34).
10. Welker (2013, 22).
11. Berkowitz (2011, 72).
12. Shulam (1998, 363, 370, 387) notes that Heb. *barakh* means both "to

use the term "commonwealth of Israel" (see Eph. 2:12). Thus the Berkowitzes say that Gentile believers "have been made part of the commonwealth of the children of Israel," although they prefer the term "citizenship" to "commonwealth";[13] "non-Jewish people . . . have now been brought near and 'grafted in' to Israel."[14] What they want to say is not that Gentile Jesus-believers have become part of ethnic Israel, but that Gentile Jesus-believers find themselves on the same spiritual footing as the "Israel of God" (cf. the terminology of Welker just quoted). In fact, in my view, the Berkowitzes come to a rather precise and correct conclusion: "Jewish and gentile believers are united together in one body — the Body of Messiah. . . . The inclusion of the gentiles together with the Jews as participants in the covenants of promise . . . now, because of the blood of Messiah, we are all one family . . . [Gentile believers] who have been grafted into the holy community."[15] Likewise, Wilson asserted that Gentile Jesus-believers had been "grafted into Israel,"[16] but later in his argument, "Israel" turns out to mean "that mysterious remnant which walked in loving obedience with the living God" and "the family of God," and "the believing family of Abraham."[17]

The Berkowitzes draw certain conclusions from this as to how Gentile believers now may participate in the observance of the Mosaic Torah, that is, "worship, dress, think, do business, and live in the manner described by the Torah (as did the ancient holy community) and simply let the Brit Hadasha [New Testament] be its God-inspired interpreter."[18] That is fine if they are referring to the Messianic Torah. Gentile Je-

---

bless" and "to graft" (see Yevamot 63a).
13. Berkowitz (1999, 107, 111, 120).
14. Berkowitz (2011, 71).
15. Berkowitz (1999, 127; cf. 181).
16. Wilson (1989, 14).
17. Wilson (1989, 15, 89).
18. Berkowitz (1999, 130).

sus-believers are never obligated to practice circumcision (on the contrary, see 1 Cor. 7:18), observe Shabbat, the Jewish festivals (on the contrary, see Col. 2:16–17), *kashrut*, and the like, that is, maintain the very elements in which the Mosaic Torah and the Messianic Torah differ.[19] Messianic Jews are under both the Mosaic Torah and the Messianic Torah—which are substantially identical anyway—whereas Gentile believers are under only the Messianic Torah.

To say the least, it is inaccurate to claim that the olive tree represents Israel. It is not the *tree* that represents Israel here, but the "natural branches" (vv. 21, 24)—not the stem and the roots. In a similar way, Jesus is the vine, and believers are the branches (John 15:1–6). Every Jew is a "natural branch." The branches that were broken off are the non-Messianic Jews. Should this be taken to mean that Jews were broken off from *Israel*? That would be absurd! Paul never says that non-Messianic Jews are no longer Israelites (on the contrary, cf. Rom. 9:4, 31; 10:1; 11:1, 7, 25; 1 Cor. 10:18; 2 Cor. 11:22)—just as he never says that Messianic Gentiles have become Israelites. If it is impossible to say that the "natural branches" were broken off from Israel, the olive tree cannot be Israel.

But then what is it? Notice that before speaking of the tree Paul refers to the "root" (v. 16b). Just as the "firstfruits" precede the "whole batch" (v. 16a), the "root" seems to represent something that preceded the "branches." Therefore, many expositors assume that Paul is thinking of Abraham, the physi-

---

19. From their book, it is not entirely clear how far the Berkowitzes go when encouraging Gentile believers to embrace the Torah, but this seems to include at least the Jewish festivals, the *tzitzit*, Shabbat, *zimrot* (Jewish songs), Messianic dance, and the like (Berkowitz 1999, 258, 263, 266, 270, 277–78, 285). However, they rightly assure us that Gentile believers do not have to be circumcised, although they may be circumcised in order to fully join the Messianic Jewish community—if personally called by the Lord to do so—as long as they realize "that his act of circumcision neither earns salvation nor wins merit with God" (249).

cal father of the non-Jesus-believing circumcised, the spiritual father of the Jesus-believing uncircumcised, and the father, both physical and spiritual, of the Jesus-believing circumcised (Rom. 4:11-12).[20] In the wider sense, he may be referring to "the patriarchs," for he says, "to them [i.e., Israel] belong the patriarchs" (Rom. 9:5), and "as regards election, they [i.e., the Israelites] are beloved for the sake of their forefathers" (11:28). From this, it naturally follows that the olive tree represents God's entire polity of patriarchal promises and blessings, from the Abrahamic covenant to the New Covenant. In the Tanakh, he granted these blessings to Israel but in the patriarchs he also promised them to the Gentiles (Gen. 12:3; 18:18; 22:18; 28:14). Of special interest in this context are Jewish sources in which Abraham and the patriarchs are called a root.[21]

Messianic Jews who, in my opinion, have understood this well are Arnold Fruchtenbaum and H. L. Ellison. The former interprets the olive tree as "the place of blessing rooted in the Abrahamic Covenant rather than being Israel as such." It is "the place of blessing as contained in the Jewish covenant."[22] Ellison expresses himself with more reserve: "What is the olive tree? Is it Israel? Paul does not say so, nor does he ever suggest elsewhere in the Letter that Gentiles can be grafted into Israel. Is it the Church? Paul does not say so, and he seems deliberately to refrain from using that term for the people of God in earlier ages.... The olive tree is in fact neither the official Church nor official Synagogue, but the body of those in whom the grace of Christ has been truly operative. If we place Israel and the Church side by side, we find that they do not merge, except as individuals experience the Messiah,

---

20. Cf. Murray (1968, 85); Moo (1996, 699).
21. E.g., 1 Enoch 93, 5, 8; Philo, *Heir* 279 (Abraham); Jubilees 21:24 (Isaac) (cf. Moo 1996, 699n13).
22. Fruchtenbaum (1992, 97, 175; cf. 744).

Appendix I: Is the Church "Spiritual Israel"?

who is the root of their being."[23]

The tree's natural branches are the Israelites, who "by nature," because of their election as God's people, share in the blessings of the patriarchs' promises. However, that blessing can truly become theirs solely by trusting in Jesus as their Messiah and Savior. The great majority of the Jews are destitute of God's blessing because they have not accepted their Messiah. Therefore, God has broken them off from the tree. The branches that have been left on the tree are the Messianic Jews. Among them, branches from a wild olive tree have been grafted in. These are Gentile believers who have received a share in the promises of the fathers because they have come to believe in Messiah, in whom the promises are being fulfilled. They are "supported" (borne, carried) by the "root" (v. 18); that is, they are spiritual children and heirs of Abraham, "children of promise" (Rom. 4:11, 16; Gal. 3:7, 29; 4:28), through which they have received justification and divine life (Gal. 3:6, 11–12, 21, 24).

Very importantly, Paul implicitly indicates that one day the "natural branches" that had been broken off would "not continue in their unbelief" but would be "grafted in" again (vv. 23–24). Subsequently, he explicitly reveals that one day "all Israel will be saved" (v. 26).[24] What concerns us here is that Romans 11 does not teach that Gentile Jesus-believers are incorporated into Israel—which would imply that they have become Israelites—but rather that the Messianic Gentiles share in the same spiritual blessings as the Messianic Jews. This is due to the promises made to the patriarchs, whereas the hardened majority of Israel is destitute of these blessings as long as they persist in their unbelief. Gentile believers share in the same blessings as Jewish believers; that is something

---

23. Ellison (1976, 88–89).
24. Dunn (1998, 526–29) strangely recognizes that "all Israel" in Rom. 11:26 can mean only historical, ethnic Israel, and yet he wants to view Gentile believers as included in this "all Israel."

very different from being incorporated into Israel.

2) Ephesians 2

In this study, I have referred to Ephesians 2 several times; what verses 12 and 13 explicitly say is this:

(1) At one time, those who are now Gentile Jesus-believers were "separated from Christ," now they "who once were far off have been brought near by the blood of Messiah."

(2) Once, they were "alienated from the commonwealth [or, citizenship] of Israel and strangers to the covenants of promise," now they are "no longer strangers and aliens, but . . . fellow citizens with the saints" (v. 19), "fellow heirs, members of the same body, and partakers of the promise in Messiah Jesus through the gospel" (3:6).

(3) Once, they were "having no hope and without God in the world" (2:12), now they are "members of the household of God" (v. 19).

Notice the NIV in Ephesians 3:6: "heirs *together with Israel.*" Here we encounter the same problem as in Romans 11: "grafted into Israel" is inaccurate wording because Gentile Jesus-believers have not become Israelites. Equally inaccurate is the phrase "heirs together with Israel." The Greek text has the word *synklēronoma*, "fellow heirs" — but fellows of whom? We are members of the same body, but with whom? It is not the "body of Israel," whatever that may mean, but the Body of the Messiah, the Ekklesia, consisting of both Jewish and Gentile believers, on equal footing. Gentile Jesus-believers are fellow heirs not with Israel, but with Jesus-believing Jews, not within Israel, but within the Ekklesia.

The text nowhere says that we have become citizens of (or together with) ethnic Israel, as if the distinction between Israel and (believing) Gentiles had been abolished. According to the prophecies, even in the Millennial kingdom the distinction between Israel and the Gentiles will be maintained (e.g., Isa. 2:1-5; 60:10-12; Zech. 6:15; 8:23; 14:16-21). What then does

Appendix I: Is the Church "Spiritual Israel"?

Paul mean in Ephesians 2? In other words, who are "the two" in verse 15? They are not *the* Jews and *the* Gentiles but the *Jesus-believing* Jews and the *Jesus-believing* Gentiles, who now have become one Body. Since the resurrection of the Messiah, there is an entirely new community in this world, in which Jesus-believing Jews and Jesus-believing Gentiles have been brought together on one footing. This community is not at all called "Israel" here—or anywhere—but "one new man," "one body," "a holy temple in the Lord," a "dwelling place for God by [or, in] the Spirit" (vv. 15-22).

This community is not ethnic Israel, nor is it some "spiritual Israel" (an expression unknown in Scripture). It does not even include the Jewish people, but only Messianic Jews from Israel, who within the Ekklesia have been joined to Messianic Gentiles as equal partners. Never in the New Testament is this community called "Israel" or something like that. Paul's argument seems to proceed rather like this. At that former time, you, Gentile believers, were excluded from citizenship in Israel, but now you have been brought near, and *you have received something better than literal citizenship in ethnic Israel*. You have not become proselytes of Israel but you are now fellow heirs, fellow citizens, and fellow household members with the Messianic Jews *within a better community*. What you inherit is even better than Israel will inherit in the Messianic Kingdom. The Body of which you are now members is a greater body than ethnic Israel ever was, or ever will be. The household of God of which you are now members is the greatest household that history has ever seen. It is the Ekklesia of the living God. Of that community we are now citizens or, if one so wishes, "our citizenship is in heaven" (Phil. 3:20)—which was never said of ethnic Israel. The Gentile Jesus-believers never were citizens of ethnic Israel, and never will be. The Messianic Jews are citizens of ethnic Israel, and always will be. But spiritually, God took them *out of* unbelieving Israel (cf. Acts 2:40), just as he took the Gentile believers *out of* the unbelieving nations (15:14; Rom. 11:5). Together he turned them into something entirely new, the Ekklesia of God, plainly distinct from both the Jews and the Greeks (1 Cor. 10:32).

Paul clearly considered himself to be a Jew until the end of his life (see §5.3 above) and he had great sorrow about the unbelieving Jews, whom he called his "kinsmen according to the flesh" (Rom. 9:3). But that is precisely the point: "kinsmen according to the flesh," not according to the Spirit. The Messianic fellow believers had become his "spiritual kinsmen," whether they came from the Jews or from the Gentiles. Paul himself said, "From now on, therefore, we regard no one according to the flesh. Even though we once regarded Messiah according to the flesh, we regard him thus no longer. Therefore, if anyone is in Messiah, he is a new creation" (2 Cor. 5:16–17). This is what matters. Messianic Jews should never abandon their unbelieving "kinsmen according to the flesh"; they should always feel close kinship with them for historical covenantal reasons and in order to win them for Jesus. But for the time being, their kinship with their Gentile fellow believers is exceedingly greater. Not that Gentile believers have become citizens of Israel, nor that Jewish believers for the time being have become part of the Gentile world (or even the "Gentile church"), but Gentile as well as Jewish believers have become citizens of the entirely new "commonwealth of the Ekklesia."

Jewish and Gentile believers are "fellow heirs," *not* of the promised land but of the entire world and of a heavenly portion (Rom. 4:13–14; 8:17; Gal. 3:18, 29; 4:7; Eph. 1:3, 11, 14, 18; 2:4–6; 5:5; Col. 1:12–13; 3:24; Titus 3:7; Heb. 6:17; 9:15; James 2:5; 1 Pet. 1:4; 3:7). Jewish and Gentile believers are "fellow citizens," *not* of ethnic Israel but of the Ekklesia, the new, heavenly city of God (cf. Phil. 3:20; Rev. 21:9–11). Jewish and Gentile believers are "fellow members of the body," *not* of some body of Israel but the Body of Messiah (Eph. 1:23; 2:16; 4:4, 12, 16; 5:23, 30–32; Col. 1:18, 24–27; 2:19; 3:15). Jewish and Gentile believers are "fellow household members," *not* in the house of Israel but in the house of God, that is, the Ekklesia of the living God (Eph. 2:19–22; 1 Tim. 3:15; 1 Pet. 2:5; Heb. 3:6; 10:21). Jewish and Gentile Jesus-believers are "fellow participants of the promise," *not* only the promise given to the patriarchs but also, for example, the promise of eternal life (Titus 1:2; 1 John 2:25).

3) Other Scriptures[25]

Please note the following.

(1) The terms "Israel" and "Ekklesia" are clearly distinguished in the New Testament. The apostle Paul puts the two side by side: there are the Jews (Israel), there are the Greeks (the Gentile world), and there is the Ekklesia of God (1 Cor. 10:32). In what sense could the Ekklesia then ever be Israel? In the book of Acts, the impression is never given that, henceforth the Ekklesia is now actually (the true) Israel. On the contrary, the two remain carefully distinguished. The non-Jesus-believing Jews are considered to be erring, but they definitely are not viewed as former Jews. Conversely, Jesus-believing Gentiles are considered to be on the right track, but they are never viewed as Jews-in-a-certain-sense. Israel is Israel, and the Ekklesia is the Ekklesia. Messianic Jews are viewed as belonging to *both* communities. The Jewish Paul says, even after his conversion to Jesus, "I *am* [not *was*] an Israelite" (Rom. 11:1). But no Gentile believer is ever reported to have said, "I have now *become* an Israelite." There is only one way to become an Israelite, and that is to join Judaism through circumcision and the *mikveh*. But that is *not* God's prescribed way for the Gentile Jesus-believer.

(2) Astonishingly, the following statement of Paul has been adduced as an argument: "[N]o one is a Jew who is merely one outwardly, nor is circumcision outward and physical. But a Jew is one inwardly, and circumcision is a matter of the heart, by the Spirit, not by the letter" (Rom. 2:28–29). Against the rules of logic, this is understood to mean that Paul is claiming

---

25. See, e.g., Fung (1988, 311n67).

that every person with a circumcised heart is a Jew. The truth is that Paul does not speak of non-Jews here at all, but only of the difference between a true and a false Jew (see further in §9.4.1).

(3) Another statement of Paul is taken as a standard proof as well: "[A]s for all who walk by this rule, peace and mercy be upon them, and upon the Israel of God" (Gal. 6:16). Some think that here the Ekklesia is being referred to as the "Israel of God," but that cannot be correct. The text distinguishes between *two* groups: "all who walk by this rule" *and* "the Israel of God." The first group consists of Jesus-believing Gentiles, who must not subject themselves to the Mosaic Torah but exclusively to the "rule" belonging to the "new creation" (v. 15), that is, the Messianic Torah. The second group, the "Israel of God," either consists of Jesus-believing Jews of the present age, or the expression prophetically anticipates "all Israel" that in the end will be saved (Rom. 11:26).[26] Of course, supersessionists have tried to view *kai* ("and") as epexegetical here: "[A]ll who walk by this rule, peace and mercy be upon them, *even* the Israel of God" (cf. RSV, NIV).[27] This is a stark example of eisegesis, though, because (1) it is hard to find clear-cut examples of this epexegetical *kai* in Paul's writings, and (2) the repetition of *epi* ("upon") makes this rendering highly unlikely. Stern observes: "The consequence of this wrong interpretation [of Gal. 6:16] has been immeasurable pain for the Jews" in lending support to cessationism.[28]

(4) It is strange that Paul's speaking of an "Israel according to the flesh" (1 Cor. 10:18) is taken as evidence that there also must be an "Israel according to the Spirit."[29] Does a "fore-

---

26. *Contra* Fung (1988, 310).
27. See Boice (1976, 507).
28. Stern (1999, 574).
29. See, e.g., Findlay (1979, 857, 863) on this verse and on v. 1, "our fathers": "the phrase identifies the N.T. Church with 'Israel'." Cf. Stern (1999, 471–72).

Appendix I: Is the Church "Spiritual Israel"?

father according to the flesh" (Rom. 4:1) imply that there also must be "forefather according to the Spirit," or "masters according to the flesh" that there also must be "masters according to the Spirit" (Eph. 6:5; Col. 3:22)? Sometimes the one does imply the other. Thus, Paul refers to his "kinsmen according to the flesh" (Rom. 9:3; cf. 11:14 "my fellow Jews," i.e., literally, "my flesh"); these are non-Jesus-believing Jews. Jesus-believing Jews were, so to speak, his "kinsmen according to the Spirit," whether they were originally Jews or Gentiles. But this does not turn the latter into Jews. Gentile believers have not become citizens of Israel, but Gentile and Jewish believers have become citizens of the totally new commonwealth of the Ekklesia.

(5) Paul's statement, "[T]hey are not all Israel who are of Israel" (Rom. 9:6 KJV), has been explained as if here an *extension* of the term "Israel" is intended, in this sense: there are those who are "of [the new, true] Israel [of God]" who originally were not of (ethnic) Israel. The context makes clear, however, that precisely the opposite is intended, namely, a *restriction* of the term. There are those who are "of Israel," that is, were born of the patriarchs, yet fall outside the patriarchal blessings, like Ishmael, son of Abraham, and Esau, son of Isaac (Rom. 9:7–13). Conversely, being "Abraham's offspring" in the spiritual sense (Gal. 3:29; cf. Rom. 4:11b) does not mean one belongs to "Israel."

(6) Paul says, "Look out for . . . those who mutilate the flesh. For we are the circumcision, who worship by the Spirit of God and glory in Christ Jesus and put no confidence in the flesh" (Phil. 3:2–3). Sometimes when Paul uses the phrase "the circumcision," he means the whole of the *literally* circumcised, namely, Israel, and "the uncircumcision" refers to the Gentiles (Rom. 2:26–27; 3:30; 4:9; Gal. 2:9, 12; Eph. 2:11; Col. 4:11; Titus 1:10). However, in the verse just quoted, Paul includes in the "we" all Jesus-believers, and thus refers to the *spiritual* circumcision. Paul turns here against the Judaizers, that is, those who teach that male Gentile believers cannot be

saved unless they are circumcised (Acts 15:1; contrast: Gal. 5:2). In a derogatory way, he calls them not *peritomē* ("circumcision," here: the circumcisers) but *katatomē* ("concision" [KJV], here: the flesh-mutilators) (see further §9.4.1).

(7) Another error is the argument by Poythress. From the facts that, first, the New Covenant is made with "Israel" (Jer. 31:31; Heb. 8:8) in the "Israelite" Jesus, and that, second, Gentile Jesus-believers also come under this New Covenant, he infers that the church is "true Israel."[30] However, if A enjoys the blessings of B, this does not mean that A has *become* B. Though Gentiles share in the patriarchal blessings of Israel, this does not make them "Israel" themselves (cf. point [5] above).

(8) 1 Peter 2:9–10 has been adduced as an argument as well: "[Y]ou are a chosen race, a royal priesthood, a holy nation, a people for his own possession, that you may proclaim the excellencies of him who called you out of darkness into his marvelous light. Once you were not a people, but now you are God's people; once you had not received mercy, but now you have received mercy." Peter alludes to identity features that in the Tanakh apply to Israel (Exod. 19:6; Hos. 1:10; 2:23), and are here applied to the Ekklesia. Peter's allusion to Hosea is also found with Paul, who applied the Hosea prophecy even more explicitly to the Gentiles (Rom. 9:24–26). However, if we read the Hosea statement in its context, we will easily see that the reference there is to ethnic Israel, whom God, because of their sins, has temporarily called "Not My People" (*Lo-Ammi*). For a time, God chastised his people, but through Hosea he has promised that one day he would restore them. It would be absurd to assume that God would grant this restoration not to that same ethnic Israel, but to some "spiritual" Israel, more than 99% of which consists of Gentiles. The *principle* behind the promised restoration—those who formerly were not God's people now become precisely this—can very well be applied to Gentile believers, as Peter and Paul were doing.

---

30. Poythress (1987, 106).

Appendix I: Is the Church "Spiritual Israel"?

But that does not make these Gentiles to be "Israel." That is not what Peter and Paul were claiming at all; it is the adherents of the "spiritual Israel" notion who do that. The "people of God" under the New Covenant (cf. Titus 2:14) include the believing *remnant* of Israel (cf. 11:5) just as they include the believing *remnant* of the Gentiles. Conversely, in Romans 9:31 "Israel" is not the nation as a whole, but the unbelieving majority of the nation.

In summary:

(1) The New Testament calls the non-Jesus-believing Jews "Israel," and they continue to be called "Israel"; the name is not taken away from them, and handed over to the Ekklesia.

(2) The Jesus-believing Jews are still "Israelites"; they have not stopped being Jews. Quite the opposite. At the same time, they are a constitutive part of the Ekklesia.

(3) The Jesus-believing Gentiles are the other constitutive part of the Ekklesia; they are called "sons of Abraham," but never "Jews" or "Israelites." The idea of the Ekklesia as some kind of "spiritual Israel" is read into the New Testament by theologians whose position requires that notion.

Appendix II
The Torah in First-Century Judaism

1) Covenantal Nomism

IN THE PRESENT STUDY, I point out that the New Testament, particularly the apostle Paul, refers to the *nomos* ("law") generally in two senses, a positive and a negative sense (see particularly §§1.3.2, 4.3.1, and 4.3.2). In the positive sense, *nomos* is the Torah of God, specifically in a more spiritual-transcendent sense, of which the Sinaitic Torah was only one temporary-immanent manifestation: the Torah of love, the Messianic Torah, the Torah of God, the royal Torah, the Torah of freedom. Love, the divine *agapē*, is the sum and fulfillment of the Torah in this sense. In Jesus, this love of God has been revealed in its most perfect form. In believers, this love of God receives its form in their keeping his commandments (John 14:15, 21-24; 1 John 2:3; 5:2-3; 2 John 6), that is, the Messianic Torah.

Negatively, *nomos* refers to the legalistic or ethnocentric context in which the Torah can function. Legalism is the system demanding legalistic works through which people try to earn points for heaven, yes, even try to bring about their own salvation. Ethnocentrism is the system boasting in Israel as God's covenantal people and demanding that repentant Gentile males be circumcised in order to join God's chosen nation and thus share in its blessings.[1] Sometimes, for brevity's sake this legalistic and/or ethnocentric system as such is called *nomos*, too. In *this* sense, *and in this sense only*, the term *nomos* refers to "the ministry of death" and "of condemnation" (2 Cor. 3:7, 9), a system that "brings wrath" (Rom. 4:15), that brings a person "under a curse," *not* because there is anything wrong with the Torah as such, but because no one can keep the Torah in his own strength (Gal. 3:10).

The question we want to investigate now is what enemy Paul was fighting when he described and condemned such a system of legalism and ethnocentrism. Who were the people in those days who really believed that one could earn salvation by accomplishing works of the Torah in one's own strength? Was this indeed the general attitude toward the Torah among the Jews in the days of Jesus and the apostles? Or does the New Testament not at all suggest that this was the general picture of contemporaneous Judaism? It is noteworthy that Luther and Calvin not only viewed New Testament Judaism as a legalistic system of works-righteousness but also considered it to be identical with the Roman Catholic way of salvation in their own times.[2] For centuries, this identification became a constitutive element in Protestant theology. This view betrayed not only a strong hostility toward Roman Catholic thinking but also a certain amount of anti-Semitism.

Two works have greatly enhanced this negative attitude toward Judaism. One was by Ferdinand Weber, *Jewish Theology on the Basis of the Talmud and Related Writings*.[3] Through a very prejudicial selection of passages from rabbinic writings composed in post-New Testament times, Weber tried to confirm the stark picture of Judaism as a strict legalistic system

---

1. See §4.3.1n29, on the view represented by Dunn (1998).
2. See Thielman (1995, 18–24) for a summary of the Reformers' viewpoints.
3. Weber (1880/1897).

Appendix II: The Torah in First-Century Judaism

of works-righteousness. At the same time, Emil Schürer gave a similar, gloomy view of Judaism, in which virtually all true piety in Israel was denied.[4] These and other works corroborated and further darkened the portrait of Judaism as it had been drawn earlier by the Reformers and their followers. It seemed to be corroborated by the apostle Paul's own allegedly negative view of Judaism.

At the beginning of the twentieth century, the picture changed drastically. The first protester was the Jewish theologian Claude G. Montefiore who, in an article at the turn of the century and afterward in a full-fledged book, dismantled Weber's view.[5] He emphasized that rabbinic literature contains almost every conceivable opinion. Therefore, one could prove anything one wished from these writings. Instead, one should ask: what is the *general* opinion, what is the *prevailing* view among the rabbis? Weber depicted a caricature, Montefiore claimed; the Torah was not a legalistic burden for the Jews at all, but a benefit and a delight. It was the rabbis themselves who time and again emphasized that in true Torah-keeping, good intentions were as important as good actions, and that any Torah-trespassing, if followed by sincere repentance, would be met by God's forgiving mercy. Similar protests against Weber and Schürer came from a non-Jewish scholar who specialized in rabbinic Judaism, George Foot Moore.[6]

The effect of Montefiore's and Moore's writings was not very widespread at the time. This changed when, half a century later, E. P. Sanders published his *Paul and Palestinian Judaism*.[7] He corroborated the views of Montefiore and Moore, but did so from the perspective of New Testament scholarship. He compared Paul's view of Judaism with the picture of Judaism emerging from contemporaneous Jewish literature.

---

4. Schürer (1885–1891).
5. Montefiore (1900–01, 1914).
6. Moore (1921, 1927–30).
7. Sanders (1977; also see 1983, 1985, 1992).

Sanders called the latter picture *covenantal nomism*, that is, "the view that the covenant requires as the proper response of man his obedience to its commandments, while providing means of atonement for transgression."[8] In other words, despite its diversity, genuine Judaism is a *religion of grace*, first, because getting into a covenant is a matter of God's *electing* grace, and second, because staying in the covenant is indeed a matter of obedience, but also of God's *atoning* grace, supplying forgiveness after failure and repentance.[9] As Orthodox Jew Pinchas Lapide, a New Testament scholar, once wrote: "The rabbinate has never considered the Torah as a way of salvation to God. . . . [We Jews] regard salvation as God's exclusive prerogative, so we Jews are the advocates of 'pure grace.'"[10] He added that "all masters of the Talmud taught that salvation can be attained 'only through God's gracious love.'"

Frank Thielman said of Sanders' book: "Seldom in the history of New Testament scholarship has a single book effected such a dramatic change. . . . [M]any New Testament scholars found his conclusions about the gracious character of ancient Judaism difficult to resist."[11] However, this new conception raised the problem as to how to understand Paul's apparent presentation of Judaism as a legalistic system of works-righteousness. Following and elaborating the ideas of Moore, Sanders' own solution was that Paul's point was not at all to depreciate Judaism as such. Rather, he wished to emphasize that salvation comes only through Jesus and his sacrifice, and that *therefore* salvation by means of obedience to the Torah alone is necessarily excluded. In Galatians 2 and 3, Paul's

---

8. Sanders (1977, 75).
9. This difference between "getting in" and "staying in" also has consequences for the doctrine of justification, which we are not discussing here (for which, see Wright [1997, chapter 7: "Justification and the Church"]).
10. Quoted in Wilson (1989, 21).
11. Thielman (1995, 31).

Appendix II: The Torah in First-Century Judaism

point is not so much that Torah-keeping is impossible or that human efforts lead only to carnal arrogance, but rather that if works-righteousness were possible, Jesus Messiah died in vain.

This is corroborated by 2 Corinthians 3:9, where Paul recognizes that in the old administration of the covenant, although it was one "of condemnation," there was definitely "glory"; however, in the new administration of the covenant there is a "glory that surpasses it." In Philippians 3:6-9, Paul does not argue that Torah-righteousness — which verse 9 proves to exist in principle — is bad, but only that it became "loss" and "rubbish" the moment he found the Messiah.[12] Basically, Paul's problem with Judaism was not so much legalistic works-righteousness, but the fact that it could not bring about true salvation, which is possible only through the Messiah. Sanders summarized this in the following way: "[T]his is what Paul finds wrong in Judaism: it is not Christianity."[13] I would prefer to say: this is what Paul finds wrong in Judaism: it lacks Christ.

Since the epoch-making work by Sanders, several authors have pursued his line of thinking. They accept Sanders' assessment of first-century Judaism, but go much further in criticizing Paul's assessment of it. Among them was especially Heikki Räisänen,[14] who explicitly accused Paul of misrepresenting Judaism and cast doubt on Paul's status as a profound theologian.[15] Likewise, the well-known German Jewish scholar, Hans Joachim Schoeps, said of "the Pauline view, the Christian evaluation of the law": "Seen from a vantage point within Judaism, it is a misconception of monstrous proportions; for all Christian polemic — and especially modern Prot-

---

12. Sanders (1977, 482–85, 492–93, 505, 551; 1983, 17–27, 43–44, 137–41).
13. Sanders (1977, 552).
14. Räisänen (1983, 1986, 1992).
15. Räisänen (1983, 266–67); see the refutation by Van Spanje (1999).

estant polemic against the law—misconstrues the law of the Jews as a means of attaining justification in the sight of God (so-called 'justification by works'). . . . And all this because, after his experience on the road to Damascus, Paul was no longer able to understand what he, as a scholar, had surely known previously: that the law of the Torah was given, not to make the Jews righteous and acceptable before their Father in Heaven, but precisely because it proclaims the holy will of their Father in Heaven."[16]

2) New Testament Judaism

In contrast both to such a condemnation of Paul himself and to the presumed development in the Pauline Letters (revealing several alleged contradictions),[17] several New Testament scholars have chosen a different approach. Though accepting Sanders' more balanced view of first-century Judaism, they have undertaken to defend a more positive assessment of Paul. James D. G. Dunn, one of the most renowned representatives of the new approach, believes that Paul was not fighting Jewish legalism but Jewish ethnocentrism. That is the notion that New Testament Judaism associated Israel's being "under the Torah" with being God's chosen, covenantal people, so that penitent Gentiles who wished to share God's covenantal promises necessarily had to join Israel through circumcision.[18] This view had considerable consequences for Dunn's view of justification by faith as well; as he put it: "Justification by faith is Paul's fundamental objection to the idea that God has limited his saving goodness to a particular people."[19]

Other New Testament scholars accepting Sanders' view

---

16. Schoeps (1963); see extensively on this subject, Schoeps (1961), especially chapter 6 on Paul's view of the Torah.
17. See especially Hübner (1984).
18. Dunn (1990b, 1996, and especially 1998); see more extensively §§4.3.1 and 4.3.2.
19. Dunn, in Dunn and Suggate (1993, 28).

Appendix II: The Torah in First-Century Judaism

of first-century Judaism have undertaken to defend a more Reformational assessment of Paul. Among them are Stephen Westerholm, N. T. Wright, Thomas Schreiner, and Frank Thielman.[20] They point out that, especially since Sanders and Räisänen, "the pendulum has now swung so far the other way that scholars stand in danger of pillorying Luther and the Protestant tradition in retaliation for what they did to Judaism."[21] These authors, as well as Dunn, do not doubt that the Mosaic Torah cannot be severed from the Sinaitic covenant, which was rooted in God's electing grace demonstrated by his delivering Israel from Egypt (Exod. 20:5; Deut. 5:6). This covenant was not based upon God's demand of Torah-keeping—although Torah-keeping was important for the *maintenance* of the covenant—but on God's unconditional love (Deut. 7:6-8). The Old Covenant was a "closed system" of mercy: it began with electing mercy, and only then placed the redeemed people on the foundation of obedience, and finished with atoning mercy by dealing with their failures in obedience.

The problem with regard to Paul's view of contemporaneous Judaism is not with this "covenantal nomism" as such, but with the way it was viewed by first-century Jews. Both Jewish literature (I) and the New Testament (II) presents us with (a) Jews who fully embraced "covenantal nomism," as well as (b) Jews who had replaced it with a legalistic system of salvation through mere Torah-keeping. Let us briefly look at these four groups.[22]

(Ia) Judaism certainly was aware of the fact that "all our

---

20. Westerholm (1988); Wright (1991, 1997, 2009); Schreiner (1993); Thielman (1995); also cf. the contributions by Davies (1984, 91–122: "Paul and the Law: Reflections on Pitfalls in Interpretation"), Moo (1987, 1996 passim), Gaston (1987), Klinghardt (1988), Snodgrass (1988), Liebers (1989), Martin (1989), Swidler et al. (1990), Segal (1990), Winger (1992), Wenham (1995), Finsterbusch (1996), Thompson (2002), Yinger (2010), Kim (2011).
21. Thielman (1995, 46).
22. Ibid., 65–68.

righteous [!] deeds are like a polluted garment" (Isa. 64:6), so that a common prayer (*Avinu Malkeinu*, sung on and between *Rosh haShanah* and *Yom Kippur*) says: "Our Father, our King, hear our voice, we have sinned before you. Have compassion upon us and upon our children." Many Jews realized that salvation could only be rooted solely in the love and mercy of God, who asks for Torah-obedience but also supplies the means for restoration after Torah-breaking. Good examples are prayers of repentance and signs of confidence in God's mercy, such as in Baruch 1:15–3:8 and the apocryphal Prayer of Manasseh (cf. 2 Chron. 33:12-13), composed some time before AD 70 by a pious Jew.

(Ib) Other apocryphal passages such as Sirach 15:15-18 ("He added his commandments and precepts. If you will keep the commandments and perform acceptable fidelity forever, they shall preserve you. He has set water and fire before you: stretch out your hand to which you will. Before man is life and death, good and evil, that which he shall choose shall be given him") and the Psalms of Solomon, although not displaying any legalistic arrogance, or legalistic fear of God's judgment for that matter, do present us with the idea that salvation at least to some extent is dependent on man's willingness to do good and avoid evil, and to put this into practice.

(IIa) Over against the traditional view of New Testament Judaism, there is no doubt that "covenantal nomism" was known and practiced in New Testament times. We find several faithful Jews who did observe the Torah but realized that salvation was dependent upon God's merciful forgiveness and deliverance. Zechariah and Elizabeth were both "righteous before God, walking blamelessly in all the commandments and statutes of the Lord" (Luke 1:6; cf. vv. 74-77). Other examples were Mary (1:38, 46-55; 2:22-24, 27, 39, 41), Simeon (2:25, 29-32), Anna (vv. 36-38), Nathanael (John 1:47), and even Gentiles such as the centurion in Luke 7 ("he loves our nation, and he is the one who built us our synagogue," v. 5) and Cornelius in Acts 10 ("an upright and God-fearing

Appendix II: The Torah in First-Century Judaism

man, who is well spoken of by the whole Jewish nation," v. 22). As to the priests, the teachers of the Law, and the Pharisees, not all of them were hypocrites; some took a positive attitude to Jesus or the apostles, and some converted to Jesus (Mark 12:28-34; Luke 13:31; Acts 5:34-39; 6:7; 15:5; 23:9). The tax collector's plea, "God, be merciful to me, a sinner" (Luke 18:13), was just as authentic an utterance of contemporaneous Judaism as the Pharisee's legalistic arrogance (vv. 11-12).

(IIb) Over against Sanders, Räisänen, Dunn, and others, there is no doubt that there were legalistic Jews in New Testament times who trusted in their own works-righteousness. I just mentioned the Pharisee in Jesus' parable as an example. The reason for this parable was that there were those "who trusted in themselves that they were righteous" (Luke 18:9). Jesus' woes upon the teachers of the Torah and the Pharisees were intended to expose their hypocrisy (Matt. 23:1-36; Luke 11:37-52). In addition to hypocrisy, there was real self-deceit in that they believed themselves to be righteous and distinguished themselves from the tax collectors, the sinners and the whores (Matt. 9:10-17 and par.; 11:19 and par.; 21:31-32; Luke 7:36-50; 15:1-2; 19:7).

Paul's double presentation of the Torah was fully in line with this. On the one hand, he presented the Torah as the guideline for those who, under God's gracious covenant, wanted to serve him (Rom. 2:13; 8:4; 13:8-10; 1 Cor. 9:20-21; Gal. 5:14; 6:2; Eph. 6:2-3). On the other hand, Paul sternly rejected any system propounding the Torah as a way of gaining works-righteousness, thereby earning salvation (legalism) (Rom. 2:17-27; 3:19-31; 4:13-15; 6:14-15; 7:1-8:4; 9:30-32; 10:4; 1 Cor. 15:56; Gal. 2:16-19; 3:1), or as a system of Jewish arrogance (ethnocentrism) (Gal. 5:4, 18; Phil. 3:6, 9; 1 Tim. 1:7-10). There is no doubt that Jews holding to such a system really existed; Paul himself had been one of them (Acts 22:3-5; Gal. 1:13-14; Phil. 3:2-11). These were those who were boasting in the Torah (Rom. 3:27), whether (1) for legalistic reasons (as claimed by the Reformers, Westerholm, Thielman, etc.), or (2) for ethnocentric reasons (as claimed by Dunn).

(3) There may have been a third group, pointed out by Sanders, who did not necessarily boast in the Torah but simply kept following the way of works-righteousness instead of the sole and only gospel of salvation (Rom. 9:30-10:4). They may have done so in an earnest and humble way. However, by refusing salvation in Messiah they were left with their own works of legalistic righteousness. The point was not only that such works did not suffice—Jews who understood what Sanders calls "covenantal nomism" should and did know that—but also that they had stumbled over Jesus (9:32-33).[23]

(4) Paul recognized the existence of a fourth group: those Jews who fully realized the import of "covenantal nomism," and for this very reason had come to trust Jesus. He said, "We ourselves are Jews by birth and not Gentile sinners; yet we know that a person is not justified by works of the Torah but through faith in Jesus Messiah, so we also have believed in Messiah Jesus, in order to be justified by faith in Christ and not by works of the Torah, because by works of the Torah no one will be justified" (Gal. 2:15-16). This way of salvation involved the ushering in of the blessings of the New Covenant. But basically this New Covenant is a "closed system" of mercy, entirely according to the pattern of the Old Covenant; that is, it begins with God's electing mercy, then places the redeemed on the pathway of obedience to the Messianic Torah, and finishes with atoning mercy by dealing with their failures in obedience. Both the electing and the atoning mercy are based upon Jesus' atoning work. Here we see the deep coherence of the two Covenants: both are "closed systems" of mercy, the Old pointing forward to the Messiah, the New presenting fulfillment in the Messiah (see chapter 4).

---

23. I will not undertake here to further compare the views of Sanders, Westerholm (Thielman, etc.), and Dunn, and choose between them. At the moment, I see valuable elements in each of the three positions.

Appendix II: The Torah in First-Century Judaism

Perhaps this deep coherence comes to light nowhere more clearly than in Deuteronomy 30:11–14, referred to in Romans 10:5–8, where Paul says, "Moses writes about the righteousness that is based on the Torah, that the person who does the commandments shall live by them. But[24] the righteousness based on faith says, 'Do not say in your heart, "Who will ascend into heaven?"' (that is, to bring Messiah down) 'or "Who will descend into the abyss?"' (that is, to bring Messiah up from the dead). But what does it say? 'The word is near you, in your mouth and in your heart' (that is, the word of faith that we proclaim)." The very thing that Moses said of the righteousness based on the Torah was said by Paul of the righteousness based on faith. No righteousness of faith without works of the Torah flowing from it, and no righteousness of the Torah without faith in God, trusting his grace and mercy. As Thielman puts it, "[T]he old covenant and the new can speak with one voice. . . . While drawing a contrast between law and gospel, [Paul] nevertheless makes the gospel speak in the language of the law. . . . The Mosaic law is absorbed by the gospel, but only under the transforming influence of the eschatological Spirit."[25] And he rightly summarizes, "The difference between Paul and common Judaism, then, was not in the way each struck the balance between God's grace and human achievement but in the position of each within salvation history. The Old Testament looked forward to the restoration of Israel and the establishment of a new covenant, Judaism carried that hope forward into the first century, and Paul proclaimed that it had been fulfilled."[26]

---

24. Or rather, "Moreover," or "Furthermore," or "*A fortiori*" (Gk. *de*, not *alla*), because there is no real contrast here, but agreement" (cf. Stern 1999, 397–400).
25. Thielman (1995, 243).
26. Thielman (1995, 245).

Appendix III
The Sacred Day of the Week

1) Four Positions

Probably no topic is more appropriate for illustrating the theological and practical differences between covenant theology, dispensational theology, and Messianic theology with regard to the Torah than the issue of whether Shabbat observance has been replaced with Sunday observance. The Fourth of the Ten Words says: "Remember the day of Shabbat, to keep it holy" (Exod. 20:8-11; Deut. 5:12-15; cf. Exod. 31:13-16; 35:2-3; Lev. 19:3, 30; 23:3; 26:2; Num. 15:32-36; 28:9-10). What should be the attitude of Jewish and Gentile Jesus-believers toward this commandment? Basically, at least four views are conceivable.[1]

(a) *Seventh-Day Adventist, or Messianic, or any other defense of Saturday observance.* This view implies that the New Testament Ekklesia is still formally under the Mosaic Torah, either with or without the ceremonial and civil parts of it. That is, Jesus-believers are formally under the Ten Commandments, including the Fourth Commandment. This is to be taken lit-

---

1. Cf. Eskenazi et al. (1991), in which, e.g., S. Bacchiocchi (see also 1977, 1998) and J. B. Doukhan defend the first view, J. H. Primus and J. F. Baldovin defend the second view, and C. Blomberg defends the fourth view.

erally; therefore, Saturday is the sacred day of the week, both for Jewish and for Gentile Jesus-believers. This is the view, for example, of the Seventh-Day Adventists, but also of those Messianic Jews who feel that, because they have not ceased being Jews, they are still under the literal Fourth Commandment. Some Messianic Jews who have written about the matter are David Stern and the couple Ariel and D'vorah Berkowitz, all of whom take a lenient stand, though, regarding Gentile Jesus-believers celebrating the first day of the week.[2]

(b) *Roman Catholic or Reformational theologians advocating Sunday observance.* This view implies, too, that the New Testament church is still formally under the Fourth Commandment. However, these theologians believe that in the New Testament era, Saturday has been formally replaced by the first day of the week as the sacred day. Therefore, allegedly, Sunday is the sacred day of the week for both Jewish and Gentile Jesus-believers. This is the view generally held by a majority of the theologians of mainline churches. Some of them, however, do not accept the replacement notion; they argue for an independent ecclesiastical origin of Sunday as the sacred day.

(c) *Dispensational theologians advocating Sunday observance.* These theologians hold that the New Testament church is not under the Mosaic Torah, and therefore not under the Fourth Commandment. Yet, like the latter group mentioned under (b), they believe that God has formally appointed Sunday as the sacred day of the week for both Jewish and Gentile Jesus-believers. This is the view, for example, of Lewis Sperry Chafer.[3]

(d) *Dispensational theologians advocating no sacred day at all.* These theologians, too, hold that the New Testament church is not under the Mosaic Torah, and therefore not under the

---

2. Stern (1997, 54, 164–65, 170; 1999, 212, 297–98, 490–91, 558, 673); Berkowitz (1999, 241–42).
3. Chafer (1948, 100–22).

Fourth Commandment. Moreover, they believe that in the New Testament era God actually has not set aside any sacred day of the week at all. This view does not necessarily object to regularly meeting as believers on Sunday, as long as one does not consider Sunday to be any more sacred than any other day. This is the view, for instance, of Hebrew Christian Arnold Fruchtenbaum.[4]

Some matters are taken for granted in this Appendix because they are dealt with elsewhere in the present study. First, Messianic Jews have every right, if not duty, to keep Shabbat (see chapters 6 and 8). Second, I claim that, although the Mosaic Torah and the Messianic Torah are historical manifestations of the same transcendent, eternal Torah, the Mosaic Torah is not identical with the Messianic Torah (see especially §§5.2 and 7.1). Consequently, I argue that the (Gentile) Jesus-believers formally are not under the Fourth Commandment. This leaves us with three possibilities: first, the Messianic Torah, too, includes a Shabbat commandment; second, the Messianic Torah has its own sacred day, namely, Sunday; third, the Messianic Torah has no sacred day at all. Consequently, there are two questions to be asked, one exegetical and the other historical.

1. *Exegetical:* Is there a sacred day formally instituted in the New Testament for Gentile Jesus-believers, and if so, is this the seventh or the first day of the week?

2. *Historical:* Which day of the week was set aside by the early Jesus-believers (that is, historically speaking, irrespective of alleged New Testament regulations), and how does the present celebration of the first day of the week relate to this?

As I said earlier, I believe that (Gentile) Jesus-believers are not formally under the Fourth Commandment. Therefore, if some believe that no sacred day of the week was set aside in the New Testament for the Gentile Jesus-believers (view-

---

4. Fruchtenbaum (1992, 478–89, 651–80); also cf. Stern (1999, 212, 297–98, 490–91, 558).

point [d]), this cannot be countered by asserting that an explicit New Testament command to observe Shabbat was not needed because the Fourth Word had already commanded it. On the contrary, theologians propounding viewpoint (b) have the burden of proving from the New Testament that Sunday was substituted for Saturday as the sacred day of the week. It is obvious to anyone who has investigated the matter that the New Testament does not provide us with such evidence. Nowhere in the New Testament is Saturday explicitly, or even implicitly, replaced by Sunday.[5] So from where, then, do theologians from mainline churches derive this idea?

The main reasons for claiming such a replacement are the following two presuppositions: (1) Jesus-believers are under the Fourth Commandment, and (2) the New Testament seems to identify Sunday as the new day of worship. Conclusion: Sunday must be the new "Shabbat" to be observed. My answer to this is: (1) Gentile Jesus-believers are *not* under the Mosaic Torah, and, (2) even if they were, a special day of *worship* is not the same as a special day of *rest*, such as Shabbat is. Shabbat is a *mandatory* day of worship and, even more so, a *mandatory* day of *rest*.[6] Sunday is at best an *obvious day of worship*. There is no New Testament evidence that Gentile Je-

---

5. As said before, not all Reformational theologians accepted the replacement idea; some argued for an independent ecclesiastical origin of Sunday as the weekly sacred day (see, e.g., Bacchiocchi 1998, 73–74, 97–98, on the intense debate in the Netherlands, particularly at the Synod of Dort, 1618–19).

6. *Shabbat* comes from the verb *sh-b-t*, "to cease (working)," often translated "to rest"; cf. the verb in Gen. 2:2; Exod. 16:30; 23:12; 31:17; 34:21, and *shabbaton*, "day of rest" in Exod. 16:23; Lev. 23:24,39; *shabbat shabbaton*, "Shabbat of rest" (Exod. 31:15; 35:2; Lev. 23:3; of *Yom Kippur*: Lev. 16:31; 23:32; of the Sabbatical year: Lev. 25:4). In Exod. 20:11, 23:12, and Deut. 5:14, "to rest" is *n-v-ch*. In Exod. 23:12 and 31:17, the NIV translates *sh-b-t* as "not work" and "abstain from work," and the niphal of *n-ph-sh* (cf. *nephesh*, "breath, soul") as "be refreshed" and "rest" (lit. "take a breath").

Appendix III: The Sacred Day of the Week

sus-believers are to celebrate "Shabbat" on Sunday as a *mandatory* day of *worship*, and even less as a *mandatory* day of *rest*.

Of course, no one denies that the New Testament marks the first day of the week in a special way. It was on this day that Jesus rose from the dead, that the risen Lord first met with his disciples, and repeated this exactly a week later, that is, on the next Sunday (Mark 16:2, 6; Luke 24:36-49; John 20:19-29). It was seven weeks after Resurrection Day, again on the first day of the week, that the risen Lord poured out the Holy Spirit on the Day of Pentecost (Acts 2). It was on the first day of the week that the believers at Troas assembled, as was presumably their custom (Acts 20:7). It seems that Paul, apparently having arrived on a Monday, waited at Troas "seven days" (v. 6) until the first day of the week because he knew that the believers at Troas assembled on Sundays. There are more occasions where Paul stayed "seven days," presumably to be able to attend the weekly meeting of the believers (21:4; 28:14). The Corinthians were told to set aside money on the first day of the week for Paul's collection (1 Cor. 16:2), which some take to suggest that they were in the habit of meeting on that day.[7] That is all true and good, but it does not prove that the first day of the week was set aside in the present dispensation as the new sacred day, even less of a new *mandatory day of rest*, a new "Shabbat."

Although it is quite possible that when referring to "the Lord's Day" (*hē kyriakē hēmera*, Rev. 1:10[8]), John meant the first day of the week,[9] there is no proof or evidence for this. Therefore, it cannot be used to defend the claim that the New Testament has set aside a sacred day of the week. To appeal

---

7. Cf. the arguments by Fee (1987, 813–14).

8. Not to be confused with "the day of the Lord" (*hē hēmera [tou] kyriou*, 1 Cor. 5:5; 1 Thess. 5:2; 2 Thess. 2:2; 2 Pet. 3:10), which is an eschatological notion (Isa. 13:6, 9; 58:13).

9. Ouweneel (1995, 153–54); *contra* Fruchtenbaum (1992, 285, 483, 674–75); cf. Stern (1999, 791–92).

to Revelation 1:10 is to beg the question.

We seem to have precious little material at our disposal for making a decision. On the one hand, the apostles never explicitly applied the Shabbat command to Gentile Jesus-believers. On the other hand, they never explicitly instituted Sunday as a mandatory day of worship, and even less as a mandatory day of rest. So what are we to conclude? I am confident that we can make at least the following two observations.

First, even if Gentile Jesus-believers are not under the Mosaic Torah, it is certain that nine of the Ten Commandments are also part and parcel of the Messianic Torah (see §6.1.3 above); so why not the remaining one, the Shabbat commandment? Moreover, the latter is not just part of the Ten Words but has a much wider impact by going back to the creation week (Gen. 2:2–3). It will not do to argue that in Genesis 2, God did not explicitly institute the Shabbat as a day of rest *for Man*. If God "blessed the seventh day and made it holy," what else could the Israelite readers of the Torah have inferred than that this day was meant as a day of blessing and holiness *for Man*? It is true that we never read that the patriarchs observed Shabbat. But Shabbat was not totally unknown either, for in Exodus 16:23–29, that is, *before* the Torah-giving on Sinai, we read four times of the Shabbat: ". . . a day of solemn rest [one word: *shabbatôn*], a holy Shabbat to the LORD . . . the seventh day, which is a Shabbat. . . . See! The LORD has given you the Shabbat." This clearly indicates that the Shabbat has a wider significance than just within the framework of the Mosaic Torah. It was made, not just for the Jews but, "for man" (Gr. *anthrōpos*, "human person") (Mark 2:27), that is, for the physical and spiritual well-being of all mankind.

Second, I am not aware of the slightest indication in the New Testament that Gentile Jesus-believers ever kept Shabbat, whereas we do have evidence, though meager, that they met on the first day of the week (Mark 16:2, 6; Luke 24:36–49; John 20:19, 26; Acts 2:1; 20:7 four times). So why not accept

Appendix III: The Sacred Day of the Week

Sunday as a most appropriate day of *worship*, even if we reject the idea that it should also be a mandatory day of *rest*? By the way, if Gentile Jesus-believers indeed keep the first day of the week as a sacred day of worship, is it not reasonable to combine this day with that regular day of rest that every human being needs?

The advantage of the Saturday view is that it guarantees the continuous validity of the Ten Commandments in their entirety within the Messianic Torah, and honors the fact that the Shabbat has an even wider (creational) significance than the Ten Words. The advantage of the Sunday view is that we have far more evidence of *Gentile* Jesus-believers observing the first day than of those celebrating the seventh day. And no wonder: that first day is the day of the resurrection of Jesus and of the outpouring of the Holy Spirit. No day of the week is more "Messianic" than the first day.

A few things must be clear. First, no one can deny the right, if not duty, of Messianic Jews to keep Shabbat. Second, one may deny the *duty* of Gentile Jesus-believers to keep Shabbat, but one cannot deny their *right* to do so. Third, one may deny the *duty* of Gentile Jesus-believers to observe Sunday as a day of worship, and even of rest, but one cannot deny their *right* to do so. *We simply have no direct biblical evidence with regard to the duty of Gentile Jesus-believers in this respect.* We will therefore have to leave room for viewpoint (d), namely, that in the New Testament era God has not set aside any sacred day of the week at all. On the other hand, there is no direct evidence for the notion that, of *all* dispensations, this present one would be the *only* dispensation without a sacred day of the week.

Another point must be absolutely clear: whatever one may think of a possible sacred day in the present dispensation, God has not abolished Shabbat. First, if Jesus in the Gospels, the apostles, and all the Messianic Jews in the book of Acts kept the whole Mosaic Torah (see §5.3 above), this necessarily included Shabbat. Paul visited Gentile congregations that apparently were accustomed to meeting on the first day of the week (Acts 20:7); but all the evidence points to his personal observance of Shabbat.

Second, Shabbat is going to be observed in the Millennial kingdom of the Messiah, not only by Israel but by all the nations (Isa. 56:1–7; 66:23; Ezek. 44:24; 45:17; 46:1, 3–4, 12). What could illustrate more clearly that Shabbat (I mean of course Shabbat on Saturday!) has never been abolished?

Third, with regard to God's prophetic ways with the earth, the ark of the covenant is seen in the heavenly temple (Rev. 11:19), implying the "[stone] tablets of the covenant" (Heb. 9:4), and thus implying the Ten Words, including the Shabbat Commandment.

Fourth, the Messianic kingdom itself will be the great Shabbat of world history; God is working his way through history to this ultimate "Shabbat-rest" (Heb. 4:9) (see below). This notion is found not only in rabbinic sources but also in the writings of the church fathers and the Reformers (see §2.3.2 above). So even many outstanding Gentile Jesus-believers, though observing Sunday as the sacred day, recognized that God himself still "keeps" Shabbat, so to speak, as he did at creation (Gen. 2:2–3; Exod. 20:11; 31:17). Whatever day Gentile Jesus-believers may use as their common day of worship, Shabbat is a spiritual reality to be reckoned with, and will be a reality as long as the earth will last.

2) Relevant Scriptures

A few Scriptures come to mind that have to be considered in this respect:

(a) Gentile believers often have little understanding of how great a delight Shabbat is for Jewish believers, Messianic or not. One of the most enlightening Scriptures is this one: "If you turn back your foot from the Sabbath, from doing your pleasure on my holy day, and call the Sabbath a delight and the holy day of the Lord honorable; if you honor it [or, him], not going your own ways, or seeking your own pleasure, or

Appendix III: The Sacred Day of the Week

talking idly; then you shall take delight in the LORD, and I will make you ride on the heights of the earth" (Isa. 58:13–14).

(b) Sometimes, we find in the New Testament the word *sabbaton* (appearing often as a plural, *sabbatōn*) in the sense of "week," for instance, in the expression "twice a week" (Luke 18:12), and especially "the first day of the week" (Matt. 28:1; Mark 16:2, 9; Luke 24:1; John 20:1, 19; Acts 20:7; 1 Cor. 16:2). Of course, the Greek word *sabbaton* is derived from the Hebrew *Shabbat*; the word can therefore mean "Shabbat" (seventh day), but also a period of seven days, the first day of this period being Sunday. This meaning is confirmed by the context: "*after* the Shabbat, *toward* the dawn of the first day of the week [*sabbatōn*] . . . " (Matt. 28:1 and par.; italics added). Amazingly, some Shabbat-observers want to understand "first of the *sabbatōn*" as referring to Shabbat, not Sunday! This points to a lack not only of knowledge of Greek language, but also of logical thinking. Matthew 28:1, Mark 16:1–2, and Luke 23:56–24:1 all clearly show that "the first of the *sabbatōn*" *followed immediately after* Shabbat.

(c) Paul wrote to the Roman believers: "One person [i.e., the "weak" one] esteems one day as better than another, while another person [i.e., the "strong" one] esteems all days alike. Each one should be fully convinced in his own mind. The one who observes the day, observes it in honor of the Lord" (Rom. 14:5–6). In my view, it clearly follows from the context that, according to Paul, it is a sign of a "strong" faith if the Jesus-believer "considers every day alike."[10] I can see no reason why this should include any legalistic or pagan (e.g., superstitious) interpretation of a specific "sacred day of the week." Legalism would include the notion that Sunday is special because

---

10. *Contra* Fruchtenbaum (1992, 670), according to whom v. 5 says that "one man is free to esteem a day as being more important than another, *be it Saturday or Sunday*, while another can view all days equally alike. Both options are valid options" (italics mine). Neither the text nor the context suggests anything of the kind.

it is the "New Testament Shabbat," to which all the Mosaic Shabbat regulations apply. Paganism would include the notion that the Sunday is special because this day was devoted to the sun god, as the name indicates.

In §9.3.1, I explained that Torah-keeping by a Messianic Jew, including Shabbat observance, is not necessarily "weakness," as long as it is not done out of a legalistic striving for works-righteousness. But the passage does seem to argue against any *formal* idea of a special sacred day during the new dispensation. It is interesting to see how John Murray circumvents this inference.[11] He argues that, if Shabbat would come within the scope of Romans 14:5, the "first day of the week would have no prescribed religious significance," and observance "of a day commemorating our Lord's resurrection would be a feature of the person weak in faith." Because Murray believes that neither statement could possibly be true, he concludes that "the abiding sanctity of each recurring seventh day [Saturday or Sunday] is not to be regarded as in any way impaired by Romans 14:5." Of course, that is begging the question. Murray does not prove the starting-point of his argument, namely, "the distinctive significance of the first day of the week as the Lord's day."

On the other hand, I think it would be going too far to use Romans 14:5 as an argument *against any* celebration of the first *or* the seventh day of the week, as long as this is not done for legalistic, ethnocentric, or pagan reasons (see again §9.3).[12] Likewise, Colossians 2:16 — "let no one pass judgment on you ... with regard to ... a Shabbat" — is evidence neither against a Messianic Jew keeping the Shabbat out of sound motives (see §9.3.2), nor against a Gentile Jesus-believer observing Sunday or Shabbat from sound motives. The statement with which the verse commences, "let no one pass judgment on you in questions of food and drink," is not a warning against

---

11. Murray (1968, 257–59); cf. Moo (1996, 841–42).
12. Bacchiocchi (1998, 250–52).

Appendix III: The Sacred Day of the Week

eating and drinking in general but against *wrong* eating and drinking. Likewise, there is here no warning against Shabbat observance in general but against *wrong* Shabbat observance. More accurately, the "judge" in this verse is probably someone who asserted that the Colossians had to eat and drink, and keep Shabbat and the festivals, in a more ascetic way.[13]

Interestingly, Joseph Shulam detects in Romans 14 a reference to the debates between Beit Hillel and Beit Shammai (the followers of the great Rabbis Hillel and Shammai, respectively): "The controversy between the two Pharisaic schools suggests that Beit Hillel granted to 'profane' weekdays the same sanctity given to Shabbat. Beit Shammai, on the other hand, regarded granting sanctity to 'secular' days as a degradation of God's sovereignty and glory. . . . Paul's description of the 'weak' in faith (love) corresponds to Beit Shammai's position, which held that men must strengthen God's hand, as it were, by defending His statutes; the 'strong' in faith (love) correspond to Beit Hillel, who judged God to be strong enough to bear the priorities established by each individual's conscience and convictions."[14] No matter how this is to be taken, neither Beit Hillel nor Beit Shammai would ever have thought of belittling the significance of Shabbat as such. This is not at stake in Romans 14.

(d) Galatians 4:10, "You observe days . . .," cannot be used as an argument against Shabbat observance as such, because the context points to a legalistic or pagan celebration of special days.[15] The passages do not lend any support to the notion of a special sacred day under the new dispensation, but they do not necessarily condemn any celebration of the first or the seventh day either, as long as any form of legalism or paganism is avoided.[16]

---

13. Ibid., 245–46; also see §9.3.2.
14. Shulam (1998, 463); see Betzah 16a; Pesikta Rabbati 23.
15. Cf. Stern (1999, 557–58).
16. Bacchiocchi (1998, 253–56).

(e) David Stern interestingly interprets Acts 20:7 and 1 Corinthians 16:2 as showing that "the Jewish believers evidently met on Saturday nights," that is, the evening called by the Jews *Motza'ei-Shabbat*, "departure of the Shabbat."[17] Apparently, the knife cuts both ways here. On the one hand, according to Jewish custom, the restful spirit of Shabbat is often preserved well into Saturday evening, after the official Shabbat is over (which occurs at sunset). Stern argues that it would be natural for Jewish believers, who had rested on Shabbat with the rest of the Jewish community, to assemble afterward with Messianic Jews and Gentiles. It would still be a meeting in the Shabbat atmosphere. On the other hand, literally, at sunset the first day of the week would have started; therefore, Acts 20:7 and 1 Corinthians 16:2 speak of this day as a special day. And because Gentile Jesus-believers used a midnight-to-midnight calendar it is feasible that afterward they kept meeting on the first day of the week, but then in the daytime.

(f) Astonishingly, Stern translates Hebrews 4:9 as follows: "So there remains a Shabbat-*keeping* for God's people," and comments: "Christians often assume that the New Testament does not require God's people to observe *Shabbat* and go on to claim that Sunday has replaced Shabbat as the Church's day of worship (see 1C 16:2N). But this [v. 9] shows that Shabbat-observance is expected of believers . . . as v. 10 explains, the *Shabbat*-keeping expected of God's people consists in resting from one's own works, as God did from his; it consists in trusting and being faithful to God (vv. 2–3)."[18] In my view, Fruchtenbaum is right in emphasizing that in Hebrews 3 and 4 the "rest" of the Shabbat is meant in a typological (*midrashic*) way, which seems to be clear from Hebrews 4:3–4. On the "day of Shabbat," that is, the future Messianic Kingdom,

---

17. Stern (1999, 212, 297–98, 490–91); cf. Fruchtenbaum (1992, 675–77).
18. Stern (1999, 673); cf. Berkowitz (2011, 36–37).

Appendix III: The Sacred Day of the Week

when God will rest from all his works throughout the dispensations, the believer will rest from his own works, too.

Fruchtenbaum drew a conclusion from this that was exactly opposite to that of Stern: "It is noteworthy that in this epistle [Hebrews], written especially to Jewish believers, nothing is said anywhere about mandatory keeping of the Shabbat."[19] But, of course, these Messianic Jews were the last to need such a reminder because at least they were the ones who kept the Shabbat commandment anyway (see §5.3 above).

My own conclusion is that the New Testament contains neither an explicit commandment to keep a sacred day of the week, either Shabbat or Sunday, nor any prohibition against doing so. The reason why most Jesus-believers consider the Sunday to be a special day is not based on a special commandment or institution but (a) on the special character of that day as the Lord's resurrection day, and (b) on a tradition that goes back to the first centuries. It is *not* true that the Sunday was instituted for the first time by the emperor Constantine, in his Sunday Law of AD 321, or by the Council of Laodicea in AD 364. Therefore, celebrating the Lord's resurrection day cannot be discarded simply for this reason, or because of the alleged anti-Semitism behind this fourth-century institution. Rather, the observance of the Sunday as a day of worship was universally practiced outside the land of Israel already by the beginning of the second century.[20] Subsequent church councils merely ratified a practice already common; their supposed anti-Semitism does not change the noble age of the custom.

What the councils did decree, however, under the influence of emerging covenant theology, was definitely wrong. They turned Sunday, as a suggested day of worship, into a *mandatory day of rest* as well, to which they applied all the Shabbat regulations from the Tanakh. This was a major mis-

---

19. Fruchtenbaum (1992, 671–72).
20. See on this matter extensively Rordorf (1968), Bacchiocchi (1977); Carson (1982).

take, both theologically and practically. There is nothing against observing the first day of the week voluntarily as a special day of *worship*; there is everything against observing it as a *mandatory day of rest*. I am not saying that a day of rest every week could not be very useful to hard-working humans. It could and would. But that is something else than asserting that Sunday is the "New Testament Shabbat," on which day it is biblically forbidden to work.

In passing, I note that covenant theologians seem to encounter inevitable problems with Acts 20:7 if they want to view the first day of the week as a mandatory day of rest. Either believers met on *Sunday* night, as many expositors assume,[21] but then the breaking of bread (the Lord's Supper, as many—in my view correctly—take it), which was celebrated after midnight, actually took place on Monday morning, not on Sunday (vv. 7, 11). Or believers met on *Saturday* night, but then Paul set out on his distant journey on Sunday morning (v. 11), which many who believe in the "New Testament Shabbat" would consider to be a capital sin. Which is worse: to eat the Lord's Supper on Monday, or to travel on Sunday? This whole dilemma vanishes once the prejudice of covenant theology is rejected.

Interestingly, Fruchtenbaum points out that first-day observance may have begun with Jewish believers.[22] In a Talmud tract it is supposed that Jews do not fast before or on a Shabbat because, naturally, that day is a special day of eating.[23] But the tract goes on to say: "Why did they not fast on the day after the Shabbat? Rabbi Johanan says, 'Because of the Nazarenes'," that is, Messianic Jews of the first centuries (see §1.2.1 above). Apparently, the non-Messianic Jews did not want to fast on the first day of the week, in order to avoid showing any respect to the day that was regarded as special

---

21. E.g., Bruce (1988, 384–85).
22. Fruchtenbaum (1992, 677–78).
23. Ta'anit 27b.

Appendix III: The Sacred Day of the Week

by the Nazarenes. This does not imply, however, that the Nazarenes knew any "Shabbat transference theology," as if they celebrated "Shabbat" on Sunday. All the evidence shows that Shabbat remained Shabbat to them, as it had always been. But Sunday was special to them apparently because it was the Lord's resurrection day, not because it had anything to do with Shabbat. In the Gentile Western world, we may be grateful for Sunday as a day of worship and rest. But any assertion that Sunday is the "New Testament Shabbat," and thus a mandatory day of rest, is false for three reasons: it is neither a "Shabbat," nor mandatory, nor a day of rest.

Appendix IV
Mosaic and Messianic Ordinances

Rabbinic tradition considers the Mosaic Torah to contain 613 ordinances (*tariag*[1] *mitzvoth*). This number was first mentioned by Rabbi Simlai: "613 precepts were communicated to Moses, 365 negative precepts, corresponding to the number of solar day [in the year],[2] and 248 positive precepts, corresponding to the number of the members[3] of man's body."[4] As evidence for this, he quoted Deuteronomy 33:4, "Moses commanded us *torah*," the latter word consisting of the letters *tav* (400), *yod* (6), *resh* (200) and *he* (5), which makes 611, plus two more, which, according to the rabbis, the people did not hear from the mouth of Moses but directly out of the LORD's mouth: "I am the LORD your God . . ." and "You shall have no other gods before me" (Exod. 20:2-3). Many rabbis have

---

1. *Tariag* (four consonants) is T (*tav*) = 400, R (*resh*) = 200, I (*Yod*) = 10, G (*gimel*) = 3; together 613.
2. Cf. Ginzberg (1968, 96).
3. These are the "members" that Paul refers to as being checked either by the Torah of sin and death or by the Torah of the Spirit of life (Rom. 6:13, 19; 7:5, 23; cf. 8:2). Several Jewish sources refer to these members, singling out ten in particular: the eyes, ears, hands, feet, mouth, and male organ (see references in Shulam 1998, 222–24, 250, 257).
4. Talmud: Makkot 23b–24a.

attempted to explain these 365 positive and 248 negative precepts; the listing by Maimonides (twelfth century) is by far the best known.

Messianic Jew Dan Juster has enumerated all 613 of them.[5] He distinguishes the following categories (listed with my own circumscriptions):

(1) **T** (Temple): the Temple sacrificial system.

(2) **UM** (Universal-Moral): ordinances that in their unchanged form remain valid in the Messianic Torah for all believers.

(3) **UR** (Universal-Revised): ordinances that remain valid in the Messianic Torah, but in an intensified and deepened form for all people.

(4) **J** (Jewish): ordinances that in the Messianic Torah remain valid for Jews as part of Israel's national and cultural heritage.

(5) **AJ** (Ancient Jewish): ordinances applying to the ancient nation of Israel; not applicable today.

(6) **UA (Unclear Application)**: partly or entirely unclear as to their application.

(7) **C** (Combination): a combination of above categories.

(8) **NA** (Not Applicable): no longer can any application be found.

I am omitting the categories **T**, **AJ**, **UA**, and **NA**, even though a number of cases of ceremonial uncleanness still have a certain medical or hygienic importance.[6] In §1 the commandments under the labels **J** and **C** are listed in combination, and in §2 those under the labels **UM** and **UR** are listed together with a distinct category: ordinances that apply to Gentiles, though not in a literal but in a figurative-moral

---

5. Juster (1995, 259–87).
6. Ibid., 265.

Appendix IV: Mosaic and Messianic Ordinances

way.[7] Please notice that the New Testament mentions many more Messianic ordinances, which are not listed here.

I follow Juster's numbering, but not always his categorization. Of course, my own categorization is also debatable; in many cases, sharp distinctions are hardly possible.

To prevent cumbersome reading, I am identifying each Torah Book by its first letter in this Appendix: G = Genesis, E = Exodus, L = Leviticus, N = Numbers, D = Deuteronomy, f = plus following (verse or commandment).

1) Ordinances Preserving Jewish Identity

N.B. It is not always easy to distinguish between this category 1 and category 2. Some of the commandments and prohibitions mentioned here have a moral, if not a literal, meaning for Gentile Jesus-believers as well.

1.1 Mandatory Commandments

[10] Remember the *Shema*[8] each morning and evening (D6:7). [12–15] Bind *tefillin*[9] on your head and arm, make *tzitziyot*[10] for your garments, and fix a *mezuzah*[11] on your door (N15:38; D6:8f.). [16] The people are to be assembled every seventh year to hear the Torah read (D31:12); you shall know and sing the song of Moses (D31:12,19).

---

7. In fact, the phenomenon of applying certain commandments in the Messianic Torah in a more figurative-moral way is not entirely new. Sanders (1985, 248) wrote, "From Philo [*De Migratione Abrahame* 89] we learn that some Jews allegorized parts of the law and did not keep it literally."
8. *Shema Yisrael*, "Hear, O Israel: The LORD our God, the LORD is one" (Deut. 6:4).
9. Phylacteries (black leather boxes containing scrolls with Bible verses; from the root *f-l-l*, "to pray").
10. Sing. *tzitzit*, lit. "offshoot" (cf. Ezek. 8:3: "lock" of hair); from *tz-v-t*, "to blossom."
11. Actually "doorframe"; here it means the little scroll containing Bible verses, attached to the doorframe in a little box.

[54] Rejoice on the festivals (D16:14). [55-58] Celebrate *Pesach* with *matzah*[12] and bitter herbs (E12:8). [59] Sound trumpets at the festivals and in times of tribulation (N10:9f.). [154-170] Observe Shabbat, *Pesach, Omer, Shavu'ot, Rosh haShanah, Yom Kippur,* and *Sukkot* (L23).

[134f, 141f] Keep the Sabbatical Year (E23:11; 34:21; D15:3) and [136-140] the Jubilee Year (L25:8-10,24,29).

[146] To be fit for consumption, beast and fowl must be slaughtered properly (D12:21) and [149-152] examined properly (L11:2, 21; D14:11).

[215] Circumcise male infants (G17:10; L12:3).

1.2 Prohibitions

[43f] Do not shave the sides of your head or beard (in the sense of bodily disfigurement) (L19:27).

[172-179] Do not eat animals that are "unclean" by nature (L11; D14) or [180f] have died naturally or are torn or mauled (D14:21; E22:31). [182-185] Do not eat a limb taken from a living animal, the tendon of the hip (G32:32), blood (L7:26), nor certain types of fat (L7:23). [186f] Do not cook a young goat in its mother's milk, nor eat it (E23:19b; 34:26b). [188] Do not eat of a stoned ox (E21:28).

[189-191] Do not eat new grain, roasted or green, or bread made of it, before the *Omer* offering (week of *Pesach*) (L23:14). [192] Do not eat forbidden fruit (L19:23) or [193] the growth of mixed planting in the vineyard (D22:9).

[196] Do not eat on *Yom Kippur* (L23:29). [197-201] During *Pesach* do not eat yeast or anything containing it; do not even have it in your possession (E12:15,19f; 13:3b,7; D16:3).

[202-209] The Nazirite shall not eat or drink anything from the vine, nor touch a corpse, nor shave his hair (N6:3-5).

[220-226] Do not till, prune or reap in the Sabbatical Year, nor in the Jubilee Year (L25:8-10,24,29; cf. E23:11; 34:21;

---

12. Unleavened bread; from *m-tz-tz*, "to be without taste."

Appendix IV: Mosaic and Messianic Ordinances

L25:4f,11; D15:3). [230f] Do not demand repayment of a loan after the Sabbatical Year, but do not refuse to lend to the poor because that year is approaching (D15:2,9).

[320-322] Do not work, travel excessively, or light a fire (for cooking and baking?) on Shabbat (E16:29; 20:10; 35:3). [323-329] Do not work on the first and seventh day of *Pesach* (E12:16), on *Shavu'ot, Rosh haShanah,* on *Yom Kippur,* and on the first and eighth day of *Sukkot* (L23:21,25,28,35f).

[330-345] Do not enter into an incestuous relationship with a close relative or relative-in-law, or with two women who are parentally related (L18:6-18,20). [346] Do not have sexual intercourse with a menstruous woman (L18:19). [347-52] Do not commit adultery, bestiality, homosexuality (L18:20, 22f). [353] Do not have intimate physical contact with forbidden women. [354] A *mamzêr*[13] shall not marry one of God's people (D23:2). [355] Do not commit prostitution (D23:17).

Note: I would not know which of the above commandments does not hold for Messianic Jews, although several need careful exegesis. When one day the Temple will have been rebuilt, many more commandments, not listed here, are to be observed. They are characteristic of the Jewish religious, cultural, and national heritage, and consequently are not given to Gentile believers.

2) Ordinances of Universal Significance

2.1 Mandatory Commandments

2.1.1 Basically Unchanged Ordinances, Thus Applying to All Jesus-Believers

[1] Believe that God exists (E20:2), and [2] acknowledge his unity (D6:4); [3-5] love, fear and serve him (D6:5,13; 11:13). [6] Hold fast to him (D10:20). [8] Walk in God's ways (D28:9) and [9] hallow his name (L22:32). [11] Study the Torah [in the

---

13. Bastard, "one born of a forbidden marriage"; from *m-z-r,* "to be rotten."

widest sense, Scripture] and teach it to others. [19] Praise God after eating (D8:10).

[73] Repent and confess your sins before God (N5:6f).

[194] Stolen property must be restored to its owner (L6:4). [195] Give charity to the poor (L25:35f; D15:8). [199] Restore a pledge to its owner if he needs it (E22:26f; D24:13). [200] Pay the worker his wages on time (D24:15); [201] permit him to eat of the produce with which he is working (D23:24f). [204] Lost property must be restored to its owner (E23:4; D22:1).

[205f] Rebuke the trespasser, but love your neighbor as yourself (L19:17f); [207] love the sojourner (D10:19).

[208] Use honest weights and measures (L19:36).

[209] Show respect for the elderly (L19:32).

[218] If someone has violated a virgin, he shall marry her and never divorce her (D22:28f).[14]

[220] Fine the seducer (E22:16).

[232–235] Treat slaves (in the wider sense: employees) well (E21:2, 8; L25:46).

[236–248] Repair torts the best way you can (many passages especially in E21 and 22).

2.1.2 Ordinances Intensified by Jesus and the Apostles

[7] Take your oaths only in God's name (D10:20), [94] honor your vows and oaths—*but it is better not to take oaths at all* (Matt. 5:33-37).

[185f] Idolatry in the Holy Land is to be (actively) destroyed (D7:5; 12:2; 13:16); that is today, in the Messianic Community's Diaspora context, (passively) *fled from* (1 Cor.

---

14. The father may refuse to give her (E22:17), which shows that the duty to marry the girl is more of a social nature—in antiquity no man would marry a girl who was no longer a virgin—than of a judicial nature as if sexual intercourse as such already constitutes a marriage, which allegedly is only to be legitimized. Therefore, it is highly questionable whether, under the present social circumstances, this commandment can be applied literally.

Appendix IV: Mosaic and Messianic Ordinances

10:14).

[210f] Honor and respect your parents (E20:12; L19:3) — *but your love to God or Jesus should surpass even that to your parents* (Luke 14:26).

[212f] Perpetuate the human race by marrying, and marry properly (G1:28); [214] bring happiness to your wife the first year of marriage (D24:5) — *but under the New Covenant it is the higher way to remain unmarried if thus called by the Lord* (1 Cor. 7:1, 6f).

[219] If someone unjustly accuses his wife of premarital promiscuity, he shall be punished and may never divorce her (D22:13-19).[15] [222] If you insist on divorcing your wife, you may only do this by means of a written document (D24:1) — *but Jesus teaches us in principle not to divorce at all* (Matt. 5:32; 19:4-9).

2.1.3 Ordinances to Be Applied Figurative-Morally

[120-124] When reaping your fields, leave the corners, gleanings etc. (L19:9f; D24:19), that is, *take care of the poor*; [127-130] pay tithes to the Levites, the priests and the poor (L27:30; N18:24,26; D14:22, 28); that is, *provide amply for the needs of God's servants and the poor* (Matt. 19:21; Luke 14:13; Rom. 15:26; 1 Cor. 9:4-14; Gal. 2:10).

[147] After having slaughtered a "clean" animal of a non-domesticated species, cover its blood with earth (L17:13); [148] when taking a nest, set the parent bird free (D22:7); that is, *revere all life*.

[172] Obey a prophet (D18:15); that is, *respect prophecies* (1 Thess. 5:20).

[174-180, 224-231] Obey the Sanhedrin, institute proper courts of justice and proper juridical procedures (E23:2; L5:1; 19:15; D13:14; 16:18; 17:11; 19:19) and execution methods

---

15. In the broad moral sense, it remains always true that a man who falsely accuses his wife—as well as a woman who falsely accuses her husband!—is to be rebuked.

(E21:16 strangulation; L20:14 fire; N35:25 exile; D21:22 hanging; 22:24 stoning; 25:2 flogging); that is, *obey your elders* (1 Thess. 5:12-13; Heb. 13:17; 1 Pet. 5:3), *let justice reign in your congregations* (Matt. 18:15-17; 1 Cor. 5; 6:1-8; 1 Thess. 5:12-14; 1 Tim. 5:17), *and obey the civil authorities* (Rom. 13:1-7; Titus 3:1; 1 Pet. 2:13-14).

[184] Build a fence around your roof (D22:8); that is, *remove potential hazards from your home.*

[192f] Keep the military camp clean (D23:14); that is, *keep evil out* (1 Cor. 5:13).

[197] Lend to the poor without interest (E22:25); [198] to the "foreigner" (who is no part of the covenant) you may lend with interest (D23:20); that is, *"do good to everyone, and especially to those who are of the household of faith"* (Gal. 6:10).

[202f] Help unload or load an animal when necessary (E23:5; D22:4); that is, *be ready to assist your neighbor.*

2.2 Prohibitions

2.2.1 Basically Unchanged Ordinances, Thus Applying to All Jesus-Believers

[1] Do not believe in the existence of any but the One God (E20:3). [2-4] Make no images for yourself (E20:4), or for others to worship, or for any other purpose (E20:4,20; L19:4). [5f] Do not worship anything but God (E20:5).

[7] Do not sacrifice children to Molech (L18:21). [8f] Do not practice necromancy or resort to "familiar spirits" (L19:31). [10] Do not take idolatry or its mythology seriously (L19:4). [11-13] Do not construct a sacred stone or image or grove in the Temple (in the wider sense: anywhere) (D16:21f).

[14-16] Do not swear by idols or instigate an idolater to do so, nor encourage or persuade any Gentile or Jew to worship idols (E23:13; D13:12ff).

[20f] Do not defend someone trying to convert you to idolatry, nor conceal the fact (D13:8). [22] Do not benefit from the ornaments of idols (D7:25). [23f] Do not rebuild that which

Appendix IV: Mosaic and Messianic Ordinances

was destroyed as a punishment for idolatry, nor benefit from its wealth (D13:16f). [25] Do not use anything connected with idolatry (D7:26). [26f] Do not prophesy in the name of idols, nor falsely in the name of God (D18:20). [28] Do not listen to anyone prophesying for idols (D13:3f); [29] do not fear the false prophet or hinder his punishment (D18:20). [30-8, 194] Do not practice the customs of idolaters: divination, sorcery, interpreting omens, witchcraft, casting spells, being a medium or spiritist, or consulting the dead, wine libations (D18:10f; 32:38). [41] Do not tattoo yourself as idolaters do (L19:28). [45] Do not cut yourself in grief about your dead (D14:1).

[47] Do not go after the lusts of your own hearts and eyes (N15:39b).

[58] Do not fear the enemy (D7:21).

[60] Do not blaspheme the Holy Name (L24:16), [61] do not break an oath made by it (L19:12), [62] do not misuse it (E20:7), nor [63] profane it (L22:32). [64] Do not try the Lord God (D6:16). [65] Do not erase God's name from Scripture, nor destroy institutions devoted to his worship.

[157] Do not break your word (N30:2f).

[195] Do not yield to profligacy and drunkenness (D21:20).

[232] Do not deny charity to the poor (L23:22; D15:11).

[234] Do not dun your debtor when you know he cannot pay (E22:22-24).

[238] Do not delay payment of wages (L19:13).

[239-42] Do not take a pledge from a debtor by violence, nor keep a poor man's pledge when he needs it, nor from a widow, nor from any debtor if he earns his living with it (D24:6, 10-12, 17).

[243-6] Do not kidnap, nor steal or rob by violence, nor remove a landmark, nor defraud (E20:15; L19:11, 13; D19:14).

[248f] Do not deny receipt of a loan or a deposit, nor swear falsely regarding another's property (L19:11).

[250f] Do not deceive anyone in business, nor mislead a

man even verbally (L25:14, 17).

[252f] Do not mistreat or oppress the stranger among you in trade (E22:21).

[256] Do not take advantage of a widow or an orphan (E22:22).

[265f] Do not covet, or even desire, another's possessions (E20:17). [267f] Do not cut down another's standing grain, nor take more fruit from his vineyard than you can eat on the spot (D23:25f).

[269] Do not ignore a lost item that is to be returned to its owner (D22:3).

[271f] Do not use dishonest weights and measures (L19:35), nor even possess them (D25:13).

[288] Do not accept the testimony of one witness only (D19:15; cf. Matt. 18:16; John 8:17; 2 Cor. 13:1; Heb. 10:28).

[289] Do not murder (E20:13). [301–305] Do not slander, hate, or shame your brother, or seek revenge or bear a grudge against him (L19:16–18).

[297–299] Do not hesitate to save another from danger, nor leave a stumbling block in the way, nor mislead another (L19:14, 16b).

[315–319] Do not curse a judge, a ruler, or any brother, nor curse or strike a parent (E21:15, 17; 22:28).

2.2.2 Ordinances Intensified by Jesus and the Apostles

[17–19] Do not listen to or love anyone who disseminates idolatry, nor withhold yourself from hating him; do not pity him (D13:9) — *but the higher way is to love your neighbor, though you may hate his works* (Matt. 5:43–47).

[355] A divorcee shall not remarry her first husband if after her divorce she has married another (D24:4); [358–359] do not divorce a wife whom you have married after having raped or slandered her (D22:19,29) — *but the higher way is not to remarry after divorce, and not even to divorce at all* (Matt. 5:32; 19:4–9).

Appendix IV: Mosaic and Messianic Ordinances

2.2.3 Ordinances to Be Applied Figurative-Morally

[39f] Do not wear clothing meant for the other sex (D22:5); that is, *do not intermingle the distinct creational roles of males and females* (1 Tim. 2:11f).

[42] Do not wear garments made of both wool and linen (D22:11); [215-218] do not plant your field with two kinds of seed, nor mate different kinds of animals, nor plow with an ox and a donkey yoked together (L19:19; D22:9f); that is, *do not get yourself in all kinds of unholy mixtures* (2 Cor. 6:14-16).

[50] Do not show mercy to idolaters (D7:2); that is, by *applying not the death penalty but congregational excommunication* (cf. 1 Cor. 5:13 with D13:6; 17:7, 12).

[52-6] Do not intermarry with Canaanites, Ammonites, Moabites, do not even make peace with them; but do not refuse (for genealogical reasons alone) an Edomite or Egyptian converted to Judaism (D7:3; 23:3, 6f); that is, *do not intermarry with unbelievers* (1 Cor. 7:39b), *but do not abhor of those who are "brothers," although of a different conviction.*

[57] Do not destroy the trees of a besieged city (D20:19); that is, *do not waste good time, energy, and materials in your spiritual warfare.*

[59] Do not forget the evil done by Amalek (D25:19); that is, *the evil wrought in our lives by the devil and by our own sinful nature.*

[210-214] Do not reap the corners of your fields, do not gather up fallen ears of grain etc. (L19:9f; D24:19); that is, *do not neglect the care for the poor.*

[219] Do not muzzle an ox while it is treading out the grain (D25:4); [229] do not leave the Levites without support (D12:19); that is, *do not withhold from the Lord's servants what is due to them* (1 Cor. 9:7-12).

[233] Do not send a Hebrew slave away empty-handed (D15:7, 13). [254f] Do not return nor oppress a runaway slave (D23:16f), nor [257-260] misuse or sell or ruthlessly treat a He-

brew slave, nor allow others to mistreat him (L25:39,42f,53). [261-264] Do not sell your Hebrew maidservant, nor, if you marry her, withhold food, clothing and marital rights from her; do not sell a female captive, nor treat her as a slave (E21:8,10; D21:14). *The slave or maidservant is here the man or woman of God's people who is in your debt, financially or morally, or is otherwise dependent on you.*

[235-237] Do not lend to or borrow from God's people at interest, or participate in agreements involving interest (L25:37; D23:20); that is, *do not withhold your help from others.*

[270] Do not refuse to help a man or an animal collapsing under its burden (E23:5); that is, *do not refuse any assistance to your neighbor.*

[273-280] A judge shall not pervert justice, accept bribes, be partial or afraid, nor show favoritism to the poor or against the wicked, nor pity the guilty, nor deprive the aliens and orphans of justice (E23:3, 6, 8; L19:15; D1:17; 19:13; 24:17). [281-283] He shall not hear one litigant without the other being present, nor decide a capital case by a majority of one, nor accept a colleague's opinion unless being convinced of its correctness (E23:1f). [284] Do not appoint as a judge someone who is ignorant of the Torah. [285-287] Do not give false testimony, nor accept it from a wicked person or from relatives of the incriminated person (E20:16; 23:1; 24:16). [290] Do not convict anyone on circumstantial evidence alone (E23:7). [291f] A witness shall not sit as a judge in capital cases; do not execute anybody without proper trial and conviction (N35:12, 30). [293] Do not pity or spare the convicted (D25:12). [294] Do not punish an act committed under duress (D22:26). [295f] Do not accept ransom for a murderer or a manslayer (N35:32f). [300] Do not administer more than the assigned number of lashes to the guilty (D25:2f).[16] [310] Do not spare a witch (E22:17).

---

16. Cf. 2 Cor. 11:24: "Five times I received at the hands of the Jews the forty lashes less one"—the last words referring to the fact that the Jews, in order not to trespass this commandment, administered one

Appendix IV: Mosaic and Messianic Ordinances

[312–314] Do not rebel against judicial decisions, nor add to or detract from the ordinances (D13:1; 17:11). In summary, *do not disobey your elders and let not injustice reign in your congregations.*

[306] When you take young birds, do not take the mother (D22:6), that is, *do not show disrespect to life.*

[311] Do not force a bridegroom to perform military service during the first year of his marriage (D24:5), that is, *do not bereave him of time to bring happiness to his wife* (cf. the same verse!).

[360] An emasculated person shall not marry a woman of God's people (D23:1), that is, *do not contract unnatural marriages*—if at least the rabbis have correctly deduced this from Deuteronomy 23:1. And if the non-married state is the higher way under the New Covenant (1 Cor. 7), is it not conceivable that, conversely, a man and a woman could marry out of love, even if sexual intercourse were physically impossible?

---

lash fewer than the prescribed number.

Bibliography

Adamson, J. B. 1976. *The Epistle of James.* New International Commentary on the New Testament. Grand Rapids, MI: Eerdmans.

Aland, K. M. Black, C. M. Martini, B. M. Metzger, and A. Wikgren, eds. 1983. *The Greek New Testament.* 3rd ed. New York: United Bible Societies.

Alexander, R. H. 1986. *Ezekiel.* Expositor's Bible Commentary. Vol. 6. Grand Rapids, MI: Regency.

Arndt, W. F., F. W. Danker, and W. Bauer. 2000. *A Greek-English Lexicon of the New Testament and Other Early Christian Literature.* Chicago: The University of Chicago Press.

Bacchiocchi, S. 1977. *From Sabbath to Sunday: A Historical Investigation of the Rise of Sunday Observance in Early Christianity.* Rome: Pontifical Gregorian University.

———. 1998. *The Sabbath Under Crossfire: A Biblical Analysis of Recent Sabbath/Sunday Developments.* Berrien Springs, MI: Biblical Perspectives.

Badenas, R. 1985. *Christ the End of the Law: Romans 10.4 in Pauline Perspective.* Sheffield: JSOT.

Bagatti, B. 1971. *The Church from the Circumcision: History and Archaeology of the Judaeo-Christians.* Jerusalem: Franciscan Printing.

Bahnsen, G. L. 1977. *Theonomy in Christian Ethics.* Nutley, NJ: Craig.

Barker, K. L. 1982. "False Dichotomies Between the Testaments." *Journal of the Evangelical Theological Society* 25: 3–16.

Barker, W. S. and W. R. Godfrey, eds. 1990. *Theonomy: A Reformed Critique.* Grand Rapids, MI: Zondervan.

Bavinck, H. 2004. *Reformed Dogmatics.* Edited by John Bolt. Translated by John Vriend. Vol. 2. Grand Rapids: Baker Academic.

Benamozegh, E. 1995. *Israel and Humanity.* Translated by M. Luria. Mahwah, NJ: Paulist.

Berger, K. 1984. *Exegese des Neuen Testaments: Neue Wege vom Text zur Auslegung.* 2nd ed. Heidelberg: Quelle und Meyer.

Berkhof, L. 1939. *Systematic Theology.* Grand Rapids, MI: Eerdmans.

Berkowitz, A. and D. 1999. *Take Hold: Embracing Our Divine Inheritance with Israel.* Littleton, CO: First Fruits of Zion.

———. 2012. *Tora Rediscovered.* 5th ed. Richmond, MI: Shoreshim Publishing.

Betz, H. D. *Galatians.* Hermeneia. Philadelphia, PA: Fortress, 1979.

Bivin, D. 2005. *New Light on the Difficult Words of Jesus.* Holland, MI: En-Gedi Resource Center.

Bivin, D. and R. B. Blizzard. 1984. *Understanding the Difficult Words of Jesus.* Shippensburg, PA: Destiny Image Publishers.

Boice, J. M. 1976. *Galatians.* Expositor's Bible Commentary Vol. 10. Grand Rapids, MI: Zondervan.

Brandon, S. G. F. 1957. *The Fall of Jerusalem and the Christian Church.* London: SPCK.

Bruce, A. B. 1979 (repr.). *The Synoptic Gospels.* Expositor's Greek Testament. Vol. 1. Grand Rapids, MI: Eerdmans.

Bruce, F. F. 1984 (repr. 1985). *The Epistles to the Colossians, to Philemon, and to the Ephesians.* New International Commentary on the New Testament. Grand Rapids, MI: Eerdmans.

———. 1964 (repr. 1985). *The Epistle to the Hebrews*. New International Commentary on the New Testament. Grand Rapids, MI: Eerdmans.

———. 1988. *The Book of the Acts*. New International Commentary on the New Testament. Grand Rapids, MI: Eerdmans.

Buber, M. 1963. *Werke*. Vol. 3: *Schriften zum Chassidismus*. München: Kösel/Heidelberg: Lambert Schneider.

Buswell, J. O. 1962. *A Systematic Theology of the Christian Religion*. 2 vols. Grand Rapids, MI: Zondervan.

Calvin, J. (1559) 1960. *Institutes of the Christian Religion*. The Library of Christian Classics. 2 vols. Louisville, KY: Westminster John Knox Press.

Carson, D. A., ed. 1982. *From Sabbath to Lord's Day: A Biblical, Historical, and Theological Investigation*. Grand Rapids, MI: Zondervan.

Carson, D. A.1984. *Matthew*. Expositor's Bible Commentary. Vol. 8. Grand Rapids, MI: Regency.

Cashdan, E. 1957. *Malachi*. Soncino Books of the Bible. London: Soncino.

Chafer, L. S. 1936. *Dispensationalism*. Dallas, TX: Dallas Seminary.

———. 1948. *Systematic Theology*. Vol. 4. *Ecclesiology, Eschatology*. Dallas, TX: Dallas Seminary.

Christ, F. 1970. *Jesus–Sophia: Die Sophia-Christologie bei den Synoptikern*. Zürich: Zwingli-Verlag.

Christiansen, E. J. 1995. *The Covenant in Judaism and Paul: A Study of Ritual Boundaries as Identity Markers*, Leiden: Brill.

Chumney, E. 1994. *The Seven Festivals of the Messiah*. Shippensburg, PA: Destiny Image Publishers.

Cohen, A. 1984. *The Five Megilloth*. Rev. by A. J. Rosenberg. Soncino Books of the Bible. London: Soncino.

———. 1985. *The Soncino Chumash*. Rev. by A. J. Rosenberg. Soncino Books of the Bible. London: Soncino.
Craigie, P. C. 1976. *The Book of Deuteronomy*. New International Commentary of the Old Testament. Grand Rapids, MI: Eerdmans.
Cranfield, C. E. B. 1959. *St. Mark*. Cambridge: Cambridge University Press.
———. 1981. *Romans*. International Critical Commentary. Vol. 2. Edinburgh: T. and T. Clark.
———. 1991. "'The Works of the Law' in the Epistle to the Romans." *Journal for the Study of the New Testament* 43: 89–101.
Dake, F. J. 1996. *Dake's Annotated Reference Bible: New Testament*. Lawrenceville, GA: Dake Publishing.
Daube, D. 1956. *The New Testament and Rabbinic Judaism*. London: Athlone.
Davies, W. D. 1952. *Torah in the Messianic Age and/or the Age to Come*. Philadelphia, PA: Society of Biblical Literature.
———. 1955. *Paul and Rabbinic Judaism: Some Rabbinic Elements in Pauline Theology*. London: SPCK.
———. 1966 (repr. 1969). *The Sermon on the Mount*. Cambridge: Cambridge University Press.
———. *Jewish and Pauline Studies*. Philadelphia, PA: Fortress, 1984.
Delling, G. 1971. "*Stoicheion*." In *Theological Dictionary of the New Testament*. Edited by G. Kittel et al. Grand Rapids, MI: Eerdmans. 7:670–86.
Dibelius, M. 1956. *Studies in the Acts of the Apostles*. London: SCM.
Dodd, C. H. 1954. *The Bible and the Greeks*. 2nd ed. London: Hodder and Stoughton.
———. 1968. *More New Testament Studies*. Manchester: University Press.
Dunn, J. D. G. 1988. *Romans*. Word Biblical Commentary. Vol. 38. Dallas, TX: Word.
———. 1990a. *Unity and Diversity in the New Testament: An*

Inquiry into the Character of Earliest Christianity. 2nd ed. London: SCM/Philadelphia, PA: Trinity Press International.

———. 1990b. *Jesus, Paul, and the Law: Studies in Mark and Galatians*. Louisville, KY: Westminster.

———. 1992. "Yet Once More—'The Works of the Law': A Response." *Journal for the Study of the New Testament* 46: 99–117.

———, ed. 1996. *Paul and the Mosaic Law*. Tübingen: Mohr Siebeck.

———. 1998. *The Theology of Paul the Apostle*. Edinburgh: T. and T. Clark.

Dunn, J. D. G. and A. M. Suggate. 1993. *The Justice of God: A Fresh Look At the Old Doctrine of Justification By Faith*. Carlisle: Paternoster.

Edersheim, A. 1971 (repr. 1883–1890). *The Life and Times of Jesus the Messiah*. Grand Rapids, MI: Eerdmans.

Ellison, H. L. 1976. *The Mystery of Israel: An Exposition of Romans 9–11*. 3rd ed. Exeter: Paternoster.

Enns, P. 2008. *The Moody Handbook of Theology: Revised and Expanded*. Chicago: Moody Publishers.

Eskenazy, T. C., D. J. Harrington, and W. H. Shea, eds. 1991. *The Sabbath in Jewish and Christian Traditions*. New York: Crossroad.

Falk, H. 1982. "Rabbi Jacob Emden's Views on Christianity." *Journal of Ecumenical Studies*. 19.1: 105–111.

Falk, H. 2003. *Jesus the Pharisee, A New Look at the Jewishness of Jesus*. Eugene, OR: Wipf and Stock.

Fee, G. 1987. *The First Epistle to the Corinthians*. New International Commentary on the New Testament. Grand Rapids, MI: Eerdmans.

Feinberg, C. L. 1961. *Premillennialism or Amillennialism?* New York: American Board of Missions to the Jews.

———. 1985. *Millennialism: The Two Major Views*. 2nd ed. Chicago: Moody.

Feinberg, J. S., ed. 1988. *Continuity and Discontinuity: Perspectives on the Relationship of the Old and New Testaments.* Westchester, IL: Crossway Books.

Findlay, G. G. 1979 (repr.). *St. Paul's First Epistle to the Corinthians.* Expositor's Greek Testament. Vol. 2. Grand Rapids, MI: Eerdmans.

Finsterbusch, K. 1996. *Die Thora als Lebensweisung für Heidenchristen: Studien zur Bedeutung der Thora für die paulinische Ethik.* Göttingen: Vandenhoeck and Ruprecht.

Fisch, S. 1950. *Ezekiel.* Soncino Books of the Bible. London: Soncino.

Fischer, J. 1992. *Messianic Services for Festivals and Holy Days.* Clearwater, FL: Menorah Ministries.

Fischer, J. and Bronstein, D. 1988. *Siddur for Messianic Jews.* Clearwater, FL: Menorah Ministries.

Flusser, D. 1988. *Judaism and the Origins of Christianity.* Jerusalem: Magnes.

———. 1998. *Jesus.* 2nd ed. Jerusalem: Magnes.

Fohrer, G. 1971. "Sophia." In *Theological Dictionary of the New Testament.* Edited by G. Kittel et al. Translated by G. W. Bromiley. Grand Rapids, MI: Eerdmans. 7:476–96.

Freeman, H. 1962. "The Problem of Efficacy of Old Testament Sacrifices." *Bulletin of the Evangelical Theological Society* 5: 73–79.

Friedman, D. 2001. *They Loved the Torah.* Clarksville, MD: Messianic Jewish Publishers.

Friedman, D., with B. D. Friedman. 2012. *James the Just Presents Applications of Torah: A Messianic Commentary.* Clarksville, MD: Messianic Jewish Publishers.

Froom, L. E. 1948. *The Prophetic Faith of Our Fathers.* Vol. 2. Washington, DC: Review and Herald.

Fruchtenbaum, A. G. 1985. "The Quest for a Messianic Theology." *Mishkan* 2: 1–17.

———. 1992. *Israelology: The Missing Link in Systematic Theology.* 2nd ed. San Antonio, TX: Ariel Ministries.

———. 1993. *Hebrew Christianity: Its Theology, History and Philosophy*. San Antonio, TX: Ariel Ministries.

———. 2003. *Footsteps of the Messiah: A Study of the Sequence of Prophetic Events*. Revised ed. San Antonio, TX: Ariel Ministries.

Fung, R. Y. K. 1988. *The Epistle to the Galatians*. New International Commentary on the New Testament. Grand Rapids, MI: Eerdmans.

Furnish, Victor P. 1968. *Theology and Ethics in Paul*. Nashville, TN: Abingdon.

Gaebelein, A. C. 1970. *The Annotated Bible: Matthew to Ephesians*, Neptune, NJ: Loizeaux.

Gaston, L. 1987. *Paul and the Torah*, Vancouver, BC: University of British Columbia Press.

Geldenhuys, N. 1983. *The Gospel of Luke*. New International Commentary on the New Testament. 2nd ed. Grand Rapids, MI: Eerdmans.

Ginzberg, L. 1968. *The Legends of the Jews*. Vol. 3. Philadelphia, PA: Jewish Publication Society of America.

Goldberg, L. 1980. "*Hokmah*. Wisdom." In *Theological Wordbook of the Old Testament*. Edited by R. L. Harris, et al. Chicago: Moody. 1:283–84.

Grant, F. W. 1901. *The Numerical Bible: Acts to 2 Corinthians*. Neptune, NJ: Loizeaux Brothers.

Greene, C. J. D. 2004. *Christology in Cultural Perspective: Marking Out the Horizons*. Grand Rapids, MI: Eerdmans.

Grosheide, F. W. 1963. *De Handelingen der Apostelen*. Korte Verklaring der Heilige Schrift. Vol. 2. Kampen: Kok.

Gutbrod, W. 1967. "*Nomos*." In *Theological Dictionary of the New Testament*. Edited by G. Kittel et al. Translated by G. W. Bromiley. Grand Rapids, MI: Eerdmans. 6:1036–91.

Halkin, A. S., ed. 1952. *Moses Maimonides' Epistle to Yemen: The Arabic Original and the Three Hebrew Versions*. Translated by B. Cohen. New York: American Academy for Jewish Research.

Hamerton-Kelly, R. 1973. *Pre-Existence, Wisdom, and The Son of Man: A Study of the Idea of Pre-Existence in the New Testament.* Cambridge: Cambridge University Press.

Hamilton, F. E. 1942. *The Basis of Millennial Faith.* Grand Rapids, MI: Eerdmans.

Harris, J. R. 1917. *The Origin of the Prologue to St. John's Gospel.* Cambridge: Cambridge University Press.

Harris, R. L., G. L. Archer Jr., and B. K. Waltke, eds. 1980. *Theological Wordbook of the Old Testament.* 2 vols. Chicago: Moody.

Harvey, W. 1972. "Torah." *Encyclopaedia Judaica.* Jerusalem: Encyclopaedia Judaica, 15: 1235–1246.

Hendriksen, W. 1978. *The Covenant of Grace.* Rev. ed. Grand Rapids, MI: Baker Book House.

Herford, R. T. 1962. *Ethics of the Talmud: Sayings of the Fathers.* New York: Schocken Books.

Hertz, J. H., ed. 1938. *The Pentateuch and Haftorahs: Hebrew Text, English Translation and Commentary.* London: Soncino.

Hillar, M. 2012. *From Logos to Trinity: The Evolution of Religious Beliefs from Pythagoras to Tertullian.* Cambridge: Cambridge University Press.

Hillers, D. R. 1969. *Covenant: The History of a Biblical Idea.* Baltimore, MD: Johns Hopkins Press.

Hodge, C. 1960. *Systematic Theology.* 3 vols. London: James Clarke and Co.

Horton, M. 2006. *God of Promise.* Grand Rapids, MI: Baker Book House.

Hübner, H. 1984. *Law in Paul's Thought.* Edinburgh: T. and T. Clark.

Jocz, J. 1981. *The Jewish People and Jesus Christ After Auschwitz.* Lanham, MD: University Press of America.

Jukes, A. 1875. *The Types of Genesis: As Revealing the Development of Human Nature.* London: Longmans, Green and Co.

Juster, D. 1995. *Jewish Roots: A Foundation of Biblical Theology.* Shippensburg, PA: Destiny Image Publishers.

Kac, A. W., ed. 1986. *The Messiahship of Jesus: Are Jews Changing Their Attitude Toward Jesus?* 2nd ed. Grand Rapids, MI: Baker Book House.

Kaiser Jr., W. C. 1978. *Toward an Old Testament Theology.* Grand Rapids, MI: Academie Books.

———. 2008. *The Promise-Plan of God: A Biblical Theology of the Old and New Testaments.* Grand Rapids, MI: Zondervan.

Karlberg, M. W. 1986. "Reformation Politics: The Relevance of OT Ethics in Calvinist Political Theory." *Journal of the Evangelical Theological Society* 29: 179–91.

Kaufmann, Y. 1988. *Christianity and Judaism: Two Covenants.* Jerusalem: Magnes.

Kelly, W. 1872. *Lectures on the Book of Revelation.* London: G. Morrish.

Kim, Yung Suk. 2011. *A Theological Introduction to Paul's Letters: Exploring a Threefold Theology of Paul.* Eugene, OR: Cascade Books.

Kissane, E. J. *The Book of Isaiah.* Vol. 2. Dublin: Browne and Nolan, 1943.

Kittel, G. 1967. "*Legō.*" In *Theological Dictionary of the New Testament.* Edited by G. Kittel et al. Translated by G. W. Bromiley. Grand Rapids, MI: Eerdmans. 6:100–143.

Kittel, G., G. Friedrich, and G. W. Bromiley, eds. 1964–1976. *Theological Dictionary of the New Testament.* Translated by G. W. Bromiley. 10 vols, Grand Rapids, MI: Eerdmans.

Kjær-Hansen, K. and B. F. Skjøt. 1999. *Facts and Myths: About the Messianic Congregations in Israel.* Jerusalem: United Christian Council.

Klausner, J. 1925. *Jesus of Nazareth: His Life, Times, and Teaching.* London: Allen and Unwin.

———. 1955. *The Messianic Idea in Israel from Its Beginning to the Completion of the Mishnah.* New York: Macmillan.

Klijn, A. F. and G. J. Reinink. 1973. *Patristic Evidence for Jewish-Christian Sects*. Leiden: Brill.

Kline, M. 1963. *Treaty of the Great King*. Grand Rapids, MI: Eerdmans.

———. 1967. Kline, M. *By Oath Consigned*. Grand Rapids, MI: Eerdmans.

Klinghardt, M. 1988. *Gesetz und Volk Gottes*. Tübingen: Mohr Siebeck.

Knowling, R. J. 1979 (repr.). *The Acts of the Apostles*. Expositor's Greek Testament. Vol. 2. Grand Rapids, MI: Eerdmans.

Ladd, G. E. 1959. *The Gospel of the Kingdom*. Grand Rapids, MI: Eerdmans.

Lancaster, D. T. 2011. *Restoration: Returning the Torah of God to the Disciples of Jesus*. 3rd ed. Marshfield, MO: First Fruits of Zion.

Lane, W. L. 1974. *The Gospel of Mark*. New International Commentary on the New Testament. Grand Rapids, MI: Eerdmans.

Lapide, P. 2004. *Er predigte in ihren Synagogen: Jüdische Evangelienauslegung*. 8th ed. Gütersloh: Mohn.

———. 2011. *Mit einem Juden die Bibel lessen*. Münster: LIT Verlag.

Lapide, P. and P. Stuhlmacher. 1984. *Paul: Rabbi and Apostle*. Minneapolis, MN: Augsburg Publ. House.

LaSor, W. S. 1972. *The Dead Sea Scrolls and the New Testament*. Grand Rapids, MI: Eerdmans.

Layton, B. 1987. *The Gnostic Scriptures: A New Translation with Annotations and Introductions*. Garden City, NY: Doubleday.

Lehne, S. 1990. *The New Covenant in Hebrews*. JSNT, Supplement Series 44. Sheffield: JSOT.

Lichtenstein, A. 1981. *The Seven Laws of Noah*. New York: Rabbi Jacob Joseph School.

Liebers, R. 1989. *Das Gesetz als Evangelium: Untersuchungen zur Gesetzeskritik des Paulus*. Zürich: Theologischer Verlag.

Lindars, B. 1988. "All Foods Clean: Thoughts on Jesus and the Law." In *Law and Religion*. Edited by B. Lindars. Cambridge: James Clarke. 61–71.
Linss, W. C. 1988. "Exegesis of telos in Romans 10:4." *Biblical Research* 33: 5–12.
Lipson, J. G. 1990. *Jews for Jesus: An Anthropological Study*. New York: AMS.
Lohfink, N. 1991. *The Covenant Never Revoked: Biblical Reflections on Christian-Jewish Dialogue*. New York: Paulist.
Lohse, E. 1971. "*Sabbaton, sabbatismos, paraskeuē*." In *Theological Dictionary of the New Testament*. Edited by G. Kittel et al. Translated by G. W. Bromiley. Grand Rapids, MI: Eerdmans. 7:1–35.
———. 1991. *Theological Ethics of the New Testament*. Minneapolis: Fortress.
Longenecker, R. N. 1981. *The Acts of the Apostles*. Expositor's Bible Commentary. Vol. 9. Grand Rapids, MI: Regency.
McCarthy, D. J. 1972. *Old Testament Covenant: A Survey of Current Opinions*. Oxford: Blackwell.
Marböck, J. 1976. "Gesetz und Weisheit: Zum Verständnis des Gesetzes bei Jesus ben Sira." *Biblische Zeitschrift* 21: 1–21.
Marshall, I. H. 1978. *The Epistles of John*. New International Commentary on the New Testament. Grand Rapids, MI: Eerdmans
Martin, B. L. 1989. *Christ and the Law in Paul*. Leiden: Brill.
Medema, H. P. 1994. *De heerlijkheid en de verbonden: De openbaring van God in het oude en het nieuwe verbond: Een evangelische visie*. Vaassen: Medema.
Meijer, L. E. 1997. *Terugkeer uit de ballingschap: Een onderzoek naar Messiasbelijdende gemeenten in Israël*. Driebergen: Gereformeerde Zendingsbond in de Nederlandse Hervormde Kerk.
Mendenhall, G. E. 1955. *Law and Covenant in Israel and the Ancient Near East*. Pittsburgh, PA: Biblical Colloquium.

Metzger, B. M. 1971 (rev. 1975). *A Textual Commentary on the Greek New Testament*. London/New York: United Bible Societies.

Miskotte, K. H. 1956. *Als de goden zwijgen: Over de zin van het Oude Testament*. Amsterdam: Uitgeversmaatschappij Holland

Montefiore, C. G. 1900-1901. "Rabbinic Judaism and the Epistles of St. Paul." *Jewish Quarterly Review* 13: 161-217.

———. 1914. *Judaism and St. Paul: Two Essays*. London: M. Goschen.

Moo, D. 1987. "Paul and the Law in the Last Ten Years." *Scottish Journal of Theology* 40: 287-307.

Moo, D. J. 1996. *The Epistle to the Romans*. New International Commentary on the New Testament. Grand Rapids, MI: Eerdmans.

Moore, G. F. 1921. "Christian Writers on Judaism." *Harvard Theological Review* 14: 197-254.

———. 1927-1930. *Judaism in the First Centuries of the Christian Era: The Age of the Tannaim*. 3 vols. Cambridge, MA: Harvard University Press.

Morris, H. M. 1976. *The Genesis Record*. Grand Rapids, MI: Baker Book House.

Morris, L. 1971. *The Gospel According to John*. New International Commentary on the New Testament. Grand Rapids, MI: Eerdmans.

Moseley, R. 1998. *Yeshua: A Guide to the Real Jesus and the Original Church*. Baltimore, MD: Messianic Jewish Publishers.

———. 2000. *Kingdom Relationships: God's Laws for the Community of Faith*. Baltimore, MD: Messianic Jewish Publishers.

Müller, K. 1994. *Tora für die Völker: Die Noachidischen Gebote und Ansätze zu ihrer Rezeption im Christentum*. Berlin: Institut Kirche und Judentum.

Murray, J. 1968. *The Epistle to the Romans*. New International Commentary on the New Testament. Grand Rapids,

MI: Eerdmans.
Neumann, E. 1955. *The Great Mother: An Analysis of the Archetype*. New York: Pantheon Books.
Neusner, J. 1983. *Judaism in the Beginning of Christianity*. Philadelphia, PA: Fortress.
———. 1986. *Judaism in the Matrix of Christianity*. Philadelphia, PA: Fortress.
———. 1990. *Jews and Christians: The Myth of a Common Tradition*. New York: Trinity Press International.
———. 1993. *A Rabbi Talks with Jesus: An Intermillennial, Interfaith Exchange*. New York: Doubleday.
———. 1995. *Children of the Flesh, Children of the Promise: A Rabbi Talks with Paul*. Cleveland, OH: The Pilgrim Press.
Neusner, J. and B.D. Chilton. 1995. *Christianity and Judaism: The Formative Categories*. Vol. 1: *Revelation: The Torah and the Bible*. Philadelphia, PA: Trinity Press International.
Nicholson, E. W. 1986. *God and His People: Covenant and Theology in the Old Testament,*. Oxford: Clarendon.
Novak, D. 1983. *The Image of the Non-Jew in Judaism: An Historical and Constructive Study of the Noahide Laws*. New York: E. Mellen.
O'Collins, G. 2009. *Christology: A Biblical, Historical, and Systematic Study of Jesus*. Oxford: Oxford University Press.
Oegema, G. S. 1999. *Für Israel und die Völker: Studien zum alttestamentlich-jüdischen Hintergrund der paulinischen Theologie*. Leiden: Brill.
O'Neill, J. C. 1972. *The Recovery of Paul's Letter to the Galatians*. London: SPCK.
Ouweneel, W. J. 1995. *Das Buch der Offenbarung*. Bielefeld: Christliche Literatur-Verbreitung.
———. 1997. *De vrijheid van de Geest: Bijbelstudies bij de Brief van Paulus aan de Galaten*. Vaassen: Medema.
———. 1998. *De zevende koningin: Het eeuwig vrouwelijke en de raad van God*. Heerenveen: Barnabas.

———. 1999. *Jeruzalem, de stad van de grote Koning*. Vaassen: Medema.

———. 2000a. *De zesde kanteling: Christus en 5000 jaar denkgeschiedenis: Religie en metafysica in het jaar 2000*. Heerenveen: Barnabas

———. 2000b. *Het Jobslijden van Israël: Israëls lijden oplichtend uit het boek Job*. Vaassen: Medema.

———. 2001. *Hoogtijden voor Hem: De bijbelse feesten en hun betekenis voor Joden en christenen*. Vaassen: Medema.

———. 2006.*'Geneest de zieken!': Over de bijbelse leer van ziekte, genezing en bevrijding*. 5th ed. Vaassen: Medema.

———. 2010. *De Kerk van God (I): Ontwerp van een elementaire ecclesiologie*. Evangelische Dogmatische Reeks. Vol. 7. Heerenveen: Medema.

———. 2011a. *De Kerk van God (II): Ontwerp van een historische en praktische ecclesiologie*. Evangelische Dogmatische Reeks. Vol. 8. Heerenveen: Medema.

———. 2011b. *Het verbond en het koninkrijk van God: Ontwerp van een verbonds-, doop- en koninkrijksleer*. Evangelische Dogmatische Reeks. Vol. 9. Heerenveen: Medema.

———. 2012. *De toekomst van God: Ontwerp van een eschatologie*. Evangelische Dogmatische Reeks. Vol. 10. Heerenveen: Medema.

———. 2018b. *The Ninth King: The Last of the Celestial Empires, The Triumph of Christ over the Powers*. Jordan Station, ON: Paideia.

———. 2019a. *Power In Service: An Introduction to Christian Political Thought*. Jordan Station, ON: Paideia.

———. 2019b. *The Eternal Word: God Speaking To Us*. Toronto: Ezra Press.

Peake, A. S. 1979 (repr.). *The Epistle to the Colossians*. Expositor's Greek Testament. Vol. 3. Grand Rapids, MI: Eerdmans.

Pentecost, J. D. 1964. *Things to Come: A Study in Biblical Eschatology*. Grand Rapids, MI: Academie Books.

Poythress, V. S. 1987. *Understanding Dispensationalists*. Grand Rapids, MI: Academie Books.
———. 1991. *The Shadow of Christ in the Law of Moses*. Brentwood, TN: Wolgemuth and Hyatt.
Pritz, R. A. 1988. *Nazarene Jewish Christianity: From the End of the New Testament Period Until Its Disappearance in the Fourth Century*, Leiden: Brill/Jerusalem: Magnes.
Quispel, G. 1979. *Het geheime boek der Openbaring*. Amerongen: Gaade.
Räisänen, H. 1980. "Legalism and Salvation by the Law." In *Die Paulinische Literatur und Theologie*. Edited by S. Pedersen. Aarhus: Aros. 63–83.
———. 1983. *Paul and the Law*. Wissenschaftliche Untersuchungen zum Neuen Testament 29. Tübingen: Mohr Siebeck.
———. 1986. *The Torah and Christ: Essays in German and English on the Problem of the Law in Early Christianity*. Helsinki: Finnish Exegetical Society.
———. 1992. *Jesus, Paul and Torah: Collected Essays*. JSNT Supplement Series 43. Sheffield: JSOT.
Rausch, D. A. 1982. *Messianic Judaism: Its History, Theology, and Polity*. Lewiston, NY: E. Mellen.
Reinmuth, E. 1985. *Geist und Gesetz: Studien zu Voraussetzungen und Inhalt der paulinischen Paränese*. Berlin: Evangelische Verlagsanstalt.
Ridderbos, H. 1960. *Aan de Colossenzen*. Commentaar op het Nieuwe Testament. Kampen: Kok.
———. 1965. *Het evangelie naar Mattheüs*. Korte Verklaring der Heilige Schrift. Vol. 1. Kampen: Kok.
Robertson, O. P. 1981. *The Christ of the Covenants*. Phillipsburg, NJ: P and R Publishing.
Robinson, J. A. T. 1952. *The Body: A Study in Pauline Theology*. Studies in Biblical Theology 5. London: SCM.
Rordorf, W. 1968. *Sunday: The History of the Day of Rest and Worship in the Earliest Centuries of the Christian Church*. London: SCM.

Ross, A. P. 1991. *Proverbs*. Expositor's Bible Commentary. Vol. 5. Grand Rapids, MI: Zondervan.

Roth, A. G. 2012. *Aramaic English New Testament*. Annotated by A. G. Roth. Mount Vernon, WA: Netzari.

Rudin, A. J. 2010. *Christians and Jews Faith to Faith: Tragic History, Promising Present, Fragile Future*. Woodstock, VT: Jewish Lights Publishing.

Rudin, A. J. and M. R. Wilson. 1987. *A Time to Speak: The Evangelical-Jewish Encounter*. Grand Rapids, MI: Eerdmans.

Rushdoony, R. J. 1973. *Institutes of Biblical Law*. Nutley, NJ: Craig.

———. 1978. *Thy Kingdom Come*. Fairfax, VA: Thoburn.

Ryrie, C. C. 1965. *Dispensationalism Today* Chicago: Moody.

Saldarini, A., ed. 1975. *The Fathers According to Rabbi Nathan*. Leiden: Brill.

Sanders, E. P. 1977. *Paul and Palestinian Judaism: A Comparison of Pattern of Religion*. Philadelphia, PA: Fortress.

———. 1983. *Paul, the Law, and the Jewish People*. Philadelphia, PA: Fortress.

———. 1985. *Jesus and Judaism*. London: SCM.

———. 1990. *Jewish Law from Jesus to the Mishnah: Five Studies*. London: SCM/Philadelphia, PA: Trinity Press International.

———. 1992. *Judaism: Practice and Belief: 63 BCE – 66 CE*. Philadelphia, PA: Trinity Press International.

Schipflinger, Th. 1988. *Sophia-Maria: Eine ganzheitliche Vision der Schöpfung*, München/Zürich: Neue Stadt. English translation: 1998. *Sophia–Maria: A Holistic Vision of Creation*. Newburyport, MA: Red Wheel/Weiser.

Schiffman, M. 1996. *Return of the Remnant: The Rebirth of Messianic Judaism*. Clarksville, MD: Messianic Jewish Resources.

Schnabel, E. J. 1985. *Law and Wisdom from ben Sira to Paul: A Traditional Historical Enquiry into the Relation of Law, Wisdom, and Ethics*. Tübingen: Mohr Siebeck.

Schoeps, H. J. 1949. *Theologie und Geschichte des Judenchristentums*. Tübingen: Mohr Siebeck.

———. 1950. *Gottheit und Menschheit: Die großen Religionsstifter und ihre Lehren*. Stuttgart: Steingrüben-Verlag.

———. 1961. *Paul: The Theology of the Apostle in the Light of Jewish Religious History*. Philadelphia, PA: Westminster.

———. 1963. *The Jewish-Christian Argument: A History of Theologies in Conflict*. New York: Holt, Rinehart and Winston.

Scholem, G. 1960. *Zur Kabbala und ihrer Symbolik*. Zürich: Rhein-Verlag.

———. 1971. *The Messianic Idea in Judaism and Other Essays on Jewish Spirituality*. New York: Schocken Books.

———. 1977 (repr. 2001). *Von der mystischen Gestalt der Gottheit: Studien zu Grundbegriffen der Kabbala*. Frankfurt, Suhrkamp.

Schonfield, H. J. 1936. *The History of Jewish Christianity from the First to the Twentieth Century*. London: Duckworth.

Schrage, W. 1988. *The Ethics of the New Testament*. Philadelphia, PA: Fortress.

Schreiner, T. R. 1993. *The Law and Its Fulfillment: A Pauline Theology of Law*. Grand Rapids, MI: Baker Books.

Schürer, E. 1885–1891. *A History of the Jewish People in the Time of Jesus Christ*. 5 vols. New York: Scribner.

Schweizer, E. 1971. *Jesus*. London: SCM.

Scofield, C. I. 1909. *Scofield Reference Bible*. New York: Oxford University Press.

Scott, W. 1920. *Exposition of the Revelation of Jesus Christ*. London: Pickering and Inglis.

Segal, A. F. 1984. "Torah and Nomos in Recent Scholarly Discussion." *Studies in Religion/Sciences Religieuses* 13.1:19–27.

Segal, A. F. 1990. *Paul the Convert: The Apostolate and Apostasy of Saul the Pharisee*. New Haven, CT: Yale University Press.

Selter, F. 1986. "Avarice, Greed, Love of Money." In *Dictionary of New Testament Theology*, Edited by C. Brown. Carlisle: Paternoster. 1:137–38.

Shulam, J., with H. Le Cornu. 1998. *A Commentary on the Jewish Roots of Romans*. Baltimore, MD: Messianic Jewish Publishers.

Sigal, Ph. 1987. *The Halakhah of Jesus of Nazareth According to the Gospel of Matthew*. Lanham, MD: University Press of America.

Snell, H. H. 1878 (repr. 2010) *Notes on the Revelation: With Practical Reflections*. Charleston, NC: Nabu.

Snodgrass, K. R. 1988. "Spheres of Influence: A Possible Solution to the Problem of Paul and the Law." *Journal for the Study of the New Testament* 32: 93–113.

Söding, Th. 1995. *Das Liebesgebot bei Paulus: Die Mahnung zur Agape im Rahmen der paulinischen Ethik*. Münster: Aschendorff.

Stein, L. 1867–1910. *Die Schrift des Lebens: Inbegriff des gesammten Judenthums*, Bd. I–III, Mannheim: J. Schneider.

Stern, D. 1985. "The Quest for a Messianic Theology (Response)." *Mishkan* 2:18–23.

———. 1989. *Jewish New Testament*. Clarksville, MD: Jewish New Testament Publications, 1989.

———. 1997. *Messianic Jewish Manifesto*. 3rd ed. Clarksville, MD: Jewish New Testament Publications.

———. 1999. *Jewish New Testament Commentary*. 6th ed. Clarksville, MD: Jewish New Testament Publications.

———. 2007. *Messianic Judaism: A Modern Movement with an Ancient Past*. Clarksville, MD: Messianic Jewish Publishers.

———. 2009. *Restoring the Jewishness of the Gospel*. 3rd ed. Clarksville, MD: Messianic Jewish Publishers.

Strachan, R. H. 1979 (repr.). *The Second Epistle General of Peter*. Expositor's Greek Testament. Vol. 5. Grand Rapids, MI: Eerdmans.

Strack, H. L. and P. Billerbeck. 1922–1928. *Kommentar zum Neuen Testament aus Talmud und Midrasch*. München: C. H. Beck.

Susman, M. 1996. *Das Buch Hiob und das Schicksal des jüdischen Volkes,*. Frankfurt: Jüdischer Verlag.

Swidler, L., L. J. Eron, G. Sloyan, and L. Dean. 1990. *Bursting the Bonds? A Jewish-Christian Dialogue on Jesus and Paul*. Maryknoll, NY: Orbis Books.

Tan, P. L. 1974. *The Interpretation of Prophecy*. Winona Lake, IN: BMH Books.

Thielman, F. 1995. *Paul and the Law: A Contextual Approach*. Downers Grove, IL: InterVarsity.

Thompson, M. B. 2002. *The New Perspective on Paul*. Cambridge: Grove Books.

Tomson, P. J. 1990. *Paul and the Jewish Law: Halakha in the Letters of the Apostle to the Gentiles*. Assen: Van Gorcum/ Minneapolis, MN: Fortress.

Van Gemeren, W., ed. 1997. *Dictionary of Old Testament Theology and Exegesis*. 4 vols. Carlisle: Paternoster.

Van Spanje, T. E. 1999. *Inconsistency in Paul? A Critique of the Work of Heikki Räisänen*. Wissenschaftliche Untersuchungen zum Neuen Testament. 2. Reihe 110. Tübingen: Mohr Siebeck.

Vermes, G. 1973. *Jesus the Jew: A Historian's Reading of the Gospels* London: Collins.

———. 1993. *The Religion of Jesus the Jew*. London: SCM.

Von Lips, H. 1990. *Weisheitliche Traditionen im Neuen Testament*. NeukirchenVluyn: Neukirchener Verlag.

Voorhoeve, H. C. (1866) 1922. *De toekomst onzes Heeren Jezus Christus*. 8th ed. Den Haag: J. N. Voorhoeve.

Walvoord, J. F. 1959. *The Millennial Kingdom*. Grand Rapids, MI: Dunham Publ. Co.

———. 1966. *The Revelation of Jesus Christ*. Chicago: Moody.

———. 1991. *Major Bible Prophecies: 37 Crucial Prophecies that Affect You Today*. Grand Rapids, MI: Zondervan.

Weber, F. 1880. *System der altsynagogalen palästinischen Theologie oder Die Lehren des Talmud.* Re-edited 1897 as *Jüdische Theologie auf Grund des Talmud und verwandter Schriften.* Published by F. Delitzsch and G. Schnedermann. Leipzig: Dörffling Franke.

Welker, C. 2013. *Should Christians Be Torah Observant?* 4th ed. Colorado Springs, CO: Sapphire Publications.

Wenham, D. 1995. *Paul: Follower of Jesus or Founder of Christianity?* Grand Rapids, MI: Eerdmans.

Westerholm, S. 1985. "*Torah, Nomos,* and Law: A Question of Meaning." *Studies in Religion/Sciences Religieuses* 15, 3: 327–36.

Westerholm, S. 1988. *Israel's Law and the Church's Faith: Paul and His Recent Interpreters.* Grand Rapids, MI: Eerdmans.

Wilckens, U. 1971. "*Sophia, sophos, sophizō.*" In *Theological Dictionary of the New Testament.* Edited by G. Kittel et al. Translated by G. W. Bromiley. Grand Rapids, MI: Eerdmans. 7:496–528.

Williams, M. 2005. *The Covenant Story of Redemption.* Phillipsburg, NJ: P and R Publishing.

Wilson, M. R. 1989. *Our Father Abraham: Jewish Roots of the Christian Faith.* Grand Rapids, MI: Eerdmans/Dayton, OH: Center for Judaic-Christian Studies.

Windisch, H. 1914. "Die göttliche Weisheit der Juden und die paulinische Christologie." In *Neutestamentliche Studien: Heinrici zu seinem 70. Geburtstag.* Leipzig: J. C. Hinrichs. 220–34.

Winger, M. 1992. *By What Law? The Meaning of* Nomos *in the Letters of Paul.* Atlanta: Scholars.

Witherington, B. 1995. *The Jesus Quest: The Third Search for the Jew of Nazareth.* Downers Grove, IL: InterVarsity.

Wright, N. T. 1991. *The Climax of the Covenant: Christ and the Law in Pauline Theology.* Edinburgh: T. and T. Clark.

———. 1997. *What Saint Paul Really Said: Was Paul of Tarsus the Real Founder of Christianity?* Oxford: Lion Publishing.

———. 2009. *Paul: In Fresh Perspective*. Minneapolis, MN: Fortress.

Wyschogrod, M. 2000. *The Body of Faith: God in the People of Israel*. Lanham, MD: Jason Aronson.

———. 2004. *Abraham's Promise: Judaism and Jewish-Christian Relations*. Grand Rapids, MI: Eerdmans.

Yinger, K. L. 2010. *The New Perspective on Paul: An Introduction*, Eugene, OR: Cascade Books.

Scripture Index

OLD TESTAMENT

Genesis
1	94
1:2	47, 130, 132, 373
1:26	132
1:27	95
1:28	94
1:29	94
2	94, 508
2:2	506
2:2-3	47, 99, 508, 510
2:7	251
2:9	177
2:10	79
2:15	94
2:16-17	94, 97, 177
2:24	95, 251, 308
2:25	98
3:5-6	105
3:7	98
3:10-11	98
3:11	94, 97
3:16	411
3:16-19	98
3:17	94, 97
3:23	95
6:22	97
7:5	97
7:9	97
7:16	97
9:1-17	418
9:4	419, 420
9:8-17	103
9:12-13	161
9:22-23	98
9:24	98
12	323
12:1	46, 96
12:3	251, 392, 480
12:10-20	98
13:10	98
14:17-20	83, 249
14:18	329
15:5	251
15:6	251
15:8	222
16	98
16:4	98
16:15	249, 251
17	160
17:1	97, 98
17:1-2	104
17:5	251
17:7	175
17:10-11	97, 251
17:10-14	320, 466
17:12-14	97
17:13	175
17:19	175
18:10	251
18:14	251
18:18	480
20:1-18	98
20:13	174
21:2	249, 251
21:9-10	249
21:10	251
21:12	252
22:14	320
22:18	249, 252, 480
25:13	98
25:23	252
25:31-34	99
26:5	3, 41, 97
26:6	97
28:14	480
38	383
38:8	99
40:15	356
45:3	85
48	99
49:1	5
49:10	3, 111, 312
49:33	373

Exodus
1:1-5	374

1:11	374	16:23	506	23:6	175
1:14	374	16:23-30	99, 508	23:9	175
1:16	374	16:26	46	23:11	175
1:22	374	16:28	41	23:12	506
2:2	374	16:30	506	23:16	124, 148, 313
2:3-4	375	17:6	252, 371		
2:5	375	18:5	320, 326	23:19	440
2:21-22	13	18:2-4	14	23:25	263
3:1	320, 326	19	162	24	161, 162, 323
4:20	371	19:1	148		
4:22	56, 255, 323	19:3-6	47, 371	24:1	369
4:25	13	19:4	358	24:3	172
4:25-26	267	19:5-6	186	24:4-8	321
4:27	320, 326	19:5-8	182	24:8	159
5:6-9	374	19:6	46, 224, 488	24:9	369
6:6-7	404	19:8	172	24:9-15	333
6:12	244, 469	19:9	173	24:12	249
6:15-19	374	19:10	400	24:13	320, 326
6:19	295	19:10-15	149	24:15-18	321
6:30	244, 469	19:16	173	24:16-18	47, 173
7:16	296	19:16-19	320	24:17	320
9:16	252	19:22	99, 149	25:8	122
9:31-32	313	19:24	99	25:9	295
10:9	296	20	323	25:16-20	336
10:25-27	296	20:2	46, 47, 103, 165, 321	25:22	336
12:7	321			25:40	295
12:22	321	20:1-17	371	26:30	47
12:40	252	20:5	497	28:1	224, 319
12:43-49	423	20:7	440	29:4	401
12:46	402	20:8-11	47, 503	29:9	227
12:48	465	20:11	506, 510	29:42-45	122
12:49	41	20:12	252	29:45	252
13:9	42, 45, 237	20:13	252	30:18-21	445
13:16	237	20:14	356	30:30	319
13:21	252	20:17	252, 356	31:12-17	47
14:14	46	20:18	320	31:13	161
14:22	252	20:18-21	149	31:13-16	503
15:13	355	20:21	172	31:15	506
15:17	355	21:10	409	31:17	161, 506, 510
15:18	318	21:12-17	322		
15:26	333	21:16	356	32:6	252
16:4	371	22:10-11	237	32:27	382
16:10	321	22:21-22	175	32:31-34	339
16:15	252	22:26-27	309	32:32	368
16:18	252	23:4-5	309	33:9-10	321

Scripture Index

33:12-23	339	10:1	386		252, 345
33:19	252	10:9	454	19:20	356
34	161	10:10	330	19:26	419, 420
34:1	249	10:10-11	319, 338	19:30	503
34:2	148	10:11	42	19:33	175
34:6-7	163, 347	11	14, 440	19:33-34	309
34:21	506	11:44-45	43, 182, 252	20:6	321
34:22	124, 313	11:46	45	20:7	43
34:26	440	12:1-4	399	20:8	182
34:27-28	171	12:3	320	20:10	356
34:28	363	12:6-8	399	20:11	409
34:29-35	333	12:7	45	20:26	43
34:29-30	372	13	355	21:8	43, 182
34:33	252, 373	14	355	21:12	409, 410
34:35	372	14:2	45	21:14	236
35:2	506	14:32	45	21:15	182
35:2-3	503	14:57	45	21:23	182, 409, 410
40:13	319	15:32-33	45		
40:15	227	16	103	22:9	182
40:33	373	16:4	401	22:11-19	381
40:34-35	47	16:16	181	22:16	182
40:34-38	321, 323	16:17	342	22:32	182
40:35	334	16:19	321	23	45, 182
		16:21-22	181	23:3	503, 506
Leviticus		16:29	181	23:15-21	246
1	445	16:31	181, 506	23:22	175
1:4	288	16:42	321	23:24	506
2:13	446	17:10	419	23:29-32	181
3	445	17:10-14	420	23:32	506
3:17	419, 420	17:11	420	23:39	506
5:4	237	17:12	420	24:7	48
6:9	41	17:14	419	24:9	381
6:12-13	46	18:5	80, 165, 166, 220, 252, 392	25:4	506
6:14	41			25:39-46	358
6:25	41			26	162
7	410, 451	18:8	409	26:2	503
7:1	41	18:16	45	26:3-6	348
7:7	41	18:20	45	26:11-12	252
7:11	41	18:26-28	219	26:15	48, 171
7:11-34	446	19:2	43	26:41	244, 468
7:13	451	19:3	503	34:28	60
7:15-18	410	19:10	175	34:38	48
7:26-27	419, 420	19:12	263		
8:6	401	19:14-15	175	**Numbers**	
9:23-24	321	19:18	50, 186, 204,	1:44	369

3:3-4	319	20:11	252	4:19-20	150
4:7	381	20:12	99	4:35	409
5:19	237	21:4	252	4:44	46
5:21	237	22:6	112	5:5	363, 370
5:30	45	23:7	112	5:6	46, 165, 321, 497
6:1-21	244	23:18	112		
6:3	454	23:21-22	318	5:12-15	503
6:13	45	24:3	112	5:14	506
6:14	256, 289	24:15	112	5:16-21	252
6:20	454	24:20-23	112	5:18	356
6:21	45	25:1	252	5:22	321
6:22	245, 407	25:8	383	5:27-29	173
6:22-27	407	25:9	252	5:33	166
9:6-12	386	25:10-13	383	6:4	234
9:10	399	25:11-13	161, 319	6:4-5	345
9:13	399	25:13	200	6:5	388
9:15	154	26:3-13	223	6:4-9	237
9:15-22	321	26:64-65	225	6:7	234
9:18	252	27:1-11	198	6:13	237
10:11-12	321	27:4	387	6:13-15	263
10:33	171, 320, 326	27:23	367	7:2	46
10:34	321	28-29	45	7:3	45
11:4	252	28:9-10	503	7:6	182
11:12	358	30:2	237	7:6-8	497
11:16	369	30:10	237	7:6-12	172
11:24-25	369	30:13	237	7:6-14	174
11:25	321	31:21	45	7:9	174
12:5	321	35:6-34	355	7:10-11	178
12:6-8	319	35:30	252, 410	7:11-20	172
12:7	138	36:3-4	387	7:12	162, 347
12:13	368	36:5-6	387	8:1	166
13:17-18	46	42:15	387	8:5	358
14:2	252			8:5-6	44, 148
14:14	321	**Deuteronomy**		8:7-10	99
14:18	347	1:5	46	9:9	171
14:36	252	1:31	44, 358	9:11	171
14:44	179	1:33	252, 321	9:15	171
15:30	178	2:10-23	219	10:1-5	122
15:31	363	3:25	99	10:2	249
15:32-36	503	4:2	293	10:4	60, 363
15:37-41	238	4:5-6	44	10:8	171
17:7-8	154	4:8	46, 176	10:12	263
18:2	154	4:13	48, 60, 171, 363	10:14	252
19:2, 21	45			10:16	244, 252, 320, 468
19:21	227	4:14	295		

10:17	252	17:7	252, 410	29	161, 162, 323
10:18-19	175	17:8-13	310		
10:20	237, 263	17:9	252	29:1	171
11	182	17:11	41, 45	29:3-4	253
11:8-15	99	17:12	410	29:7	181
11:9	166	17:18-19	310	29:9	171
11:13	263	17:19	398	29:16	150
11:13-20	237	18:1	410	30:1-10	103, 223, 324
11:22	135	18:15	319, 368		
11:26-27	172	18:18	319	30:5	15
12:5	355	19:1-13	355	30:6	244, 320, 468
12:11	355	19:15	253, 410		
12:16	419, 420	19:19	253, 410	30:1-10	473
12:21	294	21:10-13	357	30:11-14	501
12:23	419	21:10-14	309	30:12	248
12:23-25	420	21:15	266	30:12-13	392
12:25	421	21:17	99	30:12-14	253
12:32	294	21:21	410	30:15-16	172
13:4	263	21:23	253, 392	30:16	166
13:5	252, 410	22:10	409, 410	30:19-20	176-177
14	14, 440	22:21-22	410	31:9	171
14:1	323	22:23-24	356	31:12	411
14:1-2	182	22:30	409	31:15	321
14:8	346	23:3	312	31:16	171
14:23	355	24:1-4	308, 358	31:20	171
14:21	440	24:7	253, 356, 410	31:25-26	171
14:26	454			32	322
14:29	175	24:12-13	309	32:4	346
15:4-5	172	24:14	175	32:8-9	150, 151
15:7-11	175	24:17-21	175	32:11	47, 130
15:10	409	25:4	49, 253, 389, 397, 409, 410	32:17	153, 253
15:23	419, 420			32:21	253
16	45			32:35	253
16:2	355	25:5-10	313, 384	32:43	253
16:6	355	25:15	166	32:45	373
16:9-12	246	25:26	384	32:47	176
16:10-11	422	26:2	355	33:1	320
16:11	175, 355	26:12-13	175	33:2	320, 321
16:13-15	127	27:15-26	322	33:4	150
16:14	175	27:18-19	175	33:3-5	318
16:14-16	422	27:26	54, 253, 392	33:9	382
16:16	246	28:1-14	172, 223	33:10	68, 319
16:18	419	28:45-47	177	34:9	367
16:20	166	28:49	248	34:10	320
17:6	410	28:61	42, 45		

Joshua
1:8	427
2:3-5	384
2:18-20	384
2:25-26	384
6:25	384
8:31	42, 45
14:4	99
14:6	320
20	355
23:6-8	310
24:20-22	263
24:26	42, 45

Judges
2:1	175, 199
4	83
18:30	14

Ruth
2:23	313
4:12	384
4:17-22	14
4:18-22	312, 384

1 Samuel
2:35	161
4:4	336
4:21-22	327
7:2	327
8:7	318
13:14	324
14:33	419
14:33-34	421
15:23	263
16:1-13	161
17:26	326
17:36	326
18:25-27	326
20:8	174
21:2	381
21:6	302, 381
21:7	312
22:9	312

2 Samuel
3:18	324
5:7	326
6:2	336
6:10	326
6:12	326
6:16	326
6:19	329
7:1-17	103
7:5	324
7:8	324
7:13	162
7:14	104, 329
7:16	162
8:17	161, 338
12:24-25	329
14:11	355
23:1	326, 328
23:5	329
24:16-17	328

1 Kings
2:3	329
2:35	161
3:3-12	111
3:9	114, 326
3:12	114, 326
4:29-34	111
5:12	111
8:1	327
8:1-2	125
8:6	327
8:9	122, 327
8:10-11	327
8:21	327
8:23	327, 347
8:66	324
9:5	162
10:1-13	111
11:13	324
11:32	324
11:34	324
11:36	324
11:38	324
14:8	324
16:31	14
17:18	320
17:24	320
19:8	320, 326
19:9-18	339
19:10	320
19:14	320

2 Kings
1:9-13	320
5	83
8:19	324
8:25-26	14
10:31	68
11	14
12	14
17:26-27	280
17:34	69
19:15	336
19:34	324
20:6	324
21:8	398
22-23	310

1 Chronicles
2:3-15	312
2:4-15	384
2:12-17	14
5:1	99
6:3-8	338
6:3-12	385
9:20	383
9:32	381
16:3	329
16:12-18	329
16:17	175, 200
16:34	328
16:39	385
16:40	68
16:41	328
17:4	324
17:7	324
17:12	162
17:13	329
17:14	162
18:16	161, 385

Scripture Index

21:15-16	328	**Nehemiah**		19:5	173
22:10	162	1:5	347	19:7-8	259, 413
22:11-13	329	8-9	295	19:7-11	124
23:14	320	8:2	69	19:8	147
23:15-17	14	8:7-8	319	19:8-15	93
24:3	161	8:13-14	45	19:9	413
24:6	161	8:17	127	22:30-31	85
25	198, 328	9:29	80	24:1	439
26:24	14	9:32	347	24:3	320, 326, 340
29:17	267	9:36-37	374		
29:18	329	10:29	42	30	328
		10:34	46	32:6	348
2 Chronicles		13:19	308	33:3	342
3:1	328			33:6	131, 132
5:13	328	**Esther**		36:9	79
5:13-14	327	3:10	33	37:27-28	348
6:1	327	9:20-32	198	37:27-29	353
6:10-11	327			37:30-31	9, 347
6:14	327, 347	**Job**		37:31	413
6:16	162, 329	9:6	141	40:3	342
7:1-3	327	19:25	355	40:6-8	288
7:6	328	24:13	398	40:7	312
9:8	162	28:12-14	116	40:8	212, 336
20:21	328	28:20-27	116	42	295
30:16	320, 398	28:28	111, 114, 326, 330	47:6-7	318
33:12-13	498			50:5	348
		42	83	51	181
Ezra				51:6	267
1:3	295	**Psalms**		68:17	321
1:3-5	296	1:1-2	372	68:18	369
3:2	320	1:2	42, 413	69:22-23	392
5:9-10	131	1:2-3	363	72:17	324
7:1-5	295	1:6	135	74:2	323
7:6	295	2:6	57, 327, 340	74:3	291
7:10	111, 295	2:6-9	338	74:7	291
7:12	51	2:7	100, 329	75:3	141
7:14	51	2:10-12	57	78	112
7:21	51	5:16	124	78:1	46
7:25	51	7:13	124	78:1-4	63
7:26	51	12:1	348	78:5	69
9-10	295	15:2-5	269	78:10	48
9:8-9	374	16:8-11	391	78:14	321
10	13	16:10	391	78:67-72	327
10:3	45	17:5	135	78:70	324
		19:1-7	93	79:1	291
		19:4	248		

561

80:1	122, 336	111:10	111	132:16	348
80:2	327	112:1	363, 372	136	353
82:6	389	116:13	404	144:9	342
83	98	118:2-4	353	145:10-13	354
89:3	162	118:26	87	147:19-20	150
89:3-4	160	118:29	353	149:1	342, 348
89:3-5	329	119	131	149:5	348
89:4	324	119:1-2	372	149:5-9	354
89:6	160	119:14	127, 178		
89:6-7	342	119:16	43, 178	**Proverbs**	
89:19-20	407	119:18	82	1:7	111, 113
89:21	324	119:24	43, 178	1:8	43
89:26-27	329	119:35	43, 135, 178	1:20	115, 136
89:28	162	119:44	59, 104	1:22	113
89:35	162	119:47	43, 178	1:28	131
89:35-37	329	119:70	43, 178	1:32	113
89:38-40	160	119:75	346	2:16	137
90	320	119:77	43, 178	2:17	357
90:2-3	324	119:89-91	43, 47, 93	2:21-22	113
90:4	102	119:92-96	43	3:1	41, 44, 111
93:2	323	119:92	43, 178	3:1-2	348
94:12	42, 372	119:93	147	3:3	111
95:7	57	119:97	413	3:5	114
96:1	342	119:99	8	3:6	214
98:1	342	119:111	127, 363	3:7	114
99:1	122, 336	119:113	43	3:13	43, 111, 372
99:7	321	119:121	347	3:17	362
100:3	57	119:123	346	3:18	43, 95, 133, 177
100:5	353	119:138	346	3:18-20	111
101:8	286	119:142	346	3:19-20	43, 47, 93, 135
102:25-27	139	119:143	43, 178	3:22	133
104:19	141	119:144	346	3:27-28	267
104:30	132	119:159	178	4:2	41, 43, 111, 362
105:7-11	157	119:162	127	4:13	134
105:8	175, 200	119:165	348	4:22	134
105:10	175, 200	119:172	346	5:3	137
105:39	334	119:174	43, 178	5:20	137
106:3	372	119:176	57	6:20	41, 43, 44, 111
106:28-31	383	122	328	6:23	41, 44, 111, 134
106:30-31	200	128:1	372	6:24	137
107:1	353	132:8-9	353		
110:1	391	132:10-18	327		
110:4	198, 300	132:11-12	162, 329		
111:5	175	132:11-14	327		
111:9	175, 329	132:15	371		

Scripture Index

6:26	137	23:26	366	**Isaiah**	
6:32	137	24:11	113	2:2-4	42, 43
7:1-2	44, 111	24:23	112	2:2	5
7:2	41	26:4-5	112	2:2-3	277
7:5	137	28:4	44, 111	2:3	42, 59, 154,
8	4, 132	28:7	44, 111		320, 326,
8:1	115	28:9	44, 111		340, 341,
8:1-2	136	29:4	113		343
8:12	115, 136	29:14	113	2:4	3
8:22-25	137	29:18	44, 111	5:24	42
8:22-31	114	30:24-31	113	9:6	111, 338,
8:22-32	139	31:10-31	113		354
8:23	138	31:26	41	9:7	162, 285,
8:30-31	128, 131,	**Ecclesiastes**			338, 354
	134	1:9	371	11:1	338
8:32	372	2:24-26	127	11:3-5	285, 338
8:34	372	3:12-13	127	13:6	507
8:35	134	5:18-20	127	13:9	507
9:1	115, 140	9:7-9	127	14:2	358
9:1-6	109, 136	11:2	124	14:13-14	105
9:2	316	11:8	127	16:5	285
9:10	111	11:9	127	19:23-25	223
9:13	115, 136	12:10	126	24:5	48, 175
10:22	112	12:11	126	24:5-9	342
11:18	113	12:12	126	24:23	340
11:21	113	12:13	111	25:6-10	343
11:30	95	12:13-14	125	26:3	354
13:12	95	**Song of Solomon**		26:12	354
14:8	114	1:2	123	26:13	151
14:23	112	1:3	407	28:11	249
14:32	113	1:5	123	29:10	392
15:4	95	1:8	123	29:11-14	113
15:8	112, 113	2:3-4	123	29:13	179, 311
15:11	113	4:5	123	29:14	111
15:33	111	4:7	123	30:9	111
16:12	113	4:12	122	30:23-26	223
16:16	130	4:13-15	123	30:18	372
16:20	372	5:1-7	123	30:29	320, 326
20:26	113	5:10-16	123	30:29-30	341
20:28	113	7:1	114	31	87
21:3	112, 113	8:10	124	31:4-5	341
21:16	398	8:13	124	32	87
21:27	112, 113			32:1	285, 338
22:8	113			32:15	154
22:17	112			32:15-20	223

33:5	340	53:11	352	66:17	286
33:14	286	54:6	121	66:17-18	283, 449
33:15	269	54:6-8	358	66:21	224
33:24	398	54:6-10	353	66:23	222, 281, 510
37:35	324	54:10	353, 354		
40:3	295, 331, 472	54:13	353	**Jeremiah**	
		55:1-8	161	2:2	57, 121, 174
41:18	295	55:3	175, 329, 341, 391	2:8	57
42:1	100, 407			3:3-4	351
42:1-4	99, 280	55:12	354	3:33	351
42:1-7	99	56:1	269	4:4	244, 320, 468
42:3-7	42	56:1-2	372		
42:4	277, 342	56:1-7	222, 281, 510	4:10	349
42:10	342			5:4	280
42:13-44:23	99	56:9-57:13	286	6:10	244, 469
42:21	342, 346, 377	57:2	354	6:14	349
		57:15	181	6:16	135
43:2	295	57:19	354	8:8-9	111, 315
43:16	295	57:21	349	8:11	349
43:19-20	295	58:2	353	8:15	349
44:3	79, 154	58:13	507	9:24	191
45:25	85, 286, 352	58:13-14	511	9:25	320, 340, 468
47:3-4	355	59:8	349		
48:18	349, 353	59:20	340	9:26	244, 320, 340, 468
48:20-21	295	59:21	161, 341		
48:22	349	60:7	98	12:12	349
49:1-7	99	60:13	223	14:11-12	179
49:9-12	295	60:14	340	16:5	349
49:18	121	60:21	85, 286, 352	16:14	340
50:2	295	61:1	407	17:7-9	363
50:4-11	99	61:6	224	17:12	323
51:3	99, 223	61:8	161, 175	17:21-22	307
51:4	277, 285, 338	61:10	121	18:18	112
		62:5	121	23:5	340, 352
51:4-9	43	63:10-11	147	23:6	352
51:7	259, 277, 353	63:11	369	23:7	340
		63:11-14	295	30:3	340
52:1	162, 222, 281, 340, 449	64:6	498	30:5	349
		65:20	286, 457	30:9	169
		65:20-25	85	31	168
52:13-53:12	99	65:22	457	31:12	223
53:4-10	341	66:1-6	291	31:31	55, 340, 488
53:4-5	406	66:5-6	291	31:31-32	175
53:5	354	66:12	354	31:31-34	6, 103, 161,
53:6	57	66:12-14	223		

Scripture Index

	343	33:25	419, 421	45:18	222, 282
31:33	48, 106, 249, 365	34:25	161, 354	45:19	288
		34:30	249	45:21	316
31:33-34	279	34:35	249	45:21-25	222, 282
31:35-36	141	36:24-31	164	45:23-24	284, 288
31:38	340	36:24-32	473	45:25	316
32:40	161, 175	36:26	249	46:1	222, 282, 510
32:42	343	36:27	147, 154, 195	46:3-4	222, 282, 510
33:6	354				
33:9	354	36:35	99	46:6	282
33:11	353	37:26	161, 175, 354	46:9	316
33:14	340, 343			46:11	316
33:15	285	40:39	288	46:12	510
33:17	162	40:46	161, 198, 224, 338, 385	46:12-15	284
33:20	160			46:20	288
33:20-21	162			48:11	161, 198, 224, 338, 385
33:21	329	41:22	410, 445		
33:25	141, 160	42:13	288		
36:4	296	43:1-5	341, 343		
38-39	83	43:12	45	**Daniel**	
50:5	161, 175	43:19	161, 198, 224, 288, 338, 385	2:9	51
52:15	114			2:13	51
55:3-5	343			6:9	51
56:4-7	343	43:21-22	288	6:13	51
		43:25	288	6:16	51
Ezekiel		43:27	284	7	87
1:28	162	44:5	45	7:8	290
5:11	409	44:7	244, 468	7:13	131, 341
11:19	249	44:9	162, 222, 244, 281, 340, 449	7:21	290
13:10	349			7:22	341
13:16	349			7:25	51, 290
16	357	44:15	161, 198, 224, 338, 385	9:4	347
16:8	57, 172			9:24	342
16:8-13	121			9:27	290
16:59-63	57	44:16	410, 445	10:13	151
16:60	161, 176	44:23	284, 319, 330	10:20-21	151
20:11	80			12:1	151
20:12	161	44:24	222, 282, 316, 510	12:3	114
20:13	80			12:11	291
20:20	161	44:25	284		
28:17	105	44:27	288	**Hosea**	
31:33	271	44:29	288	1:9	5
32:19-32	326	45:15	288	1:10	248, 343, 488
33:18	224	45:17	284, 288, 316, 510	2	357
33:21	224			2:17	161

2:19-20	121	3:9	73	1:16	374
2:23	248, 488	3:16-18	352	1:16-18	329
3:4	473			1:18-25	373
6:6-7	179	**Haggai**		1:19	347
8:1	48	2:5	79	1:20	329, 336, 376
9:10	324	2:11-13	41		
11:1	56			1:20-23	376
12:9	222, 283, 316	**Zechariah**		2:1-18	375
		6:13	198, 338	2:2	329
Joel		8:3	340	2:4	329
2:3	99	8:4-5	85	2:13	336
2:16	173	9:9	371	2:13-15	375
2:23-27	223	9:10	354	2:16	374
2:28	154	9:11	159	2:19	336
3:16	340	11:10	161	3:3	331
3:18	371	12:10	85, 341	3:13-17	367
		12:10-14	473	4:10	263
Amos		14	87	4:11	336
1-2	219	14:3-5	341	5-7	329
5:4	269	14:5	342	5:2-16	372
5:21-24	179	14:16	316	5:3	233
6:5	198, 328	14:16-19	222, 283	5:9	337, 351
		14:20-21	285	5:10	233
Obadiah				5:12	372
1:17	340	**Malachi**		5:17	54, 59, 201, 209, 228, 261, 365, 455
1:21	340	1:7	410, 445		
		1:11	284		
Micah		1:12	410, 445		
3:5	349	2:4-6	383		
4:1	54	2:6-7	41, 319	5:18	55, 201, 228
4:1-2	277	2:16	308	5:19-20	233
4:1-4	85	3:1	296, 331, 472	5:20	350
4:2	59, 154, 320, 326, 340, 343			5:21-26	308
		3:1-4	284	5:22	262, 266
4:7	340	3:6	224	5:23	236
5:2	324, 343	3:18	347	5:23-26	236
5:5	354	4:2	352	5:25	309
6:8	269, 347, 352	4:4	277	5:28	262, 266
7:15	371	4:5-6	331	5:32	262, 357
7:20	15			5:33-37	440
		NEW TESTAMENT		5:34	262
Habakkuk		**Matthew**		5:38-42	308
2:4	269	1:1	329, 373	5:39	262, 309
2:16	340	1:3	384	5:40	309
		1:5-6	385	5:43-47	309
Zephaniah		1:6	329	5:44	262
3:5	285				

Scripture Index

5:48	56, 184	12:38-42	233	19:21	360
6:1-2	305	12:42	111	19:28	369
6:5	305	13:3	112	21:5	329
6:16-18	305	13:10-17	112	21:11	332
6:30	389	13:16-17	472	21:23	367
6:33	233, 349	13:19-23	233	21:23-27	367
7:1-2	203	13:34-35	112	21:26	331
7:2	392	13:37-38	233	21:31	233, 499
7:12	54, 261	13:41	106, 342, 404	21:32	397, 499
7:21-23	233			21:43	233
7:23	107	13:52	124, 367	21:46	332
7:28-29	366	13:57	332	22:29	114
8:2-3	373	14:5	331, 332	22:36-40	59, 79
8:4	373	15:1-20	216, 367	22:39	268
8:5-13	76	15:2	301	22:40	54, 261
8:10-12	233	15:2-3	399, 445	22:42-45	329
8:17	406	15:8	179	23	130
9:8	367	15:19-20	311	23:1-36	499
9:10-17	499	15:21-28	76, 98, 233	23:2-3	49
9:13	373	15:29-30	333	23:2-4	234, 301
9:20-22	373	16:16	329	23:3	444
10:5	405	16:17	233	23:5	238
10:5-6	233	16:19	367, 393	23:8	300
10:7-8	398	16:20	329	23:10	329
10:8	373, 405	16:27	342	23:15	18
10:10	396	17:1-2	334	23:23	107, 237, 448
10:25	57, 360	17:1-6	333		
11:2	329	17:2	372	23:23-24	306
11:5	373	17:3-5	368	23:28	107, 304
11:9	331	17:4	333	23:34	129
11:10	331, 472	17:8	334	23:37-39	87, 130
11:11-13	472	17:12	332	24	87
11:14	332	17:14	334	24:5	329
11:19	129, 499	17:24-27	236	24:12	106, 172
11:25-26	129	17:25-26	233	24:14	150
11:27	234	18:3-4	233	24:15	291
11:28	129	18:16	410	24:23	329
11:29-30	413, 426	18:18-20	335, 367, 394	24:31	250, 342
11:30	177			25:34	329
12:1-8	302, 382	19:3-9	308	25:40	329
12:1-12	367	19:4-8	95	26:17-29	402
12:4-5	373	19:8	358, 370	26:26	404
12:7	373	19:9	357, 370	26:26-28	158
12:25	366	19:14	233	26:26-29	398
12:28	148	19:19	268	26:28	164, 335,

567

	404, 406	7:19	229, 238,	2:23-24	54
26:29	404		445	2:25	347, 498
26:63	329	8:38	342	2:27	498
26:64	248, 335	9:12-13	332	2:29-32	498
26:68	329	9:50	351, 446	2:36-38	498
27:11	329	10:5	358	2:39	54, 498
27:17	329	10:5-9	95	2:41	498
27:18	366	10:9-12	357	2:51	374
27:19	212, 347	10:21	360	3:4	331
27:22	329	12:28-34	345, 499	3:21-22	334
27:24	212, 347	12:29	234, 302	3:22	130
27:29	329	14:24	164	3:24	374
27:37	329	14:61-62	233	4:1	334
27:42	329	16:1-2	511	4:8	263
28:1	511, 511	16:2	507, 508,	4:14	335
28:16-20	333		511	5:32	233
28:18-20	367, 398	16:6	507, 508	6:8	366
28:19	61, 150, 332,	16:9	511	6:35	337
	365	16:15-16	398	6:40	360
28:19-20	398	**Luke**		7	444, 498
28:20	395	1:6	191, 251,	7:16	332
			347, 498	7:19	444
Mark		1:11	336	7:27	331
1:1-3	472	1:17	332, 339	7:35	129
1:2	331	1:26	336	7:36-50	499
1:3	331	1:35	334	9:8	332
1:13	336	1:38	498	9:19	332
1:27	368	1:46-55	498	9:30-31	339
1:40-44	236	1:56	374	10:1	369, 405
2:23-28	236	1:69	250	10:7	49, 396
2:27	307, 508	1:74-75	350	10:8-9	405
6:13	405	1:74-77	498	10:9	398
6:15	332	1:75	350	10:21	129
6:20	347	1:76	331	10:23-24	472
7	446	1:79	351	10:25-28	192
7:1-7	49, 306	2:1	374	10:25-37	310, 360
7:1-13	293	2:4	376	10:26	54
7:1-23	216	2:7	375	10:30-35	236
7:3	399	2:9	336	11:20	148
7:6	180	2:12	375	11:29-32	233
7:7-8	311	2:16	375	11:31	111
7:9-13	216	2:19	374	11:37-52	499
7:14-15	448	2:22	399	11:38	445
7:15	238, 447	2:22-24	498	11:49	129
7:15-19	446			13:10-17	236

Scripture Index

13:28-30	233	1:1-3	116, 363	6:57	177
13:31	499	1:3	131, 140, 364	6:61	366
13:33	332			6:64	366
13:34-35	87, 130	1:14	335, 341	7:15	367
14:24	159	1:17	133, 260, 336, 370	7:22	320, 388
14:26	383			7:22-23	382
15:1-2	499	1:21	332	7:23	388
15:7	233	1:23	331	7:28-29	367
15:18	264	1:29	335, 402	7:37-39	301
15:21	265	1:33	335	7:38	134, 371
16:16	54, 472	1:36	402	7:38-39	79
16:17	55	1:45	54, 368	7:40	332, 368, 371
16:18	357	1:46	54		
16:31	370	2:6	301, 399, 445	7:49	366
18:9	499			8:12	134
18:12	511	2:19	334	8:16-19	367
18:13	499	2:19-22	233	8:25	213
18:22	360	2:24-25	366	8:28-29	367
19:7	499	3:3-5	233	8:29	361
19:38	250	3:14	369	8:33	84
20:36	337	3:25	399	8:34-36	191
21	87	3:28	331	8:37	84
21:20-24	19	4:9	79	8:39	84
22:7-20	402	4:10	134	8:37-40	15
22:17-20	337, 404	4:14	79	9:17	332
22:18, 20	169	4:19	332	10:4	57
22:19	186, 398	4:24	386	10:11	266
22:20	7, 164, 335, 337, 404, 458	4:34	263, 361	10:18	56, 361
		4:36	113	10:24-25	233
		5:10	307	10:34	55
22:30	369	5:27	367	10:34-36	389
22:43	336	5:30	263, 361	11:20	302
23:31	389	5:36-47	367	11:55	399
23:47	347	5:44-47	305	12:14-15	371
23:50	347	5:45-47	370	12:23-24	76
23:56-24:1	511	5:46	368	12:34	55
24:1	511	6:11	371	12:44-50	367
24:4-6	336	6:12	302	12:49-50	56, 361, 364
24:19	332	6:14	332, 368, 371	12:50	397
24:36-49	507, 508			13:3-5	301
24:44	55	6:32	369	13:11	366
		6:35	134	13:13-17	57
John		6:38	263, 361	13:34	61, 79, 208, 365
1	60, 132, 139	6:41	403		
1:1	138	6:48	403	13:34-35	349

14:1	77	20:26	508	5:33-39	253
14:6	134, 135			5:34-39	499
14:15	61, 208, 349, 365, 465, 491	**Acts**		6:5	18
		1:11	341	6:7	499
		1:12	302	6:11-14	306
		1:15	394	6:13	424
14:16-18	149	1:27	350	6:14	18, 335
14:21	61, 114, 208, 349, 364, 365, 465, 472	2	85, 148, 153, 225, 238, 464, 507	7:3	322
				7:8	160
				7:20	374
		2:1	508	7:20-28	369
14:21-24	491	2:4	395	7:22	369
14:23	472	2:6-12	149	7:23-29	369
14:23-24	60, 364	2:8	150	7:35-43	306
14:26	79, 147, 149	2:11	18, 150	7:37	332, 368
14:27	351	2:14	394	7:38-51	148
14:31	56, 361	2:22	18	7:51	244, 369, 468, 469
15:1-6	479	2:23	106		
15:3	360	2:25-28	391	7:52	212, 347, 369
15:5	361	2:30	326		
15:8	362	2:34-35	391	7:53	53, 424
15:10	56, 61, 208, 349, 360, 365	2:37	149	8:12	332
		2:38	332, 394, 398, 406	8:16	332
15:10-17	465			8:20	394
15:12	61, 208, 349, 365	2:40	86, 483	8:26	336
		2:42	395	8:36	398
15:12-13	204	2:46	253, 257, 407	9:2	18
15:13	266			9:18	402
15:25	55	3:1	253, 257, 289, 436	9:20	257
15:26	149			9:32	394
16:8	148	3:4	394	9:38	394
16:13	79, 147	3:6	18	10	442, 498
16:13-15	149	3:12	394	10:2	18, 423
16:19	366	3:13	249, 257	10:3	336
16:33	351	3:14	212, 347	10:5	394
17:20-23	iii	3:22	368	10:9-16	390
17:26	61	3:22-23	332	10:10-16	435, 443
18:37	268	4:8	394	10:22	18, 336, 347, 423
19:33	402	4:10	18		
19:36	402	4:12	85	10:28	390
20:1	511	5:3	394	10:35	18, 423
20:12	336	5:8	394	10:38	18, 367
20:19	508, 511	5:15	394	10:48	332, 398
20:19-29	507	5:19	336	11:2	394
20:23	393, 408	5:29	394	11:3	320, 332

Scripture Index

11:5-10	435, 443	17:17	423			406
11:26	11, 435	17:28	8		22:17	257
12:3	394	18:4	257, 424		22:30	86
12:7-11	336	18:7	423		23:3	424
12:23	336	18:13	51, 424		23:6	437
13:5	257	18:18	230, 256		23:9	499
13:14	257	18:19	257		23:20	86
13:15	54, 424	18:24	86		23:29	424
13:16	18, 423	18:26	257		24:5	18
13:23	250	19:5	332		24:6	424
13:26	18, 423	19:8	257		24:14	249, 424
13:34	350	20:6	246		24:15	350
13:34-35	350, 391	20:7	407, 507,		24:16	245
13:35	350		508, 510,		25:8	81, 245, 424
13:39	424		511, 514,		25:10	86
13:43	18		516		26:2	86
13:50	423	20:16	230, 245		26:7	86
14:15-17	153	20:28	310		26:9	18
15	73, 412, 418,	20:32	311		26:28	11
	419, 421,	21	254		27:9	246
	431, 459	21:4	507		27:23	336
15:1	428, 488	21:10	332		28:14	507
15:2	432	21:17-26	230		28:17	81, 245, 332,
15:5	253, 424,	21:20	18, 31, 36,			438, 452,
	499		215, 225,			454
15:7	394		253, 424,		28:23	424
15:10	129, 260,		428, 429,		**Romans**	
	426		436		1:4	184
15:14	86, 414, 483	21:20-21	86		1:16	32
15:19-21	377	21:20-26	81		1:17	350, 393
15:20	80, 215, 429	21:21	452		2	244
15:20-21	216, 231	21:23-24	245		2:1	392
15:21	421, 463	21:24	424		2:6-16	271
15:29	215, 429,	21:25	429		2:10	32
	434	21:26	289		2:12	106, 193
16	467	21:28	424		2:12-13	106
16:3	86, 332, 467	21:39	86, 239		2:13	184, 192,
16:14	423	22:3	86, 239, 392,			350, 499
16:20	86		424, 437		2:14	50
16:21-22	51, 424	22:3-5	499		2:15	102
17:1-2	257	22:4	18		2:17-18	53
17:4	423	22:8	18		2:17-24	57
17:7	51, 424	22:12	250, 424		2:17-27	499
17:10	257	22:14	212, 347		2:24	393
17:16-31	438	22:16	398, 402,			

2:25	188		337, 458,		185	
2:26-27	487		481	7:12-13	199	
2:27	273	4:17	249, 393	7:14	185, 273	
2:28-29	243, 468,	4:18	251	7:16	185, 199	
	477, 485	4:22	251	7:21-8:2	52	
2:29	273, 320	5:5	61, 271, 426	7:22	42, 53, 59	
3:2	60	5:10	389	7:25	59	
3:4	267, 393	5:11-21	389	7:26	53	
3:5	350, 393	5:12-21	102	8:1-8	270	
3:6	393	5:13	53	8:2	53, 58, 71,	
3:10	393	5:15	250		78, 154	
3:19	54, 55, 193	5:19	350	8:3	187	
3:19-21	58	5:20	54, 58, 148,	8:4	38, 54, 59,	
3:19-26	216		187, 250,		78, 147, 168,	
3:19-31	499		260		184, 212,	
3:20	54, 59, 148,	6:1	393		273, 279,	
	181, 187,	6:3	369		351, 499	
	188, 193,	6:3-4	332, 398,	8:6	351	
	260		406	8:7	53	
3:21	54, 193, 346	6:5-8	393	8:9	212, 361	
3:21-22	350	6:14	59, 193, 209,	8:10-11	393	
3:24-25	165		211, 260,	8:14	147, 148,	
3:25-26	85, 350		499		195	
3:27	51, 56, 71,	6:15	193, 211,	8:14-15	337	
	78, 184, 188,		260, 499	8:17	484	
	499	6:19	106	8:19	337	
3:27-31	427	6:22	362	8:23	337, 390	
3:28	193	7:1	53	8:29	195, 393	
3:28-31	58	7:1-8:4	499	8:31	393	
3:30	187, 487	7:2	51	8:36	393	
3:31	60, 196	7:2-3	357	9	87	
4:1	393, 487	7:4	78, 193, 228,	9:1	393	
4:2	188		260	9:3	437, 484,	
4:3	251	7:5	54, 260		487	
4:6	188	7:6	78, 193, 228,	9:4	5, 56, 57,	
4:7	106		260		255, 452,	
4:9	487	7:5-14	58		479	
4:11	7, 458, 481,	7:6	38, 59	9:4-5	317, 322,	
	487	7:7	59, 209, 248,		329, 343,	
4:11-12	85, 337, 480		393		473	
4:13-14	53, 55, 484	7:7-8	54, 260, 276	9:5	250, 324,	
4:13-15	499	7:7-11	148		480	
4:14-16	58	7:7-13	177	9:6	84, 487	
4:15	58, 188	7:8-9	106	9:6-8	15	
4:16	7, 53, 85,	7:12	59, 78, 176,	9:7	252	

Scripture Index

9:7-13	487	11:24	389	15:10	253
9:11	188	11:25	32, 479	15:16	184
9:12	252	11:26	85, 87, 90, 286, 344, 393, 486	15:21	393
9:13	393			15:26	379
9:14	393			15:33	250, 351
9:15	252	11:28	480	16:4	86
9:17	252	11:28-29	87, 249, 343	16:20	250, 351
9:24-26	488	11:29	103, 473	16:27	250
9:25-26	248	11:36	250	18	248
9:30	393	12	271		
9:30-32	499	12:1	271, 446	**1 Corinthians**	
9:30-33	58	12:1-2	224, 270	1:2	396
9:30-10:4	500	12:2	263, 379	1:10	378
9:31	212, 272, 479	12:3	195	1:13	435
		12:3-8	378	1:24	112, 128, 129, 364
9:32	188, 272, 500	12:13	379		
		12:16	378	1:30	128, 129, 350
9:33	393, 500	12:18	351, 379		
10	87, 228	12:19	253	1:31	191, 393
10:1	479	13:4	309	2:6	114, 330
10:4	59, 363, 446, 499	13:8	212	2:6-10	129
		13:8-10	60, 64, 78, 209, 228, 269, 271, 273, 345, 499	2:9	393
10:5	80, 185, 252			2:10-16	79
10:5-8	501			3:6	458
10:6	185			3:16	154, 223, 330
10:6-8	248, 253, 390	13:9	50, 252, 268, 275, 276	3:17	409, 410
10:12	241, 431	13:10	54, 59, 184, 195	4:15	300
10:15	393			4:17	396
10:19	253	13:14	271, 360	4:20	112
11	87	14	215, 454, 513	5:1	86, 275, 409
11:1	239, 431, 437, 479			5:5	507
		14:1-15:7	453	5:7	335, 402
11:5	86, 483	14:2	453	5:7-8	247, 403
11:6	188	14:5	453, 512	5:9-11	275
11:7	479	14:5-6	511	5:10	418
11:8	253, 393	14:15	273	5:10-11	273, 276
11:8-10	392	14:17	273	5:12-14	378
11:11	32	14:17-18	330, 351	5:13	252, 253, 410
11:12	389	14:19	351		
11:13	86, 323	15	454	6:7	309
11:14	487	15:3	393	6:9	273
11:15	389	15:5	378	6:9-10	275
11:16-24	7, 458, 475	15:9	393	6:10	276, 418
11:23-24	32, 90			6:12	379

6:13	275		208, 337,	15:28	56
6:16	251		459, 499	15:33	8
6:18	275	9:22	438	15:45	98, 251
7	243	9:23	438	15:50-54	85
7:2	275	10:1	252	15:50-55	457
7:3	409	10:2	369	15:52	250
7:8	449	10:3	252, 350	15:56	54, 187, 260,
7:10-11	365, 396	10:4	248		499
7:10-16	357	10:7	252, 273,	16:2	507, 511,
7:12-14	396		393		514
7:17	396	10:8	252, 275	16:8-9	246, 391
7:17-20	75	10:10	252		
7:18	222, 239,	10:14	273	**2 Corinthians**	
	432, 479	10:16	404	1:3	249
7:18-19	468	10:16-17	435	1:12	195
7:18-20	241	10:18	410, 479	2:2-11	408
7:19	61, 187, 365,	10:19-20	153	2:14-16	247
	469	10:20	253, 273	3:2-11	228
7:21	358	10:25	415, 450	3:3	147, 249,
7:25	396	10:25-27	396		272, 365
7:38	449	10:25-29	439	3:3-6	316
8-10	379	10:28	252	3:6	7, 38, 67,
8:4	409	10:31	186, 421		147, 154,
8:4-13	414	10:32	87, 438, 465,		337
8:5	151		484, 485	3:7	58, 492
8:5-6	263, 273	11:2	216, 304	3:7-8	188, 370
8:7	450	11:16	396	3:7-11	390
8:7-12	438	11:23-25	337, 396	3:9	58, 492, 495
8:8	450	11:24-26	169, 186,	3:13	252
8:10	450		398	3:14	17, 55
8:37	186	11:25	67, 164, 337	3:15	32
9	437	11:26	398, 402,	3:17	147
9:2	389		406, 407	3:18	195, 360
9:8-9	53	12	378	4:2	437
9:9	54, 253, 410	12:7-8	79	4:13	393
9:9-10	248, 389,	12:12-13	85	5:1-10	270
	409	12:13	240, 425	5:10	271
9:13-14	409, 410	12:28	310	5:14-15	393
9:14	365, 396	14	378	5:16-17	337, 484
9:19-21	437	14:1	272	5:21	350
9:20	193, 211,	14:21	55, 248	6:14	106, 409,
	499	14:24-25	335		410
9:21	2, 59, 64, 68,	14:34	396, 411,	6:16	223, 252,
	77, 106, 107,		412		273, 330
	184, 195,	14:37	61, 365	6:18	337

Scripture Index

7	249	2:20	361, 393	3:26	337	
7:14	393	2:21	58, 185, 188	3:27	332, 398	
8-9	379	3	494	3:28	39, 85, 89,	
8:9	267	3:1	499		239, 425,	
8:15	252, 393	3:2	58, 188, 193		431	
9:6	113	3:4	188	3:29	7, 48, 85,	
9:7	409	3:5	58, 193		337, 458,	
9:9	393	3:6	481		481, 484,	
9:10	362	3:7	7, 48, 337,		487	
11:2-3	57		458, 466,	4	152	
11:22	239, 437,		481	4:4	193	
	479	3:7-9	85	4:4-5	56, 58, 188	
12:6	393	3:8	251, 252	4:5	193, 260,	
12:10	184	3:9	337		337, 360	
12:21	275	3:10	53, 54, 58,	4:6	147, 271,	
13	249		188, 193,		337	
13:1	252, 253,		212, 253,	4:7	484	
	410		392, 492	4:10	513	
13:11	351	3:10-13	58, 188	4:16	393	
		3:11-12	185, 481	4:19	360	
Galatians		3:12	80, 165, 212,	4:21	54, 56, 58,	
1:4	361		252		193	
1:5	250	3:13	253, 392	4:21-31	249	
1:13-14	499	3:14	48, 85, 337	4:22	251	
1:14	311	3:15	160	4:24-26	48, 340	
1:19	18	3:15-4:7	169	4:26	457	
2	437, 494	3:16	249	4:28	7, 337, 458,	
2:3	469	3:17	53, 54, 160,		481	
2:4	4		252	4:30	251	
2:6	252	3:17-19	58, 188	4:40	166	
2:7-8	15, 394	3:18	484	5	243	
2:9	487	3:19	53, 54, 148,	5:1	413	
2:11-13	434		187, 255,	5:2	243, 488	
2:11-14	390, 422,		260, 322,	5:2-6	469	
	436, 454		370	5:3	188, 397	
2:11-16	461	3:19-4:7	4	5:3-4	58	
2:12	469, 487	3:21	58, 188, 190,	5:4	499	
2:13	86		481	5:6	187, 469	
2:14	86	3:22	337	5:13	379	
2:15	86, 500	3:23	193, 211,	5:13-14	78, 269, 345,	
2:16	58, 188, 193,		216		379	
	216, 500	3:23-24	58, 188	5:13-15	228	
2:16-19	499	3:23-25	152, 190	5:13-6:2	147	
2:19	58, 79, 188,	3:23-4:7	358	5:14	50, 54, 59,	
	195, 260	3:24	481		184, 212,	

	252, 268, 499	2	430, 482	5:1	56, 184
		2:4-6	393, 484	5:2	195, 361
5:16-18	361	2:6	457	5:3-4	275
5:18	58, 193, 260, 499	2:8-10	168	5:5	263, 273, 379, 484
		2:11	487		
5:19	275, 362	2:11-22	6, 84	5:6-10	270
5:20	273	2:12	37, 476, 478, 482	5:9	362
5:20-22	378			5:17	263
5:22	195, 351, 362	2:13	482	5:18-19	336
		2:14	183, 186, 429, 436, 461	5:22-24	57
5:23	58, 362			5:23	57, 484
5:25	361			5:25	266, 361
6:2	2, 9, 10, 49, 54, 59, 65, 68, 71, 77, 78, 184, 195, 208, 212, 269, 337, 360, 362, 459, 499	2:14-16	57, 58, 228, 229	5:25-27	400
		2:14-18	240	5:30-32	484
		2:15	53, 87, 98, 188, 483	5:31	251
				6	86
		2:15-22	483	6:1-3	270
		2:16	484	6:2-3	209, 228, 250, 252, 499
		2:19-22	485		
6:6	50	2:20-22	223	6:5	487
6:7-8	113	2:21-22	154	6:5-9	358
6:10	379	3:1	86	6:6	263
6:13	53, 58	3:6	337, 482	6:9	252
6:15	187, 469	3:10	128, 135, 457	6:12	457
6:16	84, 90, 91, 250, 351, 465, 475, 477, 485, 486			6:17	79, 148
		3:16-19	79, 361	**Philippians**	
		4:1-6	378	1:1	310
		4:3	351, 461	1:11	362
		4:4	484	1:19	361
Ephesians		4:5	398	1:27	195
1:3	223, 249, 457, 484	4:7-16	378	2:1-4	378
		4:8	370	2:5	361
1:5	337	4:11-13	310	2:6	105
1:7-8	250	4:11-16	395	2:15	56
1:8	249	4:12	484	3:2-3	470, 488
1:11	484	4:13	iii, 361	3:2-11	499
1:14	484	4:15-16	57	3:3	187, 361
1:17	135, 249	4:16	484	3:6	53, 499
1:17-18	147	4:17	86	3:6-9	347, 495
1:18	484	4:24	350	3:9	53, 188, 393, 499
1:20	457	4:25	268, 275		
1:22-23	57	4:28	267	3:15-21	270
1:23	484	4:31	274		
		5	86		

3:20	457, 483, 484		431, 458	2:15	216, 304
		3:15	351, 484	3:6	216, 304
3:20-21	85, 457	3:16	336	3:16	250
4:3	250	3:18	274		
4:7	351	3:20	274	**1 Timothy**	
4:9	250, 351	3:22	487	1:2	250
4:20	250	3:22-4:1	358	1:5	272, 397
		3:24	484	1:7-10	499
Colossians		3:25	252	1:8-9	54, 59, 187, 260
1:9	249, 263, 270	3:5	263	1:10	275
1:10	263, 270	3:10-11	361	1:9	106, 274
1:12-13	484	4:3	50	1:10	356
1:15	116	4:10	396	1:14	250
1:15-16	132	4:11	487	1:15	209
1:15-17	118	4:12	263	1:17	250
1:16	140	**1 Thessalonians**		1:20	274
1:17	132	1:6	50, 195	2:1-2	378
1:18	57, 116, 484	1:9	273	2:5	370
1:24-27	484	2:11	300	2:6	361
1:27	86	2:13	50, 311	2:7	300, 393
2	453, 455	2:14	86	2:9	186
2:2-3	364	3:13	342	3:1-7	310
2:3	248	4:1-8	270	3:1-13	378
2:6-8	455	4:3	263	3:2	395
2:8	152, 311	4:3-7	379	3:6	105
2:11	187, 252, 466	4:3-8	184, 186, 275	3:15	224, 485
		4:4-6	271	4:3	449
2:11-12	332	4:5	86	4:4	449
2:11-13	470	4:13-18	457	5:17	310, 395
2:11-15	401	4:16	250	5:18	49, 410
2:12	398	5:2	507	5:19	410
2:14	58, 188	5:12-13	310, 378	6:1-2	358
2:16	512	5:13	351	6:11	272
2:16-17	455, 479	5:15	272	6:10	276
2:16-23	216	5:18	186, 263	6:14	397
2:17	425, 455	5:23	250, 351	6:15	248
2:19	57, 484			6:20	397
2:20	455	**2 Thessalonians**			
2:22	311	1:7	342	**2 Timothy**	
3	86	2:2	507	1:2	250
3:4	342, 455	2:3	105	1:9	323
3:5	273, 275	2:4	87, 291	1:11	300
3:9-10	275	2:7	106	1:14	397
3:11	85, 187, 425,	2:8	105	2:11	50
				2:12	457

2:22	272, 351	4:1	337	9:14-15	164
3:1	5	4:3-4	514	9:15	162, 337, 370, 484
3:2	274, 276	4:9	462, 510		
3:2-4	274	4:14-15	330	9:16-17	160
3:8	369	4:16	250, 401	9:18	162
4:2	50	5:1	330	9:18-23	370
4:7-8	247	5:5	330	9:20	159
4:18	250	5:6	330	9:25	330
		5:10	330	9:26-28	164

Titus

		5:14	114, 330	9:26-10:14	288
1:2	323, 337	6:5	398	10	401
1:5-9	310, 378	6:12	337	10:1	456
1:8	350	6:17	337, 484	10:10	164
1:9	395	6:20	330	10:11-12	330
1:10	488	7:1-10	329	10:14	164, 288
1:12	8, 438	7:3	249	10:16	106
1:14	311	7:11-18	228	10:17	106
2:5	274	7:11	330, 452	10:19-22	400
2:9-10	358	7:12	201, 224	10:21	330, 485
2:11-14	350	7:15	330	10:26-28	410
2:14	106, 361, 414, 489	7:17	330	10:28	54
		7:18	199	10:29	159
3:1	378	7:21	330	10:36	337
3:4-8	168	7:22	162	11:14	457
3:7	484	7:23-28	330	11:16	86, 457
3:9	53	7:25	401	11:19	249
		7:26	350	11:23	374

Philemon

		7:27	288	11:31	385
v. 10-16	358	8	168, 337	12:5-8	337

Hebrews

		8:1	330	12:11	362
1:2	133, 140	8:5	456	12:14	272, 351
1:2-3	132	8:6	162, 337, 370, 452	12:18-22	340, 370
1:3	143			12:22	457
1:9	106	8:7	162	12:24	162, 370
1:10-12	139	8:8	55, 488	12:25	390
1:23-25	139	8:10	106, 147, 271, 452	13:4	186, 379
2:2	53, 322			13:7	310, 395
2:3-4	31	8:13	55, 162, 200, 203	13:9	451
2:10	337			13:14	457
2:11	401	9:1	162	13:15	224, 362, 401
2:17	330	9:4	171, 510		
3	514	9:9-10	450	13:17	310, 378, 395
3:1	330	9:11	330		
3:1-6	370	9:12	288	13:20	57, 159, 162, 250, 351
3:6	224, 485	9:13-14	390		

Scripture Index

13:21	250, 263, 351		330, 485	2:3-4	61
		2:9	186, 330, 414	2:5	61
James				2:7-8	61, 204
1:1	405	2:9-10	488	2:8	205
1:25	60, 128, 379	2:11-12	379	2:15	61
1:27	331	2:13-14	378	2:15-17	379
2:1-2	299	2:13-3:7	86	2:17	263
2:1-16	379	2:16	379	2:25	323, 337
2:2	257	2:18	358	2:29	350
2:5	129, 337, 484	2:25	57	3:7	350
2:6	398	3:7	484	3:10	56
2:8	60, 128, 209, 268, 398	3:11	351	3:16	266
		3:18	212, 347	3:17	61, 267, 277
		3:21	398	3:22	61
2:8-11	346	4:2-3	263	3:23	349
2:11	209	4:3-4	12	3:23-24	349
2:12	60, 128, 147, 379	4:7	209	3:24	61
		4:11	250	4:7	61, 349
2:14-26	168, 350	4:16	11	4:8	61, 349
3:13-17	109-110	4:17	224	4:12	61
3:15	128	4:18	168, 350	4:16	61, 349
3:17	128	5:1-5	310	4:21	349
3:17-18	362	5:11	250	5:2	277
4:4	379			5:2-3	57, 61, 491
4:12	452	**2 Peter**		5:3	349, 413, 426
5:3	5	1:4	337		
5:6	212, 347	1:17	334	5:19-21	379
5:7-8	405	2:8	106	5:20	364
5:14	407	2:21	397, 398	5:20-21	263
5:14-15	405	3:1-2	311		
5:15-16	406	3:2	61, 366, 397, 465	**2 John**	
5:16	350			3	250
		3:8	102	5	61, 205, 349
1 Peter		3:10	507	6	61, 349, 491
1:3	249	3:13	458	9	369
1:4	484	3:14	351		
1:9	209	3:15-16	49	**Jude**	
1:11	332, 361	3:18	250	2	250
1:16	252				
1:18-19	335	**1 John**		**Revelation**	
1:19	402	1:1-2	364	1:5	332
1:23	250	1:9	330	1:6	224, 250, 330
2:2	56	2:1	132, 212, 347	1:10	507, 508
2:4-5	224	2:1-2	330	3:5	250
2:5	186, 224,	2:3	491	3:14	116, 332

4:3	162	22:5	457
5:6-13	402	22:11	350
5:8-9	335	22:17	143
5:9	85		
5:9-10	336		
5:10	224, 330, 457		
5:13	250		
7:12	250		
7:15	341		
9:20	153		
10:1	162		
11:1	87, 290, 292		
11:5-6	339		
11:15	250, 405		
11:19	510		
12:17	292		
13:8	250		
13:11-18	291		
14:3	336		
14:4-5	342		
14:12	292		
15:3	342, 369		
15:4	350		
16:5	350		
17:8	250		
17:14	342		
19:10	272		
19:14	342		
20:4-6	85, 457		
20:6	224, 330, 457		
20:15	250		
21:1	457		
21:2	83		
21:3	341		
21:7	337		
21:8	418		
21:9-10	83		
21:9-11	484		
21:24-26	83		
21:27	250		
22:1-2	79		
22:2	162		
22:3	104, 365		

Subject Index

A
Aaron 121, 191, 197, 198, 199, 200, 223, 234, 319, 322, 325, 338, 385, 386, 401
Aaronic 99, 161, 162, 199, 200
Abandon 21, 118, 119, 131, 309, 447, 451, 470, 471, 484
Abel 99
Abolished 3, 4, 69, 74, 77, 81, 89, 200, 201, 206, 207, 208, 209, 211, 213, 215, 217, 219, 221, 229, 231, 288, 316, 443, 444, 466, 475, 482, 509, 510
Abraham 3, 7, 15, 30, 41, 48, 54, 67, 84, 85, 86, 88, 96, 97, 98, 100, 101, 114, 119, 143, 157, 160, 162, 169, 170, 176, 241, 249, 257, 328, 350, 392, 458, 466, 477, 478, 479, 480, 481, 487, 489
Abrahamic 3, 4, 86, 92, 96, 97, 103, 104, 158, 161, 169, 170, 175, 187, 215, 320, 480
Afraid 348, 375, 530
Apostle 2, 4, 8, 11, 16, 49, 51, 60, 70, 128, 212, 214, 232, 239, 246, 250, 251, 253, 269, 309, 311, 330, 389, 405, 428, 431, 449, 467, 485, 491, 493
Aspect v, 3, 31, 43, 126, 142, 144, 163, 167, 171, 176, 260, 286, 348, 359, 397
Assembly 28, 29, 35, 124, 125, 196, 257, 258, 294, 312, 318, 438
Athaliah 14

Athanasius, St. 135, 137

Atonement 16, 24, 103, 122, 181, 191, 199, 246, 283, 284, 288, 316, 321, 336, 350, 383, 420, 494

Augustine, St. 101, 102, 135, 140, 379

Authority 42, 49, 53, 117, 132, 232, 276, 297, 300, 303, 310, 325, 366, 367, 394, 417

Azariah 42, 411

B

Baptism i, 16, 18, 23, 299, 332, 333, 359, 378, 398, 399, 401, 402, 405, 406, 407, 423, 460, 462, 463, 464, 470

Baptist 35, 251, 331, 339, 347, 367, 459, 471, 472

Beast 96, 290, 522

Beatitudes 149, 333, 371, 372

Beautiful 99, 121, 122, 135, 141, 144, 271, 281, 292, 303, 322, 346, 374, 388, 456, 462, 464

Believers ii, 2, 4, 5, 6, 7, 9, 10, 11, 12, 15, 16, 17, 18, 19, 20, 21, 22, 23, 24, 29, 32, 34, 35, 36, 37, 38, 39, 41, 49, 50, 58, 59, 61, 64, 65, 66, 67, 68, 69, 71, 72, 73, 74, 77, 78, 80, 81, 84, 85, 87, 89, 90, 91, 100, 104, 107, 114, 126, 150, 151, 152, 168, 169, 170, 184, 185, 189, 205, 206, 208, 211, 215, 216, 217, 218, 219, 220, 221, 222, 223, 224, 226, 231, 232, 233, 239, 240, 243, 244, 246, 253, 254, 255, 256, 257, 258, 292, 299, 303, 311, 332, 335, 337, 342, 350, 351, 360, 369, 378, 379, 380, 381, 389, 390, 393, 395, 396, 401, 402, 403, 405, 410, 412, 414, 416, 417, 419, 420, 421, 422, 423, 424, 425, 427, 428, 429, 430, 431, 432, 433, 434, 435, 436, 437, 438, 439, 441, 443, 445, 446, 447, 449, 450, 451, 453, 454, 455, 456, 457, 458, 459, 460, 461, 462, 463, 464, 465, 466, 467, 468, 469, 470, 471, 472, 473, 476, 477, 478, 479,

Subject Index

	481, 482, 483, 484, 485, 487, 488, 491, 503, 504, 505, 506, 507, 508, 509, 510, 511, 514, 516, 520, 521, 523, 526	Boaz	413, 427, 491, 499, 500 14, 312, 314, 385	Builder Building Built	338, 343, 349, 382, 388, 400, 425, 434, 441, 471, 487, 523 119, 120, 128, 146 37, 290 109, 115, 231, 290, 325, 327, 328, 351, 498
Biblical	ii, iii, 2, 14, 15, 29, 35, 38, 47, 50, 79, 114, 138, 140, 142, 145, 158, 159, 174, 194, 195, 232, 235, 298, 299, 300, 302, 309, 339, 344, 362, 378, 379, 437, 438, 440, 442, 463, 475, 509	Body	4, 5, 34, 39, 42, 57, 82, 84, 85, 88, 122, 127, 146, 157, 202, 216, 224, 226, 229, 233, 240, 268, 275, 334, 335, 336, 368, 388, 399, 401, 404, 406, 416, 431, 435, 448, 450, 456, 460, 470, 478, 480, 482, 483, 484, 519, 547, 552	Burden **C** Caiaphas Cain Cake Calling	170, 177, 413, 417, 426, 493, 506, 530 233 99 328 38, 39, 66, 84, 85, 86, 87, 136, 300, 343, 431
Binding	22, 53, 147, 231, 378, 393, 394, 415, 418, 420, 434, 442	Books	iii, vi, 45, 46, 112, 116, 119, 126, 127, 148, 178, 248, 262, 298, 316, 372, 373	Capital Captive Century	419, 516, 530 27, 52, 190, 357, 370, 530 2, 5, 7, 13, 20, 25, 29, 36, 93, 100, 138, 142, 196, 211, 227, 234, 258, 262, 298, 302, 303, 333, 359, 372,
Bipartite Bishop Boast	429 26, 27, 135, 311 56, 57, 109, 178, 183, 185, 188, 191, 192, 193, 194,	Booths Born	45, 124, 125, 282, 283 13, 14, 25, 26, 27, 55, 56, 75, 77, 86, 88, 134, 142, 243, 300, 334,		

583

391, 405,
418, 434,
446, 491,
493, 495,
496, 497,
499, 501,
515, 520

Cephas 434

Ceremonial 45, 69,
70, 80,
81, 82,
100, 208,
214, 215,
218, 221,
231, 260,
280, 293,
301, 305,
378, 398,
399, 407,
408, 409,
410, 450,
451, 460,
471, 503,
520

Christ i, ii, iii,
iv, 2, 3,
9, 10, 11,
12, 21, 49,
52, 59, 60,
64, 65, 66,
68, 70, 71,
77, 78, 84,
116, 129,
130, 131,
142, 147,
162, 165,
170, 180,
190, 195,
209, 214,
222, 233,
242, 245,
248, 264,
271, 275,
315, 323,

335, 351,
363, 390,
400, 406,
414, 469,
470, 474,
480, 482,
487, 495,
500

Circumcision
5, 7, 13, 14,
15, 18, 29,
30, 54, 58,
72, 75, 160,
161, 162,
183, 185,
187, 188,
193, 195,
215, 218,
222, 239,
240, 242,
243, 244,
255, 281,
320, 326,
332, 333,
340, 378,
388, 397,
399, 401,
423, 429,
432, 434,
448, 449,
453, 460,
461, 464,
465, 466,
467, 468,
469, 470,
471, 475,
477, 479,
485, 487,
488, 496

City 19, 117,
130, 131,
136, 231,
264, 281,
286, 290,
302, 326,

377, 421,
451, 457,
484, 529

Civil 45, 69, 70,
80, 81, 208,
214, 215,
218, 219,
231, 241,
260, 278,
280, 284,
285, 287,
292, 293,
407, 408,
410, 460,
471, 503,
526

Commandments
3, 4, 7, 9,
35, 37, 41,
43, 44, 46,
48, 53, 56,
60, 61, 63,
70, 72, 73,
74, 75, 76,
78, 80, 81,
88, 93, 94,
95, 96, 97,
98, 112,
114, 119,
124, 125,
159, 167,
170, 171,
172, 173,
178, 182,
185, 188,
191, 194,
203, 206,
208, 215,
221, 228,
229, 232,
234, 235,
240, 241,
251, 256,
260, 262,
264, 268,

Subject Index

269, 271,
273, 276,
277, 278,
286, 292,
293, 294,
317, 321,
322, 345,
346, 348,
349, 356,
359, 360,
361, 364,
365, 366,
371, 372,
377, 378,
380, 382,
385, 386,
387, 388,
396, 398,
408, 409,
410, 412,
413, 414,
415, 416,
418, 419,
420, 421,
424, 425,
429, 445,
458, 459,
460, 465,
466, 468,
471, 472,
491, 494,
498, 501,
503, 508,
509, 520,
521, 523

Congregation
5, 26, 28,
29, 30, 34,
35, 36, 38,
39, 40, 91,
92, 121,
232, 299,
300, 303,
310, 323,
378, 394,
395, 412,
417, 425,
433, 434,
438, 442,
460, 461,
509, 526,
529, 531

Contrast
34, 39, 43,
49, 52, 55,
64, 66, 83,
90, 110,
130, 133,
147, 150,
153, 154,
181, 191,
204, 209,
244, 259,
261, 268,
316, 338,
358, 364,
370, 380,
396, 402,
410, 411,
420, 426,
447, 488,
496, 501

Covenant
i, v, 3, 4, 5,
6, 7, 10, 17,
47, 48, 49,
54, 55, 56,
57, 58, 64,
65, 66, 67,
68, 69, 70,
72, 76, 80,
82, 83, 86,
89, 90, 91,
92, 97, 103,
104, 106,
112, 113,
117, 119,
134, 157,
158, 159,
160, 161,
162, 163,
164, 165,
166, 167,
168, 169,
170, 171,
172, 173,
174, 175,
176, 177,
178, 179,
180, 181,
182, 183,
194, 197,
199, 200,
201, 203,
205, 208,
219, 220,
221, 227,
243, 255,
263, 266,
267, 268,
271, 277,
278, 279,
281, 286,
288, 303,
304, 316,
317, 320,
321, 322,
324, 325,
326, 327,
329, 330,
331, 335,
336, 337,
338, 341,
342, 343,
344, 345,
346, 347,
348, 349,
350, 351,
352, 353,
354, 357,
360, 366,
368, 370,
380, 382,
383, 400,
401, 404,

585

	407, 408,		284, 364,		404, 405,
	410, 419,		375, 399,		406, 410,
	420, 433,		412		466, 492,
	434, 452,	David	14, 82, 84,		498, 519,
	458, 459,		112, 161,		529
	471, 473,		169, 179,	Deed	125, 213,
	475, 480,		191, 197,		273, 304,
	488, 489,		198, 224,		384
	494, 495,		285, 286,	Deity	40, 127, 280
	497, 499,		302, 311,	Divine	5, 10, 40,
	500, 501,		317, 324,		42, 43, 49,
	503, 510,		325, 326,		50, 59, 60,
	515, 516,		327, 328,		83, 103,
	525, 526,		329, 338,		104, 105,
	531		339, 341,		113, 126,
Cup	157, 337,		376, 381,		127, 133,
	404		382, 385,		135, 138,
Curse	58, 98, 164,		387		142, 145,
	176, 188,	Davidic	103, 104,		146, 153,
	212, 342,		161, 162,		165, 166,
	392, 492,		175, 324,		167, 168,
	528		325, 327,		170, 177,
Customs	22, 35, 50,		329, 352,		190, 196,
	235, 245,		384, 472,		216, 234,
	254, 256,		473		248, 251,
	292, 297,	Death	47, 52, 53,		266, 310,
	300, 303,		58, 154,		311, 321,
	306, 398,		160, 164,		323, 329,
	407, 423,		167, 169,		334, 335,
	433, 442,		176, 180,		337, 340,
	448, 452,		187, 190,		341, 343,
	453, 454,		218, 219,		364, 365,
	456, 462,		247, 249,		368, 391,
	477, 527		267, 268,		394, 406,
			275, 276,		411, 417,
D			285, 289,		422, 431,
Dairy	440, 441		292, 302,		461, 481,
Daughter	14, 110, 120,		332, 335,		491
	121, 122,		342, 343,	Dispensation	
	128, 131,		356, 357,		35, 66, 67,
	133, 134,		358, 368,		84, 89, 93,
	136, 142,		370, 376,		94, 158,
	143, 146,		382, 389,		169, 171,
	153, 155,		390, 402,		173, 198,

Subject Index

	208, 222, 224, 227, 229, 262, 318, 324, 327, 329, 336, 337, 338, 359, 425, 449, 507, 509, 512, 513		86, 94, 96, 98, 100, 104, 116, 119, 121, 127, 128, 129, 139, 141, 151, 157, 158, 167, 172, 176, 198, 202, 207, 222, 228, 229, 233, 249, 261, 263, 264, 273, 277, 283, 285, 288, 310, 324, 328, 332, 335, 336, 341, 342, 343, 354, 365, 367, 390, 393, 394, 405, 439, 442, 457, 471, 510, 511, 525	Ekklesia	295, 321, 322, 327, 344, 371, 374, 375, 497 66, 83, 84, 85, 86, 87, 89, 90, 91, 125, 128, 135, 145, 146, 149, 154, 222, 223, 225, 226, 229, 240, 241, 244, 255, 266, 330, 335, 336, 337, 359, 400, 436, 457, 458, 460, 461, 465, 471, 473, 475, 476, 482, 483, 484, 485, 486, 487, 488, 489, 503
Distinction	24, 66, 83, 97, 135, 166, 194, 210, 214, 215, 240, 270, 289, 297, 320, 347, 431, 435, 443, 445, 448, 460, 463, 482
Dualism	181
Dutch	v, 25, 86, 124, 240, 241, 348, 431
Duty	7, 29, 34, 125, 193, 204, 222, 231, 265, 284, 299, 310, 383, 399, 420, 425, 437, 439, 440, 441, 454, 466, 505, 509, 524	Ebionites	20, 23	Elders	49, 125, 216, 232, 293, 294, 301, 306, 310, 311, 312, 322, 367, 369, 378, 395, 405, 425, 445, 448, 526, 531
		Ecclesiastical	18, 504, 506
		Edersheim	27, 279, 340, 372, 373, 395, 420
		Effect	160, 190, 216, 265, 305, 447, 454, 493
E		Egypt	46, 82, 117, 165, 166, 172, 283,	Elements	89, 138, 140, 154, 164, 173,
Earth	10, 47, 48, 76, 84, 85,

	200, 231, 277, 280, 298, 303, 310, 317, 351, 359, 387, 401, 408, 440, 449, 453, 479, 500	Ezekiel	400, 413, 472, 519, 527 45, 280, 282, 288, 290, 291, 316, 317, 338		98, 111, 115, 129, 132, 134, 137, 140, 144, 149, 151, 155, 184, 198, 240, 242, 263, 264, 265, 270, 273, 274, 283, 300, 305, 308, 328, 330, 331, 332, 334, 335, 339, 361, 362, 366, 367, 369, 372, 382, 383, 387, 389, 394, 403, 467, 472, 480, 487, 496, 498, 524
Elijah	100, 191, 280, 320, 331, 332, 339, 340, 368	**F** Faith	iii, 1, 6, 15, 19, 23, 25, 27, 30, 40, 51, 55, 56, 60, 75, 76, 78, 80, 165, 182, 184, 185, 186, 190, 191, 196, 209, 210, 211, 212, 216, 217, 220, 227, 234, 242, 243, 244, 245, 247, 254, 269, 272, 302, 303, 350, 384, 391, 392, 397, 398, 401, 405, 406, 424, 427, 430, 431, 438, 460, 469, 470, 496, 500, 501, 511, 512, 513, 526		
Elisha	191				
Empire	6, 21, 22, 290, 421				
Epoch	495				
Essence	11, 56, 59, 60, 61, 78, 105, 107, 164, 175, 182, 196, 201, 208, 211, 212, 213, 220, 262, 268, 269, 272, 302, 306, 319, 325, 329, 330, 345, 349, 360, 362, 432, 448, 450, 473			Family	12, 25, 26, 95, 159, 161, 198, 199, 200, 265, 283, 371, 387, 415, 441, 445, 477, 478
Erroneous	53, 86, 182, 206			Faraway Feast	74 16, 45, 124, 125, 127, 148, 198, 245, 246, 282, 283, 312, 313, 343
Eyes	16, 82, 85, 129, 147, 189, 234, 259, 285, 328, 335, 346, 392,	Father	4, 13, 14, 40, 43, 44, 56, 57, 72, 84, 88, 97,	Festivals	5, 7, 14, 29,

Subject Index

30, 34, 45, 72, 82, 200, 215, 221, 222, 247, 254, 255, 278, 282, 283, 292, 298, 316, 346, 378, 422, 432, 452, 453, 460, 461, 463, 471, 475, 479, 513, 522

Figurative 115, 137, 401, 403, 408, 410, 466, 520, 521, 525, 529

Food 14, 39, 45, 72, 94, 96, 182, 215, 238, 302, 343, 375, 403, 409, 414, 415, 416, 418, 428, 437, 440, 442, 443, 444, 445, 446, 447, 448, 450, 455, 512, 530

Foundation 35, 57, 73, 79, 117, 120, 139, 160, 164, 181, 196, 324, 341, 343, 497

Fragrance 124, 180, 247

Framework 46, 47, 48, 49, 103, 172, 201, 508

Freedom 4, 36, 60, 147, 185, 230, 249, 255, 356, 379, 380, 381, 450, 491

Fulfilled 59, 60, 63, 66, 87, 89, 147, 154, 211, 212, 217, 225, 256, 260, 261, 269, 279, 288, 324, 325, 331, 345, 351, 361, 362, 365, 371, 481, 501

Function 44, 54, 57, 59, 89, 176, 179, 180, 181, 182, 183, 184, 187, 191, 192, 229, 319, 326, 333, 461, 491

Future 4, 29, 60, 66, 68, 72, 81, 82, 83, 85, 87, 89, 97, 111, 198, 200, 217, 221, 225, 231, 255, 277, 286, 287, 288, 289, 291, 292, 314, 316, 318, 324, 325, 340, 359, 423, 514

G

Garden 94, 95, 98, 99, 120, 122, 123, 323

Garment 82, 238, 357, 498

Gentile 1, 2, 5, 6, 11, 15, 16, 17, 20, 21, 22, 23, 24, 29, 30, 32, 33, 34, 36, 37, 38, 39, 48, 58, 67, 69, 73, 76, 80, 81, 84, 86, 87, 89, 90, 91, 106, 152, 168, 170, 189, 198, 206, 208, 211, 215, 216, 217, 218, 219, 220, 222, 223, 224, 225, 226, 231, 238, 239, 240, 241,

243, 244, 246, 251, 255, 256, 258, 292, 296, 299, 320, 332, 335, 390, 402, 412, 413, 414, 416, 418, 419, 420, 421, 422, 423, 424, 425, 428, 429, 430, 431, 432, 433, 434, 435, 436, 439, 444, 445, 447, 450, 453, 454, 455, 456, 457, 458, 459, 460, 461, 462, 463, 464, 465, 466, 467, 468, 469, 470, 471, 473, 475, 476, 477, 478, 479, 481, 482, 483, 484, 485, 487, 488, 500, 503, 504, 505, 506, 508, 509, 510, 514, 517, 521, 523, 526

Gift 127, 135, 145, 147, 170, 196, 265, 308, 438

Giver 43, 79, 112, 316, 336, 359, 360, 368, 409, 421

Godly 42, 84, 86, 120, 127, 147, 190, 191, 196, 251, 339, 348, 350, 354, 359, 363, 415, 462, 473

Good 4, 14, 42, 43, 44, 56, 58, 59, 75, 76, 78, 90, 94, 106, 109, 110, 111, 114, 125, 126, 127, 140, 152, 162, 164, 167, 168, 176, 177, 178, 183, 185, 187, 190, 192, 193, 197, 199, 201, 202, 204, 209, 216, 217, 229, 234, 236, 247, 256, 270, 271, 272, 304, 309, 326, 330, 331, 343, 347, 348, 351, 352, 353, 357, 360, 362, 363, 366, 384, 388, 419, 424, 438, 439, 450, 451, 454, 455, 493, 498, 507, 526, 529

Gospel ii, 1, 24, 26, 31, 32, 33, 133, 134, 136, 144, 145, 181, 209, 231, 247, 257, 268, 329, 332, 372, 373, 374, 390, 391, 396, 409, 438, 444, 447, 482, 500, 501

Greek 11, 12, 13, 17, 22, 27, 46, 50, 56, 105, 110, 115, 125, 128, 136, 138, 140, 145, 152, 159, 184, 192, 209, 210, 239, 240, 241, 242, 350, 366, 367, 391, 403, 415, 425, 458, 467,

Subject Index

Guard	469, 470, 482, 511 304, 319, 397		425, 448, 449, 451, 466, 467, 468, 469, 470, 485, 486, 501		356, 371, 375, 398, 414, 431, 432, 433, 438, 451, 459, 470, 505, 511, 529, 530
Guardian	150, 151, 152, 190	Heaven	6, 37, 38, 104, 118,		
Guidance	298, 439				
Guilt	45, 341		120, 121, 122, 127,	Heidelberg	264
H			128, 129, 131, 146,	Heirs	7, 60, 170, 337, 458,
Hair	244, 245, 264, 521, 522		150, 176, 189, 196, 207, 208,		476, 481, 482, 483, 484
Harvest	124, 148, 312, 313, 362		211, 222, 228, 261, 263, 264,	Hesed	172, 174, 178, 344, 347, 348,
Heart	9, 26, 44, 53, 74, 95, 102, 106, 107, 122, 127, 147, 163, 167, 168, 171, 173, 177, 178, 179, 180, 181, 187, 188, 189, 192, 196, 207, 220, 237, 243, 244, 259, 263, 272, 276, 277, 281, 295, 298, 302, 320, 324, 333, 336, 340, 345, 346, 347, 348, 360, 362, 365, 366, 374, 387, 401, 409, 413, 423,	Hebrew	273, 293, 322, 327, 328, 335, 339, 341, 342, 360, 366, 367, 369, 371, 390, 393, 394, 413, 443, 457, 463, 472, 483, 491, 496, 501 2, 12, 16, 17, 23, 25, 27, 28, 29, 30, 31, 33, 34, 35, 38, 41, 68, 93, 110, 112, 125, 144, 145, 160, 163, 174, 199, 201, 241, 248, 262, 277, 303, 319,	Hindrance Hippolytus History Hokmah	350, 352, 353, 391 36, 428, 430 101 ii, 18, 22, 31, 46, 47, 54, 64, 67, 89, 101, 102, 123, 130, 205, 229, 278, 319, 359, 367, 383, 402, 404, 458, 483, 494, 501, 510 v, 4, 43, 60, 79, 93, 109, 110, 111, 114, 115, 116, 117, 118, 119, 120, 121, 124, 125,

591

	127, 128,		377, 383,		168, 171,
	129, 130,		384, 397,		172, 173,
	131, 132,		408, 414,		175, 176,
	133, 134,		415, 419,		178, 180,
	135, 136,		467		182, 183,
	137, 138,	Immortal	85		185, 189,
	139, 142,	Innovation			190, 191,
	143, 145,		76, 278		192, 193,
	146, 154,	Irenaeus	84, 101,		195, 198,
	155, 177,		102, 135,		209, 210,
	272, 323,		177		211, 212,
	325, 330,	Iron	177, 338,		219, 222,
	347, 362,		354		223, 224,
	364, 368	Irrelevant			225, 227,
Humanity			88, 357,		228, 234,
	94, 98, 134,		416, 425,		241, 243,
	154, 162,		448		244, 247,
	359, 376	Israel	i, 3, 5, 6, 11,		248, 249,
Husband	51, 72, 347,		13, 14, 18,		250, 255,
	356, 357,		21, 28, 29,		262, 263,
	396, 397,		30, 31, 32,		269, 277,
	409, 411,		33, 34, 35,		278, 279,
	525, 528		36, 37, 38,		281, 284,
I			41, 42, 44,		286, 287,
Iconium	242		47, 48, 54,		292, 293,
Iconographer			56, 57, 58,		294, 295,
	140		66, 67, 68,		302, 303,
Icons	140		69, 70, 73,		304, 310,
Idol	263, 409,		76, 77, 81,		311, 312,
	450		83, 84, 85,		318, 319,
Idolatry	75, 96, 153,		86, 87, 88,		321, 322,
	263, 273,		89, 90, 91,		323, 326,
	275, 382,		98, 99, 100,		327, 328,
	383, 409,		106, 111,		329, 336,
	415, 418,		117, 119,		337, 338,
	419, 450,		121, 122,		340, 343,
	524, 526,		123, 124,		345, 351,
	527, 528		125, 130,		355, 357,
Ignorant	13, 129,		134, 146,		358, 363,
	173, 439,		147, 149,		368, 369,
	530		150, 151,		371, 373,
Immorality			152, 153,		374, 375,
	96, 256,		157, 161,		383, 384,
	274, 275,		162, 165,		392, 400,
	276, 357,		166, 167,		410, 416,

Subject Index

J

Jacob 15, 19, 26, 30, 47, 69, 74, 75, 84, 88, 99, 117, 143, 150, 157, 176, 234, 249, 257, 277, 318, 319, 324, 344, 373, 374, 418, 474, 477

Jew 11, 13, 14, 15, 16, 20, 25, 26, 29, 32, 34, 35, 36, 40, 55, 75, 76, 77, 88, 91, 100, 105, 170, 175, 196, 206, 216, 217, 226, 232, 233, 234, 235, 238, 239, 240, 241, 242, 243, 244, 250, 254, 256, 257, 262, 292, 298, 307, 314, 337, 378, 413, 414, 419, 422, 425, 428, 430, 431, 432, 433, 434, 436, 437, 438, 439, 441, 442, 443, 444, 450, 451, 452, 454, 456, 458, 461, 462, 467, 468, 470, 472, 473, 474, 476, 477, 479, 484, 485, 486, 494, 498, 512, 520, 526

Joachim 26, 229, 234, 495

Joash 14

Joy 121, 127, 173, 176, 179, 181, 182, 196, 313, 346, 351, 353, 354, 362, 413, 414, 418, 420, 422, 423, 428, 433, 439, 441, 452, 456, 457, 458, 460, 462, 464, 465, 466, 473, 474, 475, 476, 477, 478, 479, 480, 481, 482, 483, 484, 485, 486, 487, 488, 489, 491, 493, 497, 501, 510, 515, 520, 521

Judaism 2, 7, 13, 14, 18, 19, 20, 21, 22, 23, 24, 25, 27, 29, 37, 39, 69, 73, 76, 88, 92, 142, 147, 211, 231, 239, 245, 247, 253, 261, 302, 303, 368, 388, 399, 400, 411, 421, 423, 434, 446, 468, 485, 491, 492, 493, 494, 495, 496, 497, 499, 501, 529

Judge 38, 131, 241, 247, 276, 285, 303, 309, 338, 346, 394, 513, 528, 530

Judgment 106, 125, 127, 131, 148, 194, 256, 274, 321, 332, 354, 370, 377, 393, 396, 414, 455, 461, 498, 512

Juridical 208, 297, 366, 525

Justice 6, 9, 65, 97, 100, 114,

K

Kashrut 14, 29, 30, 34, 39, 72, 82, 200, 206, 215, 218, 221, 229, 238, 254, 278, 283, 293, 346, 378, 390, 424, 428, 429, 430, 432, 434, 435, 437, 438, 440, 441, 442, 443, 444, 445, 448, 449, 450, 451, 452, 453, 460, 461, 463, 467, 471, 475, 477, 479

Keeper 241, 251, 428, 436

Kinds 30, 31, 140, 176, 187, 123, 179, 197, 237, 259, 269, 277, 280, 281, 284, 285, 287, 306, 307, 309, 338, 346, 347, 348, 352, 353, 395, 418, 441, 444, 448, 525, 526, 530

King 3, 11, 33, 35, 41, 43, 51, 57, 73, 74, 110, 111, 118, 119, 121, 125, 128, 129, 132, 143, 161, 162, 165, 169, 172, 174, 201, 224, 249, 264, 283, 285, 310, 311, 312, 316, 317, 318, 319, 324, 325, 326, 328, 329, 331, 337, 338, 344, 352, 368, 374, 375, 381, 421, 425, 438, 457, 472, 473, 498

Kingdom v, 1, 4, 6, 33, 46, 60, 65, 66, 68, 72, 81, 82, 83, 85, 87, 89, 96, 98, 111, 112, 129, 139, 162, 166, 168, 169, 185, 192, 198, 200, 237, 276, 421, 442, 443, 454, 529

208, 217, 221, 222, 223, 231, 233, 247, 250, 260, 265, 274, 275, 277, 278, 279, 281, 282, 283, 284, 285, 286, 287, 316, 317, 329, 330, 333, 336, 338, 340, 341, 342, 343, 345, 349, 351, 352, 353, 356, 357, 366, 378, 393, 398, 404, 413, 421, 423, 449, 457, 458, 465, 466, 471, 472, 482, 483, 510, 514

Kisses 123

Kosher 14, 215, 416, 419, 437, 438, 442, 443, 444, 445, 448, 454

L

Lamb 83, 141, 160, 246, 321, 335, 336, 342, 369, 402, 403

Lament 357

Subject Index

Land 6, 15, 31, 32, 46, 68, 82, 85, 87, 100, 116, 150, 157, 163, 164, 165, 167, 176, 221, 222, 223, 224, 225, 246, 270, 274, 278, 280, 282, 283, 285, 286, 292, 293, 309, 318, 327, 328, 342, 348, 353, 373, 387, 416, 421, 457, 466, 484, 515, 524

Language 115, 116, 149, 150, 192, 210, 268, 335, 336, 363, 475, 501, 511

Law i, iv, v, 1, 2, 3, 7, 9, 10, 21, 22, 34, 36, 41, 42, 43, 46, 51, 52, 53, 56, 57, 58, 59, 66, 67, 68, 70, 71, 72, 78, 84, 93, 97, 99, 100, 101, 102, 103, 104, 105, 106, 110, 113, 121, 128, 147, 148, 153, 158, 162, 167, 170, 173, 177, 181, 183, 185, 192, 194, 196, 202, 209, 210, 218, 219, 229, 235, 236, 237, 238, 241, 245, 253, 261, 262, 265, 273, 277, 280, 305, 307, 308, 309, 313, 318, 320, 321, 356, 362, 364, 378, 382, 384, 397, 410, 413, 414, 418, 419, 424, 433, 434, 444, 446, 447, 452, 472, 491, 495, 496, 497, 499, 501, 515, 521, 523

Lebanon 122

Legalism 4, 22, 38, 53, 54, 58, 73, 147, 152, 153, 170, 178, 192, 193, 194, 195, 208, 210, 211, 212, 222, 242, 245, 304, 438, 441, 455, 464, 491, 492, 496, 499, 511, 513

Levitical 161, 200, 278, 287, 382

Liberty vi, 60, 128, 185, 186, 213, 270, 381, 439

Lifeblood 96, 420

Lifestyle 22, 23, 29, 30, 244, 422, 431, 432, 454, 456

Living 4, 20, 24, 38, 44, 50, 71, 80, 94, 104, 113, 114, 116, 118, 122, 134, 147, 187, 191, 195, 196, 214, 215, 232, 240, 255, 257, 269, 271, 278, 301, 306, 315, 329, 349, 360, 371, 390, 396, 409, 421, 422, 433,

	434, 436, 441, 444, 446, 448, 457, 478, 483, 485, 486, 522, 527	192, 197, 201, 220, 225, 240, 242, 247, 249, 251, 259, 263, 264, 265,		435, 440, 442, 443, 452, 457, 463, 465, 474, 479, 483, 498, 507, 508, 510, 511,
Loan	523, 527	269, 270,		519, 521,
Logos	v, 4, 50, 56, 60, 104, 109, 116, 130, 131, 132, 133, 134, 135, 136, 137, 138, 139, 142, 145, 146, 148, 155, 363, 364, 365, 472	272, 273, 274, 275, 276, 277, 280, 281, 282, 283, 284, 285, 286, 294, 295, 300, 301, 302, 303, 311, 312, 315, 319, 320, 321, 322, 323, 325, 326, 327, 328, 329, 331, 336, 338, 340, 341, 343, 344, 345, 346, 347, 348, 351, 352, 353, 354, 355, 357, 360, 363, 368, 370, 376, 377, 381, 382, 384, 385, 386, 387, 389, 396, 397, 398, 400, 404, 405, 406, 407, 409, 410, 414, 421,	Lust Luther Lutheran **M** Mankind Manifestation Marriage	525, 527 275 100, 101, 102, 160, 492, 497 26, 35, 181, 459 58, 96, 128, 134, 149, 150, 249, 339, 404, 425, 508 61, 64, 79, 81, 82, 94, 96, 104, 133, 139, 170, 203, 208, 220, 221, 230, 271, 316, 354, 359, 360, 365, 408, 473, 491 51, 95, 121, 172, 173, 174, 312, 313, 384, 416, 449, 450, 523, 524, 525, 531
Lord	i, iii, 3, 11, 12, 39, 42, 44, 46, 47, 48, 54, 63, 69, 73, 76, 87, 94, 97, 98, 99, 111, 113, 114, 115, 116, 117, 118, 121, 122, 125, 127, 129, 130, 134, 139, 143, 148, 154, 157, 162, 163, 165, 166, 167, 171, 172, 173, 175, 176, 177, 178, 180, 181, 182, 191,			

Subject Index

Master	56, 57, 114, 119, 120, 128, 146, 196, 300, 366, 463		282, 284, 286, 291, 292, 301, 303, 315, 316, 317, 323, 324,		65, 67, 68, 81, 82, 83, 84, 86, 89, 93, 175, 191, 203, 204, 205,
Messiah	vi, 2, 3, 4, 5, 6, 9, 10, 11, 12, 16, 17, 18, 19, 20, 23, 25, 27, 28, 29, 30, 31, 32, 34, 39, 40, 65, 68, 71, 73, 74, 76, 81, 84, 85, 87, 88, 89, 98, 99, 100, 102, 107, 120, 133, 139, 146, 147, 153, 154, 160, 162, 163, 164, 168, 185, 186, 187, 189, 191, 198, 202, 208, 210, 212, 213, 216, 217, 224, 226, 227, 231, 232, 233, 239, 240, 241, 243, 244, 246, 247, 254, 255, 263, 266, 268, 270, 271, 273, 277, 278, 279, 280,		325, 326, 329, 330, 331, 332, 336, 337, 338, 339, 340, 342, 343, 349, 351, 352, 354, 359, 360, 361, 362, 364, 366, 368, 369, 370, 372, 373, 384, 385, 392, 393, 400, 403, 404, 405, 413, 414, 416, 423, 425, 430, 431, 432, 433, 434, 435, 437, 438, 442, 451, 452, 455, 456, 457, 458, 459, 460, 462, 470, 471, 472, 473, 474, 478, 480, 481, 482, 483, 484, 495, 500, 501, 510		208, 221, 222, 223, 224, 259, 260, 262, 278, 279, 280, 286, 287, 288, 289, 316, 317, 320, 324, 326, 327, 337, 338, 339, 340, 341, 342, 343, 351, 352, 354, 355, 358, 359, 365, 385, 423, 453, 457, 458, 465, 466, 482, 510
			Millennial	3, 4, 6, 7,	Ministry	2, 25, 45, 58, 113, 179, 181, 182, 187, 205, 236, 237, 257, 284, 286, 287, 288, 289, 290, 291, 292, 293, 316, 317, 318, 319, 325, 328, 330, 338, 370, 387, 390, 405, 446,

597

	449, 450, 466, 473, 492		231, 233, 248, 254, 261, 262,		100, 104, 106, 149, 150, 151,
Miracle	262, 358		277, 294, 295, 296,		152, 153, 161, 163,
Miriam	248, 375		301, 305,		168, 183,
Mirrors	118, 187, 213		306, 308, 312, 316,		217, 219, 223, 257,
Mishnah	8, 42, 97, 119, 122, 128, 132, 149, 294, 297, 301, 318, 368, 371, 395, 399, 413, 445		318, 319, 320, 321, 322, 325, 327, 331, 333, 336, 338, 339, 340, 342, 367, 368, 369, 370,		277, 280, 283, 284, 290, 337, 338, 343, 352, 354, 356, 358, 367, 373, 449, 457, 462, 465,
Mishpat	100, 196, 277, 280, 323, 346, 347, 352		371, 372, 373, 374, 375, 376,	Nabal Naval	483, 510 114 113
Missionary	25, 26, 27, 28, 242, 246		377, 382, 383, 386, 387, 397, 399, 400,	Negative	6, 31, 54, 57, 58, 59, 73, 129, 177, 180,
Mitigation	306, 307		412, 419, 421, 429,		183, 187, 191, 192,
Money	275, 379, 507		433, 452, 459, 467,		193, 210, 260, 262,
Moses	2, 3, 9, 10, 13, 22, 26, 36, 42, 45, 47, 48, 49, 53, 54, 55, 64, 75, 76, 78, 94, 95, 96, 99, 100, 101, 102, 107, 119, 122, 125, 126, 133, 134, 142, 147, 149, 167, 171, 172, 177, 191, 198, 202, 224,	Murder Muslim Muzzle N Nations	501, 519, 521 53, 60, 63, 96, 228, 266, 269, 274, 346, 383, 415, 418, 419, 528 74 389, 397, 409, 529 15, 33, 42, 43, 45, 74, 83, 84, 87,	Neighbor	263, 264, 265, 266, 267, 418, 491, 492, 493, 519, 520 60, 64, 175, 186, 192, 204, 212, 265, 267, 268, 269, 270, 273, 275, 276, 286, 309, 345, 346, 356, 382, 385, 524,

Subject Index

Noah   526, 528, 530
Noah   3, 72, 97, 98, 102, 160, 418, 419, 420
Noahic   3, 4, 75, 76, 92, 95, 97, 103, 104, 158, 161, 169, 418, 419, 420
Numbering   7, 161, 262, 521
Nurse   140
Nurture   115, 124

O

Oak   123
Oath   172, 264, 344, 440, 527
Obedience   3, 4, 17, 25, 51, 99, 163, 166, 167, 170, 177, 194, 238, 256, 272, 361, 385, 468, 478, 494, 497, 498, 500
Object   36, 76, 83, 84, 137, 174, 242, 254, 291, 344, 348, 403, 429, 444, 455, 456, 505
Objective   105, 107, 126, 385

Observance   39, 71, 97, 152, 167, 186, 238, 245, 246, 250, 256, 276, 303, 382, 385, 392, 408, 423, 435, 441, 446, 452, 478, 503, 504, 510, 512, 513, 514, 515, 516
Offerings   179, 231, 281, 282, 284, 286, 287, 288, 321, 325, 345, 409, 410
Omer   247, 313, 522
Omissions   316
Opposite   3, 21, 39, 40, 55, 84, 121, 131, 137, 166, 188, 229, 251, 279, 287, 306, 308, 356, 430, 444, 471, 476, 487, 489, 515
Opposition   52, 72, 103, 158, 226, 303, 305, 308
Ordinances   14, 42, 44,

   53, 79, 100, 132, 229, 280, 299, 378, 417, 420, 519, 520, 521, 523, 524, 525, 526, 527, 528, 529, 531
Orthodox   14, 22, 24, 27, 28, 30, 37, 73, 74, 75, 76, 77, 138, 140, 144, 183, 231, 234, 245, 253, 257, 292, 297, 303, 307, 317, 440, 441, 442, 466, 494
Outward   4, 84, 179, 243, 305, 320, 366, 448, 468, 485
Ox   356, 389, 397, 409, 522, 529
Oxen   321, 389, 397, 409

P

Parallel   86, 93, 102, 107, 112, 115, 129, 134, 149, 152, 190, 215, 271, 325, 334, 364, 369, 372, 445

Patriarchs 15, 73, 83, 84, 87, 88, 97, 98, 249, 323, 329, 337, 343, 473, 480, 481, 485, 487, 508

Paul, the apostle 2, 4, 8, 9, 11, 13, 23, 42, 49, 51, 52, 53, 54, 56, 57, 58, 59, 60, 61, 70, 71, 75, 76, 78, 81, 94, 118, 128, 147, 151, 183, 184, 185, 187, 188, 189, 190, 191, 192, 193, 195, 196, 208, 209, 210, 211, 212, 214, 220, 228, 229, 230, 238, 239, 240, 241, 242, 243, 244, 245, 246, 247, 248, 250, 251, 253, 254, 255, 256, 257, 264, 268, 269, 270, 271, 272, 273, 274, 289, 300, 308, 309, 311, 322, 330, 362, 389, 390, 391, 392, 393, 401, 402, 403, 404, 409, 411, 412, 414, 418, 422, 424, 425, 428, 430, 432, 434, 435, 436, 437, 438, 449, 450, 452, 454, 455, 456, 465, 466, 467, 468, 469, 470, 479, 480, 481, 483, 484, 485, 486, 487, 488, 489, 491, 492, 493, 495, 496, 497, 499, 500, 501, 507, 509, 511, 516, 519

Peace 6, 45, 65, 110, 111, 179, 217, 250, 256, 272, 284, 285, 287, 288, 289, 316, 321, 325, 338, 339, 341, 344, 348, 349, 351, 353, 354, 362, 383, 410, 445, 446, 451, 465, 486, 529

Perfect 56, 60, 61, 98, 99, 118, 128, 151, 184, 186, 197, 199, 200, 201, 213, 259, 270, 326, 346, 354, 360, 364, 451, 456, 491

Period 31, 83, 85, 102, 116, 224, 236, 290, 291, 296, 511

Person 4, 13, 14, 15, 40, 61, 76, 77, 105, 120, 127, 130, 135, 136, 153, 155, 159, 164, 165, 167, 168, 174, 180, 190, 191, 195, 212, 213, 234, 237, 242, 283, 291, 300, 307, 309, 316, 319, 334, 350, 357, 363, 364, 367, 383, 385, 388,

Subject Index

	400, 406, 407, 410, 415, 441, 443, 453, 456, 465, 468, 472, 477, 486, 492, 500, 501, 508, 511, 512, 530, 531	Plague Polity	498 283, 327, 328 53, 55, 56, 57, 58, 67, 147, 153, 181, 183, 185, 188, 193, 195, 201, 209, 210, 211, 212, 216, 224, 228, 260, 261, 284, 318, 361, 450, 451, 480		262, 263, 264, 266, 267, 268, 270, 276, 298, 302, 303, 393, 455, 456, 491, 496, 499, 519, 520
Pesach (Passover)	16, 21, 45, 149, 198, 246, 247, 282, 292, 316, 321, 336, 386, 399, 402, 403, 404, 406, 423, 462, 463, 465, 522, 523			Power	53, 88, 112, 114, 118, 132, 147, 152, 153, 155, 168, 170, 172, 185, 187, 188, 189, 191, 192, 194, 196, 199, 201, 204, 205, 211, 212, 217, 248, 272, 295, 296, 319, 331, 334, 335, 339, 344, 350, 353, 361, 367, 368, 374, 380, 394, 406, 407, 441, 474
Pesachim	120, 132, 323, 412	Position	3, 30, 34, 36, 37, 38, 45, 64, 68, 72, 80, 81, 83, 86, 89, 92, 105, 106, 169, 171, 175, 203, 205, 206, 210, 219, 221, 225, 226, 230, 240, 249, 277, 279, 305, 319, 394, 428, 438, 447, 453, 457, 460, 475, 489, 501, 513		
Pharisee	189, 192, 241, 304, 412, 499				
Physical	15, 30, 84, 223, 233, 243, 448, 466, 468, 475, 477, 480, 485, 508, 523				
Picture	87, 141, 153, 167, 213, 291, 356, 462, 492, 493, 494			Practice	14, 16, 23, 31, 49, 56, 67, 86, 90, 99, 110, 183, 234, 238, 253, 264, 298, 300, 301, 319, 330, 332, 350,
Pious	106, 174, 208, 249, 348, 391,	Positive	31, 57, 59, 60, 74, 76, 80, 106, 164, 185, 190, 191, 192, 210, 229, 261,		

601

THE ETERNAL TORAH: LIVING UNDER GOD

	367, 395, 396, 397, 406, 425, 437, 456, 479, 498, 515, 526, 527		362, 379, 380, 385, 390, 392, 410, 425, 435, 439, 442, 488, 495, 525		27, 28, 33, 41, 55, 73, 74, 75, 76, 93, 115, 121, 165, 180, 196, 204, 212, 214, 234, 268, 269, 280, 295, 297, 300, 316, 339, 352, 359, 368, 381, 388, 391, 399, 406, 411, 418, 441, 516, 519
Praise	47, 224, 243, 249, 250, 264, 305, 330, 354, 445, 468, 524	Promises	5, 15, 85, 87, 159, 162, 166, 169, 174, 225, 255, 264, 323, 324, 329, 337, 343, 348, 404, 433, 460, 473, 480, 481, 496		
Priest	11, 26, 106, 112, 144, 160, 161, 162, 164, 198, 199, 224, 233, 236, 289, 316, 319, 320, 325, 326, 328, 330, 338, 340, 342, 344, 368, 381, 383, 401, 445, 446				
		Prophecy	87, 130, 261, 272, 296, 331, 332, 398, 488	Ram	282
				Ratified	160, 515
				Reality	5, 117, 134, 139, 181, 279, 304, 364, 455, 458, 510
		Prophets	17, 33, 54, 55, 59, 74, 112, 129, 130, 131, 170, 179, 207, 209, 261, 294, 311, 326, 332, 340, 346, 358, 407, 472	Reconciliation	88, 389
				Reconstructionism	217, 219
				Redemption	46, 47, 49, 95, 167, 198, 260, 280, 299, 313, 316, 321, 327, 335, 341, 404
Principle	32, 40, 51, 52, 53, 56, 58, 64, 78, 98, 99, 140, 142, 143, 146, 154, 182, 184, 191, 195, 196, 208, 213, 214, 221, 230, 237, 268, 269, 272, 273, 307, 308, 310, 311, 346,				
		Psalmist	87, 139, 328		
		Psychology	40		
		Q		Redemptive	149, 163, 243, 460
		Qabbalah	142, 143		
		Quail	165		
		R		Regulations	80, 81, 82, 220, 221,
		Rabbi	7, 20, 26,		

Subject Index

	232, 245, 294, 305, 355, 358, 359, 365, 380, 450, 456, 505, 512, 515
Relationship	9, 47, 48, 50, 51, 56, 57, 73, 77, 78, 90, 94, 98, 104, 113, 117, 123, 131, 140, 149, 158, 159, 171, 174, 242, 271, 279, 395, 400, 523
Religion	13, 19, 41, 42, 50, 88, 101, 219, 241, 296, 305, 331, 399, 431, 432, 433, 456, 474, 494
Renewal	158, 175, 181, 200, 203, 227
Restoration	33, 66, 68, 87, 91, 139, 327, 408, 488, 498, 501
Resurrection	67, 149, 170, 202, 235, 247, 289, 335, 336, 373,

	391, 393, 405, 457, 474, 483, 507, 509, 512, 515, 517
Rich	123, 125, 135, 267, 343, 360
Righteousness	54, 56, 97, 114, 148, 158, 165, 179, 184, 185, 188, 189, 190, 193, 194, 195, 196, 197, 212, 213, 215, 217, 241, 242, 247, 259, 268, 269, 272, 277, 281, 284, 285, 314, 316, 338, 342, 344, 346, 347, 348, 349, 350, 351, 352, 353, 354, 362, 377, 390, 391, 392, 393, 397, 469, 492, 493, 494, 495, 499, 500, 501, 512
Risk	236, 237, 440, 441
Ritual	13, 235, 288, 289,

	293, 305, 306, 399, 400, 403, 405, 415, 418, 419, 420, 424, 445, 447, 448, 465
Rock	248, 290, 346
Rotten	523
Royal	60, 111, 128, 141, 185, 186, 270, 324, 328, 344, 345, 398, 407, 477, 488, 491
Rule	32, 50, 52, 53, 74, 88, 128, 182, 184, 191, 196, 228, 232, 285, 307, 308, 309, 338, 344, 351, 352, 386, 388, 391, 396, 410, 411, 418, 465, 486

S

Sabbath	231, 235, 236, 281, 282, 307, 372, 377, 381, 382, 408, 421, 455, 510
Sabbatical	125, 355, 506, 522, 523

603

Sacrifice	20, 83, 159, 160, 161, 164, 165, 170, 179, 181, 196, 199, 200, 201, 224, 236, 267, 271, 273, 284, 287, 288, 289, 290, 316, 321, 327, 330, 335, 341, 348, 399, 401, 439, 451, 472, 473, 494, 526		162, 168, 187, 188, 189, 194, 196, 197, 199, 200, 209, 210, 211, 212, 216, 220, 240, 242, 243, 244, 249, 250, 281, 343, 346, 349, 404, 422, 430, 431, 433, 455, 459, 461, 470, 479, 491, 492, 494, 495, 497, 498, 499, 500, 501		321, 323, 325, 327, 329, 331, 333, 335, 337, 339, 341, 343, 344, 345, 347, 349, 351, 353, 355, 357, 359, 361, 363, 365, 367, 368, 369, 371, 373, 375, 445
Sacrificial	44, 81, 113, 161, 164, 179, 181, 182, 186, 218, 231, 236, 257, 278, 284, 286, 287, 288, 289, 290, 291, 292, 293, 317, 319, 325, 330, 338, 446, 450, 453, 466, 473, 520	Satanic	152	Sinai	41, 42, 52, 53, 54, 67, 75, 83, 97, 98, 102, 117, 118, 121, 149, 161, 171, 173, 175, 180, 277, 294, 295, 314, 318, 320, 321, 322, 326, 327, 333, 334, 339, 340, 365, 370, 371, 400, 508
		Sea	94, 96, 150, 165, 196, 246, 333, 348, 352, 380		
		Season	186, 323, 348, 363		
		Sect	18, 21, 253		
		Secular	214, 378, 513		
		Sick	236, 265, 378, 398, 405, 406, 407, 463, 464	Snake	369, 443
				Snare	222, 365
Sadducees	19, 113, 149, 235			Society	25, 26, 50, 138, 146, 218, 375, 442
Salt	446				
Salvation	12, 20, 24, 31, 46, 57, 58, 64, 67, 68, 79, 83, 87, 89, 102, 152, 158,	Similarities	85, 98, 110, 160, 173, 203, 234, 295, 315, 317, 319,	Sociological	417
				Sophia	110, 117, 127, 128, 130, 131,

Subject Index

Sophianic 146
Soul 82, 100, 132, 135, 136, 140, 141, 142, 143, 144, 145, 146, 270
Soul 82, 100, 143, 146, 178, 192, 259, 341, 342, 345, 368, 376, 387, 413, 506
Sound 249, 522
Subject 1, 17, 43, 57, 77, 95, 153, 159, 174, 226, 233, 263, 288, 305, 357, 399, 414, 464, 465, 486, 496
Sunday 21, 31, 70, 186, 408, 475, 503, 504, 505, 506, 507, 508, 509, 510, 511, 512, 514, 515, 516, 517
Supersessionism 90, 91, 475
Supper 169, 186, 335, 336, 359, 378, 398, 402, 405, 406, 407, 410, 417, 435, 462, 463, 464, 465, 516
Symbol 140, 142, 322
Synagogue 19, 28, 36, 43, 175, 183, 236, 246, 249, 250, 257, 258, 299, 303, 412, 424, 480, 498
System 52, 180, 188, 192, 193, 198, 236, 278, 285, 287, 307, 381, 413, 425, 434, 441, 491, 492, 494, 497, 499, 500, 520

T

Tabernacle 47, 123, 143, 145, 153, 223, 294, 318, 321, 325, 327, 333, 334, 335, 341, 355
Tableware 441
Talmud 22, 33, 42, 55, 93, 95, 101, 126, 149, 160, 175, 196, 198, 247, 268, 291, 295, 297, 298, 300, 304, 307, 322, 335, 370, 388, 394, 395, 406, 412, 418, 462, 492, 494, 516, 519
Tanakh 6, 7, 9, 13, 18, 26, 41, 42, 45, 49, 50, 54, 55, 64, 66, 80, 83, 103, 110, 119, 122, 131, 133, 147, 160, 171, 176, 196, 197, 198, 203, 220, 228, 244, 254, 261, 263, 277, 280, 281, 288, 295, 297, 298, 301, 302, 310, 311, 332, 339, 341, 356, 375, 381, 388, 391, 395, 399, 412, 423, 448, 458, 472, 475, 480, 488, 515
Teaching ii, 41, 42,

	43, 44, 50, 76, 101, 112, 234, 235, 260, 271, 274, 305, 316, 319, 325, 330, 338, 339, 366, 367, 372, 395, 397, 413, 429, 431, 432, 447, 452		399, 401, 409, 415, 445, 449, 472, 473, 483, 510, 520, 523, 526
		Testify	245, 272, 346, 397, 469
		Testimony	i, 35, 56, 135, 153, 245, 259, 292, 303, 332, 410, 414, 433, 528, 530
Temple	14, 19, 45, 65, 80, 82, 87, 112, 124, 130, 131, 145, 153, 154, 162, 183, 189, 200, 223, 225, 231, 233, 236, 237, 253, 255, 256, 257, 258, 278, 280, 281, 284, 287, 288, 289, 290, 291, 292, 293, 316, 318, 319, 323, 325, 326, 327, 328, 329, 330, 334, 335, 336, 337, 338, 339, 342, 343, 344, 352, 355, 368, 382, 387,	Textual	543
		Theological	iii, 1, 7, 8, 10, 17, 24, 29, 39, 40, 64, 65, 72, 77, 83, 91, 92, 166, 193, 205, 216, 226, 245, 257, 287, 300, 304, 417, 458, 503
		Theophany	316, 317, 320, 327, 333, 334, 340
		Theophilus	12, 135
		Thunder	116, 320
		Time	1, 5, 6, 9, 13, 18, 19, 21, 24, 28, 31, 37, 49, 67, 68, 76, 78, 80, 82, 83, 87, 89, 94, 95, 96, 97, 101, 102, 113, 117, 119, 125, 127, 134, 137, 139, 143, 144, 145, 149, 164, 167, 168, 170, 175, 179, 182, 187, 191, 192, 198, 201, 204, 205, 208, 210, 216, 218, 221, 222, 224, 235, 237, 238, 240, 242, 244, 245, 246, 250, 255, 262, 264, 266, 271, 277, 278, 283, 284, 285, 289, 290, 291, 296, 306, 307, 310, 311, 312, 322, 324, 326, 332, 336, 342, 352, 355, 356, 358, 359, 364, 367, 368, 371, 374, 381, 384, 385, 387,

Subject Index

	390, 399, 410, 417, 431, 432, 435, 443, 444, 450, 454, 457, 462, 468, 472, 473, 474, 482, 483, 484, 488, 489, 493, 498, 515, 524, 529, 531	Uriah	385			203, 236, 301, 363, 371, 399, 400, 401, 405, 498
		V				
		Value	117, 170, 181, 200, 235, 241, 242, 288, 456, 469	Weak	152, 184, 187, 190, 198, 199, 202, 215, 352, 433, 438, 450, 453, 454, 511, 512, 513
		Venerable	26		
		Vengeance	354		
		Vessel	445		
Timeless	46	Vicinity	442		
Token	420	Victorious	413, 414	Weakness	4, 177, 197, 199, 203, 216, 255, 257, 358, 452, 453, 474, 512
U		Viewpoint	30, 104, 166, 167, 168, 243, 418, 432, 506, 509		
Umbrage	416				
Uncircumcised	74, 183, 187, 222, 240, 281, 320, 326, 332, 340, 423, 427, 449, 458, 465, 468, 470, 480			Welcome	29, 225, 385, 447
		Vile	110, 153	White	48, 264, 365, 456
		W		Wisdom	4, 9, 43, 44, 46, 60, 79, 93, 109, 110, 111, 112, 113, 114, 115, 116, 117, 118, 119, 120, 121, 124, 126, 127, 128, 129, 130, 131, 132, 133, 135, 136, 137, 138, 140, 141, 143, 177, 248, 270, 296, 315, 326, 330, 331,
		Walk	15, 48, 96, 104, 109, 147, 154, 158, 164, 178, 191, 195, 207, 211, 254, 270, 277, 297, 331, 347, 348, 351, 352, 452, 454, 465, 468, 486, 523		
Understanding	1, 2, 8, 44, 50, 58, 109, 111, 114, 115, 116, 117, 124, 126, 129, 136, 187, 216, 224, 235, 249, 270, 274, 326, 345, 395, 411, 453, 468, 510				
		Washing	399, 400, 401, 445, 448		
		Water	13, 45, 122, 134, 149, 163, 171,		
Urgent	1, 463				

347, 362, 364, 424, 456

Y

Yahweh	260
Yoke	38, 75, 129, 152, 172, 177, 181, 409, 412, 413, 414, 425,
Young	109, 127, 131, 141, 242, 243, 282, 285, 325, 360, 375, 440, 441, 522, 531

Z

Zadok	198, 224, 338
Zeal	179, 241, 339, 428, 429
Zion	2, 42, 59, 112, 117, 124, 146, 149, 154, 277, 281, 295, 320, 325, 326, 327, 328, 334, 337, 340, 343, 352, 370
Zipporah	13, 14
Zodiac	152

www.ingramcontent.com/pod-product-compliance
Lightning Source LLC
Chambersburg PA
CBHW060646150426
42811CB00086B/2443/J